PASCAL

WITH PROGRAM DESIGN

JAMES F. PETERS III

St. John's University
Collegeville, Minnesota

HOLT RINEHART AND WINSTON

New York Chicago San Francisco Philadelphia Mexico City
Rio de Janeiro Madrid Montreal Toronto London Sydney Tokyo

To
Verner J. Hoggatt, Ruth Devolder, and Margaret Dumont,
three great persons,
with love

Address correspondence to:
383 Madison Avenue, New York, NY 10017

Trademarks

Apple Computer Company: Apple IIe
IBM: System 360/370, IBM PC, IBM PC AT
Microsoft: MS Pascal 2.0
Boreland International: Turbo Pascal
Digital Equipment Corporation:VAX Pascal, VAX-11, PDP-11
University of California at San Diego Board of Regents:
UCSD Pascal
Oregon Software: OS Pascal

Library of Congress Cataloging in Publication Data

Peters, James, F.
Pascal with program design

Bibliography: p.
Includes index.
1. PASCAL (Computer program language) 2. Structured programming. I. Title.
QA76.73.P2P477 1986 005.13'3 85-24861
ISBN 0-03-003282-2

Printed in the United States of America

Published simultaneously in Canada

6 7 8 032 9 8 7 6 5 4 3 2 1

CBS COLLEGE PUBLISHING
Holt, Rinehart and Winston
The Dryden Press
Saunders College Publishing

QUICK CONTENTS

EXPANDED CONTENTS

PREFACE

This text is designed for a first course in introductory programming that emphasizes a structured approach and the development of problem-solving strategies to design programs. It follows closely the guidelines for CS1 described in "Recommended Curriculum for CS1, 1984," in the *Communications of the Association of Computing Machinery*, October, 1984, *27*, 998–1001. It also has been written to satisfy the requirements for the first half of an Advanced Placement course in Computer Science described in Advanced Placement Program of the College Board, Advanced Placement Course Description: Computer Science, Educational Testing Service, Princeton, NJ, 1983. Since this text will be used in a variety of settings and varying time spans, it includes some CS2 topics.

- Sorting and searching techniques
- File management techniques
- Dynamic data structures (singly linked and multilinked lists)
- List processing

These topics are included to provide students with more reach and help build some perspective on coming attractions in CS2. In a semester-long or longer course, there would be time to cover some of these topics.

The main goal of this book is to show how to use a top-down approach to designing programs. It relies on the use of pseudocode to present all algorithms that are used. As a rule, a graphical interpretation of collected algorithms to be used in a program is given in structure charts. Strong emphasis is placed on the importance of identifying the required input, output, and processes used to implement the algorithms written in pseudocode. Standard Pascal has been used to implement chapter algorithms.

This text has the following features:

ALGORITHMS

Algorithms are finite step-by-step methods of solving problems. Each chapter introduces problems with accompanying algorithms. The algorithms are always presented in pseudocode and implemented in Standard Pascal.

ABSTRACT PROGRAMS

An abstract program presents algorithms using ordinary language to present instructions for an ideal machine. These programs are translatable into any programming language. They are slanted in the direction of Pascal because they use the same control structures that Pascal uses. Abstract programs usually lead to procedures. Interdependent procedures used in a single program are represented using structure charts.

STRUCTURE CHARTS

Starting in Chapter 1, the use of structure charts (a variation of what is also known as a *hierarchical input process output* (HIPO) *chart* to represent programs is encouraged. A structure chart resembles an organizational chart and is used to show the connections between procedures. Procedures are presented early in this book.

EARLY USE OF PROCEDURES

Procedures define new instructions for a machine to perform. Procedures are used to present algorithms. Each procedure represents a method of performing a task, which we ask a machine to carry out. The trick in developing algorithms is to separate out major (and, often, small) things for a machine to do. In this book, procedures are used in every chapter. This technique of programming starts in Chapter 1 with what are known as *parameterless procedures*—just action words like SketchRobot, which are defined for a machine by a procedure. Procedures are usually presented as parts of complete programs.

COMPLETE PROGRAMS

Every chapter includes complete programs, both abstract programs and Pascal programs. Most Pascal programs have sample runs to show how a program works. Often by seeing what a program does, it is easier to understand the program that produces the results in a sample run. At least we know what to look for, what to expect when we check out the source text that produced the sample run.

EXPERIMENTS

In most chapters experimental programs are given to demonstrate features of Pascal and make it easier for students to see how information is stored inside a machine.

LONGER PROGRAMS

In addition to a variety of short programs which can be checked at a glance and are easy to implement, many of the chapter case studies include longer, more complete programs which reflect the program design techniques that have been discussed. The goal of these longer programs is to show more completely how software can be developed and show the unfolding of the top-down programs design technique. In parallel with these longer programs you will find companion structure charts that have been developed in stages. In addition to the complete programs, each chapter also includes a variety of learning aids.

FLOWCHARTS Flowcharts of the fundamental Pascal control structures are given as an alternative way of viewing what happens inside a program.

CHAPTER AIMS Each chapter begins with a set of aims. These aims give a quick look at what to expect in each chapter.

CHAPTER INTRODUCTIONS Each chapter begins with an introduction to the terminology needed to go further in a chapter. New parts of the Pascal language are usually accompanied by syntax diagrams, which show the legal arrangements of the tokens used in a language structure.

CHAPTER SUMMARIES Chapter summaries say in a different way just what has been covered in each chapter. You can tell whether you need to read a chapter by looking at a summary.

CHAPTER KEYWORD REVIEWS The keywords used in each chapter are collected together at the end of each chapter. These call attention to chapter highlights in another useful way. They help organize the knowledge you will need to go further in the book.

CHAPTER REVIEW QUIZZES At the end of each chapter you will find a self-test, review quiz. These are collections of statements that are either true or false. They will measure your understanding of the subtler points covered in each chapter. You can check your answers by looking at the back of the book where a complete quiz key is given.

SELECTED SOLUTIONS Selected solutions to chapter exercises are given at the back of this book.

CHAPTER CASE STUDIES At the end of many of the chapters, you will find case studies. These are more extensive developments of problems and uses of the language.

REFINEMENTS OF MOST PROGRAMS

Most programs are followed up by refinements, which are aimed at improving, fine-tuning, and broadening the reach of the programs. These are especially valuable. They give you ways to stretch proven programs and ways to make them better.

PROBLEM-SOLVING STRATEGIES

Ever and again problem-solving strategies are given in and around chapter algorithms. These are high points in any program development you will do. These are ways to tackle typical problems, both abstractly and directly in Pascal programs. Throughout this book, programs are put at the end of a set of problem-solving strategies and algorithms. Most programs contain one or more procedures, each representing ways to solve problems. These problems range from ways to format output to ways to express solutions to real-world problems like earnings on investments or ways to organize information.

STANDARD PASCAL

The Pascal used throughout this book is level 0 of Pascal described by the International Standards Organization (ISO). This standard is given in the draft standard, IOS/DIS 7185. This vintage of Pascal is available on most machines. Most versions of Pascal have their own bells and whistles. Even if a Pascal compiler implements the ISO standard, there are usually many bells and whistles in each version of Pascal that get treated in this book. Programs in this book have been tested with four different compilers on five different machines.

Apple Pascal on an Apple IIe (except for files)
IBM PC Pascal 2.00 on an IBM PC/AT
Oregon Software Pascal V2.1 on a PDP-11/70
Oregon Software Pascal V2.0 on a PDP-11/24
VAX Pascal 2.0 on a VAX-11/785

Common extensions of standard Pascal are given in Appendix C. These extensions include Apple Pascal (UCSD ™ Pascal), IBM Pascal, VAX ™ Pascal, and Turbo ™ Pascal. The methods you will need to use, especially the many special features of Turbo Pascal and Apple Pascal, to implement these extensions are given in Appendix C. In each case, the changes that need to be made to chapter programs are given. This is especially true of files and strings, which are handled differently in each version of Pascal.

GRADED EXERCISES

The exercises have been graded using the following forms of the Towers of Hanoi icon:

Intermediate  Advanced 

ICONS FOR PROGRAMS AND RUNS

The following two icons are used to call attention with program listings:

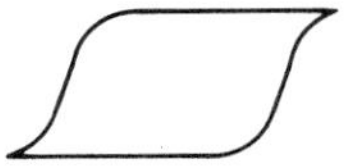

Marks beginning of a source text

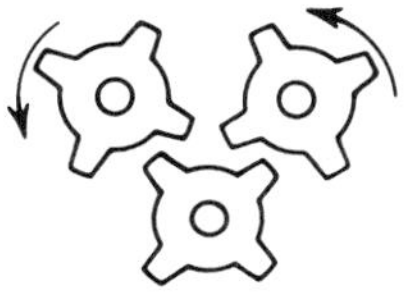

Marks beginning of a run

SOFTWARE

The Software for this book is available without charge from the publisher. This software is distributed on either VAX-11 1600 BPI magnetic tape or IBM PC 360 KB, two-sided, double density, soft sectored diskettes, which can be accessed by an IBM PCjr, IBM Personal Portable Personal Computer, IBM Personal Computer, IBM Personal Computer XT and IBM Personal Computer AT. Using these diskettes, this software has been successfully ported to a Digital Equipment Corporation VAX-11 computer system, a PDP-11/70 and PDP-11/24, and to an Apple Corporation Apple IIe. Each of these machines had a standard Pascal compiler and accepted the source code on IBM diskettes. With file-handling programs, changes were necessary to accomodate the special features of each system. Otherwise the programs ran without change. You can obtain this software by writing to

Holt, Rinehart and Winston
383 Madison Avenue, 4th floor
New York, New York 10017

USER'S GUIDE

Also available from the publisher is a User's Guide, which accompanies the software for this book. This Guide gives the details on how to implement and use the software.

ACKNOWLEDGMENTS

I wish to thank the following reviewers for their many suggestions and criticisms during the development of this text:

Robert P. Anderson (Marietta College, Ohio)
Sharon Burrowes (Wooster High School, Ohio)
James Collofello (Arizona State University)
Donald Cooley (Utah State University)
Peter Henderson (State University of New York College at Stony Brook)
Barabara Owens (Mercy College, NY)
Kulathur Rajasethputhy (State University of New York College at Brockport)
Brenda Wideman (Pennsylvania State University)
Stanley York (Iona College)

I also wish to thank the following persons for their various suggestions and generous help: Karl Glander, Ken Hortsch, Cindy Khria, Rupert Lee, Terri Hager, Tracy Gauthier, Dave Weigel, Richard Wittman, and Ted Collins (SJU CS students), Dr. Charles Lavine and Dr. Dan Steck (Physics, St. John's University) for their graphs, Professor Melchior Freund (Computer Science, St. John's University), Dr. Sylvester Theisen (SJO Sociology), Dr. Hamed M. Sallam (Computer Science, Mankato State University), Leon J. Schilmoeller (3M Corporation), Hank Marvin (Western Electric), Richard Pletcher (Boeing, Seattle, Washington), Pat Holmay, Lori Kaufenberg, Geoffrey Brunkhorst (Academic Computing, St. John's University), Mike Marrin (Computerland, St. Cloud, MN), Tom Gornick and Paul Becker (Holt, Rinehart and Winston), Maureen P. Conway (Cobb/Dunlop Publisher Services, NY), Ruth Devolder (retired teacher, Cape Cod, MA) for sharing her insights about language, James F. Peters Sr. for the art work, Patricia Peters for the word processing, Ruth Peters for her insights about trees.

I also wish to pay special tribute to Shelly Langman, development editor at Holt, Rinehart and Winston, for her many suggestions, criticisms, insight and incredible energy in discussions about Computer Science and this project. I also wish to thank Myles Thompson and Howard Wiener at Holt, Rinehart and Winston for their energy, insights and generous help during the final stages in this project. Finally, I wish to thank my wife Kathie for her suggestions and for listening and for her love.

CHAPTER 1

COMPUTERS, COMPILERS, AND PROGRAMS

The more ambitious plan may have more chance of success.

George Polya, 1957

A programming language is a formalism suitable for expressing algorithms and data structures . . .

Niklaus Wirth, 1985

AIMS

- Introduce the structure of a Pascal program with a procedure.
- Look briefly at computer organization, types of storage used.
- Look at steps leading from a source text to machine readable code using text editors, programming languages, compilers, and interpreters.
- Introduce the program development cycle, problem-solving techniques, and the use of pseudocode to write abstract programs.
- Suggest ways to verify program correctness.
- Discuss types of programming errors.
- Introduce stepwise refinement as a way to develop programs.

1.1 The Pascal Landscape

Pascal was developed by Dr. Niklaus Wirth in 1968 at the Swiss Federal Institute of Technology (ETH) in Switzerland. It is a descendent of ALGOL 60, which is a programming language designed for the study of ALGorithms (or methods of solving problems). Wirth designed Pascal with two principal goals in mind.

1. Provide a language suitable for teaching.
2. Shift the focus in programming *from* the peculiarities and features of a programming language *to* the structures and concepts to be used in programming.

Pascal was used for the first time in computer science classes at ETH in 1974.

That same year Wirth introduced a new version of Pascal called Pascal-P. The purpose of p-code (the name for the formalisms used by Pascal-P) was to make it easier to implement Pascal on various kinds of computers. Shortly after that Kenneth Bowles at the University of California at San Diego introduced UCSC Pascal. This new version of Pascal made it possible to implement Pascal on microcomputers.

A hallmark of Pascal is the procedure, which is a subprogram that can be defined within a program. Procedures make it possible to organize programs in terms of the subtasks needed to solve a problem. We show a sample Pascal program with a procedure in Section 1.2.

1.2 A Sample Pascal Program with a Procedure

A *computer* is a device designed to carry out instructions. A *computer program* is a collection of one or more instructions. A sample Pascal program is given in Figure 1.1. Every Pascal program has two parts: a program heading and a program block:

Features of every Pascal program:

1. Heading, which starts with the word *program* followed by the program name;
2. Block with (optional) declaration part and (required) action part.

For example, the heading in the program in Figure 1.1 has the name **sample** and it also indicates that this program will have output. The program block in

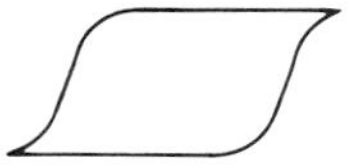

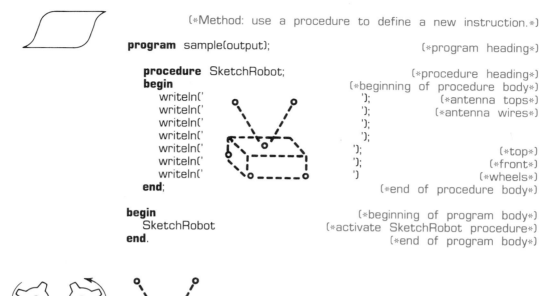

```
        (*Method: use a procedure to define a new instruction.*)
program sample(output);                          (*program heading*)

  procedure SketchRobot;                       (*procedure heading*)
  begin                               (*beginning of procedure body*)
    writeln('                 ');                    (*antenna tops*)
    writeln('                 ');                   (*antenna wires*)
    writeln('                 ');
    writeln('                 ');
    writeln('                 ');                             (*top*)
    writeln('                 ');                           (*front*)
    writeln('                 ')                           (*wheels*)
  end;                                   (*end of procedure body*)

begin                                   (*beginning of program body*)
  SketchRobot                         (*activate SketchRobot procedure*)
end.                                       (*end of program body*)
```

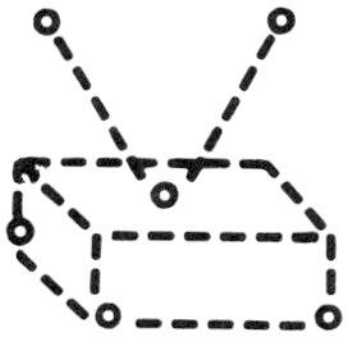

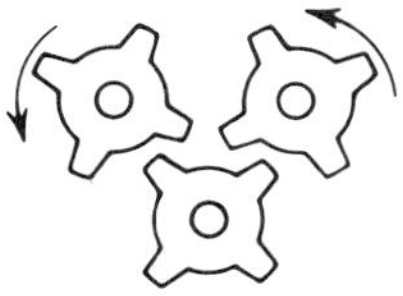

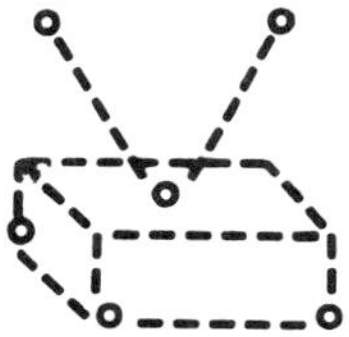

FIGURE 1.1 Sample Pascal source text

Figure 1.1 has two parts:

1. Presentation of the SketchRobot procedure.
2. Action part (in between the words **begin** and **end**) which is called the *program body* and which gives the computer an instruction-SketchRobot.

A *procedure* is a named sequence of instructions. For example, SketchRobot is the name of the sequence of instructions which tells the computer to sketch a picture of a robot. This procedure uses a built-in writeln instruction to "explain" the SketchRobot instruction given in the program body.

> **How a writeln works in Pascal:**
>
> **A writeln tells a machine to print to a screen (or printer) the characters inside the single quotes. Any of the characters you see on your keyboard can be put inside the single quotes for a machine to print out.**

Instructions in a Pascal program are called *statements*. The key idea with Pascal statements is as follows:

> **A Pascal statement tells a machine what to do, what actions to perform.**

Finally, the sample program in Figure 1.1 has an added feature: comments. A *comment* in a Pascal program is any characters enclosed between a left (* and a right *) symbol. Some versions of Pascal like VAX-11 Pascal or UCSD Pascal allow a left { and right } brace to be used to enclose comments. (You will have to check what system your version of Pascal uses.) A comment is used to explain a line of program code.

> **The term *code* refers to the symbols used to represent either data or instructions for a computer.**

An example of Pascal code (the symbols required by Pascal) is shown in Figure 1.1.

In this chapter we look more closely at the organization of a typical computer. This is followed by a look at what are known as compilers (or translators) and at Pascal, which is an example of a programming language. Finally, we look at some problem-solving strategies and a framework which can be used to develop computer programs.

1.3 Computers

A picture of the first electronic, stored-program computer and its designer, John Von Neumann, are shown in Figure 1.2. The Von Neumann machine was called the *Electronic Discrete Variable Automatic Computer* (EDVAC) and was conceptualized in 1946 and turned on for the first time in 1951 at the Aberdeen proving ground. Most computers nowadays employ the Von Neumann machine design principles. Von Neumann's machine was the first one to store instructions and data in the same storage area of the computer. That machine had the basic building blocks shown in Figure 1.3. A keyboard or card reader is an example of an input device. A printer or screen is an example of an output device. The central processing unit (CPU) takes care of the arithmetic and the comparisons that need to be made by a program. The CPU also controls the sequencing of program instructions and the flow of information to and from its storage and input/output devices. The CPU has two basic parts.

FIGURE 1.2
John Von Neumann and the EDVAC computer. Courtesy of Institute for Advanced Study, Princeton, NJ.

Main features of a CPU:

1. **Computation unit.** This unit takes care of the arithmetic and logic operations carried out by the processor.
2. **Control unit.** This unit regulates the operation of the computer. It sends signals to the storage unit when either data or instructions are needed for a program. It tells the input and output units when to transfer information, where the information is stored and where the information should go.

The primary storage unit of a computer is used to store program instructions and data. In addition, there is usually secondary storage connected to the processor. Examples of personal computers with secondary storage units are shown in Figure 1.4. These machines use floppy diskette units to provide needed secondary storage. These units provide inexpensive, low-capacity storage of programs and data used intermittently by a machine. The IBM PC AT shown in Figure 1.4 also has a more costly, high-capacity fixed disk to store programs and data. Both of these auxiliary storage devices rely on a magnetic recording surface to record data taken from primary memory.

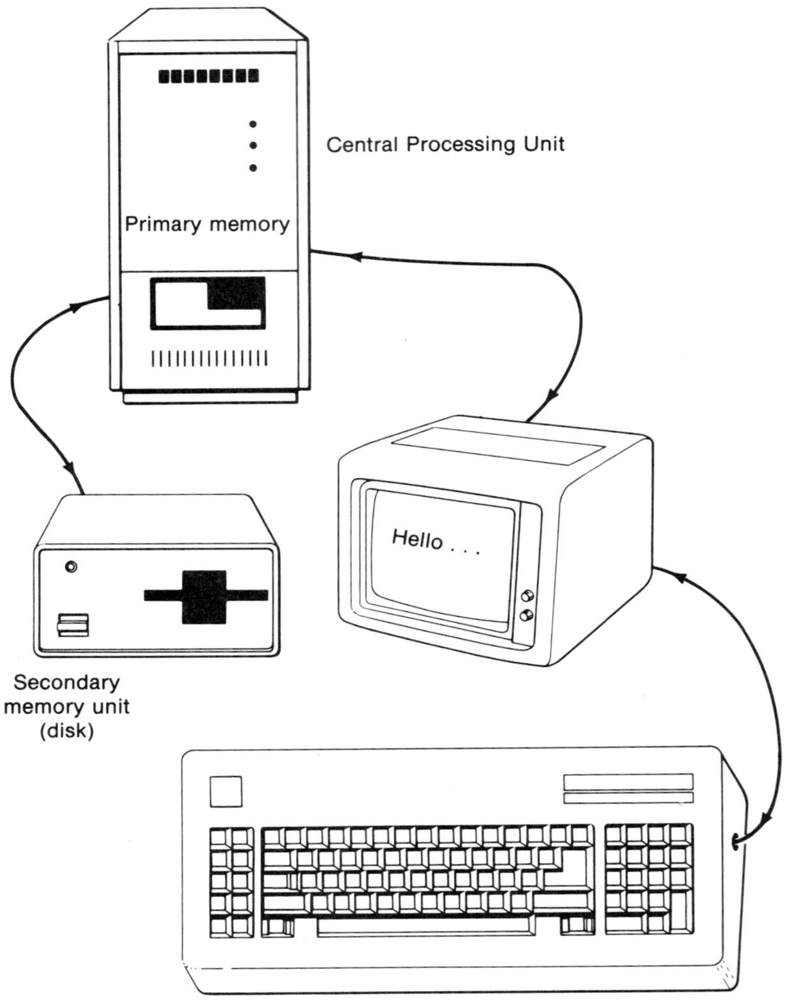

Legend: *Central Processing Unit* (CPU) handles computations, logic operations, and control of the system.

Primary memory provides storage for programs and data being used by the CPU.

Secondary memory provides storage for programs and data not currently being used by the CPU.

Symbol: ——→ (flow of information)

FIGURE 1.3
Building blocks for a computer system Courtesy of Institute for Advanced Study, Princeton, NJ.

FIGURE 1.4

All information inside a computer is stored in what are known as *bit-strings.* A bit-string is just a sequence of 0s and 1s like the following one used on an IBM PC:

Example of a bit-string.

When you hit the return (or enter key) on your Apple IIe or IBM PC, the following two bit-strings will be entered into computer memory:

Bit-String	*Meaning*
0000 1101	Carriage return
0000 1010	Line feed

FIGURE 1.4 (a)
Courtesy of International Business Machines Corporation.

FIGURE 1.4 (b)
Sample computer system. Courtesy of Computerland, St. Cloud, MN.

FIGURE 1.4 (c)
Sample computer system. Courtesy of Public Information Office, St. John's University, MN.

FIGURE 1.4 (d)
Sample computer system. Courtesy of Public Information Office, St. John's University, MN.

A processor always gets the bit-strings it needs from its primary memory. So any information on a secondary storage device must first be moved into primary memory before it can be processed. There is a constant need to move information back and forth between primary and secondary storage. This is done because the primary storage unit (also called *primary memory*) has low-capacity as a rule and is expensive by contrast with the high capacity of less expensive secondary storage devices.

Storage capacity is often measured in multiples of 8 bits called *bytes*. For example, primary memory on an IBM PC AT can have up to 3 million bytes. This same machine can have up to 40 million bytes of fixed disk storage. Typically, a machine like this will have just 512 thousand bytes of main memory and 20 million bytes of fixed disk storage. This means primary storage must be used conservatively and protectively; only absolutely necessary bit-strings are kept in primary memory. Usually this means often no more than three programs are in main memory of a small system at any one time.

1. **Operating system.** A program to control the operation of the machine.

2a. **Editor.** A program used to prepare a program text.

2b. **Compiler.** A program used to translate a symbolic program down to the binary bit-string level of a machine.

3. **User Program.** A program created to tell a machine what actions we want it to perform.

We are constantly using editors and compilers, which we consider next.

1.4 Editors Programming Languages and Compilers

Typically our relation to a computer is through a keyboard. The symbols on a keyboard make up what is known as the *character set* usable on a machine. A program like the one in Figure 1.1 is written entirely with keyboard symbols like those shown in Figure 14(e). The program in Figure 1.1 is an example of what is called a *source text*—just a collection of ordinary keyboard symbols. A source text is made up of symbolic codes taken from a programming language known to a compiler. A *programming language* is a formalism used by us to communicate instructions to a computer.

A text editor like EDLIN on an IBM PC or EDT on a VAX-11 is used to prepare a source text.

> **A *text editor* is a program that makes it possible to compose a source text using keyboard symbols.**

FIGURE 1.4 (e)
Courtesy of International Business Machines Corporation.

An editor will set up a file to save our text. A *file* is an organized collection of elements that can be held either in primary or secondary storage. When we type a keyboard symbol like *b* in the word *begin,* an editor puts a character code corresponding to *b* into our text file. You can think of a text file as a collection of character codes.

Character codes are bit-strings like the following one:

Keyboard Character	*Bit-String (Used by IBM PC)*
b	0110 0010 (in base 2)

This is character code for a *b* on an Apple IIe, IBM PC, or VAX-11, for example. The coding system used by these machines is called *ASCII,* which is an acroynm for American Standard Code for Information Interchange. This code is not a universal one! Different machines use different coding systems for their character sets. For example, on an IBM 360/370, the following code is used for its lower case *b:*

Keyboard Character	*IBM 360/370 Character Code*
b	1000 0010 (in base 2)

This IBM coding system is called *EBCDIC* (Extended Binary Coded Decimal Interchange Code). This system and the ASCII coding system are discussed in more detail in Chapters 2 and 3. Complete ASCII and EBCDIC code tables are also given in Appendix A.

After we have prepared a source text written in a programming language with an editor, a compiler can translate it into machine language. A source text must use the grammar and vocabulary of a programming language so that it can be translated by a compiler.

> **A *compiler* is a program that takes a source text and converts it into machine language.**

A text in machine language form is written entirely in base 2 or binary. This idea is shown graphically in Figure 1.5.

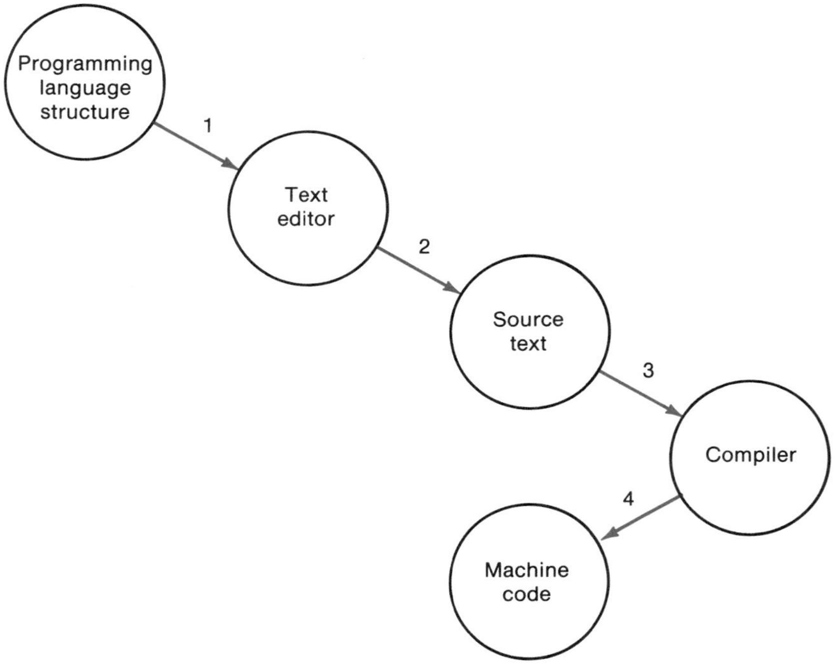

Legend:
Edge 1: input to text editor (programming language structures)
2: output from editor = source text
3: input to compiler = source text
4: output from compiler = machine code

FIGURE 1.5
Steps leading to translated program

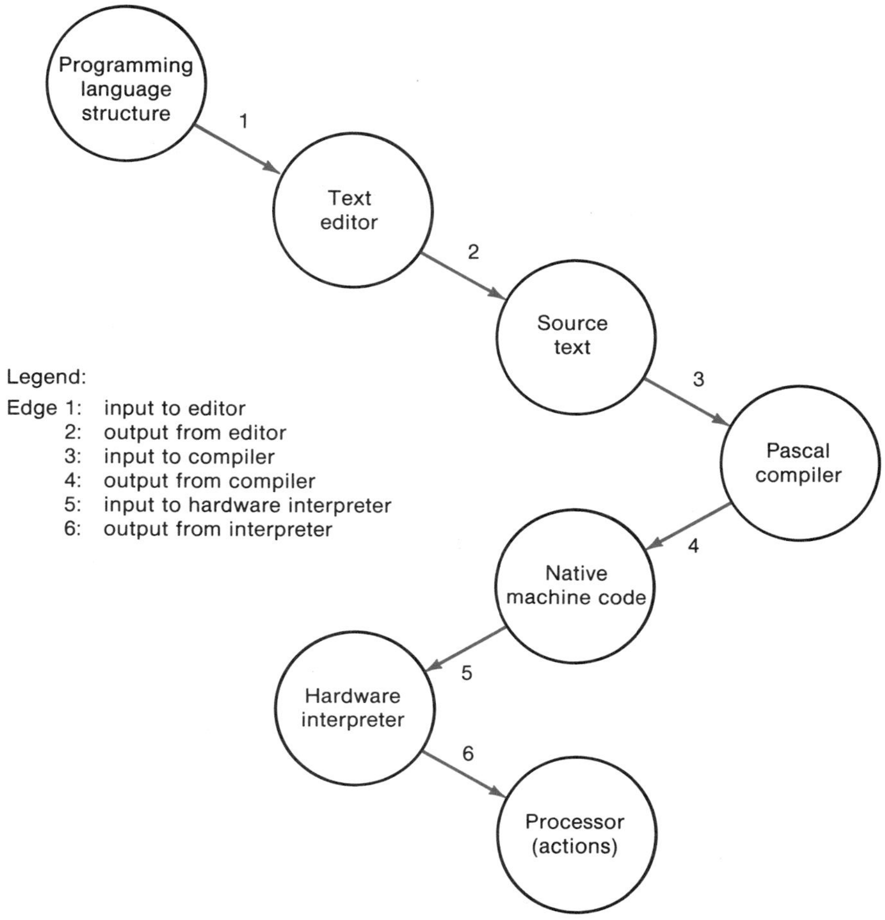

FIGURE 1.6
Compiling Pascal programs on large computer systems

1.5 What is Pascal?

Pascal is an example of a programming language. A *programming language* provides a vehicle that makes it possible to communicate methods of solving problems to a computer. A program written in Pascal must be compiled. The output from a compiler is sent to an interpreter when a program is run. An *interpreter* is also a program. There are two kinds of interpreters, hardware and software. These two interpreters differ in terms of the input they receive. The input to a *hardware interpreter* is a complete machine readable program, which is transformed into machine actions by the interpreter. The input to a *software interpreter* is an intermediate text or just a text prepared with a text editor. A software interpreter translates the input text line by line into machine code, which is run immediately, if possible.

Pascal programs must be compiled before they can be run. On bigger machines, the work of compiling a Pascal source text into a runnable program is shown in Figure 1.6. Pascal works differently on most small machines. That is, the Pascal language on an Apple IIe, for example, does not translate a Pascal source text down to the machine level. Instead, this Pascal translates a source text down to an intermediate level called the *p-code level.* A p-coded text then becomes the input to a software interpreter, which translates the p-code down to the machine level. These steps are summarized in Figure 1.7. Why use p-code? This makes Pascal easier to install on different small machines. To install Pascal on a new computer, it is only necessary to write a new p-code interpreter in terms of the requirements of the new machine. This is easier than building an entirely new Pascal compiler for each new machine. We have Pascal on smaller machines using p-code thanks to work done on UCSD Pascal by Kenneth Bowles in 1978.

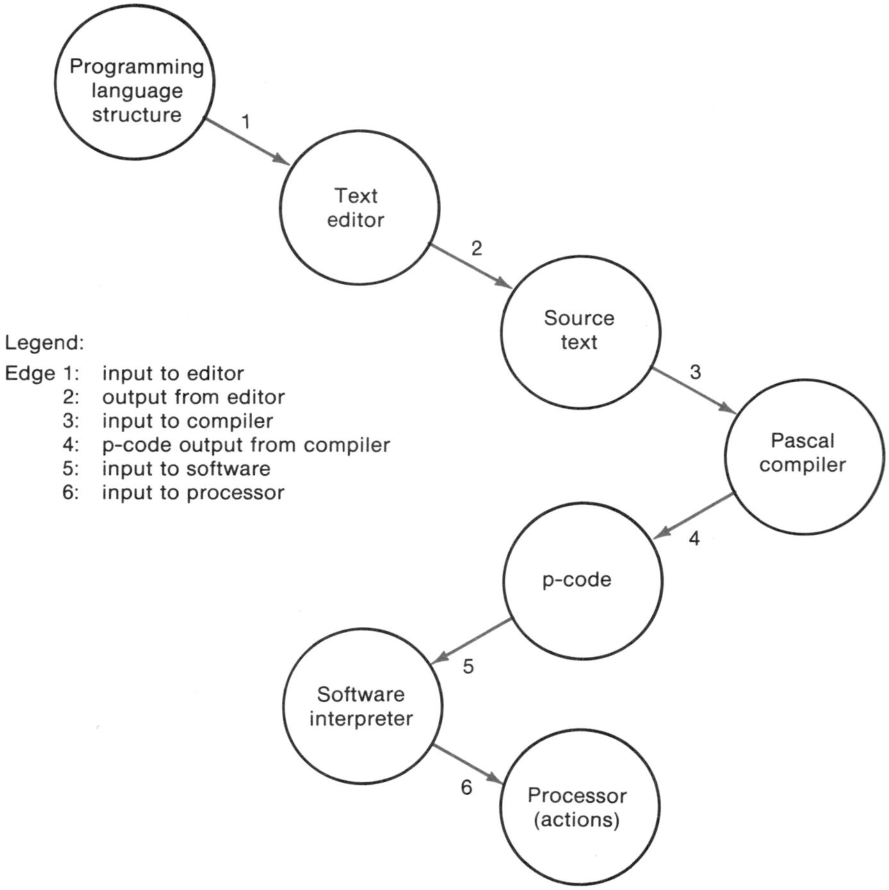

FIGURE 1.7
Compiling Pascal programs on small computer systems

1.6 How to Design Programs

A *computer program* is a set of instructions for actions that a computer is able to perform. Programs represent solutions to problems. An *algorithm* is a finite, step-by-step solution to a problem. Good algorithms have the following features:

1. **Input.** An algorithm should contain a precise description of the data to be used ("three characters" rather than "some characters," for example).
2. **Finite process.** An algorithm should specify a finite number of steps to complete the solution to a problem.
3. **Definite steps.** Each step of an algorithm should be crystal clear; each step should tell exactly what should be done.
4. **Output.** An algorithm should contain a precise description of the result(s) that will be produced.
5. **Effectiveness.** An algorithm must work, be effective, and produce the required result.

A program can embody one or more algorithms. Usually, each individual algorithm is put into a separate procedure in Pascal programs. Before we can write programs, we need to develop some problem-solving strategies. Here is a concise, overall problem-solving strategy suggested by George Polya (1957), which works beautifully.

How to solve it:

1. Understand the problem. Identify the unknowns, the data needed, and the conditions required for a solution. Try making a sketch (do some doodling with your pencil). Rough in a visual interpretation of the pieces of a problem. Separate the parts of a problem—this is a divide-and-conquer approach to getting at a problem. Try "standing above a problem"—get some perspective. Don't worry about the individual steps of the solution, at first.

2. Devise a plan. Find the connections between the unknowns and the data. Try looking at related problems, ones you have already solved. Examine the unknowns. Can you think of problems with similar or the same unknowns?

3. Carry out the plan. In computer science, this means using a text editor to prepare a source text that can be run on a machine.

4. Look back. Test your program! Do the results of your program match your expectations? Try different sets of data. Make sure your algorithm works all the time.

These same steps go into what is commonly known as the program development cycle. This cycle has five steps.

1. **Specificiation.** Specify the problem.
2. **Design.** Design a solution to the problem.
3. **Code.** Express the steps of your solution in code.
4. **Test.** Check your program for accuracy.
5. **Document.** Explain your program.

It is helpful to take the time to examine closely each of these steps. Even if these steps are familiar, it is probably a good idea to look at the following sections for alternative ways to carry out these steps.

1.6.1 Design Stage: Problem-Solving Strategies

Everybody who solves a problem is an inventor. Polya (1957) points out that it is sometimes easier to solve a more difficult problem rather than a simpler one that is part of the more difficult one. This is what Polya calls the *inventor's paradox.*

Inventor's paradox:

Sometimes a larger problem is easier to solve than a simpler one. The more ambitious plan may have more chance of success.

In other words, striving for an overview, seeing one problem in the context of a larger problem, leads to the solution of the simpler problem. For example, before trying to get a picture of a river flowing down a gorge by standing next to the flowing water, climb to high ground to study the terrain. Again, for example, suppose we want to unravel the following anagram:

he got duglb

An *anagram* is a rearrangement of the parts of an expression to form a new expression. The problem is to discover the original expression by unraveling the anagram. We might first try a brute-force technique to solve this anagram by making random rearrangements of the letters of the anagram. If we are lucky we might spot the original expression quickly. However, in a more complex anagram the brute-force method would be time-consuming and frustrating. Another approach would be to put the letters of the anagram into alphabetical order.

bdegg holtu

This at least shows us more clearly repeating letters. Notice that we separated the alphabetized letters into two smaller (more manageable) groups. This separation of the letter makes them a little easier to examine. Now try tackling this set of letters by looking at the larger problem of endings of common words.

1. *-ion* group (leads nowhere)
2. *-e* group (*the*, possibly)
3. Words ending in *G* (*hug, dug, bug, tug*, for example)
4. Words ending in *ed* (*hugged*, for example)
5. Words ending in *d* (*god, gold*, for example)

To help decide which of these trial words makes sense, it is helpful to get an overview of the problem (find a hilltop!). For example, this anagaram is derived from one Edgar Allen Poe's stories. Which one? In trying to find the original expression, keep in mind that an apostrophe can be used in words like he'll or don't in place of one or more letters. You can check your findings by looking at the solution to this anagram at the end of this chapter.

Implicit in the attempts to solve the above anagram is a divide-and-conquer technique. Not only did we put the letters into alphabetical order, we also separated the ordered letters into two groups. Separating a problem into pieces is helpful. The idea is to separate out tasks (working with the groups of letters instead of all the letters), which can lead to a solution to the problem. These separated tasks can lead to new instructions like SketchRobot, which can be expressed inside procedures. In general, the following rule is helpful in problem-solving:

Divide-and-conquer rule:

Divide a problem into separate tasks, which can lead to procedures.

1.6.2

Other Problem-Solving Strategies

Here are three other commonly used problem-solving strategies.

1. **Solution by analogy.** Try drawing on the features of solutions to previous problems in solving the current problem. For example, the methods you use to solve an anagram might be useful in decoding messages written in secret code (this is called the *cryptography problem*).

2. **Solving a special case of a general problem.** Try developing the solution to a part of a larger problem. For example, suppose we start with the following problem:

Problem: Write a program to print equilateral symbol triangles with varying dimensions and symbols like the following ones:

```
     columns              columns                 columns
row  1   2           row  1   2   3          row  1   2   3   4
 1   !                1   *                   1   a
 2   !   !            2   !   *               2   b   c
                      3   *   !   *           3   d   e   f
                                              4   g   h   i   j
```

You might try tackling a special case for this problem.

Special Case

Problem: Write a program to print a dot triangle with a fixed number of rows and columns like the ffollowing one:

```
      columns
row   1   2   3   4   5
 1    .
 2    .   .
 3    .   .   .
 4    .   .   .   .
 5    .   .   .   .   .
```

3. **Generalizing a specific solution.** Once you have a specific solution, try making the solution the basis for a more general solution. For example, if you develop a method of solving one anagram, it is very likely that the same methods can be made part of the general problem of solving any anagram.

We illustrate the use of these problem-solving techniques in Sections 1.6.3 and 1.6.4.

1.6.3

Pseudocode: Plain Talk About Algorithms

The code used to express the steps of an algorithm does not have to be in computer language like Pascal. In fact, it is better if these steps are first written out in what is known as *pseudocode,* a specialized language that contains a selection of key words imported from English. In effect, pseudocode is plain talk about algorithms.

The pseudocode used in this book has the following features:

1. Action words that specify operations like *assign, add,* and *subtract;*
2. Selection control words: *if, then,* and *else* are used to select an action to be performed based on the evaluation of some condition.

   Example:
   if he likes ice cream
   then give him some
   else give him our limited dessert menu;

   Example:
   if Ravel's Bolero is available
   then play it

   In general, a selection control structure will have the following form:

   if <condition>
   then <action>
   else <action>

3. Block words *begin* and *end* mark the beginning and end of a sequence of instructions.
4. Iteration control words *while, do, repeat,* and *until* are used to limit the repetition of an action.
   4.1. We can specify repetition using a **while** loop like the following one:

   while border pieces of a puzzle remain **do**
   construct the outside edges of the puzzle

   A **while** loop has the following form:

   while <condition> **do** <action>

   Notice that if the **while** condition is false, the action inside a **while** loop never gets performed.
   4.2. We can also set up a **repeat** loop to specify a repetition like the following one:

   repeat
   alphabetize the letters left in anagram;
   construct words with common endings from anagram;
   remove used letters from anagram
   until zero anagram letters remain

In general, a repeat loop has the following form:

repeat <action> **until** <condition>

Unlike a **while** loop, a **repeat**-loop action always gets carried out at least once, since the until condition gets checked after the action is carried out the first time. Also notice that repetition of the repeat action occurs as long as the repeat-loop condition is false. In the above example, we go back a second time and continue working with the anagram as long as there are unused anagram letters.

1.6.4 Example: A Program Written in Pseudocode

When a program is written in pseudocode, it is called an *abstract program*. For example, suppose we want to write a program to print the following triangle:

a
b c
d e f
g h i j
k l mn o

Here is the pseudocode to do this for this specific problem.

```
                    (*input: selected letter and upper limit on number of rows;
                                                      output: letter triangle*)
begin
   initialize letters;                                          (*start with a*)
   initialize RowMax;                                         (*upper limit = 6*)
   assign 1 to row and to column;
   repeat
      repeat
         print letter;
         assign next letter to letter;
         add 1 to column
      until column is greater than row;                          (*inner loop*)
      assign 1 to column;
      move cursor to next line;
      add 1 to row
   until row is greater than RowMax                              (*outer loop*)
end                                            (*algorithm to print letter triangle*)
```

An pseudocoded algorithm is also called an *abstract program*.

> **An *abstract program* is an algorithm written in pseudocode. It is abstract because it is written for no particular machine. An abstract program presents all the steps needed to solve a problem.**

You might wonder how to generalize the abstract program to print a letter triangle. This is an instance where we want to use the solution to a specific problem to build the solution to a more general problem. What changes need to be made to this program so that the following things will be possible?

1. Print more than six rows (try 20 rows, for example).
2. Repeat the lower case letters over again starting at *a* after each occurrence of a lower case *z*.

We can add these new features to the letter-triangle program by using an if statement inside the inner repeat loop. This if statement can be used to check the letter variable after each time a letter is printed. The inner repeat loop will have the following form:

```
repeat                                          (*inner repeat loop*)
   print letter;
   if letter equals 'z' then
      assign 'a' to letter
   else
      assign next letter to letter;
   add 1 to column
until column is greater than row;
```

This change in the letter-triangle program will allow RowMax to be as large as you wish. In Chapter 2 we will return to this letter-triangle problem. What we have done to print letter triangles is analogous to what we will need to do to print triangles built with numbers instead of letters. Again using the solution-by-analogy technique, we can use the print-letter algorithm to show how to construct symbol triangles. These symbol triangles can be filled with any of the characters you see on the keyboard of your terminal or microcomputer.

Pseudocode frees us from the restrictions of a particular programming language. An abstract program is easily coded in more than one programming language. The programming language we might want to use remains hidden. In addition to this, an abstract program is written for humans, not machines. It is descriptive. It makes it easier to express the algorithm in a specific programming language like Pascal after an attempt has been made to write the algorithm in pseudocode.

1.7 Three Ways to Verify Program Correctness

There are three common methods used to verify the correctness of a program:

1. **Use and check assertions.** An assertion is a claim about a result that can be expected from a part of a program. It is important to look for relations that never change in a program. Claims about program relationships that never change are called *invariant assertions.* These asser-

tions should be checked after a program is run. This calls for lots of experimenting and checking the pieces of a program. A good programmer will often spend generous amounts of time tracking down failures to produce results which match assertions that have been made.

2. **Use test data.** This gets into a touchy area, since most programs will fail if the wrong set of test data is fed to them. The goal is to create a program that runs for all sets of test data. You can expect to spend lots of time trying out various test data. You should also call attention to any restrictions on the data to be used in a program.

3. **Walk-through method.** Step through a program by hand, and use print instructions to show what the parts of your program in fact do. It is commonplace to believe a program does one thing, while in reality it does another. Make the parts of your program talk, when you are not sure what is happening.

1.7.1 Invariant Assertions

It is helpful to look for relations in a program that do not vary. Then try to predict results that should be obtained every time your program is run. These predictions are known as *invariant assertions.* For example, in the abstract program given earlier to print a letter triangle, we can make the following assertions:

1. **Assertion.** This program always prints a letter triangle with at least one letter. This happens because repeat loops are used—the condition

   column is greater than row

   gets checked the first time, *after* the first letter is printed.

2. **Assertion.** In the original program, the following relation must hold true, otherwise the program will crash:

   $$0 <= \text{RowMax} <= 6$$

   If RowMax is greater than 6, then we will run out of *next* letter values. For example, if RowMax is given a value of 7, here is what happens.

```
a
b c
d e f
g h i j
k l mn o
p q r s t u
v w x y z ? ? <- - - - - - - - - - -now  what?
```

   If RowMax is less than zero, then the letter triangle will be limited to printing a single letter, since the value of row starts with 1.

Again, for example, suppose we want to print a row of stars like the following one:

****

The idea is to write an abstract that will print a star row with varying lengths, depending on the star count we specify. Here is an abstract program to do this.

```
                                             (*input: value of count;
                                          output: printed row of stars*)
begin
   initialize count;
   while (count <= 50) and (count > 5) do begin
      print a star;
      subtract 1 from count
      end                                              (*while block*)
end                                  (*algorithm to print row of stars*)
```

We can make the following invariant assertions about this block:

1. **Assertion.** At most 45 stars get printed, if the count is an integer between 6 and 50.
2. **Assertion.** No stars get printed, if count <= 5 or if count > 50.

Notice that you can verify the first assertion by varying the inequalities in the while condition. We know the following things:

$5 < \text{count} <= 50$ must hold true to allow any output

which is another way of saying

$5 - 5 < \text{count} - 5 <= 50 - 5$

or

$0 < \text{count} - 5 <= 45$

This says, for example, that if count = 6, then one star will be printed. What value of count produces the largest number of stars?

Invariant assertions are useful tools. They not only give us claims to check for correctness when a program is run, they also help produce meaningful test data to use. Using invariant assertions, we are forced to look for extreme values that satisfy our assertions. For example, count = 6 is the minimum value to make the above abstract program produce something. In the above assertion, we also need to look for the largest value of count that will make this program print the largest number of stars. This is left for an exercise.

1.7.2 Using Test Data

Test data give us a way to check the correctness of our programs. The trick is to look for test data that will push a program to its outer limits. In other words, extreme values are helpful. For example, we can use the following test data in the abstract program in Section 1.7.1:

Test Data	*Expected Results*
Count = 5	Nothing gets printed
Count = 6	1 star gets printed
Count = ?	45 stars get printed
Count = 95	Nothing gets printed

1.7.3 *Using Print Statements to Trace the Actions in a Program*

Inserting print statements into program sections helps trace what happens when the program is run. For example, we can modify the abstract program to print stars as follows:

```
                                          (*input: value of count;
                                       output: count, row of stars*)
begin
   initialize count;
   while (count <= 50) and (count > 5) do begin
      print a star;
      subtract 1 from count;
      print count                           (*display value of count*)
      end                                                   (*while*)
end.                                 (*revised star-printer algorithm*)
```

This gives us a way to see what the program is doing. This also gives us a way to track down our logic errors—the program may be doing one thing, while we think it is doing something entirely different.

> **Rule of thumb with walk-through method:**
>
> **When you are in doubt about what a program is doing, insert one or more print statements to trace what a program is doing, especially the changes made by a computer in the values of program variables.**

1.8

Three Types of Programming Errors

There are three types of programming errors:

1. **Syntax errors.** The syntax of a programming language concerns the legal arrangements of the symbols and words of a language. These legal arrangements are spelled out by the grammatical rules of a language.

2. **Run-time errors.** Run-time errors occur when we ask a computer to do the impossible. Our syntax might be fine but we tell a computer to do something it cannot do. For example, we might tell a computer to use a number that is too big or too small.

3. **Logic errors.** Logic errors result from either a faulty implementation of an algorithm (this is usually the case) or a faulty algorithm (steps will be missing, data will be used incorrectly, and so on).

1.8.1

Syntax Errors

Syntax errors result from not following the rules of a programming language. This can mean misspellings like

be**ing** instead of be**gin**

or incorrect uses of symbols like

writeln**)**'Whoops!') instead of writeln**(**'Whoops!)
↑
backward parenthesis

Syntax errors can result from missing symbols like the missing semicolon in the following sequences of statements:

```
writeln('Try');
writeln('This')                    (*<--------missing semicolon!*)
writeln('on your machine)
```

Finally, syntax errors can result from incorrect constructions in the statements of a program. For example, here is a program heading that is riddled with syntax errors:

```
NewProgram TryThis[output]:
```

- NewProgram: invalid word-use **program**
- TryThis[: invalid symbol-use (
-]: invalid symbol-use)
- ":": invalid symbol-use ;

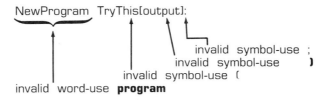

Here are two of the most common syntax errors in Pascal programs.

Three common syntax errors:

1. Missing semicolon needed to separate one statement from the one that follows.
2. Missing end for a sequence of statements that start with a begin.
3. Putting a semicolon in the wrong place.

Unfortunately, one missing semicolon (one syntax error in your eyes) may cause error messages to multiply like rabbits. A missing semicolon forces a compiler to second-guess what is meant by a source text. Separate statements of a source text will be run together by a compiler. Try the following experiment on your computer to see what happens:

Experiment 1

```
program TryThis(output);
begin;                                         (*unwanted semicolon*)
   writeln:('Oh, oh!');                        (*unwanted semicolon*)
   writeln('Try this. . .')                      (*missing semicolon*)
   writeln('And this.')
end.
```

This experiment will give you some early experience with syntax error messages printed by Pascal. As a follow-up to this experiment, try the following corrected program on your system:

Experiment 2

```
program TryThis(output);
begin                                           (*semicolon removed*)
   writeln('Oh, oh!');                          (*semicolon removed*)
   writeln('Try this. . .');                      (*semicolon added*)
   writeln('and this.')
end.
```

So, in trying to find the source of a syntax error, start by checking the source of the error at the beginning of a list of error messages. Here is what this message will look like.

Use ';' to separate statements

Experience is the best teacher in combating syntax errors. A sampler of error messages suggested by the ISO for Pascal is given in Appendix B.

1.8.2

Run-Time Errors

Usually run-time errors are easiest to correct. They usually result from trying to use faulty data. For example, if we tell a computer to compute a fraction that involves the division of a number by 0, then a run-time error will result. A computer will stop processing your program, if you ask a computer to divide a number by 0. You can also cause run-time errors by asking a computer to save too many values—it may run out of storage space.

1.8.3

Logic Errors

Logic errors are the most elusive errors to identify. Practice will help you learn to detect logic errors. Usually it is fairly easy to identify incorrect results produced by a program. The trick is to find the source of a logic error that causes the faulty results. You will probably have to cross-check the steps of your original algorithm against its implementation in your program. All in all, removing logic errors will keep you very busy.

1.9

Stepwise Refinement as a Way to Develop Programs

Taking Polya's idea again, if we start with a more general problem, we can refine the initial solution to a general problem until we reach a level of detail that is acceptable. This is actually not as difficult as it may seem. For example, suppose we want to develop an *expert system,* which is a program capable of playing the role of an expert, fielding questions, evaluating responses made by someone. We can try out this idea by building an expert system to play the role of a doctor capable of evaluating the symptoms of a new patient. This program can be developed with the help of a doctor starting at the most general level (call it level 0) as follows.

```
Level 0:
                                        (*input: patient symptoms;
                                        output: doctor's diagnosis*)
          begin
            build symptoms dictionary
          end;
```

Level 0 describes a very general plan of attack. This plan can be refined on the next level (call it level 1). The idea on the next level is to identify the tasks required to carry out the level 0 plan. Here is a sample level 1 program.

Level 1:

```
                              (*input: patient history, symptoms;
                        output: diagnosis and diagnosis dictionary*)
begin
   repeat
      introduce patient;
      determine symptoms;
      make diagnosis;
      enter diagnosis in dictionary
   until symptoms dictionary is complete
end;
```

The main idea (on level 0) is to build a dictionary. On level 1 we begin getting more specific. We specify the needed input data and expected output from a program. In addition, we list the separate actions that a program will need to perform. In this example, the expert system gets started by repeatedly performing the tasks inside the repeat loop shown in the level 1 program. The level 1 idea can be shown graphically using what is known as a structure chart like the one in Figure 1.8. Each box in the structure chart represents a procedure to be carried out by a machine. The lines connecting the boxes in the structure chart represent control lines (you can imagine a processor transferring control along these lines between the BuildDictionary procedure and the other procedures). This structure chart can be enhanced by indicating the data that are passed between the procedures. For example, we can use the following techniques to show the flow of data:

1. Left arrow (←————————————) to show data coming from a procedure

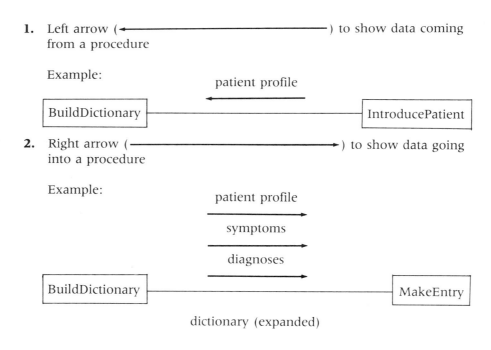

Example:

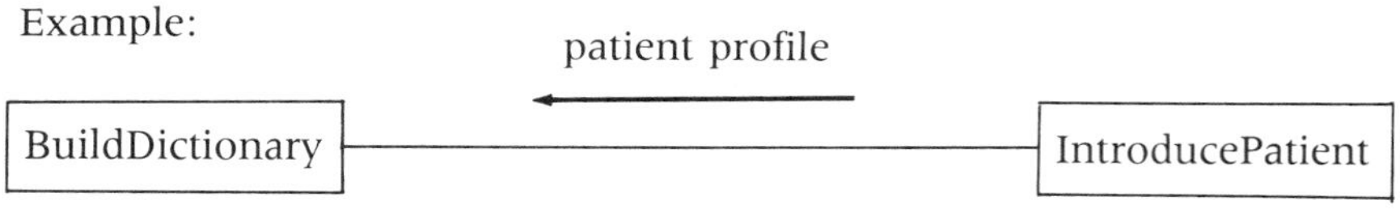

2. Right arrow (————————————→) to show data going into a procedure

Example:

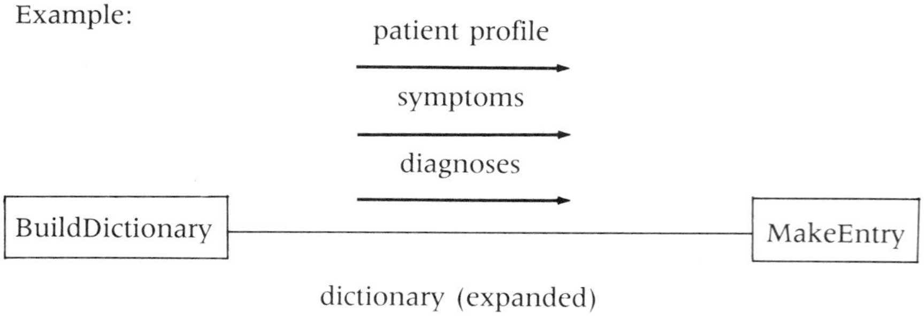

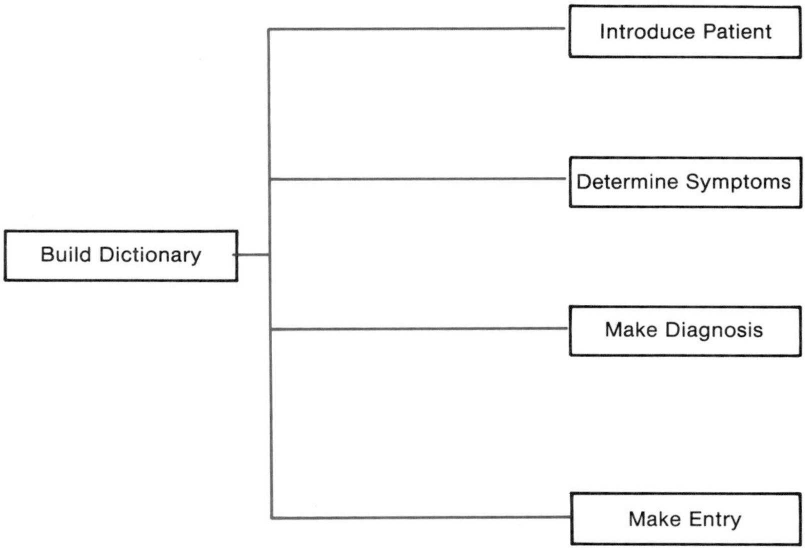

FIGURE 1.8
Structure chart for an expert system

The enhanced structure chart for this program is shown in Figure 1.9. We can refine the level 1 program by specifying what goes on inside each of the level one procedures. This will give us a level 2 program like the following one:

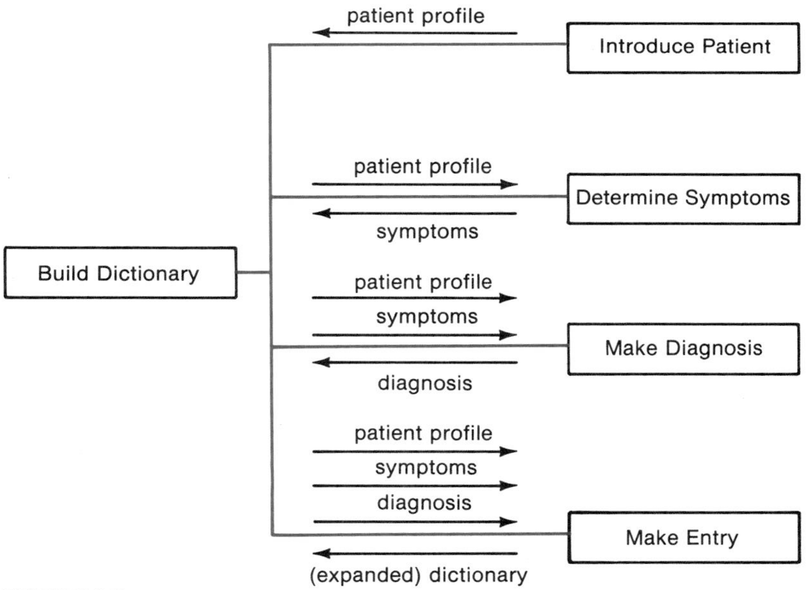

FIGURE 1.9
Structure chart showing input, output, processes

Level 2:

(*input: patient profile items, symptoms, diagnoses;
output: diagnosis dictionary*)

```
        begin
          repeat
            repeat
              read patient profile item;
              save item
            until patient profile is complete;
o i         repeat
              read patient symptom;
u n           save symptom
            until all sysmptoms are obtained;
t n         repeat
              search dictionary for diagnosis with
e e             matching symptom;
              if symptom not found then begin
r r             start new diagnosis;
                add diagnosis to dictionary;
                add preliminary diagnosis to patient profile
l l             end
              else
o o             add preliminary diagnosis to patient profile
            until all symptoms are covered;
o o         repeat
            get patient profile, symptoms;
p p         select most likely diagnosis from list
              of preliminary diagnoses in profile;
  s         make entry in dictionary
            until all diagnoses have been saved
          until dictionary is complete
        end;
```

Notice that this level 2 program still deals with the big picture. There still is no indication of how the until-condition in each of the four repeat loops will be satisfied. In fact, none of the actions inside each of the four repeat loops are detailed. So far, we just have an indication of what needs to be done. We can start fleshing out each of these repeat loops on the next level of refinement.

> **Secret of stepwise refinements:**
>
> **We proceed by stepwise refinement of an ambitious plan. In early refinements, the aim is to isolate the separate tasks that can be with separate procedures. The details of each procedure are left for later refinements.**

Why use stepwise refinements? They help us establish a context for procedures we will develop. They provide frameworks for programs.

1.10 Summary

Computers are devices designed to carry out our instructions. Usually our instructions are written in symbolic form using combinations of keyboard characters using the formalism provided by a programming language. This means that instructions written in symbolic form like

PrintList

must be translated into a machine-readable form. An instruction is in machine-readable form, if it is written as a bit-string. Text editors are used to set the initial source text we want to have translated. Compilers are translators. The input to a compiler is a source text prepared using a text editor. A *compiler* translates a source text into bit-strings, which tell a machine which actions to perform, which data to use.

On smaller computers, a Pascal compiler is used to translate source texts into an intermediate language called *p-code*. The p-code is still not on the machine level. A p-code text is the input to a software interpreter, which is also a translator. A software interpreter will translate the p-code into a machine readable form to tell a machine what to do.

Computer programs are sets of instructions. There is both a science and an art to developing noteworthy programs. We have started looking at the science of programming. There are identifiable milestones in the development of every program. For example, we can isolate the stages in the program development cycle.

1. Specify the problem.
2. Design an algorithm to solve the problem.
3. Code the algorithm.
4. Test the code.
5. Document your code.

The art of programming is something more elusive. This develops with practice. This has to do with programming style, the procedures we use, the methods we use in commenting a program, and so on.

It is a good idea to use ordinary language to rough in the general conceptions for an algorithm. This leads to abstract programs. Abstract programs are pseudocoded algorithms.

1.11 Keywords Review

Keywords	*Related Ideas*
abstract program	program written in pseudocode
algorithm	finite, step-by-step method of solving a problem

algorithm features	characteristics found in working algorithms
input	precise description of data needed
definite	precise description of actions to be performed (the process to use)
finite	algorithm produces results after a finite number of steps
output	precise description of results
effective	the algorithm works!
character set	keyboard characters usable on a computer
code	binary representation of keyboard symbols
ASCII	American Standard Code for Information Interchange
EBCDIC	Extended Binary Coded Decimal Interchange Code
compiler	a program used translate a source text into binary form
computer	device designed to carry out our instructions
processor	arithmetic and logic unit plus memory
program	set of instructions for computer
primary memory	storage inside a processor
secondary memory	storage outside a processor
interpreter	program that translates code into machine actions
hardware	translates machine code into machine actions
software	translates source text or intermediate text line by line into machine actions
problem-solving strategy	an approach to take in solving a problem
divide and conquer	subdivide a problem into manageable parts
inventor's paradox	the more ambitious plan may have more chance of success (Polya, 1957)
solution by analogy	the solution to one problem may have features that will be helpful in solving other problems
solve special case	try solving a special case (with fixed values) before trying to solve the solution to a problem for all possible values
specific to general	use your experience with a specific problem (this anagram, for example) to generalize how the problem can be solved in general (all anagrams, for example)
stepwise refinement	get a global view of what is needed to solve a problem, instead of worrying about the details (also called the top-down approach), then proceed step-by-step to reach a level of detail which is useful and desirable
p code	intermediate code used with Pascal on small computers
procedure	tells a machine how to carry out a task
body	specifies one or more actions for a machine to perform
heading	specifies procedure name, optional list of parameters, with trailing semicolon
program	set of instructions for computer
body	specifies one or more actions for a machine to perform
correctness tests	ways to check correctness of program
assertions	claims about relations and/or results produced by a program
test data	data used to measure correctness of output
walk-through method	tracing through parts of a program, following the logic and checking the output of the parts of a program with print statements
development cycle	steps used to develop a program

specify	give details of problem, the needed data, and required output
design	plan a solution
code	express solution in a source text
test	compile, run, and check program
document	explain your program
errors	mistakes in design or in coding
syntax	violations of compiler rules
run-time	impossible requests in running program
logic	faulty design or rendition of algorithm
heading	specifies program name, optional list of files to be used, and required, trailing semicolon
programming language	a formalism used to communicate algorithms to a computer
source text	text prepared by an editor
statement	Pascal term for an instruction for a machine to carry out
structure chart	way of representing processes (inside procedures), input and output to processes, needed to for a solution to a problem
text editor	program used to prepare a source text

1.12 Exercises

1. What is the main difference between a Pascal compiler and a text editor?
2. What things need to be specified in the first step of the program development cycle?
3. The stages in a mystery novel like *The Hound of the Baskervilles,* a Sherlock Holmes's story by Sir Arthur Conan Doyle, parallel the stages in the program development cycle. Describe them.
4. A Pascal block that specifies a single action has three parts. What are they?
5. What symbol marks the end of a program block?
6. What is the last symbol in every Pascal procedure?
7. What is the purpose of a Pascal procedure?
8. In Pascal, what is an instruction called?
9. Using the built-in writeln procedure, give a complete Pascal source text to print your name.
10. Using a new procedure and the built-in writeln procedure in Pascal, define the instruction TellMyStory, which tells a machine to print a 20-line story of your life (prints your autobiography).
11. Write a Pascal program to implement the TellMyStory instruction defined in exercise 10.
12. Using a comment, what would be a good way to separate one procedure from

another in a Pascal source text with two or more procedures? Illustrate your answer with the outline of a source text.

13. Using stepwise refinements, develop an abstract expert systems program that could be used by an airline to handle airline reservations. The program will perform the functions normally handled by an airline ticket agent. To do this, start with the big picture and invent your own instructions for each of the major functions you imagine a ticket agent would need to make an airline reservation for you. Do not worry about the details. You should show two levels of refinement beyond the first, very general level (level 0).

14. Give a structure chart for the level 1 refinement of the expert systems program in exercise 13. Be sure to indicate the flow of data to and from each procedure in your chart.

15. Give a structure chart for the level 2 refinement of the expert systems program in exercise 13. Be sure to include the flow of data to and from each procedure.

16. The expert systems program in exercise 13 should have included a PromptPassenger procedure. This would be used to prompt a passenger for information that will be used to make a reservation. Write a Pascal program with a procedure to define the prompt instruction so that it prints out the first question. Do not worry about the rest of the question-answer session handled by the prompt procedure—we will expand this procedure later.

17. Make one or more invariant assertions about each of the following abstract programs:

(a)

```
begin
   assign EPA number to ThreshHold;
   repeat
      assign carbon monoxide meter reading to count;
      if count > ThreshHold then sound alarm
   until 1 < 0                                          (*forever*)
end                                         (*smog control algorithm*)
```

(b)

```
begin
   initialize weight;
   initialize CalorieCount;
   repeat
      if (weight ≥ 120) or (CalorieCount ≥ 300) then begin
         exercise;
         repeat
            subtract 1 from CalorieCount
         until CalorieCount < 300
     end                                           (*then instruction*)
  until weight < 120
end.                                     (*weight watchers algorithm*)
```

1.13 Review Quiz

Determine whether the following are true or false:

1. A compiler is a translator.
2. Compilers are used to build source texts.
3. The built-in Pascal writeln procedure handles input to a processor.
4. p-code is an intermediate code between a source text and machine-executable code.
5. p-code is usually used to implement Pascal compilers on large computers.
6. An interpreter translates a compiled text into code, which allows a program to be run by a processor.
7. The lines of code produced by a compiler are immediately run line by line by a processor.
8. An invariant assertion is a claim about a relation in a program that will vary.
9. Invariant assertions are used to test the correctness of a program.
10. Faulty use of the grammar of a programming language will produce syntax errors when a program is run.

1.14 Readings

Hawsley, C. *Pascal Programming: A Beginner's Guide to Computers and Programming.* New York: Cambridge University Press, 1983. See Chapters 1–4.

Nash, J. C. The Birth of a Computer. *Byte,* 1985, *10,* 177.

Pattis, R. E. *KAREL the ROBOT: A Gentle Introduction to the Art of Programming.* New York: Wiley, 1981. See, especially, Chapters 4 and 5.

Polya, G. *How to Solve It: A New Aspect of Mathematical Method.* Garden City, New York: Doubleday Anchor, 1957. See, especially, Part I, Sections 6–11.

Wirth, N. History and Goals of Modula 2. *Byte,* 1984, *14,* 145–152.

Wirth, N. From Programming Language Design to Computer Construction, *Communications of the Association for Computing Machinery.* New York: ACM, February, 1985, *28,* 2, 160–164.

1.15 Solution to Anagram

The gold bug

CHAPTER 2

BEGINNING PASCAL PROGRAMMING

A program is worthless, unless it exists in some form in which a human can understand it and gain confidence in its design.

Niklaus Wirth, 1983

AIMS

- Present Pascal vocabulary and elementary syntax.
- Introduce the simple data types.
- Distinguish between variables and constants.
- Take another look at the structure of blocks.
- Give more features of writeln statements and introduce the built-in write procedure.
- Show how to format three kinds of output: real values, character strings, and integer values.
- Show how Pascal expressions are evaluated.
- Introduce the assignment statement
- Introduce five elementary control structures: compound statements, **if, for, repeat,** and **while** statements.

- Show the logic of control structures with flowcharts.
- Revisit the Chapter 1 abstract program to print letter triangles.
- Introduce various Pascal experiments.
- Consider ways to design a readable source text.

2.1 Introduction to Tokens, Data Types, and Control Structures

Every programming language has its own vocabulary and its own grammar. The smallest individual units of a programming language are called *tokens.* Pascal has the following four types of tokens:

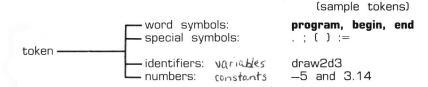

		(sample tokens)
token	word symbols:	**program, begin, end**
	special symbols:	. ; ( ) :=
	identifiers: variables	draw2d3
	numbers: constants	–5 and 3.14

Pascal source texts are written entirely with tokens. Each part of a Pascal program has a required syntax.

← no exceptions

> **The *syntax* of a programming language is a set of rules that specify the sequences of tokens, which can be used to form the parts of a program.**

For example, Pascal identifiers have the following required syntax:

> A Pascal identifier must always begin with a letter, which can be followed by a combination of zero or more letters and/or digits.

This says

draw2d3 has legal Pascal syntax;
Spring.time violates Pascal syntax because of the '.'

Identifiers can be used, for example, to name constants and variables. A *variable* represents a memory location whose content can be changed. By contrast, a *constant* represents a memory location whose content remains fixed (after a constant is defined, its value remains the same).

Before a variable can be used in a Pascal program, it must first be declared. A declaration of a variable presents the following crucial information:

1. Identifier (the name) for a variable
2. Data type of a variable

The *data type* of a variable specifies the kind of values a variable can have and the operations that can be performed on these values. Pascal has four simple data types: char, Boolean, integer, and real. We will see that each *simple data type* is defined by a specific scale of values. The simple data types are introduced in this chapter.

We also introduce some of the control structures available in Pascal.

> **A *control structure* is a programming language facility that can be used to make a computer depart from its normal sequential execution of a program.**

The following control structures are given in this chapter:

1. Sequential control using compound statements
2. Conditional control using an **if** statement
3. Iteration control using a **for**
4. Iteration control using a **repeat**
5. Iteration control using a **while**

Finally, this chapter begins a quest for the elements of programming style, which is concerned with the techniques that can be used to present programs. These techniques can be used to make your programs more readable and useful. For example, we suggest ways to comment a source text to help make it easier to read. We also suggest ways to select meaningful identifiers for the various objects you will be using routinely in your programs.

2.2 Pascal Tokens

Pascal programs are put together using tokens, which are organized as follows:

Type of Token	*How Token Is Used*
Word symbols	Reserved words of Pascal
Special symbols	; (statement separator)
Identifiers	Names of objects
Numbers	Quantities such as 5555

Pascal word symbols fall into the following groups:

Groups of reserved words:

1. Words in every program:	**program, begin, end**
2. Declaration words:	**array, const, file, function label, packed, procedure record, set, type, var**
3. Statement words:	**case, do, downto, else, for goto, if, repeat, then, to until, while, with, of**
4. Operation words:	**and, div, in, mod, not, or**
5. Special value:	**nil**

Special symbols make up the second group of tokens in Pascal.

Special symbol tokens:

Those in every program:	**. (period) ; (semicolon)**
Arithmetic operation symbols	+ − * /
Delimiters:	**, ( ) [ ]** { } **′**
Others:	**ˆ (up hat) :=** = <> < <= >= > **..**

The third group of tokens are identifiers, which are used to name objects in Pascal programs. Naming objects in a Pascal source text is one of the more demanding and important things you will do. An identifier is constructed using letters and digits and has the following form:

identifier = letter followed by zero or more letters and/or digits

For example, *writeln* is an identifier for a built-in procedure. Identifiers are constructed by us to name constants, variables, procedures, and any other objects we want to use in a program. You will get a syntax error if you use a reserved word as an identifier. For example, the following procedure heading is illegal:

```
procedure record;                    (*'record' is a reserved word*)
```

Numbers make up the final group of Pascal tokens. These include both signed and unsigned numbers like 144, 1.61803, −5, and the following numbers in exponential form: 21*e*+23 (this is shorthand for 21000000000000000000000000).

Pascal syntax can be shown graphically using syntax diagrams that look like the charts found in a railroad switching station.

2.3 Syntax Diagrams: Railroad Charts

Syntax diagrams offer a visual interpretation of language syntax. For example, a syntax diagram for an identifier is given in Figure 2.1. A syntax diagram is always read from left to right. The curved arrows leading from the central arrow (the main track) suggest alternative paths that can be followed to pick up additional parts of the same identifier. These diagrams have the appearance of railroad charts. Using this analogy, you can imagine a language being built up progressively from left to right. This idea is illustrated in Figure 2.2.

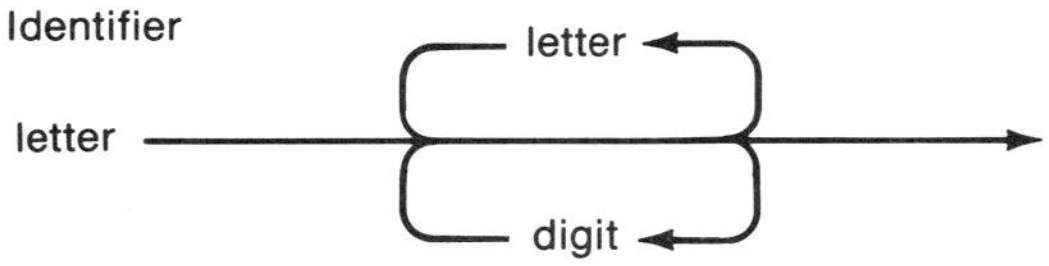

FIGURE 2.1
Syntax for an identifier

2.3.1 A Closer Look at the Syntax for Pascal Identifiers

The syntax for a Pascal identifier has a severe limitation: only letters and digits can be used and a Pascal identifier must always begin with a letter. The syntax diagram for an identifier says nothing about how many letters and digits can be used to set up an identifier. This will vary, depending on the Pascal compiler being used. As a rule only the first 8 to 10 letters and digits are significant, even though most Pascal compilers allow identifiers with up to 50 letters and digits.

You will have to check your compiler to see what the limitations are for identifiers. Notice also that the syntax formula for an identifier says nothing about the types of letters that can be used. Can both upper and lower case letters be used? As a rule, yes. For example, on systems using the ASCII character set, both kinds of letters can be used. This is so because ASCII character set has the following noncontrol symbols:

! " # $ % & ' ( ) * + , - . / 0 1 2 3 4 5 6 7 8
9 : ; < = > ? @ *A B C D E D E F G H I J K L M N*
O P Q R S T U V W X Y Z* [\ ] ^ _ ' *a b c
d e f g h i j k l m n o p q r s t u v w x y z

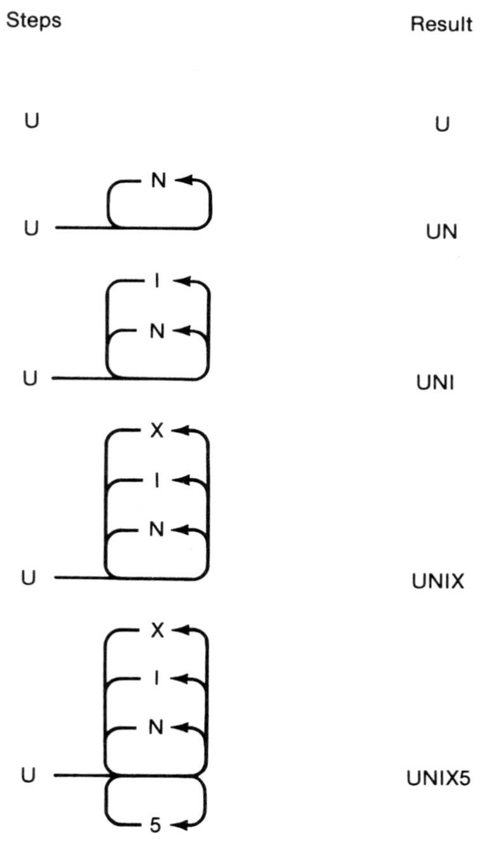

FIGURE 2.2
Constructing an identifier

So the following types of identifiers are possible using ASCII:

Identifier	*Parts*
TRUELOVE	All uppercase letters
truelove	All lowercase letters
TrueLove	Mixture, which is preferred

Using EBCDIC, we can do the same thing (see this character set in Appendix A). It is not always possible to use both upper and lower case letters in identifiers. For example, on CDC 6000 computers systems, only upper case letters are used. Again, you will have to check on the rules for identifiers set up for your local Pascal compiler.

Why bother with syntax diagrams? They show the legal arrangements and legal parts of a language structure. For example, the syntax formula for an identifier tells us that an identifier cannot begin with a digit. So, for example, the following identifiers are illegal (violate standard Pascal syntax):

Illegal Identifier	*Illegal Part(s)*
2010	Leading digit
See_2010	Illegal underline
4Sale	Illegal leading digit
4_Seasons	Illegal leading digit *and* Illegal underline

Some compilers do allow an underline. VAX-11 Pascal V2.0 or Oregon software Pascal for PDP-11 machines or IBM PC Pascal V2.00 permit the use of the underline character in identifiers. For example, Tic_Tac_Toe is a legal identifier with these compilers. However, it is unwise to use this syntax for your identifiers, if it is legal.

> **If you use nonstandard identifiers in your Pascal programs, you will limit the use of your programs to your local compiler. The idea is to invent identifiers that are recognized by *any* Pascal compiler, *not* just your local compiler.**

2.3.2 *A Closer Look at the Syntax for Pascal Numbers*

The fourth class of tokens in Pascal are numbers. We can use a syntax diagram to represent, for example, a signed integer as shown in Figure 2.3. This describes the syntax for number tokens of the form –233, +21, and plain 32766, for example. Signed reals in Pascal can have the following forms:

Signed Real	*Meaning*
1.5	$1 + 0.5 = 1 + \frac{1}{2}$
–2	Negative whole number
+7.2	Positive real
–7.2	Negative real
3*e*+02	3×10^{2}
233*e*+05	233×10^{5}
2.5*e*–07	2.5×10^{-7}
–3.14*e*–02	-3.14×10^{-2}

The *e* format for a signed real gives a compact way to express very large and very small numbers. This is called *exponential notation.* A syntax diagram for a signed real has the form shown in Figure 2.4. You should try constructing syntax diagrams for unsigned numbers. There will be two of them, one for integers and one for reals. These are left as an exercise.

Signed integer

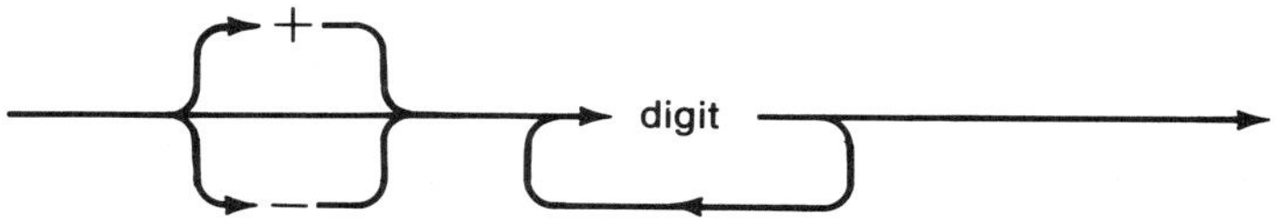

FIGURE 2.3
Syntax for a signed integer

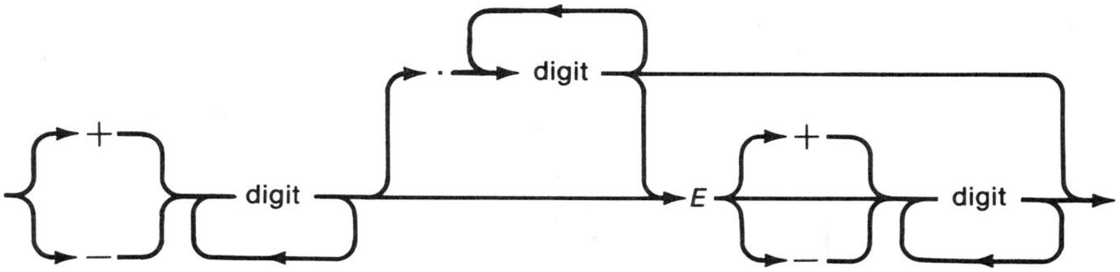

FIGURE 2.4
Syntax for a signed real

2.4 Simple Data Types

Pascal has the following four simple data types:

Simple Types

Ordinal Type	*Scale Used*
Boolean	False, true
Char	Character set of your system
Integer	−maxint, . . . , −1, 0, 1, . . . , maxint.
Nonordinal Type	*Scale Used*
Real	*−xEn* . . . −1.0, 0, 1.0 . . . *xEn*

The ordinal data types each represent scales with elements that can be completely listed. That is, the elements used to define an ordinal type can be enumerated. This is not the case with type real, since the elements of this scale cannot be completely listed.

In this chapter, we are chiefly interested in the elementary operations that can be performed with the simple types. We start with type Boolean.

2.4.1

Type Boolean

If a variable or constant is of type Boolean, then it can have either of two values, the logical truth values represented by the identifiers *true* and *false*. It is also possible to set up an expression which is either true or false.

> **An *expression* represents a value. A Boolean expression, for example, represents either a true or false value.**

For example Boolean expressions can be set up in the following ways:

1. variable logical operator variable;

2. expression logical operator variable

3. variable logical operator expression

4. variable relational operator variable

5. variable relational operator constant

6. constant relational operator constant

7. constant relational operator variable

The words **and** (conjunction), **or** (disjunction) and **not** (negation) are called the logical operators. The relational operators are the symbols > (greater than), >= (greater than or equal), < (less than), <= (less than or equal) and the equality symbol (=). For example, suppose we have use the following variables:

variable	*value*	*variable*	*value*	*variable*	*value*
x	55	y	2	z	99
found	true	complete	false	Big	32000

We can use these variables to construct the following sample Boolean expressions:

operator(s)	*Boolean expression*	*meaning*	*value*
<	x < 5	x less than 5	false
<=	x < y	x less than y	false
<=	x < z	x less than z	true
>	y > 2	y greater than 2	false

>=	y >= 2	y greater than or equal to 2	true
=	z = 5000	z equals 5000	false
not	not complete	negates complete	true
not	not found	negates found	false
and	found and complete	both true	false
or	found or complete	either found or complete is true	true
not, or	not found or complete	either not found or complete is true	false
not, >	(not found) and (Big < 2)	not found is true Big less than 2	false

The variables x, y, *found, complete* must be defined beforehand. We can do this using the **var** token in the following declaration:

```
var
   x, y: integer;               (*x and y are variables which
                                 can have only whole number
                                 values like 5*)
   found, complete: Boolean;    (*found and complete can
                                 have either the value
                                 true or false*)
```

If a variable is of type Boolean, its value can be either true or false. An expression is Boolean if its only values can be either true or false. Boolean expressions are used to control what parts of a program a computer carries out. For example, we can set up the following Pascal **if** statement:

if found **or** complete **then** writeln('Listen to Springsteen!')

which reads as follows:

"if the expression 'found **or** complete' is true, then perform the **then** statement"

When will the expression 'found **or** complete' be true? The evaluation of this expression by a computer will depend on the use of a truth table. Here is a composite truth table which will be used by your computer to evaluate Boolean expressions (p and q are expressions in the following table):

p	*q*	*p* **and** *q*	*p* **or** *q*	**not** *p*	**not** *q*
true	true	true	true	false	false
true	false	false	true	false	true
false	true	false	true	true	false
false	false	false	false	true	true

Using this truth table, you can interpret the expression *'p* **or** *q'* as follows:

> "if either *p* or *q* is true or both p and q are true, then the expression *'p* **or** *q'* is true."

Try using this table yourself to evaluate the sample Boolean expressions in the table at the beginning of this section.

2.4.2 Type Char

The scale used to define type char will vary, depending on the computer system being used. There is an ISO character set that has 128 characters. The first 33 characters in this ISO table are for control characters. The remaining 95 of the ISO characters are the visible keyboard characters. The most widely used version of the ISO character scale is the ASCII table. This is the one used in this text. The visible ASCII characters were given earlier and the entire ASCII table is given in Appendix A.

If a variable or constant or an expression is of type char, then its value is limited to a *single* character from the char scale. For example, if *letter* is a variable of type char, then we can use this variable in the following assignments:

```
letter := '!';                  (*assign ! to letter*)
letter := '5';            (*assign digit 5 to letter*)
letter := 'k';                  (*assign k to letter*)
```

In Pascal, there are four built-in functions that can be used to inspect the character scale used on your computer. In general, a function is a subprogram that returns a single value. Here are the four built-in functions:

Function	*Argument*	*Meaning*	*Example*
pred(*x*)	*x* = character	Predecessor of *x*	pred(*'c'*) is *'b'*
succ(*x*)	*x* = character	Successor of *x*	succ(*'c'*) is *'d'*
chr(*x*)	*x* = integer	Character whose code is *x*	chr(7) gives bell sound
ord(*x*)	*x* = character	Code for *x*	chr(*'c'*) is 99 (ASCII)

Except for the chr function, the argument *x* for each of these functions is type char.

2.4.3 Type Integer

The size of the scale for type integer will vary, depending on the computer system being used. This scale is a subset of the whole numbers. The ends of this scale can be determined by examining the values of the built-in constant identifier *maxint*. That is, type integer is defined in terms of the following scale:

–maxint, . . . , –1, 0 , 1, . . . , maxint

On an IBM PC, for example, maxint equals $2^{15} - 1$ or 32767, whereas on a VAX-11, maxint equals $2^{31} - 1$ or 2,147,483,647.

There is a set of arithmetic operators used with operands of type integer. An *operator* tells a machine to perform a specific operation. An *operand* is a value to be operated on. The integer arithmetic operators are

Arithmetic Operator	*Meaning*	*Sample Usage*
+	Addition	32766 + 1 = 32767
–	Subtraction	maxint – maxint = 0
*	Times	2 * 233 = 266
div	**div**	11 **div** 5 = 2 (quotient)
mod	**mod**	11 **mod** 5 = 1 (remainder)

The *div* operator uses only type integer operands and it always produces the quotient after division of the left operand by the right operand. The *mod* operator also is limited to type integer operands and always produces the remainder after division of the left operand by the right operand. Notice that in both cases the result is always an integer.

2.4.4 Type Real

The scale for type real will vary, depending on the computer being used. This scale is a subset of the real numbers. A constant of type real is written with a decimal point and a possible decimal scale factor. A *decimal scale factor* consists of the letter *e* (or *E*, usually) followed by an integer. For example, the following constant are type real:

233.0 –2.71828 7*e*–09 2.37*e*+32

The following arithmetic operators that can be used with reals:

Arithmetic Operator	*Meaning*	*Sample Operations*
+	Addition	233 + 5.2 = 238.2
–	Subtraction	233.1 – 0.2 = 232.9
*	Times	5 * 11.1 = 55.5
/	Division	(2.33*e*+02)/5 = 4.66*e*+01

Notice that type integer operands can be used to produce a result which is type real. With the arithmetic operators, if one of the operands used is type real, then the result will always be type real. With the division operator (/), both operands can be type integer. Pascal will convert the result to a type real value. It does this by internally changing the integer operands used to type real and then the processor produces a result that is type real. Knowing this, try making a table of all possible ways to have operands with these arithmetic operators and still produce a real result. This is left as an exercise.

2.4.5 *Formatted Real Values*

Reals are always stored inside a computer using a decimal scale factor. So when reals are printed out in Pascal, they normally will be printed with a decimal scale factor. It is possible to force reals to be printed without a decimal scale factor. This is called *formatted real output,* which is used with one of the built-in output procedures. For now, we will illustrate this idea using writeln statements. A real value can be formatted in the following way:

Formatted real value:

Real value : total width : fraction digits

total width — **total number of columns (not digits) used in printing real value**

fraction digits — **number of digits used by fraction**

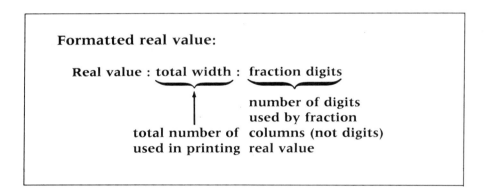

A formatted real always has two format fields.

1. Total-width field is an integer used to specify the columns to be used to print the real value (as a rule, this format field should allow a column for the sign on the number and for the decimal point).
2. Fraction-digits field is an integer used to specify the number of digits in the fraction part of the number.

Notice that each format field must be type integer. Here are some examples of formatted reals.

Formatted Real Values

Statement	Printed Result: col 1	2	3	4	5	6	7	8	9	10	11	12
writeln(1/5:10:1);								0	.	2		
writeln(2/3:12:2);									0	.	6	7
writeln(1/2:5:1,5/3:7:2);			0	.	5				1	.	6	7
writeln(43*e*+02:10:0);							4	3	0	0		
writeln(2.7*e*-03:8:~~5~~ 4);			0	.	0	0	2	7				

Notice that the total-width field number specifies the right-most column to be used to print a real value. The last fraction digit will be printed in this right-most column. It is a good idea to get comfortable working with both forms of reals. Try not to be intimidated by the scale factor! When a scale factor is used to represent a real, it is said to be in *floating point form*. The decimal scale factor is handy; it makes is easier to represent very large or very small numbers like the following:

Floating Point Form	Nonfloating Point Form
32*e* + 30	32000000000000000000000000000000
32*e* − 30	0.000000000000000000000000000032

The simple data types can be implemented in Pascal programs using constants and variables.

2.5 Constants and Variables

Constants are defined at the top of the block where they are used. A constant definition specifies the following information:

1. Identifier (or name) of a constant
2. Fixed value given to a constant

The **const** token is to set up the definition of a constant. Some examples of constant defitions are

```
const
  yes = true;                              (*type Boolean constant*)
  aha = '!';                                  (*type char constant*)
  AlmostMaxint = 32766;                    (*type integer constant*)
  e = 2.71828;                                (*type real constant*)
  BigNo = 3e+35;                              (*type real constant*)
```

The syntax for a **const** definition is given in Figure 2.5. Constants should be given suggestive names to make their purpose in a program more evident. If the identifier for a constant is defined at the top of a program block, it can be used throughout a program.

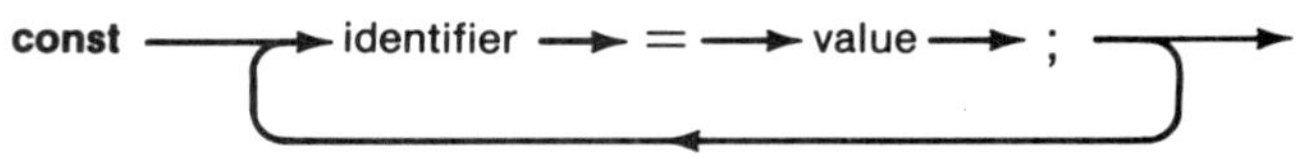

FIGURE 2.5
Syntax for the definition of a constant

> **Usefulness of constant definitions:**
>
> **It is often convenient to use the same fixed value throughout a program. If a constant definition is used, then the name of the constant can help indicate the purpose of the constant. In addition, it may become necessary to change the value of a constant. If a constant definition is used, then it will merely be necessary to change the definition rather than change the same fixed value everywhere it appears in a source text. In other words, constant definitions help make a source text easier to read and they are timesavers, if a constant must be changed.**

Notice that the equals sign (=) is used to define constants.

Variables are always declared at the top of the block where they are to be used. The **var** token is used to set up the declaration of one or more variables. A declaration of a variable gives the following information:

1. Identifier (or name) of a variable
2. Data type for a variable

Here are some sample variable declarations.

```
var
   found : Boolean;                        (*variable of type Boolean*)
   This, That : integer;                   (*variables of type integer*)
   DeepWell, WindVelocity : real;              (*type real variables*)
   letter, symbol : char;                      (*type char variables*)
```

Notice that each variable has its own data type. For example, the variables *This* and *That* are type integer. This says the values that can be assigned to This or to That must be from the integer scale. In addition, it implicity specifies which operators can be used with these variables. The syntax for a variable declaration is given in Figure 2.6. Notice that unlike a constant definition, a variable declaration does not specify any value for a variable. Instead, a variable declaration sets up the machinery that can be used later to give a variable a value. Also unlike a constant, the value of a variable can be changed. A variable can be given a value using the simplest of the Pascal statements, the assignment statement.

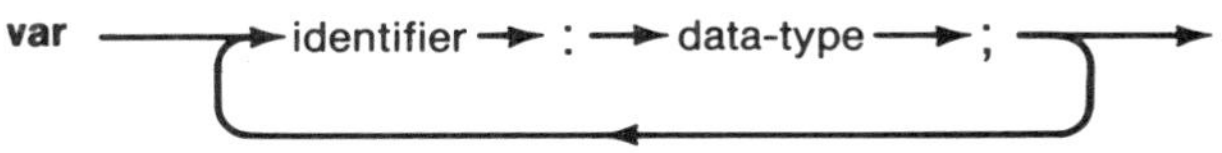

FIGURE 2.6
Syntax for the declaration of a variable

2.6 Assignment Statement

Statement specify actions for a computer to perform. An assignment statement tells a computer to assign a value to a variable. This is done using the assignment operator (:=). Some examples of assignment statesments are

Statement	*Result*
amps := 2.5	Assign 2.5 (a real value) to amps
total := 7001	Assign 7001 (an integer) to total
symbol := '!'	Assign '!' (a character) to symbol
choice := true	Assign true (Boolean value) to choice

The first assignment is explained graphically in Figure 2.7. In effect, when a machine carries out an assignment statement, it will do the following:

> **An *assignment statement* tells a machine to replace the old value in the storage area identified by the variable to the left of the assignment operator used with the value of the expression to the right of the assignment operator.**

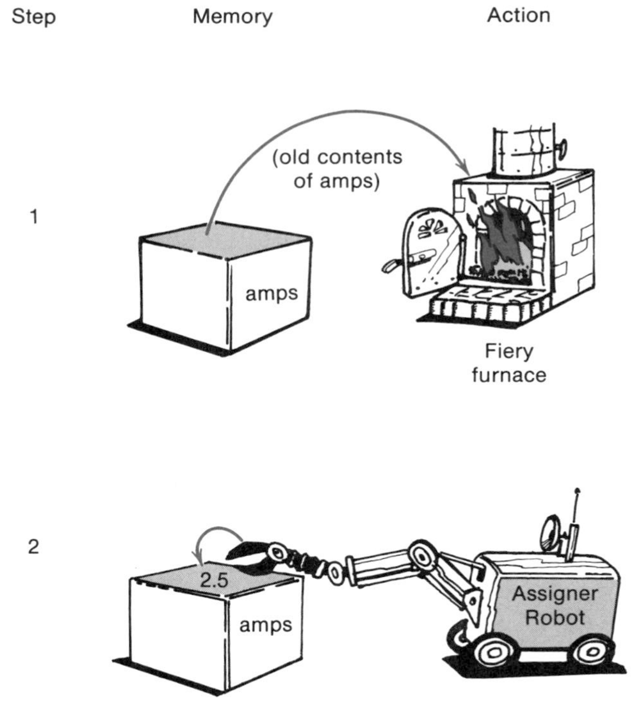

Legend:

1 The old contents of amps perishes (is thrown) into a fiery furnace inside every computer.

2 Assigner robot puts 2.5 into location amps := 2.5

FIGURE 2.7
Graphical interpretation of amps := 2.5

The syntax for an assignment statement is given in Figure 2.8. You might wonder what happens if the same variable is used more than once in a sequence of assignment statements. For example, what value does the variable amps have as a result of the following three statements?

```
amps := 7.56;              (*assign 7.56 to amps*)
amps := 3 * amps;          (*assign  ?   to amps*)
amps := amps + 5000;       (*assign  ?   to amps*)
```

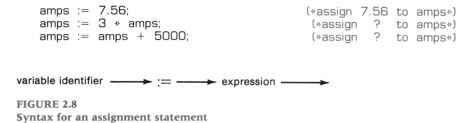

variable identifier ——→ := ——→ expression ——→

FIGURE 2.8
Syntax for an assignment statement

Remember that the old value of a variable gets replaced by the value to the right of the assignment operator. You can analyze these three statements as follows:

Analysis of Assignments

Assignment	*Old Value*	*Assigned Value*	*Result*
amps := 7.56;	Not known	7.56	amps gets 7.56
amps := 3 * amps;	7.56	3 * 7.56	amps gets 22.68
amps := amps + 5000;	22.68	22.68 + 5000	amps gets 5022.68

The third of the above assignment statements will probably seem strangest. It reads as follows:

Replace the old value of amps by the old value of amps plus 5000

In effect, the assignment

amps := amps + 5000

adds 5000 to the old value of amps, and then this result becomes the new value of amps. After the third assignment has been performed by a machine, 5022.68 will be stored in the memory location identified by the variable amps.

What these three assignment statements do to the value of amps can be seen in another way. The variable amps identifies a location in primary memory. Assume, for example that amps represents location 2000. Here is a walk through these assignments and a look at what is happening inside primary memory.

	Computed	**Primary Memory**	
Actions	**Value**	**Address**	**Content**
(before first assignment)		2000	[?!]
amps := 7.56			
1. replace old value		2000	[7.56]
amps := 3 * amps			
2. Compute value	22.68		
3. Replace old value		2000	[22.68]
amps := amps + 5000			
4. Compute value	5022.68		
5. Replace old value		2000	[5022.68]

2.7 Evaluation of an Expression

An *expression* always represents a value. An expression can have various forms. It can either be a constant like 7.56 or be "glued together" with a combination of operators (like + and *) and operands (like amps itself or a constant like 5000). Every assignment statement, for example, has an expression that must be evaluated by a computer before an assignment can be made.

In effect, every assignment statement has an implied instruction that is given to a machine.

> **An *assignment statement* tells a machine to determine the value (or evaluate) of the expression being used in the assignment.**

In an expression without parenthesis, a machine will evaluate an expression from left to right using the following operator precedence rules:

Operator Precedence Rules

Level	*Operator(s)*	*Precedence*
1	**not**	(Highest level)
2	* / **div mod and**	
3	+ − **or**	
4	= <> (not equal) < <= > >= **in** (Set operator)	
5	:=	(Lowest level)

In other words, an assignment statement assigns a value to a variable *last*. (Notice that the assignment operator has lowest precedence.) First the machine must determine the value of the expression in an assignment statement following the above precedence rules. Some examples of expressions and their evaluations are

25 + 3 * 2	becomes 25 + 6	becomes 31 (final value)
25 * 3 * 2	becomes 75 * 2	becomes 150 (final value)
25 + 3 **div** 2	becomes 25 + 1	becomes 26 (final value)
25 **div** 3 **mod** 2	becomes 8 **mod** 2	becomes 0 (final value)
25 **mod** 3 **div** 2	becomes 1 **div** 2	becomes 0 (final value)
25 **mod** 3 + 5 **mod** 2	becomes 1 + 5 **mod** 2, which then becomes 1 + 1, which then becomes 2 (final value)	

You can change the way a machine evaluates an expression by using parentheses. The parts of an expression inside parenthese will always be evaluated first by a machine, starting with the expression inside the innermost pair of parentheses. Here are some rewrites of some of the above expressions.

```
(25 + 3) * 2                becomes 28 * 2 becomes 56 (final value)
25 + (3 * 2)                becomes 25 * 6 becomes 150 (final value)
25 mod (3 + (5 mod 2))      becomes 25 mod (3 + 1), which then
                            becomes 25 mod 4, which then
                            becomes 1 (final value)
```

The built-in output procedures can be used to print values of variables. This will make it possible for you to trace what a machine does with variables in assignment statements.

2.8 Writeln Revisited and the Built-in Write Procedure

A writeln can be used to print both character strings (characters inside single quotes like those in Figure 1.1) and numbers. A writeln can also be used to move the cursor or printhead to the beginning of the next output line. Here are some sample writeln statements.

```
writeln('pi is approximately equal to', 3.14);          (*mixed output*)
writeln('pi is approximately equal to', pi);            (*mixed output*)
writeln(x, '+', y, ' = ', x + y);                       (*mixed output*)
writeln('Aha!');                                        (*string by itself*)
writeln(25, 32.7);                                      (*constants by themselves*)
writeln(pi, This, That);                                (*variables by themselves*)
writeln;                                                (*sends cursor to next line*)
```

The last sample statement suggests a powerful feature of this built-in procedure.

Special feature of a writeln statement:

A writeln by itself can be used to insert blank lines into your output. In other words, a writeln by itself produces white space on your printed page, which can make it more readable. When a writeln contains an output list, it always moves the cursor or printhead to the beginning of the next line after the specified values have been printed.

Notice that a writeln statement can also contain a mixture of items in its output list. For example, it can have character strings and constants (first example), strings and variables (second and third examples), character strings by themselves (fourth example), constants by themselves (fifth example), or variables by themselves (sixth example). Finally, notice that expressions requiring evaluation (arithmetic operations) can be used in a writeln output list (third example). The syntax for a writeln statement is given in Figure 2.9.

Pascal also has a second built-in output procedure, the write procedure. When the write procedure is used in a statement, it always necessary to specify an output list. After the items in the output list for a write statement have been printed, the cursor or printhead is not moved to the beginning of the next line. As a rule, the write procedure is used whenever it is desirable leave the cursor or printhead on the same line. The syntax for a write statement is given in Figure 2.10. Examples of both kinds of output statements are given in Section 2.9.

2.9 More on Formatted Output

The output to a screen or printer produced by either a write or writeln statement can be formatted. *Formatted output* tells a machine which print columns to use when it prints a value. Both character strings like 'Yes' and numbers can be formatted. This is done by using a single format number for the total number of columns to be used in printing a value. The following table gives some sample formatted values:

Statement		**Output**
write('yes!':20);		| | | | · · · | | y | e | s | ! |
	col:	1 2 3 16 17 18 19 20
write('x=':10, 25:10);		| | · · · | x | = | | · · · | 2 | 5 |
	col:	1 9 10 11 18 19 20
writeln('Hello, world!':15);		| | · · · | o | r | l | d | ! | · · · | |
	col:	1 11 12 13 14 15 20
		| |
	col:	1 (final position of cursor)
writeln(233:20);		| | | | · · · | | | 2 | 3 | 3 |
	col:	1 2 3 16 17 18 19 20
		| |
	col:	1 (final position of cursor)

In each of the above examples, the format number specifies the right-most column to use to print a value. The formatted numbers in the above examples are integers. The right-most digit of the integer value 25 in the second example will be printed in column 20. This is so because the right-most character in '*x* = ' (the space) uses column 10, and the formatting of the value

25 starts in column 11.

Notice that each of the items in the output lists in the sample write and writeln statements is either a character string or an integer value. In each of these cases, only a single format number is used. This format number is called the *total-columns* number. This is used to format nonreal values. In general, here is how to format a nonreal value.

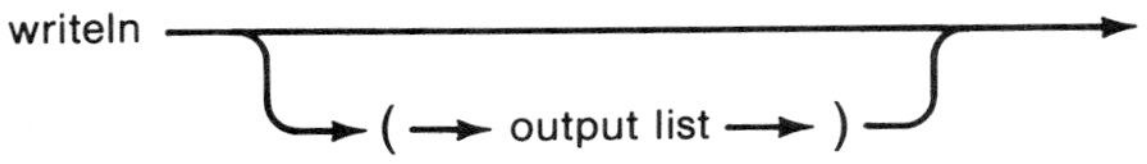

FIGURE 2.9
Syntax for a writeln statement

FIGURE 2.10
Syntax for a write statement

How to format a nonreal value:

nonreal value: total columns

specifies the right-most column to use in printing a nonreal value

Pascal statements are always part of what is known as a *block,* which is explained in Section 2.10.

2.10 Blocks

A block consists of two parts.

1. Optional definition part as well as an optional declaration part
2. Required action part (the body of the block)

So far we have seen examples of two kinds of blocks (a program block and a procedure block given in Figure 1.1). A minimal block will tell a machine to do nothing. For example, the following procedure does this:

```
procedure TryThis;
begin
                                        (*empty statement*)
end;                                             (*TryThis*)
```

The TryThis procedure body does contain a statement (an empty statement). An *empty statement* tells a machine to do nothing. Try the following experiment on your system to see an empty statement in action:

Experiment 1

```
program SampleEmptyStatement;
   procedure TryThis;
   begin
                                        (*empty statement*)
   end;                                          (*TryThis*)
begin
   TryThis;                             (*activate TryThis*)
   writeln('echo. . .')
end.
```

You can think of the TryThis procedure as a shell for a future procedure. You will see later that it is sometimes helpful to have procedure shells included in programs that are being developed. In this example, you should find that

echo. . .

gets printed. This supplies evidence that the TryThis procedure was activated, the machine was told to do nothing, then it returned to the program body to print the message.

The blocks used in Figure 1.1 and in Experiment 1 do not have any definitions or declarations. Here is an example of a program block with constant definitions and variable declarations.

Experiment 2

Line Number	*Program*	
1	**program** TryThis(output);	
2	**const**	(*start program block, here*)
3	pi = 3.1415927;	(*1st constant definition*)
4	*e* = 2.71828;	(*2nd constant definition*)
5	symbol = '!';	(*3rd constant definition*)
6	**var**	

```
7        letter: char;                              (*1st variable declaration*)
8        sum: real;                                 (*2nd variable declaration*)
9     begin                                         (*begin program body*)
10       letter := symbol;                          (*initialize letter variable*)
11       sum := pi + e;                             (*initialize sum variable*)
12       writeln('letter = ':10, letter:10);        (*print value*)
13       writeln; writeln;                          (*skip 2 lines!*)
14       writeln('pi + e = ':10, sum:10:5)          (*print value*)
15    end.
```

The program block in this example starts on line 2 and extends to line 15. Notice that it is necessary to initialize each variable before it is used. A variable is *initialized* when it is given a value. Here is another experiment you can try with this program.

Experiment 3 (with run-time errors)

1. Drop lines 10 and 11.
2. Compile the program in Experiment 2. (It should compile without any difficulty, if you have no syntax errors.)
3. Try running the program. (This will produce run-time errors because the letter and sum variables are undefined.)

This is a good experiment to try early, since it will give you some experience with run-time error messages. Here is another experiment you might want to try with this sample program.

Experiment 4

1. After you have compiled and run the original program in Experiment 2, then use your editor to change the values assigned to the constants pi and *e*. Try using

```
const
   pi  =  3.1;                                   (*new definition*)
   e   =  2.7182818;                             (*new definition*)
```

2. Recompile the source text with the new constants.
3. Run the new program to see what changes, if any, there are in the output.

It is just as easy to set up constant definitions and variable declarations inside a procedure block. Here is another experiment for you to try.

Experiment 5

Line Number — *Program*

```
1    program NowTryThis(output);
2       procedure RunExperiment;
3       const                              (*begin procedure block, here*)
4          symbol = 't';
5       var
6          ThisCharacter : char;
7       begin
8          ThisCharacter := symbol;                  (*initialize variable*)
9          write('The successor of', ThisCharacter:5);
10         write(succ(ThisCharacter):5)               (*print successor*)
11      end;                                          (*RunExperiment*)
12   begin
13      RunExperiment                        (*activate RunExperiment*)
14   end.
```

In this example, the RunExperiment procedure block starts on line 3 and extends to line 11. This program will give you some experience using the built-in successor function. Try the following experiment with this program:

Experiment 6

1. After compiling and running the program in Experiment 5 with the RunExperiment procedure, then use your editor to change the value of the symbol constant. Try, for example, the following definition:

```
const
   symbol = 'z';                                      (*new definition*)
```

2. Compile and run the new program.

Here is another experiment you can try with this program.

Experiment 7

Use your editor to add the following lines to the RunExperiment procedure in Experiment 5, starting with line 11.

Line	*Modified Lines of Program*
11	`writeln(succ(succ(ThisCharacter)):10);`
12	`writeln(succ(succ(succ(ThisCharacter))):15);`
13	`writeln(succ(succ(succ(succ(ThisCharacter)))):20);`
14	`writeln; writeln;                    (*skip 2 lines*)`
15	`writeln(pred(ThisCharacter):10);`
16	`writeln(pred(pred(ThisCharacter)):15);`
17	`writeln(pred(pred(pred(ThisCharacter))):20);`
18	`writeln(pred(pred(pred(pred(ThisCharacter)))):25)`
19	`end;                                  (*RunExperiment*)`
20	`begin`
21	`Run experiment              (*activate RunExperiment*)`
22	`end.`

This new experiment will give you some experience using the various forms of the successor and predecessor functions. The syntax for a Pascal block is given in Figure 2.11. This is a turning point in this chapter. In Sections 2.11 through 2.16, new statements are given that can be used to control what a machine does.

Block

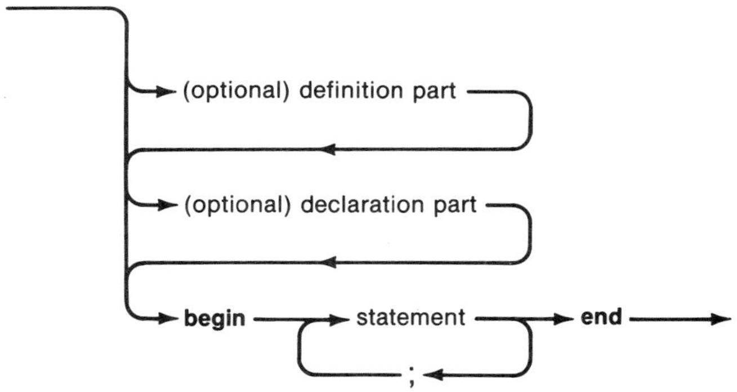

FIGURE 2.11
Syntax for a block

2.11 Sequential Control with Compound Statements

The body of a Pascal block is an example of what is known as a *compound statement.* A compound statement specifies one or more actions for a processor to perform. Here are two more examples.

```
begin
   SketchRobot          (*tells processor to carry out actions
                                    specified by a procedure*)
end.
```

and

```
begin
   count := count + 1;                         (*assignment*)
   writeln('count = ', count)               (*specifies output*)
end.
```

The syntax for a compound statement is given in Figure 2.12. The **begin** and **end** tokens mark the boundaries of the compound statement. Processing of the statements inside these boundaries will continue until the **end** token is reached.

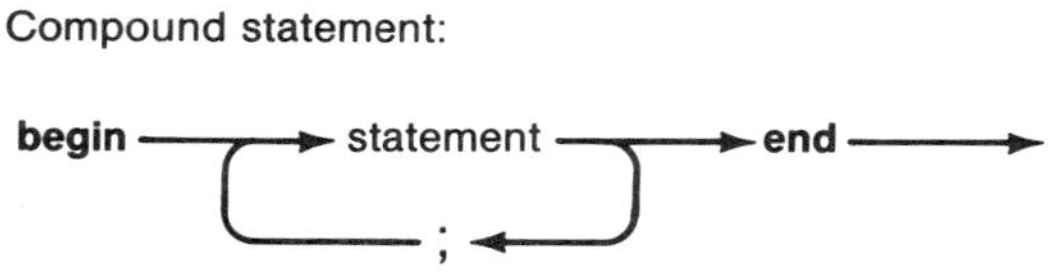

FIGURE 2.12
Syntax for a compound statement

2.12 Conditional Control with the If Statement

We can make a computer perform an action conditionally. That is, we can set up a Boolean expression that a computer must evaluate to determine what to do next. Here is an example of an **if** statement.

if count < 5 **then** writeln('!')

The Boolean expression in this example is

count < 5

which a computer must evaluate and find to be true before the writeln statement is executed. If this expression is found to be false (this happens if count is not less than 5), the computer will ignore the then statement and go on to the next statement in the program. In other words, this **if** statement tells a computer to print a ! provided count is less than 5.

Notice that the structure of a Pascal **if** statement is the same as the **if** used in the pseudocode used in Chapter 1. The Pascal **if** statement can also be set up with an **else** clause. Here is an example of an **if** statement with an **else** clause.

Sample If-Then-Else Statement

```
Line    Statement
1       if count < 5 then begin
2          writeln('!');
3          count := count - 1
4          end                          (*boundary of then statement*)
5       else begin
6          writeln('Try this!');
7          count := count + 1
8          end;                         (*boundary of else statement*)
```

Notice that the then part of this sample if statement uses a compound statement (lines 1–4). The then part of this statement works in the following way:

Actions of **then** part

If the count is less than 5, then the following actions are performed:

1. An exclamation point is printed (line 2).
2. Subtract 1 from count (line 3).
3. Else part of the **if** statement is ignored (lines 5–8).

Again, notice that the else part of this if statement also uses a compound statement (lines 5–8). Here is how the else statement comes into play.

Actions of **else** part

If the count is not less than 5, then the following actions are performed:

1. Then part is ignored by the computer.
2. The character string 'Try This!' is printed (line 6).
3. Add 1 to count (line 7).

The syntax for a Pascal **if** statement is given in Figure 2.13. The logic of an **if** statement can be shown graphically using the flowchart symbols given in

if statement:

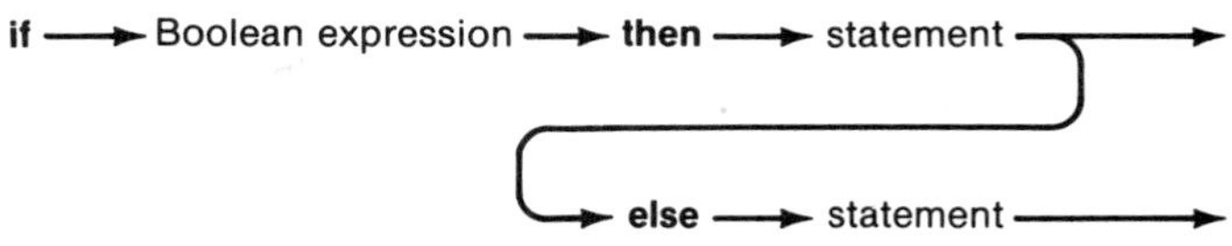

FIGURE 2.13
Syntax for an if statement

Figure 2.14. The flowchart for a Pascal **if** statement is given in Figure 2.15. It is also possible to tell a machine to iterate (or repeat) an action.

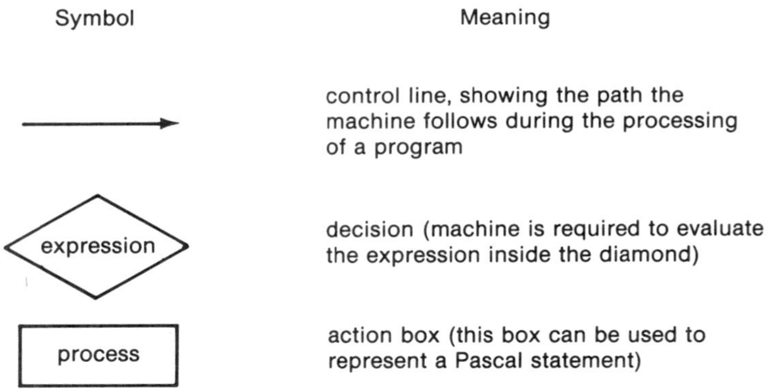
Symbol
Meaning
control line, showing the path the machine follows during the processing of a program
expression
decision (machine is required to evaluate the expression inside the diamond)
process
action box (this box can be used to represent a Pascal statement)

FIGURE 2.14
Flowchart symbols

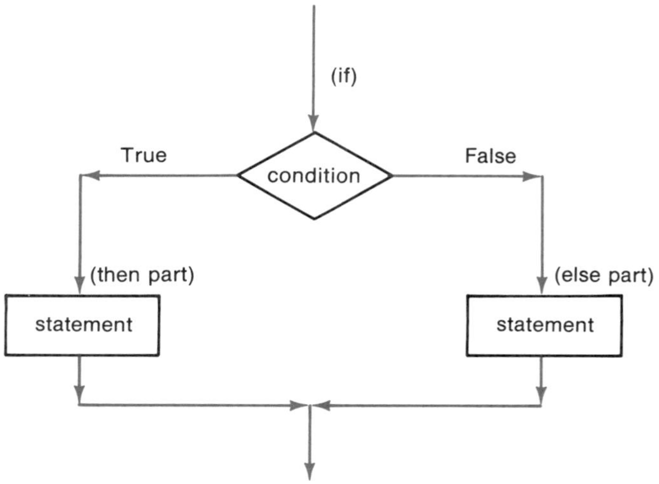

FIGURE 2.15
Flowchart for an if statement

2.13 Iteration with a For Statement

We can use a **for** statement to specify how many times we want a processor to repeat an action. For example, we can use the following **to** form of a **for** statement to tell a processor to print a row of 20 stars:

for StarCount := 1 **to** 5 **do** write('*');

which works in the following way:

Action	*StarCount*	*Output Line*
StarCount := 1	1	*
add 1 **to** StarCount	2	**
add 1 **to** StarCount	3	***
add 1 **to** StarCount	4	****
add 1 **to** StarCount	5	*****
add 1 **to** Star Count	6 (stop!)	

In other words, the machine will keep adding 1 to StarCount until the value of StarCount is greater than 5. StarCount is an example of a for statement control variable. Each time a for statement is executed, a computer will perform the following actions:

To form of for statement actions:

1. **Assign minimum value to control variable.**
2. **Compare value of the control variable with the maximum value. If the value of the control variable is <= the maximum value, then perform the do statement. Otherwise the iteration stops.**
3. **Perform do statement.**
4. **Add 1 to the control variable and repeat step 2.**

The token **to** tells a machine to add 1 to the control variable repeatedly. There is a second form of the **for** statement, which uses the **downto** token to tell a machine to subtract 1 from the control variable repeatedly. For example, the following **for** loop prints the descending values of StarCount:

for StarCount := 20 **downto** 15 **do** writeln(2 * StarCount);

which produces the following actions:

Action	*StarCount*	*Output Line*
assign 20 **to** StarCount	20	40
subtract 1 from StarCount	19	38
subtract 1 from StarCount	18	36

subtract 1 from StarCount	17	34
subtract 1 from StarCount	16	32
subtract 1 from StarCount	15	30
subtract 1 from StarCount	14 (stop!)	

The iteration stops when StarCount is less than 15. The syntax for both forms of a **for** statement is given in Figure 2.16. The flowchart for a Pascal **for** statement is given in Figure 2.17 The control variable of a **for** loop must be an ordinal type. This means it is possible to use, for example, a control variable that is type char. This fact makes the Pascal **for** statement a powerful tool. Here is an experiment you can try on your machine, which illustrates this idea.

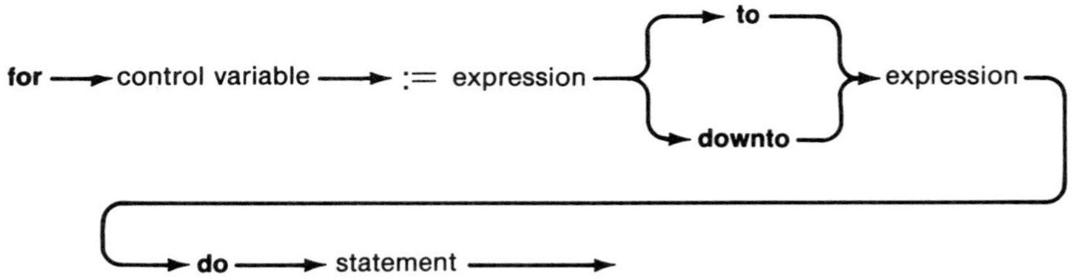

FIGURE 2.16
For statement syntax

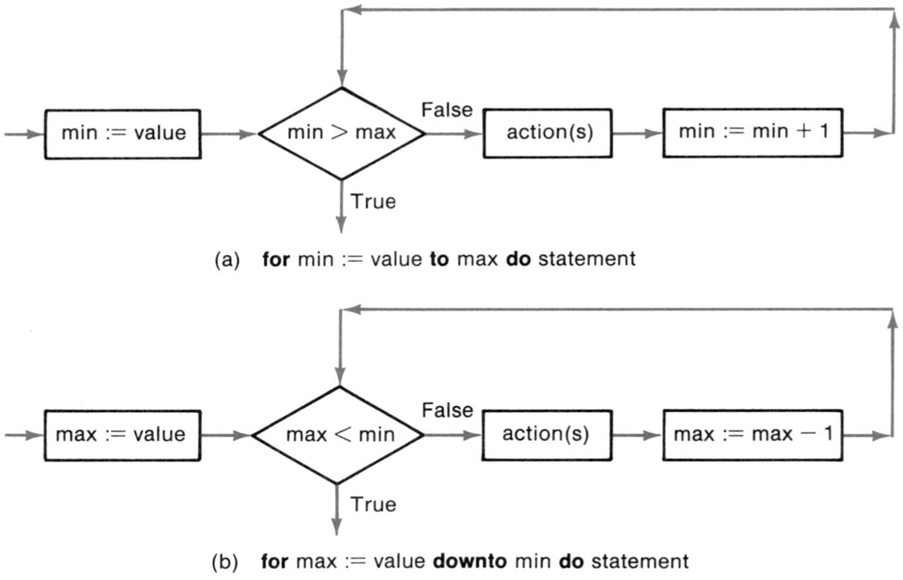

FIGURE 2.17
Flowchart for each form of the for statement

Experiment 8a (for ASCII users, only)

Line / *Source Text*

```
1   procedure InspectCharTable;
2   var
3      letter : char;                              (*control variable*)
4      count : integer;                            (*counts characters*)
5   begin
6      count := 1;                                 (*initialize count*)
7      for letter := ' ' to '~' do begin
8         if count mod 25 = 0 then writeln;        (*safety measure*)
9         write(letter:2);
10        count := count + 1                       (*add 1 to count*)
11        end
12  end;                                           (*InspectCharTable*)
```

We leave it as an exercise for you to implement the procedure in this experiment on your machine. It is limited to those machines that use the ASCII character table. It will not work with a machine that has EBCDIC because the printable characters in this table are *not* arranged consecutively. This procedure uses the mod operator to advantage. Here is how this procedure works.

Analysis of Experiment 8a

Action	*Letter Value*	*Count Value*	*Count* **mod** 25 Value	Output
assign ' ' **to** letter	' '	1	1	' '
assign '!' **to** letter	'!'	2	2	'!'
.		.	.	.
.		.	.	.
.		.	.	.
assign '7' **to** letter	'7'	24	24	'7'
assign '8' **to** letter	'8'	25	0	'8' Cursor moved to next line
and so on				

In other words, the **for** statement in Experiment 8a will tell the machine to scan the ASCII table, starting with a space and moving to the right character by character up to the tilde (~). The **mod** operator in the **if** statement in line 8 of this experiment is used to count how many characters have been printed on a line. The idea is to force the machine to print no more than 25 characters per line. This experiment will print out the printable characters in the ASCII table. You may find the output surprising.

The procedure in Experiment 8a illustrates the combined use of five different statements.

1. **For** statement to produce an iteration.
2. Compound statement to produce a sequence of actions following the **do** of the **for** statement.
3. Write statement to produce output.
4. **If** statement to control how many characters are printed on each line.
5. Assignment statement used to increment count each time the **do** compound statement is performed.

There is a variation of the program in Experiment 8a that uses the built-in chr function as follows:

Experiment 8b (for ASCII Users)

Line	*Source Text*

```
1    procedure DisplayCodeTable;
2    var
        code: integer;                          (*control variable*)
3    begin
4       for code := 32 to 126 do
           writeln(code:20, chr(code):20);      (*show code and
                                                    symbol*)
5    end;                                       (*DisplayCodeTable*)
```

The **for** loop (lines 3 and 4) in this procedure will print a character code on the same line with the corresponding character. Some samples rows of the table that will be printed are

Sample Rows of Printed Table

Code	*chr(code) = character*	*Column 20*	*Column 40*
32	chr(32) = ' '	32	' '
33	chr(33) = '!'	33	'!'
and so on			

We leave it as an excercise to implement this procedure. Perhaps you have already guessed that one **for** statement can be put inside another **for** statement. In other words, **for** statements can be nested (put inside each other). Here is a problem that can be solved using nested **for** loops.

Experiment 9

Print a daisy chain like the following one:

```
-
- -
- - -
- - - -
- - - -*
- - - -*-
- - - -*- -
- - - -*- - -
- - - -*- - - -
- - - -*- - - -* (and so on)
```

The idea is to set up an iteration that can handle printing the rows of a growing daisy chain. An inner iteration can be set up that uses the row count to tell how many stem pieces (- - - - -) and daisies (the *'s) to print. Here is the pseudocode to do this.

```
                (*Method: print a daisy chain, using an if statement to check
                          when to print a daisy (represented by a star) each
                          time the control variable is a multiple of 5. Notice
                          the use of the mod operator in the if condition.*)

program iteration(output);                                  (*specify output*)
 (*- - - - - - - - - - - - - - - - - - - - - - - - - - - - - - - - - - - - -*)
                                  (*Tell machine how to print daisy chains.*)

   procedure PrintDaisyChain;                           (*define instruction*)
   const
      max = 15;                                     (*number of daisy chains*)
   var
      row, DaisyChain: integer;                          (*control variables*)
   begin
      writeln('row':10, 'DaisyChain':20); writeln;                 (*heading*)
      for row := 1 to max do begin
         write(row:10, ' ':10);                          (*print row number*)
         for DaisyChain := 1 to row do
            if DaisyChain mod 5 = 0
            then write('*')
            else write('—');                          (*end of inner for loop*)
         writeln                                          (*start next chain*)
         end                                                (*outer for loop*)
   end;                                                    (*PrintDaisyChain*)

 (*- - - - - - - - - - - - - - - - - - - - - - - - - - - - - - - - - - - - -*)
```

```
begin
   PrintDaisyChain                                    (*activate procedure*)
end.
```

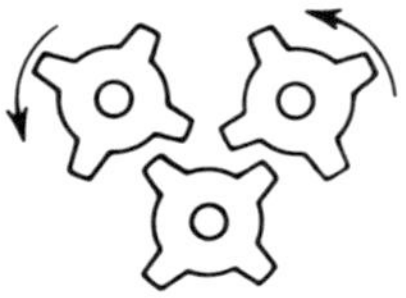

Row	DaisyChain
1	-
2	- -
3	- - -
4	- - - -
5	- - - -*
6	- - - -*-
7	- - - -*- -
8	- - - -*- - -
9	- - - -*- - - -
10	- - - -*- - - -*
11	- - - -*- - - -*-
12	- - - -*- - - -*- -
13	- - - -*- - - -*- - -
14	- - - -*- - - -*- - - -
15	- - - -*- - - -*- - - -*

FIGURE 2.18 Using a for-loop control variable

```
                        (*input: RowMax for maximum number of rows;
                                     output: printed daisy chain*)
begin
   initialize RowMax;
   for row going from 1 to RowMax do begin
      print row value;
      for DaisyChain going from 1 to row do
         if DaisyChain mod 5 equals 0 then print daisy
         else print stem piece;
      move cursor to next output line
      end
end;                                 (*algorithm to print daisy chain*)
```

Notice that the stem pieces will continue to be printed as long as the row value is not divisible by 5. Also notice that the row value determines the total number of things that get printed in each row. In effect, the row variable determines how much the daisy chain will grow in each row. A program to carry out this idea is given in Figure 2.18. At times it is desirable to increment or decrement an iteration control variable by fractional amounts. A **for** statement cannot be used to do this. A Pascal **repeat** statement can be used to handle such cases.

2.14 Iteration with a Repeat Loop

Here is an example of a **repeat** loop to handle fractional increments of a control variable.

```
begin
   controller := 0;                              (*initialize controller*)
   repeat
      controller := controller + 0.5             (*controller must be
                                                     type real!*)
   until controller > ValueYouChoose
end
```

The controller variable must be type real in this block, since this variable is incremented by fractional amounts, which are type real. This loop will continue until the value of controller exceeds ValueYouChoose. This is called the *exit condition* for the repeat loop. To guarantee that a repeat loop does not continue forever, great care is needed in setting up the exit condition. The syntax for a **repeat** loop is given in Figure 2.19. A **repeat** statement tells a machine to perform the following actions:

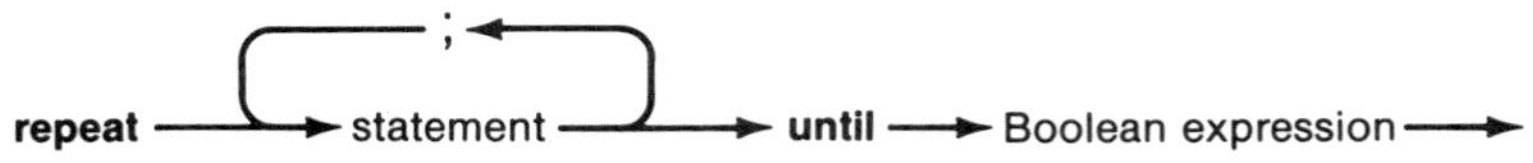

FIGURE 2.19
Repeat statement syntax

> **Repeat statement actions:**
>
> **1. Perform repeat statement(s).**
> **2. Evaluate Boolean expression. If expression is false, perform repeat statement(s) again. Otherwise go on to next line of program.**

The flowchart for a Pascal **repeat** statement is given in Figure 2.20. Pascal repeat statements can also be nested. That is, one repeat statement can be put inside another repeat statement. We can use this idea to implement the abstract letter-triangle program given in Chapter 1 to print a triangle like the following one:

```
a
b  c
d  e  f
g  h  i  j
k  l  m  n  o
```

Here is a procedure to do this alongside the original pseudocode given earlier.

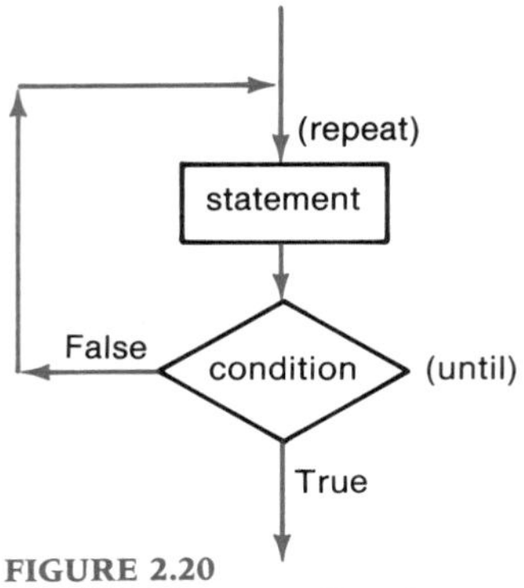

FIGURE 2.20
Repeat statement flowchart

Experiment 10

Pascal Procedure

```
procedure PrintTriangle;
const
   RowMax = 5;
var
   row, column: integer;
   letter : char;
begin
   row := 1;column := 1;letter:= 'a';
   repeat
      repeat
         write(letter:2);
         letter := succ(letter);
         column := column + 1
      until column > row;
      column := 1;
      writeln;
      row := row + 1
   until row > RowMax
end;                    (*PrintTriangle*)
```

Pseudocode

```
begin
   initialize letter;
   initialize RowMax;
   assign 1 to row and to column;

   repeat
      repeat
       print letter;

         assign next letter to
            letter;
         add 1 to column
      until column > row;
      assign 1 to column;
      move cursor to next line;
      add 1 to row
   until row > RowMax
end                       (*algorithm*)
```

Notice how the Pascal procedure uses RowMax as a constant. When this procedure is put into a Pascal program, it will print the same letter triangle each time. It is left as an exercise to implement this procedure (Experiment 10). Once you have this program set up in a Pascal program, try the following experiment:

Experiment 11

1. After compiling and running a program that uses the procedure in Experiment 10, then use an editor to make the following change:

```
const
   RowMax = 10;
```

2. Recompile and run the revised program. The last row of the newly printed triangle will contain non-lower case letters.

The idea in Experiment 10 is to print a letter triangle. You can fix up the program in Experiment 11 so that only lower-case letters are printed by using an **if** statement in the inner repeat statement. Try the following experiment:

Experiment 12

1. Use an editor to modify the inner **repeat** statement of Experiment 10 as follows:

```
repeat
   write(letter:2);
   if letter = 'z' then letter := 'a'
   else
      letter := succ(letter);
   column := column + 1
until column > row;
```

2. Recompile and run the revised program.

Carrying out this experiment is left for an exercise. There are times when **repeat** statements are not desirable. For example, whenever it is necessary to test a condition before an iteration can begin, it is better to use a **while** statement.

2.15 Iteration with a While Statement

A **while** statement has the following form:

while condition **do** statement

A **while** statement tells a computer to do the following things:

1. Test the **while** condition.
2. If the **while** condition is true, then perform the **do** statement. Otherwise, ignore the **do** statement and perform the statement following the **while** statement.

Notice that the **do** statement will not be performed at all, if the computer finds that the **while** condition is false initially. Some sample **while** statements are given in the following table:

Sample While Statements

Line	*Statement*	*Actions*
1	**while** 1 > 0 **do** write('!');	print '!' forever
2	count := 2;	initialize count
3	**while** count > 1 **do** write('!');	print '!' forever
4	now := 5;	initialize now
5	**while** now > 3 **do begin**	
6	write ('!');	print '!'(only twice)
7	now := now – 1	subtract 1 from now
8	**end**;	

Two of these **while** statements (lines 1 and 3) will produce iterations that continue forever. The iteration in line 1 continues forever, since the condition $(1 > 0)$ is always true. The second iteration (line 3) does nothing to change the value of count, so count will continue to be greater than 1. A shutoff mechanism is lacking in these first two iterations. By contrast, the third **while** statement (lines 5–8) has the following shutoff mechanism:

now := now − 1

Assuming the variable now is type integer, this iteration will eventually terminate regardless what initial value we assign to the variable now.

The flowchart for a **while** statement is given in Figure 2.21.

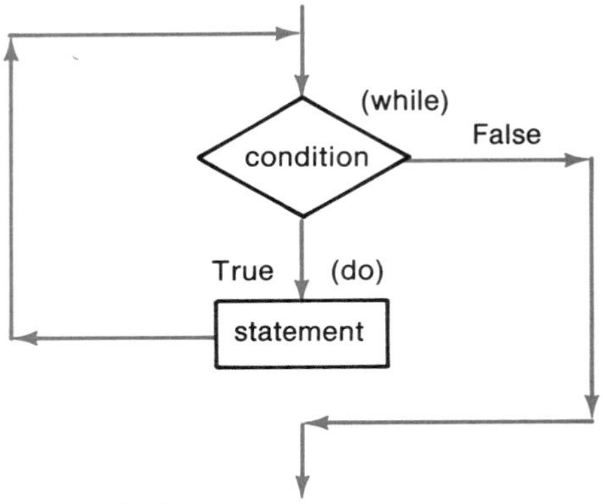

FIGURE 2.21
While statement flowchart

2.16

In Search of Programming Style

There are several things you can do immediately to cultivate a programming style.

1. Use indenting to make the lines of your source texts more readable.
2. Use comments to explain your variables, constants, and key statements, and to identify the boundaries of blocks you use, especially compound statements, which are usually numerous.
3. Use comments to separate procedure blocks.

First, we examine some rules for indenting your programs. These rules are advisory, not mandatory even though they are commonly used.

2.16.1

Rules for Indenting

Indenting should be done conservatively. If you indent too much, your source text can move too far to the right-hand side of the page. This is especially true on an Apple IIe, for example, which is normally restricted to a 40-column display. Here is a rule of thumb to try out.

> **Rule of thumb for indenting:**
>
> **Indent no more than three columns at a time, if it is necessary to indent a source text line.**

Where are some good places not to indent? Leave the following tokens in the same column: **var** and **const.** If these tokens are used in a program block, they should be lined up with the token program. If these tokens are used in a procedure block they should be lined up the token procedure. The tokens **begin** and **end,** which mark the boundaries of a program or procedure body, should be lined up with the beginning of the heading for the block they are in. Here is an example with a program block.

```
program sample;                                   (*heading*)
const                                          (*no indenting*)
   e = 2.71828;                   (*notice: indent 3 columns*)
var                                            (*no indenting*)
   This, That:integer;                    (*indent 3 columns*)
begin                                          (*no indenting*)
   This := 5;                             (*indent 3 columns*)
   That := This;                          (*indent 3 columns*)
   writeln(This:20:0, This*That*e)        (*indent 3 columns*)
end.                                           (*no indenting*)
```

It is helpful to line up all comments with the right-hand side of the page. Otherwise it gets hard to distinguish between comments and other parts of your text.

It is also helpful to line up in the same column the tokens used for a statement like the if statement. For example, try using the following format:

```
if ItIsFriday then
   GetReadyForWeekend
else
   writeln('Are you sure?');
```

Whenever a compound statement is used, it should be indented three columns. The statements inside a compound statement block should also be indented three columns. Here is an example.

```
if ItIsFriday then begin
   GetReadyForWeekend;                    (*indent 3 columns*)
   writeln('yesyesyesyes!')
   end                                    (*then statement*)
else
   writeln('Are you sure?');              (*else statement*)
```

You should put a comment at the end of every compound statement. You will be using a lot of them. This technique is used with the above then statement, which is a compound statement. This will help distinguish what compound statement each **end** belongs to.

2.16.2 *Self-Documenting Feature of Identifiers*

You can think of a meaningful name for a program or procedure block or constant or variable as a hidden comment. For example, SketchRobot in Figure 1.1 is a meaningful name of the procedure in that figure. It also employs a technique that is helpful in setting up identifiers.

> **Useful technique in setting up identifiers:**
>
> **Use a mixture of upper and lower case letters in your identifiers.**

This technique will allow you to call attention to words embedded inside a single identifier. The identifier itself becomes a comment on how it is being used in a program.

Every constant and every variable in a source text should be commented. This will tell you later how you intended to use your constants and variables. These comments can and should be cryptic. Just one or two words will usually be enough. If you use a list of variables of the same type, they should all serve the same purpose (one comment is enough for the list).

2.17 Summary

Every Pascal program has a program block that may contain declarations and definitions *and* always contains a compound statement. In other words, Pascal programs are block structured. The compound statement of a program block tells a processor what to do—what instructions (including procedures) to carry out. The minimal block is a compound statement, which specifies zero or more actions for a processor to perform. A compound statement never contains declarations or definitions.

A token is the smallest unit of a programming language. These are used to build source texts. For example, the pair of tokens, *begin* and *end,* are used to mark the boundaries of a compound statement. There are four types of tokens in Pascal.

1. Word symbols like **procedure**.
2. Special symbols like **(** and **)**.
3. Identifiers like *SketchRobot* (we invent these using letters and digits).
4. Numbers like *233* and *15e+023.*

Identifiers are used to name constants, variables, program blocks, procedure blocks, and so on. The characters available to build identifiers will vary depending on the computer system being used. There is an ISO standard character set with 128 characters available on most computers. The ASCII character set is an implementation of the ISO standard.

Statements are used to give a processor instructions. Statements specify actions for a processor to perform. Many statements contain expressions. An expression represents a value.

A compound statement is an example of a control structure. Once a processor begins executing a compound statement, it is forced to carry out the actions specified inside the compound statement. For this reason, a compound statement represents a sequential control structure. Statements can also be conditionally executed when they are made part of an **if** statement. An **if** statement is a conditional control structure. Finally, we can tell a processor to iterate an action by using an iteration control structure. The **for** statement is an example of an iteration control structure. It uses a control variable to specify how many times an action is iterated. If it is necessary to have change a control variable by fractional amounts during an iteration, then try a repeat loop.

The **repeat** and **while** statements provide two additional Pascal control structures. Both statements must be set up with shutoff mechanisms to avoid infinite iterations. The action part of a **repeat** statement is always performed at least once, since the **until** condition is tested after the action part is performed each time. By contrast, the action part of a **while** statement may not be performed at all, if the **while** condition is false initially.

Pascal has four simple data types: Boolean, char, integer, and real. These simple types are divided into two groups: ordinal and nonordinal. Each of these types are defined in terms of a scale of values. The values used to define an ordinal type can be completely listed. The values of an ordinal type are enumerable. This is the case with the following three simple types:

1. Boolean: false, true
2. Char: character scale (look at your keyboard!)
3. Integer: –maxint, . . . , –1, 0, 1, . . . , maxint

The scales for type char and integer are implementation dependent. The range of allowable characters and integer values will vary, depending on the computer system being used. Your first task is to find out about the scales used to define these types on your computer system. The values on the type integer scale are a subset of the integers. This subset is bounded by the values –maxint and maxint (–32768 and 32767 on an IBM PC, for example).

Type real is not an ordinal type. The values on the scale used to define type real are not considered enumerable. This scale is a subset of the real numbers.

Every constant and variable in a Pascal program has an implied (with constants) or declared (with variables) data type. The tokens *const* and *var* are used to make these declarations.

Finally, there is the question of programming style, which you should start pursuing. You can help establish a meaningful style by experimenting with identifiers that say something and comments that isolate and explain what you are doing. You can also make a source text more readable by carefully indenting the lines of your text.

2.18

Keywords Review

Keywords	*Related Ideas*
block	optional definition and declaration parts plus required compound statement
compound statement	specifies sequence of one or more actions
const	token to specify constant definition

decimal scale factor	letter *e* followed by integer
expression	representation of a value
flowchart	graphical way to represent a program structure like a **for** loop
identifier	name of an object
iteration	repetition
control structure	specifies action to be performed
compound statement	sequential control structure
for statement	iteration governed by a control variable
if statement	condition tested to determine if an action is to be performed
repeat statement	iteration governed by a condition tested after each iteration
while statement	iteration governed by a condition tested before each iteration
simple types	data types defined by scales
ordinal types	Boolean, char, integer
nonordinal type	real
statement	specifies action to be carried out by a machine
syntax	arrangement of the parts of a language structure
token	smallest part of a language
var	token for variable declaration
write	built-in output procedure that is always used with an output list and does not move the cursor to the beginning of a new line after the last value in its output list has been printed

2.19 Exercises

1. What are the differences between a program block and a procedure block?
2. What is a constant?
3. What is a variable?
4. What are the differences between a constant definition and a variable declaration?
5. What are the differences between the scales used to define type integer and type real?
6. How are the scales for type real and type integer identical?
7. How many characters are in the scale used to define type char on your computer system? Specify them, completely!
8. Implement the following procedure on your computer:

```
procedure DisplayMaxint;
begin
  writeln('maxint equals', maxint)
end;                                        (*DisplayMaxint*)
```

9. Give a complete syntax diagram for the following items:
   a. An English family name
   b. The title of a book
   c. Unsigned integer
   d. Unsigned number

10. Give flowcharts for each of the following:
   a. Experiment 1 (Section 2.10)
   b. Procedure in Experiment 8a (Section 2.13)
   c. Daisy chain program in Figure 2.18
   d. Procedure in Experiment 10 (Section 2.14)
   e. While statement

11. Based on the program headings you have already seen (see Figures 1.1 and 2.1, for example) give a syntax diagram for a program heading. *Hint:* The identifier output is the name of a file; allow for more than one file identifier in a program heading (if there is more than one, the list of identifiers will be separated by commas).

12. Assume that the type real variable amps identifies location 2000 in primary memory of your computer. Show step by step the changes in the content of location 2000 as a result of the following assignments:

```
amps := 1;
amps := (amps/5) * 7 + 20;
amps := amps + 25
```

13. Write Pascal procedure to print a line with 70 hyphens using a single **for** loop (call your procedure PrintLine).

14. Using the PrintLine procedure, write a procedure to print the following heading:

Passenger Name	*Airline Flight*	*Weight of Baggage*	*Origin*	*Destination*	*ETD Time*	*ETA Time*

Call your procedure PrintHeading. *Hint:* You can activate the PrintLine procedure from inside the PrintHeading procedure. That is, you can tell a processor to carry out the actions specified by PrintLine from inside the PrintHeading procedure.

15. Write a program to implement the procedures from exercises 13 and 14 in the following way:
   a. Print the heading to be used by a ticket agent.
   b. From the program body, activate the PrintHeading procedure, then
   c. Activate a new procedure called PrintNames. Use this procedure to print a *fixed* list of five passengers (you choose them and related ticket information for imaginary airlines).

16. Using write and writeln procedures to print the logo for your computer system. The output should have the following form:

Name of your computer system

Do this in the following way:

a. Using a **for** loop, write a procedure called PrintStars to print a row of stars.
b. Using a procedure called PrintLogo, print a centered logo.
c. Use a **for** loop inside the program body to activate the PrintStars and PrintLogo procedures, when they are needed. Try using an **if** statement to decide when to activate the PrintLogo procedure.

17. Write a procedure called ShowReals to print sample values of several real variables in floating point and fixed point forms. Declare these variables inside this procedure. *Hint.* When variables are declared inside a procedure block, the variable declaration is given between the procedure heading and the token **begin** of the procedure body. Do this with good program style. Careful: You must assign values to these variables before you can print them. See samples given earlier.

18. Write a program to implement the ShowReals procedure given in exercise 17.

19. Construct a table showing all possible operands with the arithmetic operators (Section 2.4.4) to produce a real result.

20. Try out Experiment 1 (Section 2.10) on your system. Comment on what you find.

21. Try out Experiment 2 (Section 2.10) on your system.

22. Implement Experiments 3 and 4 (Section 2.10) on your system and comment on the results.

23. Implement the program in Experiment 5 (Section 2.10). Then do the following things:

a. Try Experiment 6 given in Section 2.10.
b. Try Experiment 7 given in Section 2.10.
c. Redo Experiment 7 to print the sixth character to left of *'t'* and the eighth character to the right of *'t'*.
d. Comment on your findings.

24. Implement the InspectCharTable procedure in Experiment 8a (Section 2.13) in a Pascal program. Then

a. Change the program so that it prints three columns of characters in each row of the table printed.
b. Change the **for** loop so that only the lower case letters are printed.
c. Implement Experiment 8b in the same section.

25. Implement the PrintTriangle procedure in Experiment 10 (Section 2.14) in a Pascal program. Then

a. Try Experiment 11 given in Section 2.14.
b. Try Experiment 12 given in Section 2.14.

26. Write a program to print successive values of the following series of numbers:

$$1 + \tfrac{1}{2} + \tfrac{1}{3} + \tfrac{1}{4} + \cdots + 1/n$$

This is called a harmonic series (it continues to grow forever). Here is an algorithm to produce it.

```
begin
   draw a line;                          (*do this with a procedure*)
   assign 1 to term;
   repeat
      display the terms 1 + ··· + 1/term;
      assign 0 to sum;
      assign 0 to copy;
      repeat
         add 1/copy to sum;
         add 1 to copy
      until copy > term;                     (*inner repeat loop*)
      print the sum;
      add 1 to term                        (*prepare for next sum*)
   until term > max;                          (*outer repeat loop*)
   draw a line                           (*do this with a procedure*)
end                                       (*harmonic series algorithm*)
```

Try implementing this algorithm with two procedures, one to draw the necessary lines and a second to compute the terms of the harmonic series so that the program produces the following output:

$\tfrac{1}{1}$ + = 1.000000
$\tfrac{1}{1}$ + $\tfrac{1}{2}$ + = 1.500000
$\tfrac{1}{1}$ + $\tfrac{1}{2}$ + $\tfrac{1}{3}$ + = 1.833333 (and so on)

Run your program with denominators ranging from 1 to 10.

27. (Refinement: improving the output). Notice that each line of the output for the program in exercise 26 has an unnecessary trailing + sign. This can be suppressed by printing the + sign conditionally. That is, use an **if** statement to determine when to print the + sign. Modify the program in exercise 26 to eliminate this trailing + sign.

2.20 Review Quiz

Determine whether the following are true or false:

1. Variable declarations can be given inside a compound statement.

2. Blocks can be nested.

3. Every Pascal program has at least one block.

4. The last thing in every Pascal procedure is a token.

5. A token represents a value.

6. A constant like 233 is an expression.
7. Type real is an ordinal type.
8. There are at most three simple types in Pascal.
9. The values of a scale used to define an ordinal data type can be enumerated.
10. There are three standard ordinal data types in Pascal.
11. The **if** statement is an example of an iteration control structure.
12. There are three tokens in the syntax diagram for an **if** statement.
13. Expressions can be used in assignment statements.
14. The **write** identifier is a shorthand form of the **writeln** identifier.
15. A **write** statement must always have an output list.

2.21 Readings

Hawksley, C. *Pascal Programming: A Beginner's Guide to Computers and Programming.* New York: Cambridge University Press, 1983. See Chapters 5 and 7.

Martin, J., and McClure, C. *Diagramming Techniques for Analysis and Programmers.* Englewood Cliffs, NJ: Prentice-Hall, 1985. See Chapter 13 on flowcharting.

Pollack, S. V. *Programming UCSD Pascal.* New York: Holt, Rinehart and Winston, 1984. See Appendix A on Railroad diagrams for Pascal and Section 4.3 on program structure and appearance.

CHAPTER 3

PROCEDURES AND PROGRAM DESIGN

[Procedures] provide the functional "nuts and bolts" of a software system. They allow a complex system to be partitioned into a set of functional software components.

Richard Wiener and Richard Sincovec, 1984

AIMS

- Introduce the top-down approach to program design.
- Distinguish between bottom-up and top-down methods used to test procedures.
- Introduce procedures with parameters.
- Begin using two additional built-in procedures, read and readln.
- Show how to use the eoln and eof functions.
- Introduce the notion of an input file.
- Suggest more experiments useful in exploring the chapter ideas.
- Show how to use forward references.
- Look at the scope of program identifiers.
- Suggest two additional programming style techniques.

3.1

Introduction to Procedures

A *procedure* specifies a sequence of actions for a computer to perform. In effect, a procedure is a subprogram. Typically, each procedure tells a machine how to perform a sequence of actions to carry out a specific task like the following ones:

Task	Pascal Procedure

Ring keyboard bell	**procedure** RingBell;
	const
	  bell = 7;
	begin
	  write(chr(bell)) (*rings bell*)
	end; (*RingBell*)

Imitate Amadeus	**procedure** ImitateAmadeus;
	const
	  bell = 7;
	var
	  sound, silence: integer;
	begin
	  for sound := 1 **to** 50 **do begin**
	    write(chr(bell));
	    for silence := 1 **to** sound **do**
	      (*do nothing, here*)
	    end
	end; (*ImitateAmadeus*)

Each of these procedures tells a machine how to carry out a task. Procedures are used to organize programs and to separate the tasks a program needs to perform. This separation of program tasks is beneficial. It makes it easier to troubleshoot a program that is misbehaving—not doing what you expected or wanted. This separation of tasks also makes it much easier to follow the logic of a program, especially after time has passed and you find it necessary to dust off an old program to do some fine tuning. The following program body illustrates the use of the above procedures:

```
begin
   repeat
      RingBell;                    (*activate procedure*)
      ImitateAmadeus               (*activate procedure*)
   until 1 > 2                            (*endlessly*)
end.
```

This program body endlessly activates these two procedures. With considerable refinement, you might be able to produce some interesting sounds. The term *procedure call* is another way of saying that a procedure has been activated from somewhere inside a program. Since procedures can be declared inside other procedure (or nested), it is important to know when a procedure call is legal. For example, the procedure calls in the above program body are legal only if the RingBell procedure is not declared inside the ImitateAmadeus procedure. That is, a program containing these procedures must have a structure like the following one:

```
program TryThis(output);
   procedure RingBell;
         .
         .
         .
   end;
   procedure ImitateAmadeus;
         .
         .
         .
   end;
begin
   repeat
      RingBell;                                  (*call RingBell*)
      ImitateAmadeus                       (*call ImitateAmadeus*)
   until 1 > 2                                      (*endlessly*)
end.
```

If the RingBell is declared inside the ImitateAmadeus block, then it would be inaccessible from the program body. Here is a sample rewrite of the TryThis program, which reflects this idea.

Experiment 1

```
program NowTryThis(output);
   procedure ImitateAmadeus:
   var
      sound, silence: integer;
      procedure RingBell;
      const
         bell = 7;
      begin
         write(chr(bell))
      end;                                           (*RingBell*)
   begin
      for sound := 1 to 50 do begin
         RingBell;                             (*procedure call*)
         for silence := 1 to sound do
                                            (*do nothing, here*)
   end;                                        (*ImitateAmadeus*)
```

```
begin
   repeat
      ImitateAmadeus;                          (*procedure call*)
      write('Amadeus. . .')                    (*trace action*)
   until 1 > 2                                 (*endlessly*)
end.
```

In the NowTryThis program, the range of meaning of RingBell is limited by the ImitateAmadeus procedure. It can be called from inside the ImitateAmadeus procedure but not from the program body. In effect, the RingBell procedure is known only to ImitateAmadeus. This is another way of saying that the scope of a procedure is limited by the block in which it is declared. The *scope* of a procedure is the range of meaning of the procedure.

As it stands, the NowTryThis program does produce some interesting sounds because an empty statement is used in the following for loop in the ImitateAmadeus procedure:

```
for silence := 1 to sound do
                                               (*do nothing, here*)
```

This do statement is an example of what is known as an *empty statement*, which is legal in Pascal. An empty statement just tells the machine to do nothing. Because it takes time to tell a machine to do nothing, this statement gives us a way to change the interval between the rings of the keyboard bell in the ImitateAmadeus procedure. The write statement in the program body of this sample program provides a trace of what happens while this program is running. Each time the machine finishes with the ImitateAmadeus procedure, a trace of this return to the program body is given by

Amadeus. . .

The scope of a procedure is part of the larger topic of the scope of an identifier in a Pascal program. This is a key topic in this chapter.

3.2 Top-Down Approach to Program Design

What we called *stepwise refinment* in Chapter 1 is also called *top-down program design*. The basic idea of top-down design of programs is to identify a principal task. Once the principal task has been determined, this is followed up by identifying subtasks, which are required to implement the main task. Top-down design of a program proceeds in successive sets of steps. Each new set of steps will reflect greater refinement and a more detailed analysis of the subtasks. The end result of stepwise refinement is a set of statements that are easily translatable into a computer program.

For example, we could start with the ambitious idea of setting up an expert system to act as an agent for an airline in making ticket reservations.

The principal task will be

Set up airline reservation.

You can think of this as level 0 of a program design. In developing an expert system to do this, we can start by identifying the tasks that need to be performed to implement this principal task. The first set of tasks stemming from the level 0 are the level 1 tasks in the program design. We can represent this idea using pseudocode in the following way:

```
                              (*input: passenger requirements;
                          output: available flights, reservation*)
begin
   get passenger information;
   check airline schedules;
   display available flights;
   make reservation
end                                         (*display of subtasks*)
```

Each one of the level 1 tasks will probably have needed subtasks. These new subtasks will be on level 2. Some suggested level 2 subtasks are suggested in the structure chart in Figure 3.1. There is more than one way to translate this structure chart into a working program. You can think of each of these structure chart boxes in terms of a Pascal procedure. In the Section3.3 we suggest two ways to develop the procedures that will be used in a program to implement this airline reservation program.

3.3 Bottom-Up vs. Top-Down Procedure Testing Techniques

We set up the following program to develop and test the procedure to get passenger information:

```
program TrialRun(input, output);
   procedure GetInformation;
   begin
      writeln('Your name: ');
            (*store the response somewhere for future reference*)
      writeln('date and time you wish to leave: ');
                                          (*store responses*)
      writeln('destination: ');
                                          (*store response*)
                    (*this question-answer session will continue*)
   end;                                   (*GetInformation*)
begin
   GetInformation                         (*activate procedure*)
end.
```

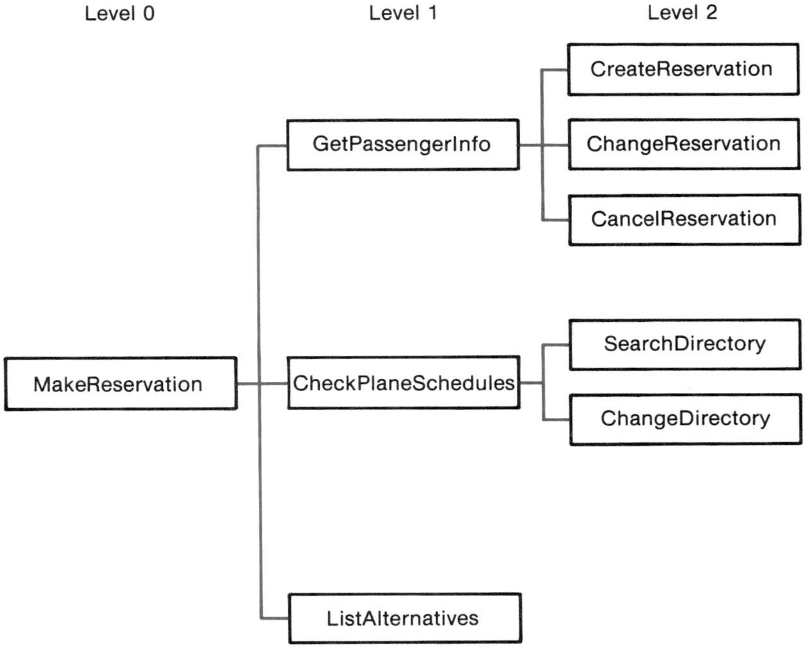

FIGURE 3.1
Structure chart for an airline reservation program

In other words, we develop and test this procedure apart from its companion procedures needed by the expert system to make an airline reservation. This is an example of the *bottom-up* approach to procedure development. It is done apart from a larger program. Each praocedure is handled initially in a separate program. This approach is commonly used in the development of longer programs like the proposed expert system since it makes it easier to divide the workload among a team of programmers. The alternative is a *top-down* testing strategy, which uses the following steps:

Top-down testing strategy

1. Develop the level 1 procedures.

2. After all level 1 procedures are working together, then begin appending the necessary level 2 procedures.

This means we would start the following skeletal structure:

```
Program agent(input, output);
  procedure GetInformation;
  begin
                                       (*flesh out in a preliminary way*)
  end;                                                  (*GetInformation*)
  procedure CheckPlaneSchedules;
  begin
                                       (*flesh out in a preliminary way*)
  end;                                             (*CheckPlaneSchedules*)
  procedure ListAlternatives;
  begin
                                       (*flesh out in a preliminary way*)
  end;                                                (*ListAlternatives*)
  procedure MakeReservation;
  begin
    GetInformation;                                 (*activate procedure*)
    CheckPlaneSchedules;                            (*activate procedure*)
    ListAlternatives                                (*activate procedure*)
  end;                                                 (*MakeReservation*)
begin
  MakeReservation                                   (*activate procedure*)
end.
```

This sample program is just a skeleton for what someday might be an expert system. The idea is to go after the big picture first. In a top-down program design the level 1 procedures would be fleshed out and tested in a preliminary way first. After you have a workable program framework, then you can start adding new procedures to meet the needs of the level 1 procedures. The top-down procedure testing strategy is illustrated graphically in Figure 3.2. In this chapter, we will show how to get information from a terminal and store it in computer memory for later use in a program. This will allow us to replace the comments in the GetInformation procedure, for example, with meaningful Pascal statements.

This is the beginning of the top-down design of a program to handle airline reservations. It starts with a subdivision of the principal task into smaller, more manageable subtasks. You probably can imagine how each of three procedures in the above skeleton can also be subdivided into subtasks. In other words, more stepwise refinement is possible. In effect, top-down design of a program uses a *divide-and-conquer* approach to programming.

The perfect tool to use in employing this top-down approach is a Pascal procedure. You probably have already guessed that the above sample program says nothing about the variables and constants that will be used by each procedure. In fact, you might begin to wonder if it is possible for Pascal procedures to share information, to pass data between procedures. In effect, you might begin to wonder if procedures can be wired together in some way so that information can be passed between them. This is possible. We show how to do this in this chapter.

In this chapter we also demonstrate how to set up procedures that can receive data when a machine is told to carry out the actions specified by a

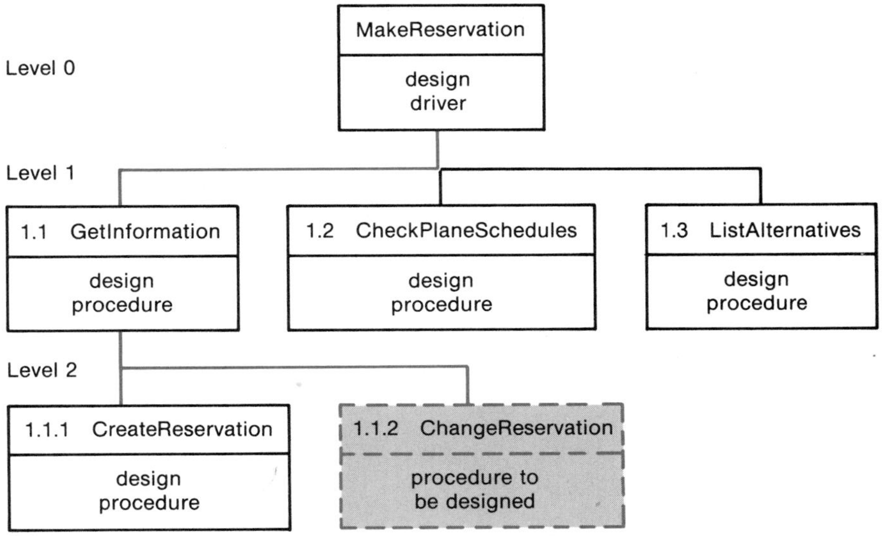

FIGURE 3.2
Top-Down Program Design

procedure. First we show how to use two built-in Pascal procedures to handle input of data from a keyboard.

3.4 Two More Built-In Procedures: Read and Readln

Pascal has the following two built-in procedures to handle input from a terminal keyboard:

Built-In Input Procedures

Procedure	*Result*
read(answer);	Waits for value of *answer* variable to be typed using your keyboard
read(this, that);	Waits for two values, usually before a *return* is typed
readln(this); readln(that);	Takes a typed value for *this,* waits for value of *this* to be typed on next line

Each of these built-in procedures relies on the use of computer memory to store the entered values. This memory can either be primary (it usually is) or secondary (on a disk, for example, in a time-share system that is very busy). This problem is handled by Pascal and your computer system, not by you. You merely need to specify that *input* will be used in your program.

Input is the name of the storage area (the *input store* or *input file*) used by these two built-in procedures. An *input file* is a temporary storage area used to hold the values you type into the system with your keyboard. The word *input* is specified in your program heading, if you want to use either a read or readln statement. Here is a sample program to illustrate this idea.

Experiment 2

```
program sample2 (input, output);                    (*notice input*)
var
   x1, x2, x3, x4, x5: integer;                     (*for data entry*)
begin
   write('Enter integers: ');                       (*prompt for input*)
   read(x1, x2, x3, x4, x5);                        (*get values*)
end.
```

When this program is run, the following prompt will be displayed:

Enter integers:

Then the machine will wait for you to enter five integers. This can be done in different ways. For example, you can type

10 20 30 40 50 <return>

As a result, these five integers are placed in the input file and then assigned to the variables *x*1–*x*5. A graphical interpretation of this idea is shown in Figure 3.3.

To handle the reading from the input file, Pascal maintains an input pointer. An *input pointer* identifies the memory location where the next input value can be stored. When *x*1 is read, the input pointer is moved to the next part of the input file, which contains the next value or an end-of-line character. Each time we type a <return>, an end-of-line character is put into the input file. When the input pointer is pointing to an end-of-line character, this fact is recorded by assigning *true* to a built-in *eoln* function. Otherwise, when the input pointer is not pointing to an end-of-line character in the input file, the *eoln* function has a value of *false*.

The eoln function guides the read procedure. You are probably wondering how this works. Here is an example. If you have told a computer to read five numbers and it finds less than five numbers before it reaches an eoln character, then the read procedure moves the input pointer to the next input line and continue reading until it finds all five numbers. For example, we could have type five integers for the above program in the following way:

Entered Values	*Entries in Input File*
10 20 <return>	| 10| | 20| |**eoln**|
30 <return>	| 30| |**eoln**|
40 50 <return>	| 40| | 50| |**eoln**|

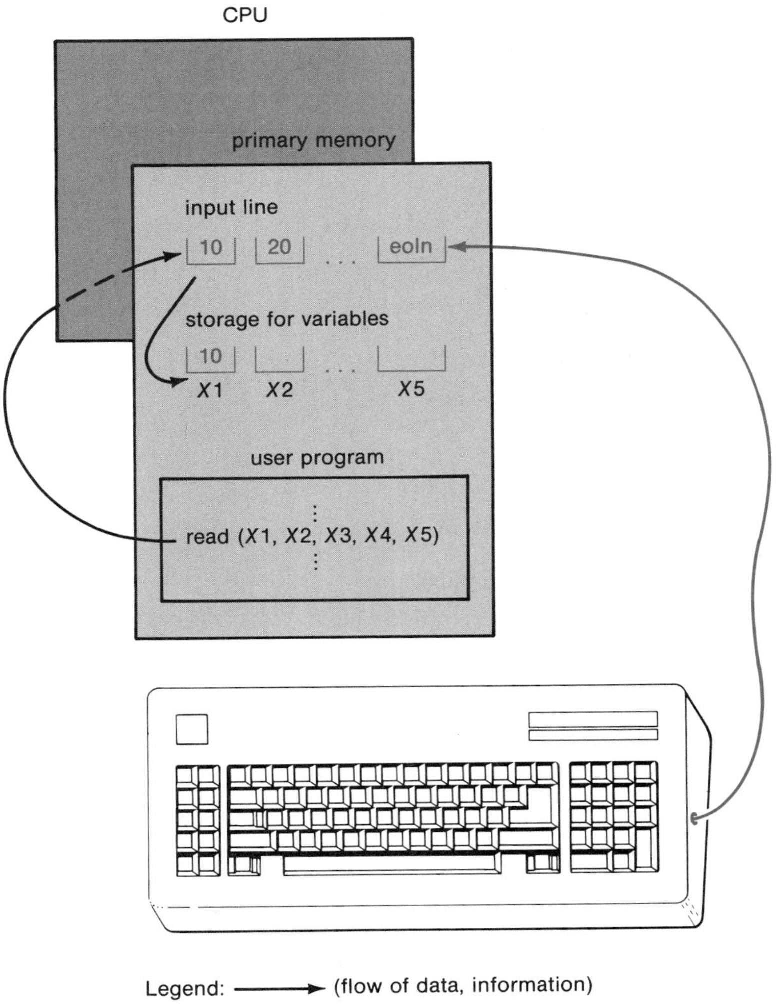

FIGURE 3.3
Graphical interpretation of read(*x*1)

Taken together, this gives us the following input file:

| 10| | 20| |**eoln**| | 30| |**eoln**| | 40| | 50| |**eoln**|

↑ input pointer ends up here

The read procedure will read past the first two eoln characters to assign all five integers specified in the sample program. After the read procedure has assigned values to each of its specified parameters, it leaves the input pointer pointing to the next entry of the input line, even the input pointer is pointing to an eoln character. In this second sample set of entered values, the input pointer is left pointing to the third eoln character.

The significance of this last feature of the built-in read procedure will become clearer, if we enter a different line of values. For example, suppose we enter 10 integers on the same input line.

10 20 30 40 50 60 70 80 90 100 <return>

↑

input pointer moved to storage area holding the value 60 after read(*x*1, *x*2, *x*3, *x*4, *x*5) statement has been performed by computer

This means we can go back later and pick up more values entered in the same input line. For example, we can have the following actions and results:

Sample Program Body	*Actions*
begin	
write('Enter 8 integers: ');	
read(*x*1, *x*2, *x*3, *x*4, *x*5);	Assign to first 5 integers entered to *x*1–*x*5
writeln(*x*1 + *x*2 + *x*3);	Print sum
writeln(*x*4 * *x*5);	Print product
read(*x*1);	Assign *next* input value to *x*1 (60 is assigned to *x*1)
writeln(*x*1);	Print value read
read(*x*1, *x*2);	Assign *next* input values to *x*1 and *x*2
writeln(*x*1 + *x*2)	Print sum
end.	

Notice that we keep returning to the same input line over and over in the above program block. A total of eight values are read. If we had entered more than eight integers, any integers following the first eight in the input file would be ignored. If we enter the numbers 10–100, what will printed by the above block? You can answer this question by keeping track of what happens to the input pointer after each activation of the read procedure. We know, for example, that the input pointer is pointing to 60 after the first call to the read procedure with

read(*x*1, *x*2, *x*3, *x*4, *x*5);

This tells us that 60 will be assigned to *x*1 after the second activation of the read procedure with

read(*x*1);

so 60 is printed on the second output line. The second activation of the read procedure leaves the input pointer pointing to 70 in the original input line. Then the next two values found in the input line will get assigned to *x*1 and *x*2 by

read(*x*1, *x*2);

Then what gets printed by the final writeln statement in the above block?

So far we have discussed only how the read procedure works with numeric input of type integer (it works the same way with type real). The read procedure works differently with input of type char.

3.4.1 *Using the Read Procedure with Type Char Input*

Here is a program that calls for input of type char.

Experiment 3

```
program sample2(input, output);
   procedure GetCharacters;
   var
      ch1, ch2, ch3, ch4, ch5, ch6 : char;
   begin
      writeln('Enter 6 characters: ');
      read(ch1, ch2, ch3, ch4, ch5, ch6);
      writeln(ch1, ch2, ch3, ch4, ch5, ch6)
   end;                                         (*GetCharacters*)
begin
   GetCharacters                    (*call GetCharacters procedure*)
end.
```

What gets assigned to the type char variables will depend on how we enter these characters. For example, we can enter the following characters:

Hello,world! <return>

Here is what sample2 program does with this input line.

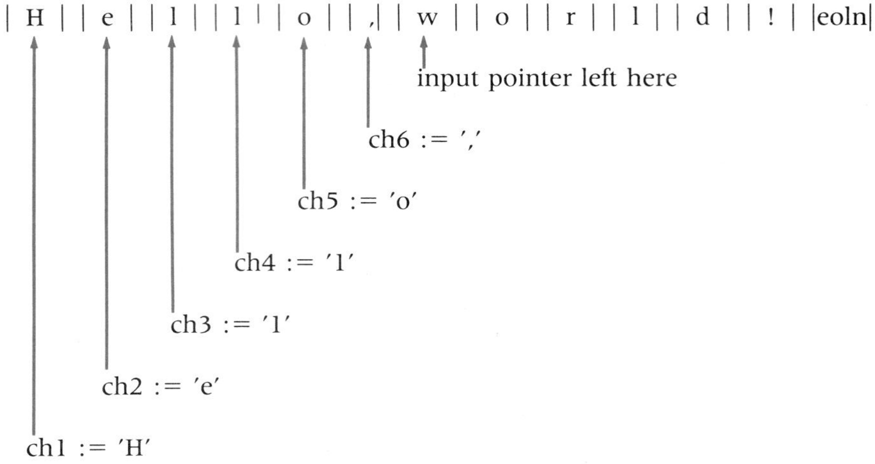

Then

Hello,

gets printed by the sample2 program. This read procedure will produce a different result, if it detects an eoln character before it finishes reading. For example, we can enter the above expression in the following way:

H<return>
e <return>
l <return>
l <return>
o <return>
World! <return>

When the read procedure in the sample2 program is activated with these input lines, we get the following results:

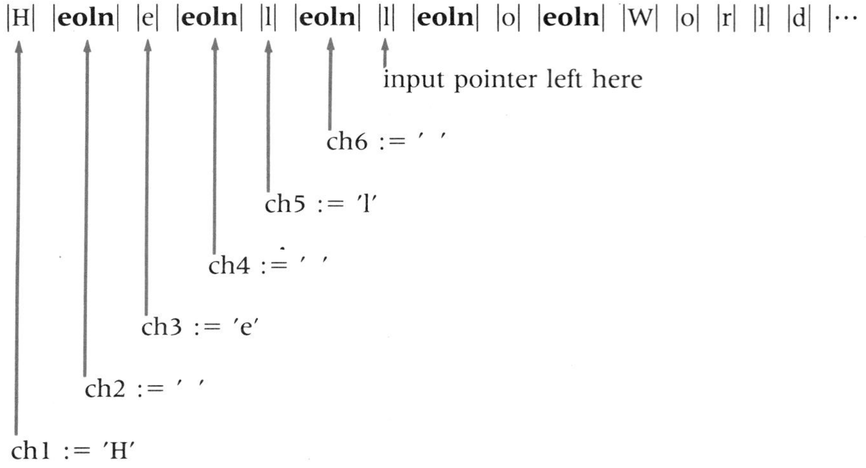

As a result, the sample2 program will produce following output:

H e l

In other words, the built-in read procedure assigns a blank (a space) to a type character variable, if an *eoln* is detected during a read operation. We can echo print what has been read after repeated visits to the same input line.

3.4.2 *Echo Printing What Is Read*

We illustrate echo printing with type character. This idea is easily extended to reading values for other data types. For example, we can use the following procedure to handle echo-printing characters that have been read:

```
procedure EchoPrint;
var
   ch:char;
begin
   repeat
      read(ch);                          (*read character*)
      write(ch)                    (*echo-print character*)
   until eoln
end;                                      (*EchoPrint*)
```

For example, if we enter

Yes! Yes! Yes! Yes! <return>

then the characters we have entered will be printed on the next output line. Besides the eoln function, there is also a second *eof* function, which can be used to determine when the end of the input file has been reached. We look at the eoln and eof functions in more detail in Section 3.4.3.

3.4.3 *Built-In eoln and eof Functions*

The eoln function will be assigned a value of true, if an eoln character is found during the activation of the read procedure. If an eoln is true and there are still more parameters that have not been assigned values by the read procedure, then the reading of the input file continues and the produces the following results:

1. The input pointer is moved to the next input line.
2. eoln is assigned *false.*
3. Reading continues on the current line until the last read parameter has been assigned a value from the input line. Repeat steps 1 and 2, if an eoln character is detected before the read procedure has assigned a value to its last parameter.

We can mark the end of the input file (after all the lines of input have been entered). We do this by inserting an end-of-file (eof) character into the input line. For example, in IBM Pascal 2.00 or VAX Pascal, a control *z* is used as the eof character. By contrast, Apple Pascal uses a control *c* as the eof character. You will have to check which eof character your system uses.

The built-in eof function has a value of *false* when the input pointer is not pointing to the eof character. If an eof character is detected, then eof becomes *true*. This fact can be used to advantage in setting up prolonged input from a keyboard. For example, we can set up the following procedure, which continues reading from the input file until we type an eof character:

Experiment 4

```
program TryThis(input, output);
  procedure ExtendedInput;
  var
    ThisChar : char;                          (*type char variable*)
  begin
    writeln('Enter text: ');                          (*prompt*)
    repeat
      read(ThisChar);                          (*get character*)
      write(ThisChar:3)                           (*echo print*)
    until eof                                (*continue until eof
                                             character is found*)
  end;                                         (*ExtendedInput*)
begin
  ExtendedInput               (*tell machine to activate procedure*)
end
```

Here is a sample input-output session with this program.

Sample Results

You Type	*Machine Response*
first love<return>	f i r s t l o v e
water music<return>	w a t e r m u s i c
eof character	<session ends, here>

In this experiment, the machine does not do any printing until you type a return. A graphical interpretation of what this program does is given in Figure 3.4. The write statement in the ExtendedInput procedure prints each character as it is read. You might wonder what is printed by the following experiment:

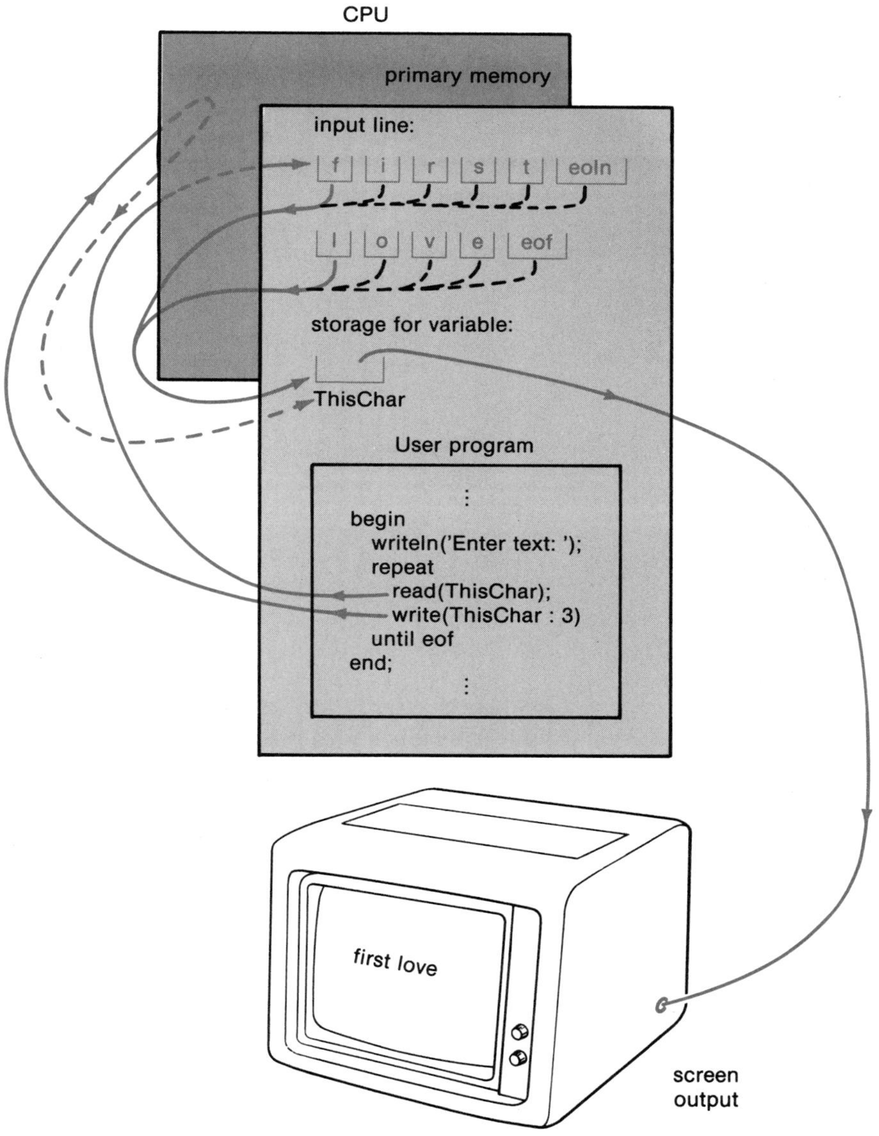

FIGURE 3.4
Graphical interpretation of reading and writing characters

Experiment 5

```
program NowTryThis(input, output);
   procedure EchoPrint;
   var
      ThatChar: char;                              (*type char variable*)
   begin
      repeat
         writeln('Enter text followed by period: ');
         repeat
            read(ThatChar);                        (*get character*)
         until ThatChar = '.';
         repeat
            write(ThatChar: 3)                     (*print character*)
         until That Char = '.'
      until eof
   end;                                            (*EchoPrint*)
begin
   EchoPrint                                       (*activate procedure*)
end.
```

After the last read in this program, ThatChar has the last character entered. So you might wonder what gets printed in the second inner repeat loop. Implementing this second experiment is left for an exercise. Pascal also has a built-in readln procedure, which can be used in two ways.

3.4.4 Readln Procedure

Unlike a read procedure, a readln procedure can be activated without any parameters. When the readln procedure is activated without parameters, the input pointer is always moved to the beginning of the next input line. This will happen regardless of where the input pointer is pointing in the current line. We can use this fact to advantage if we want to enter additional input lines after we finish the first input session. For example, we can use this idea in the ReadManyLines procedure in the following program:

Experiment 6

```
program ManyLines(input, output);
   procedure ReadManyLines;
   var
      ch: char;                                    (*char variable*)
      col: integer;                                (*format number*)
   begin
      repeat
         col := 1;
         writeln('Enter text: ');
```

```
        repeat
          read(ch);                       (*assign char to ch*)
          writeln(ch:col);                (*echo print*)
          col := col + 1
        until eoln;
        readln;                           (*move input pointer to next
                                            input line*)

        read(ch)
      until eof
    end;                                  (*NextLine*)
begin
  ReadManyLines
end.
```

This procedure will continue reading new input lines until you type an eof character. The iteration inside the inner repeat loop continues until an eoln character is detected. Implementation of this experiment is left as an exercise.

When should a readln with parameters be used instead of a read with parameters? In general, if it is necessary to have more than one input line at different times during the running of the same program, it is better to use a readln instead of a read. A readln always moves the input pointer to the next input line after the reading the specified input values is finished. This prepares the input file for more input. If it is necessary to revisit the same input line at different times during the running of a program, then it is necessary to use a read statement. When reading from the current line is complete, then use a readln by itself to move the input pointer to the next input line to prepare for any new input lines. These ideas are summarized in the following rule of thumb:

Rule of thumb with read or readln:

1. If it is necessary to revisit the same input line at different times during the running of a program, use a read statement.

2. Use a readln by itself, if it is necessary to read from another input line after repeated use of the same read statement. (This will move the input pointer to the next input line.)

3. Use a readln with parameters, if it is not necessary to revisit the same input line at different times during the running of a program.

3.4.5

Example: Sample Uses of Read and Readln

A sampler of different uses of the read and readln procedures is given in Figure 3.5. Parts 1 and 2 of the program in Figure 3.5 illustrate how the same input line can be revisited. The readln by itself at the beginning of part 3 is necessary. It takes care of moving the input pointer to the beginning of the next input line, allowing us to take data from a new input line. In the sample run for part 3, notice how a space is printed in

Yes &No

Where does this come from? A space was assigned to ch4 when the eoln character was detected after the *Yes* at the end of the first input line. Parts 4 and 5 of Figure 3.5 illustrate how an input line of numbers can be revisited at different times during the running of a program. Part 6 shows how an eoln character is ignored when numbers are being read. The reading continues until all numbers specified in the parameter list for a read or a readln are found.

```
          (*Method: Show how the input pointer can be moved and how
                         a blank is assigned to a variable of type char,
                                            if an end of line is read.*)
program ok(input, output);

 (*- - - - - - - - - - - - - - - - - - - - - - - - - - - - - - - - - - -*)
                                 (*Use all 4 bulit-in i/O procedures.*)

procedure EnterValues;
var
   ch1, ch2, ch3, ch4, ch5, ch6, ch7: char; (*sample characters*)
   no1, no2, no3, no4, no5, no6: integer;       (*sample numbers*)
begin
   write('Enter 10 characters: ');
                                                               (*1*)
   read(ch1, ch2);                        (*get first 2 characters*)
   writeln; writeln('1st 2 characters: ', ch1, ch2);
                                                               (*2*)
   read(ch3, ch4, ch5, ch6);               (*get next 4 characters*)
   writeln; writeln('next 4 characters: ', ch3, ch4, ch5, ch6);
                                                               (*3*)
   readln;                   (*move input pointer to input next line*)
   write('Enter 6 characters, 3 per line: ');
   readln(ch1, ch2, ch3, ch4, ch5, ch6, ch7);
   writeln; write('Entered characters: ', ch1, ch2, ch3);
   write(ch4, ch5, ch6, ch7);
                                                               (*4*)
   writeln; write('Enter 10 integers: ');
   read(no1, no2);
   writeln; writeln('1st 2 numbers: ', no1:10, no2:10);
                                                               (*5*)
```

```
    read(no3, no4, no5, no6);
    writeln; write('Next 4 numbers: ', no3:10, no4:10);
    write(no5:10, no6:10);
                                                                  (*6*)
    readln;                    (*move input pointer to next input line*)
    writeln; write('Enter 6 integers, 3 per line: ');
    read(no1, no2, no3, no4, no5, no6);
    writeln; write('Entered numbers: ', no1:10, no2:10);
    write(no3:10, no4:10, no5:10, no6:10)
end;                                                  (*EnterValues*)

 (*-----------------------------------------------------------*)

begin
    EnterValues                      (*activate EnterValues procedure*)
end.
```

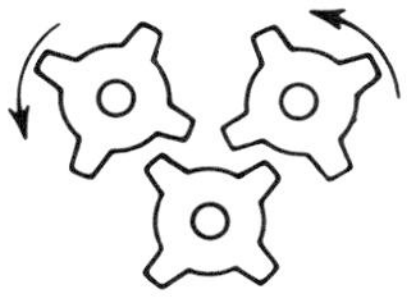

```
Enter 10 characters: Calculemus
1st 2 characters: Ca

next 4 characters: lcul

Enter 6 character, 3 per line: Yes
&No

Entered characters: Yes &No
Enter 10 integers: 199 2 3 4 8 13 21 55 34 233
1st 2 numbers:          199          2

Next 4 numbers:    3    4    8    13

Enter 6 integers, 3 per line: 55 144 2110
2000 2001 1986

Entered numbers:    55    144    2110    2000    2001    1986
```

FIGURE 3.5 Uses of the built-in input procedures

What would happen if we use a readln instead of a read in part 6? The answer to this question is left as an exercise. In Section 3.5 we show how information can be passed to and from procedures. This is made possible by setting up what are known as *procedure parameters*. A *parameter* serves as a placeholder, which is filled whenever a procedure is activated inside a program. Since parameters serve merely as placeholders, they are known as *formal parameters*.

3.5 Two Types of Formal Parameters: Value and Variable

There are two types of formal parameters: *value* parameters (these receive values when a procedure containing them is activated) and *variable* parameters (these receive references to memory locations when a procedure containing them is activated). Until now we have created procedures like *EnterValues* in Figure 3.1, which is an example of a parameterless procedure. When a procedure has parameters, these are declared in a procedure heading. For each procedure parameter, there will be a corresponding actual parameter. An *actual parameter* is used in specifying what value or reference is to be used to replace a formal parameter. A procedure heading with parameters has the syntax shown in Figure 3.6. Each type of formal parameter has its own special syntax. We show how to set up and use value parameters, first.

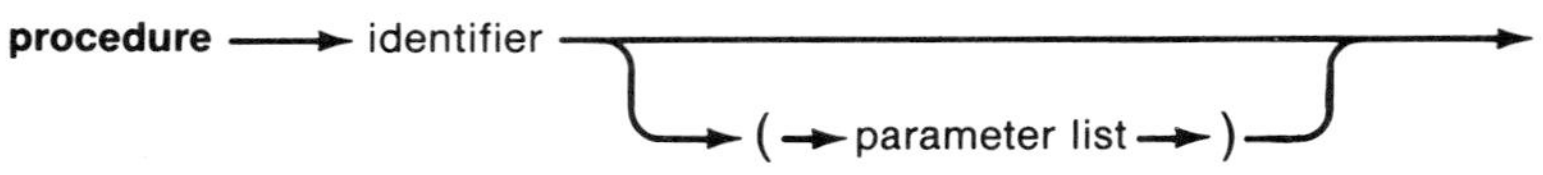

FIGURE 3.6
Syntax for a procedure heading

3.5.1 Value Parameters

A *value parameter* serves as a place marker for a value. In other words, value parameters always receive values when a procedure having them is first activated. This should tell you something about the actual parameters that must be used in a procedure call which supplies values for value parameters. In this case, each actual parameter must be an expression. (Recall that an expression always represents a value.)

Here are some examples of procedure headings with value parameters.

```
procedure ShowSamples(symbol: char;                    (*sample char*)
                              WholeNo: integer);         (*sample no*)

procedure winnings(player1, player2: real);            (*dollars won*)

procedure ok(ch1, ch2: char;                           (*two symbols*)
                 no1, no2, no3: real;               (*three numbers*)
                 decision: Boolean;            (*either true or false*)
                 yes: integer);                     (*final number*)
```

Here are some examples of procedure calls corresponding to the first of the above procedure headings.

Procedure Call	*Values Received*	
	Symbol	*WholeNo*
ShowSamples('!', 233);	'!'	233
ShowSamples(id, $x + y$);	id	$x + y$

These are two examples of calls by value. Each of the above procedure calls supplies values for the corresponding value parameters in the ShowSamples procedure. Here is a sample program that uses the ShowSamples procedure.

Experiment 7

```
program sample7(input);

            (*-------------------------------------*)
procedure ShowSamples(ch: char;              (*value parameter*)
                      no: integer);          (*value parameter*)
begin
   ch := '!';                               (*local change to ch*)
   no := no + 2010                          (*local change to no*)
end;                                                    (*Try This*)
            (*-------------------------------------*)
procedure driver;
var
   NewChar: char; NewNo: integer;            (*local variables*)
   ok: char; yes: integer;                   (*local variables*)
begin
   NewChar := 'C'; NewNo := 55;
   ShowSamples(NewChar, NewNo):             (*activate procedure*)
   readln(ok, yes);                              (*get values*)
   ShowSamples(ok, yes)                     (*activate procedure*)
end;                                                  (*driver*)
            (*-------------------------------------*)
begin
   driver                            (*activate driver procedure*)
end.
```

The NewChar, NewNo, ok, and yes variables are used as actual parameters in the driver procedure. The changes to the value parameters in the ShowSamples procedures do not change the values of the variables in the driver procedure. That is, the variables ok and yes, for example, in the driver procedure, are not changed as a result of the following call:

ShowSamples(ok, yes)

Whatever values were assigned to these variables by

readln(ok, yes);

are not changed by the ShowSamples procedure. You can verify this by inserting some write or writeln statements into the above program. This is left as an exercise.

The order of formal parameters in a procedure heading dictates the order of the actual parameters that must be used in a procedure call. In the ShowSamples procedure, for example, the ch-parameter appears first in the parameter list. For this reason, the actual parameter corresponding to ch must appear first in the actual parameter list used to activate this procedure. Here is an example of a ShowSamples call that violates this rule.

Mistaken Procedure Call

Procedure Call	*Actual Parameter*	*Formal Parameter*
ShowSamples(2010, *C*)	2010 *C*	ch (type char) no (type integer)

errors:

1. The actual parameter 2010 (type integer) does not match the formal parameter ch (type char).

2. The actual parameter *C* (type char) does not match the formal parameter no (type integer).

In general a value parameter list has the syntax shown in Figure 3.7.

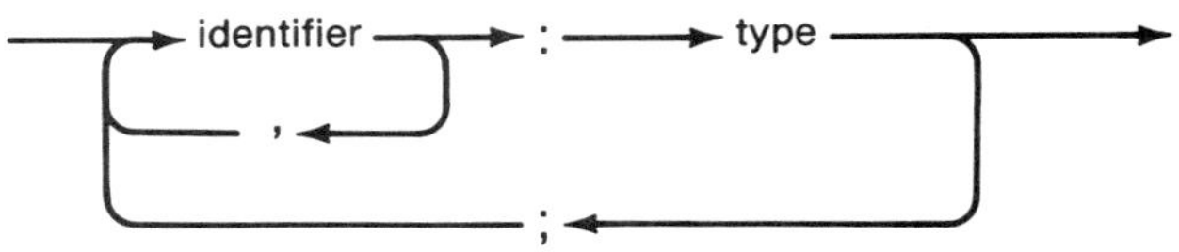

FIGURE 3.7
Syntax for a value-parameter list

Value parameters represent one-way streets. They receive values from procedure calls but they do not return values to the block containing the procedure call. Value parameters are private parameters. By contrast, variable parameters are two way streets.

3.5.2 *Two-Way Streets: Variable Parameters*

Variable parameters represent two-way streets. Whatever happens to a variable parameter inside a procedure will change the corresponding actual parameter. That is, the referenced memory location will be affected by any changes made to a variable parameter. Variable parameters are not private parameters. A procedure call that supplies a reference for a variable parameter is known as a *call by reference.* We can set up procedure headings with variable parameters. These are formal parameters that receive references to memory locations. Here are some sample procedure headings with variable parameters.

```
procedure Echo (var x, y: integer;               (*references to nos*)
                var yes: char);                   (*reference to char*)

procedure bet(var wins: integer;              (*reference to winnings*)
              var amt: real);                   (*reference to dollars*)
```

In general the syntax for a variable parameter list is given in Figure 3.8. Notice that each new variable parameter list must begin with the var token. It is often convenient to break up variable parameters of the same type, putting them on separately commented lines. For example, we can rewrite the heading for the Echo procedure as follows:

```
procedure Echo(var x: integer;                    (*reference to pitch*)
               var x: integer;            (*reference to something else*)
               var yes: char);                   (*reference to symbol*)
```

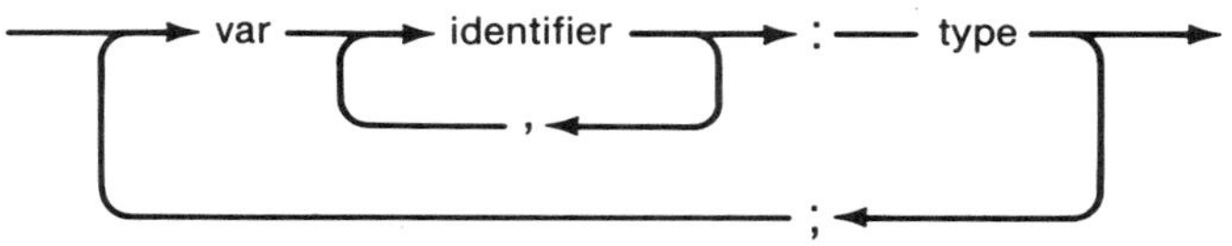

FIGURE 3.8
Syntax for a variable-parameter list

Since variable parameters receive references, not values, this should tell you something about the actual parameters that must be used to supply references in procedure calls. In this case, an actual parameter must be an identifier for a variable or, as we shall see later, for a function. We illustrate these ideas in the following example.

3.5.3 *Example: Using Value and Variable Parameters*

The program in Figure 3.9 brings together the two types of formal parameters. Notice that this program has no *global* variables (ones declared at the top of the program block). All variables are local to the procedures used. The range of meaning of a variable is limited by the block it is declared in. Both constants and values of local variables are used as actual parameters. Notice that the beginning value of *NewSymbol* is '!', which is not changed by the ShowSamples procedure because the symbol parameter in the ShowSamples procedure is a value parameter. By contrast, the variable EulerNumber in the driver procedure receives the value assigned the no parameter in the ShowSamples procedure. Why? The no parameter is a variable parameter.

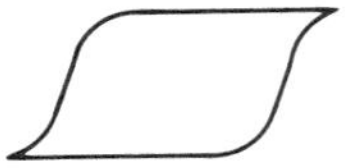

```
            (*Method: Show how constants and values of variables can be
                                              passed between procedures.*)

program constants(input, output);
 (*- - - - - - - - - - - - - - - - - - - - - - - - - - - - - - - - - - - -*)

  procedure ShowSamples(symbol: char;                      (*sample char*)
                        WholeNo: integer;                    (*sample no*)
                        var no: real);                     (*sample real*)
  const
     e = 2.71828;                                       (*Euler's number*)
  var
     col: integer;                                    (*use in formatting*)
  begin
     writeln('values obtained inside ShowSamples procedure:');
                                                                    (*0*)
     writeln('Received symbol = ', symbol);
     writeln('Received integer value = ', WholeNo);
     writeln; writeln;
     writeln('Changes in local variables: '); writeln;
                                                                    (*1*)
     col:= 10;
     repeat
        WholeNo := WholeNo * 2;
        writeln('New no.':col, WholeNo:6);
        col := col + 3
     until WholeNo > 25000;
                                                                    (*2*)
     no := e;                       (*notice!- -will change driver variable*)
     symbol := '*'                    (*notice!- -driver var not changed*)
  end;                                                       (*ShowSamples*)

 (*- - - - - - - - - - - - - - - - - - - - - - - - - - - - - - - - - - - -*)
            (*Program manager: get values, activate ShowSamples*)

  procedure driver;
  const
     ThisSymbol = '!';                                   (*local constant*)
  var
     NewSymbol: char;                                    (*local char var*)
     EulerNumber: real;                                      (*local real*)
  begin
     NewSymbol := ThisSymbol;                           (*assign constant*)
     ShowSamples(NewSymbol, 233, EulerNumber);
     writeln; writeln;
     writeln('Final values of local variables in driver procedure:');
     writeln; writeln;
     writeln; writeln('final values : ');
     writeln('Final character = ', NewSymbol);
     writeln('    Final Euler number = ', EulerNumber)
  end;                                                            (*driver*)

 (*- - - - - - - - - - - - - - - - - - - - - - - - - - - - - - - - - - - -*)
```

```
    begin
       driver                                  (*activate program manager*)
    end.
values obtained inside ShowSamples proc.:
Received symbol = !
Received integer value =           233

Changes in local variables:

   New no. 466
      New no. 932
         New no. 1864
            New no. 3728
               New no. 7456
                  New no. 14912
                     New no. 29824

Final values of local variables in driver proc.:

final values :
Final character = !
   Final Euler number = 2.718280000E+00
```

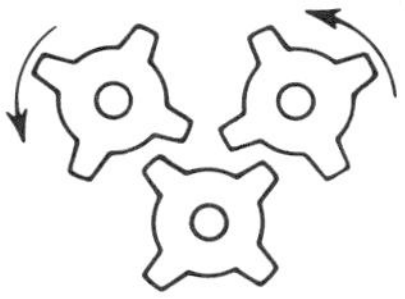

FIGURE 3.9 Working with procedure parameters

Notice that the EulerNumber variable has no value when the ShowSamples procedure is activated. Merely a reference to the memory location identified by EulerNumber is used in the procedure call. It is possible to assign a value to EulerNumber before calling the ShowSamples procedure. But this value will be lost after the activation of the ShowSamples procedure. You can verify this by adding the following actions to the driver procedure:

1. After the first ShowSamples call and the value of EulerNumber has been printed out, assign a new value to this variable, then
2. Activate ShowSamples a second time, then
3. Print out the final value of EulerNumber in the driver procedure.

This is left as an exercise. We show a more exotic example of the use of both value and variable parameters in Section 3.5.4.

3.5.4

Example: Finding the Largest Number

We can bring together the ideas we have discussed so far by setting up a procedure to scan an input line for the largest number entered. Here is a preliminary design for a program to do this.

```
                                         (*input: list of numbers;
                                           output: largest value*)
begin
   get numbers to be compared;
   find maximum value among entered numbers;
   display the largest value
end                                 (*preliminary program design*)
```

The first two lines of this preliminary program can be handled together inside one procedure. The third line can be handled separately to print a report. Controlling the use these two procedures can be handled by a driver procedure. These procedures can be "wired together" using the structure chart shown in Figure 3.10. The driver procedure will activate the FindMax procedure with two actual parameters, largest and next. In the FindMax procedure, *largest* will be a variable parameter. By contrast, the *next* parameter will be a value parameter. The driver procedure will activate FindMax with a value of the next parameter. The driver procedure will be used to manage the use of the other two procedures. We can set it up so that the user can enter more than one set of numbers. Here is the pseudocode for the FindMax procedure.

```
                                         (*input: list of numbers;
                                           output: largest value*)
begin
Enter a line of numbers;
assign the first number to largest;
repeat
   assign the next number to next;
   if next > largest then
      assign next to largest
   until an eoln character is detected
end.                  (*algorithm to find largest entered number*)
```

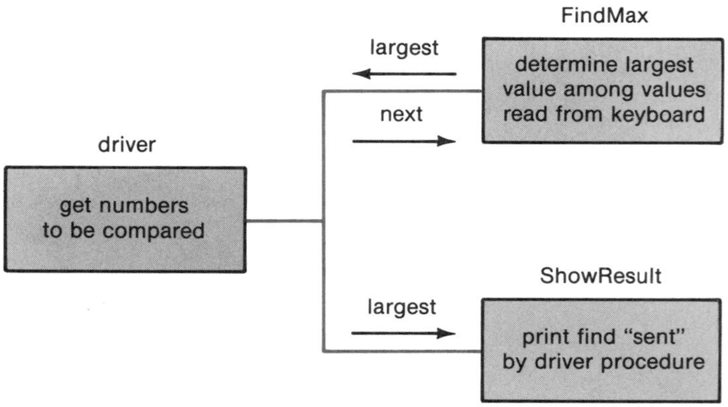

FIGURE 3.10
Structure chart for a program to find largest value

Nothing is said in this abstract program about the data type of the variables used. Both largest and next must be the same type because their values must be compared. We show a complete program to implement this FindMax procedure in Figure 3.11. Notice how a readln by itself in the driver procedure is used in Figure 3.11 to get ready for addition lines of numbers. After the processor finishes the activation of the FindMax procedure, the input pointer is pointing to the eoln character. The readln in the driver procedure moves the input pointer past the eoln character. Will this program work without the readln by itself in the driver procedure? Experiment with this program and see what happens without this statement.

```
          (*Method: Use the built-in read procedure to scan an input
                line of numbers and saving the largest entry in each
                                                 pair compared.*)

program scanner(input, output);
 (*-----------------------------------------*)
                        (*Scan input line for largest number*)

  procedure FindMax(var largest: integer;           (*number found*)
                        next: integer);              (*next entry*)
  begin
    largest := next;
    repeat
      read(next);
      if next > largest then
        largest := next                                   (*then*)
    until eoln
  end;                                                 (*FindMax*)

 (*-----------------------------------------*)
              (*Program manager: get values, activate FindMax*)

  procedure driver;
  var
    BiggestNo: integer;                              (*biggest value*)
    FirstNo: integer;                               (*leading number*)
    choice: integer;                              (*control variable*)
  begin
    repeat
      writeln('Enter two or more integers on the same line:');
      read(FirstNo);
      FindMax(BiggestNo, FirstNo);
      writeln; writeln('lgst value = ', BiggestNo:10);
      readln;                          (*move to next input line*)
      writeln; write('Again?- -1 = Y, 0 = N: '); readln(choice);
      writeln; writeln
    until choice = 0                                      (*repeat*)
  end;                                                    (*driver*)

 (*-----------------------------------------*)
```

```
begin
   driver                                    (*activate driver procedure*)
end.
```

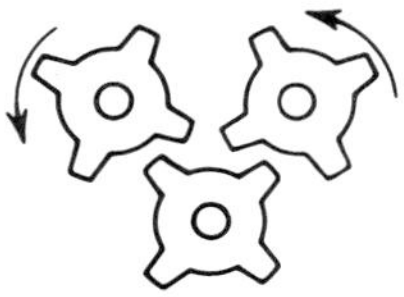

```
Enter two or more integers on the same line:
233 231

lgst value =        233

Again?- -1=Y, 0=N: 1

Enter two or more integers on the same line:
233 11 22 33 111 222 333 1111 2222 3333

lgst value =        3333

Again?- -1=Y, 0=N: 1

Enter two or more integers on the same line:
1 1 0 1 1 1 0 1 0 1 2 1 1 1 1 1 0 1

lgst value =              2

Again?- -1=Y, 0=N: 0
```

FIGURE 3.11 Finding the largest numeric entry

Is it necessary to use a read statement in the FindMax procedure? Yes. The iteration in the repeat loop in this procedure will terminate when an eoln character is detected. This will happen when we type a <return>. You might wonder what would happen if we modify the repeat statement in the FindMax procedure as follows:

```
repeat
   readln(next);
   if next > largest then
      largest := next
until eoln
```

Before you try out this modification of FindMax, see if you can guess what will happen when the following lines are entered:

```
3 44 5 99 <return>
<return>
```

Implementation of this idea is left for an exercise.

Finally, notice that largest is a variable parameter. It is used to return the largest value found among the entries in the input line. This program can be refined.

3.5.5

Refinement: Finding the Smallest Value

Try renaming the FindMax procedure FindMinMax. Then add a new variable parameter to this procedure (call it smallest). Use this new variable parameter to determine the smallest number in the entered line. This can be done by addition another assignment statement (assign the value of next to smallest). Then modify the repeat loop in the new procedure so that the smallest value is found.

Notice that you will have to introduce a new local variable in the driver procedure (call it SmallestNo). This new local variable will be needed to supply a reference in the new FindMinMax procedure call. This refinement is left as an exercise.

3.5.6

Refinement: Finding the Range and Average Value

The new FindMinMax procedure developed in Section 3.5.5 can be further refined to compute the average value. This can be done by adding a third variable parameter to this procedure (call it *sum*). In addition, introduce a fourth variable parameter to this procedure (call it *count*). Then use count to keep track of how many number have been read, including the first number, which is read inside the driver procedure. In addition, keep track of the sum of the numbers found by the FindMinMax procedure.

These changes will mean you will also have to set up new local variables inside the driver procedure, ones that can supply references for the count and sum parameters in the FindMinMax procedure. Use, for example, NewCount and NewSum as the names of the new local variables inside the driver procedure. After activating the new FindMinMax procedure, use the values of the new local variables to compute the average value found. You can obtain this average by dividing NewSum by NewCount.

The *range* of a set of numbers is the difference between the largest and smallest numbers. The following example illustrates this idea:

List of numbers: 224, 49, 72, 339, 55, 221, 70, 6, 330
Largest value: 339
Smallest value: 6
Range = 339 − 6 = 333

You have the information you need in the driver procedure to compute the range of the entered numbers. To do this, use the Smallest No and BiggestNo local variables to compute the range.

Finally, you should make the following refinement to the program in Figure 3.3 to print the new results.

3.5.7

Refinement: A New ShowResults Procedure

You should create a new procedure (call it ShowResults) for the program in Figure 3.11 that will print the following table each time you inspect a line of numbers:

Smallest Number	*Biggest Number*	*Average Value*

This new procedure should be set up with value parameters to handle the values obtained by the FindMinMax and driver procedures. In addition, this new procedure should be activated from inside the driver procedure. This refinement is left as an exercise.

Each time you add a procedure to a program, you should be concerned with where you put each procedure in the source text. We look at this problem next.

3.6 How to Order Procedures

To avoid problems in programs with more than one procedure, it is a good idea to put the driver procedure last in your source text. A driver procedure (if there is one) is your program manager. It is used to supply all the local variables you will need and to activate the other procedure you use. Secondly, think of procedure calls as "calling up" other procedures. Put called procedures *above* the ones doing the calling. Here is a sample source text organization to illustrate the idea of calling up procedures.

```
program CallingUp;
                              (*-------------------------------*)
  procedure a;
  begin
                                             (*do somthing, here*)
  end;
                              (*-------------------------------*)
  procedure b;
  begin
     a                                     (*call up procedure a*)
  end;
                              (*-------------------------------*)
  procedure driver;
  begin
     a;                                    (*call up procedure a*)
     b;                                    (*call up procedure b*)
  end;
                              (*-------------------------------*)
  begin
     driver                           (*call up driver procedure*)
  end.
```

Let the driver procedure manage the uses of the other procedures in your program. If you want to add new procedures to your source text, then add them to the top of the program block (*above* your other procedures). Then use the driver procedure to handle calls to the new procedures.

Otherwise, if one procedure "calls down" to another procedure, it is necessary to use a forward reference. There are two types of forward references.

1. Forward reference for a procedure without parameters.
2. Forward reference for a procedure with parameters.

Here is the format to use for a forward reference to a procedure without parameters.

```
program CallingDown;
   procedure b; forward;                  (*a forward reference!*)
                        (*--------------------------------*)
   procedure a;
   begin
      b                                (*call down to procedure b*)
   end;                                                     (*a*)
                        (*--------------------------------*)
   procedure b;
   begin
                                                (*do something*)
   end;                                                     (*b*)
                        (*--------------------------------*)
   begin
      a                                 (*activate procedure a*)
   end.
```

In this sample source text, procedure *a* calls down to procedure *b* because procedure *b* follows procedure *a* in the text. A very different technique is used, if it is necessary to call down to a procedure with parameters. Here is a sample source text to illustrate this idea.

Experiment 8

```
program MoreCalls;
   procedure b(var ThisNo : integer;                 (*sample no*)
                   var x, y : real;                 (*sample nos*)
                   var ok : char;                 (*sample symbol*)
                   var yes: Boolean);           (*sample decision*)
              forward;                         (*forward reference*)
   procedure c(var first, second : char); forward;
                                        (*second forward reference*)
                        (*--------------------------------*)
```

```
procedure a;
var
   result: integer;
   ThisX, This Y: real: ThisOk: char; ThisYes: Boolean;
   ThisFirst, ThisSecond: char;
begin
   b(result, ThisX, This Y, ThisOk, ThisYes);            (*call down*)
   c(ThisFirst, ThisSecond)                              (*call down to c*)
end;                                                                (*a*)
                          (*-------------------------------------------*)
procedure b;                                      (*notice!—no parameters!*)
var
   AnotherFirst, AnotherSecond: char;
begin
                        (*do something, then make the following call:*)
c(AnotherFirst, AnotherSecond)                           (*call down to c*)
end;                                                                (*b*)
                          (*-------------------------------------------*)
procedure c;                                      (*notice—no parameters!*)
begin
                                                        (*do something*)
end;                                                                (*c*)
                          (*-------------------------------------------*)
begin
   a                                                         (*call up a*)
end.
```

In other words, when a forward reference is made to a procedure with parameters, the parameter list is put into the forward reference declaration (with the term *forward*) and is omitted when the procedure itself is given in the source text. Here is a rule of thumb to keep in mind.

> **Rule of thumb with procedure calls:**
>
> **If a procedure is called up, it is not necessary to use a forward reference. It is preferable to put a procedure definition *before* a procedure call.**

3.7 Global vs. Local Variables

Each block in a Pascal program can have its own declarations of variables. This means a block becomes the defining point for variables.

The range of meaning of a variable is limited by the block that contains the variable. This is another way of saying that a block determines the *scope of a variable.*

This means that a variable declared in a program block will have widest scope. A variable declared in a program block is called a global variable. A *global variable* is a variable declared in a program block and which has unlimited scope. Global variables can be used throughout a Pascal program. By contrast, variables declared in a procedure block represent private storage for that procedure. A variable declared in a nonprogram block is called a *local variable.* The range of meaning of a local variable is limited by the nonprogram block containing it. A local variable can only be used inside the procedure block, for example, where it is declared.

The difference between local and global variables is very important. There tends to be a temptation to use global variables in setting up a Pascal program, since they are easier to use. However, global variables can help create a muddled program in two different ways.

1. Actions on a global variable by one procedure may cause unwanted side effects (unwanted or unexpected values). These side effects can cause problems when the same global variable is used in more than one procedure.
2. When procedures use globals, it is always necessary to refer back to the top of the program to get information about the data type for a variable identifier. We often need to refer back and forth between the declaration of the global and its usage in a procedure to make sense of what is being done with the global.

Globals should be avoided. If globals are not used, then it becomes necessary to pass parameters between procedures. As a rule, it is better to use procedure parameters. In this way each parameter (along with its data type) will be listed and easily referenced in each procedure heading. The use of procedure parameters and local variables makes it easier to use the same procedure in different programs. This practice helps make a procedure a complete subprogram. It is also this practice that helps explain the use of a driver procedure.

3.8 Why Use a Driver Procedure?

If procedures with parameters are activated from a program body, then it is necessary to use global variables in these procedure calls. This will build a serious problem into longer source texts. Procedures with parameters will become more difficult to follow because you will have to keep referring back to the globals set up in the program block. If you use globals, you may also be tempted to avoid procedure parameters altogether. This is an invitation to disaster! If only globals are used, then unwanted side effects may creep into your program.

Here is an example of a program with globals that will produce side effects.

Experiment 9

```
program SideEffect(input, output);
  var
    count, sum, max : integer;                                  (*globals*)
                              (*- - - - - - - - - - - - - - - - - - - - - - - - -*)
    procedure ComputeSum;
    begin
      repeat
        sum := sum + count;
        count := count + 1                               (*side effect, here*)
      until count > max
    end;                                                     (*ComputeSum*)
                              (*- - - - - - - - - - - - - - - - - - - - - - - - -*)
  begin
    write('max: '); readln(max); writeln; sum := 0;
    for count := 1 to max do begin
      ComputeSum;
      writeln(count:20, sum:20)
    end                                                             (*for*)
  end.                                                     (*program body*)
```

This program uses the global variabale count in two different ways.

1. Count is used to control the for loop inside the program body.
2. Count is used inside the ComputeSum procedure to compute a sum.

The unwanted side effect in this program occurs in the ComputeSum procedure, which changes the value of count each time it is activated. This program was run on an IBM PC with different values of max. It runs endlessly. Try this program on your machine with a value of 30000 for max.

The problem of the side effect in this program can be eliminated by making count a local variable inside the ComputeSum procedure. By making count local to this procedure, what happens to count inside the ComputeSum procedure is private to that procedure. This allows the for loop in the program body to terminate normally.

This program can be improved further by eliminating the use of global variables altogether. This can be done by introducing count, sum, and max as local variables inside a driver procedure. Then set up a variable parameter in the ComputeSum procedure to receive a reference to sum. These changes in the above program are left as an exercise. You should try experimenting with the above program on your machine to see the side effects it produces.

In this section we have been dealing indirectly with the problem of scoping variables. That is, we have been toying with the range of meaning of variables in a program, their scope in a program. We deal with this issue in more detail in Section 3.9.

3.9 Scope of Identifiers

Each block in a program determines the range of meaning of its identifiers for variables, constants, procedures, and so on. Here is the fundamental scope rule.

> **Fundamental scope rule:**
>
> **The scope of an identifier is determined by the block in which it is declared.**

We can determine the scope of an identifier by determining in which block it is. It is fairly easy to determine the scope of identifiers for variables and constants. We illustrate this idea using the outline for a source text shown in Figure 3.12. Any variable or constant declared in a program block can be referenced in any block in the program. This is not the case with variables or constants declared inside a procedure block. A block containing a declaration of a variable or constant determines the range of meaning of its variables and constants. In the above outline for a source text, for example, a variable declared in procedure *B* is a local to that procedure. Its scope is limited to the procedure *B* block. It can be referenced in any of the blocks contained inside procedure *B*, namely, *C*, *D*, and *E*. It cannot be referenced outside the procedures *B* block. Similar restrictions are put on constants and variables declared in any of the other blocks of the above source text. We summarize these ideas in the following scope table for the program in Figure 3.12.:

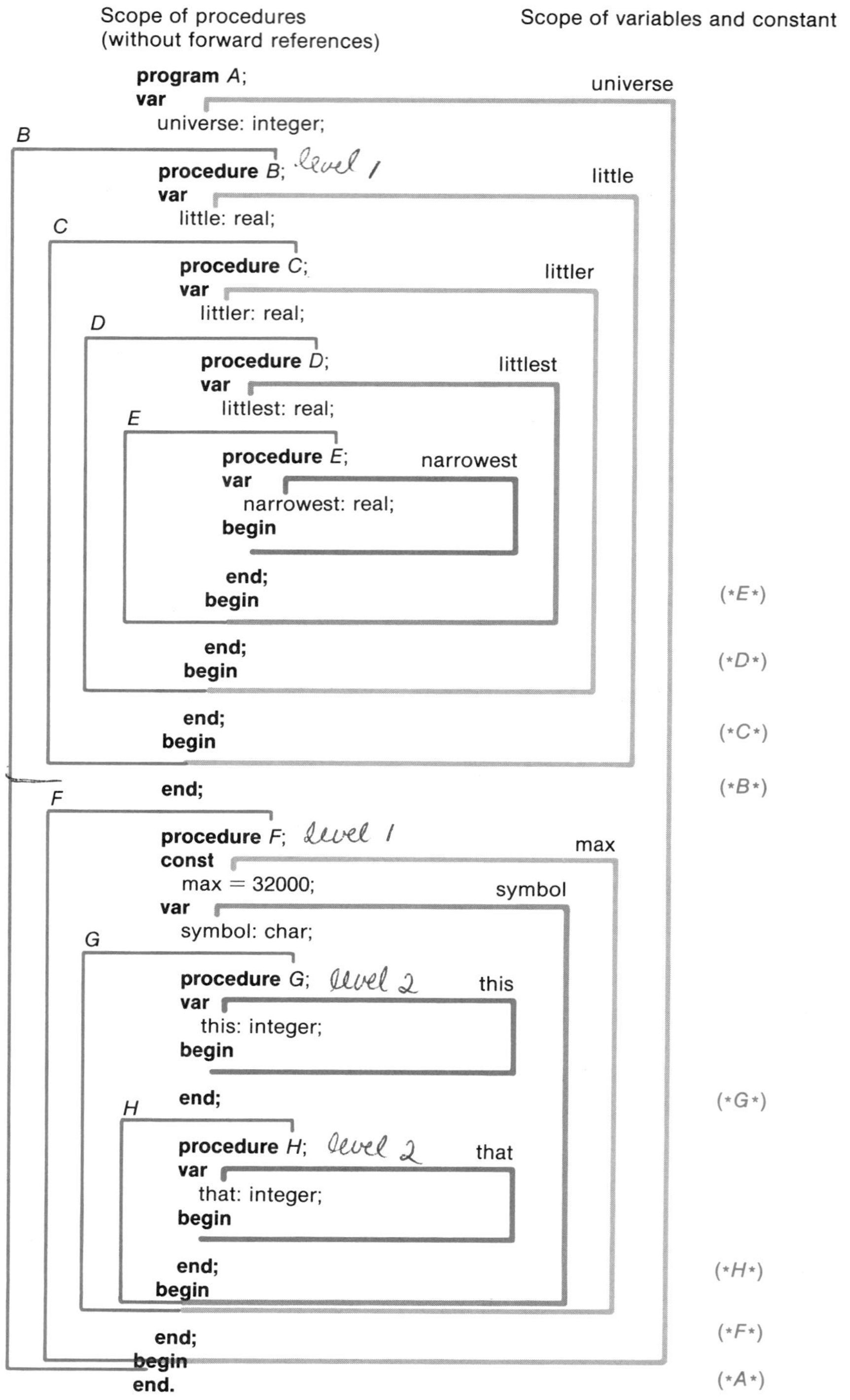
Scope of procedures
(without forward references)
Scope of variables and constant
program A;
var
universe: integer;
procedure B; level 1
var
little: real;
procedure C;
var
littler: real;
procedure D;
var
littlest: real;
procedure E;
var
narrowest: real;
begin
end;
begin
end;
begin
end;
begin
end;
procedure F; level 1
const
max = 32000;
var
symbol: char;
procedure G; level 2
var
this: integer;
begin
end;
procedure H; level 2
var
that: integer;
begin
end;
begin
end;
begin
end.
B
C
D
E
F
G
H
universe
little
littler
littlest
narrowest
max
symbol
this
that
(*E*)
(*D*)
(*C*)
(*B*)
(*G*)
(*H*)
(*F*)
(*A*)

FIGURE 3.12
Program to illustrate,

Scope Table for Variables and Constants

(Declaration) *Variables and Constants Declared Only in*	*(Scope)* *Variables and Constants Can Be Referenced in*
A (globals)	*A, B, C, D, E, F, G, H*
B (local)	*B, C, D, E*
C (local)	*C, D, E*
D (local	*D, E*
E (local)	*E*
F (local)	*F, G, H*
G (local)	*G, H*
H (local)	*H*

In other words, procedures nested inside the procedure *B* block can reference any variable or constant declared in either *B* or in the program block. Blocks can be identified by their nesting level. The program block is on level 0. Blocks declared in the program block are on level 1. A block declared in a level 1 block is on level 2, and so on. For example, in the above sample source text, we have the following nesting levels:

Nesting Levels of Blocks

Block	*Nesting Level*
A	0
B, F	1
C, G, H	2
D	3
E	4

For variables and constants declared in blocks with higher nesting levels, the scope of these variables and constants is narrower. Here is a rule of thumb for measuring the scope of a variable or constant.

> **A procedure can reference any variable or constant declared in blocks containing the procedure.**

It is also necessary to determine the scope of identifiers for procedures. We need to be able to determine range of meaning of procedure identifiers. We need to determine when a procedure can be referenced by another procedure.

A program block cannot be called. Any procedure on level 1 can be called inside a program body. Procedures on level 1 can also reference each other, either calling up or calling down to another procedure on level 1. Procedures with higher nesting levels have narrower scope. For example, in the above outline for a Pascal program, we show the scope of the procedures in this outline in the following table:

Permissible Procedure Calls

Block	*Can Be Called within the Following Procedures*
A (program)	None!
B (procedure)	*A, F, G, H*
C (procedure)	*B*
D (procedure)	*C*
E (procedure)	*D*
F (procedure)	*A, B* (with forward reference)
G (procedure)	*F, H*
H (procedure)	*F, G* (with forward reference)

Notice that procedures *C, D,* and *E* are not known and cannot be called by procedures outside procedure *B* or from the program body. These blocks are private to the *B* block. Likewise, the blocks nested inside procedure *F* cannot be referenced by procedures outside procedure *F* or from the program body. The two blocks inside the block for procedure *F* are both on the same nesting level, namely, level 2. These blocks can reference each other. Procedure *H* can call procedure *G*. If procedure *H* is given a forward reference, then procedure *G* can call procedure *H*.

It is not always the case that blocks on the same level can reference each other. Blocks *G* and *H* represent a special case. These blocks are both on level 2. These blocks are also both inside the same procedure block, namely, *F*. Notice that procedure *C* is also on level 2, but cannot be called by the other procedures on the same level. You can explain this fact in the following way. Procedure *C* is hidden from procedures *G* and *H*. Procedure *C* is inside the *B* block and not known to any block outside procedure *B*. You can use the following rule of thumb to determine when one procedure can call another one:

Rule of thumb for procedure calls:

Two procedures on the same level can call each other, if and only if they are both inside the same block or they are both on level 1.

3.10 More on Programming Style

The following two techniques have been used in programs in this chapter:

1. Procedures have been separated by a comment like the following one:

```
(*- - - - - - - - - - - - - - - - - - - - - - - - - - - - - *)
(*brief explanation of procedure, here*)
```

2. Identifiers have been given meaningful names using a combination of upper and lower case letters like the following identifiers:

Identifier	*Object Names*
ImitateAmadeus	Procedure
FindMax	Procedure
Biggest No	Variable
bell	Constant

The first technique helps show the separation of program blocks. The accompanying brief explanation will have a payoff later when it is necessary to interpret what is intended by a procedure. The second technique will help give a self-documenting character to your source texts. A meaningful identifier will "say" how the identified object is being used in a program. In general, procedure names should be made up of action words that suggest what procedures do. Names of variables and constants should be made up of one or more words that suggest how a variable or constant is used in a program. These are seemingly little stylistic techniques that will make your programs easier to follow.

3.11 Summary

A procedure call activates a procedure. When a procedure is activated by a processor, the actions specified by the procedure are carried out by the processor. Procedure calls can transmit values and references to memory locations to a procedure. Procedures with value parameters receive values when they are activated. Procedures with variable parameters receive references to memory locations when they are activated.

In between times, when a procedure is not activated, the parameters of a procedure have no meaning. For this reason, procedure parameters are called *formal parameters.* During activation, procedure parameters are used to produce results. If value parameters are used during the activation of a procedure, then any changes in these value parameters do have any affect on the corresponding actual parameters used. This is not the case with variable parameters. That is, if variable parameters are used during the activation of a procedure, then any changes in these variable parameters will change the corresponding actual parameters used. In effect, a value parameter is a one-way street. Actual parameters used to transmit values to value parameters are unaffected by changes to corresponding value parameters. This is one-way traffic.

By contrast, variable parameters are two-way streets. Traffic flows both ways. Referenced memory locations are affected by any changes made to variable parameters.

Actual parameters are used to transmit values and references in procedure calls. There are type types of actual parameters.

1. Actual parameters that transmit values are always expressions.
2. Actual parameters that transmit references are always identifiers for variables.

If a variable is used to transmit a value in a procedure call, then that variable must be initialized before the call can be made. If the identifier for a variable is used to transmit a reference in a procedure call, it is not necessary to initialize that variable. Merely the reference, not a value, is transmitted to variable parameters.

A procedure call that transmits a value is known as a *call by value.* A procedure call that transmits a reference to a memory location is known as a *call by reference.* Calls by value and calls by reference can be included in a single procedure call. The procedure calls in Figures 3.9 and 3.11 illustrate this idea.

There two built-in input procedures in Pascal, read, and readln. These can be used to take data from either a disk file or from a keyboard. When these procedures are used to read data entered from a keyboard, then a file called input is used. In this case, the *input* identifier must be put into the program heading. This tells Pascal to set up the machinery needed to allow data to be taken from a keyboard.

Activation of the read and readln procedures is guided by an *eoln* function, which either has a value of *true* if an eol character has been detected or *false* if no eol character has been detected. Both of these built-in procedures will continue reading from one input line to the next one until all of the read or readln parameters have been assigned values. The read procedure leaves the input pointer on the input line containing the last value it obtains. By contrast, the readln procedure will always move the input pointer to the beginning of the next input line after it has gotten its last value.

The read procedure is useful when it is necessary to revisit the same input line during the running of a program. When it necessary to enter new data for a new input line, then a readln by itself can be used to move the input pointer to the next input line. The readln procedure is convenient to use when it is not necessary to revisit the same input line, since the readln procedure will always leave the input pointer positioned at the beginning of the next input line. This sets up the input file for the next input line, if there is one.

Variables and constants declared in a program block are global variables with maximum scope. These variables and constants can be referenced anywhere (in any block) in a program. By contrast, the scope of variable and constants declared in a procedure block is limited by that block. These are local variables. They are private to the procedure in which they are declared. They cannot be referenced outside the procedure block in which they are declared.

It is good programming practice to use local variables. This makes it clearer what variables are being used by a procedure. The use of local rather than global variables makes it possible to avoid side effects, conflicts in the uses of variables by different procedures. It is better to pass values between procedures using local variable rather than rely on global variables and parameterless procedures.

3.12

Keywords Review

Keywords	*Related Ideas*
actual parameter	supplies value or reference in a procedure call
expression	supplies a value in a procedure call
reference	supplies a reference to a memory location using an identifier
call by reference	transmits a reference to a variable parameter in a procedure
call by value	transmits a value to a value parameter in a procedure
forward reference	used when on procedure calls down to another procedure
procedure	a subprogram
activation	begun by a procedure call. During activation, a computer carries out the actions specified by a procedure.
call	activate a procedure
level	nesting level
local constant	constant defined in procedure block
local variable	variable declared in procedure block
nesting	one procedure block declared inside another procedure block
parameter	place marker for either a value or reference to a memory location obtained from a procedure call
value	receives value at activation time
variable	receives reference to a memory location at activation time
read or readln	built-in input procedures
scope	range of meaning of an identifier
global variable	variable defined in program block
global constant	constant defined in program block
local variable	variable defined in a procedure block
local constant	constant defined in a procedure block

3.13 Exercises

1. What is the difference between an actual parameter and a formal parameter?
2. What is the scope of a variable declared in a program block?
3. What are the two types of formal parameters?
4. What are the two types of actual parameters?
5. Is it necessary to initialize a variable before a reference to that variable can be used in a call by reference?
6. What is the difference between a call by value and a call by reference?
7. Is it necessary to initialize a variable before that variable can be used in a call by value?
8. What output is produced by the following programs?

a.

```
program sample(output);
   procedure b(var x,y : integer);
   begin
      x : = 2 * x;
      y : = y + 2
   end;                                          (*b*)
   procedure c;
   var
      This, That : integer;
   begin
      This := 1; That := 5;
      b(This, This);
      writeln(This, That);
      b(That, That);
      writeln(This, That)
   end;                                          (*c*)
begin
   c
end.
```

b.

```
program TryThis(output);
var
   universe, count, max : integer;
   procedure TurnAbout;
   begin
      universe := 0;
      repeat
         universe := universe + count;
         count := count + 1
      until count > max
   end;                                          (*TurnAbout*)
begin
   max := 10;
   for count := 1 to max do begin
      TurnAbout;
      writeln(count, universe)
      end
end
```

c.

```
program NowThis(output);
var
   universe, count, max : integer;
   procedure NoSideEffect(bump : integer);
   begin
      universe := 0;
      repeat
         universe := universe + bump;
         bump := bump + 1
      until bump > max
   end;                                          (*NoSideEffect*)
begin
   max := 10;
   for count := 1 to max do begin
      NoSideEffect(count);
      writeln(count, universe)
      end
end.
```

d.

```
program TryThis(input);
const
   silence = 10000;                              (*mystery constant*)
var
   sound: integer;
begin
   for sound := 1 to silence do;
   writeln('!')
end.
```

e.

```
program NowTryThis(output);
begin
   while 1 > -1 do
end.
```

9. Write a Pascal program to do the following things:

a. Prompt for a character (use a variable of type character called *Target* to save this entered character).
b. Prompt for a line of characters to be entered at a keyboard.
c. Determine the frequency that the Target character occurs in the entered line of text.
d. Print the result.
e. Allow the user to enter a new line of text using the same Target character or using a new Target character.

10. Refine the program in exercise 9 so that the user can enter up to five target characters. Determine the frequency of each of these characters in an entered text. Allow the user to enter a new line of text using the old targets or with a new set of targets. Print the results each time in the following table form:

Target Character	*Frequency*

11. Modify program *A* in Figure 3.12, giving procedure *F* a forward reference in the following way:

```
program A;
   procedure F; forward;
                                        (*- - - - - - - - - - - - - - - - - - - - - - - - -*)
   procedure B;
       .
       .
       .
begin

end.                                                          (*program body*)
```

Then indicate which of the following procedure calls are legal:

a. Call procedure *F* from procedure *B*
b. Call procedure *F* from procedure *C*
c. Call procedure *F* from procedure *D*
d. Call procedure *F* from procedure *E*

12. Without using any forward references, complete the source text for program *A* (Section 3.12) as follows:

a. Put in all possible procedure calls.
b. Print a message each time one of the procedures in program *A* is activated. Your message should merely print out the identifier for the procedure activated.

13. Why are parameters in procedure calls referred to as *actual parameters?*

14. Using the sample2 program in Experiment 3 (Section 3.4.1), indicate what is printed by this program using the following input lines:

```
(a) Yes<return>                 (c) calculemus!<return>
     !<return>                  (d) c<return>
     <return>                       alc<return>
     <return>                       u<return>
     !<return>                      lemus!<return>
     Yes!<return>
(b) Y<return>
     e<return>
     s<return>
     !<return>
     Yes!<return>
```

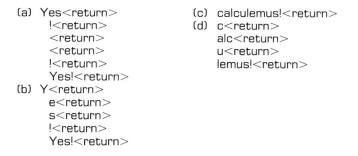

15. What is the eof character used on your computer?

16. Implement the EchoPrint procedure (Section 3.4.2) in a program. Give a sample run.

17. Implement the program in Experiment 4 (Section 3.4.3). Give a sample run.

18. Implement the program in Experiment 5 (Section 3.4.3). Give several sample runs.

19. Implement the program in Experiment 6 (Section 3.4.4). Give several sample runs.

20. What happens if a readln is used instead of a read in part 6 of Figure 3.5?

21. Insert writeln statements into Experiment 7 program (Section 3.5.1) to verify what happens to the parameters used. Give a sample run.

22. Carry out the suggested changes in Figure 3.9 described in Section 3.5.3 and explain what happens when the new program is run.

23. Carry out the refinement of Figure 3.11 described in Section 3.5.5 and give a sample run of the new program.

24. Carry out the refinement of Figure 3.11 described in Section 3.5.6 and give a sample run of the new program.

25. Carry out the refinement of Figure 3.11 described in Section 3.5.7 and give a sample run of the new program.

26. Implement the SideEffect program in Experiment 9 (Section 3.8) and explain the output when the program is run.

27. Carry out the suggested changes to the SideEffect program described in Experiment 9 (Section 3.8). Give a sample run.

3.14 Review Quiz

Determine whether the following are true or false:

1. A constant can be used as an actual parameter used in a call by reference.
2. A call by value transmits a value to a variable parameter in a procedure.
3. Variables declared in a procedure block can be referenced in the program body.
4. There are two types of formal parameters.
5. Variables declared inside a procedure block are called *local variables.*
6. Global variables can only be referenced in the program body.
7. Level 1 procedures can call each other.
8. The program block is on level 1.
9. Procedures on level 1 can call the program block.
10. The read and readln procedures are built-in output procedures in Pascal.
11. If procedure *B* follows procedure *A* in a source text, then procedure *A* must have a forward reference before it can call *B*.
12. If procedures *C* and *D* are level 2 procedures inside procedure *B*, and *D* follows *C*, then *C* can call *D* without a forward reference.

3.15 Readings

Brookshear, J. G. *Computer Science: An Overview.* Reading, MA: Benjamin/Cummings, 1985. See Section 6–5 on top-down design.

Wiener, R., and Sincovec, R. *Software Engineering with Modula-2 and Ada.* New York: Wiley, 1984. See Section 1.5 on program design.

CHAPTER 4

CONTROL STRUCTURES REVISITED

The static structure of a program should correspond in a simple way with the dynamic structure of the corresponding computations.

Bruce J. MacLennan, 1983

AIMS

- Introduce a new control structure: the **case** statement.
- Illustrate the presence and absence of exit mechanisms in **repeat** and **while** loops.
- Suggest how intentional infinite iterations can be set up and used.
- Suggest how one control structure can be rewritten using another control structure.
- Show various forms of the **case** statement and suggest the need for exception handling when **case** statements are used.

4.1 Introduction to Control Structures

A *control structure* is a statement used to control which actions are performed by a machine. The actions of a machine are channeled and guided by a control structure. For example, an **if** statement tells a machine to perform a **then** statement conditionally, provided the **if** condition is true. We can tell a machine to perform an iteration (repeat an action) using either a **repeat** or a **while** statement. The actions inside a **repeat** loop, for example, will be repeated, provided the until condition is false. We can use a compound statement with specified actions to force a machine to perform actions in sequence. Once inside a compound statement, a machine will carry out the specified actions sequentially until the end token of the compound statement is reached.

The *static structure* of a program is what you see when you read a source text. What happens when a program is activated by a machine gives a program its dynamic structure. The *dynamic structure* of a program concerns the actions carried out by a machine during its execution. The trick is to prepare a source text (the static part) so that it "says" clearly what a machine will do when a machine carries out its specified actions. This means we should look for control structures that are both readable and effective. The best control structures (the most readable ones!) are the ones that are guided by conditions, since we can read the conditions to tell when an action should be carried out by a machine.

Control structures guided by conditions help make a source text more readable. These structures give the static structure of a program a lift. They help us "see" the dynamic structure of a program—what will happen when a machine executes a program. In this chapter, we take another look at control structures we have already used. For example, we show some problems that commonly occur when an **if** statement is used. In addition, we show how **while** loops can be rewritten as **repeat** loops and vice versa. We also show how intentional and unintentional infinite **repeat** and **while** loops can be set up.

4.2 The Idea of Iteration

The term ***iteration*** belongs to the following family of words and expressions found in Roget (1852):

> **repeat, recur, reoccur, come up again, return, reappear, resume, go over the same ground, give an encore, fight one's battles over again, resound, reverberate, happen over and over, echo, battologize (keep repeating [a word or phrase]), recurrence, reissue, hammer away at**

An iteration control structure tells a machine when to repeat an action. We can tell a machine to iterate an action conditionally using either a **repeat** or a **while** loop. For example, we can set up the following **while** loops:

```
                (*repeatedly read and echo-print characters as long as
                                   an eoln character is not detected:*)
   read (symbol);
   while not eoln do begin
   write(symbol);                                    (*echo-print symbol*)
   read(symbol)                                       (*get next symbol*)
   end;                                                         (*while*)

        (*repeatedly activate a procedure to draw a robot as long as
                                count is less than the constant max:*)
count := 1;                                          (*initialize count*)
while count < max do begin
   DrawRobot;                                      (*activate procedure*)
   count := count + 1                           (*iterate this action, too*)
   end;                                                         (*while*)
```

Either a while loop or a repeat loop will continue an iteration indefinitely, if no exit mechanism is built into the loop.

4.2.1

Iterations with Exit Mechanisms

The iterations of the sample **while** loops in Section 4.2 are limited by the following exit mechanisms:

Exit Mechanism	*Result*
eoln	Iteration stops when an eoln character is detected.
count	Iteration stops when count equals max constant.

In general, an exist mechanism guarantees an iteration will stop (be finite) when the **while** expression is false. Unlike a repeat loop, the actions in a **while** loop are not performed, if the **while** expression is false right away. The iteration begun by a **while** loop will go on indefinitely unless we build into the loop a change in the **while** expression, making it eventually false. This change in the **while** expression provides a **while** loop with an exit mechanism. We can set up the second of the above **while** loops so that it has no exit mechanism.

```
                 (*iteration in a while loop without an exit mechanism*)

count := 1;                                          (*initialize count*)
while count < max do
   DrawRobot;                          (*activate procedure and make
                                          no change in the value of
                                                             count*)
```

As long as count is less than max, this iteration will continue indefinitely, since no change is made to count inside the while loop. Once this iteration begins, it has no exit mechanism. A common source of error in a program with a while loop is the absence of an exit mechanism built into the loop. This is equally a problem with repeat loops. For example, here is a repeat loop without an exit mechanism.

```
                        (*repeatedly scan input lines for integers, echo
                                                   printing what is read*)

count := 1;                                         (*initialize count*)
repeat
   read(number);                                (*read an integer value*)
   write(number)                                   (*echo-print value*)
until count = 50;                                         (*never true*)
```

The value of count is not changed inside this **repeat** loop, so it will continue the iteration indefinitely. This iteration can be given an exit mechanism by changing the value of count inside the **repeat** loop. This repeated change of the value of count must be done with the until condition in mind. A failure to do this will result in an effective exit mechanism.

If we change the value of count as follows, this iteration will still continue indefinitely.

```
                     (*iteration with an ineffective exit mechanism*)
count := 1;                                     (*count starts with 1*)
repeat
   read(number); write(number);
   count := count - 1                        (*ineffective mechanism*)
until count = 50;
```

This iteration will always fail to terminate because the value of count decreases each time, falling away from rather than approaching 50. It is left for an exercise to change this loop to make its iteration terminate.

These two control structures have important differences. To choose the appropriate one for a part of a program, it is helpful to look at how **repeat** and **while** loops differ.

4.2.2 *Differences between* **Repeat** *and* **While** *Loops*

The tokens **repeat** and **until** in a **repeat** statement serve as the boundaries for what is known as a **repeat** *block* (or the action part of a **repeat** statement). The actions of a **repeat** block are always carried out at least once, since the **until** condition does not get checked until a processor has completed the first pass through a repeat block. By contrast, the actions of a **do** statement in a **while** loop may not be performed at all because a processor must check the **while** condition and find it to be true before it can execute the **do** statement.

Notice that the actions in a **repeat** block are repeated, provided the **until** condition is false. This contrasts sharply with a **while** loop. The actions specified by a do statement are repeated by a processor, provided the **while** condition is true.

When should a **while** loop be used? If it is necessary to prevent an iteration from ever beginning under certain conditions, then use a **while** loop. For example, it is better to use a while loop that requires division, since there may be a danger of division by 0. Here is an example of a procedure that may cause problems.

```
procedure ComputeSum(term1, term2: real;
                     var result: real);
begin
  result := 0;
  repeat
    result := result + term1 / term2;
    term2 := term2 - 1
  until term2 <= 0
end;                                        (*ComputeSum*)
```

This procedure will compute the following sum:

```
term1/term2 + term1/(term2 - 1) + ···
            + term1/(term2 - 1 ··· - 1)
```

which is fine as long as term2 does not have an initial value of 0. It would be safer (and therefore better) to replace the **repeat** loop in the ComputeSum procedure with the following while loop:

```
while term2 > 0 do begin
  result := result + term1 / term2;
  term2 := term2 - 1
  end                                       (*while*)
```

The **while** condition in this statement guarantees that division by 0 is never attempted. Here is a summary of these ideas.

Rule of thumb in setting up an iteration:

If it is necessary to check a condition before beginning an iteration, then use a while loop.

Any **while** loop can be rewritten using a **repeat** loop. We show how this is done is Section 4.2.3.

4.2.3

Interchanging **While** *and* **Repeat** *Loops*

Here are some examples of iterations where **repeat** loops are used to replace **while** loops.

While Loop	Equivalent Loop

count := 1;
while count <= max **do begin**
   DrawRobot;
   count := count + 1
   end; (*while*)
	count := 1;
	if count <= max **then**
	repeat
	   DrawRobot;
	   count := count + 1
	until count > max;

while not eoln **do begin**
   write(symbol);
   read(symbol)
   end; (*while*)
	if not eoln **then**
	   repeat
	      write(symbol);
	      read(symbol)
	   until eoln;

These pairs of iterations do the same thing. The ones on the left in the above table are simpler to write, so they should be used instead of equivalent iterations using a repeat loop combined with an if statement. It is also possible to rewrite a repeat loop using a while loop. This is done by performing actions in the repeat block once before beginning a while loop. Changing various repeat loops to equivalent iterations using while loops is left as an exercise.

Sometimes it is convenient to set up infinite loops deliberately. We show how this can be done in Section 4.2.4.

4.2.4

Infinite Loops

A program can always be "shut off" or deactivated by hitting a break key or entering the right control character. For example, on an IBM PC or PDP-11 or VAX-11 a control c is used to terminate execution of a program. You will have to find out the best way to do this on your local system.

There are times when it is convenient to let a program run indefinitely. For example, we may want to let an airline ticket reservation program run indefinitely—it will probably be used 24 hours per day. We can put a program to handle reservations into an infinite loop using either a repeat or while loop. To do this with a while loop, for example, the trick is to set up a while condition that is always true. For example, the following loop is infinite:

```
while 1 > 0 do begin                    (*1 is always greater than 0!*)
   read(symbol);                                       (*check symbol*)
   if symbol = AgentPrompt then
      ProcessReservation                          (*activate procedure*)
   end;                                                      (*while*)
```

This iteration will run indefinitely. We can also set up an infinite repeat loop. To do this, the trick is to choose an until condition that is always false. Here is an example that might be used by a security system.

```
repeat
  read(sensor);                                   (*check input file*)
  if sensor = AlarmValue then
    Trigger Alarm                                 (*activate procedure*)
until 1 > 2;                                      (*impossible condition!*)
```

It is a good idea to play with infinite loops and find ways to make them finite loops. In other words, if you are given an infinite loop, find a way to install an exit mechanism in the iteration.

4.2.5

Example: Floyd Triangles and Solution by Analogy

The letter triangle presented in Chapter 1 is a variation of a triangle of numbers suggested by R. W. Floyd (1982):

1
2 3
4 5 6
7 8 9 10

The algorithm to print a letter triangle worked with consecutive letters. Now we want to work with consecutive integers. The techniques used in the letter-triangle algorithms are analogous to ones we need now. The idea is to develop an algorithm for producing a triangle of integers where the number of rows equals the number of columns. This triangle can be produced by using nested loops. Here is an algorithm to do this.

```
        (*input: initial triangle entry and maximum number of rows;
                                       output: printed Floyd triangle*)
begin
  initialize RowMax variable:                     (*for number of rows*)
  assign 1 to RowCount and ColumnCount;
  initialize RowEntry;                            (*you may not want to
                                                      start with 1*)
  while RowCount <= RowMax do begin
    while ColumnCount <= RowCount do begin
      print RowEntry;                             (*print row number*)
      add 1 to ColumnCount;
      add 1 to RowEntry                           (*key step!*)
      end;                                        (*inner while loop*)
    add 1 to RowCount;
    assign 1 to ColumnCount;
    move cursor to next line
    end                                           (*outer while loop*)
end                               (*algorithm to print Floyd's triangle*)
```

The exit mechanism for the inner while loop of this algorithm results from repeatedly adding one to ColumnCount. Eventually, ColumnCount will be greater than the value of RowCount. By repeatedly adding one to RowCount, we provide an exit mechanism for the outer while loop of this algorithm. This algorithm works with a third variable, RowEntry, which really has nothing to do with either ColumnCount and RowCount. In effect, we can modify the values of RowEntry to produce other forms of Floyd's triangle.

Before we toy with other forms of Floyd's triangle, we show a program to implement the above algorithm in Figure 4.1. The driver procedure of the program in Figure 4.1 illustrates the use of an infinite repeat loop. We leave it as an exercise to build an exit mechanism into this loop. This program was run on an IBM PC and was terminated using a control break. Notice that the algorithm used in the Floyd procedure always produces an equilateral triangle (same number of rows and columns), since printing continues inside the inner **while** loop until the ColumnCount exceeds the RowCount (the number of print columns will always equal RowCount).

```
                    (*Method: Use nested loops to produce a triangle
                     of numbers that are the integers from 1 to n.*)

program ShowFloydTriangle(input, output);

 (*-----------------------------------------------------------*)
                    (*print specified triangle using nested while loops*)

procedure Floyd(row: integer);                          (*no. of rows*)
var
   ColumnCount: integer;                             (*counts columns*)
   RowEntry: integer;                             (*entry in triangle row*)
   RowCount: integer;                                  (*counts rows*)
begin
     RowEntry := 1; ColumnCount:= 1; RowCount := 1;
     while RowCount <= row do begin
        while ColumnCount <= RowCount do begin
           write(RowEntry:3);
           RowEntry := RowEntry + 1;
           ColumnCount := ColumnCount + 1
           end;                                     (*inner while loop*)
        ColumnCount := 1;
        RowCount := RowCount + 1;
        writeln
        end                                         (*outer while loop*)
   end;                                                       (*Floyd*)

 (*-----------------------------------------------------------*)
               (*Program manager: get values and activate procedure*)

   procedure driver;
   var
     choice: integer;
```

```
begin
   repeat
      write('Enter no. of rows for Floyds triangle: ');
      readln(choice); writeln;
      writeln('Floyds triangle:':25); writeln;
      Floyd(choice)
   until 1 > 5                                          (*always false!*)
end;                                                         (*driver*)

(*- - - - - - - - - - - - - - - - - - - - - - - - - - - - - - - - - - - - - -*)

begin
   driver                                   (*activate driver procedure*)
end.
```

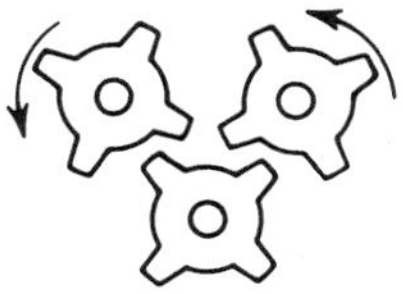

```
   Enter no. of rows for Floyds triangle: 15

Floyds triangle:

   1
   2  3
   4  5  6
   7  8  9 10
  11 12 13 14 15
  16 17 18 19 20 21
  22 23 24 25 26 27 28
  29 30 31 32 33 34 35 36
  37 38 39 40 41 42 43 44 45
  46 47 48 49 50 51 52 53 54 55
  56 57 58 59 60 61 62 63 64 65 66
  67 68 69 70 71 72 73 74 75 76 77 78
  79 80 81 82 83 84 85 86 87 88 89 90 91
  92 93 94 95 96 97 98 99100101102103104105
 106107108109110111112113114115116117118119120
```

FIGURE 4.1 Floyd's triangle

This program can be refined in several ways. We suggest one way of doing this in Section 4.2.6.

4.2.6 *Refinement: Other Forms of Floyd's Triangle*

We can modify the program in Figure 4.1 so that it prints other forms of Floyd's triangle. For example, we can print a triangle like the following one:

```
!
* !
! * !
* ! * !
! * ! * !
```

To do this we merely need to alternate between characters to be printed. Here is an algorithm to do this.

```
                     (*input: first symbol, second symbol, maximum rows;
                                  output: variation of Floyd triangle*)
begin
  initialize RowMax variable;
  assign 1 to ColumnCount and RowCount;
  assign character to FirstSymbol;
  assign character to SecondSymbol;
  assign 1 to choice;                   (*use to select FirstSymbol*)
  while RowCount <= RowMax do begin
    while ColumnCount <= RowCount do begin
      if choice = 1 then begin
        print FirstSymbol;
        assign 0 to choice
        end                                                (*then*)
      else begin
        print SecondSymbol;
        assign 1 to choice
        end;                                               (*else*)
      ColumnCount := ColumnCount + 1
      end                                     (*inner while loop*)
    assign 1 to ColumnCount;
    add 1 to RowCount
    end                                       (*outer while loop*)
  end                          (*algorithm for new Floyd triangle*)
```

The if statement used in the inner while loop of this algorithm takes the place of the following statements in Figure 4.1:

```
write(RowEntry:3);
RowEntry := RowEntry + 1
```

We leave it as an exercise to implement this new algorithm. It should be obvious that there are many forms of Floyd's triangle, depending on what entries we want to put into each triangle. It would be convenient to have some device we can use to set up a menu in the driver procedure. Then we can use this menu to choose the form of Floyd's triangle to print. We can do this with a Pascal case statement or with nested if statements. First, we show how to do this with nested if statements.

4.3 Nested If Statements

We can use nested if statements to select alternative actions. For example, we can set up the following algorithm to drive a program with a menu:

```
                                          (*input: menu choice;
                                   output: possible error message*)
begin
  print menu;                       (*assume this menu has 5 choices*)
  read menu choice;
  if choice = 1 then activate proc1
  else
    if choice = 2 then activate proc2
    else
      if choice = 3 then activate proc3
      else
        if choice = 4 then activate proc4
      else
          if choice = 5 then activate proc5
        else
          if (choice > 5) or (choice <1) then
            print an error message
end.                                      (*algorithm for a menu driver*)
```

The nested if statements in this algorithm are a little hard to follow. You might wonder where the else statements belong. Which if statement do we attach each else to? When else statements are used, the **else** clause gets attached to the nearest if statement without an **else** clause.

For small menus, this solution to the problem of setting up a menu-driven procedure is fine. For larger menus, this would be awkward and space-consuming. Pascal has a **case** statement that is simpler and will do almost the same thing. That is, except for an invalid value of the choice variable, we can use a case statement to handle lots of alternatives in a concise way.

4.4 Selection Control with a Case Statement

We can rewrite the menu-driver algorithm in Section 4.3 using a Pascal **case** statement as follows:

```
begin
  readln(choice);
  if (choice < 1) or (choice > 5) then
    write('Error—not a valid choice!')
  else
  case choice of
    1: proc1;                              (*activate proc1*)
    2: proc2;                              (*activate proc2*)
    3: proc3;                              (*activate proc3*)
    4: proc4;                              (*activate proc4*)
    5: proc5                               (*activate proc5*)
    end                                           (*case*)
end;                                      (*driver procedure*)
```

Notice that we use an **if** statement to determine when a valid menu choice has been made. We will get a fatal error message as a rule if a processor executes a case statement where the choice variable does not correspond to the case constant.

Using this technique, we can refine the program in Figure 4.1 to allow a user to choose more than one form of Floyd's triangle. We leave the implementation of this idea as an exercise.

This is a powerful statement. The expression following the token **case** is called the *case index*. For example, the variable *choice* is a case index. An expression used as case index must be an ordinal type. In addition, the value represented by the case expression must correspond to one of the case constants. More than one case constant can be used to select the same alternative. In effect, a case constant list can be used to label the same statement in the case list. For example, here is a case statement where multiple case constants are used to select the same statement.

```
    case choice of
       1: proc1;                                  (*activate proc1*)
       2, 3: proc2;                               (*activate proc2*)
       4: begin
             read(SecondChoice):
             proc3(SecondChoice)                  (*activate proc3*)
          end;                                           (*case 4*)
       5, 6, 7, 8: proc4                          (*activate proc4*)
 end;                                                     (*case*)
```

Using this case statement, a choice of 2 or 3 will tell a processor to activate proc2. Choices 5, 6, 7, or 8 will tell a processor to activate proc4. This same case statement also shows how a compound statement can be labeled by a case list. Any case list statement can be a compound statement. The syntax for a **case** statement is given in Figure 4.2.

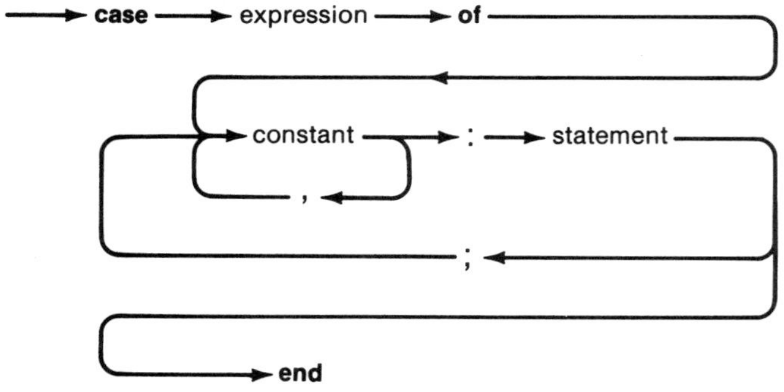

FIGURE 4.2
Syntax for a case statement

Other forms of the case statement are shown in Section 4.4.1

4.4.1 Case Statement with Boolean Constants

In Section 4.4, the sample case statement used type integer constants. Here is an example of a case statement with type Boolean constants.

```
case yes of
   true: statement1;                  (*if yes, activate statement1*)
   false: statement2              (*if not yes, activate statement2*)
   end                                                       (*case*)
```

This is really another form of the following if statement:

```
if yes then
   statement1                                      (*when yes is true*)
else
   statement2;                                    (*when yes is false*)
```

In this instance, the case statement is a little easier to read.

4.4.2 Case Statements with Arithmetic Expressions

So far the case expressions used to guide the selection of a case constant have not been arithmetic expressions. Here is an example of a case statement with an arithmetic expression for the case index.

```
case (wins + losses) div wins of
   1:  PayBonus;                                  (*activate procedure*)
   2:  begin
          EvaluatePitching;                       (*activate procedure*)
          EvaluateHitting                         (*activate procedure*)
       end;                                                  (*case 2*)
   3:  VisitFarmClub                              (*activate procedure*)
   end;                                                        (*case*)
```

The case index in this sample statement is

(wins + losses) **div** wins

which might be used to track the performance of a baseball team to produce the following results:

Wins	*Losses*	*Case Index*	*Action Taken*
55	2	(55 + 2) **div** 55 = 1	activate PayBonus
22	46	(22 + 46) **div** 22 = 2	activate procedures to evaluate pitching and hitting
22	57	(22 + 67) **div** 22 = 3	panic!

There are several things to watch out for when case statements are used. We discuss these dangers in Section 4.4.3.

4.4.3

Bug Clinic: How Not to Use a Case Statement

First, the case index expression must represent an ordinal type. For example, the following case index will produce a syntax error:

case (wins + losses) / wins **of** . . .

This case index will not work because it represents a type real value.

Second, a case constant can appear only once in a case statement. In other words, the same case constant cannot be used in more than one case-constant list. For example, the following case statement has several syntax errors:

```
case sum of
   0, 1, 2: statement1;
   1, 5, 7: statement2;                       (*1, again!*)
   0, 1, 8: statement3                    (*0 and 1, again!*)
   end;                                (*illegal case statement*)
```

Third, it is always necessary to prevent the occurrence of case index values that do not have corresponding case constants. In other words, the only valid case index values are the ones corresponding to case constants. It is a good idea to check case index values before allowing a case statement to be activated. This can be done by making a case statement part of an if statement. For example, we can put the team performance case statement from Section 4.4.2 into the following if statement:

```
performance := (wins + losses) div wins;
if (performance < 1) or (performance > 3) then
   write('Error!—check your data!')
else
   case performance of
      1: PayBonus;                          (*activate procedure*)
      2: begin
            EvaluatePitching;               (*activate procedure*)
            EvaluateHitting                 (*activate procedure*)
         end;                                           (*case 2*)
      3: VisitFarmClub                      (*activate procedure*)
      end;                                                (*case*)
```

Notice that this if statement will prevent invalid performance values ever being used in the else case statement.

Finally, the ordinal type of the case constants must be the same as the ordinal type of case index expression. Here is an example of conflict between the case index and case constants.

```
                                   (*assume sum is type integer*)
case sum of
   20, 21, 22: statement1;                          (*fine, so far*)
   55, '!': statement2;               (*whoops! '!' and sum conflict*)
   7, true: statement3               (*whoops! true and sum conflict*)
   end;                                 (*illegal case statement*)
```

Here is a summary of the case-statement rules.

> **Case statement rules:**
>
> **1. The expression used for a case index must be an ordinal type.**
> **2. A case constant cannot be used in more than one case constant list.**
> **3. Each value of a case index must have a corresponding case constant.**
> **4. Case constant values must be the same ordinal type as the case index.**

4.5 How to Use an Empty Statement in a Case Statement

Pascal has a maverick statement called an *empty statement,* which tells a machine to do nothing. The was used, for example, in the ImitateAmadeus procedure at the beginning of Chapter 3 as a way to inject intervals of silence between the rings of a keyboard bell. Even though an empty statement does nothing, it still takes time to tell a machine to do nothing. An empty statement can be used to advantage in a case statement whenever a case constant will be used as an exit condition inside a loop. Here is a sample repeat loop that illustrates this idea.

```
repeat
   writeln('menu:  ');
   writeln('- - - - >  1  make  reservation;');
   writeln('- - - - >  2  cancel  reservation;');
   writeln('- - - - >  3  list  available  aircraft;');
   writeln('- - - - >  4  exit');
   readln(choice);
   case choice of
      1: MakeReservation;                              (*case 1*)
      2: CancelReservation;                            (*case 2*)
      3: ListAircraft;                                 (*case 3*)
      4:                                      (*empty statement*)
      end                                               (*case*)
until choice = 4
```

In other words, this tells the machine to do nothing, if the exit condition is chosen. When "choice = 4" is typed, the **until** condition is true and the machine will drop out of the **repeat** loop. The only danger in this setup is the possibility of a value of choice that does not correspond to one of the case constants. This repeat loop should be refined to handle the exceptional values of choice. This refinement is left for an exercise.

If more than one empty statement is used in a case statement, then these empty statements must be separated by semicolons in the usual manner. Here is a variation of the above case statement to illustrate this idea.

```
case choice of
   1: MakeReservation;                          (*case 1*)
   2: CancelReservation;                        (*case 2*)
   3: ListAircraft;                              (*case3*)
   4: ;                                (*empty statement*)
   5: ;                                (*empty statement*)
   6:                                  (*empty statement*)
   end;                                         (*case*)
```

Empty statements can be useful in designing new programs. They can be used to set up shells (places for future code) that can be filled later. The idea of empty statements extends to procedures also.

4.6 Using Empty Statements to Set Up Procedure Stubs

In the top-down design of programs we begin with a pilot program having absolutely necessary procedures to get a program started. It is common practice to have a structure chart that suggests needed procedures which are incorporated after the fundamental procedures have been installed. It is possible to set up empty procedures, which serve as shells stubs for later program development.

> **A *stub* is a skeletal version of a final program structure. A stub merely suggests the empty framework for a program structure which can be fleshed out later.**

These stubs can be activated and they will tell a machine to do nothing. They merely serve as suggestions for future development in the framework of a developing program. We illustrate this idea with a program to set up an airline reservation system in Figure 4.3.

The program of Figure 4.3 merely serves as a suggestion for the framework of a future program. Each of the procedures are merely shells for future development, which we come back to again and again later. These stubs serve as focal points for a discussion of the framework for a program. The program in Figure

4.3 also illustrates the use of multiple empty statements in a single case statement.

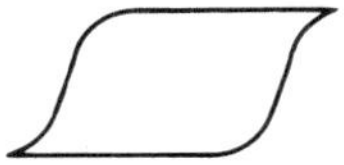

```
      (*Method: use empty statements to set up procedure stubs*)
program TryThis(input, output);
   procedure MakeReservation;
    begin
                                                   (*empty statement*)
   end;                                            (*MakeReservation*)
   procedure CancelReservation;
   begin
                                                   (*empty statement*)
   end;                                          (*CancelReservation*)
   procedure ListAircraft;
   begin
                                                   (*empty statement*)
   end;                                               (*ListAircraft*)
   procedure driver;
   var
      choice: integer;
   begin
      repeat
         writeln('menu:':20);
         writeln('---->':20, '1) make reservation;');
         writeln('---->':20, '2) cancel reservation;');
         writeln('---->':20, '3) list aircraft;');
         writeln('---->':20, '4) open;');
         writeln('---->':20, '5) open;');
         writeln('---->':20, '6) exit');
         write('Enter choice--1 to 6: '); readln(choice); writeln;
         case choice of
            1: begin
                  MakeReservation;
                  writeln('procedure is empty!')
                end;
            2: begin
                  CancelReservation;
                  writeln('procedure is empty!')
                end;
            3: begin
                  ListAircraft;
                  writeln('procedure is empty!')
                end;
            4: ;
            5: ;
            6:
            end
      until choice = 6
    end;                                                     (*driver*)
begin
    driver                                          (*activate driver*)
end.
```

FIGURE 4.3 The empty statement

You might be wondering if a Pascal program body can also be empty. To answer this question, try the following experiment on your machine:

```
Experiment
program TryThis;
begin
end.
```

You may be surprised by what happens when you compile this program (it will compile!) and then try to run it.

4.7 Summary

The actions we tell a computer to perform can be selected, repeated, or performed conditionally as a result of results that have been computed in a program. Control structures are used to channel and guide actions performed by a machine. When a program is activated, a control structure can be used to tell a machine which action to choose next, which one to perform repeatedly.

Here is a summary of the control structures we have covered.

Control Structures

Form	*Action*
	Conditional
1. **if** expression then statement	Activate **then** statement provided expression is true
2. **if** expression **then** statement1 **else** statement2	Activate **then** statement provided expression is true. Otherwise activate the else statement
	Selection
case expression **of** constant list: statement1; . . . constant list: statementk **end;**	Select statement with **case** constant equals case index (Last statement to select)

Iteration

1. **for** index := min **to** max **do** statement;	Use range of index values to control iteration
2. **for** index := max **downto** min **do** statement;	Use range of index values to control iteration
3. **while** expression **do** statement	Begin and continue interation as long as **while** expression remains true
2 **repeat** statement1; . . . **until** expression;	Perform actions in **repeat** block, then continue the iteration as long as the **until** expression is false

Each of the above control structures is governed by a condition. Evaluation of a condition is implicit in either a for loop or a case statement. With a for loop, continued activation of a for statement is dependent on the current value of a for index. Logically, a for statement can represented as follows.

For Statement	*Equivalent Statement*
for index := min **to** max **do** statement;	index := min; **while** index <= max **do begin** statement; index := index + 1 **end;** (*while*)
for index := max **downto** min **do** statement;	index := max; **while** index >= min **do begin** statement; index := index – 1 **end;** (*while*)

It is necessary to use a while loop instead of a for loop, if we want to increment or decrement an index by fractional amounts. Every for statement can be rewritten using an assignment and while-loop combination. Try this in some of your earlier programs to get comfortable with switching back and forth between these two control structures.

A case statement with two or more case lists is really a hidden set of nested if-then-else statements. Here is a case statement and its equivalent statement.

Case Statement		*Equivalent Statement*

case expr of
   c1: s1;
   c2: s2;
   c3, c4: s3;
   end;
	(*case*)	**if** expr = c1 **then**
		   s1
		else
		   if expr = c2 **then**
		      s2
		   else
		      if (expr = c3) or (expr = c4) **then**
		         s3;

Case statements have lurking sand traps. The case expression is called the *case index*. This must always be an ordinal type. This leaves out case indices that are type real. If it is necessary to use an expression that is type real to select a statement to activate, then use nested if statement instead of a case statement.

There is another case statement sand trap to keep in mind. Case constants must also be the same ordinal type as the case index type. A case constant can appear in only ane case constant list. In other words, the same case constant cannot be used to select more than one case statement.

The final case statement sand trap has to do with exception handling. You will cause a fatal run-time error, if you attempt to give a case index a value that has no corresponding case stant. In other words, every time a case statement is activated, its index must have a value that equals one of the case constants. To avoid run-time errors with case statements, it is necessary to check for exceptional values of a case index. This is an instance of what is known as *exception handling*. The trick is build into your programs checks for bad input and for unacceptable values produced by a program.

The aim in programming is to produce source texts that are readable. The static structure of a program is what you see when you read a source text. The trick is to make the static structure of a program reflect (and suggest!) what will happen when a program is activated by a computer.

4.8 Keywords Review

Keywords	*Related Ideas*
case statement	selection control structure
index	expression that always represents an ordinal type and is used to select an action
constant list	values used to label statements inside a case statement
control structure	controls which actions a processor performs next
conditional	
if statement	action specified by then statement or else statement is carried out, depending on the truth value of an if condition

iteration

- for statement — depending on the value of a control variable, an action specified by the do statement is repeated
- **repeat** statement — repeating the actions in the **repeat** block is dependent upon the evaluation the until condition, which must be false
- **while** statement — execution of the **do** statement will occur, if the **while** expression is true, and the **do** statement will be iterated as long as the **while** expression is true

selection

- **case** statement — select statement with a **case** constant label having the same value as the **case** index

sequential

- compound statement — carry out the actions in sequence specified by a compound statement

exit mechanism — device used to terminate an iteration

infinite loop — iteration without an exit mechanism

stub — A skeletal version of a program structure.

4.9 Exercises

1. How does a repeat loop differ from a while loop?
2. Which iteration control structure depends on a false condition to continue an iteration?
3. Which iteration control structure always tells a processor to carry out the actions of the iteration at least once?
4. In what ways does a case statement differ from an if statement?
5. Rewrite the following repeat loops using while loops:

a.

```
repeat
   read(choice);
   write(choice)
until choice = 0;
```

b.

```
repeat
   DrawTopView;
   DrawSideView;
   DrawFrontView;
   count := count + 1
until count > max;
```

6. Rewrite the following while loops using repeat loops:

a.

```
read(choice);
while (choice > 0)
   and (choice < 5) do begin
   write(choice);
   readln(choice)
   end;                                          (*while*)
```

b.

```
count := 3000;
readln(yes);
while (count >= 0)
   and yes do begin
   write(count);
   count := count - 1;
   readln(yes)
   end; (*while*)
```

c.

```
read(choice);
while not eoln do begin
   write(choice);
   read(choice)
   end;                                        (*while*)
```

7. Insert an exit mechanism into each of the following infinite loops, making them finite loops:

a.

```
repeat
   read(choice);
   write(choice)
until 1 > 5;
```

b.

```
count := 1;
repeat
   write(count);
until 1 < 0;
```

c.

```
while 5 < 6 do
   writeln('yes!');
```

d.

```
yes := true;
while yes do
   writeln('ok!');
```

8. Indentify which if statement each of the else clauses belong to in the following statements:

a.

```
if expr = 0.5 then
   if expr = 1.0 then
      if expr = 2.0 then
         if expr = 1.6 then
            writeln('expr is close to golden ratio')
               else
                  writeln('expr is interesting')
                     else
                        writeln('Try again!')
                           else
                              writeln('I believe so');
```

b.

```
if expr = 2 then
   if expr < 3 then
      writeln('Euler will be happy!')
         else
            if (expr > 2) and (expr < 4) then
               writeln('Perhaps!')
                  else
                     writeln('Mmmmm . . .')
                        else
                           writeln('Which if?');
```

9. Can the nested if statements in exercise 8 be rewritten with case statements? Explain your answer. *Note:* You can assume the expr variable is type real in part (a) and type integer in part (b) of exercise 8.

10. (Modified Floyd triangle) Pascal has a successor function that can be used to inspect the successor of a value (if there is one!) on a scale used to define an ordinal type. For example, the succ('a') is *b* on the type char scale and succ(1) is 2 on the type integer scale. Use this function in a program to produce the following symbol triangle:

```
a
b c
d e f
g h i j
k l m n o
p q r s t u
v w x y z a b
c d e f g h i j
```

Let the user determine how many rows this triangle will have and always have the triangle start with a lower case *a*. Notice that this triangle has a wrap-around feature: if succ(symbol) is *z*, then an *a* is printed next, then a *b* and so on. Run this program for each of the following cases:

a. rows = 1
b. rows = 5
c. rows = 50

11. Refine the program in exercise 10 so that the user can select beginning lower case letter to start the symbol triangle. Give a sample run, using

a.

```
starting letter = 'k';
rows = 10;
```

b.

```
starting letter = 't';
rows = 15.
```

12. Rewrite the repeat loop at the end of Section 4.2.1 so that it has an effective exit mechanism.

13. Insert an exit mechanism into the repeat loop in the driver procedure in the program in Figure 4.1. Give a sample run.

14. Carry out the refinement of the program in Figure 4.1, which is described in Section 4.2.6. Give a sample run using the following values for FirstSymbol and SecondSymbol:

a.
```
FirstSymbol equal to '!;;
SecondSymbol equal to '*';
rows = 10;
```
b.
```
FirstSymbol equal to '*';
SecondSymbol equal to '!';
rows = 15;
```
c.
```
FirstSymbol equal to 'U' ;
SecondSymbol equal to 'S' ;
rows = 15.
```

15. Write a driver procedure that is menu driven and gives the user to choose from the following selection of Floyd triangles:
   a. Floyd triangle from Figure 4.1
   b. Modified Floyd triangle from exercises 10 and 11
   c. Modified Floyd triangle from exercise 14

   Give a sample run that illustrates each case. Use a separate procedure to carry out each menu choice. Be sure to build into your driver procedure a provision for exception handling in case wrong menu choices are entered.

4.10 Review Quiz

Determine whether the following are true or false:

1. Repetition of the actions in a repeat block occurs as long as the until condition is false.
2. The actions in a repeat block are always executed at least once.
3. The **do** statement in a **while** loop is always activated at least once.
4. When **if** statements are nested, the last **else** clause always gets attached to the nearest **if** statement without an **else** clause.
5. One **if** statement can have more than one else clause.
6. A **case** statement can always be rewritten as nested **if** statements.
7. Every finite iteration control structure has an exit mechanism.
8. An empty statement can be used as one of the statement choices in a Pascal **case** statement.
9. An empty statement tells a machine to do nothing.
10. A **case** index can be any of the simple types.

4.11 Readings

Cooper, D. *Standard Pascal User Reference Manual.* New York: Norton, 1983. See Sections 2–4 and 2–7.

MacLennan, B. J. *Principles of Programming Languages: Design, Evaluation, and Implementation.* New York: Holt, Rinehart and Winston, 1983. See Section 5.5 on control structures.

Polya, G. *How to Solve It.* New York: Doubleday Anchor, Books, 1957. See discussion of solution by analogy, pp. 37–46.

CHAPTER 5

WHAT ARE DATA TYPES?

In almost all cases it is advisable to start the detailed examination of the problem with the questions: What is the unknown? What are the data? What is the condition?

George Polya, 1957

. . . The apparently obvious can often be deceptive.

Stephen Jay Gould, 1977

. . . Computer science can be defined as the study of data, its representation and transformation by a digital computer.

Ellis Horowitz and Sartaj Sahni, 1982

AIMS

- Explain the terms *data, type, data type, data abstraction,* and *abstract data type.*
- Look more closely at the scales used for the simple data types.

- Introduce the built-in arithmetic, ordinal, and transfer functions.
- Distinguish between the ordinal data types and type real.
- Show how to compute powers of numbers in two different ways.
- Illustrate the use of the exponential and natural log functions in computing interest earned on investments.
- Introduce the enumeration and subrange data types.
- Illustrate the use of the sqr() and trunc() functions to set up a user-defined function to generate random numbers.
- Discuss how the operator precedence rules are used by a computer to evaluate an expression.
- Examine the problem of computational errors with reals.

5.1 Introduction to Data Abstraction

The term *data* means values. In Pascal it is always necessary to specify the type of data used in a program. The term *type* basically means kind of value and is used to specify the qualities common to a group of data. The term *data type* refers both to a set of values (the data) and to the operations that can be performed on the data. This distinction between *data* and *data type* is analogous to the distinction between courses in a school curriculum and the courses offered by a department of the school.

Sample Catalogue Courses (Data)	*Department (Data Type)*
Algebra	Algebra
Discrete mathematics	Discrete mathematics
Calculus	Calculus
Accounting	Computer science 1
Anatomy	Computer science 2
Assembly language	Assembly language
Astronomy	Data structures
Compiler theory	Machine organization
Computer science 1	Compiler theory
Computer science 2	Operatining systems
Cost accounting	Compiler theory
Data structures	
Business administration	
Geology	
Health	
Machine organization	
Operating systems	
Physics	
World literature	

The courses in a computer science curriculum are related to each other. They share common characteristics. There may be courses in the complete curriculum that are not related. In addition, the courses for a department are ordered (you must take CS 1 before you take CS2, for example). You can think of the verbs **prepare, review, employ, extend, reflect** as "operations" defined on the departmental courses. This gives the following organization for the data type *computer science:*

Sample Data (Values)	*Operations (Actions)*
Discrete mathematics	PrepareFor(CS1)
CS 1	Employ(Discrete mathematics);
	Review(Discrete mathematics);
	Extend(Discrete mathematics)
	PrepareFor(CS 2)
CS 2	Employ(CS 1)
	Review(CS 1);
	Extend(CS 1);
	PrepareFor(assembly language)
(and so on)	

Similarly, the Pascal data type integer specifies a set of values (a subject of the integers) and operations that can be performed on these values.

Data Values (integers)	*Operations (Actions on Integers)*
-maxint, . . ., −1,0,1, . . ., maxint	+ to add integers
	– for subtraction
	* to multiply integers
	div for division
	mod to compute remainder
	succ(*x*) to get successor of *x*
	and so on

Here are the two characteristics associated with every data type.

Characteristics of a *data type*

1. **A set of values (the data).**
2. **A set of operations on the values (actions that can made by a machine on the data).**

A course description in a school catalogue describes the main features of a course. For example, a music history course might list the following items:

A study of musical instruments, musicians of the 17th, 18th, 19th, and early 20th century (from J. S. Bach to P. D. Q. Bach), and musical works.

Nothing is said in this music course description about where it will be taught (the building, the room), or how it will be taught (teaching methods like listening to live orchestras vs. listening to recordings), or what instruments or works will be studied (the data values of the course). In effect, the course description is an example of what is known as a *data abstraction.* This idea is represented graphically in Figure 5.1.

In computer science, a *data abstraction* specifies a data type without saying how the data values will be represented inside a computer and without specifying the computer code that will be used to implement the operations on the data values. For example, type char is a data abstraction in Pascal. In specifying this type, nothing is said about how the characters for type char will be stored inside a computer or how the operations defined on type char values will be implemented. This idea is represented graphically in Figure 5.2.

The data types used in Pascal are examples of what are known as *abstract data types.* These data types are used without concern about their representation inside the computer you are using or what machine code is used to carry out the operations on the data. Instead, we deal with these data types on an abstract level, free of concern about their inner workings inside a machine. Data abstraction is beneficial because it allows us to focus on real-world concerns rather than on the mechnaical side of how a machine manipulates our data to get a job done.

5.2 Simple Data Types

In this chapter we revisit the simple data types. A *simple data type* is defined in terms of a scale of values. For this reason, the simple data types are also known as the *scalar data types.* In Pascal, there are four simple types: type real as well as type integer, char, and Boolean. The simple types are part of a rich selection of data types available in Pascal. The various Pascal data types are given in Figure 5.3. In this chapter, we will look more closely at the scales used to define the simple data types. We will also show how new data types can be defined using an ordinal scale, the enumeration type, and the subrange data types.

Among the simple types, type real sits all by itself and is handled in a special way because of the special nature of its scale, which is a subset of the real numbers, all fractions, and whole numbers. The idea of immediate neighbor of a value has no meaning on the type real scale. It is not possible to identify the immediate neighbor (the first number of the left or right) of a real value, since we can always identify another real between any two reals.

Abstraction

Implementation

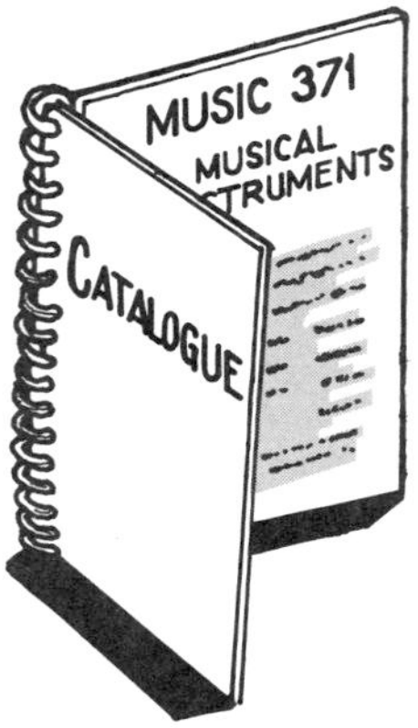

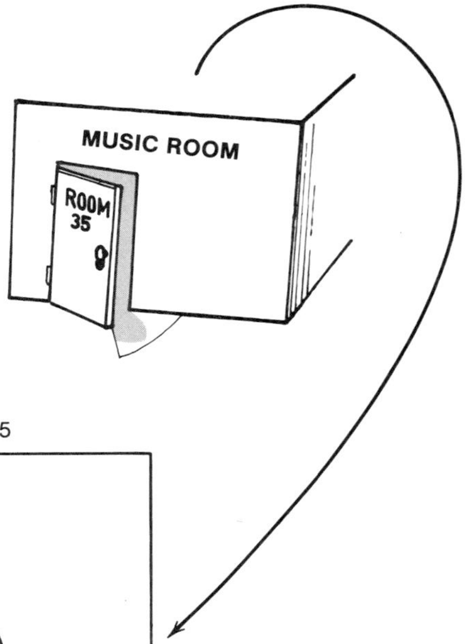

Note: The description of Music 371 does not specify how this course will be *implemented.*

Top view of classroom 35

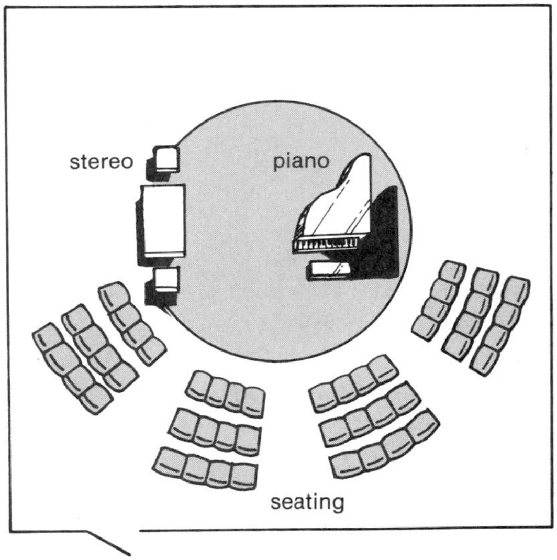

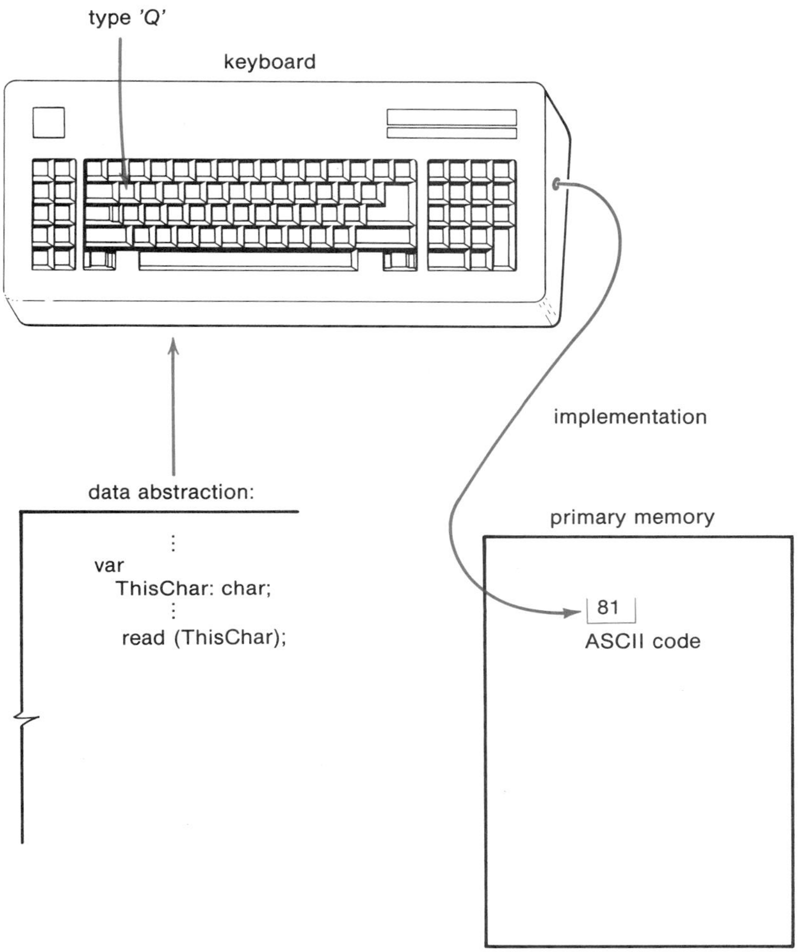

FIGURE 5.2
Data abstraction with type char

Try an experiment with reals to satisfy yourself that this idea of immediate neighbors of a real makes no sense. Just take any two reals x and y, then $(x + y)/2$ will lie between x and y. This is another way of saying that the values for the type real scale can never be completely listed. This is not the case with the other simple data types.

The idea of the immediate neighbor of a value does make sense with type integer, char, and Boolean. These three simple types are called the *ordinal data types*. The values for each of the ordinal types can be completely listed. For this reason, we can talk about the immediate neighbors of 2, which are 1 and 3 on

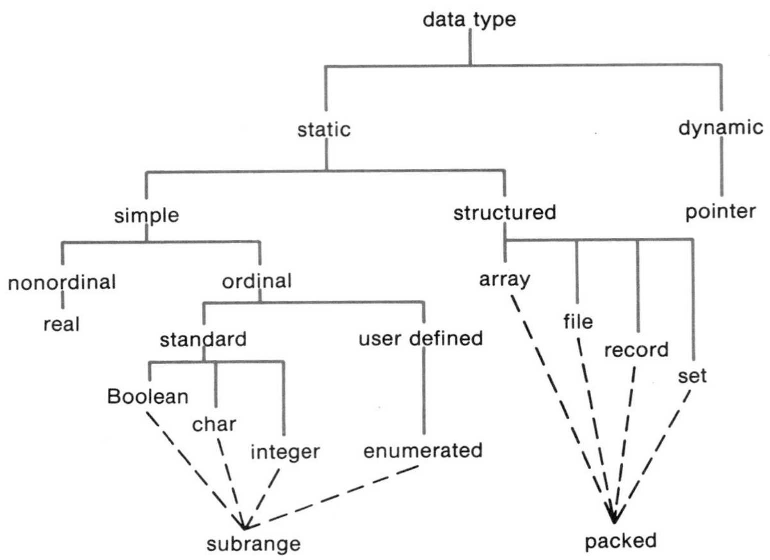

FIGURE 5.3
Pascal data types

the type integer scale. The scale used to define type integer ranges from a minimum integer value (–maxint) and maximum integer value (maxint).

–maxint, . . ., –2, –1, 0, 1, 2, . . ., maxint

The type integer scale represents a subset of all possible integers. The value of maxint will vary depending on the computer system you are using. For example, maxint on an Apple IIe is 32767, whereas maxint on a VAX-11is 2,147,483,647. A sampler of maxint values for various systems is given in Table 5.1. The identifier maxint is a built-in constant in standard Pascal. You can determine the value of maxint on your computer system by implementing the following write statement:

```
write('On this system, maxint equals', maxint);
```

Table 5.1 Maxint Implementations

Pascal Compiler	*–maxint* $\leq i \leq$ maxint	$-2^n \leq i \leq 2^n-1$
Apple IIe Pascal	$-32768 \leq i \leq 32767$	$-2^{15} \leq i \leq 2^{15}-1$
OS Pascal	$-32768 \leq i \leq 32767$	$-2^{15} \leq i \leq 2^{15}-1$
Zenith Pascal	$-32768 \leq i \leq 32767$	$-2^{15} \leq i \leq 2^{15}-1$
HP 1000 Pascal	$-2,147,483,648 \leq i \leq 2,147,483,647$	$-2^{31} \leq i \leq 2^{31}-1$
VAX-11 Pascal	$-2,147,483,648 \leq i \leq 2,147,483,647$	$-2^{31} \leq i \leq 2^{31}-1$
PDP-10 Pascal	$-34,359,738,368 \leq i \leq 34,359,738,367$	$-2^{35} \leq i \leq 2^{35}-1$
IBM PC Pascal	$-32768 \leq i \leq 32767$	$-2^{15} \leq i \leq 2^{15}-1$

In other words, the value of maxint can be printed and it can be used as a value in various ways in Pascal programs. For example, in this chapter we will use maxint to define a new data type that is a subset of the type integer scale. This is known as a *subrange type.*

The idea of immediate neighbor of a value also makes sense for the type char scale. This is a little tricky, though, since the scale used to implement type char will vary, depending on the computer system being used. For example, depending on the scale being used on your system, the immediate neighbors of the less than symbol (<) will vary. Here is a sampler of immediate neighbors of the less than symbol for two commonly used scales.

Immediate Neighbors of < Symbol

Left Neighbor	*Right Neighbor*	*Scale Used*
.	(	EBCDIC = Extended Binary Coded Decimal Interchange Code
;	=	ASCII = American Standard Code for Information Interchange

There are major differences between the EBCDIC and ASCII scales, which you should investigate. These scales are given in Appendix A. Notice that the positions of the upper and lower case letters in these two tables differ considerably. For example, notice that lower case letters are contiguous in the ASCII table, whereas these letters are presented in three noncontiguous groups in the EBCDIC table.

In this chapter we introduce four built-in functions, which can be used to inspect the ordinal scales. These are powerful functions. These ordinal functions are given in two groups.

Ordinal Functions

Function	*Result*
	Neighbor Functions
pred(*x*)	Identifies value (if it exists!) to the left of *x* on an ordinal scale.
succ(*x*)	Identifies value (if it exists!) to the right of *x* on an ordinal scale.
	Position Functions
ord(*x*)	Identifies position of the ordinal value on the scale containing *x*.
chr(*x*)	Identifies character (if it exists!) in the position in the character scale corresponding to the integer value of *x*.

In Pascal it is possible for the user to introduce new ordinal types by specifying the scale for the new type. These new ordinal types can be declared in any block. The declarations of these new data types have the following form:

type
identifier = ordinal scale;

In this chapter we show two different user-defined data types.

1. Enumeration type where the ordinal scale used is a list of identifiers that can be used as values of control variables.
2. Subrange type where the ordinal scale used to define the subrange type is part of a built-in ordinal scale or is part of a scale used to define an enumeration type.

Pascal provides a rich selection of functions that can be used with the simple types. In this chapter we show how some of these functions can be used. ISO Pascal does not have a built-in function to compute powers of numbers. In this chapter we show two ways powers of numbers can be computed.

Finally, we take a second look at the arithmetic operators. When arithmetic expressions without parentheses are evaluated, a processor will evaluate these expressions from left to right based on a set of precedence rules. This idea can be expressed by rewriting an arithmetic expression using parentheses. Here is an example.

$$a + b + c + d + 100 = (((a + b) + c) + d) + 100$$

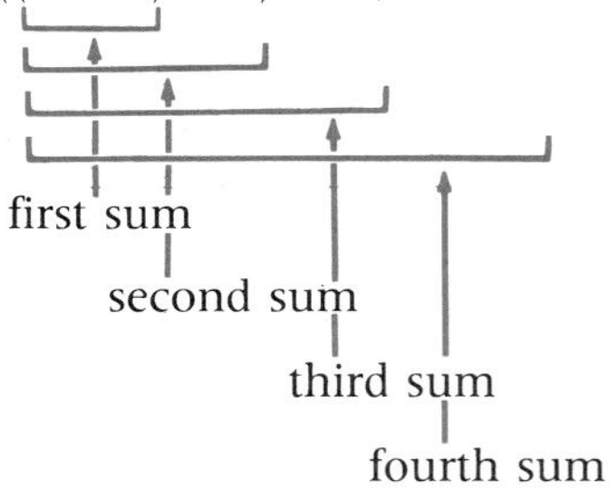

For this reason, the arithmetic operators are said to be *left associative.* That is, the evaluation of an arithmetic expression moves from left to right, starting with the operators that have highest precedence (predetermined priority). It is a little tricky to determine the final value of an arithmetic expression with a mixture of arithmetic operators. A computer uses a built-in set of rules to tell which arithmetic operators get treated first. This is another way of saying that precedence rules govern the evaluation of an arithmetic expression without parentheses. An understanding of these rules is important. We look at these precedence rules. If nothing else, this will probably motivate you to use parentheses to control how an arithmetic expression is evaluated.

Finally, whenever arithmetic expressions with reals are used, you can expect approximate results. Reals like ⅔, which have no exact value, get rough treatment inside machines. The number ⅔ can be written as follows:

$$2/3 = 0.66666666666666666666666666666 \text{ (forever)}$$

Computers have a very limited capacity for dealing with such numbers. Machines represent repeating decimals, for example, with a limited number of digits. For example, on an IBM PC, ⅔ is represented with 0.6666667, which is a rounded form of the "real" thing. In this chapter, we show some of the computational errors that can occur and techniques you can use to prevent these errors from ruining a program.

5.3 Ways to Inspect Ordinal Scales

The built-in successor and predecessor functions can be used to inspect the immediate neighbors (if they exist!) of a value on a scale. For example, here are some sample uses the succ() and pred() functions with the type char scale.

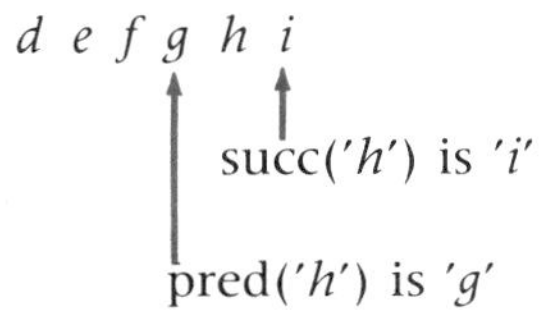

The succ() and pred() functions can only be used to inspect the immediate neighbors of ordinal scales. It is not possible, for example, to determine succ(0.5) or pred(0.5). In other words, these two functions will not accept type real arguments. Here are some sample uses (good and bad) of these functions.

Function	*Argument*	*Value*	*Scale Used*
succ('x')	'x'	'y'	ASCII
succ('A')	'A'	'B'	ASCII
succ(54)	54	55	integer
succ(maxint)	maxint	error!	integer
pred('x')	'x'	'w'	ASCII
pred('A')	'A'	'	ASCII
pred(54)	54	53	integer
pred(maxint)	maxint	maxint-1	integer
pred(−5)	−5	−6	integer
pred(−maxint)	−maxint	error!	integer

Pascal has two additional built-in functions that can be used to inspect ordinal scales.

Function	*How It Is Used*
ord(x)	gives the position of x on an ordinal scale.
chr(y)	gives the character (if it exists!), which is position y on the type char scale (notice!—the identifier y represents a value of type integer).

For now, we will illustrate the use of the ord() function using the type char scale. This built-in function is also useful with user-defined ordinal scales, which we introduce in Section 5.4. Here are some sample uses of these functions.

Function	*Argument*	*Value*	*Scale Used*
ord('*J*')	'*J*'	209	EBCDIC
ord('*J*')	'*J*'	74	ASCII
ord('*0*')	'*0*'	240	EBCDIC
ord('*0*')	'*0*'	48	ASCII
chr(209)	209	'*J*'	EBCDIC (Note: this will be error, if ASCII Is used.)
chr(48)	48	0	ASCII
chr(251)	251		ASCII scale for an IBM PC, which is not standard

You can print a copy of the non-EBCDIC type char scale used by your system by using the following algorithm:

```
                                   (*input: integer values for first, last;
                                  output: interval from type char scale*)
begin
   initialize First, Last;               (*scale for printable characters*)
   repeat
      print the value of chr(First);
      add 1 to First
   until First > Last
end                                (*algorithm to print type char scale*)
```

Notice that this algorithm is limited to integer values for the part of the type char scale having printable characters. It will not work for the EBCDIC scale. Why? There are gaps between the printable characters on the EBCDIC scale. So you will have to adjust this algorithm to take into account these gaps, if your system uses the EBCDIC scale to implement type char. This algorithm will work for the ASCII scale, which has 95 printable, consecutive characters. Here is a simplified ASCII table showing these printable characters and their corresponding position numbers:

Printable ASCII characters:

	32	48	64	80	96	112
0		0	@	P	′	p
1	!	1	A	Q	a	q
2	"	2	B	R	b	r
3	#	3	C	S	c	s
4	$	4	D	T	d	t
5	%	5	E	U	e	u
6	&	6	F	V	f	v
7	'	7	G	W	g	w
8	(	8	H	X	h	x
9	)	9	I	Y	i	y
10	*	:	J	Z	j	z
11	+	;	K	[	k	{
12	,	<	L	\	l	|
13	–	=	M	]	m	}
14	.	>	N	^	n	~
15	/	?	O	_	o	

Special cases:

chr(7) rings the keyboard bell
chr(9) prints a horizontal tab
chr(10) prints a line feed
chr(11) prints a vertical tab
chr(12) prints a form feed
chr(13) prints a carriage return
chr(32) prints a space

The ASCII scale is the one most commonly used to implement type char. This is the one we use in this book. Except for chr(7), the special ASCII characters in the above table are called the *white space characters.* They introduce white space (blank space) into a printed text. We leave it for an exercise to implement the above algorithm.

The standard ordinal scales can be used to define new data types. In addition, it is possible to define new data types with entirely new ordinal scales. We show how to do this in Section 5.4.

5.4

New Ordinal Data Types

Each block of a Pascal program can be used to define new ordinal types. We can either define a new data type using a set of contiguous values on a predefined ordinal scale or we can list the values for an entirely new ordinal scale. A data type, which is defined in terms of a predefined ordinal scale, is called a *subrange type.* A data type defined in terms of a new ordinal scale is called an *enumeration type.* We show how to set up enumeration types, first.

5.4.1

Enumeration Data Types

An enumeration data type is defined using a scale of values set up in a program. This sets up a group of named values. To do this, it is necessary to specify all possible values of the new scale. Here are some examples of enumeration types.

```
type
   temp  =  (Fahrenheit, Celsius, Kelvin, Rankine);
   greens  =  (Atlantic, absinthe, aqua, chartreuse, emerald,
                cobalt, holly, Irish, Kelly, leaf, olive, Paris,
                sea, Pacific, SouthPacific, turquoise);
   days  =  (Sunday, Monday, Tuesday, Wednesday, Thursday,
            Friday, Saturday);
   cities  =  (Albuquerque, Anchorage, Atlanta, Austin,
              Baltimore, Billings, Bismark, Boise, Boston,
              LosAngeles, Phoenix, Pittsburgh);
```

These are examples of newly defined enumeration types. Each declaration for an enumeration type enumerates (lists completely) the members of the scale used. A declaration like this is usually given in a program block. In each case, the first identifier used to set up the scale for an enumeration type is always in position 0. For example,

ord(Fahrenheit) = ord(Atlantic) = 0

In general, a declaration of an enumeration type has the following syntax:

enumeration type:

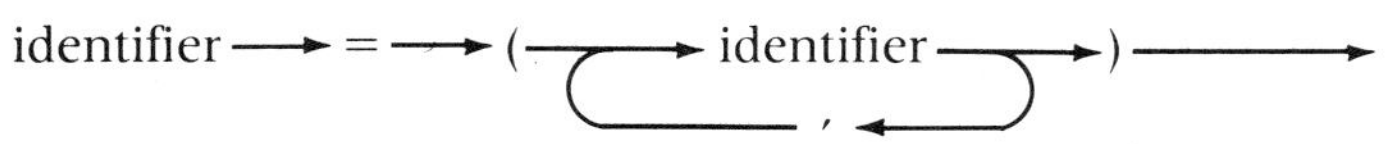

There are severe restrictions on the use of variables that are enumeration types. For example, we can have the following variables:

```
var
   reading: temp;                          (*type temp variable*)
   SingleColor: greens;                   (*type green variable*)
   AllDays: days;                          (*type days variable*)
   places: cities;                       (*type cities variable*)
```

The only values that can be assigned to places, for example, are the identifiers of the cities scale. These values have no meaning outside a program. They can neither be printed nor can they be entered from a keyboard. For example, it is not legal to do either of the following things:

```
readln(places);                    (*a cities identifier cannot be read*)
writeln(places);                (*a value of places cannot be printed*)
```

Enumeration types are used to set up control structures within a program. They are also used to make more clear what is being done in a program. Here is an example of a for loop to print temperatures in various cities.

```
for reading := Fahrenheit to Rankine do
   case reading of
      Fahrenheit: write(x:8:5);                        (*x is type real*)
      Celsius: write((5 / 9)*(x - 32):8:5);
      Kelvin: begin
                 NewX := (5 / 9)*(x - 32);
                 write((NewX + 273.25):8:5)
              end;                                           (*Kelvin*)
      Rankine: write((x + 459.67):8:5)              (*used in physics*)
      end;                                                     (*case*)
```

Notice how the values of reading are used to select the temperatures printed. The values of reading are limited to the identifiers on the temp scale. In this example, the value of *x* is a Fahrenheit temperature supplied somewhere else in a program with this for loop. Depending on the value of **reading,** either the value of *x* or its equivalent in one of the temperature scales is printed. For example, we can use this procedure to print a cross-reference table of temperatures. In Figure 5.4 we show an implementation of this idea. Refinements of the program in Figure 5.4 are possible. We suggest some of these in Sections 5.4.2 and 5.4.3.

5.4.2 *Refinement: Selecting the Increment*

The program in Figure 5.4 is limited to an increment of 0.5 between table temperatures printed. It would be better to determine what increment the user wants to have between the rows of the cross reference table. This can be changed by adding a new parameter for the driver procedure to pass to the *X*RefTable procedure. This refinement is left as an exercise.

5.4.3 *Refinement: Selecting the Temperature Scales to Use*

It is possible to introduce a parameter of type temp in the XRefTable procedure in Figure 5.4. This can be used to pass a temp scale identifier to use in this procedure. Actually two such parameters should be used in the *X*RefTable

```
              (*Method: Use a control variable that is an enumeration
                     type to set up cross-reference table entries.*)
program TempTable(input, output);
type
   temp = (Fahrenheit, Celsius, Kelvin, Rankine);

 (*-----------------------------------------------------------*)
                 (*Use supplied extremes to print a temp table*)

   procedure XRefTable(low, high : real);
   var
      reading: temp;                    (*enumeration type variable*)
      NewX: real;                       (*use to compute other temps*)
   begin
      repeat
         for reading := Fahrenheit to Rankine do
            case reading of
               Fahrenheit: write(' ':10,low:8:5, ' ':10);
               Celsius: write((5/9)*(low - 32):8:5, ' ':10);
               Kelvin: begin
                          NewX := (5/9)*(low - 32);
                          write((NewX + 273.15):8:5, ' ':10)
                        end;
               Rankine: begin
                           write((low + 459.67):8:5)
                         end
               end;                                          (*case*)
         writeln; writeln;                        (*skip to next line*)
         low := low + 0.5
      until low > high
   end;                                                 (*XRefTable*)

 (*-----------------------------------------------------------*)
            (*Program manager: get values and activate procedure*)
   procedure driver;
   var
      LowTemp, HighTemp: real;
   begin
      repeat
         write('Enter low & high Fahrenheit temperatures: ');
         readln(LowTemp, HighTemp);
         writeln('Crossreference Temperature Table':40);
         write('Fahrenheit':20, 'Celsius':16, 'Kelvin':16);
         write('Rankine':16); writeln; writeln;
         XRefTable(LowTemp, HighTemp)
      until 1 > 2                                    (*always false!*)
   end;                                                    (*driver*)
 (*-----------------------------------------------------------*)
begin
   driver                                (*activate driver procedure*)
end.
```

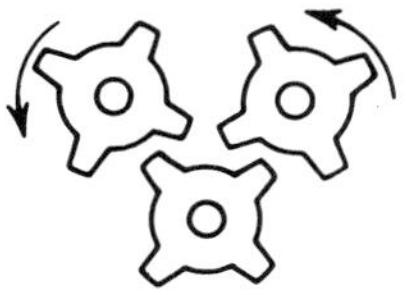

```
Enter low & high Fahrenheit temperatures: 32 35
      Crossreference Temperature Table
        Fahrenheit       Celsius        Kelvin        Rankine
        32.00000         0.00000        273.15000     491.67000
        32.50000         0.27778        273.42778     492.17000
        33.00000         0.55556        273.70556     492.67000
        33.50000         0.83333        273.98333     493.17000
        34.00000         1.11111        274.26111     493.67000
        34.50000         1.38889        274.53889     494.17000
        35.00000         1.66667        274.81667     494.67000
```

FIGURE 5.4 Printing a cross-reference temperature table

procedure, one for the beginning temp scale, the other for the ending temp scale. For example, we can use the following new *X*RefTable heading:

> **procedure** *X*RefTable(FirstScale, LastScale :temp;
>   low, high, step: real);

Then use the driver procedure to print a menu like the following one:

> menu:
>   → 1 all four scales;
>   → 2 Fahrenheit and Celsius, only
>   → 3 Celsius and Kelvin, only
>   → 4 Fahrenheit, Celsius, and Kelvin, only

Depending on the entered menu choice, values for FirstScale and LastScale can be passed to the *X*RefTable procedure. We can carry out this idea with the following repeat loop:

```
repeat
  reading := FirstScale;
  case reading of
     .
     .
     .
     end;                                              (*case*)
  if FirstScale <> NonScale then
     FirstScale := succ(FirstScale)
until FirstScale = NonScale
      or (ord(FirstScale) > ord(LastScale));
```

This will work if we redefine the temp scale as follows:

> temp = (Fahrenheit, Celsius, Kelvin, Rankine, NonScale);

This refinement is left as an exercise. In addition to enumeration types, we can also define new ordinal types using either one of the built-in ordinal scales or a previously defined scale for an enumeration type. These new ordinal types are called *subrange types.*

5.4.4

Subrange Data Types

A subrange data type is defined by setting up a scale containing contiguous values of a previously defined type. The previously defined ordinal type is known as the *host type*. For example, we can set up variables using the following subranges taken from enumeration types:

```
type
   temp = (Fahrenheit, Celsius, Kelvin, Rankine, NonScale);
   UsualScales = Fahrenheit .. Kelvin;          (*underlying scale is
                                                   the temp scale*)
   reds = (annato, Burgundy, cardinal, carnation, CasinoPink,
           cinnabar, claret, cochineal, cordovan, crimson,
           damask, EnglishRed, FuchsiaRed, Goya, maroon,
           sienna, strawberry);
   SomeReds = cardinal .. Goya;                 (*underlying scale is
                                                   the reds scale*)
var
   reading : templ                            (*type temp variable*)
   LabData : UsualScales;              (*type UsualScales variable*)
   paintings : reds;                          (*type reds variable*)
   sunsets : SomeReds;                    (*type SomeReds variable*)
```

The host type for type SomeReds is type reds and temp is the host type for the UsualScales subrange. In both cases, it is necessary to specify the host type first, if a user-defined type is being used as the host type. Here is an example of a procedure to compile a list of paintings with red sunsets using the sunsets variable.

```
procedure CompileList(kinds : SomeReds);
const
   million = 1E06;                               (*this is 1,000,000*)
var
   value : real;
begin
   for kinds := cardinal to Goya do
      case kinds of
         cardinal: begin
                      write('Enter % of cardinal in painting:');
                      read(value); writeln;
                      writeln('value =', value * million)
                   end;                                  (*cardinal*)
         .
         .                                (*put in other cases, here*)
         .
         Goya : begin
                   write('Enter % of Goya red in Painting:');
                   read(value); writeln;
                   writeln('value =', value*million)
                end                                          (*Goya*)
         end                                                 (*case*)
end;                                                  (*CompileList*)
```

Each of the colors in the SomeReds subrange would be used as case constants in the above procedure. The whimsical assumption in the CompileLIst procedure follows: The value of a painting with a sunset increases as the percentage of red in the painting increases. For example, a painting with 15% cardinal red in it will have its worth computed as follows:

```
value := 0.15 * million
      := 0.15 * 1E06
      := 15E04                                  (*or $150,000.00*)
```

We leave it for an exercise to try this procedure in a program. (It will tax your knowledge of art as well as subranges!) In terms of subranges, the thing to notice about this example is its selection of values from the reds scale. Because reds has been defined beforehand, the SomeReds scale can be set up as a subinterval of the reds scale.

Subranges can also be defined in terms of the built-in ordinal scales. For example, here are some subranges defined this way.

```
type
  NaturalNos = 1 .. maxint;                    (*positive integers*)
  NegativeNos = -maxint .. -1;                 (*negative integers*)
  LowerCase = 'a' .. 'z';
  UpperCase = 'A' .. 'Z';
  Printables = ''.. '~';
```

In general a subrange type declaration has the following syntax:

Subrange type:

identifier ⟶ = ⟶ constant ⟶ .. ⟶ constant

Subranges help make source texts more clear and more readable. In addition, a subrange can be used to limit the values a variable can have. This gives us a way to put a check on the values that a variable get. If a variable that is a subrange type is assigned a value outside its subrange, this will result in the following run-time error message:

value is out of range

and the execution of your program will stop. In other words, subranges can be used as a way to maintain a program—guarantee it is working with the correct range of values. Here is an example of a procedure that will be used to illustrate this idea.

```
procedure ListEvenValues(FirstNo, LastNo: NaturalNos);
begin
  repeat
    if FirstNo mod 2 = 0 then
     write(FirstNo:3);
    if FirstNo <> LastNo then
     FirstNo := succ(FirstNo)
  until FirstNo = LastNo
end;                                                    (*EvenValues*)
```

Notice the difference between the following two procedure calls:

Procedure Call	*Result*
ListEvenValues(5, 11);	6 8 10 (printed by procedure)
ListEvenValues(−5, 11);	error! −5 is out range

5.4.5

Bug Clinic: Parameters that Are Subrange Types

There is subtle sandtrap with procedure parameters that are subrange types, which stems from the following rule:

> **Rule for actual and formal parameters:**
>
> **The data type for an actual parameter must be the same as the data type for the corresponding formal parameter.**

For example, the subrange NaturalNos used in the above procedure is a subset of the integers. A type violation message will result if an actual parameter of type integer is passed to the FirstNo or SecondNo parameters in the ListEven-Values procedure. Here is an example to illustrate this idea:

Experiment

Line *Program*

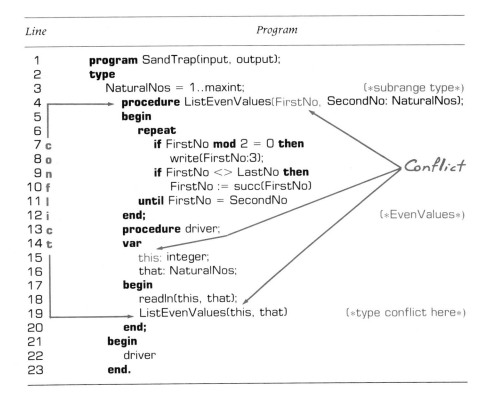

```
1   program SandTrap(input, output);
2   type
3     NaturalNos = 1..maxint;                          (*subrange type*)
4       procedure ListEvenValues(FirstNo, SecondNo: NaturalNos);
5       begin
6         repeat
7           if FirstNo mod 2 = 0 then
8             write(FirstNo:3);
9           if FirstNo <> LastNo then
10            FirstNo := succ(FirstNo)
11        until FirstNo = SecondNo
12      end;                                           (*EvenValues*)
13      procedure driver;
14      var
15        this: integer;
16        that: NaturalNos;
17      begin
18        readln(this, that);
19        ListEvenValues(this, that)                   (*type conflict here*)
20      end;
21    begin
22      driver
23    end.
```

There is a type conflict between *this* (type integer on line 15) and *FirstNo* (type NaturalNos on line 4). This program will not compile! Try experimenting with this program on your system to see how it behaves with various forms of this and that.

A subrange is restricted to values from the underlying scale of the host type. It is a fatal error to use type real to set up a subrange. The two-period ellipsis (..) represents the values in the subrange between the two constants, which indicate the extreme values of a subrange. It makes no sense to talk about a subrange of the reals because, for example, the value to the right of the lower limit will have no meaning. For example, the following subrange is illegal:

```
type
  percentages = 55.5 .. 95.5;          (*illegal subrange type*)
```

Pascal offers a rich selection of built-in arithmetic functions. We look at these in Section 5.5.

5.5 Arithmetic Functions

The standard arithmetic functions available in Pascal are given in Table 5.2. The ISO standard does not include a function to compute powers of numbers. So it is necessary to invent a way to compute powers of numbers. Here are two ways to do this.

1. Use repeated multiplication to compute the power of a number.
2. Use the exp() and ln() functions to do the same thing.

Table 5.2 Arithmetic Functions

Function	*Argument*	*Result*	*Act*
abs(x)	Either*	Same as x	Returns absolute value of x
arctan(x)	Radian Measure	Radian Measure	Returns angle whose tan is x
cos(x)	Radian Measure	Real	Cosine of angle (in radians)
exp(x)	Either	Real	Returns e^x to the power x or e^x (e = 2.718, approximately)
ln(x)	Either	Real	Returns exponent such that e^{exponent} = x or natural logarithm of x
sin(x)	Radian	Real	Sine of angle (in radians)
sqr(x)	Either	Same type as x	x^2
sqrt(x)	Either $\geqslant 0$	Real $\geqslant 0$	Square root of x

*"Either" means either integer or real argument.
†e is called the Euler number.
‡ln(x) is the same as $\log_e x$.

First, we show how to compute powers of numbers using repeated multiplication.

5.5.1 *Computing Powers with Repeated Multiplication*

If we have a base value (either type integer or type real), we want to be able to compute

$$\text{base}^{\text{exponent}} = \underbrace{\text{base} \times \text{base} \times \cdots \times \text{base}}_{\textit{exponent} \text{ copies of base}}$$

For example, we might want to compute

$$2^{15} = \underbrace{2 \times 2 \times \cdots \times 2}_{15 \text{ copies of } 2} = 32768$$

Here is an algorithm to carry out this idea.

```
                                              (*input: base, exponent;
                                              output: power of base*)
begin
   initialize base and exponent
   assign 1 to power;
   if exponent = 0 then
      print power                             (*without any change!*)
   else
      if exponent ≥ 1 then                    (*take care of positive
                                                 exponents, here.*)
         repeat
            assign power * base to power;
            subtract 1 from exponent
         until exponent equals 0
   else                                       (*take care of negative
                                                 exponents, here.*)
      repeat
         assign 1/base * power to power;
         add 1 to exponent
      until exponent equals 0
end;                                          (*algorithm to compute powers*)
```

Here are some sample computations using this algorithm.

Powers Table

Base	*Exponent*	*Computations*	
2	−1	Power := ½ ; exponent := −1 + 1	
		(stop, since exponent equals 0!)	
2	0	Power := 1	
2	1	Power := 2; exponent := 1 − 1	
		(stop, since exponent equals 0!)	
2	5	Power := 1*2;	exponent := 5 − 1
		:= 2*2;	:= 4 − 1
		:= 4*2;	:= 3 − 1
		:= 8*2;	:= 2 − 1
		:= 16*2;	:= 1 − 1
		(power is 32 and stop, since exponent is 0)	
2	−5	Power := ½;	exponent := −5 + 1
		:= (½)*(½);	:= −4 + 1
		:= (¼)*(½);	:= −3 + 1
		:= (⅛)*(½);	:= −2 + 1
		:= (1/16)*(½);	:= −1 + 1
		(Power is 1/32 = 0.03125 and stop, since exponent is 0)	

Notice that this algorithm will only work if power is a type real variable. We leave it as an exercise to implement this algorithm.

There is another way to compute powers, using two of the built-in Pascal functions. We show how to do this in Section 5.5.2.

5.5.2 *Computing Powers with the exp( ) and ln( ) Functions*

The log (short for logarithmic) function ln() is also called the *natural log function.* It was invented by the 17th century mathematician Leonard Euler, who found it convenient to use a new constant

$e = 2.71828\cdots$ (approximate value of Euler's constant)

to represent exponents. In general, a natural log of a number reads as follows:

ln(x) reads "the log of x raised to the e power"

If we assume ln(x) equals some exponent y, we can write this fact in the following way:

if $\ln(x) = y$ then $e^y = x$

In other words, ln(x) just gives us another way to represent exponents on e used to compute x. The built-in exponential function exp() is a shorthand for raising the number e to a power. That is, we can rewrite the exponential function as follows:

exp(x) is the same as e^x

The exponential function exp() can be used with the natural log function to compute powers of numbers. We can do this because the exponential and logarithmic functions are inverses of each other. That is, we can use ln(x) as an argument in the exp() function to get back x. This is done in the following way:

$$\begin{aligned} \exp(\ln(x)) &= {}_e\ln(x) \\ &= \ln(\exp(x)) = \ln(e^x) \\ &= x * \ln(e) = x * 1 = x \end{aligned}$$

There is one more fact we need before we can write a complete expression to compute a power of a number. There is a law of logs that allows us to rewrite the log of a power as follows:

$$\text{if } y = \text{base}^{\text{exponent}} \text{ then } \ln(y) = \ln(\text{base}^{\text{exponent}}) + \text{exponent} * \ln(\text{base})$$

In other words, the exponent on base can be multiplied times the log of the base. We can put these ideas together in the following expression:

$$\begin{aligned} \exp(\text{exponent} * \ln(\text{base})) &= \exp(\ln(y)) && \text{(by above identity)} \\ &= y && \text{(the inverse idea)} \\ &= \text{base}^{\text{exponent}} && \text{(by above identity)} \end{aligned}$$

For example, we can compute 2^5 power using the following technique:

$$2^5 = \exp(5 * \ln(2)) = 32$$

Here is a procedure that can be used to build a powers table.

```
procedure BuildTable(FirstExponent, LastExponent:integer;
                     base: integer);
var
  power: real;                    (*use to compute power of base*)
begin
  repeat
    power := exp(FirstExponent * ln(base)};
    writeln(power:16:0, FirstExponent, (1/power):20:1);
    FirstExponent := FirstExponent + 1
  until FirstExponent > LastExponent
end;                                              (*BuildTable*)
```

Notice that it is possible to use the exponential and natural log functions to compute negative powers of numbers directly. For example, we can use the following expression to compute a $2^{(-5)}$:

$$\exp(-5 * \ln(2)) = 2^{(-5)} = 0.03125$$

In the above procedure we simply print the reciprocal of a positive power of the base, which does the same thing in a simpler way. We leave it as an exercise to implement the BuildTable procedure. We illustrate the use of this second technique of computing powers of numbers by constructing a table to show earnings on an investment.

5.5.3 *Example: Computing Earnings on Investments*

Accountants use the following formula to compute the future value of $1.00 over n periods based on a given compound interest rate:

$$\text{future value of } \$1.00 = (1 + \text{rate})^n$$

For example, if we invest $1.00 and let it accrue interest for five interest periods at 9%, here is its future value.

$$\begin{aligned}\text{future value of } \$1.00 &= (1 + 0.09)^5 \\ &= (1.09)^5 \\ &= 1.53862\end{aligned}$$

This says we have earned 54 cents on our original dollar after five interest periods. To compute the future value of an amount greater than 1, just multiply the investment times the future value of 1 for n periods at the investment rate. For example, if we invest $12500.00 for five periods at 9%, we get the following results:

$$\text{future value of } \$12{,}500.00 = 12500 * (1 + 0.09)^5$$
$$= 12500 * 1.53862$$
$$= \$19{,}232.00$$

$$\text{earnings} = \text{future value of amount} - \text{amount}$$
$$= \$19{,}232.00 - \$12{,}500.00$$
$$= \$6732.80$$

Here is an algorithm to carry out this idea.

```
                      (*input: rate, amount, number of interest periods;
                         output: gross, future value of 1, earnings*)
begin
   initialize rate and amount;
   initialize n;                                (*for number of periods*)
   assign 1 to period;
   repeat
      assign exp((1 + rate)*ln(n)) to FutureValueOfOne;
      assign amount*FutureValueOfOne to gross;
      assign gross - amount to earnings;
      print FutureValueOfOne, gross, and earnings;
      move cursor to next line of table;
      add 1 to period
   until period > n
end;                          (*algorithm to compute future values table*)
```

This algorithm can be used to construct a complete future value table, which will let you see the stages in the growth of earnings on an investment. A program to carry out this idea is given in Figure 5.5. Refinements of the program in Figure 5.5 are possible.

```
          (*Method: Use the exp() and ln() function to compute future
                values on an investment using the following formula:
                          Future value of $1.00 = (1 + rate)^n
                                over n periods at a given rate.*)

program Earnings(input, output);

(*-----------------------------------------------------------*)
                                        (*Build an earning table*)

   procedure BuildTable(amount: real;                (*investment*)
                        rate: real;               (*compound rate*)
                        periods: integer);                (*time*)
   var
      gross:real;                        (*investment + earnings*)
      earnings:real;                       (*gross - investment*)
      n: integer;                            (*control variable*)
      FutureValueOfOne:real;                        (*for $1.00*)
```

```
begin
   n := 1;
   repeat
      FutureValueOfOne := exp(n * ln(1 + rate));
      gross := amount * FutureValueOfOne;
      earnings := gross - amount;
      write(n:10,' ':12, FutureValueOfOne:8:6,' ':4);
      write(gross:15:2, ' ':4, earnings:15:2); writeln;
      n := n + 1
   until n > periods
end;                                                    (*BuildTable*)

(*-----------------------------------------------------------------*)
          (*Program manager: get values and activate procedure*)

procedure driver;
var
   CompoundRate, investment: real;
   time: integer;                                    (*no. of periods*)
   dash: integer;                                (*control of variable*)
begin
   repeat
      write('Enter investment, compound rate, periods: ');
      readln(investment, CompoundRate, time); writeln;
      writeln; writeln;
      writeln('Future value table:':25);
      writeln('rate =':10, CompoundRate:10:8);
      write('period':10, 'future value':20);
      writeln('future value':20, 'earnings':20);
      write('of 1 dollar':30, 'of':10, investment:8:2);
      writeln; for dash := 1 to 70 do write('—'); writeln;
      BuildTable(investment, CompoundRate, time);
      writeln; writeln
   until 1 > 2                                         (*always false*)
end;                                                       (*driver*)
(*-----------------------------------------------------------------*)

begin
   driver                                (*activate driver procedure*)
end.
```

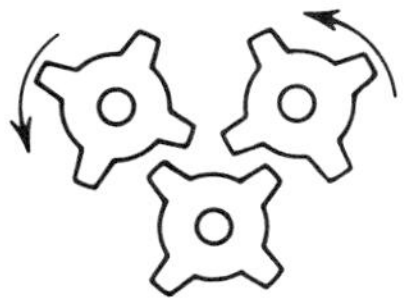

```
Enter investment, compound rate, periods: 10000 0.12 5


   Future value table:
 rate =0.12000000
 period         future value        future value        earnings
                   of 1 dollar          of10000.00
----------------------------------------------------------------------
         1           1.120000            11200.00         1200.00
         2           1.254400            12544.00         2544.00
         3           1.404928            14049.28         4049.28
         4           1.573519            15735.19         5735.19
         5           1.762342            17623.42         7623.42
```

FIGURE 5.5 Earnings on an investment

5.5.4

Refinement: Computing Earnings on Changing Investment

The program in Figure 5.5 does not allow for the possibility of adding to the original investment at the beginning of each interest period. Accountants use the following formula to compute the earnings over n periods, if we invest one additional dollar at the end of each new interest period:

$$\text{future value of ordinary annuity} = ((1 + \text{rate})^n - 1)/\text{rate}$$

The term *annuity* refers to a periodic investment. The term *ordinary* is used when a periodic investment (or rent) is made at the end of each interest period. Here is a graphical interpretation of this idea for an ordinary annuity of $5.00 over four interest periods at 12%.

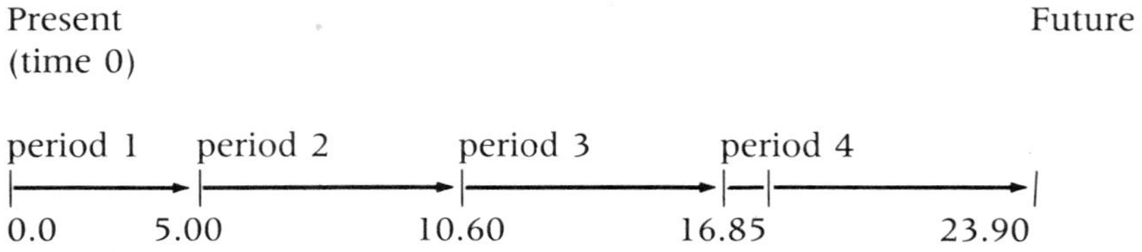

These amounts are computed using the following formula:

$$\text{future value} = (\text{periodic amount}) * ((1 + i)^n - 1)/i$$

This is a good place to set up a new data type.

```
type
  investments = (FVwithAnnuity, FVwithoutAnnuity);
```

Then use this enumeration type in a case statement to select the type of table to build, depending on a choice made by a user after viewing a printed menu of the form.

```
menu:
    → 1 Show Future Value of amount without annuity;
    → 2 Show Future Value of annuity
```

Carrying out this refinement is left as an exercise. We can add to this menu another desirable feature shown in Section 5.5.5.

5.5.5

Another Refinement: Determining the Annuity

Notice that the new future value formula given in Section 5.5.4 can be used to backtrack, if we know how much we want to end up with after n periods and do not know the amount of the periodic investment. We can use the following formulas to do this:

```
FVO := ((1 + i)^n - 1)/i;              (*Future value of ordinary
                                          annuity of $1.00*)

FutureValue := (annuity) * FVO;
annuity := FutureValue/FVO;            (*desired formula*)
```

This can be used to add another feature to the program in Figure 5.5. Carrying out this refinement is left as an exercise.

In addition to the arithmetic functions, Pascal also has two built-in functions that can be used to coerce the machine into converting type real values to type integer. These are called transfer functions.

5.6 Transfer Functions: trunc() and round()

There are two built-in functions in Pascal that can be used to force (coerce) a machine to convert a type real value to a type integer value. This is done internally by the machine whenever either of the following functions are activated:

Transfer Functions

Function	*Conversion*
trunc(x)	If x is a positive real, this function converts x to the greatest integer less than or equal to x; if x is negative, this function converts x to the least integer greater than or equal to x.
round(x)	If $x \geq 0$, then this function converts x to trunc($x + 0.5$); if $x < 0$, then this function converts x to trunc($x - 0.5$).

For example, we can make the following type conversions:

trunc(−5.67) = −5;
trunc(5.67) = 5;
trunc(5.0) = 5;
round(−5.67) = trunc(−5.67 − 0.5) = trunc (−6.17) = −6;
round(5.67) = trunc(5.67 + 0.5) = trunc(6.17) = 6;
round(−5.45) = trunc(−5.45 + − 0.5) = trunc(−5.95) = −5;
round(5.45) = trunc(5.45 + 0.5) = trunc (5.95) = 5;

There is a severe restriction on the use of these two transfer functions, which is probably obvious to you. Here is the restriction.

> **Warning:**
>
> **The trunc() and round() functions only work for real values of *x* that can be converted to integer values in the following scale:**
> **−maxint, . . ., −1, 0, 1, . . ., maxint**

So, for example, the following uses of the transfer functions are illegal:

```
x := trunc(-53001.67);            (*argument out of bounds for
                                    Apple IIe or IBM PC*)
x := trunc(4111222333.92);        (*argument out of bounds for
                                    VAX-11 Pascal and most other
                                    machines!*)
x := round(53001.92);             (*argument out of bounds for
                                    Apple and IBM PC Pascal*)
x := round (4111222333.92);       (*argument out of bounds for
                                    VAX-11 Pascal and most other
                                    machines!*)
```

In Section 5.6.1 we illustrate the use of the trunc() function to produce random numbers. We do this by showing how to set up a user-defined function.

5.6.1 *User-Defined Function to Produce Random Numbers*

We can use the following technique to construct a user-defined function to produce random numbers in the interval from 0 to 1:

```
seed := sqr(seed + 3.141597);       (*use built-in square
                                      function, here*)
seed := seed - trunc(seed);         (*chop off whole part*)
RndNo : seed;                       (*a random number*)
```

The trick is to produce values of RndNo that are as irregular as possible.

After we calculate the first random number using this technique, then the second value is obtained by using the old value of the seed. Here are some sample random numbers we get using this idea.

```
seed := 2.71828;                    (*initial value*)
```

Table of Random Numbers

seed	*sqr(seed + 3.141597)*	*seed – trunc(seed)*
2.71828	34.33815846	0.33815846
0.33815846	12.10834758	0.10834758
0.10834758	10.56213977	0.56213977

and so on. Pascal also allows user-defined functions to be set up. Here is a function to carry out this idea.

```
function RndNo: real;                                    (*result is a real*)
begin
   seed := sqr(seed + 3.141597);
   RndNo := seed - trunc(seed)                           (*chop off whole part*)
end;                                                                  (*RndNo*)
```

This is an example of a function without parameters. In general, the syntax for the declaration of a parameterless function is given in Figure 5.6. Functions differ from procedures in the following ways:

1. A function identifier is always assigned a value inside the function body.
2. When a function is activated, the identifier used to activate a function must be part of another Pascal statement (it cannot stand by itself the way a procedure identifier always does).
3. The value assigned to a function identifier can be used in calculations in a statement used to activate a function.

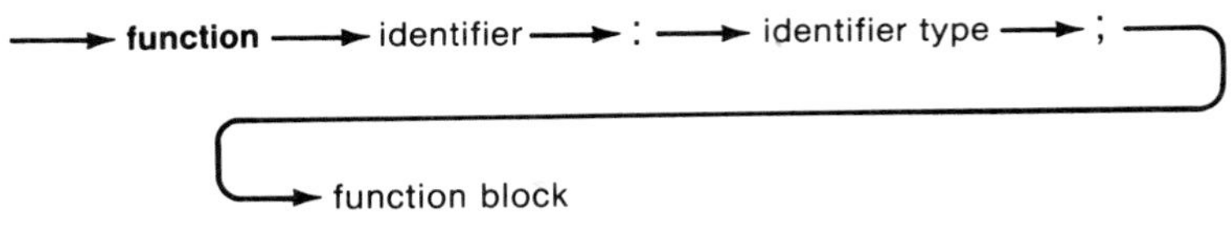

FIGURE 5.6
Syntax for a parameterless function

So, for example, the identifier for this new RndNo function can be used as the argument in the trunc() to produce integer values. Since the values of RndNo will always be in the interval from 0 to 1, this will not produce very exciting results. That is,

trunc(RndNo) will always be 0

If we use

trunc(12 * RndNo)

then we will get integer values from 0 to 11, depending on the value of RndNo. If we want to simulate the rolls of a pair of dice (the sum of pair of numbers that turn up), then we can use the following technique:

SumOfDice := trunc(12 * RndNo) + 1

This will produce integer values in the interval from 1 to 12. In Figure 5.7, we give a program to illustrate these ideas. The program in Figure 5.7 can be refined to make it more useful.

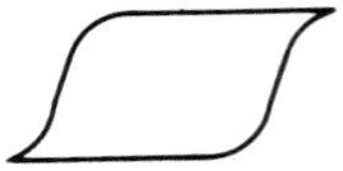

```
        (*Method: Use the trunc() function to define a new function
                   to produce random numbers from 1 to 12*)

program ShowDice(input, output);
var
  seed: real;                              (*use to start RndNo fn*)

  (*-----------------------------------------------------------*)
           (*Produce random numbers using sqr() and trunc() fns*)

  function RndNo: real;
  begin
    seed := sqr(seed + 3.1415927);
    seed := seed - trunc(seed);               (*chop off whole part*)
    RndNo := seed
  end;                                                     (*RndNo*)

  (*-----------------------------------------------------------*)
                                   (*Print table of random numbers*)

  procedure ShowTable;
  var
    no : integer;                                (*number of rolls*)
    dash: integer;                               (*control variable*)
  begin
    write('Enter value for seed: '); readln(seed); writeln;
    repeat
      write('Enter no. of rolls of dice you wish to see: ');
      readln(no);
      writeln; writeln;
      writeln('Random number table:':30);
      writeln('seed':10, 'RndNo value':24, 'roll of dice':25);
      writeln; for dash := 1 to 70 do write('-'); writeln;
      repeat
        write(seed:12:10,' ':10, RndNo:12:10, ' ':10);
        writeln(trunc(12 * RndNo) + 1);
        no := no - 1
      until no = 0;                              (*inner repeat loop*)
      writeln; writeln
    until 1 > 2                                      (*always false*)
  end;                                                 (*ShowTable*)

  (*-----------------------------------------------------------*)

begin
  ShowTable                          (*activate ShowTable procedure*)
end.
```

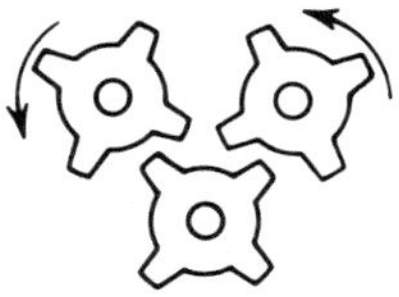

```
Enter value for seed: 2.71828

Enter no. of rolls of dice you wish to see: 10
```

```
        Random number table:
     seed              RndNo value                  roll of dice
-----------------------------------------------------------------
2.7182800000       0.3381081000                              2
0.1083174000       0.5619154000                              9
0.7159719000       0.8808050000                              3
0.1796837000       0.0308771100                              1
0.0645647000       0.2794456000                              9
0.7035036000       0.7847652000                              5
0.4162865000       0.6585045000                              6
0.4407387000       0.8330984000                             10
0.7981691000       0.5217237000                              6
0.4198875000       0.6841412000                              8
```

FIGURE 5.7 Simulating the rolls of a pair of dice

5.6.2 *Refinement: Choosing Limits on the Range of Random Numbers*

The program in Figure 5.7 is restricted to producing random numbers in the range from 1 to 12 using

trunc(12 * RndNo) + 1

It would be better if we allow the user to select the range of random number that are produced. This can be done by introducing two new type integer variables low and high and using them in the following assignments:

1. Determine maximum random number with

```
NewNo := trunc(high * RndNo);
```

2. Force the value of NewNo to be in the interval from low to high with

```
NewNo := (NewNo mod (high - low + 1)) + low;
```

For example, suppose we want random numbers in the range from 5 (the low) to 12 (the high). Here are some sample calculations using these assignments.

NewNo	*Adjusted NewNo*
2	(2 **mod** (12 – 5 + 1)) + 5 = (2 **mod** 8) + 5
	= 2 + 5
	= 7
9	(9 **mod** (12 – 5 + 1)) + 5 = (9 **mod** 8) + 5
	= 1 + 5
	= 6

Carrying out this refinement is left as an exercise.

You might wonder how a processor will evaluate an expression like the one used in the second of the above assignments. We look at how a processor does this using precedence rules in Section 5.7.

5.7

How a Processor Evaluates Arithmetic Expressions

Here is an arithmetic expression without parentheses.

$7 - 16 / 3 + 1 * 2 - 4$

Since this expression does not have grouping symbols, a processor will evaluate it from left to right, starting with the operators with highest precedence (the / and * operators). After taking care of these two operators, a processor will scan the new expression form left to right for the remaining operators on the next precedence level (the + and – operators). Here is what happens.

Step 1:
$7 - 16/3 + 1 * 2 - 4 \quad = 7 - 5.333 + 1 * 2 - 4$

Step 2:
$= 7 - 5.333 + 2 - 4$

Step 3:
$= 1.6667 + 2 - 4$

Step 4:
$= 3.6667 - 4$

Step 5:
$= -0.33333$

We can force a processor to produce an entirely different result by introducing grouping symbols into this same expression. For example, here is a rewrite of the above expression.

New expression:

$7 - (16/(3 + 1) * 2) - 4$

A processor will always evaluate an expression with parentheses from the inside out. It takes care of the expressions inside the innermost pair of parentheses before it does anything else. So even though the + operator has a lower precedence than the times (*) and divide (/) operators, a processor will evaluate the (3 + 1) term in this new expression before it does anything else. Here are the new steps that a processor will follow.

Step 1:
$7 - (16/(3 + 1) * 2) - 4 = 7 - (16 / 4 * 2) - 4$

Step 2:
$= 7 - (4 * 2) - 4$

Step 3:
$= 7 - 8 - 4$

Step 4:
$= -1 - 4$

Step 5:
$= -5$

Table 5.3 Operator Precedence Rules

Level	*Operators*	*Comment*
1	**not**	(Highest precedence)
2	* **div** / **mod and**	
3	+ − **or**	
4	= <> < <= > >= **in***	
5	: =	(Lowest precedence)

***in** is a set operator, which is explained later.

Expressions can be formed with a variety of Pascal operators, including the relational operators like < (less than) or ≤ (less than or equal). There are also the Boolean operators **and, or,** and **not,** which can be used to build expressions. Each of the Pascal operators belongs to a particular precedence level, which tells a processor which ones to treat first when it evaluates an expression. A summary of these precedence rules is given in Table 5.3. It takes time and experience to get used to using these rules. Knowing these rules is important. They can be side stepped by building expressions with parentheses. The following rule of thumb is useful in setting up expressions:

> **Evaluation of an expression with operators:**
>
> **An expression without parentheses will be evaluated from left to right using the operator precedence rules. An expression with parentheses will force a processor to evaluate expressions inside parentheses, first, starting with the innermost enclosed expression.**

When expressions include type real values, then it is important to guard against computational errors. These can crop up during the running of a program because processors routinely give approximate values for real numbers like ⅔. We discuss the problem of computational errors with reals in Section 5.8.

5.8 Computational Errors with Reals

Numbers like ⅔ are expressed in rounded form like

⅔ stored as 0.6666667 on an IBM PC/AT

Sometimes this can lead to bizarre results and completely wrong arithmetic.

For example, there is no guarantee that the following sum *computed in a program* will equal 1:

$$\tfrac{1}{7} + \tfrac{1}{7} + \tfrac{1}{7} + \tfrac{1}{7} + \tfrac{1}{7} + \tfrac{1}{7} + \tfrac{1}{7} \text{ may} = 1$$

Here is an experiment you might want to try on your machine (a calculator will do) to see how these round-off errors can crop up.

Round-Off Errors Experiment

Algorithm	*Example*
begin	
initialize term;	term := 11
assign term **to** count;	count := 11
assign 0 **to** sum;	sum := 0
repeat	
add 1/term **to** sum;	sum := sum + term
subtract 1 from count	count := count − 1
until count = 0	
end;	

This algorithm aims at computing the following sum:

$$\begin{aligned} \text{sum} &:= 1/\text{term} + 1/\text{term} + \cdots + 1/\text{term} \\ &=\mathbf{?}\ \text{term}/\text{term} \end{aligned}$$

A program to carry out this idea is given in Figure 5.8. This program was run using IBM PC Pascal. It was also run on a PDP-11/70 using OS Pascal and produced entirely different results. On the 11/70, sum became 1 when term was 11, but sum was not 1, when term was 19. Try this experiment on your machine to see what happens. On a smaller machine like the IBM PC or Apple IIe, for example, you can expect errors to crop up with smaller values of term, but not all the time!

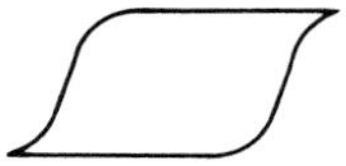

```
      (*Method: compute 1/x + ··· + 1/x (x copies of 1/x) to see
                 how close to 1 we get for different values of
                   x. Print formatted and E forms of result.*)

program sum(input, output);

 (*- - - - - - - - - - - - - - - - - - - - - - - - - - - - - - - - - - - - - - - -*)
                                              (*Check for round-off error*)

  procedure AddEmUp(bottom: integer);
  var
    term: integer;                                     (*control variable*)
    result: real;                              (*sum of fractions 1/bottom*)
```

```
begin
   result := 0;
   for term := 1 to bottom do begin
      result := result + 1/bottom;
      writeln(' ':20, result:15:13, ' ':10, result)
      end                                                        (*for*)
end;                                                         (*AddEmUp*)

(*----------------------------------------------------------------*)
        (*Program manager: get values and activate procedure*)

procedure driver;
var
   denominator: integer;                                (*for fraction*)
begin
   repeat
      write('Enter x in 1/x: '); readln(denominator);writeln;
      writeln('Partial sums':20);
      writeln('formatted form':35, 'E-form':20);
      AddEmUp(denominator);
      writeln; writeln
   until 1 > 2                                          (*always false*)
end;                                                        (*driver*)
(*----------------------------------------------------------------*)
begin
   driver                                   (*activate driver procedure*)
end.
```

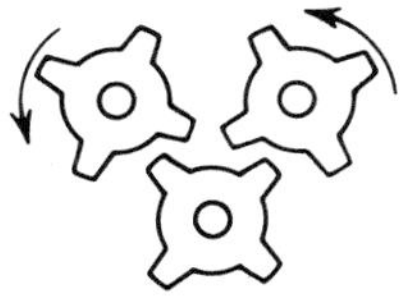

```
Enter x in 1/x: 3

          Partial sums
                        formatted form               E-form
                       0.3333333000000           3.333333000E-01
                       0.6666667000000           6.666667000E-01
                       1.0000000000000           1.000000000E+00


Enter x in 1/x: 11

          Partial sums
                        formatted form               E-form
                       0.0909090900000           9.090909000E-02
                       0.1818182000000           1.818182000E-01
                       0.2727273000000           2.727273000E-01
                       0.3636364000000           3.636364000E-01
                       0.4545455000000           4.545455000E-01
                       0.5454546000000           5.454546000E-01
                       0.6363636000000           6.363636000E-01
                       0.7272727000000           7.272727000E-01
                       0.8181818000000           8.181818000E-01
                       0.9090908000000           9.090908000E-01
                       0.9999999000000           9.999999000E-01
```

FIGURE 5.8 Round-off error

In general it is a mistake to set up control structures that depend on exact results with reals. Here is a sample control structure that will sometimes produce an infinite loop.

```
readln(term);
sum := 0;
repeat
                                        (*do something!*)
   sum := 1/term
until sum = 1;                          (*source of mistake!*)
```

You can guarantee that a loop like this will always terminate by not requiring exact results. Here is a rewrite of the above repeat loop, which illustrates this idea.

```
repeat
                                        (*do something!*)
   sum := 1/term
until sum >= 1;                         (*will always terminate*)
```

Now we are not depending on an exact result. Sometimes the sum in this loop will be 1, sometimes it will never reach 1, but the loop will always terminate. The until condition takes care of this problem. Eventually, for cases where the sum never reaches 1, the sum will slip past 1 and shut off the interation inside this loop.

There are other cases where computations with reals produce bizarre results. Here are some experiments for you to try.

Experiments

1. (x / term) $*$ term may not equal x;
2. sqrt(term) $*$ sqrt(term) may not equal term; (try this with term = 2)
3. $a * x^2 + b * x + c$ may not equal 0 for real values of x computed using the quadratic formula:

```
x := (-b + sqrt(sqr(b) - 4*a*c))/(2*a);
x := (-b - sqrt(sqr(b) - 4*a*c))/(2*a);
```

4. For reals values of a and b, you will probably find a discrepancy between the theoretical and machine results:

Theoretical Idea	*Machine Results*
$a^3 - b^3 =$	$a*a*a - b*b*b$ may not =
$(a + b)*(a^2 + ab + b^2)$	$(a - b) * (\text{sqr}(a) + a*b + \text{sqr}(b))$
$a^3 + b^3 =$	$a*a*a + b*b*b$ may not =
$(a + b)*(a^2 - ab + b^2)$	$(a +)*(\text{sqr}(a) - a*b + \text{sqr}(b))$

In general, if you rely on computations with reals in a program, you can only expect approximate results.

5.9 Summary

What are the data? That is the question George Polya (see opening quote of this chapter) suggests we ask when we want to solve a problem. In Pascal programming we are forced to answer this question before we can do anything. We always need to tell a machine the data type for each variable we use in a program. Pascal has a rich selection of data types to choose from. The complete selection of these data types for ISO Pascal is given in Table 5.1.

In this chapter the focus have been on the simple data types. Each of the simple types is defined in terms of a scale of values. Type real stands by itself among the simple types, since it is not possible to list all the values of the scale used to define type real. It is also not possible to talk about the immediate neighbors of any number on the scale for type real. Between any two reals, we can always identify another real value. Nonrepeating as well as repeating decimals are represented inside a machine in rounded form. So calculations with reals are subject to round-off errors. Try the experiment in Figure 5.8 to verify this on your machine.

The remaining simple types (type Boolean, char, and integer) are defined by scales with values that can be completely listed. These are known as the built-in ordinal types, since we can always specify the position of a value on an ordinal scale. Except for the extreme values on an ordinal scale, each ordinal value has immediate neighbors on either side of a value.

In addition to the built-in ordinal types, we can also define new ordinal data types. New ordinal types can be declared in any block in a Pascal program. An enumeration type helps make more clear out intentions in setting up a control structure. The identifiers used to define the scale for enumeration type have no meaning outside a program. It is neither possible to input or output an identifier belonging to a scale for an enumeration type.

A subrange data type is also an ordinal type. The scale for a subrange can be taken from a part (or all!) of a scale for one of the standard ordinal types, usually type integer or type char. A subrange type can also be defined in terms of a portion of a scale of identifiers for an enumeration type.

ISO Pascal also has four built-in functions, which can be used to inspect ordinal scales.

Function	*Purpose*
pred()	Predecessor function used to determine the immediate neighbor (if it exists!) to the left of an ordinal value
succ()	Successor function used to determine the immediate neighbor (if it exists!) to the right of an ordinal value
ord()	Ordinal function used to determine the position of an ordinal value
chr()	Character function used to determine the character on a type char scale corresponding to a position number (a type integer value)

In addition, Pascal has two built-in transfer functions that can be used to force a processor to convert a type real value to an integer value: trunc() and round() functions.

Expressions are evaluated by a processor according to a set of operator precedence rules. Operators with higher priority will be evaluated by a computer first. In arithmetic expressions without parentheses, a computer will follow the set of precedence rules given in Table 5.3, moving from left to right across an expression. The evaluation will start with the operators with highest precedence. The evaluation from left to right occurs whenever two or more operators with the same priority (precedence level) appear in the same expression. It is possible to circumvent the usual operator precedence rules. This can be done by using parentheses to group the parts of an expression. This will force a computer to evaluate expression inside parentheses first. Here is rule of thumb to keep in mind.

Rule of thumb in forming expressions:

When in doubt and to make an expression more readable use parentheses to tell a computer how and in what order to evaluate the parts of an expression.

5.10

Keywords Review

Keywords	*Related Ideas*
abstract data type	data abstraction
data	values
data abstraction	specification of data and operations on the data without a specification of how the data are represented inside a machine or how the operations are implemented by a machine

data type	specification of 1. set of values (the data) 2. set of operations on the data
e	Euler constant that is approximately equal to 2.71828; the base use for the ln() and exp() functions in Pascal
function	a subprogram used to produce a single value
arithmetic	abs(), exp(), ln(), and so on (see Table 5.2 for list)
ordinal	used to inspect ordinal scales: pred(), succ(), ord(), and chr() functions
transfer	used to coerce type real values into type integer values (this is done internally by a processor when a transfer function is activated)
round(*x*)	rounds *x* (type real) to nearest integer
trunc(*x*)	truncates (chops) *x* (type real) to produce either greatest integer less than or equal to *x*, if *x* >= 0, or 'east integer greater than or equal to *x*, if *x* is negative
ln(x)	natural log function, wı 'ch represents the exponent used on the base *e* to compute the value of *x*
ln(*x*) = y	says $e^y = x$
operator precedence	priority given to Pascal opε rators (see Table 5.3)
ordinal types	defined in terms of a scale ʼith values, which can be completely listed
Boolean	scale: false, true
char	scale (implementation dependent but often the ASCII or EBCDIC table); see Appendix A
enumeration	scale: (identifier list)
integer	scale: –maxint, . . ., 0, . . ., maxint
subrange	scale: section of an ordinal scale
scalar types	the four simple types (real as well as Boolean, char and integer), which are defined in terms of scales
type	specification of qualities, which are shared by a group of values, the kind of values

5.11 Exercises

1. What is the main difference between type real and the other simple data types?

2. Using the operator precedence rules in Table 5.3, mimic a processor and evaluate the following expressions:

a. 253 – 5 + 99 * 2 – 1
b. 253 – (5 + 99) * 2 – 1
c. ((253 – 5) + 99) * 2 – 1
d. 253 – 5 + 99) * 2 – 1
e. (253 – 5 + 99) * 2 – 1
f. (253 – 5 + 99) * (2 – 1)
g. 253 – (5 + (99 * 2) – 1)
h. (((253 – 5) + 99) * 2) – 1
i. 253 – (((5 + 99) * 2) – 1)

3. Imagine yourself transported to another world where all computers run a language called *lacsaP*, which uses the following new operators that are defined using Pascal operators and the operator precedence rules given in Table 5.3:

OtherWorld Operator Precedence Rules

Level 1: Rwhoops, Lwhoops (for either type real or type integer operands)
  Example:
    x Rwhoops $y = (x * y) * y;$
    x Lwhoops $y = x * (x * y);$

Level 2: *R*sum, *L*sum (for either type real or type integer operands)
  Example:
    x *R*sum $y = (x + y) + y;$
    x *L*sum $y = x + (x + Y)$

Using these rules, evaluate the following expressions in this strange new world:

a. 253 *R*sum 5 *L*sum 99 *R*whoops 2
b. 253 *R*whoops 5 *L*whoops 99 *L*sum 2 *R*whoops 1
c. 253 *R*sum 5 *R*sum 99 *R*sum 2 *R*sum
d. 253 *L*sum 5 *R*whoops 99 *R*sum 2 *L*whoops

4. Implement the algorithm (Section 5.3) in a program to print the scale used to define type char on your computer system.

5. Refine the program for exercise 4 so that both the position number (ord(x)) and corresponding character are printed in six columns. Print a table have the following form:

Scale for Type Char

Symbol	*ord(symbol)*	*Symbol*	*ord(symbol)*	*Symbol*	*ord(symbol)*

6. Using maxint, write a program to print selected actual values (the extreme values and the five middle values, for example) used by your computer system to implement type integer. For example, on an Apple IIe, your program should produce the following scale:

$$-32768, \ldots, -2, -1, 0, 1, 2, \ldots, 32767$$

7. Refine the program for exercise 6 so that the user can choose how many values below maxint and above −maxint to print in the scale printed. For now, keep the middle values the same. Then print the type integer scale in columns having the following form (possible on an IBM PC or Apple IIe):

Scale for Type Integer

Low Side	*High Side*
−32768	32767
−32767	32766
−32766	32765
.	.
.	.
.	.
−3	2
−2	1
−1	0

You should limit the amount that you will let this table grow. So give a range of choices to make. Try restricting the user to no more than 20 values below maxint, for example. Be sure to build into your program a driver procedure that allows the user to try more than one set of values to produce more than one table.

8. You can determine the largest real value your computer system can handle by repeatedly computing higher and higher powers of 2 until exponential overflow occurs. Write a program to determine the largest real your system can handle. Print successive powers of two in the following table:

Segment of Scale for Type Real

Formatted Form	*E Form*

9. Carry out the refinement of the program in Figure 5.4, described in Section 5.4.2. This is the temperature table program. Give sample runs of the new program using the following values:

a. Low = 32, high = 35, increment = 0.25;
b. low = −459, high = −418, increment = 1.0

10. Carry out the refinement of the program in Figure 5.4, described in Section 5.4.3. Try the suggested repeat loop to do this. Run the new program using the following values:

a. low = 32, high = 34, increment = 0.5
menu choice 2 (Fahrenheit and Celsius, only);
b. low = 32, high = 34, increment = 0.5
menu choice 3 (Celsius and Kelvin, only);
c. low = 32, high = 34, increment = 0.5
menu choice 4 (all but Rankine scale)

11. Implement the CompileList procedure (see Section 5.4.4) in a program. Give a sample run with either some imaginary paintings or some of your favorites (just guess the percentage of red in each painting you choose).

12. Implement the ListEvenValues procedure (see Section 5.4.4) in a program. You should allow a user to return to a driver procedure to reactivate the EvenValues procedure with an alternate value for the number parameter. Give a sample run for

a. number = maxint − 20
b. number = maxint − 35

13. Refine the program for exercise 12 as follows:

a. Change the name EvenValues to Multiples procedure.
b. Add a parameter (call it factor) to the Multiples procedure that is used to determine occurences of multiples in the range from

number,. . ., maxint

For example, if factor is 5, then your new procedure should print all multiples of 5 in the above range.

c. Prompt the user for values of number and a value to pass to factor from your driver procedure and then print out the multiples in the specified interval. Allow the user to return to your driver procedure for more choices. Give sample runs using
d. minimum = 32500 (value to pass to number)
multiple = 5 (value to pass to factor)
e. minimum = 32500
multiple = 12

14. Implement powers algorithm (see Section 5.5.1) in a program. This algorithm uses repeated multiplication to determine powers. Give a sample run.

15. Implement the BuildTable procedure (see Section 5.5.2) using the ln() and exp() functions to compute powers. Give sample runs using

a. low exponent value = 0, high = 15, base = 2
b. low exponent value = 5, high = 5, base = 5
c. low exponent value = 1, high = 5, base = 16

16. Carry out the refinement of the program in Figure 5.5, described in Section 5.5.4. This is the future values program. Give a sample run for

a. periodic amount = 5.00, periods = 5, rate = 0.0625
b. periodic amount = 50.00, periods = 5, rate 0.0625
c. periodic amount = 500.000 periods = 5, rate = 0.0625

17. Carry out the refinement of the program in Figure 5.5, described in section 5.5.5. You should allow the user to specify the final amount from an ordinary annuity over *n* periods at a given compound interest rate. Give a sample run for

a. final amount = 500.00, periods = 4, rate = 0.12
b. final amount = 10000, periods = 12, rate = 0.12

18. Carry out the refinement of the program in Figure 5.7, described in Section 5.6.2. This is the random number program. Give a sample run for

a. low = 2, high = 6
b. low = 5, high = 12

19. Experiment with the program in Figure 5.8 and report the results you obtain on your system.

20. The notation *n!* reads "*n* factorial." For an integer *n*, it represents the follow product:

$$n! = n \times (n-1) \times (n-2) \times \cdots \times 3 \times 2 \times 1$$

Here are some sample factorials.

n	$n!$
5	$5 \times 4 \times 3 \times 2 \times 1 = 120$
4	$4 \times 3 \times 2 \times 1 = 24$
3	$3 \times 2 \times 1 = 6$

Write a procedure called FactorialTable to produce a table like the above one for all factorials from 1 to *n*. Let the user supply the value of *n* (keep it small!). Write a program to implement this procedure. Give a sample run.

21. You can approximate the value of the Euler constant e using the following series:

$$e = 1 + 1/1! + 1/2! + 1/3! + 1/4! + \cdots$$

Due Monday

Write a program to which uses this series to print approximate values of *e*, depending on the number of terms requested by the user of your program. Print the results as successive approximations in a table which has the following form:

ask- How many terms do you want to approximate e?
test w/ # diff. values - (4)

Approximations of the Number *e*

Value	*Series Used*
1	1
2	1 + 1/1!
2.5	1 + 1/1! + 1/2!

procedure factorial (
N: integer,
var nfact: integer)

Give a sample run of your program.

5.12 Review Quiz

Determine whether the following are true or false:

1. Type real is not an ordinal type.
2. An enumeration type is an ordinal type.
3. Every enumeration type is defined by a scale of values.
4. The scale for type real can be used to define a new subrange of reals.

5. If MyFavoriteMovies is an enumeration type, then a new subrange type can be defined using the MyFavoriteMovies scale.
6. A subrange type is an ordinal type.
7. The values on a scale used to implement type integer can be completely listed.
8. The same scale is always used to implement type char.
9. Type Boolean is not an ordinal type.
10. If StarWars is the first identifier in the scale used to define the MyFavoriteMovies enumeration type, then the ord(StarWars) = 1

5.13 Readings

Gould, S. J. *Ever Since Darwin.* New York: Norton, 1977.

Horowitz, E., and Sahni, S. *Fundamentals of Data Structures.* Rockville, Md: Computer Science Pres, 1982. See first part of Chapter 1 for good discussion of data types.

Polya, G. *How to Solve It.* New York: Doubleday Anchor, 1957. See Chapter 7 on understanding the problem.

Stubbs, D. F., and Webre, N. W. *Data Structures with Abstract Data Types and Pascal.* Monterey, CA: Brooks/Cole, 1985. See excellent discussion of data types in Chapter 1.

CHAPTER 6

STRUCTURED DATA TYPES AND ARRAYS

[In Pascal], the array is a *data type, not* the *data type.*

Doug Cooper, 1983

Intuitively, an array is a set of pairs, index and value. For each index which is defined, there is a value which is associated with that index.

Ellis Horowitz and Sartaj Sahni, 1982

AIMS

- Introduce array data types.
- Distinguish between structured data types and data structures.
- Show how arrays can be accessed, constructed, and inspected.
- Illustrate various forms of index expressions usedto select array components.
- Introduce strings and string constants.
- Introduce multidimensional arrays.

- Show how enumerated types can be used to define array indices to clarify the mechanisms used in a program
- Give a case study on selection sorting a list of names.
- Give a case study on the binary search technique.

6.1 Introduction to Structured Data Types

Until now we have only used the simple data types. The values of a simple data type are not made up of other values of the same type. Each value of a simple type has no parts. For example, the type char value *'t'* is not decomposable into other characters. It is "simply" a single value. In addition, no relationships are imposed on the values of a simple data type, except for the scales used to define a simple type. The *'t'* of the type char scale remains fixed; it is always appears after *'s'* and always appears before *'u'* on this scale. By declaring a variable to be a simple type, we are not free to order the values of the scale used for the simple type. In other words, we have no way to fit the values of a simple type together in an arbitrary way. The simple types have the following characteristics:

Characteristics of Simple Types

Characteristic	*Example*
1. The values of a simple type are *atomic* (indecomposable or single values), not representative of other simple type values.	Type char value: *'t'*, for example, does not represent one or more other characters
2. The values of a simple type remain fixed in relation to other values of the same data type.	*'t'* always comes before *'u'* and always comes after *'s'* on the same scale

By contrast, a *structured data type* can have values that are not atomic. There are rules that allow us to fit its values together in various ways. A musical score, for example, is analogous to a structured data type. If this score has lyrics, we are free to change the timing used to sing the lyrics. Here is an example.

Changes in the Timing of the Lyrics for a Song

Lyrics	*Word*	*Key*	*Timing*	*Count*
We are the world!	world . . .	D	Whole note	2
	world . . .	D	Half	½
	world . . .	D	(gasp) Quarter notes	¼

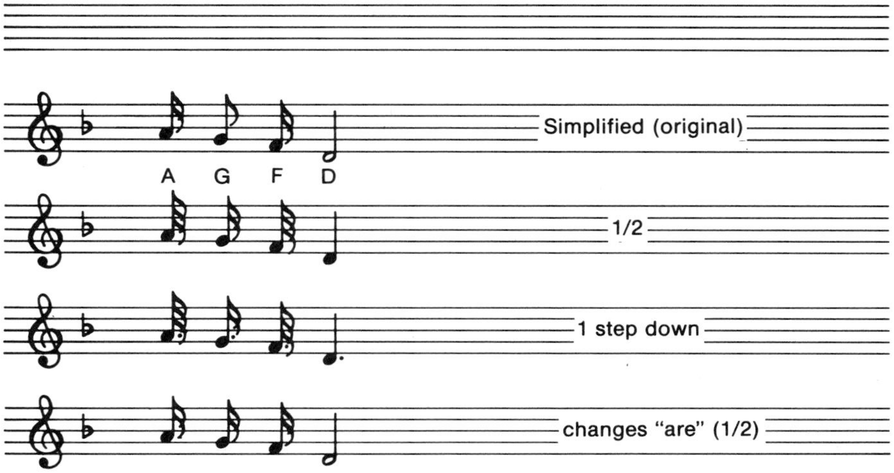

FIGURE 6.1
A Musical Structure

This idea is illustrated graphically in Figure 6.1. In other words we can change the beat used to sing the words of a song. In effect, we are free to *restructure* the song by changing the timing used to sing the lyrics of the song.

In Pascal there are four basic structured types: array, record, set, and file. An *array* is a collection of elements all of the same type. Array elements can either by *atomic* values like integers (each element is of type integer) or they can be composite. Each element of an array can also be an array, for example. Here is an example of array declaration.

```
type
   total = array [1..4] of real;
var
   sample: total;                         (*sample array variable*)
```

Up to this point, this declaration just set up the machinery to allow us to build an array of type *total.* All we have told Pascal to do is reserve memory cells to hold values for an array. This declaration produces the following result inside a storage area of the computer:

Result of Declaring an Array Variable

Memory Address (Imaginary)	*Array Element Position*	*Array Element Value*
300	[1]	?
304	[2]	?
308	[3]	?
30C	[4]	?

We can access an array cell by using a combination of the array *variable* (not type!) name and a position value. For example, we can access the second and fourth sample elements using the following technique:

Array Element Designator	*Array Element Value*
sample[2]	? (in position [1])
sample[4]	? (in position [2])
	? (in position [3])
	? (in position [4])

We are free to fill these storage cells with any allowable real values we choose. This can be done, for example, using an assignment statement like the following one:

```
sample[2] := 2.71828
```

which puts 2.71828 into the array cell in position 2. The beauty of a structure data type is the flexibility it gives us. We are free to rearrange the values inside an array. We can change the positions of the values of the array, using appropriate position numbers. These position values are called array *index* values or array *subscripts.* An array index value gives us a way to select an array data value. The array index is appended to an array variable name to select an array element.

We can, for example, set up two or more variables of the same type and fill the arrays in different ways. Here is an example.

```
var
  ResultA, ResultB: total;                    (*two array variables*)
```

Then we can assign values to the array cells in computer memory to produce arrays like the following ones:

Sample Initialized Arrays

	ResultA			Result*B*	
Memory Address	*Position*	*Value*	*Memory Address*	*Position*	*Value*
300	[1]	23.5	400	[1]	3.14
304	[2]	3.14	404	[2]	23.5
308	[3]	44.6	408	[3]	44.6
30C	[4]	2001.3	40C	[4]	2001.3

Notice that each array stores the *same* values. However, the values are stored differently in each array in two different ways

1. The values of Total$A$ and Total$B$ are in different areas computer memory.

2. The values of Total$A$ and Total$B$ are arranged differently; the values in positions [1] and [2] are switched.

This suggests some of the power available to you by using array variables. This is also an invitation to consider the power of each of the structured data types available in Pascal. This chapter is limited to a study of arrays. In Chapters 7 and 8 we will examine the remaining three structured data types. A structured data type that has been implemented with a set of values is called a *data structure.* Here are the two main characteristics of data structures.

> **Data structure:**
>
> **1. A set of possible values that are not necessarily atomic**
> **2. A set of operations and rules governing the operations that make it possible to rearrange and fit the values into a data structure in various ways and impose a structure on the values.**

6.2 Sample Arrays

Here are some other examples of array types and variables:

```
type
   index = 1..5;
   speeds = 0..55;
   SpeedLimits = array[index] of speeds;            (*notice index*)
   vowels = (a, e, i, o, u);
   voice = array[1..10000] of vowels;               (*notice: array
                                                    values are from an
                                                    enumeration type*)
   sounds = array[vowels] of char;                  (*aha!—an array
                                                    index can be an
                                                    enumeration type*)
   speech = array[1..500] of sounds;                (*array of arrays*)
var                                                 (*array variables*)
   SomeSpeeds, CityA, CityB : SpeedLimits;
   answers, fragments : sounds;
   echos : voice;
   prose : speech;
```

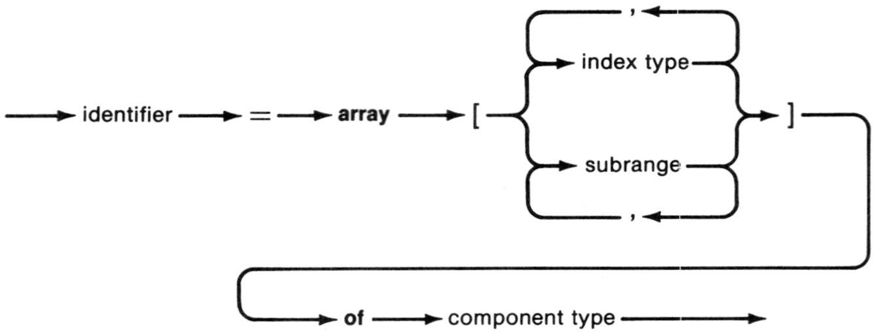

FIGURE 6.2
Array-type syntax

In general the declaration for an array type has the syntax shown in Figure 6.2. The index type for an array must be an ordinal type, which means we can use any of the simple types (except type real), an enumeration or subrange type to set up an array index. The component type of an array can be any simple type or *any* of the structured types or a pointer type (covered later). This means the components of an array can also be arrays (array type speech is an example). The only restriction on the component type for an array is that the components of an array cannot be the same type as the array itself. In the above list, we have the following examples of index and component types:

Array Type	*Index Type*	*Component Type*
SpeedLimits	1..100 (subrange)	0..55 (subrange)
Voice	1..10000 (subrange)	Vowels (enumeration)
Sounds	vowels (enumeration)	Char (simple)
Prose	1..500(subrange)	Sounds (array of Elements of type char)
Speech	1..500 (subrange)	Sounds (array)

An array variable is called a *component variable.* An array variable that has been initialized is a set of one or more pairs of values and corresponding indices. Each index value identifies the position of an array component. For example,

echos[500] identifies a vowels identifier in position 500
fragments[*a*] identifies a character like *t* in position a
speech[2] identifies a speech array in position 2

and so on. An array represents memory cells used to hold values of the array component type. For example, we can set up a *sample* SomeSpeeds array using the following sequence of assignments:

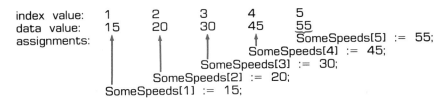

```
index value:   1      2      3      4      5
data value:    15     20     30     45     55
assignments:   ↑      ↑      ↑      ↑      SomeSpeeds[5] := 55;
               |      |      |      SomeSpeeds[4] := 45;
               |      |      SomeSpeeds[3] := 30;
               |      SomeSpeeds[2] := 20;
               SomeSpeeds[1] := 15;
```

An array index is always an expression representing an ordinal type. This means any of the expressions (including arithmetic expressions) we have used so far to represent ordinal values can be used to locate an array element. Here are some examples of index expressions using the sample SomeSpeeds array.

i	*Index Expression*	*Indexed Variable*	*Position*	*Value Located*
25	*i* **mod** 5	SomeSpeeds[*i* **mod** 5]	5	55
3	*i* + 1	SomeSpeeds[*i* + 1]	4	45
25	*i* **mod** 5 − 1	SomeSpeeds[*i* **mod** 5 − 1]	4	45
2	*i* * 4	SomeSpeeds[*i* * 4]	8	Error!
1	*i* * 4	SomeSpeeds[*i* * 4]	4	4
20	*i* **div** 2	SomeSpeeds[*i* **div** 2]	10	Error!
3	*i* **div** 2	SomeSpeeds[*i* **div** 2]	1	15

Note. The errors in this result from computing an index value outside the prescribed subrange.

The above table not only illustrates sample index expressions, it also points out a severe restriction on index expression values. The values of an index expression must fall within limits set by the array type. For example,

$i * 4$ is out of bounds for $i = 2$

since the index range is limited to integer values in the 1··5 subrange. SomeSpeeds is a SpeedLimits array type, which limits an index expression to the following subrange:

1..5 subrange limits SomeSpeeds indices

This brings up another crucial feature of array types.

> **An array type declaraction always specifies the maximum number of elements an array can have.**

In each of the above examples, the maximum number of array elements is specified: 5 for type SpeedLimits, 10,000 for type voice and so on.

6.3 Packed Arrays and String Types

It possible to conserve on the storage used by an array by declaring an array to be a *packed* type. The packed token tells Pascal to conserve, if possible, on the storage used to save array values. Here are two examples of packed array types and variables.

```
type
   name = packed array[1..15] of char;
   locations = packed array[-10..+10] of real;
var
   directory: name;                          (*type name var*)
   latitudes: locations;                (*type locations var*)
```

How much storage is saved by using the packed modifier will vary, depending on the implementation of Pascal. The packed modifier is used to set up what is known as a *string type* (type name is an example). A *string type* is a packed array of components of type character. There are two crucial restrictions on the subrange used to set up a string type.

1. A string type index must be a subrange of type integer (the negative values and zero are excluded).
2. The subrange used in a string type must always begin with 1 and 1..2 is the minimum subrange.

In this chapter, we illustrate how arrays can be built and inspected, how existing array elements can be accessed, how array elements can be ordered (sorted). Arrays offer convenient tools that can be used to hold values we need to store temporarily. The storage offered by arrays is always temporary. It lasts as long as a program that uses them remains activated.

6.4 Accessing Arrays

We can access an array element by using an appropriate value of an array index. For example, we can inspect the second array element using the following technique:

```
write(SomeSpeeds[2]);                    (*exhibit value*)
```

There are two ways to fill an array cell, either by individual component or by an entire array. For example, we can make the following assignments to initialize individual array calls:

Array	*Assignment*	*Action*
SomeSpeeds	SomeSpeeds[1] := 5;	Puts 5 into cell at position 1 of SomeSpeeds
SomeSpeeds	read(SomeSpeeds[1]);	Assigns input value to cell in position 1
SomeSpeeds	**for** *i* := 15 **to** 55 **do** read-(SomeSpeeds[*i*]);	Assigns cells 15–55 with input values
SomeSpeeds	**for** *i* := 15 **to** 55 **do** Some-Speeds[*i*] := *i*;	Assigns cells 15–55 with index values

We can inpect all the values stored in an array by specifying the correct values of the index variable. For example, we can print the values stored in the SomeSpeeds array as follows:

```
for index := min to max do
   writeln(SomeSpeeds[index]);
```

The values of min and max determine which cells of the SomeSpeeds array get inspected (printed). We can also assign the values of an entire array to another array of the same type. For example, if City*A* and City*B* are both array variables of type SpeedLimit given earlier, then, once CityA is initialized, all values of that array can be assigned to CityB in the following way:

```
CityA := SomeSpeeds;          (*put copy of all values of
                                SomeSpeeds into CityA
                                array*)
CityB := CityA;               (*put copy of all values in
                                CityA into CityB array!*)
```

Here is a sample displaying the effect of these two assignments.

Results of Assigning One Array to Another

Index	*SomeSpeeds*	*Index*	*CityA*	Index	City*B*
[1]	15	[1]	15	[1]	15
[2]	17	[2]	17	[2]	17
[3]	20	[3]	20	[3]	20
[4]	25	[4]	25	[4[	25
[5]	30	[5]	30	[5]	30

Try experimenting with the following program to see how this works:

Experiment 1

```
program TryThis(input, output);
type
   SpeedLimit = array[1..15] of 0..55;                 (*array type*)
var
   CityA, CityB  : SomeSpeeds;                  (*array variables*)
   index  : integer;                            (*index variable*)
begin
     writeln('Enter a row of speed limits for your city:');
     for index := 1 to 15 do
        read(CityA[index]);                 (*store entered values
                                                  in CityA array*)
     CityB := CityA                        (*copy of CityA is put
                                                 into CityB array*)
     for index := 1 to 15 do
        write(CityB[index])                   (*will print a duplicate
                                                        of CityA*)
end.
```

This is an example of an unfriendly program. It will not let you rest until you have entered 15 integer values every time it is activated. This is fine when it is always necessary to enter the same number of values to build an array. If we want to vary the number of values we want to store in an array each time, then we need to devise some shutoff mechanism. This is actually easier than it sounds.

For example, a simple shutoff mechanism to use in the above program would be an entered count of the number of values to be entered. Using this idea, we can modify the above program as follows:

Experiment 2 (Refinement)

```
begin
   write('Enter number of elements: ');
   readln(max);
   writeln('Enter', max, 'elements: ');
   for index := 1 to max do
      read(SomeSpeeds[index])
              .
              .
              .
end.                               (*modified TryThis program body*)
```

The drawback to this method is that it requires the user to count the number of entries before data entry can begin. There is a better way to do the same thing, using what is known as a *sentinel value*. This is a value that signals the completion of data entry.

6.5 Building Arrays Using a Sentinel Value

Here is an algorithm that uses a sentinel to control the building of an array.

```
                                  (*input: limit, empty, array elements;
                                                       output: array*)
begin
   initialize limit with 0;
   initialize empty variable;
   let info be an array variable with max components;
   repeat
      add 1 to limit;
      read(info[limit])
   until info[limit] = empty;
   subtract 1 from limit                        (*do this to compute
                                                  actual array size*)
end.                                      (*algorithm to build an array*)
```

The last step in this algorithm is crucial. Notice that the value of *empty* does get assigned to an info-array cell. If we do not want to use this sentinel value, then the actual list size is one less than the final value of limit when a processor exists from the repeat loopp. Then subtract 1 to get the actual list size. Here is a Pascal procedure to implement this algorithm.

Procedure la

```
procedure BuildArray(var info: infotype;                (*user defined*)
                     var limit: integer);                  (*list size*)
begin
   limit := 0;                                         (*use as index*)
   writeln('Enter info element—a <sentinel type> to stop');
   repeat
      limit := limit +1;                          (*point to first cell*)
      read(info[limit])                        (*assign value to array*)
   until info[limit] = empty;
   limit := limit – 1                                (*a crucial step!*)
end;                                                     (*BuildArray*)
```

This procedure is not completely general because the index type has been specified as *integer*. Notice, also, that this procedure does nothing to protect against array overflow, since data entry stops only when the sentinel value for *empty* is read. Also, notice that the last array cell is used up by the value of *empty*. This may be desirable, since it will give you a built-in indicator of when you have reached the last array value. Finally, notice that final value of limit gives the array size, excluding the cell with the empty value. In Section 6.6 we suggest ways to improve this procedure.

6.6

Bug Clinic: Array Overflow

The algorithm in Section 6.5 has a potential problem. There is no provision for detecting when a user has entered too many values and exceeded the capacity of the info array. We can avoid this problem by setting up a max constant, which gives the upper limit on an array size. Then we can compare the value of limit with the value of max each time we increment limit. Here is a revised version of the array-builder algorithm.

```
                                   (*input: empty, IndexMax, limit, info;
                                                        output: array*)
begin
   initialize empty;                                        (*sentinel*)
   initialize IndexMax;                               (*safety feature*)
   assign 0 to limit;
   declare info to be an array variable;
   repeat
      add 1 to limit;
      if limit > IndexMax then
         use algorithm to handle array overflow
      else
         read(info[limit])
   until info[limit] = empty;                      (*shutoff mechanism*)
   subtract 1 from limit                              (*a crucial step!*)
end.                            (*Improved algorithm to build an array*)
```

This is an example of a less blind algorithm. It relies on the use of another algorithm to handle the problem of array overflow, if overflow is detected by this algorithm. Here are some suggestions for this array-overflow algorithm (call it AdjustForOverflow).

1. An error message should be printed announcing the possibility of array overflow (the array index goes out of bounds).
2. A warning message (ring of keyboard bell) when an array index has reached some threshhold, a value near the out-of-bounds value.
3. Allow continued data entry by using a second, backup array to handle the excess data, if there are any.
4. Modify the original program to allow for a bigger info array (this just means the max constant would have to be increased in size).

Here is a Pascal procedure to implement this idea.

Procedure 1b

```
                    (*Note: IndexMax and empty are global constants*)
procedure BuildArray(var info: infotype;
                           var limit: integer);
begin
  limit := 0;
  writeln('Enter info—sentinel value, to stop:');
  repeat
    limit := limit + 1;
    if limit > IndexMax then
      AdjustForOverflow(info, limit)              (*procedure call*)
    else
      read(info[limit])
    until info[limit] = empty;
    limit := limit - 1
  end;                                           (*Refined procedure*)
```

The construction of the AdjustForOverflow procedure is left as an exercise. This will be included as a procedure shell in the array-handling programs shown in this chapter. Next we show how to inspect an existing array.

6.7 Inspecting an Existing Array

Once an array has been built, the values stored in array cells will be saved until we are ready to use them. To inspect an existing array, we always need to know the actual array size. This is the number of values that have been stored in an array. The number of stored values will be less than or equal to the maximum size for the array type. Using the algorithm in Section 6.6, we have the value of limit to tell us the actual size of an array. Here is an algorithm that can be used to inspect an array.

```
                                                  (*input: array;
                                   output: inspected array elements*)
begin
  BuildArray(info, limit);                        (*use build-array
                                              algorithm to initialize
                                                    info and limit*)

  repeat
    write(info[limit]);                       (*inspect array element()
    subtract 1 from limit
  until limit = 0
end                            (*algorithm to inspect an existing array*)
```

This algorithm will print the info values in reverse order, starting with the end value in the array. This algorithm is one among hundreds of algorithms that might be used to inspect the same array. The way we inspect an array will depend on our interests and the values of the index variable limit. For example, here is an algorithm to print every other element in the same array.

```
                                                   (*input: array;
                  output: array elements with even-numbered indices*)
begin
   BuildArray(info, limit);                         (*use build-array
                                                        algorithm*)
   repeat
      if limit mod 2 = 0 then
         write(info[limit];
      subtract 1 from limit
   until limit = 0
end                 (*algorithm to inspect every other array element*)
```

This algorithm will print all info entries with even-numbered index values. Both of these algorithms suggest something else.

Array parameters:

A procedure parameter can be an array type.

The values of an entire array can be passed to a procedure with a value parameter that is an array type. We will illustrate these ideas using the following algorithm to print the elements in an array forward and backward.

```
                                      (*input: array, min, max values;
                 output: array elements printed forward and backward*)
begin
   initialize info array;
   initialize min, max;                     (*use to identify extremes*)
   if min ≤ max then
      repeat                                          (*print forward*)
         print min;                               (*display index value*)
         print info[min];                       (*display indexed value*)
         add 1 to min
      until min > max
   else
      repeat                                         (*print backward*)
      print min;                                  (*display index value*)
      print info [min];                         (*display indexed value*)
      subtract 1 from min
   until min < max
end                 (*algorithm to print array forward and backward*)
```

A structure chart for a program to implement these array-handling algorithms is shown in Figure 6.3. We illustrate the use of this last algorithm in the program in Figure 6.4, which builds an array to type char and prints the array component values forward and backward.

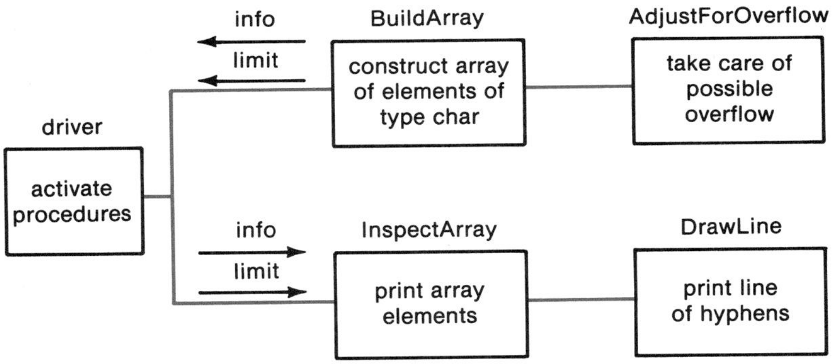

FIGURE 6.3
Structure chart for an array-handling program

```
                (*Method: Use a procedure to initialize an array of type
                          char, then print the array elements forward
                                                     and backward.*)

program Reverberation(input, output);
const
   max = 500;                                     (*limit on array size*)
   empty = '*';                                  (*sentinel character*)
type
   symbols = array[1..max] of char;                     (*array type*)

  (*- - - - - - - - - - - - - - - - - - - - - - - - - - - - - - - - - -*)
                                        (*Handle array overflow problem*)

   procedure AdjustForOverflow(var info: symbols;
                               var limit: integer);
   begin
                                                  (*empty statement*)
   end;                                     (*AdjustForOverflow shell*)

  (*- - - - - - - - - - - - - - - - - - - - - - - - - - - - - - - - - -*)
                           (*Construct an array of elements of type char*)

procedure BuildArray(var info: symbols;               (*array parameter*)
                     var limit: integer);                   (*list size*)
begin
   limit := 0;
   write(' ':10, 'Enter text--a *, to stop:');
   repeat
      limit := limit + 1;
      if limit > max then
         AdjustForOverflow(info, limit)            (*call error handler*)
      else
         read(info[limit])
   until (info[limit] = empty);
   limit := limit - 1                               (*a crucial step!*)
end;                                                    (*BuildArray*)
```

```
  (*----------------------------------------------------------*)
                                          (*draw line of hyphens*)

procedure DrawLine;
var
   hyphen: integer;
begin
   writeln; for hyphen := 1 to 70 do write('-'); writeln
end;                                                 (*DrawLine*)

  (*----------------------------------------------------------*)
                                              (*Inspect array*)

procedure InspectArray(info: symbols;               (*array param*)
                        min, max: integer);            (*extremes*)
begin
   writeln; writeln(' ':35, 'List elements:');
   DrawLine;                                (*activate DrawLine*)
   writeln('index value':35, 'indexed variable':20);
   if min <= max then
      repeat
         writeln(min:30, ' ':15, info[min]);
         min := min + 1
      until min > max
   else
      repeat
         writeln(min:30, ' ':15, info[min]);
         min := min - 1                (*same idea as in algorithm
                                                 in section 6.7*)
      until min < max;
   DrawLine
end;                                             (*InspectArray*)

  (*----------------------------------------------------------*)
          (*Program manager: get values and activate procedure*)

procedure driver;
var
   quote: symbols;                               (*array variable*)
   length: integer;                                  (*array size*)
   choice: integer;                            (*control variable*)
begin
   repeat
      BuildArray(quote, length);              (*activate procedure*)
      InspectArray(quote, 1, length);                  (*forwards*)
      InspectArray(quote, length, 1);                 (*backwards*)
      write(' ':10, 'Again?--1 = Y, 0 = N: ');readln(choice);writeln
   until choice = 0
   end;                                                  (*driver*)

  (*----------------------------------------------------------*)

begin
   driver                                       (*activate driver*)
end.
```

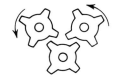

```
Enter text--a *, to stop:Tumtytum!*
                      List elements:

-----------------------------------------------------------
              index value             indexed variable
                   1                         T
                   2                         u
                   3                         m
                   4                         t
                   5                         y
                   6                         t
                   7                         u
                   8                         m
                   9                         !

-----------------------------------------------------------
                      List elements:

-----------------------------------------------------------
              index value             indexed variable
                   9                         !
                   8                         m
                   7                         u
                   6                         t
                   5                         y
                   4                         t
                   3                         m
                   2                         u
                   1                         T

-----------------------------------------------------------
   Again?--1 = Y, 0 = N:
                   0
```

FIGURE 6.4 Building a array of type char

6.8 Refinement: Error Handling

The BuildArray procedure in Figure 6.4 should be refined to cope with the threat of the array index going out of bounds. Right now, the info array can handle up to 500 characters before the array index will go out of bounds. In other words, the AdjustForOverflow procedure shell in Figure 6.4 should be fleshed out. (Right now, it consists of just an empty statement.) In doing this, you should do the following things:

1. Announce that there is a danger of overflow.
2. Announce the possibility of letting the user enter a limited number of additional values. In doing this you have the following design choices to make:
   2.1. Activate the AdjustForOverflow procedure when limit reaches a threshhold value below the IndexMax. For example, you can re-

write the if statement inside the repeat loop of BuildArray procedure as follows:

```
if limit = IndexMax – threshhold then
   AdjustForOverflow
else . . .
```

You could use threshold = 5, for example, which triggers the use of the overflow procedure, if the array being used has only five cells left.

2.2. Activate the AdjustforOverflow procedure when limit equals the IndexMax. Then allow the user to use a backup array to store a limited number of additional values.

3. Use the InspectArray procedure, first to print a copy of the info-array, then have the driver procedure activate the InspectArray a second time with the backup array (if one was used) to print the excess characters for the forwards case.

4. Reverse the steps in step 4, activating the InspectArray first with the backup array, then a second time with the info array to print the original text backward.

We leave it as an exercise to implement both forms of the Adjust-ForOverflow procedure.

6.9 Another Example: Another Form of an Array Index

Here is an algorithm to gather temperature readings from different cities, using an enumeration type.

```
                    (*input: cities scale, cities subrange, places array;
                                                output: weather table*)
begin
   set up cities, which is an enumeration type;
   set up SomeCities, which is a subrange of cities;
   set up places, which is an array type indexed by
      the SomeCities subrange;
   set up a readings array with components of type real
   which are indexed by an expression of type SomeCities;
   initialize index with an identifier from SomeCities;
   for index := <indentifier. l> to <identifier.k> do
      case index of
         <identifier.l> : readln(places[index]);
                .
                .
                .
         <identifier.k> : readln(places[index];
         end                                                 (*case*)
end                    (*algorithm to build a weather report table*)
```

The novel feature of this algorithm is its use of an index which depends on a subrange of an enumeration type. Here is what the cities and SomeCities types will look like:

```
type
   cities = (Albuquerque, Anchorage, Atlanta, Austin,
             Billings, Bismark, Boise, Boston, StPaul);
   SomeCities = Alburquerque..Atlanta;              (*subrange type*)
```

The use of the identifiers from an enumeration type as values instead of numbers for the readings array helps make clearer what is being done with the array. A program to print carry out this idea is given in Figure 6.5. The program in Figure 6.5 can be refined to make it more useful.

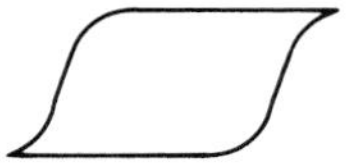

```
program Weather(input, output);
type
   cities = (Albuquerque, Anchorage, Atlanta, Austin, Baltimore,
             Billings, Bismark, Boise, Boston, LosAngeles);
   SomeCities = Albuquerque..Atlanta;
   places = array[SomeCities] of real;

(*-----------------------------------------*)
                         (*Use enumeration variable to select a city*)

   procedure WeatherReport(var readings: places);
   var
      index: SomeCities;
   begin
      for index := Albuquerque to Atlanta do
         case index of
            Albuquerque:begin
                           write(' ':10,'Enter temp of Albuequerque:');
                           readln(readings[index]); writeln
                        end;                                  (*case 1*)
            Anchorage: begin
                           write(' ':10,'Enter temp for Anchorage: ');
                           readln(readings[index]); writeln
                        end;                                  (*case 2*)
            Atlanta: begin
                        write(' ':10, 'Enter temp for Atlanta: ');
                        readln(readings[index]); writeln
                     end                                      (*case 3*)
            end                                                (*case*)
   end;                                                (*WeatherReport*)

(*-----------------------------------------*)
                                              (*Print line of hyphens*)

   procedure DrawLine;
   var hyphen: integer;                             (*control variable*)
   begin
      writeln; for hyphen := 1 to 70 do write('—'); writeln
   end;                                                    (*DrawLine*)
```

```
(*------------------------------------------------------------*)
                    (*Print table of cities with temperature readings*)

procedure GiveReport(readings: places);
var
   index: SomeCities;
begin
   writeln(' ':20, 'Partial Weather Table');
   DrawLine;
   writeln('city':18, 'temperature':20);
   for index := Albuquerque to Atlanta do
      case index of
         Albuquerque: begin
                         write('Albuquerque':20, ' ':10);
                         writeln(readings[index]:8:2)
                      end;                                   (*1*)
         Anchorage: begin
                       write('Anchorage':20, ' ':10);
                       writeln(readings[index]:8:2)
                    end;                                     (*2*)
         Atlanta: begin
                     write('Atlanta':20, ' ':10);
                     writeln(readings[index]:8:2)
                  end                                        (*3*)
         end;                                                (*case*)
   DrawLine
end;                                                         (*GiveReport*)

(*------------------------------------------------------------*)
                    (*Program manager: activate needed procedures*)

procedure driver;
var
   LocalReading: places;
   selector: integer;
begin
   WeatherReport(LocalReading),
   GiveReport(LocalReading)
end;                                                         (*driver*)

(*------------------------------------------------------------*)

begin
   driver
end.
```

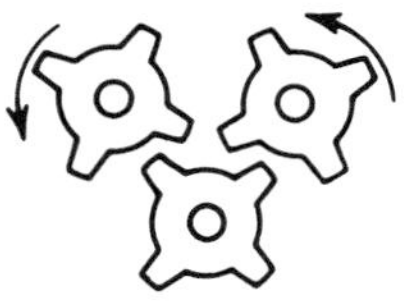

```
   Enter temp of Albuequerque:65.6

   Enter temp for Anchorage: -2

   Enter temp for Atlanta: 52.3
```

Partial Weather Table

City	*Temperature*
Albuquerque	65.60
Anchorage	–2.00
Atlanta	52.30

FIGURE 6.5 Using an enumeration type with arrays

6.10 Refinement: Computing the Average Temperature

The information stored in an array is there for us to use. For example, the readings array in Figure 6.5 holds the temperatures for several cities. We can enhance the weather report table printed by computing the average temperature using the following technique:

```
sum := 0;
for index := Albuquerque to Atlanta do
   sum := sum + readings[index]
average := sum/ord(index);
```

In addition to this refinement, it would be helpful if the user were able to choose various subranges to use to construct a weather table. A menu like the following one could be printed:

menu:
- → 1 weather table for 45 major U.S. cities given daily by the National Weather Services (NWS);
- → 2 weather table for 42 major foreign cities given daily by the NWS;
- → 3 weather table for eastern seaboard cities;
- → 4 weather table for western seaboard cities;
- → 5 weather table for middle western cities

This will mean the cities enumeration type will have to be expanded. Then different subranges can be set up for each menu choice. In addition, the following submenu should be printed for each menu choice:

submenu:
- → 1 Set up weather table for single day;
- → 2 Set up weather table for last five days

For the second choice, either five separate arrays or what is known as *two-dimensional array* (we explain two-dimensional arrays later in this chapter) can be used to save the weather information for each day. Then a composite table can be printed with daily averages and a weekly average temperature. These refinements are left as exercises.

In addition to the array types we have already considered, standard Pascal has a string type, which is set up using the *packed* modifier. In addition, it is possible to set up string constants. We show how to do this next.

6.11 Character String Constants

Here are some examples of string constants:

```
const
   Clophile = 'Hello, world!';
   yawn = 'hohum . . .';
   empty = '         ';                          (*filled with spaces*)
```

In general, a sequence of characters between single quotes is a string constant. A string constant with more than one character is automatically a packed array of type character, which is fixed forever inside a program. A string constant like empty is useful as a sentinel when arrays of strings are built, using entries from a keyboard.

6.12 Strings

A *string* is a packed array of type char with an index of type integer. The subrange used to define the index for a string must always begin with 1 and have a minimum subrange of 1··2. This is another way of saying the minimum string length is 2. Here are some examples of string types.

```
type
   length = 1..50;
   script = packed array[length] of char;          (*length 50*)
   name = packed array[1..15] of char;             (*length 15*)
   TeamName = packed array[1..20] of char;         (*length 20*)
var
   FirstName, LastName: name;            (*string variables of type
                                                          name*)
   league: array[1..10] of TeamName;             (*array of strings*)
   prose: script;                         (*string variable of type
                                                        script*)
```

The league variable is an array variable with string components. Here are some sample assignments of strings to the league array.

```
league[1] := 'Cardinals';                (*padded with 1 space*)
league[2] := 'Padres';                   (*padded with 4 spaces*)
league[3] := 'Dodgers';                  (*padded with 3 spaces*)
league[4] := 'Twins';                    (*padded with 5 spaces*)
```

Each one of these indexed variables is also a string variable. Whenever a string constant is assigned to a string variable, it must have the same number of characters as the string type used to define the string variable. For example, the string type for each indexed league variable has length 20. So it is necessary to pad a string constant with blanks, if the number of its nonblank characters is less than the string length.

Pascal makes it easy to use a read or readln statement to assign values to string variables. Pascal takes care of the blank spaces for us, if an entered string falls short of the prescribed string length. For example, here is a loop that can be used to fill the league array:

```
limit := 0;
empty := '          ';                              (*string constant with
                                                           ten blanks*)
writeln('Enter team name—a <return>, to stop:');
repeat
   limit := limit + 1;
   readln(league[limit])
until league[limit] = empty;
limit := limit - 1                                  (*actual array size*)
```

Again, it will be necessary to refine this repeat block to avoid having the league index limit go out of bounds. There is a trick being used here, which may not be obvious. If we type a simple <return>, then the corresponding string variable league[limit] will be initialized with 10 blanks. This is a handy service offered by Pascal to make string handling easier.

In general, here is string-handling tool to keep in mind.

String-handling tool:

If an entered string falls short of the length of a corresponding string variable in a read or readln statement, then the entered string will be filled out with blanks automatically. If a simple <return> is the entered string, then all blanks will be assigned to the string variable used.

In Figure 6.6 we show a program to build and print an array of strings. The BuildList procedure in Figure 6.6 can be improved with an error-handling procedure, if the value of limit goes out of bounds. Again, it is a good idea to have a backup array to handle the extra input. (This is the friendly approach to an over-ambitious team watcher with too many team names.) These refinements are left as an exercise.

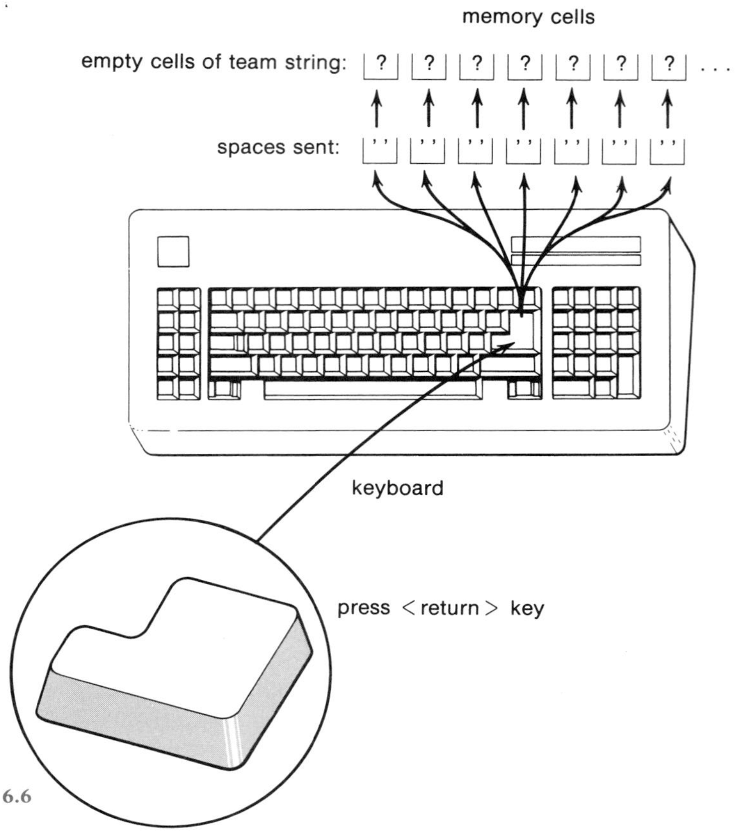

FIGURE 6.6

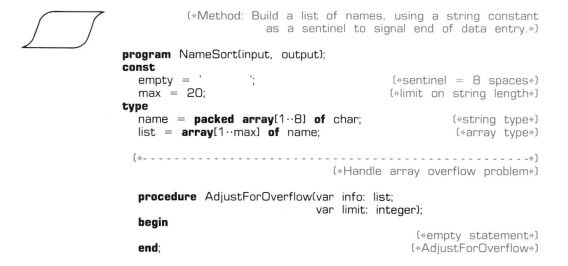

```
                    (*Method: Build a list of names, using a string constant
                              as a sentinel to signal end of data entry.*)

program NameSort(input, output);
const
  empty = '        ';                          (*sentinel = 8 spaces*)
  max = 20;                                    (*limit on string length*)
type
  name = packed array[1..8] of char;                     (*string type*)
  list = array[1..max] of name;                           (*array type*)

 (*-----------------------------------------------------------------*)
                                           (*Handle array overflow problem*)

  procedure AdjustForOverflow(var info: list;
                              var limit: integer);
  begin
                                                    (*empty statement*)
  end;                                             (*AdjustForOverflow*)
```

```
(*--------------------------------------------------*)
                        (*Save entered names in an array*)

procedure BuildList(var info: list;                  (*for names*)
                    var limit: integer);             (*list size*)

begin
  limit := 0;
  repeat
    limit := limit + 1;
    if limit > max then
      AdjustForOverflow(info, limit)
    else begin
      write(' ':10,'Enter directory name- -a <return> to stop: ');
      readln(info[limit]); writeln
      end                                            (*else*)
  until info[limit] = empty;
  limit := limit - 1                                 (*a crucial step!*)
end;                                                 (*BuildList*)
(*--------------------------------------------------*)
                                       (*Print line of hyphens*)

procedure DrawLine;
var hyphen : integer;                                (*control variable*)
begin
  writeln; for hyphen := 1 to 70 do write('—'); writeln
end;                                                 (*DrawLine*)
(*--------------------------------------------------*)
                                       (*Show list of names*)

procedure PrintList(info: list;                      (*names*)
                    limit: integer);                 (*list size*)
var
  index: integer;                                    (*name selector*)
begin
  writeln('List of names stored in array:':40);
  DrawLine; write(' ':10);
  for index := 1 to limit do begin
    if index mod 6 = 0 then begin
      writeln; write(' ':10)
      end;                                           (*to control output*)
    writeinfo[index], ' ':3)
    end;                                             *(*for*)
  DrawLine
end;                                                 (*PrintList*)

(*--------------------------------------------------*)
                  (*Program manager: activate procedures*)

procedure driver;
var
  directory: list;                                   (*array variable*)
  ListSize: integer;                                 (*directory size*)
  dash: integer;                                     (*use to print dashes*)
```

```
   begin
      repeat
         BuildList(directory, ListSize);                  (*activate procedure*)
         PrintList(directory, ListSize);                  (*activate procedure*)
      until 1 > 2                                                  (*forever*)
   end;                                                             (*driver*)

  (*-------------------------------------------------------------------------*)

begin
   driver                                                  (*activate driver*)
end.
```

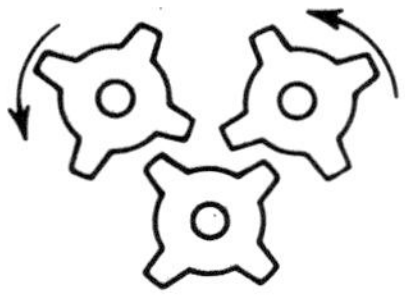

```
Enter directory name--a <return> to stop: Kathie

Enter directory name--a <return> to stop: Lori

Enter directory name--a <return> to stop: Tomas

Enter directory name--a <return> to stop: Juan

Enter directory name--a <return> to stop: Jorge

Enter directory name--a <return> to stop: Tony

Enter directory name--a <return> to stop: Ozzie

Enter directory name--a <return> to stop: Garth

Enter directory name--a <return> to stop:

List of names stored in array:
----------------------------------------
Kathie     Lori     Tomas     Juan     Jorge
Tony   Ozzie   Garth
----------------------------------------
```

FIGURE 6.6 Building an array of strings

6.13 Comparisons of Strings

Strings can be compared using any of the following operators:

<, <=, >, >=, =, <>

This is another service supplied by Pascal for string handling. Pascal will use the scale used to implement type char to make these comparisons. For example, we can use

```
league[1] := 'Cubs       ';
league[2] := 'Cardinals  ';
if league[1] > league[2] then begin
   buffer := league[1];                 (*buffer is type TeamName, also*)
   league[1] := league[2];
   league[2] := buffer
   end;                                                           (*then*)
```

In this example, the strings stored in league[1] and league[2] will be swapped, if either the ASCII or EBCDIC scale is used, since both of these scales have lower case letters and the *u* in 'Cubs' puts this string after the 'Cardinals' string. Comparison of strings can be tricky, though, depending on the scale being used for type character.

For example, the upper case letters appear after the lower case letters in the EBCDIC table, which is the reverse of the arrangement of these letters in the ASCII table. So, for example, the following expression will not always be true:

'CUBS ' < 'cubs ' (false in EBCDIC, true in ASCII)

Because strings can be compared, it is fairly easy to sort a list of names, for example. In the case study at the end of this chapter, we show how this is done.

The league array (an array of strings of type TeamName) is an example of a multidimensional array. We look more closely at multidimensional arrays in Section 6.14.

6.14 Multidimensional Arrays

The info array in Figure 6.6 is an example of a two-dimensional array. A graphical interpretation of the info array is given in Figure 6.7. In effect, each value of the index for the info array gives a row in a table of strings. In fact, the info array can be written in two different ways to reflect this idea.

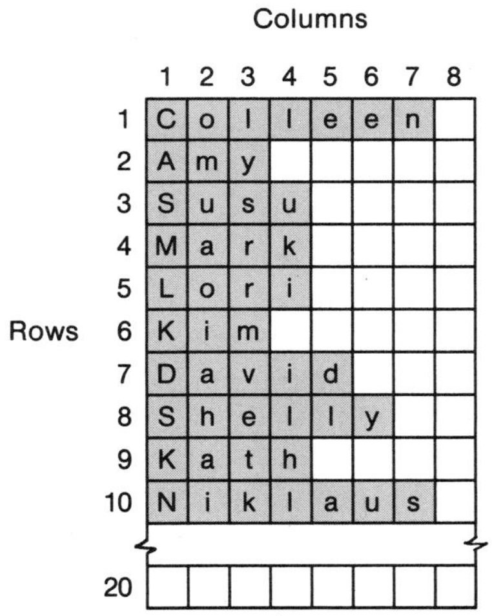

FIGURE 6.7
Graphical interpretation of a two-dimensional array

original declaration:

```
type
   name = packed array[1..5] of char;
   list = array[1..max] of name;
var
   info:list;
```

new declaration:

```
type
   list = packed array[1..max,  1..8] of char;
                       \_____/  \___/
                                 columns in Fig. 6.7
                        rows in Fig. 6.7
var
   info:list;
```

A three-dimensional array type will have three indices, a four-dimensional, four indices, and so on. Here are some other examples of multidimensional arrays.

```
type
   cities = (Albuquerque, Anchorage, Atlanta, Austin,
             Baltimore, Billings, Bismark, Boise, Boston,
             NewYork, LosAngeles);
   SomeCities = Albuquerque..Atlanta;
   days = (Monday, Tuesday, Wednesday, Thursday, Friday,
           Saturday, Sunday);
   places = array[SomeCities, days] of real;
var
   readings : places;                    (*two-dimensional array var*)
```

Notice that it is possible to have more than one ordinal type in the declaration of the index types for a multidimensional array. For example, the places array type has the following structure:

```
places = array[SomeCities, days] of real;
               \________/  \__/
                    |        ^
                    |      enumeration type for days
                    |      of the week
               subrange of cities enumeration type
               for all reporting U.S. cities
```

In other words, the ordinal types for the indices on a multidimensional array do not have to be subranges of the same ordinal type. We can use an array variable like readings, for example, to improve the program given earlier in Figure 6.2. We can do this by using the readings array to store more than one temperature reading for each reporting city. For example, we ca load this array with readings for weekdays for the reporting cities. This will allow us to build the following table:

	(Rows) Days: Monday	Tuesday	Wednesday	Thursday	Friday
(Columns) Cities:					
Albuquerque	55	62	59	55	52
Anchorage	−12	−5	−29	−20	−10
Atlanta	58	58	52	54	50
.					
.					
.					
Los Angeles	49	51	53	55	55

A structure chart for a program to implement this idea is given in Figure 6.8. The WeatherReport procedure shown in Figure 6.8 can be implemented using the following nested for loops:

```
var
   DayIndex: days                              (*for days of week*)
   CityIndex: SomeCities                       (*for reporting cities*)
   readings: places;                           (*two-dimensional array var*)
begin
for DayIndex: = Monday to Sunday do
   for CityIndex: = Albuquerque to LosAngeles do
      case CityIndex of
         Albuquerque:begin
                          write('Enter Albuquerque temp:');
                          readln(readings[CityIndex,DayIndex]);
                          writeln
                        end;                                (*Albuquerque*)
                  .
                  .
                  .
         LosAngeles: begin
                          write('Enter Los Angeles temp:')
                          readln(readings[CityIndex,DayIndex[);
                          writeln
                        end                                 (*LosAngeles*)
         end                                                (*case*)
```

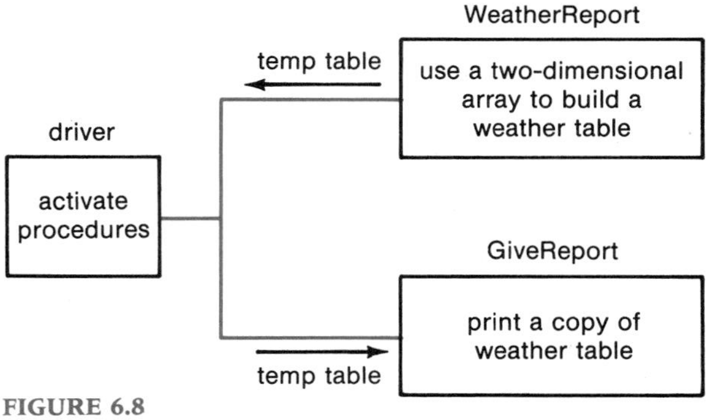

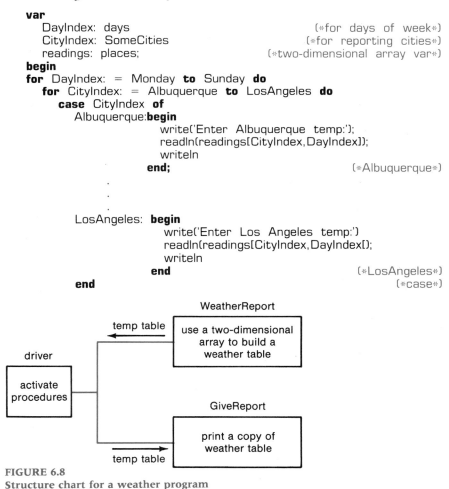

FIGURE 6.8
Structure chart for a weather program

Notice that for each value of the DayIndex (an identifier for each weekday), the inner for-loop cycles through the cities selected by the CityIndex. Temperature readings (real values) will be stored for each city. If the above case statement were fleshed out, it would have case constants for every reporting city. (The National Weather Service reports on 45 U.S. cities!) A shortened version of the above case statement has been implemented in the program in Figure 6.9. Several refinements of the program in Figure 6.9 are possible.

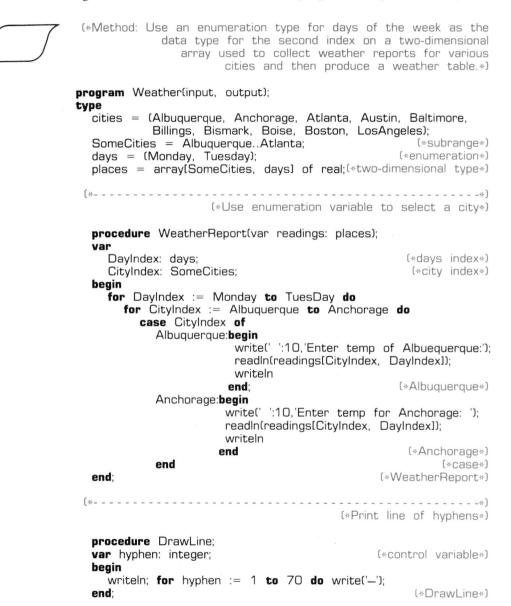

```
(*Method: Use an enumeration type for days of the week as the
                 data type for the second index on a two-dimensional
                    array used to collect weather reports for various
                          cities and then produce a weather table.*)

program Weather(input, output);
type
  cities = (Albuquerque, Anchorage, Atlanta, Austin, Baltimore,
            Billings, Bismark, Boise, Boston, LosAngeles);
  SomeCities = Albuquerque..Atlanta;                    (*subrange*)
  days = (Monday, Tuesday);                          (*enumeration*)
  places = array[SomeCities, days] of real;(*two-dimensional type*)

(*-----------------------------------------------------------------*)
                          (*Use enumeration variable to select a city*)

  procedure WeatherReport(var readings: places);
  var
    DayIndex: days;                                    (*days index*)
    CityIndex: SomeCities;                             (*city index*)
  begin
    for DayIndex := Monday to TuesDay do
      for CityIndex := Albuquerque to Anchorage do
        case CityIndex of
          Albuquerque:begin
                       write(' ':10,'Enter temp of Albuequerque:');
                       readln(readings[CityIndex, DayIndex]);
                       writeln
                      end;                            (*Albuquerque*)
          Anchorage:begin
                     write(' ':10,'Enter temp for Anchorage: ');
                     readln(readings[CityIndex, DayIndex]);
                     writeln
                    end                                 (*Anchorage*)
          end                                                (*case*)
  end;                                              (*WeatherReport*)

(*-----------------------------------------------------------------*)
                                              (*Print line of hyphens*)

  procedure DrawLine;
  var hyphen: integer;                           (*control variable*)
  begin
    writeln; for hyphen := 1 to 70 do write('–');
  end;                                                   (*DrawLine*)
```

```
(*-----------------------------------------------------------*)
                  (*Print table of cities with temperature readings*)

procedure GiveReport(readings: places);
var
   DayIndex: days;                                        (*day index*)
   CityIndex: SomeCities;                                 (*city index*)
   dash: integer;                                         (*control var*)
begin
   writeln(' ':10,'National Weather Service Temperature Readings');
   writeln;
   writeln('city':18, 'Monday':20, 'Tuesday':20);
   for dash := 1 to 70 do write('—'); writeln;
   for CityIndex := Albuquerque to Anchorage do begin
      case CityIndex of
         Albuquerque:begin
                     write('Albuquerque':20, ' ':10);
                     for DayIndex := Monday to Tuesday do begin
                        case DayIndex of
                           Monday:begin
                              write(readings[CityIndex,DayIndex]:8:2);
                              write(' ':10)
                              end;                        (*Monday*)
                           Tuesday:begin
                              write(readings[CityIndex,DayIndex]:8:2);
                              write(' ':10)
                              end                         (*Tuesday*)
                        end                               (*inner case*)
                     end                                  (*for*)
                    end;                                  (*Albuquerque*)
         Anchorage: begin
                     write('Anchorage':20, ' ':10);
                     for DayIndex := Monday to Tuesday do begin
                        case DayIndex of
                           Monday:begin
                              write(readings[CityIndex,DayIndex]:8:2);
                              write(' ':10)
                              end;                        (*Monday*)
                           Tuesday:begin
                              write(readings[CityIndex,DayIndex]:8:2);
                              write(' ':10)
                              end                         (*Tuesday*)
                           end                            (*inner case*)
                        end                               (*for*)
                     end                                  (*Anchorage*)
         end;                                             (*outer case*)
         writeln
   end                                                    (*outer for loop*)
end;                                                      (*GiveReport*)
(*-----------------------------------------------------------*)
                  (*Program manager: activate needed procedures*)
procedure driver;
var
   LocalReading: places;                      (*two-dimensional array var*)
   choice: integer;                                       (*control var*)
```

```
   begin
      repeat
         WeatherReport(LocalReading);
         GiveReport(LocalReading);
         writeln; writeln; write(' ':10,'Again?- -1 = Y, 0 = N: ');
         readln(choice); writeln; writeln
      until choice = 0
   end;                                                    (*driver*)
   (*- - - - - - - - - - - - - - - - - - - - - - - - - - - - - - -*)

begin
   driver                                         (*activate driver*)
end.
```

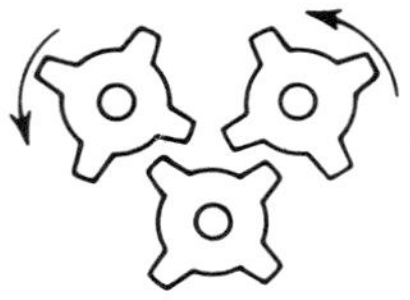

```
Enter temp of Albuequerque: 55

Enter temp for Anchorage: -12

Enter temp for Albuequerque: 59.6

Enter temp for Anchorage: -21.5
```

National Weather Service Temperature Readings

City	*Monday*	*Tuesday*
Albuquerque	55.00	59.60
Anchorage	−12.00	−21.50

```
Again?- -1 = Y, 0 = N: 0
```

FIGURE 6.9 Setting up a 2-dimensional array

6.14.1

Refinement: Expanding the Number of Report Days

The GiveReport procedure in Figure 6.9 is the beginning of a fairly major procedure. Notice how a for loop is used for part of the case statement in this procedure. This for loop allows us to pick up the temperature readings for each day. We have shortened the range covered by the DayIndex used as a control variable in each inner for loop. This can be expanded to pick off the temperature readings for additional days. If we do this, the for loop used by the Albuquerque case, for example, will have the following form:

```
Albuquerque:begin
   write('Albuquerque':20, ' ':10);
   for DayIndex := Monday to Sunday do begin
      case DayIndex of
         Monday:begin
            write(readings[CityIndex,DayIndex]:8:2);
            write(' ':10)
            end;                                   (*Monday*)
```

```
            Tuesday:begin
               write(readings[CityIndex,DayIndex]:8:2);
               write(' ':10)
               end;                                    (*Tuesday*)
                  .
                  .
                  .
            Sunday:begin
               write(readings[CityIndex,DayIndex]:8:2);
               write(' ':10)
               end                                     (*Sunday*)
            end                                          (*case*)
         end                                              (*for*)
      end;                                        (*Albuquerque*)
```

This will mean a corresponding change will have to be made in the WeatherReport procedure to allow for additional days of the week. Using this refinement, it will be possible to print a two-row table with temperature readings for 7 days. This refinement is left as an exercise.

To expand the table printed to handle additional cities, another refinement will have to be made.

6.14.2 *Refinement: Increasing the Number of Table Rows*

If we want to print an expanded table using the program in Figure 6.9, then we need to expand the case statement in the WeatherReport procedure. For example, if we want to add a third table row for the city of Atlanta, then the nested loops used in this procedure will have to be modified as follows:

```
for DayIndex := Monday to Sunday do
   for CityIndex := Albuquerque to Atlanta do
      case CityIndex of
         Albuquerque:begin
                        write('Enter Albuquerque temp:');
                        readln(readings[CityIndex,DayIndex]);
                        writeln
                     end;                         (*Albuquerque*)
            .
            .
            .
         Atlanta : begin
                      write('Enter Atlanta temp:');
                      readln(readings[CityIndex,DayIndex]);
                      writeln
                   end                                (*Atlanta*)
         end;                                            (*case*)
```

This refinement of Figure 6.9 is left as an exercise.

6.15 Summary

An array is a structured data type. An array is always made up of elements of the same type. Arrays offer a means of temporary storatge of data inside a computer. Data stored in array cells will remain in memory as long as a program that sets up an array remains activated. Array elements are selected using an indexed variable, which is a combination of index and array variable identifier. Array elements can be selected directly by using a correct value of an array index.

The array type is a built-in structured type in Pascal. An array type gives us a way to build a data structure. That is, we have a way to build a collection of elements that can be accessed using a set of operations and rules governing the usage of these operations.

Arrays can be accessed either component by component or entirely. For example, if info is an array variable with components that are strings, then the following techniques can be used to fill an individual cell of this array:

1. Assign a value to the first cell using

```
info[1] := 'Colleen                    (*string with length 10*)
```

2. Assign a value to the first cell using

```
readln(info[1]);                       (*string from input file*)
```

Arrays can also be filled completely with one assignment. For example, if NewInfo is an array variable that is the same array type as info, then the following technique can be used to initialize all elements of a NewInfo array in one assignment statement:

3. Initialize the info array, then use

```
NewInfo := info;                       (*make copy of info*)
```

In setting up a procedure to build an array using data from an input file, it is wise to set up a sentinel value that can be used to determine when data entry is complete. Since it is always necessary to specify the maximum number of cells an array type can have, it is important to guard against the possibility of an array index value going out of bounds. In other words, along with each array-building procedure, it is wise to set up a companion error-handling procedure. This will prevent your program from crashing, allowing some form of recovery from excess input.

Pascal also has a packed token that can be used as a modifier in an array type declaration. This will tell Pascal to economize on the storage used to set up an array. This also allows us to set up string types, which are packed arrays of components of type char.

Finally, Pascal also allows us to set up arrays with more than one dimension or multidimensional arrays. These are useful in setting up tables, for example.

6.16

Keywords Review

Keywords	*Related Ideas*
array	collection of elements of the same data type
access	assign or inspect individual components using an indexed variable or assign all components of one array to another array of the same type in a single assignment statement
cell	place in memory used to store an array component
component	element of an array
index	used to select an array component
declaration	specifies an ordinal type, always
indexed variable	array variable identifier plus index value
packed	token used to modify a declaration of an array type; this instructs Pascal to economize on the storage used to store array components
type	built-in structured type in Pascal
declaration	specifies ordinal type of index (or types of indices) to use and the array component type
variable	identifies an array
character string	characters inside single quotes
data structure	1. set of possible values that are not necessarily atomic; 2. set of operations and rules governing the operations that make it possible to access, rearrange and fit values in the structure and impare a structure (relationships) on the values.
sentinel	value used to mark the end of a data entry session, for example
string	packed array of components of type char
constant	defined using a character string
length	two or greater

6.17

Exercises

1. What is the difference between a structured data type and a data structure? Give an example of each.

2. What is the difference between a declaration of an array type and an array variable that has been initialized?

3. What is the difference between a string and an ordinary array of components of type char?

The next four exercises use the following declarations:

```
type
   range = 1..20;
   SomeNumbers = array[range] of integer;
var
   samples, copy: SomeNumbers;
   selector: range;
```

4. Using the above declarations, identify and explain each of the following items:
   a. Array type used
   b. Array variable used
   c. Samples[5]
   d. Selector

5. Based on the above declarations, the following loop is worng. Correct it.

```
selector := 0;
repeat
   selector := selector + 1;
   readln(samples[selector])
until selector > 20;
```

6. List the array component values for the samples and copy arrays after the following assignments:
   a.

```
for selector := 1 to 20 do
   samples[selector] := selector;
copy := samples;
for selector := 1 to 20 do
   copy[selector] := copy[selector] + 1;
```

   b.

```
for selector := 1 to 20 do
   sample[selector] := selector;
copy := samples;
selector := 1;
repeat
   copy[selector] := copy[selector + 1] + 1;
   selector := selector + 1
until selector > 19;
```

7. Write a program that does the following things with the samples array:
   a. Uses a read statement to initialize the samples array.
   b. Prints every other component value.
   c. Prints every third component value.
   d. Prints every fifth component value.
   e. Prints the average component value.
   f. Prints the smallest and largest component value.
   g. Prints the geometric mean of the component values, using the following formula:

      geometric mean $= (x1 * x2 * \cdots * xn) 1/n$

      which is the nth root of the product of the each of n numbers, from $x1$ to $x2$. *Hint.* Use exp() and ln() functions to do this.
   h. Prints the range of the component values, which is the difference between the largest and smallest component values.
   i. Prints the average amount each component value differs from the mean value (called the standard deviation), using the following formula:

$$\text{sum} = (x1 - \text{mean})^2 + \cdots + (xn + \text{mean})^2$$
$$\text{standard deviation} = (\text{sum}/(n - 1))^{1/2}$$

To do this, first compute the value of sum by adding up the squares of the differences between each component value and the mean. Then compute square root of this sum divided by n – 1.

8. Carry out the refinement of the program in Figure 6.4 described in Section 6.8. That is, introduce an error-handling procedure to take care of the possibility of the array index going out of bounds. Give a sample run.

9. Carry out the refinement of the program in Figure 6.5 described in Section 6.10 and give a sample run.

10. Using a two-dimensional array and the sample weather table given in Appendix A, carry out the refinement of the program in Figure 6.5 described in Section 6.10. That is, print a menu with tables the user can choose to have printed.

11. Carry out the refinement of the program in Figure 6.9 described in Section 6.14.1. That is, develop an expanded GiveReport and WeatherReport procedures. Use the NWS table in Appendix A to provide sample runs.

12. Carry out the refinement of the program in exercise 11, using the guidelines described in Section 6.14.2. That is, increase the number of rows in the table printed, allowing for more cities to be included in the printed table. Use the NWS table in Appendix A to provide sample runs.

6.18 Review Quiz

Determine whether the following are true or false:

1. Pascal has one structured data type.
2. An array type is another example of a simple type.
3. The expression used for an array index can be any ordinal type.
4. The indices for a multidimensional array do not have to be subranges of the same ordinal type.
5. Pascal has a string type.
6. A packed array of components of type char is a string.
7. We can economize on the storage used by an array by using the packed token in the declaration of the array.
8. Any array can be packed.
9. Strings cannot be compared.
10. All of the components of one array can be assigned to another array of the same type in one assignment statement.

6.19

Case Study: Sorting a List of Names

It is possible to sort a list of names, which are stored in a single array. Here is the level 0 idea for a program to do this.

```
begin
   sort a list of names
end                                        (*level 0 algorithm*)
```

Here are some declarations that can be used to do this.

```
const
   empty = '                               (*string constant*)
   max = 10;                               (*limit on list size*)
type
   name = packed array[1..5] of char;      (*string type*)
   list = array..max] of name;             (*array type*)
var
   info: list;                             (*array variable*)
   limit: integer;                         (*index variable*)
```

We will use the technique given earlier in Figure 6.2 to build this list of names. (You can think of them, for example, as passenger names used by an airline.) We will use the BuildArray procedure in Figure 6.4 to do this. To sort the list of names, we can use a technique favored by poker players.

Poker Player's Technique

1. Look for the name that belongs at the end of the list of alphabetized names.
2. Shuffle the names, switching the last name and the one that has been found to belong at the end of the list.
3. If more unshuffled cards remain, repeat step 1. Otherwise stop (and start the bidding!).

In step 3, think of the remaining list names as part of a new list, which has one less name in it. We will scan the new list, look for the name that belongs at the end of the list. Shuffle the list, again! Move the name found to the end of the new list. Then repeat the preceding steps with a new list with two less names than the original list, and so on. This is called a *selection sort.* Here is the beginning of the top-down design of a program to handle this sorting technique:

```
begin
   initialize limit, the list size;
   build a list of names;
   find the name that belongs at the end of the list;
   swap two names;
   print the new list of ordered names
end
```

A structure chart reflecting which reflects this level 1 algorithm is shown in Figure 6.10. In this structure chart, the PerformSort procedure will be in charge of handling the sort of the list of names. It uses the FindMax and Swap procedures to do this. The driver procedure takes care of the housekeeping

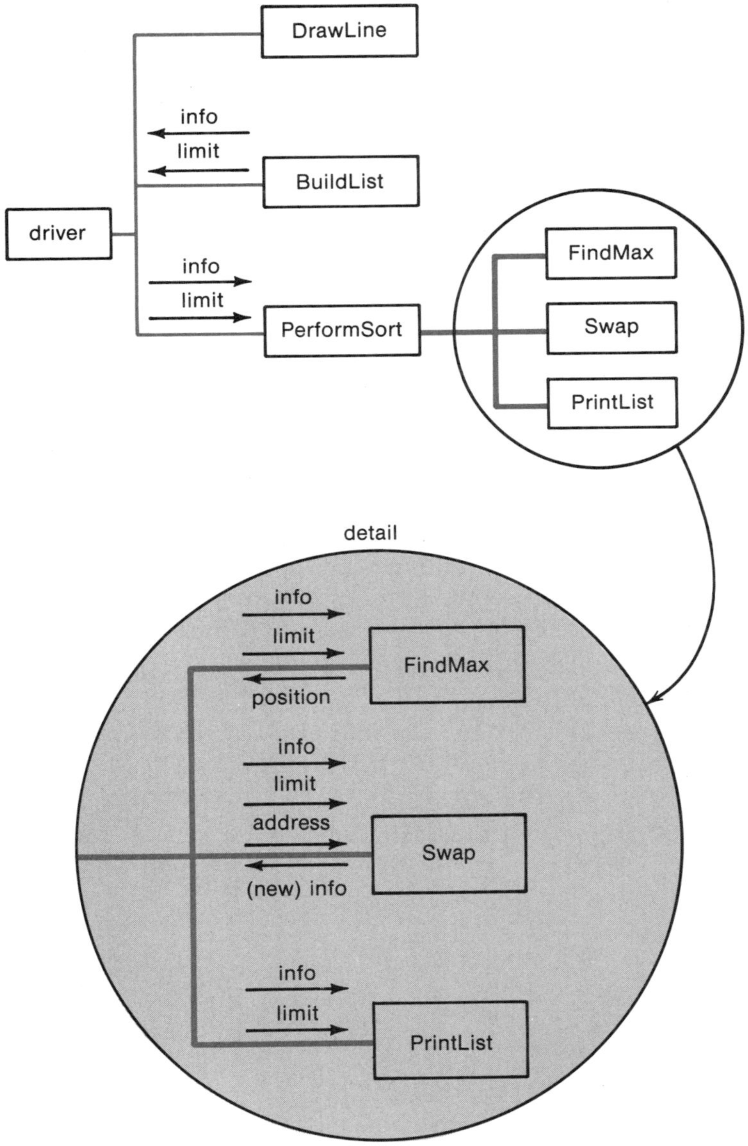

FIGURE 6.10
Structure chart for a selection sort of a list

problems: building the initial list using the BuildArray procedure and printing a copy of the list using PrintList. Notice that the PerformSort procedure also uses the PrintList procedure to print a history of the shuffling of the names. Here is an algorithm for the PerformSort procedure in the chart in Figure 6.10.

```
                                        (*input: info array, array size;
                                            output: ordered list*)
begin
   initialize info with list of names to sort;
   initialize limit with the number of names;
   assign limit to OldLimit;
   repeat
      assign limit to place;
      FindMarx(info, limit, place);          (*activate algorithm to
                                               determine position of
                                              name to move and assign
                                                 position to place*)
      swap(info, limit, place);              (*activate algorithm to
                                               swap end name with
                                                      name found*)
      PrintList(info, OldLimit);             (*activate algorithm to
                                               print changed list*)
      subtract 1 from limit                     (*shrink list size!*)
   until limit = 1
end            (*PerformSort algorithm to shuffle and sort names*)
```

This algorithm depends on three other algorithms. The FindMax algorithm takes care of the hard part, finding the name that belongs at the end of the list. Here is how this algorithm works.

```
begin
   initialize info with list of names;
   initialize limit with list size;
   assign info[limit] to highest;
   assign 1 to i;                              (*index variable*)
   while i < limit do begin
      if info[i] >= highest then begin
         assign info[i] to highest;
         assign i to position
         end;                                          (*then*)
      add 1 to i
      end                                             (*while*)
end                                  (*algorithm to find end name*)
```

This same algorithm can also be used with other lists. For example, it can be used with a list of numbers. It merely determines the position of the end entry. The value of position is passed back to the calling algorithm or procedure. It is the value of position that is used by the following swap algorithm:

```
begin
   initialize info with list of names;
   initialize limit with list size;
   initialize address with the value of position;
   assign info[address] to buffer;
   assign info[limit] to info[address];
   assign buffer to info[limit]
end                                                    (*swap algorithm*)
```

At this point, a structure chart like the one in Figure 6.10 is helpful. It shows how the procedures we need will be connected together. A driver procedure is used to set up local variables that will be used when the BuildList and PerformSort procedures are activated. The lines leading from the driver procedure show the activation paths. The driver procedure is the program manager. The PerformSort procedure is the sort manager; it activates the procedures it needs to shuffle the list of names and get them into alphabetical order. The PrintList procedure is activated each time a shuffle is made to give a history of what happened during the activation of the PerformSort procedure. This lets you "look" inside the sorting algorithm. Later, the driver procedure can be used to activate the PrintList after the PerformSort procedure has shuffled all the names.

A program to carry out these ideas is given in Figure 6.11. Several refinements of the program in Figure 6.11 are possible.

```
                    (*Method: Use a selection sorting technique to shuffle
                          a list of passenger names stored in an array*)

program NameSort(input, output);
const
   empty = '        ';                              (*8 spaces = sentinel*)
   max = 50;                                          (*limit on list size*)
type
   name = packed array[1..8] of char;                      (*string type*)
   list = array[1..max] of name;                            (*array type*)

(*-------------------------------------------------------------------*)
                                          (*Save entered names in an array*)

   procedure BuildList(var info: list;                       (*for names*)
                       var limit: integer);                  (*list size*)
   begin
      limit := 0;
      repeat
         limit := limit + 1;
         write(' ':10, 'Enter name--a <return> to stop: ');
         readln(info[limit]); writeln
      until info[limit] = empty;
      limit := limit - 1                                (*a crucial step!*)
   end;                                                      (*BuildList*)
```

```
(*----------------------------------------------------*)
                                     (*Swap names in list*)

procedure swap(var info: list;                  (*names*)
                   limit: integer;               (*list size*)
                   address: integer);         (*name to swap*)
var
   buffer: name;                          (*temporary storage*)
begin
   buffer := info[address]; info[address] := info[limit];
   info[limit] := buffer
end;                                                 (*swap*)

(*----------------------------------------------------*)
                             (*Find position of name to swap*)

procedure FindMax(info: list;                       (*names*)
                     limit: integer;              (*list size*)
                     var position: integer);
var
   i: integer;                               (*name selector*)
   highest: name;                       (*stores highest name*)
begin
   highest := info[limit]; i := 1;
   while i < limit do begin
      if info[i] >= highest then begin
         highest := info[i]; position := i
         end;                                        (*then*)
      i := i + 1
      end                                           (*while*)
end;                                              (*FindMax*)

(*----------------------------------------------------*)
                                     (*Print line of hyphens*)

procedure DrawLine;
var hyphen: integer;                     (*control variable*)
begin
   writeln; for hyphen := 1 to 70 do write('—'); writeln
end;                                             (*DrawLine*)

(*----------------------------------------------------*)
                                      (*Show list of names*)

procedure PrintList(info: list;                     (*names*)
                       limit: integer);           (*list size*)
var
   selector: integer;                        (*name selector*)
begin
   write(' ':10);                               (*for margin*)
   for selector := 1 to limit do begin
      if selector mod 8 = 0 then begin
         writeln; write(' ':10)
         end;                                          (*if*)
```

```
        write(info[selector], ' ':3)
      end;                                                    (*for*)
    writeln
  end;                                                   (*PrintList*)

(*- - - - - - - - - - - - - - - - - - - - - - - - - - - - - - - - -*)
                         (*Manages sort of list of passenger names*)

  procedure PerformSort(var info: list;                    (*names*)
                            limit: integer);           (*list size*)
  var
    OldLimit: integer;                        (*for copy of list size*)
    place: integer;                             (*place to make swap*)
  begin
    OldLimit := limit;
    repeat
      place := limit;
      FindMax(info, limit, place);
      swap(info, limit, place);
      PrintList(info, OldLimit);
      limit := limit - 1
    until limit = 1
  end;                                                 (*PerformSort*)

(*- - - - - - - - - - - - - - - - - - - - - - - - - - - - - - - - -*)
                           (*Program manager: activate procedures*)

  procedure driver;
    var
      PassengerList: list;                          (*array variable*)
      ListSize: integer;                       (*for actual list size*)
      dash: integer;                              (*control variable*)
    begin
      repeat
        BuildList(PassengerList, ListSize);
        writeln; writeln;
        writeln('History of selection sort of names:':40);
        DrawLine;
        PerformSort(PassengerList, ListSize);
        DrawLine
      until 1 > 2                                     (*always false*)
    end;                                                  (*driver*)

(*- - - - - - - - - - - - - - - - - - - - - - - - - - - - - - - - -*)

begin
  driver                                           (*activate driver*)
end.
```

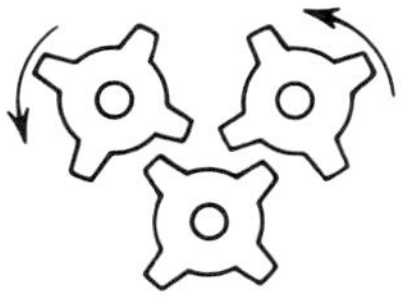

```
Enter name- -a <return> to stop: Jim

Enter name- -a <return> to stop: Amy

Enter name- -a <return> to stop: Ozzie
```

```
    Enter name- -a <return> to stop: Lou

    Enter name- -a <return> to stop: Juan

    Enter name- -a <return> to stop: Jorge

    Enter name- -a <return> to stop:

History of selection sort of names:

- - - - - - - - - - - - - - - - - - - - - - - - - - - - - - - - - - - - - - - - - - - - - - - - - -
    Jim        Amy        Jorge      Lou        Juan       Ozzie
    Jim        Amy        Jorge      Juan       Lou        Ozzie
    Jim        Amy        Jorge      Juan       Lou        Ozzie
    Jim        Amy        Jorge      Juan       Lou        Ozzie
    Amy        Jim        Jorge      Juan       Lou        Ozzie

- - - - - - - - - - - - - - - - - - - - - - - - - - - - -
```

FIGURE 6.11 Sorting a list passenger names

6.19.1

Refinement: Error Checking

The BuildList procedure in Figure 6.11 runs blind. It does not keep track of the size of the limit variable. As a result, this program can crash, if the value of limit runs out of bounds—slips past the maximum value set for subrange used to define the info index. A separate error-handling procedure, which the BuildList procedure can activate, is used if the info-index does go out of bounds. This error-handling procedure should allow the user to enter names into a backup array.

If a backup array is used, this will mean a fairly major change will have to be made in the BuildList procedure. It will be necessary to combine the info array and the backup array in a third array (call it *third array BailOut*). Then the driver procedure should activate the PerformSort procedure with either the info array (if there was no excess) or with the BailOut array (if there was excess). The PerformSort procedure remains the same! The revised program has the new structure chart shown in Figure 6.12. This refinement is left as an exercise. The program in Figure 6.11 can be refined to allow for a complete passenger name.

6.19.2

Refinement: Allowing for a Complete Name

In place of the PassengerList variable in the driver procedure in Figure 6.11, we can introduce the following array variables in the driver procedure:

```
var
   FirstNames, MiddleNames, LastNames: list;
```

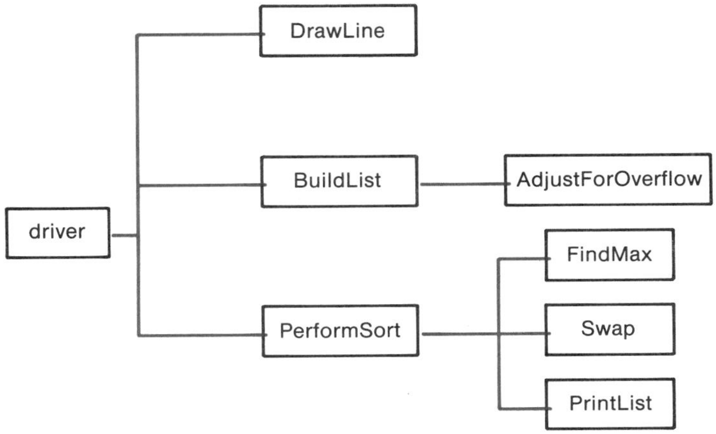

FIGURE 6.12
Expanded structure chart for selection sort

Then modify the BuildList procedure heading as follows:

procedure BuildList(var first, middle, last: list;
                        var limit);

Use the driver procedure to activate the BuildList procedure with the three array variables, which can be used to construct each passenger's complete name. It is usual to sort a list of names by last name. Even so, it will be necessary to modify the swap procedure used by the PerformSort procedure. Why? Each time a last name is shuffled, the corresponding first and middle names also must be shuffled.

It is still possible to use the PrintList procedure to print a history of what happens inside the PerformSort procedure. Just have the PerformSort procedure activate the PrintList procedure with the last array to show what happens to the last names during the shuffling. This will mean we will have to add a second print procedure (call it ShowPassengers) to print a list of each passenger's complete name. Use the driver procedure to activate the ShowPassengers procedure with the three array variables after the PerformSort procedure has completed the sort.

These changes will add a new box to the structure chart in Figure 6.12. It is left as an exercise to draw the new structure chart and to carry out this refinement.

6.19.3 Analysis of the Selection Sort

The PerformSort procedure in Figure 6.7 uses what is known as a *selection sort.* We estimate the running time of this sort by determining how comparisons are made every time the PerformSort procedure is activated, every time a selection sort is used. The chief time-consuming feature of this program is the FindMax procedure, which is activated repeatedly by the PerformSort procedure. Here is what happens.

$n - 1$ comparisons are made the first time (on n elements)
$+\ n - 2$ comparisons are made the second time (on n–1 elements)
$+\ n - 3$ comparisons are made the third time (on n–2 elements)
$+\ n - 4$ comparisons are made the fourth time (on n–3 elements)
.
.
.
$+$ 4 comparisons on 5 elements
$+$ 3 comparisons on 4 elements
$+$ 2 comparisons on 3 elements
$+$ 1 comparisons on 2 elements

Totaling these comparisons, we get the following sum:

$$\begin{aligned}\text{total comparisons} &= 1 + 2 + 3 + 4 + \cdots + (n - 2) + (n - 1) \\ &= (n - 1)((n - 1) + 1)/2 \\ &= (n - 1)(n/2)\end{aligned}$$

This total can be rewritten as follows;

$$\text{total comparisons} = n^2/2 - n/2$$

This total can be used to give us some idea how long it will take a machine to perform a selection sort. We know the running time of this sort will be roughly proportional to $n/2$ (the $n/2$ term in the above total does not contribute much to the running time estimate, when n is large). For example, with a list of 100 names, we get the following total:

$$\begin{aligned}\text{total comparisons} &= (100)/2 - (100)/2 \\ &= 10{,}000/2 - 100.2 \\ &= 5000 - 50 \\ &= 4950\end{aligned}$$

The 100/2 term has little influence on this total. That is, we can round off this total as follows:

5000 – 50 = 4950 is verý close to 5000

For this reason, the running time of a selection sort will be proportional to n for a list of n elements. If we know the time it takes a machine to make one comparison, then we can compute how long it will take that machine to carry out a selection sort. It is left as exercise to experiment with the running times of a selection sort of various array sizes. In doing this, it is best to have a machine build a list internally. This can be done by constructing arrays of random numbers and then selection sorting these random numbers. The program in Figure 6.11 can be modified to do this by adding a RndNo function. Then use the BuildList procedure to activate the RndNo function repeatedly to get values to put into an array. This can be done using the following technique:

```
const
   max = 1000;                                          (*array size*)
   SampleMax = 1000;                              (*limit on sample size*)
type
   list = array[1..max] of inteter;
var
   seed: real;                                       (*starts RndNo fn*)
      .
      .
      .
function RndNo:real;
begin
   seed := sqr(seed + 3.141597);
   seed := seed - trunc(seed);                   (*chop off whole part*)
   RndNo := seed
end;                                                          (*RndNo*)
procedure NewBuildList(var NewInfo : list;
                          var limit: inteter);
begin
   readln(seed);
   for limit := 1 to SampleMax do
      NewInfo[limit] := trunc(SampleMax * rnd) + 1
end;                                        (*new BuildList procedure*)
```

Carrying out this experiment is left as an exercise.

6.19.4 Exercises

1. Carry out the refinement of the program in Figure 6.11 described in Section 6.19.1. Give a sample run that forces the info index to go out of bounds.
2. Carry out the refinement of the program in exercise 1 using the method shown in Figure 6.19.2. Give a sample run that prints out
   a. The history of the sort of the last names of passengers handled by the PerformSort procedure and
   b. The final list of complete passenger names in sorted order.
3. Draw the new structure chart for the program in exercise 2.
4. Write an entirely new version of the program in Figure 6.7 that sorts lists of 1000 random numbers. Keep track of the number of comparisons used by the FindMax procedure. Find out how long it takes your machine to make one comparison. Use this machine time for one comparison to give an estimate of the total running time of the selection sort.

5. (Optional) Use mathematical induction to prove that the following sum holds true for n items:

$$\text{total} = 1 + 2 + 3 + 4 + \cdots + (n - 1) + n$$
$$= n*(n + 1)/2$$

6.20 Binary Search Technique: Divide-and-Conquer Searching

If we have an ordered list, the next trick is to devise a method of search a list for a given item. A simple way to do this is start at the beginning of a list and move from one item to the next one looking for the desired item. This is called a *linear* search technique. As a rule, it takes about $n/2$ comparisons to find an item in a list with n items using a linear search.

A more efficient method of searching stems from applying the divide-and-conquer principle to the problem. Instead of starting at the beginning of a list, try starting in the middle of an ordered list. Then see which side of the middle the desired item is located. This technique eliminates half a list from the search with a single comparison. On occasion, you may be lucky and find the desired item to be the middle item. Repeated application of the divide-and-conquer principle produces what is known as a *binary* search (literally, a "by halves" technique). Here is the algorithm to implement this idea.

Binary Search Algorithm

```
                                        (*input: low, high, list elements;
                                     output: position of desired element*)
begin
   initialize low with 1; high with n (the list size);
   while low <= high do begin
      assign (low + high) div 2 to middle;
      if list[middle] < target then
         assign middle + 1 to low                    (*search upper half!*)
      else
         if target < list[middle] then begin
            high := middle - 1;                      (*search lower half!*)
            middle := high
            end                                                     (*if*)
         else
            high := low - 1
      end;                                                       (*while*)
   position := middle
end;                               (*divide-and-conquer search technique*)
```

We can use this algorithm to search for a place to insert a new name into an old ordered list of names. This can be done by introducing a new procedure (call in *Insert*), which will use the position value from the BinarySearch to make an insertion of a new name into an old list. Here is an algorithm for this new Insert procedure.

```
begin
   determine target (use driver procedure to do this);
   BinarySearch(List, ListSize, target, position);
   add 1 to ListSize;
   repeat
      List[ListSize] := List[ListSize – 1];
      subtract 1 from ListSize
   until ListSize = position;
   List[position] := target                    (*insert new name here*)
end                                              (*Insertion algorithm*)
```

This will give us an expanded structure chart like the one in Figure 6.13. Now the driver procedure for the program in Figure 6.11 will have the following form:

```
begin
   repeat
      print the following menu:
         ----> 1 build list of names;
         ----> 2 print copy of list of names;
         ----> 3 sort list of names;
         ----> 4 insert a new name in an ordered list;
         ----> 5 exit;
      make menu choice;
      activate appropriate procedure to implement choice
   until choice = 5
end
```

This is good place to use a case statement to handle the menu choice made. Implementing this driver procedure and the binary search algorithm is given in the program in Figure 6.14.

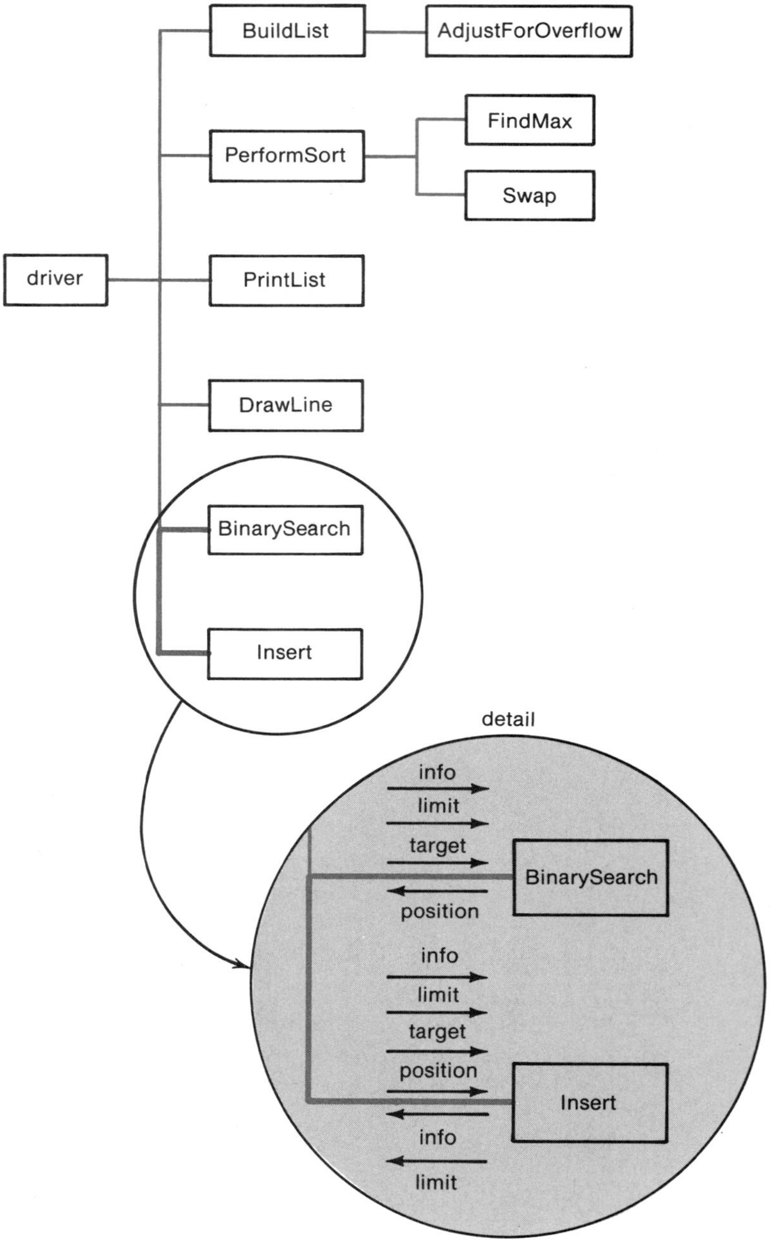

FIGURE 6.13
Refinement of structure chart

```
                    (*Method: Use a selection sorting technique to shuffle
                        a list of passenger names stored in an array
                        and binary search to insert a new name.*)

program NameSort(input, output);
const
   empty = '        ';                          (*8 spaces = sentinel*)
   max = 50;                                   (*limit on list size*)
type
   name = packed array[1..8] of char;                 (*string type*)
   list = array[1..max] of name;                       (*array type*)

 (*-------------------------------------------------------------*)
                                    (*Binary search for a list entry*)

   procedure BinarySearch(info: list;                 (*ordered list*)
                          limit: integer;                (*list size*)
                          target: name;                (*item sought*)
                          var position: integer);
   var
      middle, low, high: integer;
   begin
      low := 1; high := limit;
      while low <= high do begin
         middle := (low + high) div 2;
         if info[middle] < target then begin
            low := middle + 1;                   (*search upper half*)
            middle := low
            end
         else
            if target < info[middle] then
               high := middle - 1                (*search lower half*)
            else
               high := low - 1
         end;
      position := middle
   end;                                               (*BinarySearch*)

 (*-------------------------------------------------------------*)
                                          (*Insert name into list*)

   procedure insert(var info: list;                        (*names*)
                    var limit: integer;                (*list size*)
                    target: name;                 (*name to insert*)
                    position: integer);         (*place to put name*)
   var
      index: integer;
   begin
      limit := limit + 1;                     (*increase list size*)
      for index := limit downto position + 1 do
         info[index] := info[index - 1];
      info[position] := target
   end;                                                   (*insert*)
```

```
(*------------------------------------------------*)
                          (*Adjust for array overflow*)

procedure AdjustForOverflow(var info: list;
                            var limit: integer);
begin
                                 (*empty statement*)
end;                             (*AdjustForOverflow*)

(*------------------------------------------------*)
                       (*Save entered names in an array*)

procedure BuildList(var info: list;          (*for names*)
                    var limit: integer);     (*list size*)
begin
   limit := 0;
   repeat
      limit := limit + 1;
      if limit > max then
         AdjustForOverflow(info, limit)
      else begin
         write(' ':10, 'Enter name--a <return> to stop: ');
         readln(info[limit]); writeln
         end                                     (*else*)
   until info[limit] = empty;
   limit := limit - 1                   (*a crucial step!*)
end;                                        (*BuildList*)

(*------------------------------------------------*)
                                 (*Swap names in list*)

procedure swap(var info: list;                (*names*)
               limit: integer;            (*list size*)
               address: integer);      (*name to swap*)
var
   buffer: name;                  (*temporary storage*)
begin
   buffer := info[address]; info[address] := info[limit];
   info[limit] := buffer
end;                                           (*swap*)

(*------------------------------------------------*)
                        (*Find position of name to swap*)

procedure FindMax(info: list;                 (*names*)
                  limit: integer;         (*list size*)
                  var position: integer);
var
   i: integer;                        (*name selector*)
   highest: name;               (*stores highest name*)
```

```
begin
   highest := info[limit]; i := 1;
   while i < limit do begin
      if info[i] >= highest then begin
         highest := info[i]; position := i
         end;                                          (*then*)
      i := i + 1
      end                                              (*while*)
end;                                                   (*FindMax*)

(*-----------------------------------------------------------*)
                                        (*Print line of hyphens*)

procedure DrawLine;
var hyphen: integer;                         (*control variable*)
begin
   writeln; for hyphen := 1 to 70 do write('—'); writeln
end;                                                 (*DrawLine*)

(*-----------------------------------------------------------*)
                                          (*Show list of names*)

procedure PrintList(info: list;                         (*names*)
                    limit: integer);                (*list size*)
var
   selector: integer;                           (*name selector*)
begin
   for selector := 1 to limit do
      write(info[selector], ' ':3);
   writeln
end;                                                (*PrintList*)

(*-----------------------------------------------------------*)
                    (*Manages sort of list of passenger names*)

procedure PerformSort(var info: list;                   (*names*)
                      limit: integer);              (*list size*)
var
   OldLimit: integer;                     (*for copy of list size*)
   place: integer;                         (*place to make swap*)
begin
   OldLimit := limit;
   repeat
      place := limit;
      FindMax(info, limit, place);
      swap(info, limit, place);
      limit := limit — 1
   until limit = 1
end;                                              (*PerformSort*)
```

```
(*- - - - - - - - - - - - - - - - - - - - - - - - - - - - - - - - - - - - - - - - - -*)
                             (*Program manager: activate procedures*)

  procedure driver;
  var
    PassengerList: list;                           (*array variable*)
    ListSize: integer;                         (*for actual list size*)
    NewName: name;                      (*name to insert into old list*)
    there, choice: integer;                           (*menu choice*)
  begin
    PassengerList[1] := empty;                     (*safety measure*)
    repeat
      writeln('menu:':20);
      writeln('- - - ->':20, '1) build list;');
      writeln('- - - ->':20, '2) print list;');
      writeln('- - - ->':20, '3) sort list;')'
      writeln('- - - ->':20, '4) insert name into old ordered list;');
      writeln('- - - ->':20, '5) exit');
      write(' ':10, 'choice: '); readln(choice);
      case choice of
        1: BuildList(PassengerList, ListSize);
        2: begin
             DrawLine;
             if PassengerList[1] = empty then
               writeln(' ':10, 'passenger list is empty!')
             else PrintList(PassengerList, ListSize);
             DrawLine
           end;
        3: begin
             PerformSort(PassengerList, ListSize);
             DrawLine;
             writeln; writeln('sorted list:':30);
             PrintList(PassengerList, ListSize);
             DrawLine
           end;
        4: begin
             write(' ':10, 'Enter new name: '); readln(NewName);
             writeln;
             BinarySearch(PassengerList, ListSize, NewName,
             there);
             Insert(PassengerList, ListSize, NewName, there)
           end;
        5:                                                  (*empty*)
        end                                                  (*case*)
      until choice = 5
  end;                                                     (*driver*)

(*- - - - - - - - - - - - - - - - - - - - - - - - - - - - - - - - - - - - - - - - - -*)

begin
  driver                                          (*activate driver*)
end.
```

```
   menu:
   ---->1) build list;
   ---->2) print list;
   ---->3) sort list;
   ---->4) insert name into old ordered list;
   ---->5) exit
choice: 2

----------------------------------------
passenger list is empty!
----------------------------------------
   menu:
   ---->1) build list;
   ---->2) print list;
   ---->3) sort list;
   ---->4) insert name into old ordered list;
   ---->5) exit
choice: 1
Enter name--a <return> to stop: Garth

Enter name--a <return> to stop: Lori

Enter name--a <return> to stop: Lolita

Enter name--a <return> to stop: Lou

Enter name--a <return> to stop: Tony

Enter name--a <return> to stop:

   menu:
   ---->1) build list;
   ---->2) print list;
   ---->3) sort list;
   ---->4) insert name into old ordered list;
   ---->5) exit
choice: 2
----------------------------------------
Garth        Lori        Lolita        Lou        Tony
----------------------------------------
   menu:
   ---->1) build list;
   ---->2) print list;
   ---->3) sort list;
   ---->4) insert name into old ordered list;
   ---->5) exit
choice: 3
----------------------------------------
                      Sorted list:
Garth        Lolita        Lori        Lou        Tony
----------------------------------------
```

```
   menu:
   ---->1) build list;
   ---->2) print list;
   ---->3) sort list;
   ---->4) insert name into old ordered list;
   ---->5) exit
choice: 4
Enter new name: Zorba

   menu:
   ---->1) build list;
   ---->2) print list;
   ---->3) sort list;
   ---->4) insert name into old ordered list;
   ---->5) exit
choice: 2
---------------------------------------
Garth       Lolita      Lori      Lou      Tony      Zorba
---------------------------------------
   menu:
   ---->1) build list;
   ---->2) print list;
   ---->3) sort list;
   ---->4) insert name into old ordered list;
   ---->5) exit
choice: 4
Enter new name: Amy

   menu:
   ---->1) build list;
   ---->2) print list;
   ---->3) sort list;
   ---->4) insert name into old ordered list;
   ---->5) exit
choice: 2
---------------------------------------
Amy    Garth    Lolita    Lori    Lou    Tony    Zorba
---------------------------------------
   menu:
   ---->1) Build list;
   ---->2) Print list;
   ---->3) Sort list;
   ---->4) Insert name into old ordered list;
   ---->5) Exit
choice: 5
```

FIGURE 6.14 Maintaining a list passenger names

6.20.1

Refinement: Timing Study

You can estimate the time it takes for a binary search by keeping track of the number of comparisons made each time a search is made. This will mean adding a ComparisonCount variable to your binary search procedure. Each time a comparison is made during a binary search, add 1 to ComparisonCount. Do this for more than one search and add a procedure to print a table like the following one:

Timing Study

Target Sought	*Number of Comparisons*	*Running Total*

Note. Print the average number of comparisons made using

average = (final) running total / number of targets

Then find out how long it takes your computer to make one comparison. This information will be available in your system manual. For example, if it takes your system 0.78 microseconds to make one comparison, then use

running time of search = average * (comparison time)
= average * (0.78)

to get an estimate of the running time in microseconds.

6.20.2 Exercises

1. Refine the BinarySearch procedure in Figure 6.14 so that it maintains the following arrays:

ComparisonCount	holds number of comparisons for each binary search made
Targets	holds copies of targets sought in binary searches

So Target[1] will correspond to ComparisonCount[1] and so on. Also introduce a new BinaryHistory procedure, which prints the table shown in Section 6.20.1. Then do the following:

a. Write an expanded structure chart for the program design used for the new program.
b. Run the new program with the following list and targets and give a sample run for
c. list: Amy, Susu, Kim, Phil, Tom, Jill, Jon, Shelly, Kim
target: Amy;
d. list: same as in part (c)
target: Susu;
e. list: same as in part (c)
target: Kim
f. list: same as in part (c)
target: Zorba
g. list: same as in part (c)
target: Allan

2. Verify that an ordered list can be built from scratch using just the BinarySearch and Insert procedures. Demonstrate this with a sample run. You will be using what is known as a *binary insertion sort.* What is the running time of this sort? Contrast this running time with the Selection sort used in Section 6.20.1.

6.21 Readings

Brookshear, J. G. *Computer Science: An Overview.* Menlo Park, CA: Benjamin Cummings, 1985. See Chapter 7 on arrays.

Cooper, D. *Standard Pascal User Reference Manual.* New York: Norton, 1983. See Section 11-2.

Horowitz, E., and Sahni, S. *Fundamentals of Data Structures.* Rockville, MD: Computer Science Press, 1982. See Chapter 2 on arrays.

Peters, J. F. *Problem Solving with Pascal: Programming Methods, Algorithms and Data Structures.* New York: Holt, Rinehart and Winston, 1986. See Chapters 7, 10, and 11.

CHAPTER 7

EXPRESSION AND PROCEDURAL ABSTRACTION

A function is a kind of program which accepts input (its arguments) and produces output (its result). To be able to construct more powerful programs, then, it is necessary to be able to define new functions using old ones.

Peter Henderson, *Functional Programming: Application and Implementation*

AIMS

- Introduce expression abstraction with functions.
- Contrast and compare functions and procedures.
- Distinguish between function identifiers and function designators.
- Show how new functions can be built using old ones.
- Introduce information hiding and procedural abstraction.
- Suggest how information hiding can be used to advantage in the development of procedures with function parameters.
- Show how to set up functions with forward references.
- Introduce a new function to produce random numbers.
- Show how random numbers can be used to set up a guessing game.
- Give a case study on a game for shy persons.

7.1

Introduction to Expression Abstraction

An expression always represents a value. Here is an example of an expression that can be used to compute percentage of wins made by a team.

Wins	*Losses*	*Expression*	*Computations*	*Result*
22	5	Wins/(wins + losses)	1. (22 + 7) = 29 2. 22/29 = 0.76	76%

Our main interest is in the result, not the computations needed to obtain the result (the percentage of wins). It is possible to write the value of an expression like this one in the following way:

PctOfWins(wins, losses) (*which equals the value of an expression, which is hidden*)

You can think of PctOfWins(wins, losses) as an expression abstraction. An *expression abstraction* is used without concern about how a value is obtained or what mechanisms are used to obtain a value. The focus is on the *value,* not on the expression used to obtain the value.

In Pascal an expression abstraction is made possible by using what is a known as a *function.* A *function* is a subprogram that is used to return a single value. The structure of function is the same as a procedure, except for two things.

1. A function heading must indicate the data type of the value to be returned by a function.
2. The body of a function must include a statement of the form

FunctionName := <a value>

For example, we can write a Pascal function to take care of the computations needed to obtain a percentage of wins as follows:

```
function PctOfWins(wins, losses: integer): real;
begin
  PctOfWins := wins/(wins + losses)            (*hidden part*)
end;                                           (*PctOfWins*)
```

Expression abstraction is used to help make a procedure more concise and more readable, and focus on the results instead of the operations involved. For example, we can use a function to simplify a procedure that relies on the value of an expression to carry out its specified task. Here are two forms of the same procedure, which how this simplification can be achieved.

Two Forms of a Procedure

Procedure 1a
(without expression abstraction)

```
procedure BuildScoreCard(var results: ArrayType;
                         var limit: integer);
var
   pct, wins, losses: real;
begin
   limit := 0;
   writeln('Enter wins, losses- -a –1,–1, to stop:');
repeat
   limit := limit + 1;
   if limit > ArrayMax then
      AdjustForOverflow(results, limit)
   else begin
      readln(wins, losses);
      pct := wins/(wins + losses);
      results [limit] := pct
      end
   until wins = –1;
   limit := limit – 1
end;                                              (*BuildScoreCard*)
```

Procedure 1b
(with expression abstraction)

```
procedure BuildScoreCard(var results: ArrayType;
                         var limit: integer);
var
   wins, losses: real;                    (*notice one less variable*)
begin
   limit := 0;
   writeln('Enter wins, losses- -a –1,–1, to stop: ');
   repeat
      limit := limit + 1;
      if limit > ArrayMax then
         AdjustForOverflow(results, limit)
      else begin
         readln(wins, losses);
         results[limit] := PctOfWins(wins, losses)          (*notice!*)
         end
   until wins = –1;
   limit := limit – 1
end;                                              (*BuildScoreCard*)
```

In version 1b of this BuildScoreCard procedure, here is what we have done.

Original Expression	*Abstraction*
Wins/(wins + losses)	PctOfWins(wins, losses)

This abstraction causes the actual parameters (wins and losses) and to be used in a PctOfWins function to compute a value. The computed value will be assigned to PctOfWins(wins, losses). In effect, we have hidden the expression used to compute the needed value. We have turned our attention, instead, to what is really more important: the result produced by the function, the percentage of wins. This is our main interest.

7.2 Function Designators

A *function designator* is a function name (and any required parameters) used to activate a function. In procedure 1b, PctOfWins (wins, losses) is the function designator. Notice that it does not stand alone; it is part of a statement.

results[limit] := PctOfWins(wins, losses)

This is always true whenever a function designator is used to activate a function.

> **First cardinal rule for function designators:**
>
> **A function designator is used to activate a function and is always part of a larger statement.**

This rule for function designators contrasts sharply with what we know about procedures. That is, when a procedure name (and any necessary actual parameters) is used to activate a procedure, the procedure name (and its parameters) stands alone and is never part of a larger statement. For example, in Figure 6.7 the PerformSort procedure is activated by the driver procedure in the following way:

```
begin
   .
   .
   .
   PerformSort(PassengerList, ListSize);         (*activate procedure*)
   .
   .
   .
end;                                  (*driver procedure in Figure 6.7*)
```

The statement used to activate the PerformSort procedure stands by itself! In addition, the PerformSort identifier is never given or has any value. In the above statement, this procedure name merely serves as a means of identifying the procedure to be activated by a processor. By contrast, a function designator is always given a value by the function it activates. We have seen numerous examples of this. Here are some more examples.

1. Using the built-in succ() function in a write statement:

```
write(succ('t'));                              (*a 'u' will be printed*)
```

2. Using the RndNo function to produce a roll of a die:

```
roll := trunc(6 * RndNo) + 1;                  (*assigns a number
                                               from 1 through 6 to roll*)
```

3. Using the built-in chr() function to ring the keyboard bell:

```
for BellSound := 1 to MaxTimes do
  write(chr(7));                               (*rings bell*)
```

   (This is a handy tool in error-handling procedures like the ones discussed in Chapter 6 whenever, for example, a warning must be given that an array index is about to go out of bounds.)

4. Using the built-in ln() and exp() functions to compute the power of a number:

```
power := exp(exponent * ln(base));
```

Here is another cardinal rule for function designators.

> **Second cardinal rule for function designators:**
>
> **A function designator is always given a value by the function it activates.**

Finally, the observation made by Peter Henderson (1980) in the opening quote of this chapter gives an important hint about any new functions we want to invent. That is, it is a good strategy to build new functions atop the shoulders of old functions. A new function is made more powerful by using old functions to define new ones. Again, the RndNo function given in Chapter 5 is an example of how this is done. The RndNo function was set up using two built-in functions, the trunc() and sqr() functions. The result is a powerful tool that can be used in simulating chance events like the roll of a pair of dice in Figure 5.4.

7.3 Blocks Revisited

A Pascal program can have three types of blocks:

1. Program block, which holds all other blocks

2. Procedure block, which can have other blocks inside it, including either other procedure blocks or function blocks or both

3. Function block, which can have other blocks inside it, including either other function blocks or procedure blocks or both

This is another way of saying that blocks can be nested (one block can be inside another block). The exception is the program block, which cannot appear inside another block. If blocks are nested, they are nested inside a program block. A program block consists of everything in a program except the program heading and the trailing period (.) used to mark the end of the program block. Similarly, the heading and trailing semicolon (;) at the end of a nonprogram block are not considered a part of either a function or procedure block.

Every block has an optional part and a required part. The syntax for any Pascal block is given in Figure 7.1. The declaration and definition parts of any block are optional. The syntax for these optional parts of a block is given in Figure 7.2. Function and procedure blocks have identical syntax. However, function and procedure headings are different. In the next section we discuss a feature of a function body has a feature that is never present in a procedure body.

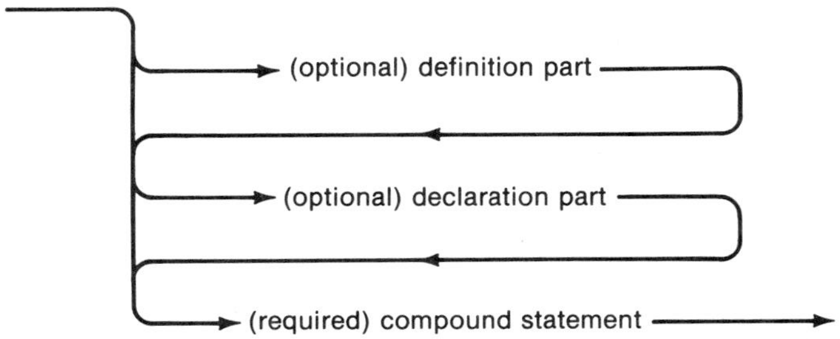

FIGURE 7.1
Syntax for a block

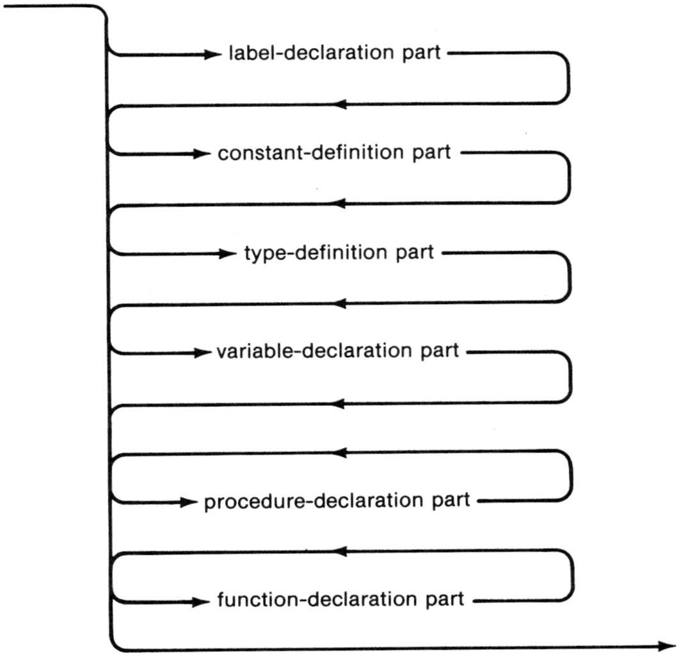

FIGURE 7.2
Syntax for optional parts of a block

7.4 Differences between Procedures and Functions

A function heading has a feature not present in a procedure heading.

> **A function heading must always specify the data type of the value returned by the function.**

Here is an example.

```
function PctOfWins(wins, losses: integer): real;
                                           result type
```

The syntax for a function heading is shown in Figure 7.3. Every function body has a feature that is never present in a procedure body.

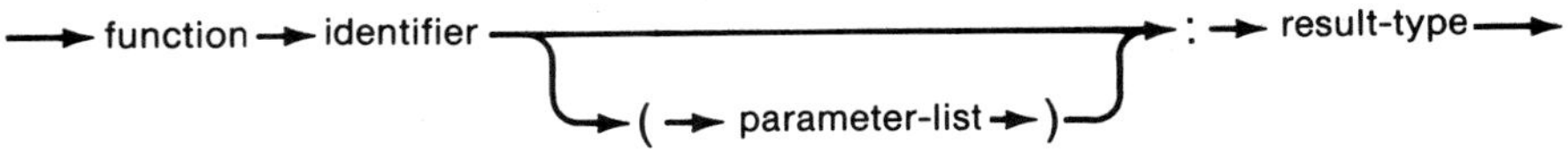

FIGURE 7.3
Syntax for a function heading

A function body is used to assign a value to the function identifier. This is the value the function designator receives.

Here are two examples of this idea.

1. RndNo := seed (*from Section 5.5.1*)
2. PctOfWins := wins/(wins + losses)

We illustrate these ideas about function headings and function designators with the example in Section 7.5.

7.5 Example: A New Way to Inspect a Type Char Scale

It is sometimes helpful to know how many characters there are between any two characters in a scale used to implement type char. This information can be used, for example, in cryptography programs to encode a message. Here is a complete function that can be used to determine how many characters there are between any two characters on the scale used to define type char on your system.

```
function distance(FirstChar, SecondChar:char):integer;
begin
   if FirstChar = SecondChar then
      distance := 0
   else
      distance := abs(ord(SecondChar) - ord(FirstChar)) -1
end;                                                    (*distance*)
```

You can implement this function in a program with the following steps:

1. Activate the distance function using a function designator; for example, a function designator to activate this function will have the following form:

   write(distance('*a*', '*c*'));

   ↑ 'c': actual parameter that supplies a value for the formal parameter SecondChar

   ↑ 'a': actual parameter that supplies a value for the formal parameter FirstChar

2. If the two characters used to activate the distance function are the same, then

```
distance := 0                    (*assign 0 to function
                                   identifier*)
```

In other words, the function designator gets a value of 0 or

3. If the two characters used to activate the distance function are not the same, then the number of characters between the two actual parameters is computed. For example, on the ASCII scale, the following computations will be made for 'a' and 'c':

```
ASCII scale:

codes: ... 97 98 99 100 101  102  103  104  105...122...
char:  ... a  b  c  d   e    f    g    h    i ...  z ...
           ↑     ↑ord('c') = 99
           ord('a') = 97
```

which gives

```
distance := abs(ord('c') - ord('a')) - 1
         := abs(99 - 97) -1
         := abs(2) - 1
         := 2 - 1
         := 1
```

You are probably wondering why the built-in absolute value function is being used in this distance function. The abs() function takes care of cases where FirstChar represents a character that comes after the character represented by SecondChar. We are interested in distance, so we always want a positive result from the above subtraction. Here is an example where the abs() function will be useful.

4. Activate the distance function as follows:

```
write(distance('z', 'a'));
                ↑    ↑
                |    value assigned to SecondChar
                value assigned to FirstChar
```

then the following calculations will be made inside distance function:

```
distance := abs(ord('a') - ord('z')) - 1
         := abs(97 - 122) -1
         := abs( -25 ) - 1
         := 25 - 1
         := 24
```

The absolute value function comes to rescue in this example. It converts abs(−25) to positive 25, which is what we need to figure the number of characters between *'a'* and *'z'* on the scale for type char. Here is a basic idea for a program to use the distance function:

```
                              (*input: two characters;
                   output: scalar distance between the characters*)
begin
   get two characters;
   determine the distance between the two characters
end
```

A structure chart to represent this idea more precisely is given in Figure 7.4. This is a good place for a function, which can be used to separate the method used to compute the desired distance from the distance itself. In other words, we can use expression abstraction. The structure chart highlights the essential idea behind this: The distance function is activated with two values (the entered characters) and it returns a single value (the desired distance). A program to implement this idea is given in Figure 7.5. The program in Figure 7.5 has several potential refinements which you might want to try.

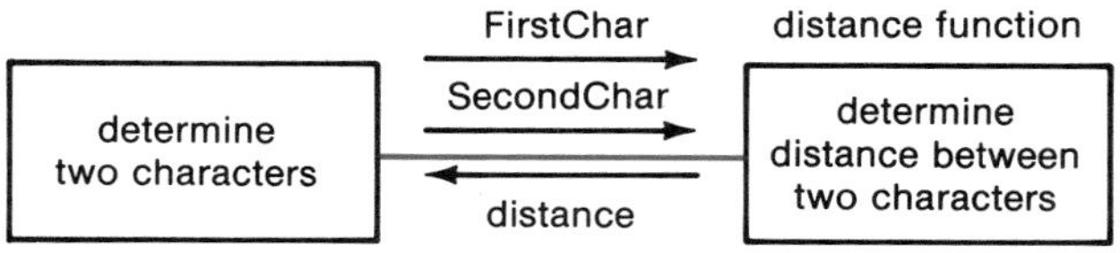

FIGURE 7.4
Structure chart for distance program

```
        (*Method: Set up a function to compute the distance between
                        a pair of entered characters using the built-in
                              absolute value abs() and ord() functions.*)

program TryThis(input, output);

  (*- - - - - - - - - - - - - - - - - - - - - - - - - - - - - - - - - - -*)
        (*Determine number of characters between entered pair*)

  function distance(FirstChar, SecondChar:char): integer;
  begin
     if FirstChar = SecondChar then
        distance := 0
     else
        distance := abs(ord(SecondChar)-ord(FirstChar)) - 1
  end;                                                        (*distance*)
```

```
(*- - - - - - - - - - - - - - - - - - - - - - - - - - - - - - - - - - - - - - - - - - - - - -*)
          (*Program manager: get values and activate procedure*)

 procedure driver;
 var
    FirstChoice, SecondChoice: char;                          (*targets*)
 begin
    repeat
       write('Enter pair of characters: ');
       readln(FirstChoice, SecondChoice); writeln;
       write('There are ', distance(FirstChoice, SecondChoice):2);
       write(' characters between the entered characters.');
       writeln; writeln
    until 1 > 2
 end;                                                           (*driver*)

(*- - - - - - - - - - - - - - - - - - - - - - - - - - - - - - - - - - - - - - - - - - - - - -*)

begin
   driver                                    (*activate driver procedure*)
end.
```

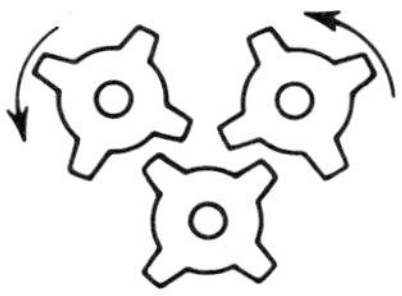

```
Enter pair of characters: az

There are 24 characters between the entered characters.

Enter pair of characters: 2a

There are 46 characters between the entered characters.

Enter pair of characters: !2

There are 16 characters between the entered characters.

Enter pair of characters: !z

There are 88 characters between the entered characters.

Enter pair of characters: ^C
```

FIGURE 7.5 Program to compute distance between characters

7.5.1

Refinement: Inventing a New Interval Procedure

The distance function in Figure 7.5 is limited to telling us the number of characters between any two entered characters. The counterpart of the distance function would be a procedure to tell what characters lie between any two characters we select. For example, it would be handy to have a machine pump out the hard-to-remember characters between the numerals and the letters or between ' ' and the numeral 0. The successor function could be used to invent a new procedure (call it *interval*) to print out the characters between any two characters we enter. This refinement is left as an exercise.

7.5.2

Refinement: Inventing a New Extreme Function

The distance function in Figure 7.5 tells us nothing about the number of characters between the ends of a type char scale and the entered characters. This information can be obtained from a pair of new functions (call them *LeftExtreme* and *RightExtreme*) or from a single function (call it *extreme*) with an integer parameter that indicates which extreme we want to check. Here is what the function heading for the extreme function would look like.

```
function extreme(FirstChar, SecondChar: char;           (*selections*)
                 choice: integer): integer;
```

The choice parameter can be used to determine which end of the character scale to check. Here is an algorithm to carry out this idea in a new driver procedure.

```
                        (*input: two characters, interval choice;
                              output: number of characters*)
begin
   initialize First Choice, SecondChoice with characters;
   print the following menu:
      menu:
         ---> 1 number of in-between characters;
         ---> 2 number of characters to left of First Choice;
         ---> 3 number of characters to right of
                SecondChoice;
   initialize choice variable;
   if choice = 1 then
      activate distance function with entered characters
   else
      activate extreme function with entered characters
      and the choice variable
end;                    (*algorithm for a new driver procedure*)
```

Here is an algorithm that can be used to set up the extreme function.

```
                        (*input: two characters, choice, max;
                              output: number of characters*)
begin
   initialize FirstChar and SecondChar with characters
   (taken from a function designator);
   initialize choice (taken from a function designator);
   if choice = 2 then
      if ord(FirstChar) <= SecondChar then
         if FirstChar <> 0 then
            assign ord(FirstChar) - 1 to function identifier
         else if ord(SecondChar) <> 0 then
               assign ord(SecondChar) - 1 to function identifier
            else assign 0 to function identifier
```

```
else
   if SecondChar >= FirstChar then
      if ord(SecondChar) <> max then
            assign max – ord(SecondChar) – 1 to function identifier
      else
            assign zero to function identifier
      else
         if ord(FirstChar) <> max then
            assign max – ord(FirstChar) – 1 to function identifier
         else
            assign zero to function identifier
end                              (*algorithm for new extreme function*)
```

This second algorithm depends on the value of max to handle the right end of the type char scale. This will be 127 (for the ASCII scale), or 256 (for the EBCDIC scale). You will have to determine the value of max for the scale used for type char on your system. Despite all the activity in this algorithm, the function identifier extreme will end up with a single value, which is returned to the driver procedure. We leave it as an exercise to implement these algorithms.

Function identifiers have some special features. We examine these features in Section 7.6.

7.6 Special Features of a Function Identifier

A function identifier is specified in a function heading. There are two things to notice about this.

1. A function identifier is used to return a single function result.
2. A function identifier data type is limited to the simple types, enumerated or subrange types, or pointer type (explained later).

A function identifier type cannot be a structured data type. It is not possible, for example, for a function identifier to be an array type. This is reasonable because a structured type leaves open the possibility of returning more than one value. This would violate the cardinal rule of functions.

Cardinal rule for function identifiers:

A function can only return a single value. A function identifier is limited to a scalar or pointer type, which can be used to return a single value.

A function identifier must be assigned the return value within the body of a function. For example, with the above choice function, we can set up the following definition:

```
function choice(x, y, z : integer): Boolean;
begin
choice := ((x <= y) and (y <= z))
end;                                              (*choice*)
```

This says the function identifier choice will be true, provided the expression

$(x <= y)$ **and** $(y <= z)$

is true, otherwise this function will return a value of false, which is assigned to choice if the above expression is false. For example, the statement

```
if choice(FirstChoice, SecondChoice, ThirdChoice) then
   TellMyFortune                              (*procedure call*)
else write('Ask Goldberry!')
```

will produce the following results for the specified values of the actual parameters:

FirstChoice	*SecondChoice*	*ThirdChoice*	*Resulting Action*
5	2	1	Ask Goldberry!
5	5	5	TellMyFortune
21	233	0	Ask Goldberry!
0	0	233	TellMyFortune

In this example, the function designator is used as the entire Boolean condition that controls which action gets executed by a processor. The trick we used to assign a value to the type Boolean function identifier is useful and is not limited to function identifiers. That is, the following rule holds true in general for a variable of type Boolean:

The Boolean result rule:

If NewIdea is a variable of type Boolean, then a computer will assign a value to NewIdea when it evaluates an expression (to see if it is true) in an assignment like the following one:

NewIdea := (Boolean expression)

We use this idea to advantage in Chapter 8 about records.

7.7

Bug Clinic: Forgetting about the Function Identifier Value

Forgetting to assign a value to a function identifier will produce an error message like the following one:

Function assignment not found

This is the syntax error message produced by IBM Pascal 2.00 in this case. It is easy to forget to assign a value to the function identifier. Pascal will let you know it, if you do forget.

7.8

Structure of a Program with a User-Defined Function

The program in Figure 7.5 typifies the program structure you can expect to find whenever a user-defined function is used. In Figure 7.6 we show this structure graphically. That is, the user-defined function *B* gets called by procedure *C* in Figure 7.6. Unlike a procedure call like *C* in

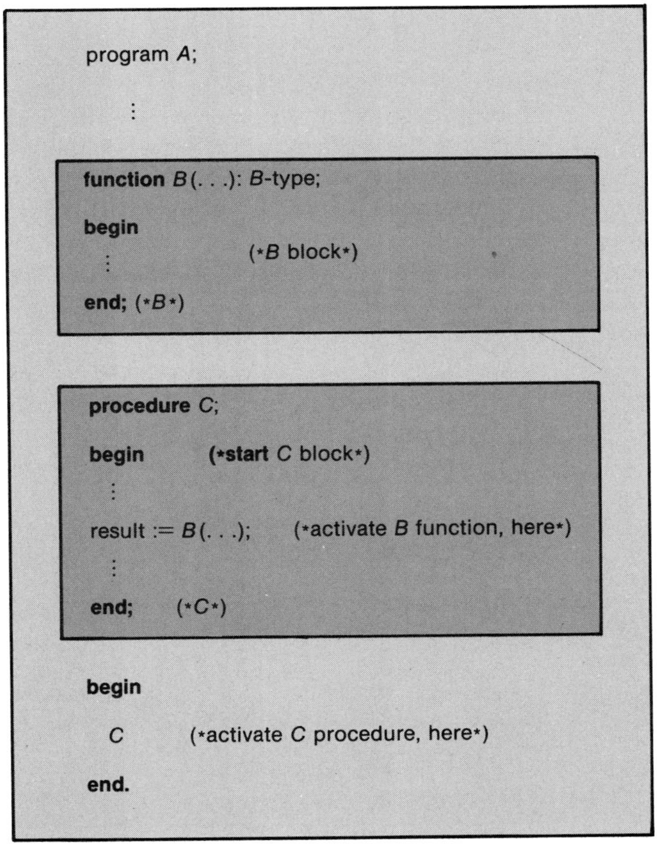

FIGURE 7.6
A user-defined function block

```
begin
   C                                                    (*procedure call*)
end.
```

a function call cannot stand alone. That is, a function designator cannot stand alone. A function designator must be included within a Pascal statement. In the above example, we used

(*the function designator is part of an assignment statement, here*)

The variable *x* gets the *B* value determined by the *B* function. Finally, functions can also have locally declared constants, data types, variables (like ChosenValue in the EvenNumber function given earlier), functions, and procedures.

7.9 Function Parameter Lists

The syntax diagram for a parameter list in a user-defined function heading is shown in Figure 7.7. In other words, the parameter list for a user-defined function can be included in either variable or value parameters. Value parameters are more usual. For example, here is a function that can be used to compute the age of an object using what is known as the *carbon dating method.*

```
function age(CarbonLeft: real): real;
begin
   age := ln(CarbonLeft)/DecayConstant
end;                                                    (*age*)
```

Depending on the value of the CarbonLeft parameter when this function is activated by a function designator like

result := age(0.6)

this function will return a value for age of type real. In Section 7.10 we illustrate the use of a user-defined function with a variable parameter.

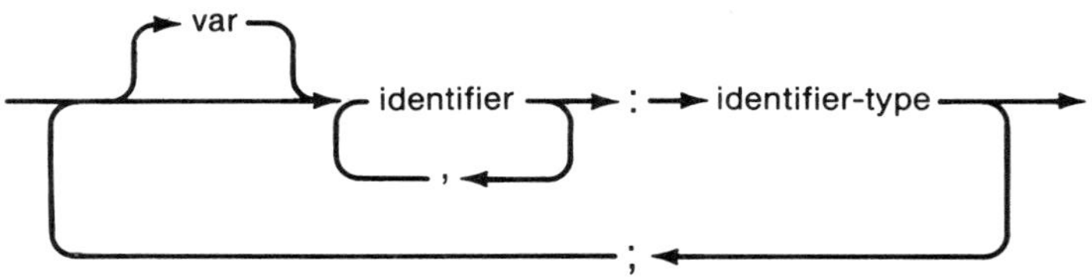

FIGURE 7.7
Syntax for a paramter list

7.10

Example: Randon Number Function Revisited

Events are random if they are equally likely to happen. In the real world, it is difficult (some would say impossible!) to find random events. For example, if there were some way to draw numbers from a hat so that each of the numbers were equally likely to be drawn, then we would have examples of random numbers. You can imagine a situation like one shown in Figure 7.8. Each marble inside the hat will have a number written on it. We can assume the marbles are perfectly spherical, each with an identical weight. We can shake this hat each time, before we draw a marble to get a number. If each marble is equally likely to be picked, we get random numbers. In general, numbers that are random are equally likely to occur.

FIGURE 7.8
Marbles in a hat

We can get close to this idea by setting up a function that produces numbers in an irregular fashion. We can do this so that there will be no apparent pattern. Here is another form of the RndNo function given earlier in Chapter 5.

```
function NewRndNo(var seed: real): real;
begin
   seed := exp(seed + 3.1415926535;          (*get fat number*)
   seed: = seed – trunc(seed);               (*chop off whole part*)
   NewRndNo := seed                          (*crucial step!*)
end;                                         (*NewRndNo*)
```

Notice that seed is a variable parameter! By using seed as a variable parameter, we eliminate the need for a global variable. Every time this function gets activated, the value of seed will be changed. The value of seed is supplied before the NewRndNo function is called. For example, if seed = 2.7 and we can activate NewRndNo 10 times as follows:

```
for trial := 1 to 10 do
  write(NewRndNo:3:2)
```

This loop produces the following numbers:

0.33, 0.10, 0.61, 0.39, 0.19, 0.89, 0.57, 0.82, 0.69, 0.23

The first of these numbers is obtained in the following way:

```
      seed  := exp(2.7 + 3.1415927)
             = exp(5.841592700)
             = 344.3273143
      seed  := seed - trunc(seed)
             = 344.3273143 - trunc(344.3273143)
             = 344.3273143 - 344
             = 0.3273143
 NewRndNo := 0.3273143
```

All of these values of the function designator are between 0 and 1. This gives us the following inequality (invariant assertion):

$0 \leq \text{NewRndNo} < 1$

A program to produce some of these numbers is given in Figure 7.9. Notice that each time the NewRndNo function is activated, the old value of seed becomes the basis for a new seed and a new random number. We can use the values of NewRndNo to produce random numbers inside a desired interval above 0 and 1. For example, suppose we want to produce random numbers in the interval from 1 to 100. We can do this as follows:

SampleNo := trunc(NewRndNo(starter) * 100) + 1

We can explain the production of random numbers in the 1 to 100 interval by tracking what happens to NewRndNo (starter) in the above assignment statement. Notice that all values of NewRndNo are in the following interval:

0 <= NewRndNo(starter) < 1

Here is what happens when the above statement is executed.

```
0 <= NewRndNo(starter) < 1                (*NewRndNo(starter) result in 0
                                                            to 1 interval*)
0*100 <= NewRndNo(starter)*100 < 100          (*argument for trunc()*)
0 <= trunc(NewRndNo(starter)*100) < 100          (*produces a number
                                                in the 0-to-99 interval*)
0 + 1 <= trunc(NewRndNo(starter)*100) + 1 < 101            (*produces
                                           a number in 1—to-100 interval*)
```

This gives us another invariant assertion, one you can test when you use the above assignment in a program.

1 <= trunc(NewRndNo(starter) * 100) + 1 < 101

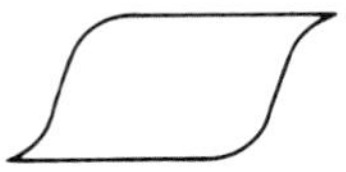

```
            (*Method: Set up a user-defined function to produce random
                              numbers in the interval from 0 to 1*)

program samples (input, output);

 (*- - - - - - - - - - - - - - - - - - - - - - - - - - - - - - - - - - - -*)
                  (*Produce a random number in 0-to-1 interval*)

  function NewRndNo(var seed:real):real;
  begin
     seed := exp(seed + 3.1415926535);            (*fat number*)
     seed := seed - trunc(seed);             (*chop off whole part*)
     NewRndNo := seed                              (*crucial step!*)
  end;                                                 (*NewRndNo*)

 (*- - - - - - - - - - - - - - - - - - - - - - - - - - - - - - - - - - - -*)
         (*Program manager: get values and activate procedure*)

  procedure driver;
  var
     starter: real;                       (*starts NewRndNo function*)
     choice: integer;                    (*how many numbers to print*)
  begin
     repeat
        write('Enter seed: '); readln(starter); writeln;
        write('Enter no. of samples to print: ');
        readln(choice); writeln;
        repeat
           writeln(NewRndNo(starter):30:2);
           choice := choice - 1
        until choice = 0
     until 1 > 2
  end;                                                     (*driver*)
begin
  driver                                  (*activate driver procedure*)
end.
```

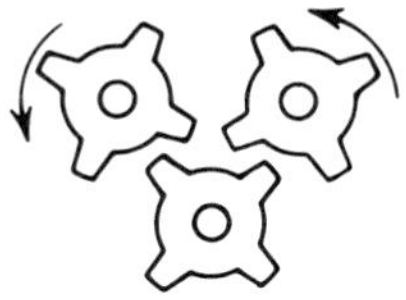

```
Enter seed: 2.71828

Enter no. of samples to print: 10
        0.68
        0.65
        0.52
        0.79
        0.77
        0.09
        0.21
        0.50
        0.09
        0.37
Enter seed: ^C
```

FIGURE 7.9 Generating random numbers

We leave it as an exercise to carry out this idea in a program to produce integer random numbers. (This will be very similar to the program already given in Figure 5.4.) You may be wondering how we can check just how reliable a random number function can be. We explore this idea in Section 7.11.

7.11 Checking for Randomness

The numbers in a sequence are considered random, if each one is equally likely to occur. For example, if we produce 1000 numbers from 1 to 10, there should be the following distribution of numbers, if they are perfectly random:

Number	*Frequency Number Occurs*
10	100
9	100
8	100
7	100
6	100
5	100
4	100
3	100
2	100
1	100

That is, even though the 1000 numbers are scattered, there should be 100 tens, 100 nines, and so on. The distribution, in other words, will be uniform. No random number will appear more often than any other random number. Here is an algorithm to measure the randomness of numbers produced by the rnd function.

```
        (*input: seed, starter, initialized array, maximum sample size;
                                      output: array of frequency counts*)
begin
  initialize a count array with 0s;
  initialize a seed for NewRndNo function;
  initialize max (try max := 1000);
  initialize SampleNo with 0;
  while SampleNo is less than max do
    begin
      assign trunc(NewRndNo(starter) * 100) + 1 to No;
      add 1 to count[No];
      add 1 to SampleNo
    end
end;                                      (*testing for randomness*)
```

In other words, each time one of the random numbers is produced between a and 100, this value is used to select the cell of the count array to increment by 1. When we implement this algorithm, it would be helpful to print a star to represent the occurrence of the same random value 1 or more times. For example, we can print a star for every 10 occurrences of a number in the interval from 1 to 10. We can do this with a sleight of hand using the count array. How? We know, for example,

count[10] contains the number of times 10 occurred,
count[9] contains the number of times 9 occurred,
and so on

If we assume, for example,

count[10] = 93

then

count[10] **div** 10 = 9

and use this to print 9 stars to represent the approximate number of times a random number has occurred. Try this in the following loop:

```
for sample := 10 downto 1 do begin
   write(sample, count[sample]);
   for sample := 1 to (count[sample] div 10) do
      write('*');
   writeln                              (*to move to next line of table*)
   end
```

The first row of the table produced by these nested loops has the following appearance:

10 93 *********

Putting these ideas together, we can set up the following driver for a program to check for randomness:

```
begin
   initialize HowMany;                          (*number of samples*)
   initialize SampleSize;                    (*largest random number*)
   initialize frequencies table with 0;
   build a table of frequencies of random numbers;
   print frequency table heading;
   print frequency table
end                                             (*driver algorithm*)
```

This algorithm leads to a structure chart like the one shown in Figure 7.10. We show a program to carry out this idea in Figure 7.11.

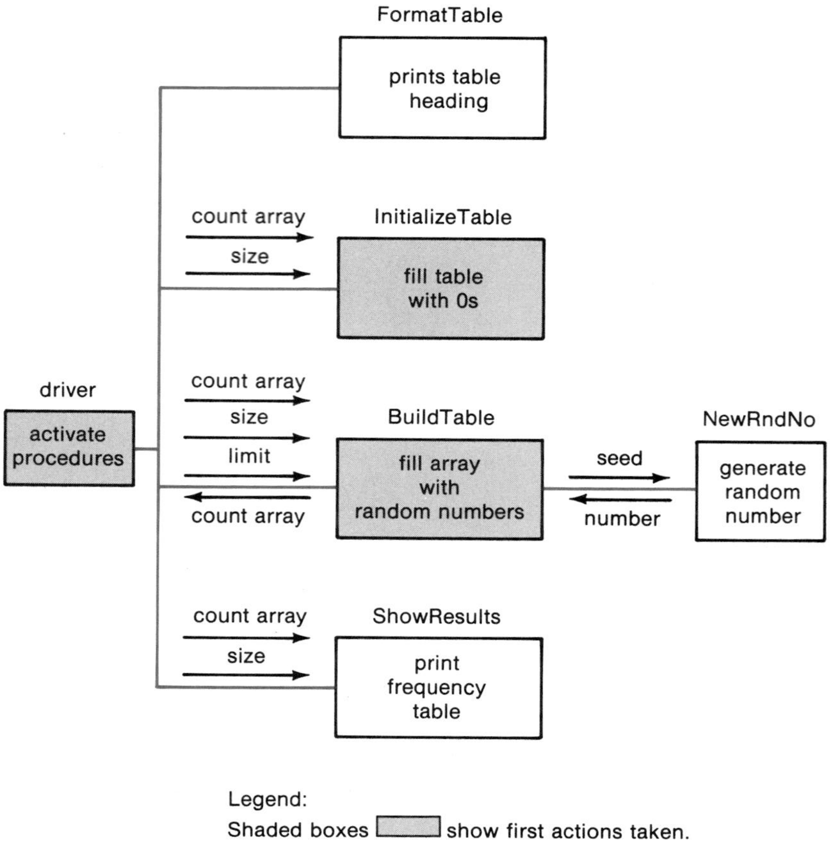

FIGURE 7.10
Structure chart for a frequency count program

```
        (*Method: Set up a user-defined function to produce random
                  numbers in the interval from 0 to 1, then keep
              track of the frequency each random number occurs*)
program samples(input, output);
  const
    max = 100;                                (*maximum array size*)
  type
    nos = array[1..max] of integer;                   (*array type*)

 (*------------------------------------------------------------*)
                         (*Produce random number in 0-to-1 interval*)

  function NewRndNo(var seed: real): real;
    begin
      seed := exp(seed + 3.1415926535);               (*fat number*)
      seed := seed - trunc(seed);            (*chop off whole part*)
      NewRndNo := seed                             (*crucial step!*)
    end;                                              (*NewRndNo*)
```

```
(*- - - - - - - - - - - - - - - - - - - - - - - - - - - - - - - - - - - - - - - - -*)
                                                          (*Print table heading*)

procedure FormatTable;
var
   dash: integer;                                          (*control variable*)
begin
   writeln; writeln('no.':10, 'count':10, 'frequency':40);
   writeln;
   writeln('note: each star represents 10 occurences.':40);
   for dash := 1 to 80 do write('–'); writeln
end;                                                           (*FormatTable*)
(*- - - - - - - - - - - - - - - - - - - - - - - - - - - - - - - - - - - - - - - - -*)
                                     (*Make sure count array is filled with 0s*)

procedure InitializeTable(var count: nos;                      (*array of nos*)
                              size: integer);                    (*array size*)
  var
     index: integer;                                 (*array index variable*)
  begin
     for index := 1 to size do count[index] := 0
  end;                                                      (*InitializeTable*)
(*- - - - - - - - - - - - - - - - - - - - - - - - - - - - - - - - - - - - - - - - -*)
  (*Use random number to select count table cell to increment*)

  procedure BuildTable(var count: numbers;                 (*array of numbers*)
                           size: integer;                        (*array size*)
                           limit: integer);               (*lgst round number*)
  var
     index: integer;                                            (*array index*)
     sample: integer;                               (*random number variable*)
     starter: real;                                     (*starts NewRndNo fn*)
  begin
     write('Enter seed: '); readln(starter); writeln;
     for index := 1 to limit do begin
        sample := trunc(NewRndNo(starter) * size) + 1;
        count[sample] := count[sample] + 1
        end
  end;                                                           (*BuildTable*)
(*- - - - - - - - - - - - - - - - - - - - - - - - - - - - - - - - - - - - - - - - -*)
                                                                (*Show results*)

  procedure ShowResults(count: numbers;                    (*array of numbers*)
                            size: integer);                      (*array size*)
  var
     FirstIndex, SecondIndex: integer;                        (*array indices*)
  begin
     for FirstIndex := size downto 1 do begin
        write(FirstIndex:9, count[FirstIndex]:9, '|':10);
        for SecondIndex := 1 to (count[FirstIndex] div 10) do
           write('*');
        writeln
        end                                                  (*outer for loop*)
  end;                                                          (*ShowResults*)
```

```
(*- - - - - - - - - - - - - - - - - - - - - - - - - - - - - - - - - - - - - - - - -*)
          (*Program manager: get values and activate procedures*)

   procedure driver;
   var
      frequencies: nos;                                  (*array variable*)
      HowMany: integer;                                (*number of samples*)
      SampleSize: integer;                     (*size of lgst random number*)
      dash: integer;                                  (*control variable*)
   begin
      repeat
         write('Enter no. of samples to print: ');
         readln(HowMany); writeln;
         write('Enter largest random no. you wish to use: ');
         readln(SampleSize); writeln;
         InitializeTable(frequencies, SampleSize);
         BuildTable(frequencies, SampleSize, HowMany);
         FormatTable;
         ShowResults(frequencies, SampleSize);
         writeln;
         for dash := 1 to 80 do write('—'); writeln
      until 1 > 2
   end;                                                          (*driver*)
begin
   driver                                     (*activate driver procedure*)
end.
```

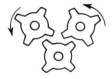

```
          Enter no. of samples to print: 1000

          Enter largest random no. you wish to use: 10

Enter seed: 2.71828

                              Random Number Distribution
```

Note. Each star represents 10 occurences.

No.	*Count*	*Frequency*
10	89	|********
9	79	|*******
8	108	|**********
7	90	|*********
6	122	|************
5	102	|**********
4	92	|*********
3	123	|************
2	93	|*********
1	102	|**********

FIGURE 7.11 Checking for randomness

7.12 Forward References with Functions

A function can have a forward reference. If a function designator is used before the corresponding function is declared in a Pascal program, then that function must be given a forward reference. There are two situations to consider, depending on whether a function has a parameter list or not.

1. A forward reference like

   function EvenNumber: integer; **forward**;

   where there is no parameter list, and

2. A forward reference like

   function choice(*x*, *y*, *z*: integer): Boolean; **forward**;

   where there is a parameter list.

We illustrate both of these situations in the following outline for a whimsical source text:

```
program PasttimeForHobbits(input, output);
  function EvenNumber: integer; forward;
  function choice (x, y, z: integer): Boolean; forward;
  (*- - - - - - - - - - - - - - - - - - - - - - - - - - - - - - - - - - - - - - - -*)
                 (*This procedure calls functions that appear after
                                                 it in the source text.*)
  procedure TryThis;
  var
    FirstNo, SecondNo, ThirdNo: integer;
  begin
    readln(FirstNo, SecondNo, ThirdNo);
    if choice(FirstNo, SecondNo, ThirdNo) then
      write('Goldberry pulled Toms beard!')
    else write('Run for', Even Number, 'number of times')
          .
          .
          .
  end;                                                         (*TryThis*)
  (*- - - - - - - - - - - - - - - - - - - - - - - - - - - - - - - - - - - - - - - -*)
              (*a parameterless function with a forward reference*)
  function EvenNumber;
  var ChosenValue: Integer;
  begin
    readln(ChosenValue);
    EvenNumber := ChosenValue * 2
  end;                                                      (*EvenNumber*)
  (*- - - - - - - - - - - - - - - - - - - - - - - - - - - - - - - - - - - - - - - -*)
              (*a function with parameters with forward reference*)
  function choice;
```

```
begin
   choice := ((x <= y) and (y <= z))
end;                                                    (*choice*)
(*-------------------------------------------------------------*)
begin
   TryThis                                  (*activate procedure*)
end.
```

In this roughed-in source text, a forward reference to the EvenNumber function is needed, since this function is called by the NeedsAnEvenNumber procedure that appears *before* this function in the source text. The EvenNumber function has no parameter list.

If a function with a forward reference has a parameter list, then this parameter list appears only once. That is, the parameter list will appear in the forward declaration, but not in the presentation of the function later in a source text. The choice function in PastimeForHobbits program illustrates this idea. Here is a rule of thumb for forward references to functions.

> **Rule of thumb for functions with forward references:**
>
> **If a function is given a forward reference, then only the function identifier is used in the function heading when the function itself is presented. A forward reference is needed whenever a function designator appears before a function is presented.**

7.13 Information Hiding

Functions make it possible to "hide" the expression(s) used to produce a value. Functions can be used to streamline procedures. The focus is on the result rather than on the machinery used to obtain a result. By using functions, we can make the source text for a procedure look more like pseudocode. This technique increases the readability and maintainability of a procedure. This technique also makes program development easier because it gives us another way separate the tasks of a program. In effect, we are making use of the divide-and-conquer principle in another way.

There are other forms of information hiding in Pascal programs. For example, each time we use a built-in input or output procedure, we are using a hidden procedure. For example, we can use the following statements:

```
writeln('Do you like ice cream?');
readln(answer);
```

These two statements use procedures that are hidden.

Our main interest is not the hidden information (the built-in writeln and readln procedures) but on the results produced by the hidden procedures. By using information hiding, we separate a hidden mechanism used to obtain a result from the result (the value) itself. This is a good programming strategy because it helps simplify our programs.

7.14 Information Hiding: Functions as Parameters

In standard Pascal, it is possible to set up procedures that use functions as parameters. This makes it possible to activate the same procedure with a different function each time it is activated. This will be legal as long as the function used as an actual parameter has exactly the same heading as the function used as a formal parameter.

In other words, a procedure can have a function parameter that is an "alias" for more than one function. Since an alias is used, the functions used to activate the procedure will remain hidden. The focus in the procedure is on using the result from the function used as an actual parameter instead of on the function itself. For example, here are some procedure headings with function parameters.

```
procedure MyStyle(function DoThis(x, y, z: real):Boolean;
                   Truth, Beauty, Goodness : real);
procedure ShowLog(function ThisLog(x: integer): real;
                  base: integer'
                  argument: integer);
```

We can activate MyStyle, for example, with more than one function as long as the functions we use have identical headings (except for the function identifier)—ones that match the structure of the DoThis formal parameter in the heading for MyStyle. Here are two functions with identical headings (except for the function identifier), which match the TryThis function parameter of the MyStyle procedure:

```
function choice(length, cost, profit: real): Boolean;
begin
  choice := ((length < cost * FudgeFactor)
                and (profit/cost > FudgeFactor))
end;                                                      (*choice*)
```

and

```
function AnotherChoice(audience, young, old:real):Boolean;
begin
  AnotherChoice := (audience - old < young)
end;                                        (*AnotherChoice*)
```

The body of each of these functions is different. Yet the structure of each heading matches the heading of the formal function parameter DoThis in the parameter list for the MyStyle procedure. So we can activate MyStyle, first using the choice function as an actual parameter, then using AnotherChoice as an actual parameter. For example, we can do this in the following ways:

MyStyle(choice, value*A*, value*B*, value*C*)

and

MyStyle(AnotherChoice, value*A*, value*B*, value*C*)

where

value*A*, value*B*, and value*C* are of type real

Notice that the function identifier *DoThis* (in the MyStyle heading) serves as a local alias, first for the choice function and then for AnotherChoice. There is a subtlety about this that still may not be apparent from the above examples. That is, even though the entire function heading appears as a formal parameter, only the function identifier of this parameter will be used within a procedure. The values of the function parameter list either must be passed separately to a procedure when it is activated or must be supplied inside a procedure. In the above example, the MyStyle procedure does not receive values for the formal parameter list for the DoThis function, so these must be supplied by MyStyle, whenever it activates the DoThis function.

This is another way of saying that when a function is used as an actual parameter, only the particular function is identified, not any of its parameters (if there are any!). Here is a rule of thumb to remember.

Function-as-parameter rule:

When an actual parameter is a function, only the specific function identifier is specified. Any function parameters must be supplied as separate actual parameters or obtained locally within a procedure.

Here is the pseudocode for a driver that uses the MyStyle procedure to go about its business.

```
begin
   make a choice from the following menu:
      Menu:
         ----> 1) evaluate classical recording;
         ----> 2) evaluate jazz recording;
         ----> 3) evaluate rock'n'roll recording;
         ----> 4) evaluate ragtime recording;
         ----> 5) exit
   if choice is 1 then begin
      initialize length, cost, profit;
      MyStyle(choice, length, cost, profit)
      end
   else if choice = 2 then begin
      initialize TotalAudience, young, old;
      MyStyle(AnotherChoice, TotalAudience, young, old)
      end
   and so on
end                                          (*algorithm for new driver*)
```

A structure chart that reflects this program design idea is shown in Figure 7.12. Notice all four MyStyle formal parameters can be varied by the driver procedure. This can be done by changing the *intent* of the actual parameters used in the driver procedure. You can do this by using a case statment in the driver procedure, which specifies different uses of the actual parameters, depending on the menu choice made. A program to carry out this idea is given in Figure 7.13.

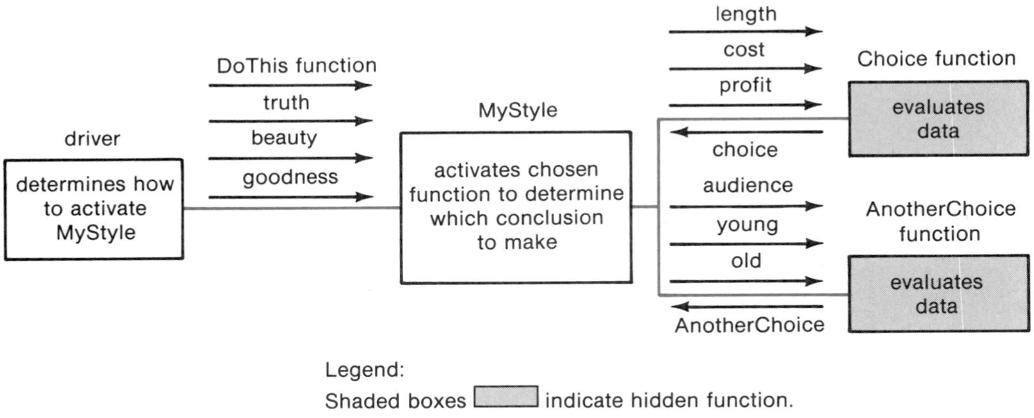

FIGURE 7.12
Structure chart for a program with function parameters

```
        (*Method: Activate a procedure with a function parameter
                       with different actual function parameters.*)

program choice(input, output);
const
  FudgeFactor = 0.5;                             (*arbitrary constant*)

 (*-----------------------------------------------------------------*)
                                           (*Hidden from MyStyle procedure*)

  function choice(length, cost, profit: real):Boolean;
  begin
    choice := ((length < cost*FudgeFactor)
              and (profit/cost > FudgeFactor))
  end;                                                      (*choice*)

 (*-----------------------------------------------------------------*)
                                           (*Hidden from MyStyle procedure*)

  function AnotherChoice(audience, young, old: real):Boolean;
  begin
    AnotherChoice := (audience - old < young)
  end;                                               (*AnotherChoice*)

 (*-----------------------------------------------------------------*)
                                   (*This procedure uses a hidden function*)

  procedure MyStyle(function DoThis(x,y,z: real):Boolean;
                    Truth, Beauty, Goodness: real);
  begin
    case DoThis(Truth, Beauty, Goodness) of
      true: writeln('Yes, record this music!');
      false: writeln('No, try some other music.')
      end                                                     (*case*)
  end;                                                     (*MyStyle*)

 (*-----------------------------------------------------------------*)
                           (*Program manager: decide which function to use*)

  procedure driver;
  var
    valueA, valueB, valueC: real;                (*actual parameters*)
    option: integer;
  begin
    repeat
      writeln('Menu':20);
      writeln('--->':20, '1 evaluate classical recording;');
      writeln('--->':20, '2 evaluate jazz recording;');
      writeln('--->':20, '3 evaluate RockNRoll recording;');
      writeln('--->':20, '4 evaluate ragtime recording;');
      writeln('--->':20, '5 exit');
      readln(option);
      case option of
```

```
            1: begin
                  write('Enter length, cost, profit: ');
                  readln(valueA, valueB, valueC); writeln;
                  MyStyle(choice, valueA, valueB, valueC)
               end;
            2: begin
                  write('Enter total audience, young, old: ');
                  readln(valueA, valueB, valueC); writeln;
                  MyStyle(AnotherChoice, valueA, valueB, valueC)
               end;
            3: ;                                  (*empty for now*)
            4: ;                                  (*empty for now*)
            5:                                    (*empty for exit*)
            end;                                          (*case*)
         until option = 5
   end;                                                 (*driver*)
begin
   driver                             (*activate driver procedure*)
end.
```

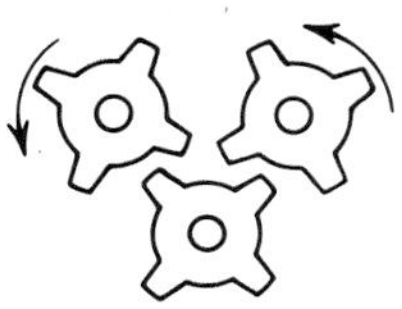

```
      Menu
      --->1 evaluate classical recording;
      --->2 evaluate jazz recording;
      --->3 evaluate RockNRoll recording;
      --->4 evaluate ragtime recording;
      --->5 exit
entry: 1

         Enter length, cost, profit: 2 14.95 1.25

   No, try some other music.
      Menu
      --->1 evaluate classical recording;
      --->2 evaluate jazz recording;
      --->3 evaluate RockNRoll recording;
      --->4 evaluate ragtime recording;
      --->5 exit
entry: 2

         Enter total audience, young, old: 5000 5900 800

   Yes, record this music!
      Menu
      --->1 evaluate classical recording;
      --->2 evaluate jazz recording;
      --->3 evaluate RockNRoll recording;
      --->4 evaluate ragtime recording;
      --->5 exit
entry: 5
```

FIGURE 7.13 Information hiding

7.14.1

Refinement: Fleshing Out the Case Statement Used

The case statement in the driver procedure in Figure 7.13 has empty statements next to some of the case labels. These empty statements serve as shells for future statements. Let your imagination roam a little and try fleshing out these empty statements in various ways. This will give you a chance to try activating the MyStyle procedure in various ways. This refinement is left as an exercise.

7.14.2

Refinement: Build Music Evaluation Table

The choice and AnotherChoice functions offer arbitrary ways to evaluate musical recordings. You might want to tinker with these functions to make them produce evaluations that you consider more reasonable. You might also introduce a different choice function for each type of music. It is probably better to use separate functions to do this, since the criteria for evaluating each type of music will probably be different. When you build these choice functions, try imagining yourself in one of the following ways:

1. A purchaser of a new record
2. A manager of a recording company
3. A recording artist

Then design functions that can be used to activate MyStyle. Use MyStyle to build an array of evaluations. Then introduce a ShowEvaluations to print a table like the following one:

		Music Evaluations		
Music Type	*ValueA*	*ValueB*	*ValueC*	*Decision*

In designing the new program, develop a structure chart that shows the framework of your program. These refinements are left as an exercise.

7.15

Procedural Abstraction

A *procedural abstraction* hides the details and method of implementation used to obtain a result in a procedure. A procedural abstraction can be used to streamline a procedure. The goal of procedural abstraction is to make the text of a procedure have the appearance of pseudocode. In other words, we want to increase the readability of a procedure. The following two procedures illustrate the use of procedural abstraction:

Procedure	*Procedural Abstraction*

procedure SketchR2D3;
begin
  writeln('- - - - - - - - -');
  writeln('   o   o ');
  writeln('   ');
  writeln('   ');
  writeln('   O   ');
  writeln('- - - - - - - - -')
end;   (*SketchR2D3*)
	procedure NewSketchR2D3;
	begin
	  DrawLine;
	  DrawAntenna;
	  DrawLine
	end; (*NewSketchR2D3*)

The NewSketchR2D3 procedure relies on user-defined procedures to "say" what is being done. This is a procedural abstraction. By using this abstraction, we have shifted the focus from the machinery used to obtain results (the various writeln statements) to the results obtained (the lines and antenna in this example). You can think of this as a black box approach to procedures. The idea is to show the outside of the "box" (*what* is being done in a procedure) and to hide what is inside the box (*how* results are obtained by a procedure). A graphical interpretation of this idea is given in Figure 7.14.

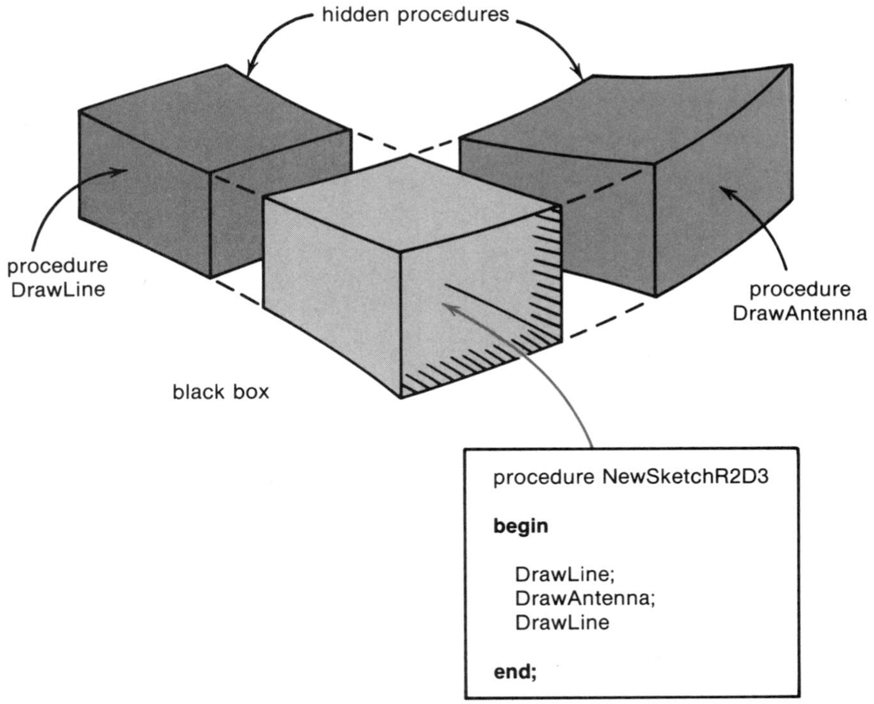

FIGURE 7.14
Graphical interpretation of procedural abstraction

Procedural abstraction is at the heart of top-down design of programs. The idea is to take preliminary versions of our procedures and streamline them. This is done by identifying the subtasks used by a preliminary procedure. This will lead to other procedures *and* to expression abstractions. Functions are especially useful in procedural abstractions. Expressions used to obtain results in procedures can be hidden by using functions. Procedural abstraction gives us the following results:

Benefits of procedural abstraction:

1. Procedures become more readable.
2. By using procedure abstraction, we make a program easier to maintain, since this makes it possible to isolate the tasks that need to be performed.
3. Procedural abstraction separates *how* something is done from *what* is to be accomplished by a procedure.

7.16 Summary

User-defined functions can be used to replace expressions with function designators. This makes expression abstraction possible. *Expression abstraction* hides the function used to compute a single value. By using the technique of expression abstraction, we can add clarity to the source text for a procedure. This technique allows us to shift the emphasis from expression(s) used to compute a result to the result itself. Usually it is the value of an expression, not the expression itself, which is the main interest in a procedure.

User-defined functions can either be parameterless or can be defined with formal parameter lists. When a function has a formal parameter list, value parameters are usually used. Variable parameters are possible. Every function heading has a function identifier, which is used for a function result. This means every function heading must always specify the data type of the function identifier. This is the function result type referenced in the function syntax diagram in Figure 7.1. It is also necessary to assign a value to the function identifier inside a function. That is, every function must include an assignment statement, which assigns the function result to the function identifier. A Pascal function is limited to producing a single result, returning a single value when a function is activated.

A function is activated with a function designator, which consists of the function identifier and actual parameters (if there are any!). Notice that when a parameterless function is activated (called from within a Pascal program), then the function designator consists of just the function identifier. However, the notion of a function designator used to activate a function should not be thought of as the same the function identier. Why? There are two good reasons for keeping these two notions separate.

1. A function designator is used to activate a function. A function identifier is used to return a function result.
2. A function designator consists of more than a function identifier, whenever a function is activated with actual parameters.

There is a severe limitation prescribed by Pascal syntax for a function identifier. That is, a function identifier is limited to being a simple type, or a subrange, or an enumerated type, or a pointer type (we explain pointers in Chapter 11). It is not possible to have a function identifier, which is a structured type. So a function identifier cannot be an array type, for example.

7.17 Keywords Review

Keywords	*Related Ideas*
activate a function	call a function
function	subprogram used to return single result
designator	consists of function identifier and actual parameters (if there are any!)
forward reference	used when a function is referenced before it is defined in a source text
identifier	used to return function result
parameter	either value (usually) or variable
parameterless	without formal parameters
result type	data type of function identifier
as parameter	can be a formal parameter where the function parameter identifier is an alias for a function identifier supplied by a function designator when a procedure with a function parameter is activated (This feature of Pascal supports the use of information hiding—the function referenced by the formal function parameter is hidden.)
information hiding	viewing an object abstractly, leaving the actual object hidden, while the result of its use allows a procedure or function to be developed. A useful tool in the development of procedures, for example, when a function is a formal parameter of a procedure.

7.18 Exercises

1. Explain the differences between a function designator and a function identifier.
2. When a function is used as a formal parameter in a procedure, what parts of the function heading must appear in the heading?

3. How is a function activated in a Pascal program?

4. How does a function differ from a procedure? (*Careful:* List all of the differences, starting with the headings.)

5. When would it be possible for a function to return more than one result?

6. Is it possible for a function to have a formal parameter that is a structured type?

7. When a function is defined, what data types can be used for the function identifier?

8. What is the last thing in every function block?

9. What is wrong with the following functions?

a.

```
function Trial: array[1..10] of char;
begin
  Trial[1] := '1'
end;                                                    (*Trial*)
```

b.

```
function NewTrial(symbol: array[1..10] of char): char;
begin
  NewTrial := pred(symbol[1]) + 1
end;                                                    (*NewTrial*)
```

c.

```
function ThisIsNotOk(one, two, three : integer);
begin
  ThisIsNotOk := chr(one + two + three)
end;                                                    (*ThisIsNotOk*)
```

d.

```
function TryThisOne(yes : Boolean; x, y : integer):real;
begin
  if yes and (y > 0)
    then x := 25 * x + ln(y)
    else x := 25 * x - ln(y)
end;                                                    (*TryThisOne*)
```

10. Write a function called ScanText that has the following features:

a. The formal parameter list for this function includes
script, which is a string type
target, which is type char

b. The result type is type integer.

c. When ScanText is activated, it will return the number of times the target occurs in the script supplied by the function designator. Notice that you will have to work out a method of determining when you have reached the end of the script during a scan of the script. You can do this by passing your own homemade eoln character (a trailing sentinel tacked onto the script when it is created) or passing a count of the number of characters in the script (a primitive way to do the same thing).

11. Write a program to implement the use of the ScanText function developed in exercise 10. Your program should include the following procedures:

a. WordProcessor procedure, which is used to obtain a text from a user and activate the ScanText function
b. Driver procedure, which is used to activate the WordProcessor procedure and determines if the user wishes to reactivate the WordProcessor procedure. Run your program with
c. Text:

   The essential methodology for data abstraction is known as *information hiding*. This approach was first proposed by Parnas in 1972. . . . He proposed that the behavior of software modules be specified completely in terms of their external effects. Such a module hides a secret, namely, the representation of the data object that the module manages. (G. F. Simons, "Data Abstraction," *Byte* October 1984)

   target = *'d'*;

d. Text:

   Old Tom in summertime walked about the meadows gathering the buttercups, running after shadows, tickling the bumblebees that buzzed among the flowers, sitting by the waterside for hours upon hours. There his beard dangled long down into the water: up came Goldberry, the river woman's daughter; pulled Tom's hanging hair. In he went a-wallowing under the water lilies, bubbling and a-swallowing. (J. R. R. Tolkien, *The Adventures of Tom Bombadil,* 1961)

   target = *'a'*

e. Text: same as part (d)

   target = ' ';

f. Text: same as part (d)

   target = *'i'*

12. Refinement of the WordProcessor procedure in exercise 11: Add a new formal parameter to the WordProcessor procedure that is a function with a heading structurally the same as the ScanText function. To do this, use

```
function CheckText(x : StringType;
                   part: TargetType): integer;
```

as the formal parameter. Then modify the ScanText heading so its parameter list matches the CheckText parameter list. In doing this, use a string type for the target, instead of type char. Why? So that a second function called CheckForWords can be set up. Then the WordProcessor procedure can be used to activate either the ScanText or CheckForWords function. You will use the ScanText function to determine the frequency a target character occurs in a text. You will use the CheckForWords function to determine the frequency that a target word occurs in a text. Notice that the driver procedure will be passing to the WordProcessor procedure a specification of which function the user wishes to use. Run your program for

a. Text: same as part (d) of exercise 10

target = 'the'

b. Text: same as part (d) of exercise 10

target = 'Goldberry'

13. Refinement of the program in exercise 12: Add to this program a ShowResults procedure that prints the following table:

First Three Words in Entered Text	*Target*	*Frequency in Text*

Since the program in exercise 12 allows the user to activate the WordProcessor procedure more than once, save the results from the WordProcessor procedure somewhere safe after each activation, then use the driver procedure to activate the ShowResults procedure to print the results in a table. For example, a table like the following one should be printed:

First Three Words in Entered Text	*Target*	*Frequency in Text*
Old Tom in	Summertime	1
Old Tom in	Hours	2
The essential design	He	1

Run your new program for

a. Text: "We're going through!" The Commander's voice was like thin ice breaking. He wore his full-dress uniform, with the heavily braided white cap pulled down rakishly over one cold gray eye. "We can't make it, sir. It's spoiling for a hurricane, if you ask me." "I'm not asking you, Lieutenant Berg," said the Commander. "Throw on the power lights! Rev herup to 8500! We're going through!" The pounding of the cylinders increased: ta-pocketa-pocketa-pocketa-pocketa-pocketa. (James Thurber, *The Secret Life of Walter Mitty,* 1937)
target: We're
target: through (second activation of WordProcessor)
target: '!' (third activation of WordProcessor)
text: same as part (d) of exercise 11;
target: hair (4th activation of WordProcessor)
target: tickling (5th activation of WordProcessor)

b. Text: one you choose;
target: your choice
target: your 2nd choice
target: your 3rd choice
target: your 4th choice
text: one from part (a) of this exercise;
target: your choice (5th activation of WordProcessor).

14. Carry out the refinement of the program in Figure 7.5 described in Section 7.5.1. Give sample runs, using

a. First character = *'a'* and 2nd character = *'z'*;
b. First character = *' '* and 2nd character = *'a'*

15. Carry out the refinement of the program in Figure 7.5 described in Section 7.5.2. Give sample runs, using

a. Same as part (a) in exercise 14 for characters on left-hand side
b. Same as part (a) in exercise 14 for characters on right-hand side

16. Define a function called *Craps* with the following heading:

```
function Craps: integer;
```

Define Craps so that it produces random numbers in the range from 1 to 6. To do this, use a random number generator like the one given in this chapter. In other words, use Peter Henderson's strategy and build your new Craps function using the old rnd function. (Keep the rnd function separate in your program and call it from inside the Craps function.)

17. Write a program that uses the Craps function in exercise 16 to simulate the rolls of a die. Your program should print the numbers that turn up when a die is rolled. Set up your program so that the user can choose the number of times to roll a die. Then run your program for 100 rolls of a die.

18. Write a program that simulates the rolls of a pair of dice. Use a case statement to print pictures of the faces of the dice that turn up. If the total rolled is a 7 or 11 on the first roll, the game is won. Print a message to that effect. A total of 2, 3, or 12 loses the game. On any other total rolled, call the total the point, and keep rolling the dice (with your program!) until you get a 7 (you lose, then!) or the same point turns up again (you win, then!). *Hint:* Just call the Craps function twice, each time, and keep track of the pairs of values produced by Craps.

19. Make an invariant assertion about the rolls of the dice in exercise 18. Test your assertion in terms of the rolls of dice produced by your program, the pairs of numbers that turn up.

20. Write a program using the random number function rnd (given earlier) to produce 1000 random numbers in the range from 1 to 500. Run your program; show the results.

21. Write a program to measure the randomness of the numbers produced by the program in exercise 20. Print a frequency table like the one in Figure 7.11.

22. The following function gives another way to generate random numbers:

```
function KnuthRnd(var seed:integer): real;
begin
  seed := (1987 * seed) mod 65063;
  KnuthRnd := seed/65063
end;                                        (*KnuthRnd*)
```

This function comes from D. E. Knuth (1981). Write a program to print sample data from this generator. Allow the user to select the number of samples produced by KnuthRnd.

23. Write a program that uses the KnuthRnd function in exercise 21 to print random numbers in the range from 1 to 10.

24. Refine the program in exercise 23 so that the user can pick the upper and lower bounds of the random numbers generated. Try using

```
no := trunc(high * rnd);
no := (no mod (high - low + 1)) + low
```

and let the user choose the values for low and high.

25. Assuming low is always less than high, which of these variables determines the upper bound of the range of random numbers generated in exercise 24?

26. Now you have another chance to try your skills with information hiding in developing a procedure. Refine the program in exercise 24 so that it has a CheckRandomness procedure with the following function parameter:

function *f*: real;

Then build into your new program both the old rnd function (the one used in Figure 7.11) and the new one given in exercise 22 (call it *KnuthRnd* in your program). Now fix up a driver procedure so that the user can select one of these random number generators to measure randomness. Then activate the CheckRandomness procedure using the actual function parameter selected by the user. Your CheckRandomness procedure should be used to activate one of the random number generator functions and build a frequency table like the one given in Figure 7.11. Run your program for

a.
generator = rnd;
sample range = 1 to 52;
number of samples = 1000;

b.
generator = KnuthRnd;
sample range = 1 to 52;
number of samples = 1000;

c.
generator = rnd;
sample range = 21 to 55;
number of samples = 1000;

d.
generator = KnuthRnd;
sample range = 21 to 55;
number of samples = 1000

7.19

Review Quiz

Determine whether the following are true or false:

1. A Pascal function can have its own local variables.
2. A function identifier is not needed in a parameterless function.
3. A function designator is used to activate a function.
4. A function designator is just another form of a function identifier used outside a function to activate a function.
5. A function designator can be used without being part of another Pascal instruction.
6. A function identifier can be an actual parameter when a procedure is activated or called.
7. When a function heading appears in a formal parameter list in a procedure heading, the function identifier serves as an alias for an actual function.
8. A function with more than one formal parameter can return (produce) more than one result.
9. If a function block consists of one statement, it must always be an assignment statement.
10. It is possible for an array type to be a formal parameter of a function.

7.20

Case Study: A Guessing Game

We can use a random number generator to get the computer to produce a number we do not see but we know ahead of time the range of numbers in which the result (found by the computer!) appears. This will give us the basis for a guessing game, using the following algorithm:

```
                                    (*input: low, high, seed, and guess;
                                          output: message and score*)
begin
start the game by initializing a seed variable;
initialize low and high;
initialize found with false;
repeat
   activate a NewRndNo function to get random number;
   prompt for a guess by the user;
   if guess = NewRndNo
      then
         begin
            print congratulations! and score;
            assign true to found
         end
      else add 1 to score
   until found = true
end;                                              (*guessing game*)
```

Notice that the higher the score, the poorer the guessing that was done. A quick way to find the number the computer has found is a divide-and-conquer approach in your guessing. That is, if we know ahead of time a random number is between 1 and 100, for example, then try using the middle of this interval for the first guess. If we assume the computer is "thinking" about 84, then here is a divide-and-conquer scenario.

You guess 50, which is low.
You guess 75, which is low.
You guess 87, which is high.
You guess 81, which is low.
You guess 84, which is correct!

This is called a binary search technique. With 10,000 possible consecutive integers to choose from, for example, you should be able to guess the hidden number (the one the compute "knows") in at most 14 guesses. Try it! Write a program to implement the guessing game algorithm.

7.21 Case Study: A Game for Shy Persons

Here is an algorithm for a game for shy persons.

```
                                   (*input: two pairs of characters;
                                              output: message*)
begin
  initialize MyFirst, Mysecond with characters;
  initialize YourFirst, YourSecond with characters;
  activate a function called AddEmUp as follows:
    assign AddEmUp(MyFirst, MySecond) to MySum;
    assign AddEmUp(YourFirst, YourSecond) to YourSum;
  if MySum > YourSum then
    print victory message: "I win!"
  else
    if MySum < YourSum then
      print victory message: "You win!"
    else
      print message: "It's a tie!"
end                         (*algorithm for a game for shy persons*)
```

This game has several wonderfully twisty levels for shy persons, especially ones who favor hiding things. The AddEmUp function activated by this algorithm has the following form:

```
function AddEmUp(first, second: char): integer;
begin
  AddEmUp := ord(first) + ord(second)
end;                                              (*AddEmUp*)
```

The above algorithm is for level 0 of this game. The idea is to pick pairs of characters and compute the sums of the character codes for each pair. If we restrict the character pairs to nonletter and non-numeral characters, then the game gets interesting for everybody. The higher levels of the same game work in the following ways:

1. **Level 1.** Have the computer randomly choose a character from the character table used by your computer system. Then guess that code. You only know the code is inside your character table. You can ask the computer for a hint and it will print out the code of the character next to the one it is thinking about. The computer keeps track of the number of guesses you need. Low score wins.

2. **Level 2.** Think of your character table as a circular list, where the ends of your table are connected. Now a hint from the computer consists of telling you the character within five characters to the right of the one it has found randomly. Each new guess will produce a hint with the character that is one place nearer to the correct one. Limit = 4 guesses. Notice that the idea of a circular list comes into play, if the computer comes up with a code near the ends of your character table. For example, if it comes up with 125 as the decimal code in the ASCII table, it can use "code = 2" in its first hint for the character code, which is five codes "above" or to the right of the randomly selected code. this adds a twist to level 2, which makes it almost baffling for the guesser. To write this level into your program, it will be necessary to use the following technique:

```
if abs(CodeFound - 127) < 5
   then hint := 4 - abs(Codefound - 127)
   else hint := CodeFound + 5
```

For example, if CodeFound (by the computer) is 125 (in the ASCII table), then we get

```
abs(CodeFound - 127) = abs(125 - 127)
                     = abs(-2)
                     = 2
then hint := 4 - abs(CodeFound - 127)
           = 4 - 2
           = 2
```

Notice where this puts you in the ASCII table:

```
···123 124 125 126 127 0 1 2 3 4 5 ···
            ↑                ↑
            |               hint
            └── CodeFound
```

We leave it as an exercise to implement these two levels of the code game in a Pascal program.

7.21.1 Exercises

1. Write the level 0 game for shy persons described at the beginning of Section 7.21. Give some sample runs.
2. (Refinement) Modify the program written for exercise 1 so that guessers can only work with nonletter and non-numeral characters. This will make the game a little more challenging. Give some sample runs.
3. (Refinement) Modify the program in exercise 2 so that it keeps score and prints out a final tally of wins and losses for each player after the last pair of guesses have been entered. Give some sample runs.
4. (Refinement) Modify the program in exercise 3 to allow players to play a level 1 guessing game, if they wish. Give some sample runs.
5. (Refinement) Modify the program in exercise 4 to allow players to play a level 2 guessing game, if they wish. Notice that you should print a menu to allow guessers to choose the game level they wish to use. Your program should keep track of what happens and it should print a report after the game is over. Give some sample runs.

7.22 Readings

Henderson, P. *Functional Programming: Application and Implementation.* Englewood Cliffs, NJ: Prentice-Hall, 1980. See Chapter 1 for discussion of programming with functions.

Shankar, K. S. "Data Design: Types, Structures, and Abstractions," In C. R. Vick and C. V. Ramomoorthy (Eds.), *Handbook of Software Engineering.* New York: Van Nostrand Reinhold, 1984. See Chapter 12 for an excellent discussion of procedure abstraction.

Simons, G. F. "Data Abstraction," Byte, October, 1984, 7, p. 130.

CHAPTER 8

RECORDS AND SETS

In an array all elements are of the same type. In contrast to the array, the record structure offers the possibility to declare a collection of elements as a unit even if the elements are of different types.

Niklaus Wirth, 1982

A set is a data object containing an un-ordered *set of* distinct *values. In contrast, a list is an ordered collection of values, some of which may be repeated.*

Terrence W. Pratt, 1984

AIMS

- Introduce the record structured type and the syntax for various record fields (components of a record type).
- Suggest ways to use the with statement to simplify the problem of accessing record elements.
- Give methods that can be used to build records as well as inspect the components of a record.

- Introduce arrays of records.
- Present variant records.
- Introduce the set data type, set constructors, and set operators.
- Give a case study on sorting arrays of records using a new version of the FindMax procedure given in Chapter 6.
- Give a case study that illustrates the use of variant records.

8.1 Introduction to Records

A *record* is a structured data type. In other words, a record is a collection of values with associated operations that can be used to access these values. Unlike an array, the values held by a record do not have to be all of the same type. Records give us a way to group together various pieces of data that are logically related.

The components of a record are called *fields*. Each record field has a field identifier. Each field identifier is the name of a record component, which can be any of the data types we have seen so far as well as record types themselves. Field identifiers are called the record component selectors. Here are some examples of record types.

```
const
  max = 100;
type
  alfa = packed array[1..16] of char;
                                              (*first record type*)
  TeamMember = record
    BallClub, player: alfa;                   (*name fields*)
    CareerHits, GamesPlayed, years: integer;  (*number fields*)
    end;                                      (*TeamMember*)
                                              (*second record type:*)
  team = record
    logo: alfa;                               (*team name*)
    wins, losses : integer;                   (*number field*)
    pct: real                                 (*number field*)
    end;                                      (*team*)
var
  club: team;                                 (*record variable*)
  league: array[1..max] of team;              (*array of records*)
  ThesePlayers: array[1..max] of TeamMember;
  person: TeamMember;
```

The declaration of a record variable will result in reserved storage for each field of the record. For example, with the person variable, here is what you can expect to find somewhere in computer memory.

Storage for a Record Variable

Record Variable	*Field*	*Memory Content*
Person	person.BallClub	| ?| ?| ··· | ?| ?|
	person.player	| ?| ?| ··· | ?| ?|
	person.CareerHits	| ?|
	person.GamesPlayed	| ?|
	person.years	| ?|

Instead of an array index, the content of a record field can be accessed by appending a point (.) and the field name to the variable name. So, for example,

> **person.years** identifies years field of person

In this example, Pascal will reserve enough storage for each field. Just as in the case with array variables, a record variable will have no values when it is declared. A record variable must be initialized before it can be used.

The record fields make up what is known as a *field list.* Each instance of one of the above records will always have exactly the same number of fields. These records are examples of *invariant records.* The number and type of fields will not vary each time a variable is defined for an invariant record type. In general, an invariant record will have the form

> **record type** identifier = **record** fixed field list **end**;

The first part of this chapter will deal with invariant records. They will become the basis for a case study on sorting records, using a new version of the FindMax procedure introduced in Chapter 6 and the use of what is known as a *sort key.* The syntax for a Pascal invariant record type declaration is given in Figure 8.1. In this chapter we will also examine how to set up variant records. In a *variant record* the number and type of record fields can vary, depending on

Invariant record:

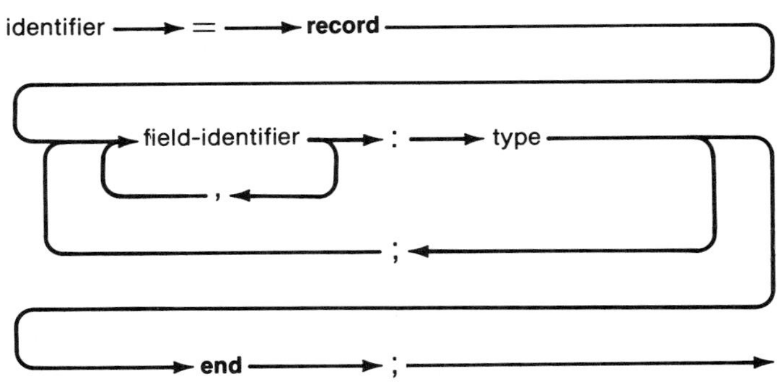

FIGURE 8.1
Syntax for an invariant record

the evaluation of a case statement built into the record. Variant records are very useful. They are well worth the trickiness required to set them up in a program. Variant records will become the basis for a case study on the construction of employee pay records given at the end of this chapter.

8.2 Record Field Designators

A record variable field can be accessed using what is known as a *field designator,* which has the following form:

record variable identifier.field identifier

For example, we can use the following field designators to assign values to the fields of the record variables declared earlier:

```
club.pct := club.wins/(club.wins + club.losses)
                              (*assigns value to last field of club
                                          variable of type team*)
readln(league[1].wins, league[1].losses);
                              (*assigns values to wins and losses
                                 fields of a league array element
                                                  of type team*)
write(person.player, person.manager, person.BallClub)
                              (*prints out string fields of person*)
```

We can use this idea to build an entire record. For example, we can initialize a person variable of type TeamMember as follows:

```
person.BallClub := 'Seattle Mariners';
person.player    := 'Jim Beattie       ';
person.CareerHits := 621;
person.GamesPlayed := 114;
person.years := 5
```

In effect, we have built a record like the one shown in Figure 8.2.

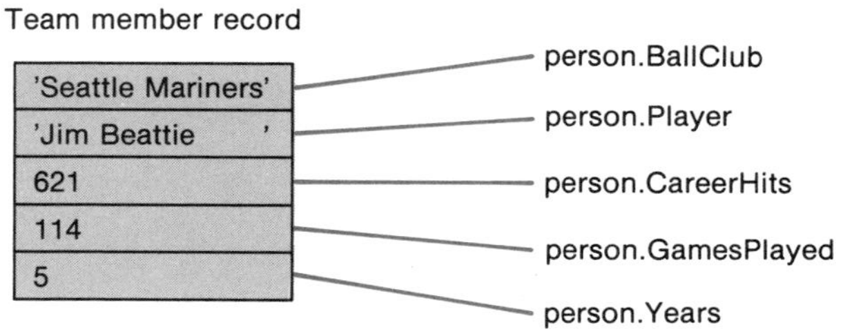

FIGURE 8.2
Sample record

8.3 Assignments between Record Variables

One record variable can be used to initialize another record variable of the same type. For example, we can set up the following variables:

```
var
      person, copy: TeamMember;
```

This says person and copy are record variables of type TeamMember. We can assign the person record to the copy variable using

```
copy := person
```

What happens as a result of this assignment is shown in Figure 8.3. Notice that this is third method we have used to build a record. That is, we have shown the following three ways to build a record:

> **Ways to build a record:**
>
> **1. Direct assignment of component values using a record field designator with the point notation.**
> **2. Assignment of component values using a read statement.**
> **3. Assignment of component values by copying one record to another using an assignment statement.**

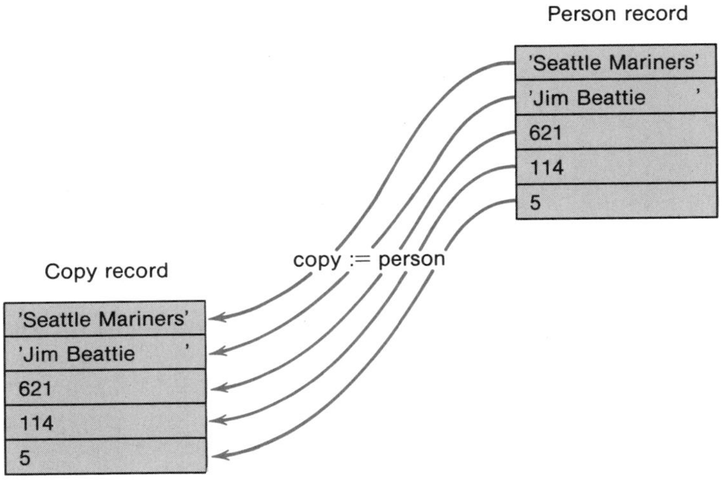

FIGURE 8.3
Making a copy of a record

8.4 Nested Records

It is possible for a record field to be a record type. For example, we can have the following record types:

```
type
   alfa = packed array[1..15] of char;                   (*string type*)
   beta = packed array[1..8] of char;                    (*string type*)
   artist = record
      name: alfa;                                        (*string field*)
      school: beta;                                      (*string field*)
      living: Boolean                                  (*decision field*)
      end;                                                    (*artist*)
   ArtCollection = record
      exhibitor : artist;                                (*record field*)
      works: array[1..max] of alfa;
      DominantColor: (red, blue, yellow, gray);
      motifs: array[1..max] of beta;
      values: array[1..max] of real
      end;                                             (*ArtCollection*)
var
       display: ArtCollection;                        (*record variable*)
```

In this example, the first component of the display record variable is itself a record, namely a record of type artist. We can make multiple use of a point ('.') to set up record designators to access the fields of the record component of the display variable. For example, we can use the following technique to build a sample record:

```
display.exhibitor.name := 'Vermeer                ';
display.exhibitor.school := 'Dutch';
display.exhibitor.living := false;
display.works[1] := 'Lacemaker';
display.works[2] := 'The Coquette';
display.works[3] := 'Love Letter';
display.DominantColor := red;
display.motifs[1] := 'grace';
display.motifs[2] := 'fantasy';
display.motifs[3] := 'message';
display.values[1] := 0.5;
display.values[2] := 0.25;
display.values[3] := 0.4
```

Notice that the first three assignments fill the leading record fields of the display variable. We can also do this using another technique. We can use the sample variable of type artist to do this. Then we can build the sample variable as follows:

```
readln(sample.name);
readln(sample.school);
readln(sample.living)
```

Then we can use a display record field designator to initialize the exhibitor field:

display.exhibitor := sample

In either case, a graphical interpretation of the display record we have built is shown in Figure 8.4.

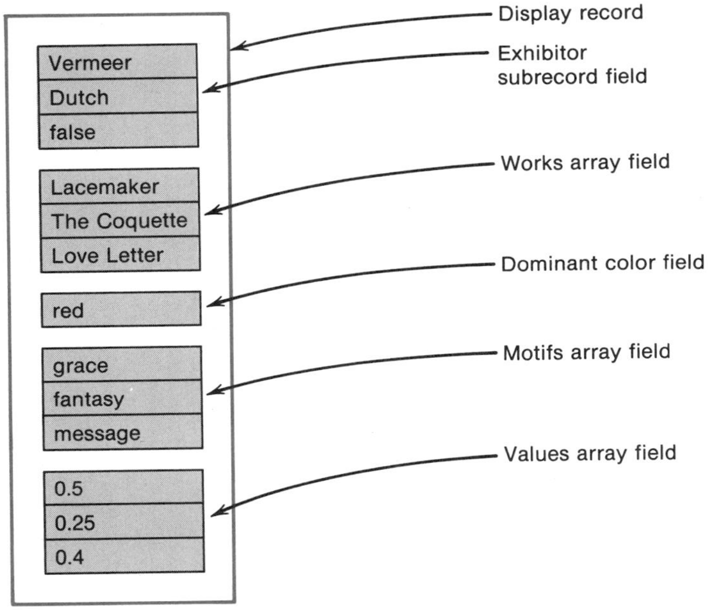

FIGURE 8.4
Sample display record

8.5 The With Statement: A Handy Shorthand

Pascal has a **with** statement that makes it possible to simplify a record designator. This statement has the following form:

with record variable identifier **do** statement

This will allow us to drop the redundant reference to the record variable name seen earlier. The do part of the **with** statement can be set up using only the field names of a record variable. For example, with the person record variable, we can use the following technique:

```
with person do begin
     readln(player);
     BallClub := 'Seattle Mariners';
     readln(CareerHits, GamesPlayed, years)
     end;                                              (*with*)
```

This gives us a handy way to access a more clumsy record like the display variable given earlier. We access the display record by using nested **with** statements to access a nested record. For example, we can use the following technique with the display variable:

```
selector := 1; choice := true;
with display do begin
   with exhibitor do begin
      readln(name);
      readln(school);
      readln(living)
      end;                                          (*with*)
   while selector <= max do begin
      readln(works[selector]);
      readln(DominantColor);
      readln(motifs[selector]);
      readln(values[selector]);
      selector := selector + 1
      end                                           (*while*)
   end;                                             (*with*)
```

8.6 Building an Array of Records

The ThesePlayers and league variables given earlier are an example of an array with elements that are records. We will use the league variable to illustrate how to build an array of records. If we start filling these league records, we get an array like the one shown in Figure 8.5. The level 0 idea for a program to build an array of records is as follows:

```
                                        (*input: records;
                                   output: array of records*)
begin
   build list;
   print list
end                                     (*level 0 algorithm*)
```

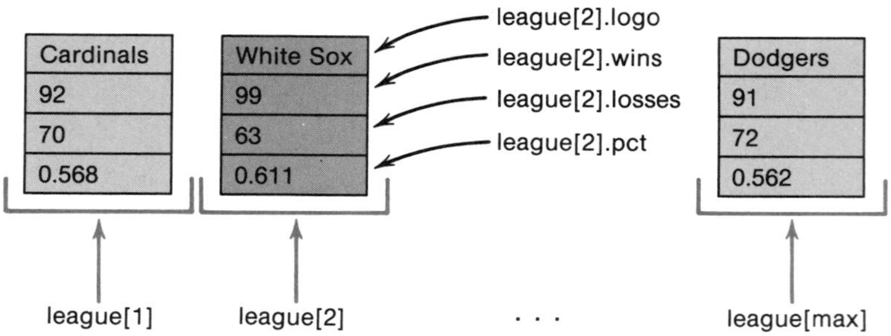

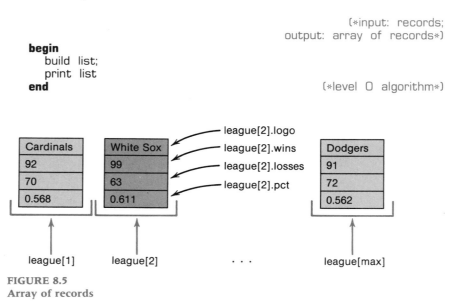

FIGURE 8.5
Array of records

We can refine this level 0 algorithm in terms of an array team record (think of the league array variable given earlier) as follows:

```
                                     (*input: values for record fields;
                                          output: array of records*)
begin
   assign 1 to selector and to choice;
   while (choice is 1) and (selector <= ArrayMax) do begin
      initialize each field of league[selector];
      determine new value of choice
      end
end                                          (*array-builder algorithm*)
```

A structure chart for this program is given in Figure 8.6. We show a program to implement these ideas in Figure 8.7.

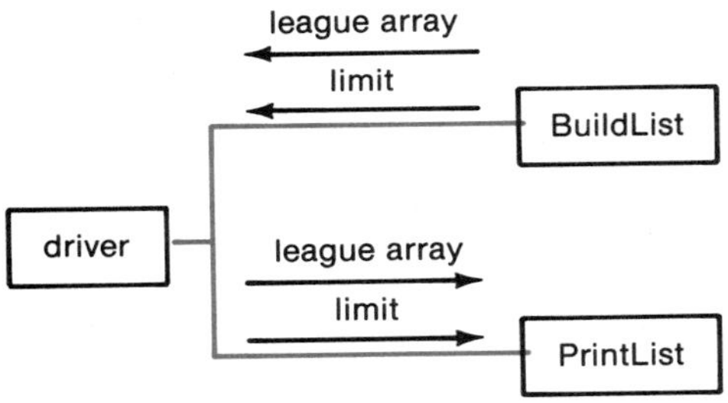

FIGURE 8.6
Structure chart for building an array of records

```
(*Method: This program builds an array of type info, which is an
    array type with components of type team, which is a record
                                                       type.*)

program TeamStandings(input, output);
const
   max = 20;                                  (*maximum array size*)
type
   alfa = packed array[1..15] of char;               (*string type*)
   team = record
      logo: alfa;                                  (*team nickname*)
      wins, losses: integer;                    (*team performance*)
      pct: real                               (*percentage of wins*)
   end;                                                   (*team*)
   info = array[1..max] of team;                       (*array type*)
```

```
(*- - - - - - - - - - - - - - - - - - - - - - - - - - - - - - - - - - - - - - - - -*)
      (*This procedure builds an array of records of type team.*)

procedure BuildList(var league: info;            (*array of records*)
                    var limit: integer);              (*array size*)
var
   choice: integer;                            (*control variable*)
   selector: integer;                               (*array index*)
begin
   selector := 1; choice := 1;
   while (choice = 1) and (selector <= max) do begin
      with league[selector] do begin
         write('Enter logo: '); readln(logo); writeln;
         write('Enter wins, losses: '); readln(wins, losses);
         writeln;
         pct := wins/(wins + losses)
         end;                                             (*with*)
      selector := selector + 1;
      write('Again- -type 1, to continue, 0, to stop: ');
      readln(choice); writeln
      end;                                               (*while*)
   limit := selector - 1                        (*A crucial step!*)
end;                                                 (*BuildList*)

(*- - - - - - - - - - - - - - - - - - - - - - - - - - - - - - - - - - - - - - - - -*)
         (*This procedure prints a copy of the league records.*)

procedure PrintList(league: info;                (*array of records*)
                    limit: integer);                  (*array size*)
var
   NewSelector: integer;                            (*array index*)
begin
   writeln;
   for NewSelector := 1 to 75 do write('-'); writeln;
   writeln('team standings:' : 45); writeln;
   writeln('team':10, 'wins':10, 'losses':10, 'pct':10); writeln;
   for NewSelector := 1 to 75 do write('-'); writeln;
   for NewSelector := 1 to limit do
      with league[NewSelector] do begin
         write(logo:10, wins:10, losses:10, pct:10:4); writeln
         end;                                              (*for*)
   for NewSelector := 1 to 75 do write('-'); writeln
end;                                                 (*PrintList*)

(*- - - - - - - - - - - - - - - - - - - - - - - - - - - - - - - - - - - - - - - - -*)
           (*This procedure activates the appropriate procedures
                 to build and then to print the league records.*)

procedure driver;
var
   OurList: info;                     (*array of records variables*)
   OurLimit: integer;                                (*array size*)
begin
   BuildList(OurList, OurLimit);
   PrintList(OurList, OurLimit)
end;                                                    (*driver*)
```

```
(*- - - - - - - - - - - - - - - - - - - - - - - - - - - - - - - - - - - - - - - -*)

begin
   driver                                        (*activate driver procedure*)
end.
```

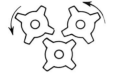

```
Enter logo: whippets

Enter wins, losses: 32 9

Again- -type 1, to continue, 0, to stop: 1

Enter logo: twins

Enter wins, losses: 55 21

Again- -type 1, to continue, 0, to stop: 1

Enter logo: avon

Enter wins, losses: 34 17

Again- -type 1, to continue, 0, to stop: 0

- - - - - - - - - - - - - - - - - - - - - - - - - - - - - -
```

Team standings

Team	*Wins*	*Losses*	*Pct*
whippets	32	9	0.7805
Twins	55	21	0.7237
Avon	34	17	0.6667

FIGURE 8.7 Building an array of records

8.7 Refinement: Expression Abstraction of a PctOfWins Function

The program in Figure 8.6 gives us an opportunity to try an expression abstraction. We can do this by replacing the line

pct := wins/(wins + losses)

with a function call like

pct := PctOfWins(wins, losses)

This means we need to set up a PctOfWins function to carry out the calculation of the pct value. This opens the possibility of the same function being used by more than one procedure. It simplifies the BuildList procedure, hiding what the PctOfWins function looks like, which is not what is important in this procedure. The main concern is with the result, namely, the percentage of wins chalked up by a team member. This refinement is left as an exercise.

8.8 Variant Records

So far we have worked exclusively with invariant records, ones with a fixed number of fields and types. In Pascal it is also possible to set up a variant record type where the number of fields will vary, depending on the way a record variable is initialized. A variant record can have a fixed (invariant) part and/or a variant part, which is specified by what is known as a *tag type*. This tag type identifies a case-constant list. For example, we can have the following record type, which has only a variant part:

```
type
   affiliation = (Hobbitville, MiddleEarth, Mars, Pluto);
   hobbit = record
      case  dweller: affiliation of
         Hobbitville: (hikes, climbs: integer);
         MiddleEarth: (burrows, digs: integer);
         Pluto, Mars: (distance, weight: real)
         end;                                              (*hobbit*)
```

In this example, dweller is a tag of type affiliation. This tag will allow to select which field of this record to activate. That is, when we build a record variable of type hobbit, we will select one of the fields tagged by the value of dweller. We can illustrate this as follows:

1. Introduce

```
var
   sample: hobbit;
```

2. Assign a tag value as follows:

```
sample.dweller := MiddleEarth;
```

3. Activate a record field using

```
with sample do
   case dweller of
      Hobbitville: readln(hikes, climbs);
      MiddleEarth: readln(burrows, digs);
      Pluto, Mars: readln(distance, weight)
   end;                                                  (*case*)
```

In this example, only the MiddleEarth field will be activated. The other fields will remain undefined during the lifetime of this record. Notice that this time the case statement has an end, whereas the case list in the declaration of the variant record does not have an end.

As a rule, only one case list can be used in a record and this case list should be given last in the list of record components. Notice that there is another way we could have declared the variant hobbit record.

```
hobbit = record
   case affiliation of
      Hobbitville: (hikes, climbs: integer);
      MiddleEarth: (burrows, digs: integer);
      Pluto, Mars: (distance, weight: real)
      end;                                               (*hobbit*)
```

Now the tag for this record is affiliation, instead of dweller. This simplifies the presentation of the record type. Then we would use the following technique in the third of the above steps:

```
with sample do
   case affiliation of
      HobbitVille: readln(hikes, climbs);
      MiddleEarth: readln(burrows, digs);
      Pluto, Mars: readln(distance, weight)
      end;                                               (*case*)
```

The sample record variable of type hobbit is an example of a record that has only a variant part. It is also possible to have a record that has both a fixed (invariant) and variant part. For example, we can have the following record:

```
type
   alfa = packed array[1..20] of char;
   PaySchedule = 1..7;
   salary = record
      name: alfa;
      earnings: real;
      case PaySchedule of
         1: (wage, hours, OverTime, OverTimeWage: real);
         2: (commission, sales: real);
         3: ();                  (*for retirement benefits package*)
         4: (rate, time, tips: real);
         5: ();                      (*for social security package*)
       6,7: ()                      (*for medical benefits package*)
      end;                                              (*salary*)
```

Notice the following things about this record type:

1. | *Fixed Part* | *Variant Part* |
|---|---|
| Name field
Earnings field | PaySchedule case list |

2. Empty fields (ones that can be used for future expansion of this record type) are presented by using empty round parentheses.

3. More than one value of a tag type can be used to select the same tag field to activate. In this example, integer values 6 and 7 will both activate the trailing tag field of this record type.

4. Each tag field list, empty or not, is enclosed by round parentheses.

We illustrate the use of this record type in a case study at the end of this chapter. We now have a considerable expanded view of the field list for a record type. A syntax diagram to bring together these ideas about the structure of a field list is given in Figure 8.8. Variant records are ideal to use in situations where exceptions are common, where the same record is ideally utilized in more than one way. You can imagine a personnel office wanting to store information on different types of employees in different ways. A variant record makes it easier to do this. Here are some things to keep in mind in setting up records with variant parts.

Variant record sand traps:

1. The tag type must be an ordinal type.
2. Tag field lists are always enclosed inside round parentheses and each list must include a trailing type, which tells us the type of each list element.
3. Field list identifiers must be unique (appear only once) inside the same variant record.
4. Only a variant (field list), which has been activated (selected by an appropriate value of the tag type), can be accessed.
5. Empty parentheses can be used to mark an empty field list. This is a safety mechanism and a convenience.

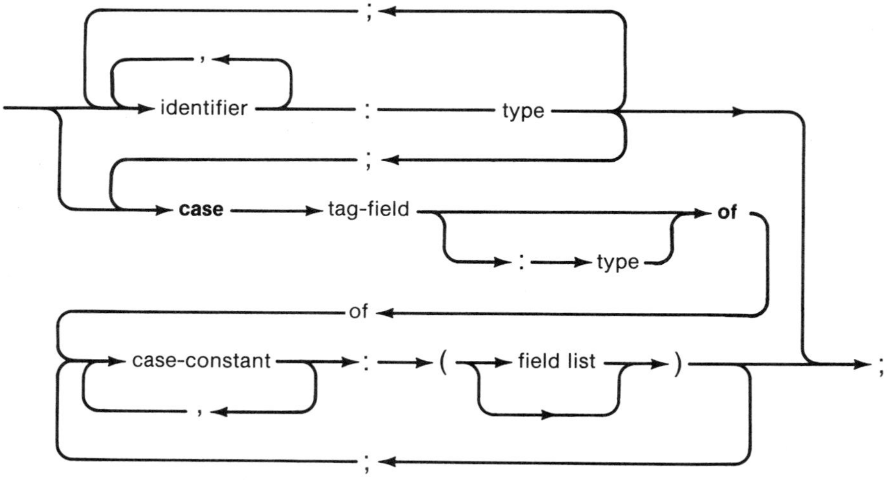

FIGURE 8.8
Syntax for a generalized field list

8.9 Another Structured Type: The Set Type

In addition to record and array types, Pascal also has a set type. This is a structured type. It gets its structure from the subsets of a set. These subsets are the members of a set type. A set type is declared using the following syntax:

set identifier = 'set of' ordinal type;

Here are some examples of set types and set variables.

```
type
   nos = 1..max;
   poets = (Arnold, Blake, Browning, Rilke, Thoreau);
   words = (water, wind, whisper, wild, night, day);
   verse = set of words;
   SchoolOfThought = set of poets;
   marks = set of numbers
var                                                (*set variables*)
   MetaphysicalPoets: SchoolOfThought;
   grades, scores: marks;
   prologue, introduction: verse;
   SomeLetters: set of 'g'..'t';
   SomeNumbers: set of 1..2010;
```

Again, the declaration of a set variable tells Pascal to set aside storage for the set components. It is necessary to initialize a set variable before it can be used. This is done with set constructors.

8.9.1 Set Constructors: Enumerating Set Members

A *set constructor* is used to initialize a set variable. A set constructor has the following form:

[list of member designators]

For example, we can have the following set variable:

```
var
   letter: set of char;
```

Then we can use a set constructor with members of the same type as letter to initialize this variable. Here are some of the ways we can do this:

Assignment	*Comment*
letter := ['a', 'h']	Initializes letter variable with a set constructor with two members
letter := [ ]	Makes letter the empty set
letter := ['g'..'t','5'..'@']	Initializes letter with a constructor with two subranges of type char

A set constructor can also be used to specify the members of a set. Here are some ways to do this.

Set Constructor	*Comment*
[ ]	Empty set
[riverrun]	Set with one member
[cribbage, poker, blackjack]	Set with three members
['!'..'*']	Subrange of character table
['a'..'g', 'A'..'G']	Two subranges of char table
[21,34,55]	Subsequence of Fibonacci nos.
[3..2010]	Subrange of integer scale
['21','34','55']	Three character strings

8.9.2 *Set Operators Used to Produce New Sets*

Set operators can be used to produce new sets. Here is a list of set operators.

Operator	*Operation*
*	Intersection of two sets
+	Union of two sets
−	Difference of two sets

The intersection operator (*) can be used to operate on two sets like sounds and keys given earlier (each with members with type char). The intersection of these two sets, for example, will produce a new set containing those elements common to set sounds and set keys. The new set may be empty. Here are some examples of intersections of set constructors.

['a'..'z'] * ['A','B','a','9'] is ['a']
[20..30] * [10..25] is [20..25]
[20..30, 35, 55] * [2..9] is [ ]

The union of two sets *x* and *y* is the set of those members in *x* or in *y* or in both *x* and *y*. Here are some examples of set unions.

['a'..'z'] + "'A','a'..'e'] is ['A','a'..'z']
[20 .. 30, 35] + [24, 25] is [20..30, 35]

The difference of two sets *x* and *y* is the set of those members in *x* which are not also in *y*. Here are some examples of the differences of two sets.

['a'..'z'] − ['A', 'a'..'e'] is ['f'..'z']
[5, 7, 19, 20] − [19, 21] is [5, 7, 20]

8.9.3 *Set Relational Operators Used to Produce a Boolean Result*

In Pascal there are relational operators that can be used to compare sets and test for set membership to produce a Boolean result. Here are the set relational operators.

Relational Operator	Comment
in	Test membership or set inclusion
=	Test for set equality
<>	Test for set inequality
<=	Tests for inclusion in (included-in operator)
>=	Tests for inclusion (includes operator)

A set relational operator can be used to check the relationship between two sets. We can use these relational operators to set up new Boolean conditions to control program execution. We show how to do this in the following examples:

Statement	Result
1. **if** [2,3] **in** [1..8] **then** PlayCribbage	PlayCribbage procedure is activated, since [2,3] is a member of [1..8]

2. read symbol; (*of type char*)
    while symbol **in** letter **do**
      begin
        drawr2d3;
        readln(symbol);
      end; (*while*)
	Letter is a set of char;
	
	Procedure to draw r2d3 will continue to be activated as long as symbol is in letter

3. **for** symbol := '!' **to** 'z' **do**
    if symbol in letter
      then drawr2d3;
	Whenever symbol is in letter, the procedure to drawr2d3 will be activated

4. **while not** eof **do**
    begin
      readln(symbol);
      letter := letter – [symbol];
      (*take symbol out of letter*)
      if ['e'..'h'] <= letter
        then drawr2d3
    end; (*while*)
	This time, the procedure to drawr2d3 will be activated, if ['e'..'h'] is included in letter

5. readln(symbol);
    while letter >= [symbol] **do**
      begin
        DealHandOfCards;
        readln(symbol)
      end; (*while*)
	Procedure to deal a hand of cards will be activated as long as the letter set includes symbol as a member

8.9.4

Example: A Text Scanner

We can use set types to build a scanner to check how many vowels, for example, there are in a coded message. Here is an algorithm to do this.

```
begin
   initialize a sentinel of type char;
   assign ['a','e','i','o','u','A','E','I','O','U'] to vowels;
   assign 0 to count and to index;
   enter text, a string type;
   repeat
      add 1 to index; read(text[index];
      if text[index] is in set of vowels then add 1 to count
   until text[index] = sentinel
end                                        (*text scanner algorithm*)
```

To implement this algorithm in Pascal, we need the following variables:

vowels, a set variable with members of type char
sentinel of type char, text (a string type)
count of type integer

Using these variables, we can implement the above algorithm as follows:

```
procedure TextScanner(var count: integer;
                         var ThisText: StringType;
                         vowels: SetType;          (*initialized set*)
                         sentinel: char);
var                                                (*index for string*)
   index: integer;
begin
   index := 0; count := 0;
   writeln('Enter text: ');
   repeat
      index := index + 1; read(text[i]);
      if text[i] in vowels then count := count + 1
   until text[i] = sentinel
end;                                               (*TextScanner*)
```

We leave it as an exercise to implement this scanner procedure in a Pascal program.

8.10

Summary

We have added two new structured data types to our toolbox: record and set types. There are three types of record types.

1. An invariant record with only a fixed part, one that always has the same number and type of fields

2. A record with only a variant part, one that has a case list of tag fields and where only one can ever be activated during the execution of a program

3. A record that has both a fixed part and a variant part

We have shown examples of all three types of record variables. When a variable is an invariant record type, it always has a fixed number of fields. These fields can be accessed using a field designator, which has the following form:

record identifier.field identifier

For example, if we have

```
type
   alfa = packed array[1..20] of char;
   CompleteAnglersGuide = record
      BaitToUse, FishToCatch: alfa;
      GoodFishingPlaces: array[1..5] of alfa;
      NoOfFlies, hooks: integer
   end;                                    (*CompleteAnglersGuide*)
var
   sample: CompleteAnglersGuide;           (*record variable*)
```

then we can use the following technique to initialize the fields of the sample record variable:

```
readln(sample.BaitToUse);
readln(sample.FishToCatch);
selector := 1;
repeat
   readln(sample.GoodFishingPlaces[selector]);
   selector := selector + 1;
   readln(choice)
until not choice;
sample.NoOfFlies := 12;
sample.hooks := 3;
```

These assignments can be simplified by using the Pascal with statement. Here is a rewrite of the above statements using the with statement.

```
with sample do
   begin
      readln(BaitToUse);
      readln(FishToCatch);
      selector := 1;
      repeat
         readln(GoodFishingPlaces[selector]);
         selector := selector + 1;
         readln(choice)
      until not choice;
      NoOfFlies := 12;
      hooks := 3
   end;                                    (*with*)
```

Records are useful because they allow us to cluster together pieces of information that are logically related. A record type is a valuable programming tool.

The set type is another example of a structure type in Pascal. A set is a collection of members of the same ordinal type. Sets can be initialized using set constructors, which are instances of set members inside square brackets. New sets can be formed out of old sets using the three set operators.

1. *, for the intersection of two sets to produce a set of all members common to the two sets in an intersection
2. +, for the union of two sets to produce a set of all members in either or both of the two sets in the union
3. –, for the difference of two sets to produce a set of all members in the first set that are not in the second set

There are various ways to test for set membership using the set relational operators.

in, to test if an ordinal value is contained in a set
=, to test for equality between two sets
<>, to test for inequality between two sets
<=, to test if one set is included in another set
>=, to test if one set contains another one

Sets are useful in building new Boolean conditions to control the execution of a program. They also can be used to simplify the method needed to check whether or not an item is contained in a list, for example. This was demonstrated with the construction of a TextScanner procedure to count the occurrences of vowels in a text.

8.11 Keywords Review

Keywords	*Related Ideas*
array of records	array elements each of the same record type
field	component of a record type
designator	record-identifier.field-identifier
fixed part	invariant number of fields
identifier	name of record field
type	can be either a record type or a simple or derived type (subrange or enumerated type) or array type
variant part	case list of fields, only one of which is ever activated
in	set relational operator to test whether or not an ordinal value belongs to a set

record type	mechanism for setting up a collection of components of one or more differing field types
field	component of a record type
identifier	record type name
set type	mechanism for setting up a collection of members of the same ordinal type
constructor	ordinal values inside square brackets
identifier	set type name
structured type	array, record, or set type
variable	can have its content varied
record	variable of record type
set	variable of set type
with statement	simplifies accessing record components

8.12 Exercises

1. How does a record type differ from an array type?
2. How does a record type differ from a set type?
3. Why is a record type a structured type as opposed to a scalar type like type char?
4. How is a record type similar to an array type?
5. What distinguishes a fixed part from a variant part in a record variable with both fixed and variant parts?
6. There are three types of records. Give an example of each type in a complete type declaration.
7. A variant record tag type is limited to what data types?
8. In what ways is a book-filled shelf comparable to a record variable with more than one field?
9. Construct a record type to characterize each of the following:
   a. Information about an airline passenger in the Trans World Airline (TWA) system
   b. Information about a dog registered with the American Kennel Club
   c. Information about an astronaut in the space shuttle program
   d. Information about architects in New York
10. What is a record field designator?
11. Why is a set type a structured type?
12. If we have

```
type
        samples  =  0..21;
        PowerSet  =  set of samples;
var
        nos: PowerSet;
```

which of the following set constructors can be used to initialize the nos set variable?

a. [5··9]
b. [ ]
c. [25]
d. ['3', '5']
e. [3, 5]
f. [9··22]

13. What is the difference between the empty set [ ] and 0?

14. What is the difference between ( ) used to mark an empty spot in a case list in a variant record and the empty set [ ]?

15. How is a case list in a variant record different from a case statement?

16. How is a record field designator constructed?

The following seven questions concern the following record type and record variables:

```
type
   alfa = packed array[1..50] of char;
   day = (M, Tu, W, Th, F, Sat, Sun);
   date = 1..31;
   time = -500··2010;
   year = record
      BirthYear: time;
      month = record
         notes: array[1..20] of alfa;
         week : record
                    WeekDay: day:
                    CalendarDay: date
                 end;                                    (*week*)
      end;                                               (*month*)
   end;                                                  (*year*)
var
   schedule: array[1..12] of year;
   LastYear, ThisYear: year;
```

17. Using record field designators, show how to fill the LastYear record variable with sample information, including three entries in the notes array.

18. Use the with statement to replace all field designators used in exercise 17 to fill the LastYear record variable.

19. Construct a loop that uses the LastYear record variable to initialize three records of the schedule array.

20. Construct a loop that loads the schedule array records directly without a separate record variable of type year like LastYear.

21. Initialize the fields of the ThisYear record variable and then initialize LastYear with ThisYear, only.

22. Write a BuildSchedule procedure to load the schedule array of records of type year used as a variable parameter. Include a variable parameter Limit to keep track of how many records have been put into the schedule array.

23. Write a ShowSchedule procedure to print a copy of the schedule array of records of type year used as a value parameter. Include Limit as a value parameter to hold the count of the number of records in the schedule array. Create a table to show the contents of each record. Devise a scheme for indicating the end of one record and the beginning of another in the table you print.

24. Write a program to implement the TextScanner procedure given in Section 8.9.4. Create a ShowResults procedure to print the following table:

First Five Words of Text	*Vowel Count*

Run your program for
a. Text from exercise 13(a) in Chapter 7 (Thurber, *Secret Life of Walter Mitty*);
b. Text from exercise 11(d) in Chapter 7 (Tolkien, *The Adventures of Tom Bombadil*).

25. Refine the TextScanner procedure from exercise 24 to maintain a history of the vowels found—use a record to do this with

field to hold vowels found
field to hold corresponding count for each vowel

Then refine the ShowResults procedure to produce the following table:

First Five Words of Text	*Vowel*	*Frequency*

Run your program for
a. Text for part (a) of exercise 24
b. Text for part (b) of exercise 24

26. Give the sets produced by the following operations:
a. [5, 6, 8] * [1, 2]
b. [5, 6, 8] * [0..6]
c. [5, 6, 8] + [1, 2]
d. [5, 6, 8] + [0..6]
e. ['a'..'t'] * ['A'..'T']
f. ['a'..'t'] + ['A'..'T']
g. ['a'..'t'] * ['d'..'t']
h. ['a'..'t'] * [ ]
i. ['a'..'t'] + [ ]
j. ['a'..'t'] − [ ]
k. [5, 6, 7] − [1, 5]
l. [5, 6, 7] − [0..9]
m. ['a'..'t'] − ['A'..'T']

8.13

Review Quiz

Determine whether the following are true or false:

1. A field designator can be used to access a record field.
2. A record variable that has only a fixed part always has the same number and type of fields.
3. A record component is a field.
4. A record can have a variant part.
5. A tag type is used to determine which field of the fixed part of a record variable will be activated.
6. It is possible to activate more than one field in a record that has only a fixed part.
7. In a variant record, a case list is used to identify the tag fields of the fixed part of the record.
8. It is possible to have more than one tag field in a variant record.
9. The intersection of two set variables always produces a new set.
10. A set constructor is a constant, which is a set type.

8.14

Case Study: Sorting an Array of Records

Sorting an array of records is made easy by the fact that one record can be assigned to another record in a single assignment statement. To sort an array of records, it is necessary to choose the record field that can be used to guide the sort. For example, if we have

```
type
   alfa = packed array[1..20] of char;
   person = record
      name: alfa;
      age: real
   end;                                                    (*person*)
var
   group: array[1..max] of person;
```

then the records in the group array in two different ways.

1. Sort group records based on the name field
2. Sort group records based on the age field

A record field used to guide and control a sort is called a *sort key*. In the first sort, name is the sort key. In the second of the above sorts, age is the sort key. We can use the idea of a sort key to construct a new FindMax algorithm. We will write this new algorithm to sort an array of team records (of type team given earlier):

```
                                (*input: list of team records, sort key;
              output: position of record with maximum sort key value*)
begin
  read list of team records;
  read a key value of type integer;
  initialize lgst of type team with list[limit];
  initialize i with 1;
  while i < limit do
    begin
      case key of
        1: check := (lgst.wins <= list[i].wins);
        2: check := (lgst.losses <= list[i].losses);
        3: check := (lgst.name >= list[i].name);
        4: check := (lgst.pct <= list[i].pct)
      end;                                                    (*case*)
      if check
        then begin
               assign list[i] to lgst;
               assign i to position variable
             end;                                               (*if*)
      add 1 to i
    end;                                                     (*while*)
  end;                                       (*new FindMax algorithm*)
```

Notice that we have used a technique with type Boolean variables introduced in Chapter 7. That is, check is of type Boolean. It assigned a value of true, if the Boolean condition inside the round parentheses in the above case statement is true. Notice, also, how the key value is used to select the comparison to make. This algorithm will allow use to sort an array of team records in four different ways! Also notice how the inequalities are arranged for the different cases. To put names in lexicographic order, we switch the inequality used in the other three cases. That is, names that begin with letters at the end of the alphabet will appear after those names that begin with letters which appear earlier in the alphabet.

Next we show an algorithm to perform a sort on an array of records using the FindMax algorithm.

```
                                (*input: list of team records, sort key;
                    output: ordered list of records relative to sort key*)
begin
  initialize a variable OldLimit with the list size n;
  read a value for key from the KeyRange;
  repeat
    assign list size n to place variable;
    FindMax(list, n, place, key);
    swap the end element and max element;
    subtract 1 from n
  until n = 1
end;                                      (*new selection sort algorithm*)
```

A structure chart, which brings together these algorithms for a record sort, is given in Figure 8.9. A program to implement these algorithms is given in Figure 8.10.

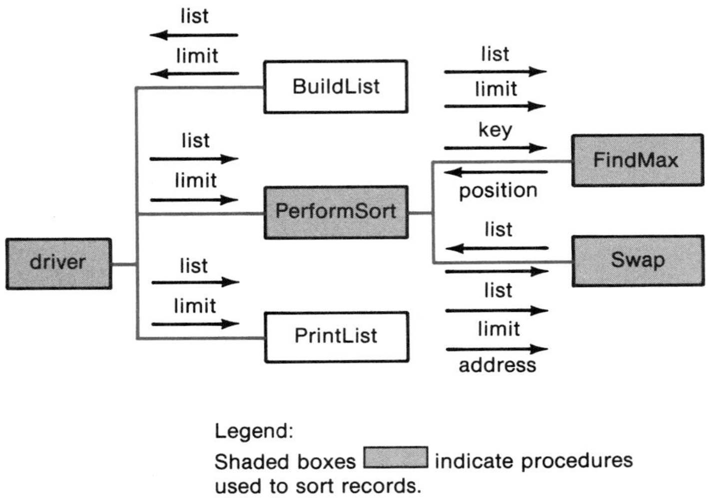

FIGURE 8.9
Structure chart for a program to sort records

```
        (*Method: This program uses the name field of each list record
                  of type team as the sort key. The records are sorted
                     using the selection sort technique from Chapter 6.*)

program NewSelectionSort(input, output);
const
   sentinel = -1;                        (*used to terminate data entry*)
   max = 100;                                (*upper limit on array size*)
type
   beta = packed array[1..10] of char;                    (*string type*)
   alfa = packed array[1..20] of char;                    (*string type*)
   team = record
      logo: beta                                             (*nickname*)
      wins, losses: integer;                         (*team performance*)
      pct: real                                    (*percentage of wins*)
   end;                                                          (*team*)
   info = array[1..max] of team;                           (*array type*)

 (*------------------------------------------------------------------*)
     (*This procedure builds an array of records of type team.*)

procedure BuildList(var list: info;                  (*array of records*)
                          var limit: integer);              (*array size*)
var
   selector: integer;                                     (*array index*)
```

```
begin
  selector := 1; list[selector].wins := 1;
  while (list[selector].wins <> sentinel) and (selector <= max) do
    with list[selector] do begin
      write('Enter team wins- -a -1, to stop: '); readln(wins);
      if list[selector].wins <> sentinel then begin
        write('Enter team logo: '); readln(logo); writeln;
        write('Enter team losses: ');readln(losses); writeln;
        pct := wins/(wins + losses);
        selector := selector + 1
        end;                                                (*if*)
      end;                                                  (*with*)
  limit := selector - 1;                                    (*a crucial step!*)
end;                                                        (*BuildList*)

 (*- - - - - - - - - - - - - - - - - - - - - - - - - - - - - - - - - - - - - - - - - - -*)
                        (*This procedure shows the sorted records.*)

procedure PrintList(list: info;                             (*array of records*)
                    limit: integer);                        (*array size*)
var
  NewSelector: integer;                                     (*array index*)
begin
  writeln;
  for NewSelector := 1 to 75 do write('-'); writeln;
  writeln('team standings: ':45); writeln;
  writeln('team':10, 'wins':10, 'losses':10, 'pct':10); writeln;
  for NewSelector := 1 to 75 do write('-'); writeln;
  for NewSelector := 1 to limit do
    with list[NewSelector] do begin
      write(logo:10, wins:10, losses:10, pct:10:4); writeln
      end;                                                  (*with*)
  for NewSelector := 1 to 75 do write('-'); writeln
end;                                                        (*PrintList*)

 (*- - - - - - - - - - - - - - - - - - - - - - - - - - - - - - - - - - - - - - - - - - -*)
               (*This procedure does a remarkable thing: It exchanges the
                 end record with the one that has the dominant sort key
                                              using a simple sort key.*)

procedure swap(var list: info;                              (*array of records*)
                   limit: integer;                          (*array size*)
                   address: integer); (*location of record to swap*)
var
  buffer: team;                                             (*record variable*)
begin
  buffer := list[address]; list[address] := list[limit];
  list[limit] := buffer
end;                                                        (*swap*)
```

```
(*------------------------------------------------*)
          (*Notice how the key value in FindMax is used to select
                              the correct comparison to make.*)

procedure FindMax(var list: info;                 (*array of records*)
                      limit: integer;                   (*array size*)
                      key: integer;                     (*search key*)
                      var position: integer); (*location of lgst element*)
var
   check: Boolean;                               (*to detect change*)
   lgst: team;                                       (*end record*)
   i: integer;                                       (*array index*)
begin
   lgst := list[limit]; i := 1;
   while i < limit do begin
      case key of                       (*assign true or false to check*)
         1: check := (lgst.wins <= list[i].wins);               (*1*)
         2: check := (lgst.losses <= list[i].losses);           (*2*)
         3: check := (lgst.logo >= list[i].logo);               (*3*)
         4: check := (lgst.pct <= list[i].pct)                  (*4*)
         end;                                                (*case*)
         if check then begin
            lgst := list[i]; position := i
            end;                                             (*then*)
         i := i + 1
      end                                                   (*while*)
end;                                                      (*FindMax*)

(*------------------------------------------------*)
          (*This procedure handles the activation of the FindMax
               and swap procedures after the user has selected a
                                                       sort key.*)

procedure PerformSort(var list: info;             (*array of records*)
                          limit: integer);                (*list size*)
var
   entry: integer;                                         (*choice*)
   place: integer;                       (*location of element to swap*)
begin
   write('Enter sort key number (1 = W, 2 = L, 3 = logo, 4 = pct): ');
   readln(entry);
   repeat
      place := limit;
      FindMax(list, limit, entry, place);
      swap(list, limit, place);
      limit := limit - 1
   until limit = 1
end;                                                  (*PerformSort*)
```

```
  (*------------------------------------------------------*)
           (*Program manager: activate procedures and get choice*)

procedure driver;
var
   OurList: info;                              (*array of records*)
   OurLimit: integer;                               (*array size*)
   choice: integer;                           (*control variable*)
begin
   BuildList(OurList, OurLimit);
   repeat
      PerformSort(OurList, OurLimit);
      PrintList(OurList, OurLimit);
      write('Again?--1 = Y, 0 = N: '); readln(choice); writeln
   until choice = 0
end;                                                    (*driver*)

  (*------------------------------------------------------*)

begin
   driver                             (*activate driver procedure*)
end.
```

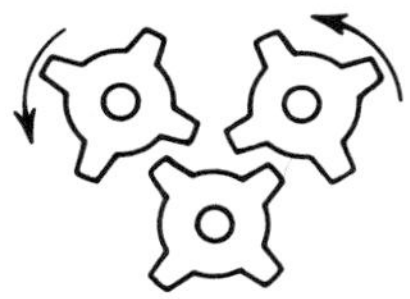

```
Enter team wins--a -1, to stop:  1
Enter team logo:  whippets

Enter team losses:  5

Enter team wins--a -1, to stop:  16
Enter team logo:  twins

Enter team losses:  12

Enter team wins--a -1, to stop:  34
Enter team logo:  lakers

Enter team losses:  55

Enter team wins--a -1, to stop:  9
Enter team logo:  cubs

Enter team losses:  2

Enter team wins--a -1, to stop:  -1
Enter sort key number (1 = W, 2 = L, 3 = logo, 4 = pct): 1
```

Team Standings

Team	*Wins*	*Losses*	*Pct*
Whippets	1	5	0.1667
Cubs	9	2	0.8182
Twins	16	12	0.5714
Lakers	34	55	0.3820

```
Again?- -1 = Y, 0 = N: 1

Enter sort key number (1 = W, 2 = L, 3 = logo, 4 = pct): 2
```

Team Standings

Team	Wins	Losses	Pct
Cubs	9	2	0.8182
Whippets	1	5	0.1667
Twins	16	12	0.5714
Lakers	34	55	0.3820

```
Again?- -1 = Y, 0 = N: 1

Enter sort key number (1 = W, 2 = L, 3 = logo, 4 = pct): 3
```

Team Standings

Team	Wins	Losses	Pct
Whippets	1	5	0.1667
Twins	16	12	0.5714
Lakers	34	55	0.3820
Cubs	9	2	0.8182

```
Again?- -1 = Y, 0 = N: 1

Enter sort key number (1 = W, 2 = L, 3 = logo, 4 = pct): 4
```

Team Standings

Team	Wins	Losses	Pct
Whippets	1	5	0.1667
Lakers	34	55	0.3820
Twins	16	12	0.5714
Cubs	9	2	0.8182

```
Again?- -1 = Y, 0 = N: 0
```

FIGURE 8.10 Sort records with more than one sort key

8.14.1 Refinement: Expanded Team Record

Make the following TeamMember record a field of the team record type:

```
type
   alfa = packed array[1..20] of char;
   TeamMember = record
      player: alfa;
      games, hits, home runs: integer;
      year: 1936..1990
   end;                                          (*TeamMember*)
```

In addition add to the team record a year field of type integer. Then expand the KeyRange to allow for key values for the new team record fields. This will mean refinements will need to be made in the FindMax and PrintList procedures to allow for the new sorts. You want to allow the user to construct team records for a single team and sort the records by player's name, by year, and so on. This will mean more than one record will probably have the same team name, one for each player. This will mean setting up a case statement inside the PrintList procedure to handle the following tables: (a) the same table printed in Figure 8.0 and (b) the following table:

Team	*Player*	*Games*	*Hits*	*Home Runs*	*Year*

Notice the program in Figure 8.8 does not do anything with the manager field of a record of type team. This should be taken care of in the refined version of this program. That is, you should also prompt for a manager's name for each team record. You should also make it possible to sort the team records by manager.

8.14.2 Exercises

1. Carry out the suggested refinements given in the previous section for the program in Figure 8.8. Run your program for team standings of your favorite sport. Then run your program to print out
   a. Team table sorted by percentage of wins
   b. Player table (see part (b) of Section 8.14.1) sorted by games played
   c. Player table sorted by home runs
   d. Player table sorted by player

2. Write a program to sort an array of records holding information about books you own. You should be able to sort this array by title or by author or by copyright year. In a trial run of your program use the following list of books:
   a. Author: Niklaus Wirth
      title: *Programming in Modula-2*
      year: 1982
   b. Author: Robert L. Kruse
      title: *Data Structures and Program Design*
      year: 1984

c. Author: Kathleen Jensen, Niklaus Wirth
title: *Pascal User Manual and Report*
year: 1974

d. Author: Isaac Asimov
title: *I, Robot*
year: 1950

e. Author: George Polya
title: *How to Solve It*
year: 1957

Run your program for

f. Sort by author (use leading author's last name)

g. Sort by title

h. Sort by year

8.15 Case Study: Business Applications for Variant Records

In a personnel office, it is necessary to maintain pay records for each employee. In the Gandalf Ring Company, it is necessary to maintain records for the following persons:

1. Persons with a straight wage
2. Sales persons who earn a commission
3. Persons who earn a fixed wage plus tips in the Gandalf coffee shop

In Figure 8.11, we show a program to build records for each of these types of persons.

```
          (*Method: This program uses a record of type salary that
           has both a fixed part (the name and earnings fields) and
                                                 a variant part.*)

program PersonnelOffice(input, output);
type
  alfa = packed array[1..20] of char;
  salary = record
    name: alfa;                                  (*employee name*)
    earnings: real;                          (*employee earnings*)
    case PaySchedule: integer of                  (*variant part*)
      1: (wage, hours, OverTime, OverTimeWage: real);
      2: (commission, sales: real);
      3: ( ):                   (*for retirement benefits package*)
      4: (rate, time, tips: real);
      5: ( );                        (*for social security package*)
      6: ( )                        (*for medical benefits package*)
end;                                                    (*salary*)
```

```
(*- - - - - - - - - - - - - - - - - - - - - - - - - - - - - - - - - - - - - - - - - - - - -*)
   (*This procedure builds a payroll record. Notice how the value
 of sample.PaySchedule determines which case field to activate.*)

procedure BuildRecord(var sample: salary);
begin
   writeln(' ':10, 'menu:');
   writeln(' ':20, '- -> 1. hourly wage with overtime');
   writeln(' ':20, '- -> 2. salary based on commission');
   writeln(' ':20, '- -> 3. retirement benefits package (future)');
   writeln(' ':20, '- -> 4. hourly wage plus tips');
   writeln(' ':20, '- -> 5. social security benefits (future)');
   writeln(' ':20, '- -> 6. medical benefits package (future)');
   writeln;
   write('Enter choice: '); readln(sample.PaySchedule); writeln;
   with sample do
      case PaySchedule of
         1: begin
               write('Your hourly wage: '); readln(wage); writeln;
               write('Hours worked: '); readln(hours); writeln;
               write('Overtime worked: '); readln(OverTime); writeln;
               if OverTime = 0
               then OverTimeWage := 0
               else begin
                  write('Overtime wage: '); readln(OverTimeWage);
                  writeln
                  end                                        (*else*)
               end;                                        (*case 1*)
         2: begin
               write('Commission rate as a percent: ');
               readln(commission); writeln;
               write('Amount sold: '); readln(sales); writeln
               end;                                        (*case 2*)
         3: writeln;                                       (*case 3*)
         4: begin
               write('Hourly wage: '); readln(rate); writeln;
               write('Hours worked: '); readln(time); writeln;
               write('Tips received: '); readln(tips); writeln;
               end;                                        (*case 4*)
         5: writeln;                                       (*case 5*)
         6: writeln                                        (*case 6*)
      end;                                                   (*case*)
   with sample do
      case PaySchedule of
         1: earnings := wage * hours + OverTime * OverTimeWage;
         2: earnings := commission/100 * sales;
         3: writeln;                                    (*open slot*)
         4: earnings := rate * time + tips;
         5: writeln;                                    (*open slot*)
         6: writeln                                     (*open slot*)
      end;                                                   (*case*)
end;                                                  (*BuildRecord*)
```

```
 (*- - - - - - - - - - - - - - - - - - - - - - - - - - - - - - - - - - - - - - - - - -*)
                                        (*This procedure prints the results.*)

procedure ShowRecord(sample: salary);
begin
   with sample do
      case PaySchedule of
         1: writeln('You have earned ', sample.earnings:5:2, ' dollars.');
         2: writeln('You have earned ', sample.earnings:5:2, ' dollars.');
         3: writeln('Retirement benefits package not available.');
         4: writeln('You have earned ', sample.earnings:5:2, ' dollars.');
         5: writeln('Social security benefits package not available.');
         6: writeln('Medical benefits package not available.')
      end                                                          (*case*)
end;                                                         (*ShowRecord*)

 (*- - - - - - - - - - - - - - - - - - - - - - - - - - - - - - - - - - - - - - - - - -*)

procedure driver;
var
   employee: salary;                                   (*a sample record*)
   choice: integer;                                   (*control variable*)
begin
   repeat
      BuildRecord(employee);
      ShowRecord(employee);
      writeln; write('Again?- -1 = Y, 0 = N: '); readln(choice); writeln
   until choice = 0
end;                                                             (*driver*)

 (*- - - - - - - - - - - - - - - - - - - - - - - - - - - - - - - - - - - - - - - - - -*)

begin
   driver
end.
```

```
menu:
                          - -> 1. Hourly wage with overtime
                          - -> 2. Salary based on commission
                          - -> 3. Retirement benefits package (future)
                          - -> 4. Hourly wage plus tips
                          - -> 5. Social security benefits (future)
                          - -> 6. Medical benefits package (future)

Enter choice:  4

Hourly wage:  3.5

Hours worked:  23

Tips received:  1299  .99

You have earned  93.49 dollars.

Again?- -1 = Y, 0 = N: 1
```

```
menu:

                    --> 1. Hourly wage with overtime
                    --> 2. Salary based on commission
                    --> 3. Retirement benefits package (future)
                    --> 4. Hourly wage plus tips
                    --> 5. Social security benefits (future)
                    --> 6. Medical benefits package (future)

Enter choice:  1

Your hourly wage:  7.5

Hours worked:  35

Overtime worked:  12

Overtime wage:  12.25

You have earned  409.50 dollars.

Again?- -1 = Y, 0 = N: 0
```

FIGURE 8.11 Variant records

8.15.1 *Refinement: More Nonempty Tag Fields*

We can expand the salary record type to include a field for the following:

1. Monthly salary for a Gandalf administrator; merit pay for an administrator; note: use

   earnings := monthly salary + merit pay

2. Fixed salary for a Gandalf ring salesperson plus commission (as a percent) plus sales of rings; note: use

   earnings := fixed salary + commission/100 * sales

Then modify the program in Figure 8.9 to handle these new cases.

8.15.2 *Another Refinement: The Name Field and Retirement Benefits*

Notice that the program in Figure 8.9 ignores the name field of each sample record. This should be fixed. In addition, for those Gandalfites that have retired, a record needs to be set up to compute the monthly retirement check to send to the retired Gandalf employee. Replace the empty number 3 field of the salary record by

> last yearly salary plus
> RRate and use

earnings := LastYearlySalary * RRate + 1500.00

to compute the retirement benefit for retirees. LastYearlySalary and RRate will be type real and in the tag-field list.

8.15.3

Exercises

1. Carry out the refinement of the program in Figure 8.9 using the instructions in Section 8.15.1. Give a sample run to display the new features.

2. Carry out the refinement of the program in Figure 8.9 using the instructions in Section 8.15.2. Give a sample run to display the new features.

8.16

Readings

Cooper, D. *Standard Pascal User Reference Manual.* New York: Norton, 1983. See Chapter 11.

Pratt, T. W. *Programming Languages: Design and Implementation.* Englewood Cliffs, NJ: Prentice-Hall, 1984. See pp. 436–437.

Wirth, N. *Programming in Modula-2.* New York: Springer-Verlag, 1982. See Chapter 19 for discussion of record types.

CHAPTER 9

FILES

The storage requirements for programs and data on which they operate customarily exceed the capacity of internal memory of most computer systems. Thus, there is the requirement to provide other storage facilities on which to store programs and data.

Billy G. Claybrook, 1983

AIMS

- Introduce the file type.
- Distinguish sequential from direct access structures.
- Distinguish text from nontext files.
- Introduce the concept of a file buffer or window.
- Illustrate the use of the built-in input and output procedures used with Pascal files.
- Give a case study on merging files.
- Give a case study on file management techniques.

9.1 Introduction

A file is an organized collection of components of the same type. A file type is also a structured data type. It is structured as a sequence of components stored on some external storage medium like a floppy diskette or a fixed disk. Unlike the other structured types in Pascal (arrays, records, and sets), the size of a file type can vary and is not specified when a file type is introduced in a program. The maximum size of a file will vary, depending on the capacity of the storage medium being used to save a file.

A file can exist on a storage medium like a Winchester disk used on an IBM PC AT or a floppy diskette. It can be stored without dependence on any one program. Its life span can be the same as the life span of the storage medium used to save it. This makes a file quite different from the other structured types (in fact, all other types) in Pascal. That is, the life span of an array or a record is the life span of a program (its execution time) that contains one of these other types.

The declaration of a file type has the form

file identifier = **file of** file component **type**

For example, here are some examples of file types.

```
type
   name = packed array[1..20] of char;
   members = file of name;
   numbers = file of real;
   BallClub = array[1..max] of name;
   league = file of BallClub;
   years = file of integer;
var
   FirstFile, SecondFile: members;
   ThisLeague: league;
   winnings: numbers
   history: years;
   musicians: file of name;
```

This example says

1. The FirstFile and SecondFile variables are members file types, with components of type name, which is a string type.
2. The ThisLeague variable is a league file type with components of type BallClub, which is array of strings.
3. The winnings variable is a numbers file type with components of type real.
4. The history variable is a years file type with components of type integer.

5. The musicians variable is a file variable with components of type name, which is a string type.

In each case, the component type of a file type must be specified. There is no indication of the file size. Except for the musicians file variable, each of the other file variables are user-defined file types. The musicians file variable is a file with a user-defined component type. In general, the component type of a file can be any of the data types we have seen so far, scalar or structured. The FirstFile, SecondFile, and ThisLeague variables are examples of file types with array components. It is also possible for a file to have components of type record. For example, we can have the following file variables:

```
type
  alfa = packed array[1..20] of char;
  years = 1930..2010;
  teams = array[1..15] of alfa;
  player = record
    name, CurrentTeam: alfa;
    PastTeams: teams;
    WorldSeriesGames: years;
    games: integer
  end;                                        (*player*)
  BallClub = file of player;       (*file type with record
                                   components of type player*)
var
  NewLeague: BallClub;
  slogans: file of alfa;               (*file with string-type
                                                  components*)
  RecordYears: file of years;        (*file with components of
                                                  type years*)
```

This says the NewLeague variable is a BallClub file type with record components of type player. There is an important restriction on the component type of a file—it cannot be a file type. So it is not possible to have a file of files. It is not possible to nest files, in other words. This means that a structured type like a record with a field that is a file type cannot be a component of a file.

Finally, the elements of a Pascal file are accessed one after the other, always starting with the first component of a file. That is, file components are accessed sequentially. This method of accessing file components is quite different from the method used to access elements of an array. To access an array element, we need to specify the position of an array element. Array elements can be accessed directly rather than sequentially. A direct access method is used to access an element of an array. In sum, here are some things to remember about file components.

File component rules:

1. **The components of a file must all be of the same type.**
2. **The number of components in a file is never specified when a file type is declared. The maximum number of components a file can have will depend on the capacity of the storage medium being used.**
3. **A file type cannot be a component of a file. If a structured type like an array or record has a file component type, then that structured type cannot be a component of a file.**
4. **The components of a file are accessed sequentially, starting with the leading file component and moving from one component to the next until the end of a file.**

In general, the syntax diagram for a file type is given in Figure 9.1. In this chapter, we start by distinguishing a file type from the other structured types we have seen so far. We have already mentioned one key difference between a file and any of the other types seen so far: A file can exist on its own outside any program. The life span of a file is not dependent on the life span of a running program. The distinction between a file type and the other Pascal types will deepen and grow sharper in Section 9.2.

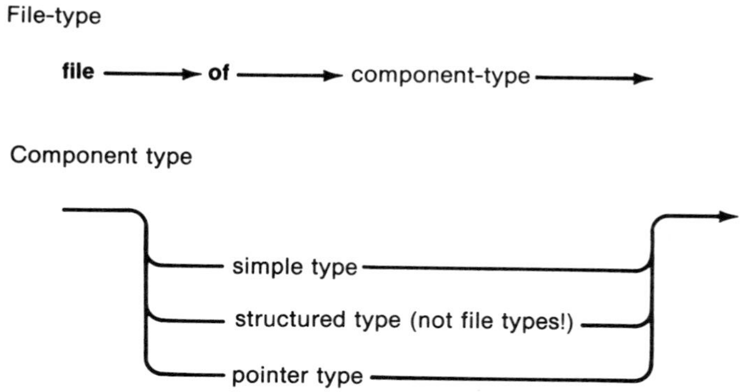

FIGURE 9.1
Syntax diagram for a file type

We will also distinguish the two kinds of files that can be used by ISO Pascal, text and nontext files. A text file has components of type char. The components of a nontext file can be any of the data types we have seen so far, except the file type itself (a file component cannot be a file type). Pascal has a generous set of built-in procedures to handle traffic of files to and from an external storage device. These are given in Table 9.1. We show how to use these built-in procedures in this chapter. Before we do this, we look first at what is known as a *file buffer variable*, a stepping-stone to understanding file handling in Pascal.

TABLE 9.1 *Pascal File Operators*

Operator	*Operation*
	Output Operators
rewrite(f)	Clears file f, making it ready for data entry. Eof(f) is set equal to true. This procedure prepares file f for *writing* or insertion of data into file f.
write(f,datum)	Write datum to file f. (used with either nontext or text files);
writeln(f,datum)	Writes datum to a text file f and terminates current line of f, moving the file pointer to the beginning of the next line of f (*restriction* f *must* be a text file);
writeln(f)	Terminates current line of textfile f. (*restriction;* f *must* be a text file);
put(f)	Appends the value of the buffer variable f^ to the file f. This works, provided eof(f) is true;
	Input Operators
reset(f)	Move the sequential file pointer back to the first cell of file f. This prepares file f for reading or inspection, bringing data from file f into memory specified by a user's program. If file f is *not* empty, then eof(f) is set equal to false.
read(f,datum)	The content of the current file buffer f^ is assigned to datum and the file pointer is moved to the *next* cell of f. (This operator can be used with either non-text or text files);
readln(f,datum)	Datum := f^ and the file pointer is moved to the *next* line of the text file f (*restriction:* this operator is used *only* with text files);
readln(f)	Skip to beginning of *next* line of text file f (f« becomes the first character of the next line). (*restriction:* this works only with text files).
get(f)	Advances the file pointer for f to the next cell of f and assigns to f^ the content of this new cell.

9.2 File Buffer Variable

Every time a file variable is declared in a Pascal program, Pascal automatically introduces a corresponding buffer variable. For example, if

NewData is a file variable

then

NewData^ is the file buffer variable

NewData^ (this reads "NewData up arrow") is also called a *file window.* A buffer variable is used to hold a single file component in main memory. A buffer variable like NewData^ serves as a window, allowing us to inspect the current file component being accessed by a Pascal program. A graphical interpretation of a file window is shown in Figure 9.2. For example, we can have the following file variables and windows:

File Variable	*Description*	*Window*
NewLeague	File of BallClub	NewLeague^
DataBase	File of real	DataBase^
IdNumbers	File of integer	IdNumbers^
Symbols	File of char	Symbols^

Values can be assigned to a file buffer variable using an assignment statement. We show how this is done next.

9.2.1 *Using a File Buffer Variable in an Assignment Statement*

A file buffer can be filled using assignment statements. For example, we can use the following assignments to fill some of the above file buffers or windows:

Assignment	*Result*
NewLeague^ := sample;	Assign a sample record of type player to the NewLeague^ buffer
DataBase^ := 2.71828;	Assign a value to DataBase^
IdNumbers^ := Number;	Assign Number (of type integer) to IdNumbers^ buffer
symbols^ := '!';	Assign a character to symbols^

We can just as easily assign the value of a buffer variable to another variable. For example, assuming

```
var
  sample: player;          (*Sample is a record variable of type
                                                         player*)
```

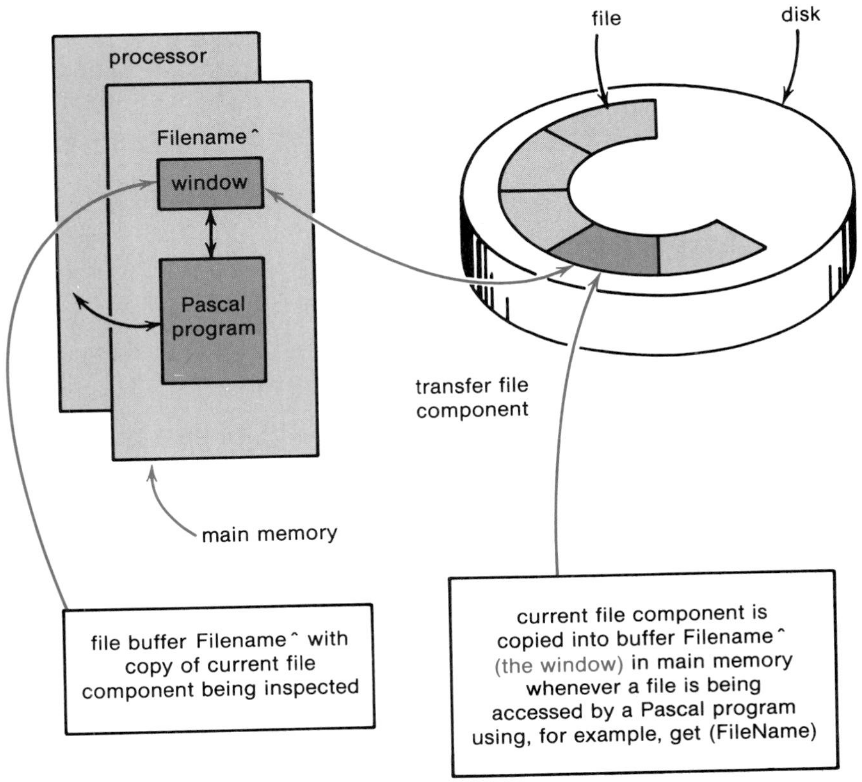

FIGURE 9.2
Graphical Interpretation of a file window

then we can fill the fields of the sample variable using the fields of the NewLeague^ window with the following assignments:

```
sample.name := NewLeague^.name;
sample.CurrentTeam := NewLeague^.CurrentTeam;
sample.PastTeams[1] := NewLeague^.PastTeams[1];
sample.PastTeams[2] := NewLeague^.PastTeams[2];
sample.WorldSeriesGames := NewLeague^.WorldSeriesGames;
sample.games := NewLeague^.games;
```

We can also use the with statement with file buffer variable of type record.

9.2.2 *Using a With Statement to Access a Window of Type Record*

The NewLeague^ variable is an example of a buffer variable or window of type record. Notice that the NewLeague^ window has enough storage in main memory to hold an entire record of type player. We can use a with statement to simplify the statements used in Section 9.2.1 to tap the contents of the NewLeague^ window. For example, suppose we want to assign the first two fields of NewLeague^ window to the first two fields of the sample record. We can use the following technique:

```
with NewLeague^ do
  begin
    sample.name := name;
    sample.CurrentTeam := CurrentTeam
  end;
```

Notice that we can use a similar technique to fill the NewLeague^ window using keyboard input as follows:

```
with NewLeague^ do
  begin
    readln(name);
    readln(CurrentTeam);
    readln(PastTeams[1], PastTeams[2]);
    readln(WorldSeriesGames, games)
  end;
```

This technique tends to make it easier to set up a procedure to load a file buffer of type record from a keyboard. The usual write, writeln, read, and readln procedures can be used with file buffer variables to handle input and output to and from a terminal.

9.2.3 Screen Output and Keyboard Input with a File Window

We can use the built-in procedures write and writeln to send the contents of a file window to a screen or printer. For example, using the NewLeague^ variable, we produce the following screen or printer output:

Statement	*Result*
writeln(NewLeague^.name)	Print copy of NewLeague^ name field.
with NewLeague^ **do** write(name, CurrentTeam)	Print copy of both NewLeague^ name and CurrentTeam fields.
with NewLeague^ **do** write(name:30, games:30)	Format output of NewLeague^ name and games fields.

Again, for example, if we have

```
var
  count: file of integer;
  Percent: file of real;
```

then we can use the following techniques to screen output and keyboard input with the count^ and Percent^ file buffers:

Statement	*Result*
readln(count^);	Assign value to count^ buffer variable, using keyboard input.
read(count^, Percent^);	Assign values to both buffer variables in one readln statement.
write('count = ', count^);	Screen output of count^ value.
writeln(Percent^:5:2);	Formatted screen output of Percent^ buffer variable.

Next we need to show how to put the contents of file buffer into a disk file and to fill a file window with a file component. This is done with built-in file-handling procedures, which are discussed next.

9.3 Rewrite and Reset File-Handling Procedures

Table 9.1 shows the built-in file handling available in standard Pascal. To prepare a new file for data entry or what is commonly called *file generation*, we use

```
rewrite(FileName);                    (*prepare for file generation*)
```

We use the rewrite procedure to clean house. This built-in procedure clears a file, making it ready for writing. When the rewrite procedure is executed, Pascal also sets up a FileName^ buffer variable. With some versions of Pascal like Apple or DEC or Oregon Software Pascal, it is necessary to include a name used to identify a user's file in a file directory. For example, we can use

```
rewrite(FileName, 'team.85');
            ↑          ↑
            |     directory name
   name of file used in Pascal program
```

This allows a user to set up a permanent reference to a disk file that will be created. This form of the rewrite procedure puts team 0.85 into a user's directory. This problem is handled differently on an IBM PC with MS Pascal 2.00. That is, IBM Pascal uses an assign procedure to associate a file name with a file directory entry. We would use the following two statements to prepare a file for data-entry on an IBM PC:

```
assign(FileName, 'team0.85');
rewrite(FileName);                    (*prepare file to receive data*)
```

In all cases, the built-in rewrite procedure prepares a file for data entry and it sets up a corresponding file buffer variable.

There is one more key thing to notice about the rewrite procedure. Suppose OldFile is the name of an existing file, then

```
rewrite(OldFile);
```

will eliminate the existing OldFile components and prepare OldFile for entirely new components. The original OldFile components will be lost, if we do not save them in another file before we activate the rewrite(OldFile).

To prepare an existing file for inspection, there is a built-in reset procedure. For example, if DataBase is the name of an existing file (an old one that resides on an external storage device), then

```
reset(NewData);                    (*prepare for file inspection*)
```

will prepare the NewData file for inspection. When the reset procedure is executed, a DataBase^ file buffer variable is created by Pascal and it is initialized with the content of the leading DataBase file component. In other words, if the DataBase file is not empty, then DataBase^ will have a value after the reset(DataBase) statement is executed. Here are some things to remember about the rewrite and reset procedures.

Guidelines for rewrite and reset procedures:

1. To prepare a file for data entry, use the rewrite procedure.

2. It will be necessary to determine how your local rewrite procedure is used to insert the name of a newly created file into your file directory.

3. The rewrite procedure will clear an existing file of its components, preparing it for entirely new components.

4. A file buffer variable is set up by Pascal each time either the rewrite or reset procedure is executed.

5. The reset procedure initializes the file buffer variable with the content of the leading component of a nonempty file that has been reset.

After we have activated either the rewrite or the reset procedure, we need some method for moving data to and from a file. In Section 9.4 we show how to do this using two other built-in procedures, get and put.

9.4 Get and Put Procedures

File input and output can be handled using the get and put built-in procedures. A

```
get(FileName);           (*assigns next file component to the
                               FileName^ buffer variable*)
```

is used to fill the file buffer variable with the next file component, if there is one. We can write the contents of a file buffer out to a file on an external storage medium using

```
put(FileName);                    (*write content of file buffer
                                     variable out to file*)
```

For example, if we have

```
var
  digits: file of integer;
```

then we can use the following technique to build the digits file:

File Operations	*Result*
rewrite(digits);	Prepare file for data entry.
digits^ := 21;	Assigns 21 to digits^ buffer.
put(digits);	Puts copy of buffer into leading component of the digits file.
readln(digits^);	Initializes digits^ buffer with value typed at a keyboard.
put(digits);	Puts copy of buffer into next component of the digits file.
close(digits);	A nonstandard procedure used to free up memory used for the file buffer and make eof(FileName) true.

The last of the above procedures is nonstandard but is commonly used by Pascal compilers. It is used to ensure that a file is ended correctly. The close procedure is used by UCSD Pascal, DEC Pascal, OS Pascal, and IBM Pascal, for example.

If digits is an existing file, we can use the get procedure in the following way to access components of this file:

File Operations	*Result*
reset(digits);	Prepares digits file for inspection and initialized the digits^ buffer with the leading (first) digits component.
First := digits^;	Assigns buffer to First of type integer.
get(digits);	Initializes digits^ buffer with the content of the next file component.
Second := digits^;	Assigns new buffer value to Second, which is of type integer.
get(digits);	Initializes digits^ buffer with the content of the next (the third) file component of this file.

With nontext and text files, the ISO standard provides a shorthand to use in reading from and writing to a file. This is done using the familiar built-in read and write procedures.

9.5 New Uses of the Read and Write Procedures

The following blocks are equivalent (accomplish the same thing):

File Generation

Long Form:

```
begin
   rewrite(digits);
   digits^ := 21;
   put(digits)
end;
```

Short Form:

```
begin
   rewrite(digits);
   write(digits, 21)
end;
```

File Inspection

Long Form:

```
begin
   reset(digits);
   First := digits^;
   get(digits);
   Second := digits^
end
```

Short Form:

```
begin
   reset(digits);
   First := digits^;
   read(digits, Second)
end
```

In general,

write(FileName, ComponentType);

is equivalent to the following block

```
begin
   FileName^ := ComponentType;          (*Fill buffer*)
   put(FileName)                        (*copy buffer to file*)
end;
```

and

read(FileName, ComponentType);

is equivalent to

```
begin
   get(FileName);                       (*initialize buffer with
                                           file component*)
   ComponentType := FileName^           (*make copy of buffer*)
end;
```

This portion of the ISO standard is implemented in both DEC Pascal and IBM

Pascal, for example. However, only the get and put procedures can be used with nontext files in Apple Pascal.

The read and write procedures are more convenient to use, if they are available. Next we show how the names of files are introduced in a program heading. We also show how variable procedure parameters of type file can be used to advantage.

9.6 File Names in Program Headings and in Parameter Lists

A variable procedure parameter can be a file type. That is, a procedure can be activated with a reference to an external file. The file itself is not passed to a procedure with a file type parameter. Only the reference to a file is passed. This is useful, since it makes it possible to make it clear what file is being used by a procedure. For example, we can have the following file type:

```
type
   nos = file of real;
```

Then this file type is referenced in the following procedure headings:

```
procedure BuildFile(var random: nos;                (*a file parameter*)
                    var seed: real);
procedure ShowFile(var random: nos);                (*a file parameter*)
```

If a variable of type file is used in a program, its name must appear in the list of identifiers in the program heading. We have been doing this all along for the input and output identifiers, which are names of files used for terminal input and output. If we want to use the random file variable in a program, for example, this file name should be listed in the program heading. For example, in a program with the BuildFile and ShowFile Procedures, we would use

program FileBuilder(input, output, random);

Again, for example, if shapes, costs, and inventory are the names of external files to be used in a program, then we would use

program sample(shapes, costs, inventory);

In effect, the sample program will introduce shapes, costs, and inventory as names of files. This heading also says there will be no terminal input and output. If this program had just terminal input, then we would use

program sample(input, shapes, costs, inventory);

If this sample program were to use both terminal input and output, then we would use

program sample(input, output, shapes, costs, inventory);

We illustrate these ideas in the following example.

9.7 Example: Building a File of Random Numbers

An algorithm to build a file of random numbers will have the following form:

```
begin
  prepare a file of type real for generation;
                                        (*call the file random*)
  initialize max with number of file entries;
  repeat
    assign rnd value to random^ buffer;
    copy random^ value out to random file;
    subtract 1 from max
  until max = 0;
  assign sentinel value to random^;
  copy random^ to random file          (*save sentinel to mark the
                                          end of the random file*)
end;                                   (*algorithm to build file of reals*)
```

The last thing we do in this algorithm is place a sentinel value in the random file. Why? This will allow us to tell when we have reached the last file entry. The sentinel value gives a way of marking the logical end of the random file. Physically, the random file can stretch past the point where we inserted our sentinel. So, instead of using

while not eof(random) **do** . . .

to check for the physical end of the random file, we can use

while random^ <> sentinel **do** . . .

to check for the logical end of a file. It is much easier to work with a file sentinel than it is to work with the eof() function when a file is being inspected. For example, none of the random numbers we will generate will ever be less than 0, so we can use

```
write(random, -1.0);                    (*put -1.0 into file*)
```

to insert −1.0 as a logical end-of-file mark in the random file.

To insert a random number into the random file, we can use the following technique:

```
write(random, rnd(seed));               (*put rnd value into file*)
```

which is equivalent to the following block:

```
begin
  random^ := rnd(seed);                 (*assign rnd value to buffer*)
  put(random)                           (*copy buffer to random file*)
end
```

In effect, each time the above write statement is executed, a number between 0 and 1 is inserted into the random file. To get a copy of the random file, we can use the following method:

```
begin
   prepare file for inspection;                    (*use reset procedure*)
   while random^ <> sentinel do
      begin
         print a copy of file buffer variable value;
         assign next file component to buffer variable
      end
end;                                              (*file inspection method*)
```

A structure chart for a program to build a file of random numbers is given in Figure 9.3. We show how to carry out these ideas in the program in Figure 9.4.

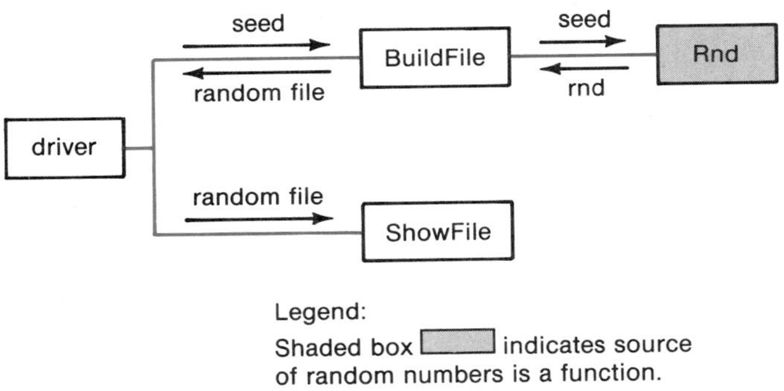

FIGURE 9.3
Structure chart for a random number file builder

```
          (*Method: This program puts random numbers out into a
             disk file, instead of storing them in an array in main
             memory. This gives us a permanent copy of a collection
                                             of random numbers.*)

program SamplesFile(input, output, random);
const
   sentinel = -1.0;          (*used to mark the logical end of file*)
   max = 50;                       (*limit on number of file entries*)
type
   nos = file of real;            (*nos is a user defined file type*)

 (*-----------------------------------------------*)
          (*This function produces random numbers of type real.*)

function rnd(var seed:real): real;  (*notice the variable parameter*)
begin
   seed := sqr(seed + 3.141592654);       (*produce a number with
                                                   fractional part*)
   seed := seed - trunc(seed);              (*chop off the fraction*)
   rnd := seed                          (*assign copy of seed to rnd*)
end;                                                          (*rnd*)
```

```
  (*----------------------------------------------*)
   (*This procedure repeatedly activates the rnd function to obtain
              random entries for the random file of type real.*)

procedure BuildFile(var random: nos;   (*entries is a type nos file*)
                    var seed: real);  (*supplied by driver procedure*)
var
   dash: integer;
begin
   rewrite(random, 'rnd.nos');                (*open random file with a
                                          directory name of rnd.nos'*)
   for dash := 1 to max do write(random,
   write(random, -1.0);                        (*insert sentinel value*)
   writeln;
   for dash := 1 to 70 do write('-'); writeln;
   writeln('A random numbers file has been created!'); writeln;
   for dash := 1 to 70 do write('-'); writeln
end;                                                         (*BuildFile*)

  (*----------------------------------------------*)
  (*This procedure moves the random file pointer to the beginning
     of the file and, then, advances through the random file entry
               by entry, until the sentinel value is reached.*)

procedure ShowFile(var random: nos);               (*a file parameter*)
var
   dash: integer;                               (*used to print dashes*)
begin
   writeln('Copy of file of random numbers:');
   for dash := 1 to 70 do write('-'); writeln;       (*print dashes*)
   reset(random, 'rnd.nos');                      (*reopen random file*)
   dash := 1;             (*use dash to control printing of numbers*)
   while random^ <> sentinel do
      begin
         if dash mod 7 <> 0
         then  write(random^:5:4, ' ':5)
         else writeln;
         dash := dash + 1;
         get(random)
      end
end;                                                          (*ShowFile*)

  (*----------------------------------------------*)
   (*This procedure gets a value of seed and activates the above
                                                        procedures.*)

procedure driver;
var
   random: nos;
   seed: real;
begin
   write('Enter a seed of type real: '); readln(seed); writeln;
   BuildFile(random, seed);
   ShowFile(random)
end;                                                            (*driver*)
```

```
(*- - - - - - - - - - - - - - - - - - - - - - - - - - - - - - - - - - - - - - -*)

begin
   driver
end.
```

```
Enter a seed of type real:  2.71828

A random numbers file has been created!
```

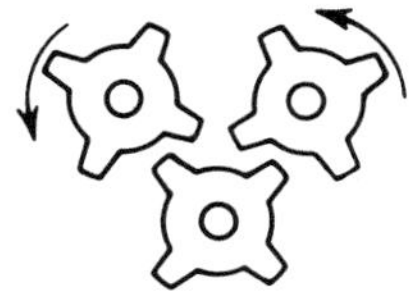

Copy of File of Random Numbers

0.3381	0.1083	0.5619	0.7160	0.8808	0.1797
0.0672	0.2965	0.8202	0.6955	0.7233	0.9372
0.2751	0.6735	0.5551	0.6658	0.4963	0.2343
0.5193	0.4024	0.5601	0.7023	0.7754	0.3428
0.7776	0.3601	0.2616	0.5818	0.8639	0.0441
0.8246	0.7305	0.9930	0.0950	0.4758	0.0859
0.6609	0.4587	0.9624	0.8428	0.8753	0.1356
0.0687					

FIGURE 9.4 Building a file of random numbers

9.8 Refinement: Changing the Random Number Entries

The above program permits little interaction with a user when it is run. It may be helpful to make it possible for the user to determine how many random numbers are put into the random file. To do this change the max constant to an integer constant local to the driver procedure, which can be used to initialize max before it is passed to the BuildFile and ShowFile procedures.

It may also be convenient to set up a second file with random entries of type integer. For example, we can use

program SamplesFile(input, output, random, copy);

to set up a copy file. Then

write(copy, trunc(Bound * rnd(seed)) + 1)

can be used to set up a file of random numbers from 1 to bound. Then the random and copy files can be built within the BuildFile procedure, using

```
reset(random);
for count := 1 to max do write(random, rnd(seed));
write(random, -1.0);                       (*to set up sentinel entry*)
reset(copy);                             (*prepare copy file for entry*)
for count := 1 to max do
   write(copy, trunc(bound * rnd(seed)) + 1);
write(copy, -1)                             (*for second sentinel entry*)
```

Carrying out these refinements is left as an exercise.

9.9

Building a File of Records

We will set up a file of records of the following type:

```
type
   alfa = packed array[1..20] of char;
   BallClub = record
      name: alfa;                                 (*team name*)
      wins, losses: integer;               (*team wins, losses*)
      pct: real                         (*percent of games won*)
end;                                               (*BallClub*)
standings = file of BallClub;
                                            (*this says standings
                                            is a file type and its
                                           components are of type
                                                       BallClub*)
```

A procedure to build a file of components of type BallClub is very much like the earlier BuildFile procedure. For example, if team is a file variable of type standings, then we can use the following technique to build a team file:

```
begin
   rewrite(team);
   repeat
      with team^ do                        (*start file generation*)
         begin
            readln(name);                (*assign entered string to
                                             name field of team^
                                                  buffer variable*)
            readln(wins, losses);          (*assign values to next
                                              two fields of team^*)
            pct := wins / (wins + losses);
                                            (*notice! this assigns
                                                the value of the
                                              expression shown to
                                              pct field of team^*)
            pct(team);                     (*copies buffer to file*)
            readln(choice)                   (*want to continue?*)
   until choice = 0;
   team^.wins := -1;                         (*assign sentinel to
                                                  buffer variable*)
   put(team)                               (*copy sentinel to file*)
end;                               (*method for building a team file*)
```

The above block employs the with statement to simplify our working with the fields of the file buffer. How? Without the with statement, each assignment would have the following form:

```
readln(team^.name);
readln(team^.wins, team^.losses)
```

which is fine! However, these statements are awkward to set up (typos can creep into your source text—it is easy to forget to type the up arrow (^)). And they are not easy to read, which may be important to you later when it is necessary to read through a source text. This gives us

> **The with tool:**
>
> **Use**
>
> **with FileName^ do**
>
> **to simplify access to a file buffer of type record.**

To see a copy of the team file, we can use the following technique:

```
begin
  reset(team);                          (*prepare file for inspection*)
  while team^.wins <> sentinel do
    begin
      writeln(name, wins, losses, pct);
      get(team)
    end                                                         (*while*)
end;                                               (*inspection method*)
```

Once we have reset the team file, we can begin inspecting by checking the content of the current file buffer. A structure chart for this new program is given in Figure 9.5. We show a program to carry out this idea in Figure 9.6.

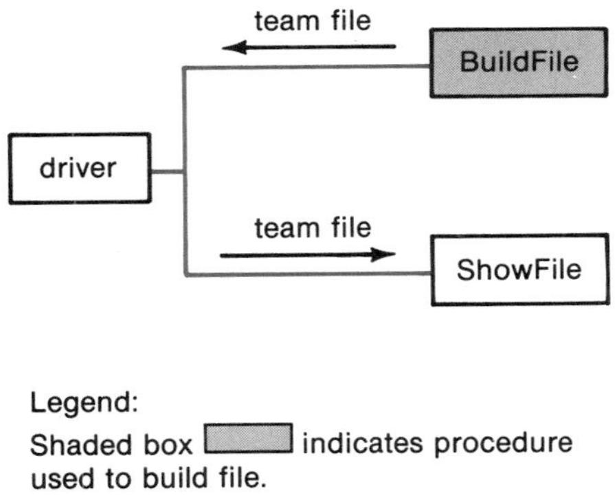

FIGURE 9.5
Structure chart for a file-record building program

```
program RecordFile(input, output, team);
const
   sentinel = -1;                              (*use to identify last record*)
type
   alfa = packed array[1..20] of char;     (*string type for names*)
   BallClub = record                        (*record type to be used in file*)
      name: alfa;                                            (*team name*)
      wins, losses: integer;                          (*team wins, losses*)
      pct: real                                    (*percentage of wins*)
   end;                                                         (*BallClub*)
   standings = file of BallClub;                  (*user-defined file type*)

 (*- - - - - - - - - - - - - - - - - - - - - - - - - - - - - - - - - - - - - -*)
       (*This procedure builds a file of records of type standings.
   Notice how the with statement is used to advantage to select
                                                    BallClub fields.*)

procedure BuildFile(var team: standings);             (*a file parameter*)
var
   choice: integer;
begin
   rewrite(team, 'team.85');
   writeln('enter team name on a separate line, then');
   writeln('enter team wins and losses on the next line.');
   repeat
      with team^ do
         begin
            readln(name); readln(wins, losses);  (*first 3 team fields*)
            pct := wins/(wins + losses);         (*calculate pct of wins*)
            put(team);                              (*write record to file*)
            write('Again?- -1 = Y, 0 = N: ');
         end                                                        (*with*)
   until choice = 0;
   team^.wins := -1;
   put(team);                                       (*aha!- -save sentinel.*)
   close(team)                                          (*a crucial step!*)
end;                                                           (*BuildFile*)

 (*- - - - - - - - - - - - - - - - - - - - - - - - - - - - - - - - - - - - - -*)
    (*This procedure reopens the team file and displays a copy of
 each file record until the dummy record with team^.wins = -1 is
     found. Again, the with statement is used to advantage here.*)

procedure ShowFile(var team: standings);
var
   dash: integer;                                  (*use to print dashes*)
begin
   reset(team, 'team.85');
   writeln('team':20, 'wins':20, 'losses':10, 'pct': 12);
   for dash := 1 to 70 do write('-'); writeln;
   while team^.wins <> sentinel do          (*notice that the sentinel
                                            guarantees we will never print
                                                    out an empty record*)
```

```
    begin
      with team^ do
        writeln(name:30, wins:10, losses:10, pct:12:3);
      get(team)
    end                                                    (*while*)
end;                                                       (*ShowFile*)

 (*- - - - - - - - - - - - - - - - - - - - - - - - - - - - - - - - - -*)
 (*Notice how much mileage we get out of the above procedures:
  (1) we can inspect an old file by merely activating the ShowFile
 procedure or (2) we can build a new team file as well as inspect
     the completed file. We also can go back for another option.*)

procedure driver;
var
  option: integer;
  team: standings;
begin
  repeat
    writeln('Enter a menu choice:');
    writeln; writeln('menu':20); writeln;
    writeln('--->':20, '1. See copy of old file');
    writeln('--->':20, '2. Build new file');
    writeln('--->':20, '3. None of these');
    readln(option);
    case option of
      1:  ShowFile(team);
      2:  begin
         BuildFile(team); ShowFile(team)
         end;
      3:  begin
         write('Again?--1 = Y, 0 = N: '); readln(option)
         end
    end                                                    (*case*)
  until option = 0
end;                                                       (*driver*)

 (*- - - - - - - - - - - - - - - - - - - - - - - - - - - - - - - - - -*)

begin
  driver
end.
```

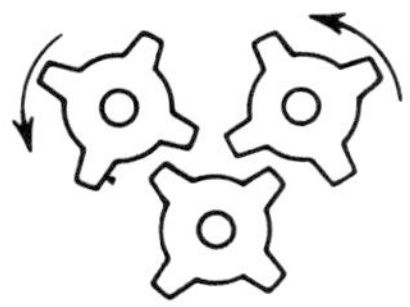

```
Enter a menu choice:

                    menu:

                    --->1. See copy of old file
                    --->2. Build new file
                    --->3. None of these
```

```
1
```

Team	Wins	Losses	Pct
Whippets	23	11	0.676
Avon	2	11	0.154
Ucsd	19	19	0.500

```
Enter a menu choice:

                         menu:

                         --->1. See copy of old file
                         --->2. Build new file
                         --->3. None of these

2
Enter team name on a separate line, then
enter team wins and losses on the next line.
whippets
33 16
Again?--1 = Y, 0 = N:  1

twins
54 21
Again?--1 = Y, 0 = N:  1

ucsd
34 19
Again?--1 = Y, 0 = N:  0
```

Team	Wins	Losses	Pct
Whippets	33	16	0.673
Twins	54	21	0.720
Ucsd	34	19	0.642

```
Enter a menu choice:

                         menu:

                         --->1. See copy of old file
                         --->2. Build new file
                         --->3. None of these

3
Again?--1 = Y, 0 = N: 0
```

FIGURE 9.6 Building a file of team records

9.10

Refinement: Changing the Content of a File

Until now, we have only illustrated how to prepare a file for generation (or data entry) and for inspection. Once a file is created, it is usually necessary to change the file. Here are some of the changes that are commonly made to an existing file.

1. **Insertion.** Adding a new component to an existing file.
2. **Deletion.** Removing a component from an existing file.
3. **Edit.** Changing the content of a file component (for example, with the team file, we will probably need to change the team wins and losses, which will also change the percentage of wins).

To change a Pascal file, it is necessary to set up a scratch file of the same type (call it *copy*). Then the components of a master file are written to a copy file until the record to changed or deleted is found (if it exists!). Similarly, if we want to add a new component to an existing file, we need to scan the existing file to determine where to insert the new component. To do this, the master file components are written to the copy file until we find the place where the insertion is to be made. Once the change is made, we continue copying the file components to the copy file until we reach the end of the master file. Then the master file is rewritten and the components of the copy file are written into the master file. These file-handling techniques are discussed more fully in the file management case study at the end of this chapter.

9.11

Text Files

A text file is a file of char. For example, the input and output files are text files. Every time we use the read or write procedures with terminal or printer, we are implicitly using the input and output files declared in a program heading. The following statements are equivalent:

Required Form	*Implied Form*
write('Hello, world!');	write(output, 'Hello, world!');
writeln('yes.');	writeln(output, 'yes.');
read(YourChoice);	read(input, YourChoice);
readln(This, That);	readln(input, This, That);

Besides the read and write procedures, the readln and writeln can also be used with any text file. In Pascal, text is a standard file type. So, for example, we can have the following text files:

```
var
  symbols, choices, essay: text;          (*this says that
                              that these three variables are
                                            text file types*)
```

We illustrate the use of text files by building a telephone directory inside a text file.

9.12 Example: A Telephone Directory in a Text File

We will use the following record type to build a telephone directory inside a text file:

```
type
   BigString = packed array[1..20] of char;
   LittleString = packed array[1..8] of char;
   entry = record
      name, address: BigString;        (*used for name and address
                                           in phone directory*)
            number: LittleString          (*for phone number*)
   end                                              (*entry*)
```

The fields a record of type entry are string types and can be written out to a text file. For example, we use the following method to build a text file containing the strings of a type entry record:

```
begin
   rewrite(phone);                             (*phone is a text file*)
   repeat
      with listing do                         (*listing is of type entry*)
         readln(name);                        (*get name from keyboard*)
         readln(address);                  (*get address from keyboard*)
         readln(number);             (*get phone number from keyboard*)
         writeln(phone, name, address, number);
                                       (*this statement writes the strings
                                          of the listing record out to the
                                                         phone text file*)
         readln(choice);              (*see if user wants to make another
                                                                  entry*)
   until choice = 0;
   writeln(phone, chr(26))                  (*put end-of-file character after
                                                   last entry in phone file*)
end;                         (*method to use in building a phone directory*)
```

The last step in this method will vary, depending on the computer system being used. That is, this procedure puts a logical *end-of-file* (eof) mark after the last file entry. The choice of the eof character will depend on the implementation of your local Pascal. Here are some examples of eof characters.

chr(26) or <control><*z*> is the *end-of-file* character used by DEC Pascal and IBM Pascal for the IBM PC;
chr(3) or <control><*c*> is the *end-of-file* character used by Apple Pascal.

The insertion of an eof character at the end of a text file gives a convenient way to detect the logical end of a file when we are inspecting a text file. We illustrate these ideas in the program in Figure 9.7.

```
                (*Method: A text file is used to store entries in a phone
                     directory. The last thing inserted into the directory
                    file is an eof character, which is a chr(26) or ctrl-z
                       for the system being used for this program. The
                       end-of-file character is used to locate the end of
                                              the phone directory.*)

program directory(input, output, phone);
type
  BigString = packed array[1..20] of char;         (*use for name,
                                                          address*)
  LittleString = packed array[1..8] of char;        (*use for phone
                                                           number*)
  entry = record                                 (*phone book entry*)
    name, address: BigString;
    number: LittleString
  end;                                                     (*entry*)

 (*-----------------------------------------------------------*)
       (*This procedure builds a phone directory on a disk file.*)

procedure BuildDirectory(var phone: text);  (*a text file parameter*)
var
  listing: entry;                              (*use to build listing*)
  choice: integer;                         (*iteration control variable*)
begin
  rewrite(phone, 'phone.dir');
  repeat
    with listing do
      begin
        write('Name: '); readln(name); writeln;
        write('Address: '); readln(address); writeln;
        write('Number: '); readln(number); writeln;
        writeln(phone, name, address, number)     (*write to file*)
      end;
    write('Again?- -1 = Y, 0 = N: '); readln(choice); writeln
  until choice = 0;
  writeln(phone, chr(26))                    (*insert end-of-file char*)
end;                                                (*BuildDirectory*)

 (*-----------------------------------------------------------*)
    (*This procedure prints a copy of the phone directory that is
                                                        on the disk.*)

procedure PrintDirectory(var phone: text);
var
  listing: entry;                               (*use for phone listing*)
  dash: integer;                                (*use to print dashes*)
```

```
begin
   reset(phone, 'phone.dir');
   for dash := 1 to 75 do write('—'); writeln;
   writeln('name':20, 'address':30, 'number':15); writeln;
   for dash := 1 to 75 do write('—'); writeln;
   repeat
      readln(phone, listing.name, listing.address, listing.number);
      with listing do
         writeln(name:20, address:30, number:15)
   until eof(phone);
   for dash := 1 to 75 do write('—'); writeln
end;                                                    (*PrintDirectory*)

  (*- - - - - - - - - - - - - - - - - - - - - - - - - - - - - - - - - - - - - - -*)

procedure driver;
var
   LittleBlackBook: text; option: integer;
begin
   repeat
      writeln('menu: ');
      writeln('- - -> 1. See old directory');
      writeln('- - -> 2. BuildNewDirectory');
      writeln('- - -> 3. None of these');
      writeln; write('Enter choice: '); readln(option); writeln;
      case option of
         1:  PrintDirectory(LittleBlackBook);
         2:  begin
            BuildDirectory(LittleBlackBook);
            PrintDirectory(LittleBlackBook)
            end;
         3:  writeln
      end                                                         (*case*)
   until option = 3
end;                                                            (*driver*)

  (*- - - - - - - - - - - - - - - - - - - - - - - - - - - - - - - - - - - - - - -*)

begin
   driver
end.
```

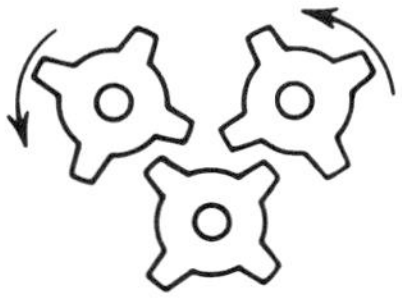

```
menu:
- - -> 1. See old directory
- - -> 2. BuildNewDirectory
- - -> 3. None of these

Enter choice: 2

Name: Whippets

Address: Lake Wobegon

Number: 13
```

```
Again?- -1  =  Y,  0  =  N:   1

Name:   Ken  Stabler

Address:   Dallas

Number:   33

Again?- -1  =  Y,  0  =  N:   0
```

Name	*Address*	*Number*
Whippets	Lake Wobegon	13
Ken Stabler	Dallas	33

```
menu:
---> 1. See old directory
---> 2. BuildNewDirectory
---> 3. None of these

Enter choice:  1
```

Name	*Address*	*Number*
Whippets	Lake Wobegon	13
Ken Stabler	Dallas	33

```
menu:
---> 1. See old directory
---> 2. BuildNewDirectory
---> 3. None of these

Enter choice:  3
```

FIGURE 9.7 How to set up a phone directory in a text file

9.13 Why Use Files?

Files give us a way to create a permanent copy of data entered into a computer. When we use one of the nonfile structured types (arrays, sets, records) for entered data, we have only a temporary copy of our data. Unless a file is used to store our data, we will lose our entered data when we stop running a program having only nonfile structured types.

With files in Pascal, we are dealing with a sequential structure with no explicit upper bound. Unlike arrays, for example, the number of components in a file is not fixed or declared ahead of time when a file type is used in a program.

The permanency and variable size of files, make files both flexible and economical to use. Files save us time, since they can be reused by different programs. In other words, by using files we make it possible to share data between programs and between users.

9.14 Summary

Until now, we have relied entirely on terminal input and output. The introduction of files gives us a way to handle input and output in alternative ways. We can use files to hold copies of information we have entered into a computer. After a data file has been set up, it can be used and reused by more than one program and by more than one user with file access privileges.

In Pascal, the input and output files are examples of text files. These are files of type char. These two files are in statements like

```
read(item)
```

which is equivalent to

```
read(input, item);
write(item)
```

which is equivalent to

```
write(output, item)
```

The writeln and readln built-in procedures can be used only with text files. The write and read procedures can be used with either text or nontext files.

Here is a key feature of Pascal files to keep in mind.

> **All files in Pascal are sequential files.**

A file is prepared for generation or data entry using the built-in rewrite procedure. A file is prepared for inspection using the built-in reset procedure. Each time either the rewrite or reset procedure is executed, a corresponding file buffer variable is set up by Pascal. For example, if team is a file name, then the corresponding buffer variable is given by team^.

Since all files in Pascal are sequential, this means we need to start at the beginning of a Pascal file each time we want to find a particular file component. To inspect a file in search of a particular file component, it is necessary to move with the leading component and move component by component until we find the component we want. In other words, a sequential access must always be used to inspect an existing file or to gain access to any file component. This contrasts sharply with an array type, since the elements of an array can be accessed directly by specifying the position of a desired array element.

Changes in a sequential file must be made with the help of a scratch file. For example, if we want to insert a component into an old file, we need to use the following steps:

1. rewrite(ScratchFile); (*prepare ScratchFile for data entry*)

2. reset(OldFile); (*prepare OldFile for inspection*)

3. Move OldFile components to the ScratchFile.

4. Insert any new file components by appending them to the ScratchFile. This can be done by using the following block:

```
begin
   readln(ScratchFile^);              (*assign value to the
                                   ScratchFile buffer variable*)
   put(ScratchFile)
end;
```

5. reset(ScratchFile); (*prepare for inspection*)

6. rewrite(OldFile); (*prepare for generation*)

7. Move components of the ScratchFile into the OldFile.

We illustrate methods that can be used to change existing Pascal files in the first case study at the end of this chapter.

When a file is declared in a Pascal program, the size of the file is not specified, just the file name and its component type. This is important. This means a file can grow or shrink, depending on our needs and the capacity of the external storage device being used.

Since files are a permanent record f what we have entered, they are time-savers. A file built one day can be reused later (the next time we activate a file-handling program) without rebuilding. Finally, the use of files makes it possible to share data between programs and between users.

9.15 Keywords Review

Keywords	*Related Ideas*
eof(FileName	true when the physical end of a nontext file is reached or when an eof character is reached in text file, false otherwise
file	collection of components of the same type; a structured type
buffer variable	automatically set up by Pascal whenever the rewrite or reset procedure is activated. It is used to hold a copy of the current file component being accessed.
file-handling procedure	a procedure used in file generation or inspection or file management

generation	begun by activating the built-in rewrite procedure; entering data into a file
get	built-in procedure used to fill a file buffer with the next file component
inspection	begun by activating the built-in reset procedure; assigning a file component to the file buffer variable
nontext	a file with components that are not of type char
put	built-in procedure used to put a copy of a file buffer out to a file
read	a built-in procedure used to inspect either a text or nontext file; form read(FileName, expression)
readln	a built-in procedure used only in the inspection of text files; form readln(FileName, expression)
reset	a built-in procedure used to prepare an existing file for inspection and to set up a file buffer variable; form reset(FileName)
rewrite	a built-in procedure used to prepare a file for data entry (a file generation procedure used to set up a new file) and to set up a file buffer variable; form rewrite(FileName)
write	a built-in procedure used to put a copy of the file buffer out to either a text or nontext file; form write(FileName, expression)
writeln	a built-in procedure used only with text files to put a copy of the file buffer out to the file
file management	generating, inspecting, or changing a file
1. build	construct a file
2. copy	set up a second file with a copy of the components of a master file
3. deletion	removing a file component. In Pascal, this is done by copying a master file to a copy file until the record to be deleted is found. Then we skip past the unwanted component and continue copying. Then we reconstruct a new master file using the components of the copy file.
4. insertion	adding a new component to a file
4.1. append	copy master to a copy file completely, then add new component(s) onto copy file and use the copy file to generate a new master file
4.2. inorder	copy master to copy file until a place to insert a new component into the copy file, then continue copying the master to the copy file
5. inspection	scan an existing file
5.1. find	scan for a particular component
5.2. global	scan entire file (print a copy)
6. sort	put file components in order. This is discussed in the second case study in this chapter.
text	standard type in Pascal, a file to type char (each file component is of type char)

9.16 Exercises

1. What is a file?

2. What is meant by the term *file* in Pascal?

3. What is the difference between a text and nontext file?

4. What is the maximum size of a file?

5. What is a file buffer variable?

6. When is a file buffer variable created?

7. If OurRecords is the name of an existing file, what happens if the following statement is executed in any program?

```
rewrite(OurRecords);
```

8. In a nontext file, when is an eof(FileName) true?

9. In a text file, what are two ways to make eof(FileName) true?

10. Is it possible for a file to have components of type Boolean? If so, give an example.

11. Is it possible for a file component to be an array of arrays? If so, give an example.

12. Which of the following would be the most likely reason for building file backup procedures into a computer system offering services to many different users?
    a. To serve the public's right to know
    b. To enable supervisors to monitor system use
    c. To improve processing speed
    d. To facilitate the interchange of information
    e. To allow recovery from system and/or user errors
    f. To free up storage in the main memory

13. Why are files used?

14. For a file *f*, what is the difference between a reset(*f*) and a rewrite (*f*)?

15. Rewrite the following statements using the file window and get and put:
    a. read(ThisFile, result);
    b. read(ThisFile, ThatFile^); (*assume that ThisFile and ThatFile are the same type*)
    c. readln(AnotherFile, symbol);
    d. write(Statistics, 2.7);
    e. write(History, 'Hello, world!');
    f. write(History, AnotherStory^); (*assume that History and AnotherStory are of same type*)
    g. writeln(Story, 'Tom went walking on up the Withywindle.');

16. Write a program to do the following:
    a. Allow the user to enter a directory file name (prompt for this name) for a file of type char.
    b. Print a copy of the contents of the file.

Run your program for
c. Phone file set up by Figure 9.7
d. Pascal program (the source text) in Figure 9.7

17. Add the following menu to the program for exercise 16:

Menu:
1. Print copy of a text file.
2. Check the syntax of the first line of a Pascal prorgram (the heading) to see if it ends with a semicolon.
3. Determine how many times a symbol occurs in a text file.

Run your program for
a. Choice 2 with the phone directory program in Figure 9.7
b. Choice 3 with left parenthesis
c. Choice 3 with single quote
d. Choice 3 with period

18. Write a program to store the names, addresses, phone numbers, hobbies, and sports activites for members of your class. Your program should allow you to do the following things:
a. Build a file.
b. Print a copy of an existing file.

19. Refine the program in exercise 18 so that the user can choose from the following menu:

Menu:
1. See old file.
2. Build new file (let user select directory file name).
3. Print ordered list of names of persons represented in an existing file. (*Hint:* Copy file names into an array and selection sort the names.)
4. Add a name to an existing file (see steps to do this in Section 9.10).
5. Drop a name from an existing file (see steps to do this in Section 9.10).
6. Change an address in an existing file.

Give a sample run to illustrate the use of each menu item.

20. Write a program to store the review word lists in each chapter of this book. Use the following record to do this:

```
type
  alfa = packed array[1..20] of char;
  beta = packed array[1..120] of char;
  idea = record
    words: alfa;                                  (*keyword(s)*)
    explanation: beta;                            (*related ideas*)
    chapter, section, page: integer
  end;                                            (*idea*)
```

Your program should have the following procedures:

a. BuildFile to set up new file
b. ShowFile to print copy of an existing file

Run your program for

c. Review lists in last two chapters

9.17 Review Quiz

Determine whether the following are true or false:

1. The input and output files are text files.
2. A component of a text file is a string type.
3. A writeln can be used to put a string into a text file.
4. The read and write procedures can be used with either text or nontext files.
5. The readln and writeln procedures can only be used with text files.
6. The components of a nontext file can be a record type.
7. The components of a nontext file can be a file type.
8. The components of a file do not have to be all of the same type.
9. A file buffer variable is not affected by the execution of the get procedure.
10. A file buffer variable is not changed by the execution of the put procedure.
11. A file buffer variable is also called a *file window.*
12. If a file component is a record type, then the corresponding file window is also a record type.
13. A file lasts only as long as a program is running.
14. It is always necessary to specify file size when a file type is declared.
15. Text and nontext files in Pascal are both sequential files.

9.18 Case Study: File Management Techniques

Here is the level 0 idea for a program to manage files.

```
begin
   construct a file;
   make necessary changes in a file;
   print a copy of a file
end                          (*preliminary idea for a program*)
```

Here are three changes we will want to be able to make with any file we set up.

1. **Insertion.** Adding a new component to an existing file.
2. **Deletion.** Dropping a component from an existing file.
3. **Editing.** Changing a component of an existing file.

These are level 1 ideas for a file-management program. A structure chart showing a framework for this new program is given in Figure 9.8. The insert,

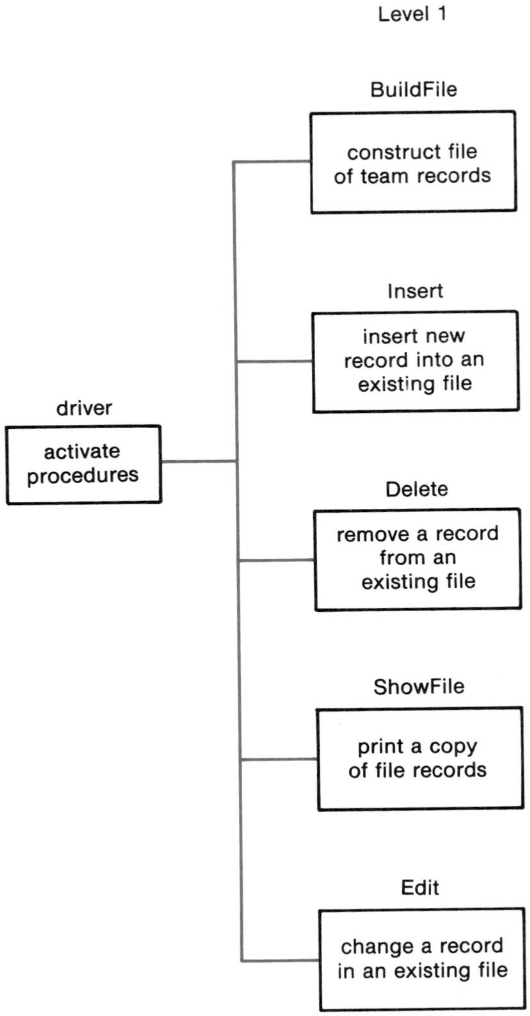

FIGURE 9.8
Framework for a file management program

delete, and edit procedures will each need to set up a scratch file to build a copy of the new file with the changes that have been made to an existing master file. We will illustrate these file management procedures using the following types:

```
type
  alfa = packed array[1..20] of char;
  BallClub = record
    name: alfa;                                    (*team name*)
    wins, losses: integer;               (*team wins and losses*)
    pct: real                             (*percentage of wins*)
    end;                                            (*BallClub*)
  teams = file of BallClub;                      (*a file type*)
```

We will use DataBase and NewData as the names of two files of type teams. DataBase will be the master file; NewData, the copy file.

9.18.1 *Inserting a New Component into an Existing File*

Here is a file-insertion algorithm.

```
begin
  prepare the NewData file for generation;         (*use rewrite*)
  prepare DataBase file for inspection;              (*use reset*)
  while DataBase^.wins <> sentinel do
    begin
      put copy of DataBase window into NewData file;
      file DataBase window with new DataBase component
    end;
  repeat
    with NewData^ do
      initialize NewData window with new component;
    put copy of NewData window into NewData file;
    read a value for a choice variable
  until choice = 0;
  put dummy record with sentinel into NewData file;
  BuildCopy(DataBase, NewData)             (*activate a BuildCopy
                                  procedure to build a new DataBase
                                         file with the NewData file*)
end;                                       (*file-insertion algorithm*)
```

Notice that this algorithm appends new file components to the end of an existing file. There is no concern for order of the file components. All appending of new components is done to the newly generated NewData file. We use the old DataBase file merely to copy its components to the NewData file. This algorithm makes use of another algorithm, one to handle rebuilding a new master file (the DataBase file) using the components of the NewData file after all insertions have been made. Here is the BuildCopy algorithm.

```
begin
   prepare NewData file for inspection;                (*use reset*)
   prepare DataBase file for generation;               (*use rewrite*)
   while NewData^.wins <> sentinel do
      begin
         put copy of NewData window into DataBase file;
         assign next NewData component to NewData window
      end;                                                   (*while*)
   put copy of NewData window with sentinel into DataBase;
end;                                          (*BuildCopy algorithm*)
```

The BuildCopy algorithm will also be useful in procedures to handle deleting and editing file components. We show how to handle deletions next.

9.18.2 Deleting a File Component

Here is an algorithm to handle deletions of file components:

```
begin
   prepare NewData for generation;                     (*use rewrite*)
   prepare DataBase for inspection;                      (*use reset*)
   read a search key value;                  (*this will be one of the
                                               fields of a DataBase
                                                        component*)
   while not eof(DataBase) do
      begin
         if DataBase^.keyfield <> key
            then copy DataBase^ to NewData file;
         fill DataBase window with next DataBase component
      end;
   BuildCopy (DataBase, NewData)
end;                                          (*deletion algorithm*)
```

For example, if we choose the name field of a DataBase component as the keyfield, then we would use the following steps:

1. readln(SearchKey); (*SearchKey will type alfa or a string type*)

2.
```
   while not eof(DataBase) do
      begin
         if DataBase^.name <> SearchKey
            then write(NewData, DataBase);
         get(DataBase)
      end;
```

9.18.3 Refinement: Multiple Deletions

Notice that the deletion algorithm allows for only one deletion. This algorithm can be refined to handle more than one deletion in complete pass through the master file. To do this, it will be necessary to expand the first of the above steps and construct a list of SearchKey values. Then the second of the above steps can be modified by inserting a while loop to determine if the current value of the DataBase^ buffer variable corresponds to any of the SearchKey values. You might try using a Boolean variable, which be assigned true, if DataBase^ matches one of the SearchKey values. Try, for example, Found of type Boolean. Then use

if not Found **then** write(NewData, DataBase);

to decide when to copy the current value of DataBase^ to the NewData file. This refinement is left as an exercise.

9.18.4 *Refinement: Error Handling for a Search Failure*

What if the item we wish to delete from an existing file is not one of the file components? The deletion algorithm we have given makes no provision for a search failure. The above deletion algorithm runs blind. It does not detect when a record to be deleted has not been found. You can add to this algorithm a Boolean variable KeyFound, which can be assigned a value of false before the

while not eof(DataBase) **do** . . .

is executed. Then, inside the while block, assign a value of true to KeyFound, if there is a match between a value of the file window keyfield (name was used) and the SearchKey value. Then print an error message, if KeyFound is still false after the execution of the while block is complete. This refinement is left as an exercise.

9.18.5 *Editing a Component of an Existing File*

Here is an algorithm to handle editing a component of an existing file.

```
begin
  prepare NewData file for generation;                    (*use rewrite*)
  prepare DataBase file for inspection;                     (*use reset*)
  read value for SearchKey;              (*use name field of DataBase
                                            file as the SearchKey, for
                                                             example*)
  while DataBase^ <> sentinel do
    begin
      if DataBase^.keyfield = SearchKey
        then read new value for DataBase^;
                (*Notice! Here is where you should add an error-
                  handling provision, in case the component to be
                                          changed is not found.*)
      copy DataBase^ to NewData file;
      assign next DataBase component to DataBase^
    end;                                                      (*while*)
  copy DataBase^ to NewData file;       (*save dummy record with
                                                   sentinel field*)
  BuildCopy(DataBase, NewData)
  end;                                               (*edit algorithm*)
```

Notice that this algorithm also makes use of the BuildCopy algorithm given earlier. Several helpful refinements of this algorithm are possible.

9.18.6

Refinements of the File Edit Algorithm

Notice also that this algorithm makes no provision for multiple file-component changes. That is, only one SearchKey value is handled during one complete scan of the DataBase file. Notice also that this algorithm also runs blind. That is, it is possible to specify a SearchKey value for a file component that does not exist. Finally, notice that this algorithm works with only one SearchKey value. There is no provision for letting the user select the search key to use: name, wins, losses. These refinements are left for exercises.

9.18.7

Example: File Management of Team Records

A structure chart showing the framework for a beginning file-management program is given in Figure 9.9. The chart in Figure 9.9 shows considerable refinement of the structure chart in Figure 9.8. Notice how edit, delete, and

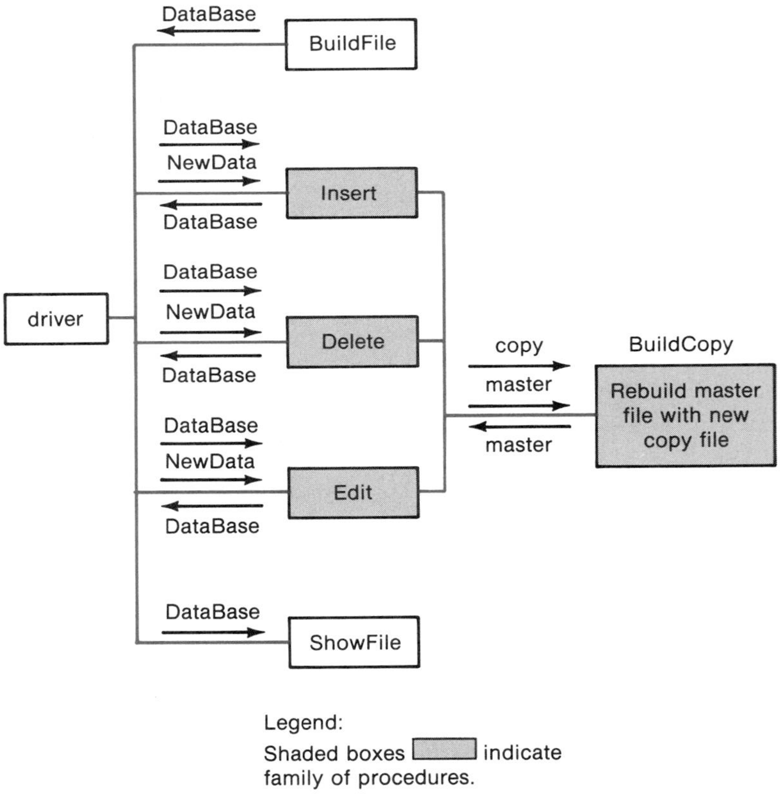

FIGURE 9.9
Structure chart for file management program

insert procedures rely on BuildCopy procedure to set up a scratch file. The BuildCopy procedure represents a level 2 procedure resulting from the stepwise refinement of these three file-management procedures. A program to implement the file management algorithms is given in Figure 9.10.

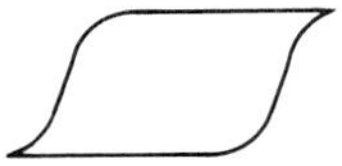

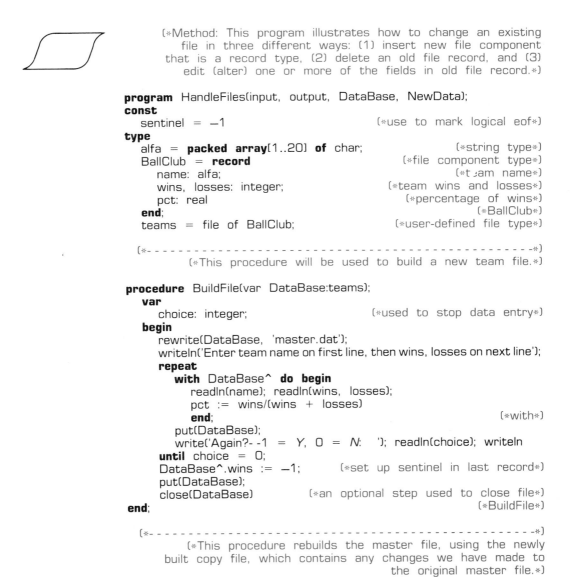

```
        (*Method: This program illustrates how to change an existing
           file in three different ways: (1) insert new file component
         that is a record type, (2) delete an old file record, and (3)
            edit (alter) one or more of the fields in old file record.*)

program HandleFiles(input, output, DataBase, NewData);
const
   sentinel = -1                              (*use to mark logical eof*)
type
   alfa = packed array[1..20] of char;                  (*string type*)
   BallClub = record                            (*file component type*)
      name: alfa;                                         (*team name*)
      wins, losses: integer;                     (*team wins and losses*)
      pct: real                                 (*percentage of wins*)
   end;                                                    (*BallClub*)
   teams = file of BallClub;                   (*user-defined file type*)

 (*-----------------------------------------------------------------*)
          (*This procedure will be used to build a new team file.*)

procedure BuildFile(var DataBase:teams);
   var
      choice: integer;                          (*used to stop data entry*)
   begin
      rewrite(DataBase, 'master.dat');
      writeln('Enter team name on first line, then wins, losses on next line');
      repeat
         with DataBase^ do begin
            readln(name); readln(wins, losses);
            pct := wins/(wins + losses)
            end;                                                   (*with*)
         put(DataBase);
         write('Again?- -1 = Y, 0 = N:   '); readln(choice); writeln
      until choice = 0;
      DataBase^.wins := -1;          (*set up sentinel in last record*)
      put(DataBase);
      close(DataBase)             (*an optional step used to close file*)
end;                                                          (*BuildFile*)

 (*-----------------------------------------------------------------*)
          (*This procedure rebuilds the master file, using the newly
        built copy file, which contains any changes we have made to
                                              the original master file.*)

procedure BuildCopy(var DataBase, NewData: teams);
```

```
begin
   reset(NewData, 'copy.dat');
   rewrite(DataBase, 'master.dat');
   while NewData^.wins <> sentinel do
      begin
         write(DataBase, NewData^);
         get(NewData)
      end;
   write(DataBase, NewData^);        (*save the dummy record, too*)
   close(DataBase); close(NewData)
end;                                                   (*BuildCopy*)

  (*- - - - - - - - - - - - - - - - - - - - - - - - - - - - - - - - - - - - - -*)
     (*This procedure allows a user to insert as many new team
                                               records as needed.*)

procedure Insert(var DataBase, NewData: teams);
var
   choice: integer;                        (*used to stop data entry*)
begin
   rewrite(NewData, 'copy.dat');
   reset(DataBase, 'master.dat');
   while DataBase^.wins <> sentinel do
      begin
         write(NewData, DataBase^);      (*write DataBase buffer to
                                                      NewData file*)
         get(DataBase)
      end;
   repeat
      with NewData^ do
         begin
            write('team name: '); readln(name); writeln;
            write('wins, losses: '); readln(wins, losses); writeln;
            pct := wins/(wins + losses)
         end;                                                (*with*)
      put(NewData);
      write('Again?- -1 = Y, 0 = N:  '); readln(choice); writeln
   until choice = 0;
   NewData^.wins := -1; put(NewData);
   BuildCopy(DataBase, NewData)
end;                                                       (*Insert*)

  (*- - - - - - - - - - - - - - - - - - - - - - - - - - - - - - - - - - - - - -*)
 (*This procedure allows a user to delete a single record from the
                                   original team (master) file.*)

procedure Delete(var DataBase, NewData: teams);
var
   cancel: alfa;                  (*used for name of team to cancel*)
begin
   rewrite(NewData, 'copy.dat'); reset(DataBase, 'master.dat');
   write('name of team you wish to drop: '); readln(cancel); writeln;
   while not eof(DataBase) do
```

```
      begin
         if DataBase^.name <> cancel
         then write(NewData, DataBase^);
         get(DataBase)
      end;
   BuildCopy(DataBase, NewData)
end;                                                        (*Delete*)

  (*---------------------------------------------------------*)
  (*This procedure allows the user to change only name field of an
                                original team (master) file record.*)

procedure Edit(var DataBase, NewData: teams);
var
   sample: BallClub; change: alfa;
begin
   reset(DataBase, 'master.dat'); rewrite(NewData, 'copy.dat');
   write('Enter team name to change: '); readln(change); writeln;
   while DataBase^.wins <> sentinel do
      begin
         if DataBase^.name = change
         then begin
            write('Enter new name: '); readln(DataBase^.name); writeln
            end;
         write(NewData, DataBase^);
         get(DataBase)
      end;
   write(NewData, DataBase^);             (*save record with sentinel*)
   BuildCopy(DataBase, NewData)
end;                                                          (*Edit*)

  (*---------------------------------------------------------*)
            (*This procedure prints a copy of the master file called
                                                         DataBase.*)

procedure ShowFile(var DataBase: teams);
var
   dash: integer;                             (*use to print dashes*)
begin
   reset(DataBase, 'master.dat');
   writeln('team':20, 'wins':20, 'losses':10, 'pct':12);
   for dash := 1 to 70 do write('—'); writeln;
   while DataBase^.wins <> sentinel do
      begin
         with DataBase^ do
            writeln(name:30, wins:10, losses:10, pct:12:3);
         get(DataBase)
      end
end;                                                      (*ShowFile*)
```

```
     (*- - - - - - - - - - - - - - - - - - - - - - - - - - - - - - - - - - - - - - - - -*)
       (*This procedure handles all the give and take among the other
                                      program procedures. It is menu driven.*)

procedure driver;
var
   HomeTeam, NewTeam: teams; option: integer;
begin
   repeat
      writeln('menu':20);
      writeln('- ->':20, '1. See copy of old file');
      writeln('- ->':20, '2. Build new file');
      writeln('- ->':20, '3. Insert new record into file');
      writeln('- ->':20, '4. Delete old record from file');
      writeln('- ->':20, '5. Edit old file record');
      readln(option); writeln;
      case option of
         1: ShowFile(HomeTeam);
         2: begin
               BuildFile(HomeTeam); ShowFile(HomeTeam)
               end;
         3: begin
               Insert(HomeTeam, NewTeam); ShowFile(HomeTeam)
               end;
         4: begin
               Delete(HomeTeam, NewTeam); ShowFile(HomeTeam)
               end;
         5: begin
               Edit(HomeTeam, NewTeam); ShowFile(HomeTeam)
               end
      end;                                                          (*case*)
      write('Again?- -1 = Y, 0 = N:   '); readln(option); writeln
   until option = 0
end;                                                              (*driver*)

  (*- - - - - - - - - - - - - - - - - - - - - - - - - - - - - - - - - - - - - - - - -*)

begin
   driver
end.
```

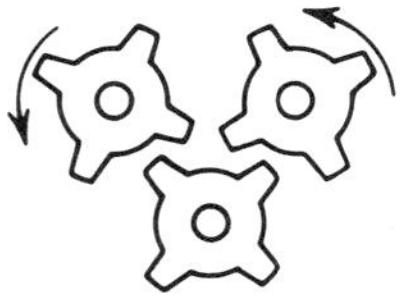

```
menu:
                    - ->1. See copy of old file
                    - ->2. Build new file
                    - ->3. Insert new record into file
                    - ->4. Delete old record from file
                    - ->5. Edit old file record
  1
```

Team	*Wins*	*Losses*	*Pct*
NewWhippets	33	4	0.892
Ucsd	9	5	0.643

```
Again?- -1  =  Y,  0  =  N:   1

                        menu:
                         -->1. See copy of old file
                         -->2. Build new file
                         -->3. Insert new record into file
                         -->4. Delete old record from file
                         -->5. Edit old file record
2

Enter team name on first line, then wins, losses on next line
whippets
45 1
Again?- -1  =  Y,  0  =  N:   1

avon
33 23
Again?- -1  =  Y,  0  =  N:   1

ucsd
20 9
Again?- -1  =  Y,  0  =  N:   0
```

Team	*Wins*	*Losses*	*Pct*
Whippets	45	1	0.978
Avon	33	23	0.589
Uscd	20	9	0.690

```
Again?- -1  =  Y,  0  =  N:   1

                        menu:
                         -->1. See copy of old file
                         -->2. Build new file
                         -->3. Insert new record into file
                         -->4. Delete old record from file
                         -->5. Edit old file record
3

team name: us c  twins

wins, losses: 44 5

Again?- -1  =  Y,  0  =  N:   0
```

Team	*Wins*	*Losses*	*Pct*
Whippets	45	1	0.978
Avon	33	23	0.589
Uscd	20	9	0.690
Twins	44	5	0.898

```
Again?--1 = Y, 0 = N:  1

                    menu:
                     -->1. See copy of old file
                     -->2. Build new file
                     -->3. Insert new record into file
                     -->4. Delete old record from file
                     -->5. Edit old file record
4

name of team you wish to drop: avon
```

Team	*Wins*	*Losses*	*Pct*
Whippets	45	1	0.978
Uscd	20	9	0.690
Twins	44	5	0.898

```
Again?--1 = Y, 0 = N:  1

                    menu:
                     -->1. See copy of old file
                     -->2. Build new file
                     -->3. Insert new record into file
                     -->4. Delete old record from file
                     -->5. Edit old file record
5

Enter team name to change:  whippets

Enter new name: N NewWhippets
```

Team	*Wins*	*Losses*	*Pct*
NewWhippets	45	1	0.978
Uscd	20	9	0.690
Twins	44	5	0.898

FIGURE 9.10 File management program

```
Again?--1 = Y, 0 = N:  0
```

9.18.8

Exercises

1. Carry out the refinement of the deletion algorithm described in Section 9.18.3, which will make it possible to delete more than one file component during a single scan of a file. Do this in terms of the deletion procedure in Figure 9.10. Give a sample run.

2. Carry out the refinement of the deletion algorithm described in Section 9.18.4, which will make it possible to detect a search failure when a file component is specified that does not exist. Again, do this in terms of the deletion procedure in Figure 9.10. Give a sample run.

3. Carry out the refinments of the edit algorithm described in Section 9.18.16. Do this in terms of the edit procedure in Figure 9.10. Give a sample run to illustrate all three cases.

4. Implement the insertion algorithm, and the refined versions of the deletion and edit algorithms in the program for exercise 21, which builds a file of records for chapter review words. Give a sample run to illustrate each feature of your program.

9.19 Case Study: Merge Sorting Files

If two files are sorted to begin with, then the following algorithm can be used to merge the two files to produce a file that is also sorted. In setting up this MergeSort, we will use two files with identical string-type components. We will call the first file *a*, the second *b*.

```
begin
  prepare existing a file for inspection;                  (*use reset*)
  prepare existing b file for inspection;                  (*use reset*)
  while (a^ <> sentinel) or (b^ <> sentinel) do
    if a^ <= b^
      then begin
        copy a^ to MergeFile;                          (*save a^ string*)
        assign next a component to a^
        end                                                  (*then*)
      else begin
        copy b^ to MergeFile;                          (*save b^ string*)
        assign next b component to b^
        end;                                                (*while*)
              (*Next, copy tails of two old files to MergeFile.*)
  while a^ <> sentinel do
    begin
      copy a^ to MergeFile;                          (*save current a^*)
      assign next a component to a^
    end;                                                    (*while*)
  while b^ <> sentinel do
    begin
      copy b^ to MergeFile;                          (*save current b^*)
      assign next b component to b^
    end;
  assign sentinel value to MergeFile^;
  copy MergeFile^ to MergeFile
end;                                            (*merge sort algorithm*)
```

The MergeSort algorithm works with a pair of existing files of the same type, which are sorted and have a trailing component used as a sentinel value. For example, if we are working with two ordered name files, then we can put a nonsense name like

'xxxxxyyyyy'

at the end of each ordered file as a sentinel to mark the logical end of each file. A program to illustrate this idea is given in Figure 9.11.

```
   (*Method: This program prepares two existing (ordered!) files for
                                        inspection and merges them.*)

program merge(a, b, NewBook);
const
   sentinel = 'xxxxxyyyyy';          (*used to mark logical end-of-file*)
type
   name = packed array[1..10] of char;
   BlackBook = file of name;                (*user-defined file type*)
var
   a, b, NewBook: BlackBook;               (*three file type variables*)

 (*- - - - - - - - - - - - - - - - - - - - - - - - - - - - - - - - - -*)
           (*This procedure does most of the work: prepares the
              ordered files for inspection, prepares NewBook for
                 generation, and merges the two name files.*)

procedure MergeFiles;
begin

   reset(a, 'a.dat'); reset(b, 'b.dat');  (*prepare a, b for inspection*)
   rewrite(NewBook, 'fold.dat');   (*prepare NewBook for generation*)
   while (a^ <> sentinel) and (b^ <> sentinel) do
      if a^ <= b^
      then begin
         write(NewBook, a^);
         get(a)
         end
      else begin
         write(NewBook, b^);
         get(b)
         end;
   while a^ <> sentinel do        (*take care of tail of the a file*)
      begin
         write(NewBook, a^); get (a)
      end;
   while b^ <> sentinel do        (*take care of tail of the b file*)
      begin
         write(NewBook, b^); get (b)
      end;
   write(NewBook, sentinel);
   close(NewBook)          (*optional, nonstandard step to make sure
                                        new file is ended correctly*)

end;                                               (*MergeFiles*)
```

```
(*-----------------------------------------------------*)
            (*This procedure prints a copy of the new file, which
            contains the merge of the original two ordered files.*)

procedure ShowMergedFiles;
begin
  reset(NewBook, 'fold.dat');
    while NewBook^ <> sentinel do
      begin
        writeln(NewBook^ : 40); get(NewBook)
      end
  end;                                        (*ShowMergedFiles*)

(*-----------------------------------------------------*)

begin

  MergeFiles;
  ShowMergedFiles

end.
```

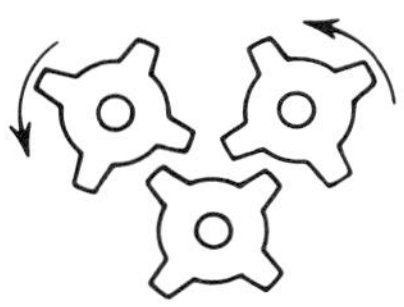

```
ty a.dat

andy    amy    arthur   susu   tim    xxxxxyyyyy

ty b.dat

enoch   malachi   sly   titus   valery   william   xxxxxyyyyy

run merge
                          andy
                          amy
                          arthur
                          enoch
                          malachi
                          sly
                          susu
                          tim
                          titus
                          valery
                          william
```

FIGURE 9.11 MergeSort of two files

Legend: 'ty' is short for 'type' used on a VAX-II to type the contents of a file.

9.19.1

Exercises

1. The MergeSort program in Figure 9.11 merges only a pair of ordered files. Refine this program so that the user can merge up to five ordered files. This means you will have no prompt for the names of the first two files to merge, then merge them, and then merge the NewBook file with the next ordered file the user might want to merge with the original pair of files. Give a sample run of your program for three ordered files.

2. Write a program to set up ordered files of type teams used in Figure 9.11. Then write another program to perform a MergeSort of the ordered team files. Give a sample run.

3. Expand the program in Figure 9.10 to include a MergeSort procedure. Then allow the user to set up more than one team file, then merge them when necessary. Do the following things:
   a. Give a new structure chart for the file management program.
   b. Give a sample run that demonstrates the MergeSort of two files that have been set up and managed with this program.

9.20 Readings

Claybrook, B. G. *File Management Techniques.* New York: Wiley, 1983.

Jensen, K., and Wirth, N. *Pascal User Manual and Report.* New York: Springer-Verlag, 1974. See Chapter 9 on files.

Loomis, M. E. S. *Data Management and File Processing.* Englewood Cliffs, NJ: Prentice-Hall, 1983. See discussion of Pascal files in Chapter 16.

CHAPTER 10

RECURSION

> *. . . Any program that can be written using assignment, the* **if-then-else** *statement and the* **while** *staement can also be written using assignment,* **if-then-else** *and recursion.*
>
> Ellis Horowitz and Sartaj Sahni, 1982

AIMS

- Introduce the notion of self-activation (also called *recursion*) in both functions and procedures.
- Suggest economies of expression that result from the use of a recursive technique.
- Show how to transform an assignment, **if-then-else, while** loop combination into an assignment, **if-then–else** and recursion combination.
- Introduce natural hunting grounds for recursive procedures and functions: recurrence relations.
- Introduce Dijkstra's greatest common divisor (GCD) machine.
- Give a case study on recursive string handling.
- Give a case study on MergeSort an array of records.
- Give a case study on quick-sorting lists.

10.1 Introduction to the Idea of Recursion

In Pascal it is possible for either a procedure or a function to activate itself. In effect either a function or procedure can call itself during its activation. For example, we can have the following function that activates itself:

```
                    (*infinite self-activation, if the following function is
                              activated with an integer less than 5*)
function aha(YourChoice: integer): real;
begin
  if (YourChoice - 1 < 5) and (YourChoice >= - 5) then
    aha(YourChoice - 1)                            (*self-activation!*)
  else
    if YourChoice < -5 then
      aha(YourChoice + 1);                    (*another self-activation*)
  aha := YourChoice
end;                                                           (*aha*)
```

The aha function calls itself endlessly, provided the function is activated with an integer value less than 5. For example, if this function is activated with

```
begin
  aha(5);                                             (*aha returns 5*)
  aha(4);                                          (*aha never returns*)
end;
```

then here is what happens.

Activation	*Result*
aha(5)	Then YourChoice is not less than 5 and the aha function identifier is assigned the value 5 (the returned value in the first line of the above block).
aha(4)	Then YourChoice is less than 5 and aha activates itself with aha(4 – 1) which means YourChoice is 3, so aha activates itself with aha(3 – 1) which leads to the following sequence of self-activations: aha(2 – 1) aha(1 – 1) aha(0 – 1) aha(–1 – 1) aha(–2 – 1) aha(–3 – 1) aha(–4 – 1) aha(–5 – 1)

Notice that now YourChoice is less than –5, so the else part of this function takes over and produces the following sequence of recursive calls:

aha(–6 + 1)
aha(–5 + 1)
aha(–6 + 1) and so on to infinity

Procedures can also activate themselves. For example, here is a procedure that works with character codes.

```
                    (*infinite self-activation, if the following procedure is
                       activated with a code for an uppercase letter*)
procedure BounceBack(YourCode : integer);
begin
  if (YourCode < ord('z')) and (YourCode > ord('A')) then
    BounceBack(pred(YourCode))                      (*self-activation*)
  else
    if YourCode <= ord('A') then
      BounceBack(succ(YourCode) + 50))              (*self-activation*)
end;                                                  (*BounceBack*)
```

The BounceBack procedure also produces an infinite recursion, if the value of YourCode is less than 122, which is the ASCII code for a lowercase *z*. For example, if we activate the BounceBack procedure with 65, the ASCII code for an uppercase *A*, then the following self-activations occur:

Activation	*Self-Activation*

begin
BounceBack(65)
end;
	BounceBack(pred(65))
	(*BounceBack activates itself with pred(65) = 64. This produces the second self-activation:
	BounceBack(succ(64) + 50) which means that YourCode now has a value of 65 + 50 = 115. This produces the following sequence of self-activations:
	BounceBack(pred(115))
	BounceBack(pred(114))
	BounceBack(pred(113))
	BounceBack(pred(112))
	BounceBack(pred(111))
	.
	.
	.
	BounceBack(pred(65)) *)

and this self-activation of the BounceBack will continue into infinity. In the real world, this theoretically infinite recursion will come to end rapidly and probably produce a fatal run-time error message like the following one on your computer:

```
Not enough memory!
(procedure Bounceback called 450 times)
```

If a recursion continues for too long, you will overflow the storage area used by Pascal to manage recursions. Pascal keeps track of what is happening during a recursion by using a linear list called a *stack*, which is governed by the last in, first out (LIFO) rule. Insertions and deletions in a stack are made at the same end. An insertion stack operation is called a *push;* a deletion stack operation, a *pop*.

Using this recursion stack, a processor will save the memory address following a recursive call as well as any parameters used in a recursive call. This takes up memory. The allowable memory used to manage these recursive calls will vary, depending on the resources of your computer. It does not take long before there is stack overflow because a function or procedure has attempted to activate itself too many times. This usually produces a run-time fatal error message like the above message.

It should also be noticed that some Pascal compilers are less forgiving, if you run a program with an infinite recursion. For example, an IBM PC/AT will crash, if an infinite recursion is run. Then it is necessary to reboot the machine to bring it back on line. You might try this on your local machine to see how forgiving (and watchful!) your Pascal compiler is.

It is necessary to build into a recursion some form of a shut-off (exit) mechanism to avoid infinite recursions. For example, we can rewrite the BounceBack procedure as follows:

```
procedure NewBounceBack(YourCode : integer);
begin
  if (YourCode < ord('z')) and (YourCode > ord('A')) then
    NewBounceBack(pred(YourCode))                (*self-activation*)
end;                                             (*NewBounceBack*)
```

The exit mechanism in this procedure results from restricting the values of YourCode, which will trigger self-activation. Even if YourCode has an initial value of 121, this NewBounceBack procedure will activate itself only a finite number of times. How many? Your might also wonder what would happen if this procedure were activated with a value of YourCode that is outside the interval from 66 (ASCII code for '*B*') to 121 (ASCII code for '*y*'). For example, what would happen if this NewBounceBack procedure were activated with a value of 2000 for YourCode?

It may not be obvious at first, but notice what happens in both of the above examples of self-activation. The aha function activates itself with a new value for the YourChoice parameter each time. In the above sample "run," with 4 as the initial value of YourChoice when the aha function is activated, then the aha function activates itself with a new value of its parameter

YourChoice, namely, 3. Notice that the BounceBack procedure activates itself with a new value of YourCode each time. In other words, a self-activation can be used to produce a desired change in the parameter(s) for a procedure or function.

Self-activating functions and procedures are easy to set up. They can be used to simplify the code in a procedure. We show how this can be done on a regular basis in this chapter. The aha function and BounceBack procedure illustrate a danger in the use of a self-activation mechanism: Self-activation will be endless unless some exit mechanism is built into a self-activating procedure or function that guarantees that the self-activation will not go on forever.

A procedure or function that has a self-activation mechanism is called a *recursive object.* The term **recursive** means return or recur (happen again). Here are some related words to keep in mind when you are mulling over recursion.

Words related to recursion:

Return; recur; happen again; do it over; reoccur; come again; reappear; resume; resound; reverberate; reverberation; echo; shout across a deep, vast canyon; revert; go back; try again; bounce back; happen over and over; turn back; another turn; the tide running to and fro; up and down the shales at Dover beach.

In general, a recursive object is defined in terms of itself. There are many real-world examples of recursive objects. Try looking in a mirror with your back turned to a second mirror. Position one mirror so that you can see yourself looking at yourself looking in a mirror (a simple recursion). An extension of this idea comes from an artist painting a picture of himself painting a picture of himself like the one in Figure 10.1. A procedure or function that activates itself is another example of a recursive object. This chapter shows how to set up recursive functions and procedures. As a result we will be able to set up a very useful and efficient method of sorting, a recursive MergeSort given in the first of the case studies at the end of this chapter. Recursion will also be useful later (in Chapter 12) when we study multilinked lists called trees.

FIGURE 10.1
Portrait of an artist painting a picture of himself

Here are some things to remember about recursion.

Design features of recursions:

1. Functions and procedures can activate themselves.

2. Recursions are managed by Pascal using a stack to save the memory address for line of code just after the one containing a recursive call and the processor is instructed to save any parameters that are part of the self-activation.

3. An exit mechanism must be built into a recursive function or procedure to prevent endless self-activation. An exit mechanism imposes a reasonable limit on the number of possible self-activations.

4. A recursive call can be used to modify the original value of a procedure parameter.

10.2 A Hidden Feature of Recursive Functions and Procedures

What happens inside a recursive function or procedure after the last self-activation and the end of the procedure block is reached? Each self-activation causes a return address to be put on a stack. When the processor reaches the **end** of the recursive procedure, it will start popping the return addresses off the stack. Remember that this return address identifies the location of the line of code immediately following the line of code containing the self-activation (recursive call). Each time the processor gets one of these return addresses off the recursion stack, it will use this address to determine which instruction to execute next. It will execute this instruction and any that follow it in sequence until it reaches the end of the procedure block. Then this process repeats itself.

1. Pop next return address off the recursion stack.
2. Execute the sequence of instructions (if there are any!), starting with the instruction specified by the return address popped from the recursion stack and proceding in sequence until the end of the procedure block.
3. Repeat step 1 until the last return address has been popped from the recursion stack.

For example, here is an algorithm that can used to set up a recursion which counts the number of characters in a string:

```
begin
   read in a script, which a string-type;
          (*note: make last character of script a sentinel char*)
   initialize count with 1;                 (*use to count characters*)
   while script[count] <> sentinel do
      begin
         assign count to tally;          (*tally holds character count*)
         add 1 to count
      end;                                                   (*while*)
end;                         (*algorithm to count characters in a string*)
```

We can use a recursive procedure to implement this algorithm. We can do this by replacing the **while** statement by an **if-then** statement. Here is a procedure to do this.

```
procedure LengthOfString(var script: StringType;           (*a string*)
                              count: integer);             (*char count*)
begin
   if script[count] <> sentinel                             (*exit mechanism*)
      then begin
         tally := count;                                    (*tally is a global*)
         LengthOfString(script, count + 1)                  (*self-activation*)
         end;                                               (*if*)
   writeln('count = ', count, ' for ', script[count]))
end;                                                        (*LengthOfString*)
```

Notice how the sentinel is used in this procedure as an exit mechanism. As long as we append a sentinel character to the end of a string we enter, this procedure will not be an infinite recursion. For example, we can activate this procedure with

LengthOfString('Susu*', 1);

The trailing asterisk (*) will be used as the sentinel character to shut off the recursion. Here is a running history of what happens during the activation of the LengthOfString procedure.

Activation	Count	Character Found
LengthOfString('Susu*', 1);	1	*'S'*
LengthOfString('Susu*', 1 + 1);	2	*'u'*
LengthOfString('Susu*', 2 + 1);	3	*'s'*
LengthOfString('Susu*', 3 + 1);	4	*'u'*
LengthOfString('Susu*', 4 + 1);	5	'*'

Now the processor begins popping the return addresses.

Action Taken	Result
Return to writeln following self-activation	Count = 5 for *
Return to writeln following self-activation	Count = 4 for *u*
Return to writeln following self-activation	Count = 3 for *s*
Return to writeln following self-activation	Count = 2 for *u*
Return to writeln following self-activation	Count = 1 for *S*
Return to driver procedure	String length = 4

The choice of parameters to be changed by a recursive call is crucial. There is a bug you should be wary of when you set up the parameters used in a recursion.

10.3

Bug Clinic: Parameters Used in a Recursive Procedure

The above procedure has a variable parameter used in this recursion, namely, *tally*. This is a reference to a memory location, which is affected by what happens inside the LengthOfString procedure but not by the self-activation. During this recursion, only the count parameter is changed during the self-activation. That is, each time procedure activates itself, it increments count by 1. Count is a value parameter. Try making count a variable parameter and see what happens.

10.4

Example: A Program with a Recursive Procedure

In Figure 10.2 we show a program to illustrate the use of the LengthOfString procedure. This program prints a history of what happens after the last self-activation by the LengthOfString procedure. You might also want to try putting the following writeln statement at the beginning of the then block of this procedure.

```
writeln('count = ', count:4, ' for ', script[count]:5);
```

```
        (*Method: Trace history of self-activation of a procedure that
                                      counts the length of a string.*)

program TraceRecursion(input, output);
const
  max = 80;                                    (*maximum string size*)
  sentinel = '*';                            (*end-of-string character*)
type
  StringType = packed array[1..max] of char;         (*type string*)

 (*-------------------------------------------*)
               (*Use recursion to find the length of a string:*)

procedure LengthOfString(script: StringType;        (*entered string*)
                         var tally: integer;          (*string size*)
                         count: integer);             (*holds tally*)
begin
  if script[count] <> sentinel then begin
    tally := count;
    LengthOfString(script, tally, count + 1)      (*self-activation*)
    end;                                               (*then block*)
  writeln('count = ':20, count:5, ' for ', script[count]:5)
end;                                               (*LengthOfString*)
```

```
  (*- - - - - - - - - - - - - - - - - - - - - - - - - - - - - - - - - - - - - - - - - -*)
                  (*Get values needed to activate LengthOfString:*)

procedure driver;
var
   LocalString: StringType;                                  (*supplied by user*)
   choice: integer;                                          (*control variable*)
   LocalTally: integer;                                      (*will hold length*)
begin
   repeat
      write('Enter string with trailing * :   ');
      readln(LocalString); writeln;
      LengthOfString(LocalString, LocalTally, 1);
      writeln; for choice := 1 to 70 do write('—'); writeln;
      writeln('String Length = ':25, LocalTally:6);
      write('Again?- -1 = Y, 0 = N:   '); readln(choice); writeln
   until choice = 0
end;                                                                  (*driver*)

  (*- - - - - - - - - - - - - - - - - - - - - - - - - - - - - - - - - - - - - - - - - -*)

begin
   driver                                          (*activate driver procedure*)
end.
```

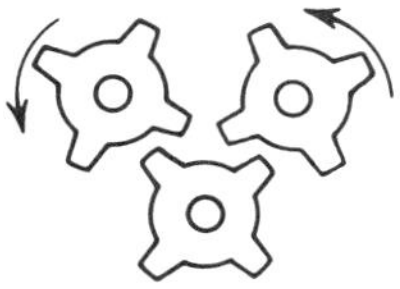

```
Enter string with trailing *: Eureka!*

               count =      8 for   *
               count =      7 for   !
               count =      6 for   a
               count =      5 for   k
               count =      4 for   e
               count =      3 for   r
               count =      2 for   u
               count =      1 for   E

            String Length =        7
Again?- -1 = Y, 0 = N:  0
```

FIGURE 10.2 History of a recursion

Why? This will show you what happens during the recursion. It will show you the changes in the count parameter after each self-activation by the LengthOfString procedure. This writeln statement plus the one already in Figure 10.2 will give you a complete trace of what happened during the activation of this procedure. It is a good idea to build into a recursive procedure a trace of what happens, especially when you are first learning to set up procedures like this. This change in the LengthOfString procedure is left as an exercise.

Here is a rule of thumb to remember.

> **Recursion rule of thumb:**
>
> **When a processor exits from a recursion, it will return to execute the statement after the self-activation statement. It will do this as many times as the self-activation occurred.**

10.5 Another Recursive Procedure: Dijkstra's GCD Machine

Edsger Dijkstra (1976) suggests a way to find the GCD of two positive integers using what he calls a *GCD machine.* He suggests thinking of a pair of positive integers you start with as the lengths of horizontal and vertical wires. These can be thought of as the width and length of a rectangle. Now imagine a 54° line shooting up from the lower left-hand corner of the rectangle. Now think of the lines opposite the 45° line as wires that can be moved. Then move the horizontal wire down and the vertical wire to the left until the two wires intersect on the 45° line. Where the two wires intersect on the 45° line will be the GCD of the two numbers the wires represent. So this is a subtraction process. Move the wire with the smaller magnitude; do this by subtracting the length of the shorter wire from the longer one (cutting the longer one, if you like). Eventually, both wires will have the same length. We show a graphical interpretation of this idea in Figure 10.3. In this picture, the vertical wire (on

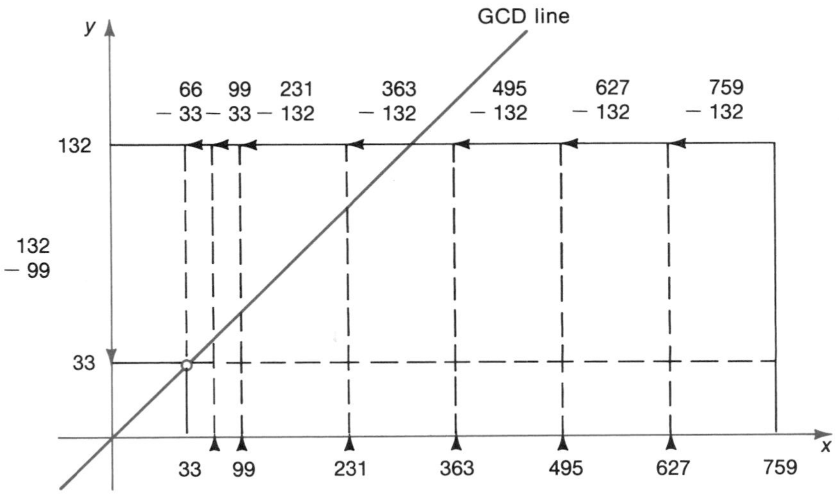

FIGURE 10.3
Moves inside Dijkstra's GCD machine

the right-hand side of the outside rectangle) has an initial length of 132 units. The horizontal wire (the top line of the rectangle) has an initial length of 759 units. Since the horizontal wire is the longer of the two wires, it gets cut by 132 units. (This moves the vertical wire in 132 units.) A horizontal wire gets cut this way five times before it is shorter than the vertical wire. Here is the whole story.

Horizontal Wire	Vertical Wire	Action
759	132	(Initial state of machine)
627	132	Cut horizontal wire
495	132	Cut horizontal wire
363	132	Cut horizontal wire
231	132	Cut horizontal wire
99	132	Cut horizontal wire
99	33	Cut vertical wire
66	33	Cut horizontal wire
33	33	Cut horizontal wire
		(Stop the machine!)

The greatest common divisor of 759 and 132 is 33, the position on the 45° line where the original two wires intersect. A nonrecursive algorithm to implement Dijkstra's GCD machine follows:

```
begin
   read values for two positive integers x and y;
   while x <> y do
      if x < y
         then y := y − x                       (*y is longer, "cut" it*)
         else x := x − y                       (*x is longer, "cut" it*)
end;                                           (*Dijkstra's GCD machine*)
```

We can implement this algorithm in Pascal as follows:

```
procedure GCD(x, y : integer);
begin
   while x <> y do
      if x < y
         then y := y − x                                  (*diminish y*)
         else x := x − y;                                 (*diminish x*)
   writeln('GCD = ', x)
end;                                                      (*GCD*)
```

Notice that we can print either *x* or *y*, once we exit from the while loop of this GCD procedure. Notice that this GCD procedure matches the situation described by Horowitz and Sahni (see the opening quote of this chapter). That is, we have an **if-then-else** statement with assignment statements inside a **while** loop. So we should be able to rewrite this procedure so that it is recursive. This can be done as follows:

```
procedure GCD(x, y: integer);
begin
   if x <> y
      then
         if x < y
            then GCD(x, y - x)                  (*a self-activation*)
            else GCD(x - y, y)                  (*a self-activation*)
      else
         writeln('GCD = ', x)
end;                                                          (*GCD*)
```

Notice that the writeln statement in this recursive procedure will only get executed once. This happens when *x* equals *y*. You might also wonder what happens when the processor starts popping the return addresses off the recursion stack after the last self-activation. This question is left as an exercise. You might also wonder what would happen if we printed the values of *x* and *y* before each self-activation. Finally, you might also wonder what would be printed if we were to put a the following statement as the last statement in this recursive procedure:

```
writeln(x, y)                     (*placed at end of GCD block*)
```

This question is also left as an exercise. We show the implementation of the recursive form of the GCD procedure in Figure 10.4. Even though the GCD procedure in the program in Figure 10.4 will always be finite, it can still have a potential for causing run-time problems. Remember that the recursion stack used by Pascal to handle a recursive procedure or function is limited in size. We take a closer look at the exit mechanism used by the GCD procedure next.

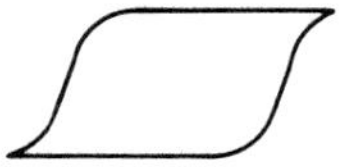

```
        (*Method: This program uses GCD, a recursive procedure,
        to determine the GCD of a pair of integers entered from
                                                   a keyboard.*)

program DijkstrasMethod(input, output);

 (*-------------------------------------------------------*)
      (*This procedure will continue to activate itself until x = y;
   it uses repeated subtraction to isolate the GCD of x and y.*)

procedure GCD(x, y: integer);
begin
   if x <> y
   then begin
      writeln(x:20, y:10);
      if x < y
      then GCD(x, y - x)
      else GCD(x - y, y)
      end
   else writeln(x:20, ' = the greatest common divisor.')
end;                                                      (*GCD*)
```

```
  (*- - - - - - - - - - - - - - - - - - - - - - - - - - - - - - - - - - - - - - - - - - - -*)
  (*This procedure activates GCD with 2 numbers supplied by the user.*)

procedure driver;
var
   FirstNumber, SecondNumber: integer;        (*get values from user*)
   choice: integer;                          (*allow for more choices*)
begin
   repeat
      write('Enter a pair of positive integers: ');
      readln(FirstNumber, SecondNumber);
      writeln('trace of what happens during recursion:');writeln;
      GCD(FirstNumber, SecondNumber);                  (*start recursion*)
      for choice := 1 to 70 do write('—'); writeln;
      write('Again?- -1 = Y, 0 = N: '); readln(choice); writeln
   until choice = 0
end;                                                              (*driver*)

  (*- - - - - - - - - - - - - - - - - - - - - - - - - - - - - - - - - - - - - - - - - - - -*)

begin
   driver
end.
```

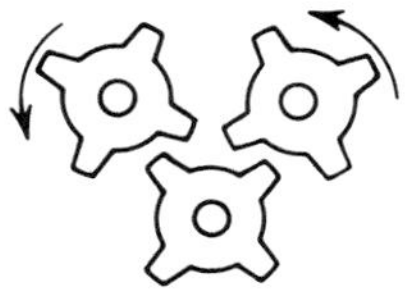

```
Enter a pair of positive integers: 220 284
trace of what happens during recursion:

                              220          284
                              220           64
                              156           64
                               92           64
                               28           64
                               28           36
                               28            8
                               20            8
                               12            8
                                4            8
                                4 = the greatest common divisor.

Again?- -1 = Y, 0 = N: 1

Enter a pair of positive integers: 32767 7000
trace of what happens during recursion:

                            32767         7000
                            25767         7000
                            18767         7000
                            11767         7000
                             4767         7000
                             4767         2233
                             2534         2233
                              301         2233
                              301         1932
```

```
301        1631
301        1330
301        1029
301         728
301         427
301         126
175         126
 49         126
 49          77
 49          28
 21          28
 21           7
 14           7
  7 = the greatest common divisor.

Again?- -1 = Y, 0 = N: 0
```

FIGURE 10.4 Dijkstra's GCD machine with recursion

10.6 Bug Clinic: A Finite Recursion Can Still Be a Problem

Even though a recursive procedure will always activate itself a finite number of times, it is possible to have a run-time error. Your recursive procedure can swamp the recursion stack, causing it to overflow. Notice that the exit mechanism used to stop the recursion in the GCD procedure in Figure 10.4 is produced by the following **if-then** statement:

if $x <> y$
  then . . .   (*exit mechanism*)

Eventually x will equal y and this will prevent further self-activation by the GCD procedure. On a computer that allows a maximum of 450 self-activations by this procedure, can you think of allowable integer values of x and y that will make the above program bomb? Try experimenting with the above program on your machine to answer this question. You will be looking for a way to overflow the recursion stack used by your processor. In other words, even though the above procedure is never infinitely recursive, it still may act up on your machine for some values of x and y.

10.7 Hunting Ground for Recursions: Recurrence Relations

A recurrence relation is a rule that defines each term of a sequence in terms of previous terms. For example, we can set up a recurrence relation to define each term of a sequence of factorials. To compute $n!$ (read n factorial), we use the following method:

$$1 \times 2 \times 3 \times 4 \times 5 \times \cdots \times (n-1) \times n = n!$$

Here are some examples of factorials.

n	n!	n	n!
1	1	7	5040
2	2	8	40320
3	6	9	362880
4	24	10	3628800
5	120	11	39916800
6	720	12	479001600

Notice that we can set up the following recurrence relation to describe a sequence of factorials:

$n! = (n = 1)! * n$ (*recurrence relation*)

This gives us the following sequence:

n	Term of factorial sequence
1	$1! = 0! * 1 = 1$
2	$2! = 1! * 2 = 2$
3	$3! = 2! * 3 = 2 * 3 = 6$
4	$4! = 3! * 4 = 6 * 4 = 24$
5	$5! = 4! * 5 = 24 * 5 = 120$
6	$6! = 5! * 6 = 120 * 6 = 720$
.	.
.	.
.	.
n	$n! = (n - 1)! * n$

Notice how each factorial is defined in terms of the previous factorial. A sequence set up with a recurrence relation makes an ideal hunting ground for recursive procedures. For example, we can use the following recursive procedure to compute factorials:

```
procedure ComputeFactorial(n, nFactorial : integer);
begin
  if n <> 1
    then ComputeFactorial(n - 1, n * nFactorial)
    else writeln('n factorial = ', nFactorial)
end;                                           (*ComputeFactorial*)
```

For example, if we activate this procedure with

ComputeFactorial(5, 1);

the following actions occur within this procedure:

Action	n	nFactorial
ComputeFactorial(5, 1)	5	1
ComputeFactorial(n–1,n*nFactorial)	4	5
ComputeFactorial(n–1,n*nFactorial)	3	20
ComputeFactorial(n–1,n*nFactorial)	2	60
ComputeFactorial(n–1,n*nFactorial)	1	120
Stop self-activation, since $n = 1$		

Print n factorial = 120

A program to implement the ComputeFactorial procedure is given in Figure 10.5. This procedure is severely limited. Why? Factorials grow fast. It will not take long for this procedure to outstrip the capacity of your machine. If you are using a 16-bit machine, you will probably find your machine cannot handle

ComputeFactorial(8, 1);

Why? On a 16-bit machine, the largest integer will be 32767 or $2^{15} - 1$ and $8! = 40320$. We can improve the yield from the above procedure by declaring the nFactorial parameter to be real. This improvement is left as an exercise.

```
          (*Method: Use recurrence relation for factorials to set
                    up recursion to produce factorials.*)

(*- - - - - - - - - - - - - - - - - - - - - - - - - - - - - - - - - - -*)
            (*Supply terms of recurrence relation in recursion:*)

program TryThis(input,output);
procedure ComputeFactorial(n: integer;                (*gives n in n!*)
                           nFactorial: integer;        (*product*)
begin
  if n <> 1
  then ComputeFactorial(n - 1, n * nFactorial)
  else writeln('n factorial = ':20, nFactorial)
end;                                            (*ComputeFactorial*)

(*- - - - - - - - - - - - - - - - - - - - - - - - - - - - - - - - - - -*)
         (*Program manager: gets values needed for recursion*)

procedure driver;
var
  choice: integer;                              (*control variable*)
begin
  repeat
    write('Enter n to compute n!   '); readln(choice); writeln;
    ComputeFactorial(choice, 1);
    write('Again?- -1 = Y, 0 = N:   '); readln(choice); writeln
  until choice = 0
end;                                                     (*driver*)
```

```
(*- - - - - - - - - - - - - - - - - - - - - - - - - - - - - - - - - - - - - - - - - - - - - - - -*)

begin
   driver                                              (*activate driver procedure*)
end.
```

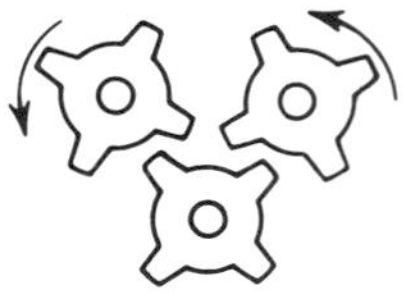

```
Enter n to compute n!  3

      n factorial =         6
Again?- -1 = Y, 0 = N:  1

Enter n to compute n!  4

      n factorial =        24
Again?- -1 = Y, 0 = N:  1

Enter n to compute n!  5

      n factorial =       120
Again?- -1 = Y, 0 = N:  0
```

FIGURE 10.5 Factorials from a recursion

10.8 Replacing a Recursion by an Iteration

Any recursive procedure can be rewritten as a nonrecursive one. It is good to practice undoing recursive procedures, using an iteration like the while loop in the first form of the GCD procedure in Section 10.7. For example, we can rewrite the ComputeFactorial procedure so that it is nonrecursive. Here is a nonrecursive version of the same procedure.

```
procedure ComputeFactorial(n : integer;                        (*for n!*)
                           nFactorial: real);              (*for bigger
                                                       factorial values*)
begin
   while n <> 1 do
      begin
         nFactorial := nFactorial * n;
         n := n - 1
      end;                                                     (*while*)
   writeln('n factorial = ', nFactorial:18:0)
end;                                                (*ComputeFactorial*)
```

Because a recursive procedure or function depends on the use of a recursion stack, using an iteration instead of a recursion will sometimes be desirable. An iteration will take less time and less memory than a corresponding recursion.

10.9 Why Use Recursion?

Recursions are useful tools for the following reasons:

1. **Simplification.** Procedures that depend on iterations can usually be simplified with a recursion.

2. **Readability.** Recursive procedures tend to be easier to follow and shorter than their iterative counterparts.
3. **Natural adaptation.** There are structured data types with definitions that are recursive. This is especially true of lists of items where each item in the list is defined in terms of preceding list items. For example, in a family tree (a list showing parents and their offspring) there is a natural recursive relationship between a child and its ancestors.

In deciding whether to use a recursive procedure, you will have to balance off the above features against the storage overhead and extra time required by a recursion. Every recursion has storage overhead, since each recursion depends on the use of a stack. How much stack storage will be needed will depend on the number of recursive calls made during a recursion. In addition, a recursion will take more time than the corresponding iteration. So a lengthy recursion will be slower than the corresponding iteration.

Recursions take more time because of the stack management problem. It takes a processor time to push and pop the return addresses it uses. Even with these two problems, we are talking about very little storage and time, if a recursion is not lengthy. You can gauge which method is better to use after you have had some experience with both recursions and iterations. For this reason, it is a good idea to try both methods with the same procedure. You will quickly find out which method is more reasonable.

10.10 Summary

Pascal procedures and functions can activate themselves. A procedure or function that activates itself is recursive. A recursion will be infinite unless an exit mechanism is built into a recursive procedure or function.

During the activation of a recursive procedure or function, a recursion stack is used to manage the recursion. This stack guarantees that a processor will return to the line of code that follows a self-activation. If recursion inside a procedure is terminated in a normal way, then a processor will pop the last return address and any parameters from the recursion stack. This return address leads the processor to the line of code immediately following the statement responsible for a recursion.

Execution continues until the procedure **end** is reached. Then the processor pops the next return address and any parameters off the recursion stack. This leads the processor back to the line of code immediately after the line of code responsible for a self-activation. This process continues until the recursion stack is empty, which terminates activation of the recursive procedure.

Because the activation of a recursive procedure depends on the use of a stack, there is always a danger that this stack will overflow before a recursion is complete. In other words, a recursive procedure can bomb, if it is allowed to go on too long. This problem needs to be considered when a recursive procedure is set up. That is, the exit mechanism used to guarantee a finite recursion should also guarantee that a recursion will terminate after a reasonable number of self-activations.

A procedure that relies on the use of an **if-then-else** and assignment statements inside a while loop, can be rewritten as a recursive procedure. This is both easy and sometimes useful to do to produce a procedure that is more readable. it is also possible to go back the other way: Replace a recursive procedure by a nonrecursive one that depends on an iteration.

Sequences defined by recurrence relations make natural hunting grounds for recursive procedures and functions. We illustrated this idea in Figure 10.5.

10.11 Keywords Review

Keywords	*Related Ideas*
exit mechanism	used to terminate a recursion
GCD	greatest common divisor
GCD machine	Dijkstra's way of finding the GCD
recurrence relation	rule used to define the current term of a sequence in terms of preceding terms
recursion	self-activation within a procedure or function
recursive object	defined in terms of itself
self-activation	recursive call

10.12 Exercises

1. What is meant by the term *self-activation* or *recursive call?*
2. What is an exit mechanism?
3. What is the exit mechanism in the picture of the artist painting a picture of himself in Figure 10.1?
4. Give an example of an activation of a recursive procedure that has an exit mechanism and still produces a run-time fatal error (the recursion stack overflows).
5. When will a recursive procedure be infinite?
6. Sketch the operation of Dijkstra's GCD machine for the following pairs of numbers:
   a. 255, 990
   b. 660, 3795
   c. 1980, 2556
7. Using Dijkstra's method, write a program to compute the GCD of two or more positive integers, not just a pair of positive integers. Run your program for
   a. 220, 284, 32
   b. 220, 284, 500, 32

8. Put writeln statements into the following figures to trace what happens during a recursion:
   a. Figure 10.2
   b. Figure 10.5

   Give a sample run in each case.

9. Write recursive procedures to produce terms of the sequences defined by the indicated recurrence relations.

Sequence	*Recurrence Relation*
(a) 1, 1, 2, 3, 5, 8, 13, . . .	Fibonacci sequence where $F(1) = F(2) = 1$ and $F(n) = F(n-1) + F(n-2)$
(b) 2, 1, 3, 4, 7, 11, 18, . . .	Lucas sequence where $L(0) = 2$, $L(1) = 1$ and $L(n) = L(n-1) + L(n-2)$

10. Write a program to implement the procedures in exercise 9 so that the your program does the following things:
   a. Prints a menu:

      → 1. Fibonacci sequence
      → 2. Lucas sequence

   b. Prompts for initial two terms of the chosen sequence.
   c. Determines how many terms of the chosen sequence to print.
   d. Allows the user to make another choice from the menu. Give samples runs using
   e. Fibonacci sequence with leading terms 3, 5 and prints 10 terms.
   f. Fibonacci sequence with leading terms 1, 1 and prints 20 terms.
   g. Lucas sequence with leading terms 7, 11 and prints 10 terms.
   h. Lucas sequence with leading terms 2, 1 and prints 20 terms.

11. Refinement. The program for exercise 10 can be simplified. Except for the initial two terms, the recurrence relations in exercise 9 are the same. The terms of either the Fibonacci or Lucas sequence are each obtained from the preceding two terms. Replace the two Fibonacci and Lucas procedures in the program for exercise 10 by one procedure. Run the new program for the values in parts (a)–(d) of exercise 10.

12. (Ackermann) The Ackermann function Acker(m, n) is defined as follows:

```
if m = 0 then Acker(m, n) := n + 1
   else
      if n = 0 then Acker(m, n) := Acker(m - 1, 1)
         else
            Acker(m, n) := Acker(m - 1, Acker(m, n - 1))
```

Write a program to implement this function. Include in your program a trace of what happens during the recursion. Give a sample run for the following values of *m* and *n*:

a. Acker(0, 0)
b. Acker(0, 7)
c. Acker(1, 7)
d. Acker(2, 0)
e. Acker(2, 5)
f. Acker(3, 0)
g. Acker(3, 2)
h. Acker(4, 0)

What can you say about higher values of *n*, if $m = 4$?

13. (Towers of Hanoi) Imagine three needles used to hold disks. Further imagine that the first needle has five disks and the remaining two needles are empty. Each of the five disks on the first needle is a different size and they are arranged in order from smallest (on top) to largest (on the bottom). Write a procedure that simulates moving all the disks from the first needle to the third one subject to the condition that no disk is ever allowed to be placed on top of a smaller disk. This can be done using recursion. Implement your procedure in a program. Allow the user to choose how many disks are on the first needle. Give some sample runs.

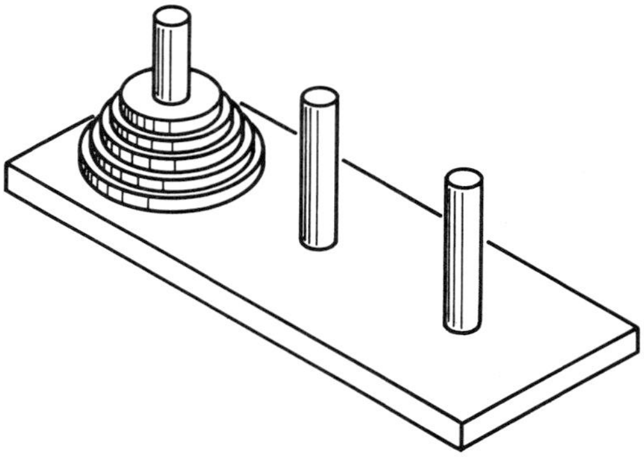

14. (Graphical Towers of Hanoi) Use the Towers of Hanoi procedure in exercise 13 in a program which prints the disks after *each* move. Allow up to 4 disks to be used.

10.13 Review Quiz

Determine whether the following are true or false:

1. Every finite recursion has an exit mechanism.
2. In Pascal, both procedures and functions can be recursive.
3. Recursion begins in a recursive procedure when the procedure activates itself.

4. Only value parameters can be changed when a procedure activates itself.

5. A recursive procedure can have both variable and value parameters.

6. Pascal relies on the use of a queue to manage a recursive procedure or function.

7. After the last self-activation inside a recursive procedure, all activity inside the procedure terminates.

8. If the last line of a recursive procedure is

   writeln('Yes!')

   and this procedure calls itself 20 times, then 'Yes' will be printed 21 times by this procedure.

9. A recursive procedure takes less time and memory than a nonrecursive procedure.

10. A nonrecursive procedure that relies exclusively on an **if-then-else** and assignment statement combination inside a **while** loop, cannot be rewritten as recursive procedure.

10.14 Case Study: String Handling

Here is an algorithm to concatenate two strings:

```
                                        (*input: two strings;
                                        output: joined strings*)
begin
   read StringA and StringB;
   assign to CountA the length of StringA;
   assign to CountB the length of StringB;
   assign 1 to selector;
   while selector ≤ countB do
      string[countA + selector] := StringB[selector];
      add 1 to selector
      end;                                           (*while*)
end;                         (*algorithm to concatenate two strings*)
```

Notice that StringA will hold the concatenated (attached) strings when the execution of the **while** loop is finished. Also notice that we can implement the **while** loop of this algorithm using a recursive procedure. Here is a procedure to do this.

```
procedure concatenate(var StringA, StringB: StringType;
                          countA, countB: integer;
                          selector: integer);
begin
   if selector ≤ countB then begin
      StringA[countA + selector] := StringB[selector];
      concatenate(StringA,StringB,countA,countB,selector+1)
      end
end;                                              (*concatenate*)
```

In this procedure, both variable and value parameters are used. During the activation of this procedure, String*A* is used to build the concatenated string. Whatever characters that are in second string are loaded into the array cells trailing after the last entered character of String*A*. To start this recursion, it will be necessary to start the selector parameter with a value of 1. We show a program to carry out this idea in Figure 10.6. In this program, notice how the **if** statement inside the repeat loop of the ShowString procedure is used to suppress the printing of the sentinel character (a '*'). Actually, String*A* will end up holding two copies of the sentinel. The use of a sentinel can be eliminated in this program. This leads to the refinement explained in Section 10.14.1.

```
      (*Method: This program uses a recursive procedure called
         concatenation to attach one string onto another. The
         string type used has a length big enough to hold both
            strings. Using the lengths of two entered strings,
         the empty positions following the last character of the
           first entered string are filled with the characters of
                                                  the second string.*)

program BuildStrings(input, output);

const
   max = 160;                                (*maximum length of string*)
   sentinel = '*';                                 (*mark end of string*)
type
   StringType = packed array[1..max] of char;          (*use for both
                                                              strings*)

  (*-----------------------------------------------------------------*)

procedure concatenate(var StringA, StringB: StringType;  (*pair of strings*)
                            countA, countB: integer;       (*sizes of strings*)
                            selector: integer);          (*select characters*)
begin
   if selector <= countB
   then begin
      StringA[countA + selector] := StringB[selector];
      concatenate(StringA, StringB, countA, countB, selector + 1)
      end
end;                                                       (*concatenate*)

  (*-----------------------------------------------------------------*)

procedure initialize(var script: StringType;                   (*a string*)
                         limit: integer);                (*size of string*)
var
   selector: integer;
begin
   for selector := 1 to limit do script[selector] := ' '
end;                                                        (*initialize*)
```

```
(*------------------------------------------*)

procedure BuildString(var script: StringType;          (*a string*)
                      var limit: integer);             (*string size*)
var
   selector: integer;
begin
   writeln('Enter string with end-of-string character * :');
   selector := 1;
   while not eoln do
      begin
         read(script[selector]); selector := selector + 1
      end;                                              (*while block*)
   readln;                          (*move input pointer to next line*)
   limit := selector - 1                          (*true string length*)
end;                                                   (*BuildString*)

(*------------------------------------------*)

procedure ShowString(script: StringType;                (*a string*)
                     limit: integer);                   (*string length*)
var
   selector: integer;
begin
   selector := 1;
   writeln('Concatenated string:   ');
   repeat
      if script[selector] <> sentinel then
         begin
            write(script[selector]); selector := selector + 1
         end                                            (*then block*)
      else selector := selector + 1;
   until selector = limit
end;                                                    (*ShowString*)

(*------------------------------------------*)

procedure driver;
var
   FirstString, SecondString: StringType;        (*2 string variables*)
   FirstCount, SecondCount: integer;              (*sizes of 2 strings*)
   choice: integer;                                (*control variable*)
begin
   repeat
      BuildString(FirstString, FirstCount);
      BuildString(SecondString, SecondCount);
      concatenate(FirstString, SecondString, FirstCount, SecondCount, 1);
      ShowString(FirstString, FirstCount + SecondCount);
      writeln; writeln;
      write('Again?- -1 = Y, 0 = N:   '); readln(choice); writeln;
      if FirstCount = 1
      then begin
         initialize(FirstString, FirstCount);
         initialize(SecondString, SecondCount)
         end                                            (*then block*)
   until choice = 0
end;                                                        (*driver*)
```

```
(*- - - - - - - - - - - - - - - - - - - - - - - - - - - - - - - - - - - - - - - -*)

begin
   driver
end.
```

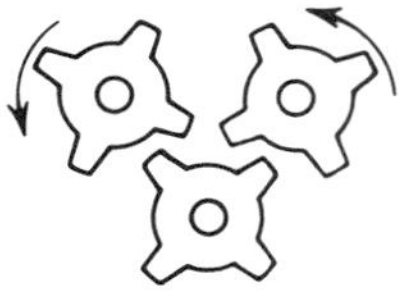

```
Enter string with end-of-string character * :
        Tom went walking  *
Enter string with end-of-string character * :
on up the Withywindle.*
Concatenated string:
        Tom went walking on up the Withywindle.
Again?- -1 = Y, 0 = N:  1

Enter string with end-of-string character * :
        kkkkkkkkkkkkkkkkkkkkkkkkkkkkkkkkkkk and     *
Enter string with end-of-string character * :
pppppppppppppppppppppppppppppppppppppppppppppppppppppppppppppppp!!!!!!!!!*
Concatenated string:
kkkkkkkkkkkkkkkkkkkkkkkkkkkkkkkkkkkkkkkkkkkk and ppppppppppppppp-
ppppppppppppppppppppppppppppppppppppppppppppppppp!!!!!!!!!*

Again?- -1 = Y, 0 = N:  0
```

FIGURE 10.6 String handling

10.14.1 *Refinement: Eliminating the Sentinel*

The concatenate procedure in Figure 10.6 relies on the use of the lengths of the two strings (count*A* and count*B*). A combination of the eof and eoln Boolean functions can be used in a while loop to load one or more lines of characters into String*A* and String*B*. Then the LengthOfString procedure in Figure 10.2 can be used to determine the lengths of the two entered strings. These two changes will simplify the Build String procedure in Figure 10.6. The LengthOfString procedure can be called from the driver procedure before the concatenate procedure is called. It will be necessary to call LengthOfString more than once. This refinement is left as an exercise.

10.14.2 *Refinement: Concatenating More than Two Strings*

A slight change in the program in Figure 10.6 (after the previous refinement, preferably) will make it possible for the user to concatenate two or more strings. This can be done by reusing String*B* to load another string from the keyboard. Then the concatenate procedure can be reactivated with the new pair of strings. As long as String*A* has the room, then two or more strings can be attached together.

It may be desirable to insert a space or some other character between a pair of attached strings. This should be done before the concatenation procedure is activated. These refinements are left as an exercise.

10.14.3 *Exercises*

1. Carry out the refinement given in Section 10.14.1 for the program in Figure 10.6. Give a sample run for

a. first string = 'Day broke, '
   second string = 'gray.'
b. first string = 'Programming is designing, '
   second string = 'creating programs (Wirth).'

2. Carry out the refinement given in Section 10.14.2 for the program in Figure 10.6. Give a sample run for

a. first string = 'Divide'
   second string = 'and' (*put trailing space in String*A**)
   third string = 'conquer.' (*put trailing space in String*A**)
b. first string = 'This'
   second string = 'is' (*put chr(10), chr(13), and 2 spaces at end of String*A*.*)
   third string = '*a*' (*put chr(10), chr(13), and 4 spaces at end of String*A*.*)
   fourth string = 'staircase.' (*put chr(10), chr(13), and 6 spaces at end of String*A*.*)

3. Add to the program in Figure 10.6 (with above refinements) a procedure that allows a user to insert one string into another string. You will have to prompt for a target (one or more characters supposedly found together one after the other) in String*A*, for example, to identify where to start inserting String*B*. Make it a rule that String*B* will always be inserted immediately after the target supplied by the user. Run your program for

a. String*A* = 'Divide and conquer'
   String*B* = '!'
   target '*r*'
b. String*A* ='Why is it that most hackers confuse Halloween and Christmas? Because 31 (octal) = 25 (decimal).'
   String*B* = '(octal)'
   target = '1'
c. String*A* ='An assertion is an expression inserted, which the programmer claims is true whenever control reaches that point (Evans, 1984),'
   String*B* = 'in the code'
   target = 'inserted'

10.15 Case Study: Merging Unordered Arrays of Records

We can use the following algorithm to merge the upper and lower halves of an array of records:

```
                    (*input: unordered array of records from file, sort key;
                                          output: ordered list of records*)
begin
  initialize a list array;
  assign to first the position of the leading list entry;
  assign to midpoint the position of the middle list entry;
  assign to last the position of the last list entry;
  assign first to i;
```

```
   assign midpoint + 1 to j;
   assign first - 1 to k;
   while (i <= midpoint) and (j <= last) do
     begin
       if list[i].searchkey <= list[j].searchkey
       then begin
         add 1 to k;
         assign list [i] to list[k];
         add 1 to i
         end                                              (*then*)
       else begin
         add 1 to k;
         assign list[j] to list[k];
         add 1 to j
         end;                                   (*else and while*)
          (*Now, copy the rest of old list into the copy array*)
   while i <= midpoint do begin       (*get leftovers in lower half*)
     add 1 to k; assign list[k] to copy[k]; add 1 to i
     end;
   while j <= last do begin           (*get leftovers in upper half*)
     add 1 to k; assign list[j] to copy[k]; add 1 to j
     end;
   assign copy array to list array
 end;                                             (*merge algorithm*)
```

To use this algorithm to sort an unordered list, it is first necessary to determine values for first, midpoint, and last. We want to separate a list into pairs and let this algorithm operate on the unordered pairs. Then we want to activate this algorithms for all sublists with four elements (all the pairs from the first round with the merge algorithm). Then we want to identify all the sublists with eight elements and so on until we have obtain a sublist that is the same size as the original list. A graphical interpretation of this idea using an unordered list of integers is shown in Figure 10.7. The production of the values of first, midpoint, and last for the different sized sublists can be obtained using the following recursive procedure:

```
procedure MergeSort(var list: info;                 (*list of records*)
                        first: integer;          (*beginning of sublist*)
                        last: integer);                (*end of sublist*)
var
  middle: integer;
begin
  if first < last
    then begin
      middle := (first + last) div 2;
      MergeSort(list, first, middle);
                        (*Next self-activation will occur after the
                  reduction of last to 1, which exhausts all the
                         sublists in the lower half of the original
                       list. The next self-activation takes care of
                                          the upper half of the list:*)
```

```
            MergeSort(list, middle + 1, last);
                    (*now repeatedly call the merge procedure until
                         the recursion stack has been emptied.*)
            merge(list, first, middle, last)
            end                                            (*if*)
    end;                                            (*MergeSort*)
```

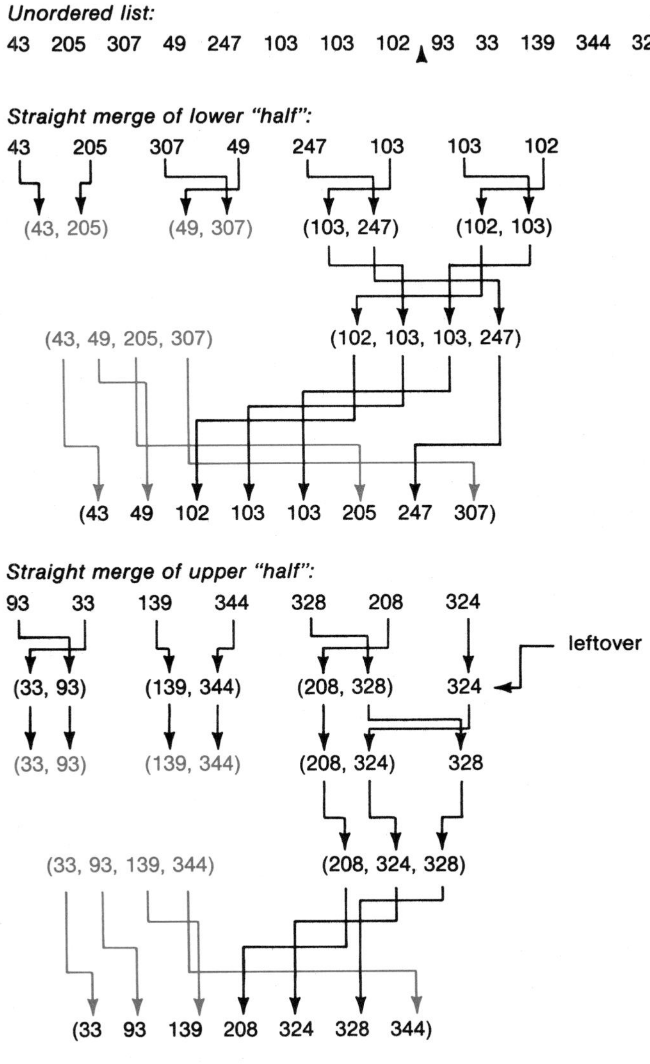

This procedure begins by identifying the halves of a list. For example, in a list with nine elements, we get the following results:

First	*Middle*	*Last*	*MergeSort* *First*	*MergeSort* *Middle*	*Middle + 1*	*Last*	*Merge* *First*	*Middle*	*Last*
1	5	9	1	5					
1	3	5	1	3					
1	2	3	1	2					
1	1	2	1	1	(Now first = last!)				
1	1	2			2	2	(First = last)		
1	1	2					1	1	2
							(Merge first pair)		
(Pop next set of values off stack:)									
1	2	3			3	3	(First = last)		
1	2	3 (pop)					1	2	3
							(Merge second pair)		
(Pop next set of values off stack:)									
1	3	5			4	5			
4	4	5	4	4	(First = last)				
4	4	5 (pop)				4	4	5	
							(Merge third pair)		
(Pop next set of values off stack:)									
1	3	5				1	3	5	
							(Merge first four elements)		
(Pop next set of values off stack:)									
1	5	9			6	9			
6	7	9	6	7					
6	6	7	6	6	(First = last)				
6	6	7 (pop)					6	6	7
							(Merge fourth pair)		
6	7	9 (pop)			8	9			
8	8	9	8	8	(First = last)				
8	8	9			9	9	(First = last)		
8	8	9 (pop)					8	8	9
							(Merge fifth pair)		
6	6	7 (pop)					6	7	9
							(Merge second four elements)		
1	5	9 (pop)					1	5	9
							(Merge the two halves)		

The key to the use of the MergeSort and merge procedures is the production of the values of first, middle, and last during the recursion inside the MergeSort procedure. The above trace on the MergeSort of a list of nine integers shows the following things:

1. The MergeSort merges the pairs of integers in the lower half of the list, first. Then, before any attempt is made to merge the pairs of the upper half, the lower four elements (from position 1 to 5) are merged.
2. Next, the MergeSort works on the upper half of the list, first with the pairs, then with the upper four elements.
3. Finally, the MergeSort procedure activates the merge procedure with the entire list, which means the two halves of the list will be merged.

A refinement of the above MergeSort is possible, which will make it possible to trace what the MergeSort procedure does each time it is run.

10.15.1 *Refinement: Tracing the MergeSort Recursion*

It is helpful to modify the MergeSort procedure so that it gives us a trace of the values of first, middle, and last that it works with during its activation. To do this, writeln statements should be added to the MergeSort procedure so that we can see what values are used in each self-activation. For example, we can use the following modification of the MergeSort if statement:

```
if first < last
   then begin
      middle := (first + last) div 2;
      writeln('*':5, first:20, middle:10, last:10);
      MergeSort(list, first, middle);
      writeln('**':5, first:20, middle:10, last:10);
      MergeSort(list, middle + 1, last);
      writeln('***':5, first:20, middle:10, last:10);
      merge(list, first, middle, last)
      end                                                    (*if*)
```

When this version of the MergeSort is activated, it will now be possible to see which values are being used to change first and last during the recursion. This refinement is left as an exercise.

10.15.2 *Example: Merging an Array of Records*

We will use the old DataBase file from Chapter 9 to supply records for an array that we will merge. A program to do this is given in Figure 10.8. In this program the MergeSort procedure is still the same but the merge procedure has been changed, slightly. Since we are merging records, we need to select a sort key that can be used to decide when two records need to be swapped. A sort key is just one of the fields of a record used to control the merge sort. In this case, we used the name field of the list of records of type BallClub.

```
                (*Method: This program uses a recursive procedure to
                   merge the elements of an unordered list of random
                                         numbers into an ordered list.*)

program AnotherSort(input, output, DataBase);

const
   max = 10;                                      (*maximum size of list*)
   sentinel = -1;                  (*used to check for logical end-of-file*)
type
   alfa = packed array[1..20] of char;                  (*a string type*)
   BallClub = record
      name: alfa;                                           (*team name*)
      wins, losses: integer;                      (*team wins and losses*)
      pct: real                                    (*percentage of wins*)
   end;                                                      (*BallClub*)
   teams = file of BallClub;                    (*user-defined file type*)
   info = array[1..max] of BallClub;                           (*array of
                                                   records to be merged*)

 (*- - - - - - - - - - - - - - - - - - - - - - - - - - - - - - - - - - -*)
  (*This procedure uses an existing master file to build an array
                                        of file records of type BallClub.*)

procedure BuildList(var DataBase: teams;                   (*a file type*)
                    var list: info;                   (*list of records*)
                    var limit: integer);                    (*list size*)
var
   selector: integer;                                      (*list index*)
begin
selector := 1;                               (*give selector initial value*)
   reset(DataBase, 'master.dat');          (*prepare file for inspection*)
   while DataBase^.wins <> sentinel do       (*check of last record*)
      begin
         list[selector] := DataBase^;
         selector := selector + 1;
         get(DataBase)
      end;
   limit := selector -1                                 (*true list size*)
end;                                                        (*BuildList*)

 (*- - - - - - - - - - - - - - - - - - - - - - - - - - - - - - - - - - -*)
     (*This procedure prints a copy of the list of file records.*)

procedure ShowList(list: info;             (*array type value parameter*)
                   limit: integer);                        (*array size*)
var
   selector: integer;                                 (*list-cell selector*)
begin
   for selector := 1 to 70 do write('-'); writeln;
   selector := 1;
   while selector <= limit do
```

```
      begin
        with list[selector] do
          writeln(name:30, wins:10, losses:10, pct:12:3);
        selector := selector + 1
      end                                                    (*while*)
end;                                                      (*ShowList*)

  (*-----------------------------------------------------------*)
   (*This procedure merges the list of records. It is controlled by
      the upper limit (last) and lower limit (first), the extremes of
             the sublist, which the MergeSort procedure activates
                                            this procedure with.*)

procedure merge(var list: info;                    (*list of records*)
                    first: integer;            (*beginning of sublist*)
                    midpoint: integer;            (*middle of sublist*)
                    last: integer);                  (*end of sublist*)
var
  copy: info;                         (*will hold copy of merged records*)
  i, j, k: integer;                  (*hold copy of first, midpoint, last*)
begin
  i := first; j := midpoint + 1; k := first -1;
  while (i <= midpoint) and (j <= last) do
    if list[i].name <= list[j].name
    then begin
      k := k + 1; copy[k] := list[i]; i := i + 1
      end                                                      (*then*)
    else begin
      k := k + 1; copy[k] := list[j]; j := j + 1
      end;                                                     (*else*)
  while i <= midpoint do                   (*get leftovers in left half*)
    begin
      k := k + 1; copy[k] := list[i]; i := i + 1
    end;                                                      (*while*)
  while j <= last do begin
    k := k + 1; copy[k] := list[j]; j := j + 1
    end;                                                      (*while*)
         (*copy merged records from buffer back into list array*)
  for i := first to j - 1 do list[i] := copy[i]
end;                                                          (*merge*)

  (*-----------------------------------------------------------*)
    (*This procedure uses recursion to identify the sublists to use
                          when it activates the merge procedure.*)

procedure MergeSort(var list: info;                (*list of records*)
                        first: integer; (*beginning of sublist*)
                        last: integer);          (*end of sublist*)
var
  middle: integer;                               (*marks middle of list*)
```

```
begin
   if first < last
   then begin
      middle := (first + last) div 2;
      MergeSort(list, first, middle);
      MergeSort(list, middle + 1, last);
      merge(list, first, middle, last)
      end                                                (*then*)
end;                                               (*Merge Sort*)

  (*-------------------------------------------------------*)

procedure driver;
var
   DataBase: teams;                         (*team records file*)
   LocalList: info;                    (*array of team records*)
   LocalLimit: integer;                             (*array size*)
begin
   BuildList(DataBase, LocalList, LocalLimit);
   MergeSort(LocalList, 1, LocalLimit);
   ShowList(LocalList, LocalLimit)
end;                                                  (*driver*)

  (*-------------------------------------------------------*)

begin
   driver                          (*activate driver procedure*)
end.

     NewWhippets45        1        0.978
     Twins        44      5        0.898
     Ucsd         20      9        0.690
```

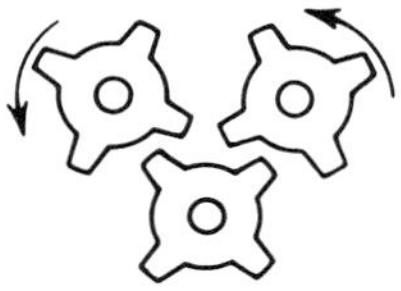

FIGURE 10.8 Recursive MergeSort

A merge sort is more efficient than a selection sort, which we have used earlier. We look at the running time of a MergeSort in Section 10.15.3.

10.15.3 *Running Time of a MergeSort*

In the above sort, the MergeSort procedure subdivides the original list by 2 repeatedly to get down to the level of single list elements. In a list of nine elements, for example, the MergeSort procedure starts with

$$\text{ListSize } \mathbf{div}\ 2^1 = (9 + 1)\ \mathbf{div}\ 2 = 5$$

This identifies the "halves" of the list. Dividing by 2 again, we get

$$(\text{ListSize } \mathbf{div}\ 2)\ \mathbf{div}\ 2 = \text{ListSize } \mathbf{div}\ 2^2 = 2$$

This partitions the lower half of the list. Dividing by 2 again, we get

$$((\text{ListSize } \mathbf{div}\ 2)\ \mathbf{div}\ 2)\ \mathbf{div}\ 2 = \text{ListSize } \mathbf{div}\ 2^3 = 1$$

This isolates the first pair of the original list from positions 1 to 2. We have reached the level of single elements and are ready to activate the merge procedure, which first orders single elements into ordered pairs.

The secret to understanding this sort is in the powers of 2 used to subdivide the list to be merged. Notice that we reach the level of single elements in three tries, using 2^3. Also notice that the binary log of the ListSize is also approximately 3. That is,

$$\begin{aligned} \lg 9 &= \text{exponent to use on 2 to get 9} \\ &= (\ln 9)/(\ln 2) \\ &= 2.20/0.69 \\ &= 3.17 \\ &= 3 \text{ (if take the trunc(lg 9))} \end{aligned}$$

In general, it will take lg n subdivisions of a list of n elements to get down to the level of single elements. This tells us how many scans of a list are necessary to complete a MergeSort. That is, a list of n elements will require lg n scans to complete a MergeSort. Since each scan is in terms of n elements, there will be at most $n * \lg n$ comparisons needed to complete the sort. That is, the running time of a MergeSort can be expressed in the following way:

Time required by a MergeSort:

The running time of a MergeSort will be proportional to $n * \lg n$.

What does this mean when we MergeSort large lists? Suppose we want to MergeSort a list of one million records. We can compute the number of comparisons made by a MergeSort on this list.

$$\begin{aligned} n * \lg n &= 1{,}000{,}000 * \lg 1{,}000{,}000 \\ &= 1{,}000{,}000 * (\ln 1{,}000{,}000)/(\ln 2) \\ &= 1{,}000{,}000 * 19.93 \\ &= 1{,}993{,}000 \end{aligned}$$

That is, each scan of the MergeSort on one million elements will require 19 passes. This gives us roughly two million comparisons to make to complete the MergeSort. If we assume it takes 0.78 microseconds to do one comparison by a machine, it will take 14.82 seconds to complete a MergeSort of one million elements.

This contrasts sharply with the running time required by a selection sort. Why? It takes

$n^2/2 - n/2$ comparisons

to complete a selection sort. If we plot the expected running times of these two sorts for different list sizes, the running time of the MergeSort will grow along a logarithmic curve. By contrast, the running times of a selection sort will grow along the sharply rising curve of a parabola. The running time of a selection sort is given by a second degree or quadratic expression, so the running time of a selection sort is said to grow quadratically. A sketch of these two curves is given in Figure 10.9. For example, with the same list of one million records, a selection sort will require the following number of comparisons:

$$
\begin{aligned}
n^2/2 - n/2 &= (1{,}000{,}000)^2/2 - (1{,}000{,}000)/2 \\
&= 500{,}000{,}000{,}000 - 500{,}000 \\
&= 499{,}999{,}500{,}000
\end{aligned}
$$

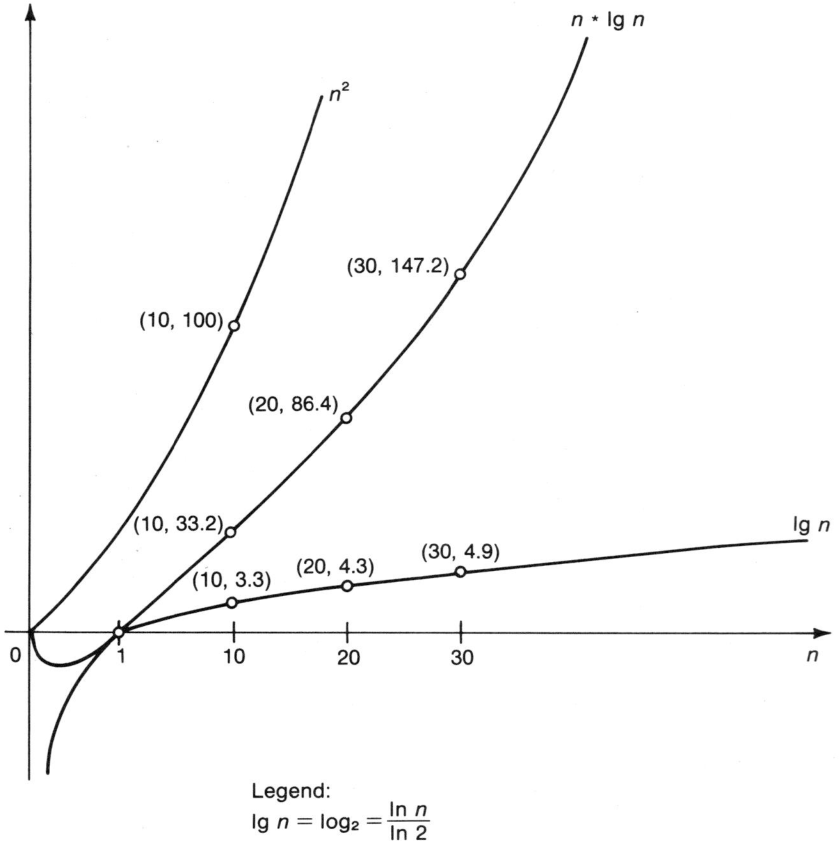

FIGURE 10.9
Comparison of running time growth rates

Assuming it takes 0.78 microseconds for one comparison by a machine, a selection sort of a million elements will require the following time:

$$\begin{aligned}\text{running time} &= 390{,}000 \text{ seconds}\\ &= 6500 \text{ minutes}\\ &= 108 \text{ hours}\\ &= 4.51 \text{ days}\end{aligned}$$

10.15.4

Exercises

1. Write a program to MergeSort lists of integer random numbers (You choose the range). Your program should do the following things:
   a. Prompt for ListSize and value of seed and range (used by your random number generator).
   b. Use a BuildList procedure to build a list of ListSize random numbers.
   c. Activate a MergeSort procedure to MergeSort the list.
   d. Print a copy of the merged list.

   Run your program for
   e. ListSize = 9, seed = 2.71828, low = 1, high = 200.
   f. ListSize = 50, seed = 2,71828, low = 100, high = 2000.

2. Refinement. Modify the program in exercise 1 so that your MergeSort procedure prints a trace of the values of first, middle, and last. *Hint.* See suggestions for doing this in Section 10.15.1.

3. Refinement. Modify the program in exercise 2 so that your MergeSort procedure prints
   a. Values of first, middle, and last that are pushed
   b. Values of first, middle, and last that are popped

4. Refinement. Modify the program in Figure 10.8 so that the new program does the following things:
   a. Prompts for file name to be merged (create more than one file of BallClub records, beforehand, in another program).
   b. Prompts for the sort key to use (the program in Figure 10.X is restricted to one sort key, namely, the name field).
   c. MergeSorts the chosen file of records using the chosen sort key.
   d. Allows the user to rerun the program with a new set of choices.

   Give a sample run.

10.16

Case Study: Quick Sorting

A quick sort of a list of items uses the following divide-and-conquer technique:

```
                                                   (*input: list;
                                            output: ordered list*)
begin
   repeat
      if list has more than 1 entry then begin
         partition the list into low and high lists;
         sort the low list;
         sort the high lists
         decrease the size of the list to sort
   until no more than 1 entry is left to sort
end                                     (*algorithm for a quicksort*)
```

For example, we can apply this sorting technique to the following list of numbers:

6 42 122 55 94 18 5 44
(low = 1) (high = 8)

1. Scan list from left to right until an entry is found that is greater than or equal to list[low].

   6 **42** 122 55 94 18 5 44
   →

2. Scan list from right to left until an entry is found that is less than or equal to the entry found in the low list.

   6 **42** 122 55 94 18 **5** 44
   → ←

3. Swap the two list entries found.

   6 **5** 122 55 94 18 **42** 44

4. Continue the scanning and swapping in the first three steps until the scans cross each other.

5. Shrink the list to be scanned.

6. Repeat steps 1–5 until no more than one entry is left to scan.

Step 5 of this algorithm can be handled recursively. We can set up a quick-sort procedure that calls itself. Each time a recursive call is made, we can diminish the value of the high limit and increase the value of the low limit. The recursion will continue until the values of low and high meet each other. A structure chart for a program to carry out quick sort is given in Figure 10.10. Here is the pseudocode for a quick-sort algorithm:

```
                    (*This algorithm starts with a list L of n elements and
                                        with low = 1 and high = n.*)
begin
   if low < high then begin
      assign low to head and high to tail;
      repeat
         repeat add 1 to head until L[head] >= L[low];
         repeat subtract 1 from tail until L[tail] <= L[low];
         if head < tail then swap L[head] and L[tail]
      until head is greater than tail;
      swap L[low] and L[tail[;                          (*each time*)
      quick sort(low, tail – 1);              (*replace high by tail – 1*)
      quick sort(tail + 1, high)               (*replace low by tail + 1*)
end                                               (*quick-sort algorithm*)
```

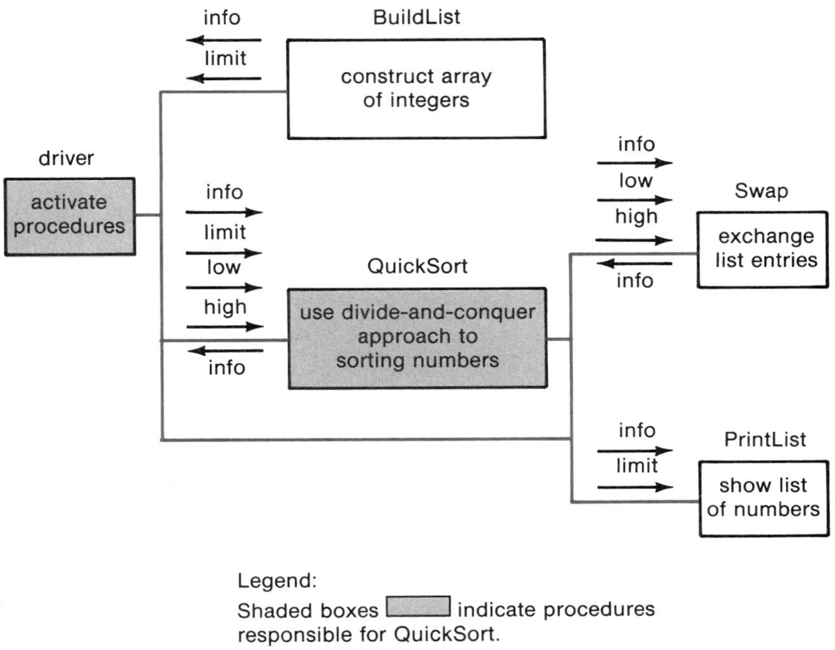

FIGURE 10.10
Structure chart for a QuickSort program

The scans of the list take place inside the inner repeat loop of this algorithm. The swapping continues until the scans cross each other. After that one last swap is made

swap *L*[low] **and** *L*[tail]

then the recursive calls are used to shrink the size of the list for the next set of scans. This sort works best when a list is very disorganized. It will be very inefficient if the list is almost sorted to begin with, since it must continue scanning (making comparisons) until the list has been shrunk down to one entry. Here is a walk through this algorithm with the sample list of numbers.

Low	*High*	*ThisLow*	*ThisHigh*	*List*
1	8	1	9	6 42 122 55 94 18 5 44
(Scan right)		2	9	6 **42** 122 55 94 18 5 44
				⟶ (Stop)
(Scan left)		2	7	6 42 122 55 94 18 **5** 44
				(Stop) ⟵
	(Swap)			6 **5** 122 55 94 18 42 44
(Scan right)		3	7	6 5 **122** 55 94 18 42 44
				⟶ (Stop)
(Scan left)		3	2	6 5 122 55 94 18 42 44
			(Stop)	⟵
	(Swap)			5 6 122 55 94 18 42 44
1	1	1	2	(Nothing happens)
3	8			(No swaps in inner loop)
	(Swap in outer loop)			5 6 **122** 55 94 18 42 **44**
				⟶ ⟵
				5 6 44 55 94 18 42 122
4	7	4	8	
(Scan right)		4	8	5 6 44 **55** 94 18 42 122
				⟶ (Stop)
(Scan left)		4	7	5 6 44 55 94 18 **42** 122
				(Stop) ⟵
	(Swap)			5 6 44 **42** 94 18 **55** 122
(Scan right)		5	7	5 6 44 42 **94** 18 55 122
				⟶ (Stop)
(Scan left)		5	6	5 6 44 42 94 **18** 55 122
				(Stop) ⟵
	(Swap)			5 6 44 42 **18** **94** 55 122
3	5	3	6	(No swap in inner loop)
(Swap in outer loop)				5 6 **18** 42 **44** 94 55 122
				⟶ ⟵
6	7	(From recursion)		5 6 18 42 44 **94** **55** 122
				⟶ ⟵
(Final swap in outer loop)				5 6 18 42 44 **55** **94** 122

A program to implement this algorithm is given in Figure 10.11.

```
                    (*Method: Use a quick-sorting technique to put a list
                                                    of integers in order*)

program QuickSortNos(input, output);
const
   empty = -1;
   max = 20;                                        (*limit on list size*)
type
   list = array[1..max] of integer;                     (*array type*)
```

```
(*-----------------------------------------------------*)
                              (*Save entered numbers in an array*)

procedure BuildList(var info: list;              (*for numbers*)
                    var limit: integer);          (*list size*)
begin
  limit := 0;
  repeat
    limit := limit + 1;
    write(' ':20, 'Enter count--a -1, to stop:   ');
    readln(info[limit]); writeln
  until info[limit] = empty;
  limit := limit - 1                             (*a crucial step!*)
end;                                                  (*BuildList*)

(*-----------------------------------------------------*)
                                          (*Swap numbers in list*)

procedure swap(var info: list;                         (*numbers*)
               low: integer;                          (*list size*)
               high: integer);                   (*number to swap*)
var
  buffer: integer;                            (*temporary storage*)
begin
  buffer := info[high]; info[high] := info[low];
  info[low] := buffer
end;                                                       (*swap*)

(*-----------------------------------------------------*)
                                         (*Show list of numbers*)

procedure PrintList(info: list;                        (*numbers*)
                    limit: integer);                  (*list size*)
var
  selector: integer;                             (*name selector*)
begin
  write(' ':20);
  for selector := 1 to limit do
    write(info[selector]:2, ' ':2);
  writeln
end;                                                  (*PrintList*)

(*-----------------------------------------------------*)
                                 (*QuickSort of a list of names*)

procedure QuickSort(var info: list;                    (*numbers*)
                    limit, low, high: integer);
var
  ThisLow, ThisHigh: integer;
begin
  if low < high then begin
    ThisLow := low; ThisHigh := high + 1;
    repeat
```

```
            repeat
               ThisLow := ThisLow + 1
            until (info[ThisLow] >= info[low]) or (ThisLow > limit);
            repeat
               ThisHigh := ThisHigh - 1
            until (info[ThisHigh] <= info[low]);
            if ThisLow < ThisHigh then begin
               swap(info, ThisLow, ThisHigh);
               PrintList(info, limit)
               end
         until ThisLow > ThisHigh;
         swap(info, low, ThisHigh);
         PrintList(info, limit);
         QuickSort(info, limit, low, ThisHigh - 1);
         QuickSort(info, limit, ThisHigh + 1, high)
         end
end;                                                        (*QuickSort*)

  (*-------------------------------------------------------------*)
                                 (*Program manager: activate procedures*)

procedure driver;
var
   ThisList: list;                                      (*array variable*)
   ListSize: integer;                                 (*for actual list size*)
   choice: integer;                                        (*menu choice*)
begin
   repeat
      writeln('menu:':20);
      writeln('---->':20, '1) build list;');
      writeln('---->':20, '2) print list;');
      writeln('---->':20, '3) sort list;');
      writeln('---->':20, '4) exit');
      write('choice: ':15); readln(choice); writeln;
      case choice of
         1: BuildList(ThisList, ListSize);
         2: PrintList(ThisList, ListSize);
         3: begin
                QuickSort(ThisList, ListSize, 1, ListSize);
                writeln; writeln('sorted list:':30);
                PrintList(ThisList, ListSize)
             end;
         4:                                                        (*empty*)
         end                                                        (*case*)
      until choice = 4
end;                                                              (*driver*)

  (*-------------------------------------------------------------*)

begin
   driver                                     (*activate driver procedure*)
end.
```

```
                   menu:
                   ---->1) Build list;
                   ---->2) Print list;
                   ---->3) Sort list;
                   ---->4) Exit
choice: 1
                         Enter count--a -1, to stop:  6

                         Enter count--a -1, to stop:  42

                         Enter count--a -1, to stop:  122

                         Enter count--a -1, to stop:  55

                         Enter count--a -1, to stop:  94

                         Enter count--a -1, to stop:  18

                         Enter count--a -1, to stop:  5

                         Enter count--a -1, to stop:  44

                         Enter count--a -1, to stop:  -1
                   menu:
                   ---->1) Build list;
                   ---->2) Print list;
                   ---->3) Sort list;
                   ---->4) Exit
choice: 2
                              6   42   122   55   94   18    5   44
                   menu:
                   ---->1) Build list;
                   ---->2) Print list;
                   ---->3) Sort list;
                   ---->4) Exit
choice: 3
                              6    5   122   55   94   18   42   44
                              5    6   122   55   94   18   42   44
                              5    6    44   55   94   18   42  122
                              5    6    44   42   94   18   55  122
                              5    6    44   42   18   94   55  122
                              5    6    18   42   44   94   55  122
                              5    6    18   42   44   94   55  122
                              5    6    18   42   44   55   94  122

                         sorted list:
                              5    6    18   42   44   55   94  122
                   menu:
                   ---->1) Build list;
                   ---->2) Print list;
                   ---->3) Sort list;
                   ---->4) Exit
choice: 4
```

FIGURE 10.11 Quick sorting

10.16.1

Exercises

1. Modify the program in Figure 10.11 to trace what happens to low, high, ThisLow, and ThisHigh during the quick sort. Print the trace in a table like the one given in the walk through in Section 10.16. Give a sample run.

2. Add the following features to the program in Figure 10.11:
   a. A selection sort procedure
   b. Random number generating function
   c. Random generation of lists of numbers to be sorted (allow the user to pick the range of random numbers produced and the list size)
   d. Maintain a count of the number of comparisons made by both sorts and print the following table:

List Size	*Selection Sort Comparisons*	*Quick Sort Comparisons*
10	?	?
100	?	?
1000	?	?
10000	?	?

   e. Estimate the running time of each sort. You can do this by finding out how long it takes your computer to make one comparison (your system manual should have this time). Then use the following formula:

   approximate running time = ComparisonCount∗ComparisonTime

3. Write a program to perform a quick sort by last name on an array of airline passenger records like the following one:

```
StringType  =  packed array[1..10] of char;
HalfString  =  packed array [1..5] of char;
passenger  =  record
   LastName, FirstName: StringType;
   Initial: char;
   DepartureCity, destination: StringType;
   ETA, ETD: HalfString;
   FlightNumber: HalfString
   end;
```

Print the results of the quick sort in table form like the following one:

Last Name	*First Name*	*I*	*City*	*ETD*	*City*	*ETA*	*Flight Number*

10.17 Readings

Kruse, R. L. *Data Structures and Program Design.* Englewood Cliffs, NJ: Prentice-Hall, 1984. See Chapter 7 on recursion.

Sahni, H., and Horowitz, S. *Fundamentals of Data Structures.* Rockville, MD: Computer Science Press, 1982. See Chapter one.

Stubbs, D. F., and Webre, N. W. *Data Structures with Abstract Data Types and Pascal.* Monterey, CA: Brooks/Cole, 1985. See Chapter 6 on sorting, especially Section 6.3.1, which presents the version of the quick sort used in the final case study of this chapter.

CHAPTER 11

POINTERS

[A linked list] uses the same idea as a children's treasure hunt, where each clue that is found tells where to find the next one.

Robert L. Kruse, *Data Structures and Program Design*

AIMS

- Distinguish between pointer types and domain types.
- Distinguish between pointer variables and referenced variables.
- Show ways to introduce and use pointer types.
- Show uses of pointer variables as procedure parameters.
- Show uses of referenced variables with the built-in input and output procedures.
- Show how to set up singly linked lists.
- Suggest how recursive procedures can be used with linked lists.
- Discuss the advantages of linked lists as opposed to arrays.

11.1 Introduction to Pointers and Heap Storage

Pascal maintains a certain amount of computer storage for allocation during the operation of a program. This storage area is called a *heap*. During the operation of a program, it is possible to allocate a portion of the heap for use by a program. This is called *dynamic allocation*. To make dynamic allocation possible, Pascal has dynamic data type called a *pointer*. If a variable ThisPointer is a pointer type, then it is used to identify a portion of the heap.

Here is how to set up a pointer variable.

```
type
  name = packed array[1..3] of char;
  Pointer = ^name;                              (*pointer type*)
var
  ThisPointer: Pointer;                         (*pointer variable*)
```

Until now, no storage from the heap has been allocated in connection with ThisPointer. Before a pointer variable can be used, some necessary apparatus for heap storage allocation must be set up. This apparatus includes the hidden creation of a new variable called a *referenced variable*. It is this hidden referenced variable that will be allocated storage from the heap. A referenced variable always has a two-part name.

referenced variable name = <pointer name><up hat>

For example, if we tell Pascal to create a reference variable for ThisPointer, it will have the following form:

ThisPointer^ (name of a referenced variable)

A referenced variable is not created by declaring a variable to be a pointer type. A special built-in Pascal *new* procedure must be used to do this. The declaration of a pointer variable is limited to setting up storage for that pointer variable. A pointer variable has a single purpose in life.

> **A pointer variable is used to hold a reference to an area of heap storage.**

Without worrying yet about how heap storage itself is allocated during the operation of a program, imagine that the referenced variable for ThisHeap has been allocated heap storage. Here is the situation inside the computer.

Heap Storage Area Addresses	Heap Content	ThisPointer (Pointer variable)
2000	?	2005
2001	?	
2002	?	
2003	?	
2004	?	
2005	?	<---- ThisPointer^[1]
2006	?	<---------- ThisPointer^[2]
2007	?	<---------------- ThisPointer^[3]
2008	?	
2010	?	

In other words, ThisPointer holds the beginning heap address for the storage used by ^ThisPointer. In this example, the pointer is used to identify the heap storage used to store a string. You can assign a value to the referenced variable using an assignment statement like the following one:

```
ThisPointer^ := 'Amy'
```

This assignment procedures the following result:

Heap Storage (Address)	Heap (Content)	ThisPointer
2000	?	2005
2001	?	
2002	?	
2003	?	
2004	?	
2005	'A'	<---ThisPointer^[1]
2006	'm'	<------ThisPointer^[2]
2007	'y'	<----------ThisPointer^[3]

11.2 Built-In New Procedure

Pascal has a built-in *new* procedure used to allocate heap storage. This procedure has one actual parameter, a pointer variable. For example, suppose we want to allocate heap storage for ThisPointer^. We can do this in the following way:

```
new(ThisPointer);                    (*allocates heap storage*)
```

Three things happen when the new procedure is activated.

What the new procedure does:

1. **The pointer variable is assigned a heap storage address.**
2. **A referenced variable is created.**
3. **Heap storage is allocated to the referenced variable.**

Even though it may be a bit awkward to handle at first, you can manipulate a referenced variable just the way you would manipulate any other variable of the same type. For example, you can try the following experiment on your system:

Experiment 1

```
program TryYourHeapOut(input, output);
const
  empty = '   ';
type
  ThisPointer = ^ShortName;
  ShortName = packed array[1..3] of char;
var
  MyName, YourName: ThisPointer;                    (*pointer variables*)
begin
  new(MyName); new(YourName);
  repeat
    write('Enter name—a <return> to stop: ');
    readln(YourName^); writeln; writeln;
    MyName^ := YourName^;                           (*xerox copy in heap*)
    writeln(YourName^:20, MyName^:20)                        (*evidence!*)
    writeln(MyName^[1]:25);                               (*first letter*)
    writeln(MyName^[2]:30);                              (*second letter*)
    writeln(MyName^[3]:35;                                (*third letter*)
  until YourName^ = empty
end.
```

Pascal is very protective about its pointer variables. It will not let you inspect the value of a pointer variable. You cannot print out its value. This is another way of saying you cannot print out the heap address used by a referenced variable. Try the following experiment to verify this on your system:

Experiment 2 (You will get an error message!)

```
program ThisIsTabu(output);
type
   ptr = ^node;
   node = array[1..5] of integer;
var
   byte: ptr;                          (*pointer variable*)
begin
   new(byte);                (*create referenced variable*)
   write(byte)                    (*illegal statement!*)
end.
```

11.3 Operations with Pointer Variables

In general the syntax for the declaration of a pointer type has the following syntax:

> pointer **type** = ^domain **type**
> domain **type** = **type** identifier

In other words, each declaration of a pointer type specifies the domain type. The *domain type* is the data type of the referenced variable that will be created by the new procedure. For example, we can set up the following pointer types:

```
type
   RowPtr = ^quantities;             (*RowPtr = pointer type*)
   SelectorRange = 1984..2010;
   quantities = array[SelectorRange] of real;
   ThisSymbol = ^char;                         (*pointer type*)
   ThisNumber = ^integer;              (*another pointer type*)
var
   YourName, MyName: ThisSymbol;(*2 pointer variables of the same type*)
   Nos: RowPtr;                            (*pointer variable*)
   choice: ThisNumber;             (*another pointer variable*)
```

When a pointer variable is declared, it has no reference to a memory location. A pointer variable is given a value, a reference to a memory location, in several ways:

1. A pointer variable can be initialized by using the built-in new procedure.
2. We can initialize one pointer variable with the value of another pointer variable of the same type.
3. A pointer variable can be made to point to nothing, to no memory address, using the nil token.

The symbols used for each of these cases are given in Figure 11.1.

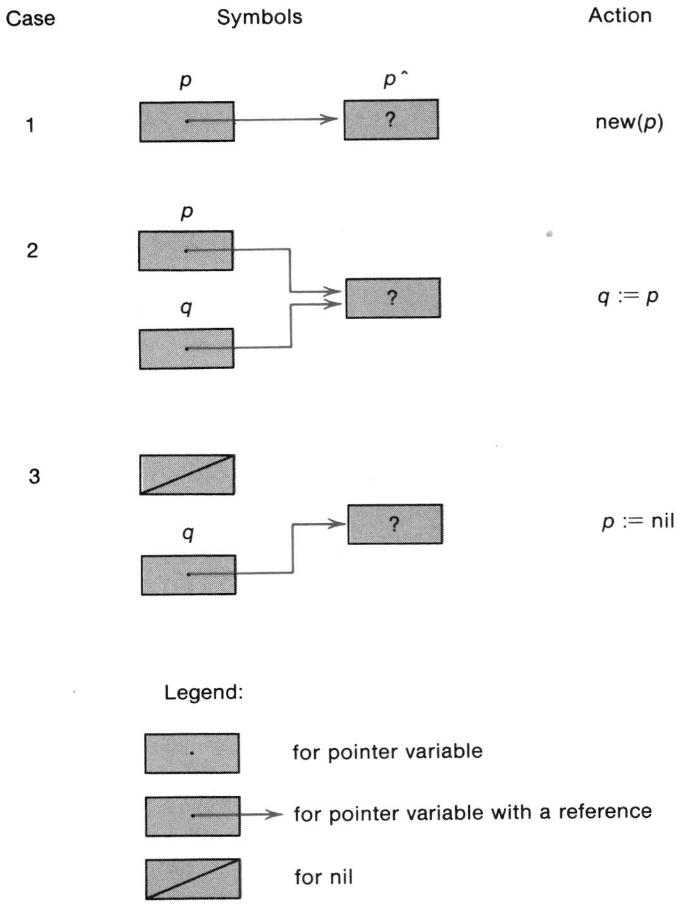

FIGURE 11.1
Giving a pointer variable a reference

11.3.1 *Examples with Pointers*

In this section we will use the following pointer type and variables:

```
type
   PointerType = ^name;
   name = packed array[1..3];
var
   YourPassword, MyPassword: PointerType;
```

To allocate heap storage to these pointer variables, we use

new(YourPassword)

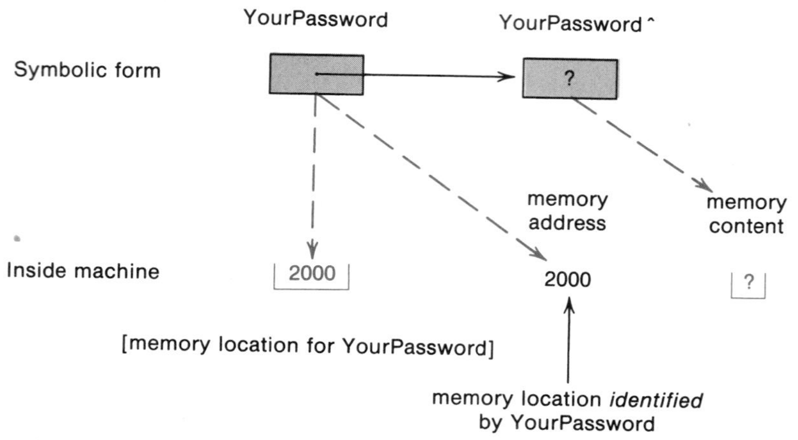

FIGURE 11.2
Two "points of view"

A graphical and analytical interpretation of what has happened so far inside the machine is shown in Figure 11.2. The box filled with a question mark in Figure 11.2 represents the content of memory location pointed to by YourPassword after the new procedure has been activated with this pointer variable. Then, for example, we can use this heap storage as follows:

YourPassword^ := 'Kim';

This assignment produces the result shown in Figure 11.3.

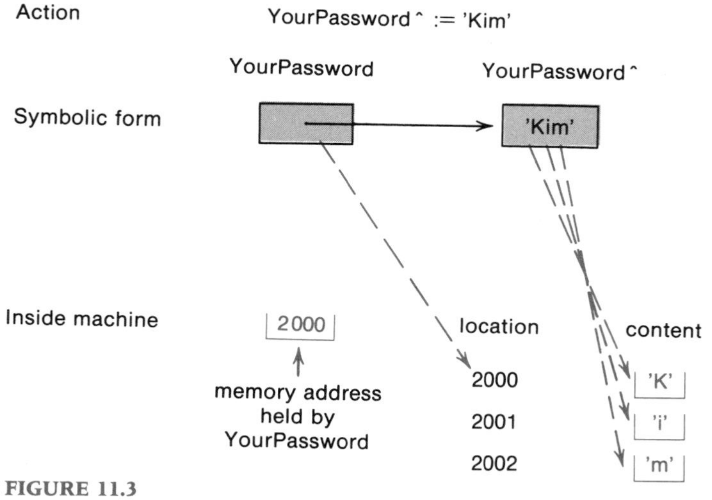

FIGURE 11.3
Using heap storage

One pointer variable can be initialized with the value of a another pointer variable of the same type. For example, we can make MyPassword point to the same memory location that YourPassword points to in the following way:

MyPassword := YourPassword;

This assigns the heap address held by YourPassword to Mypassword. This produces the result shown in Figure 11.4. In effect, YourPassword and MyPassword now both point to the same location in memory.

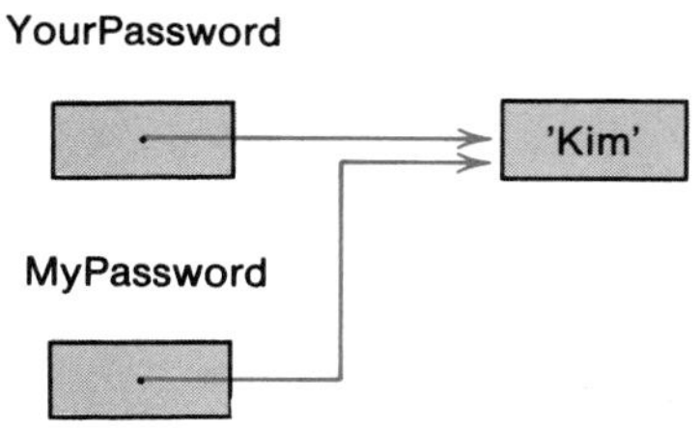

FIGURE 11.4
Copying pointers

11.3.2 *The Nil Pointer*

We can also make a pointer variable point to nothing. We do this by assigning nil (it has a value supplied locally on your system) to a pointer variable. For example, we can do this as follows:

MyPassword := **nil**; (*now MyPassword points to nothing*)

This idea is represented graphically in Figure 11.5.

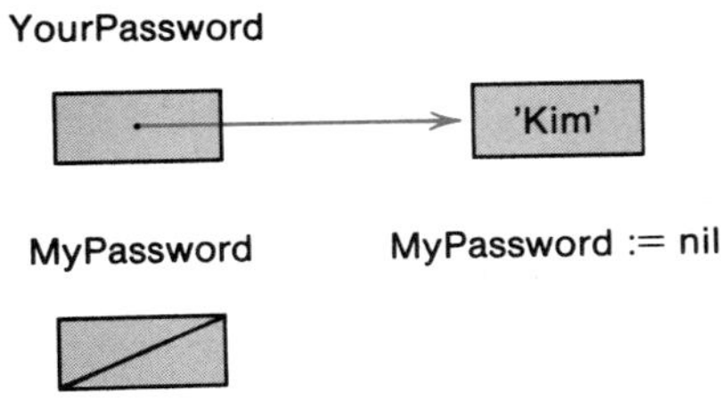

FIGURE 11.5
Making a pointer point to nil

The value of a pointer variable can be changed during the running of a program. For example, we can make the following changes to the above variables:

```
new(MyPassword);                    (*allocate storage for MyPassword^*)
MyPassword^ := 'Tom';                   (*assign name to MyPassword^*)
YourPassword := MyPassword;            (*make YourPassword point to
                                                         MyPassword^*)
```

These statements produce the results shown in Figure 11.6. Associated with every pointer type is a domain type. We look at domain types in Section 11.3.3.

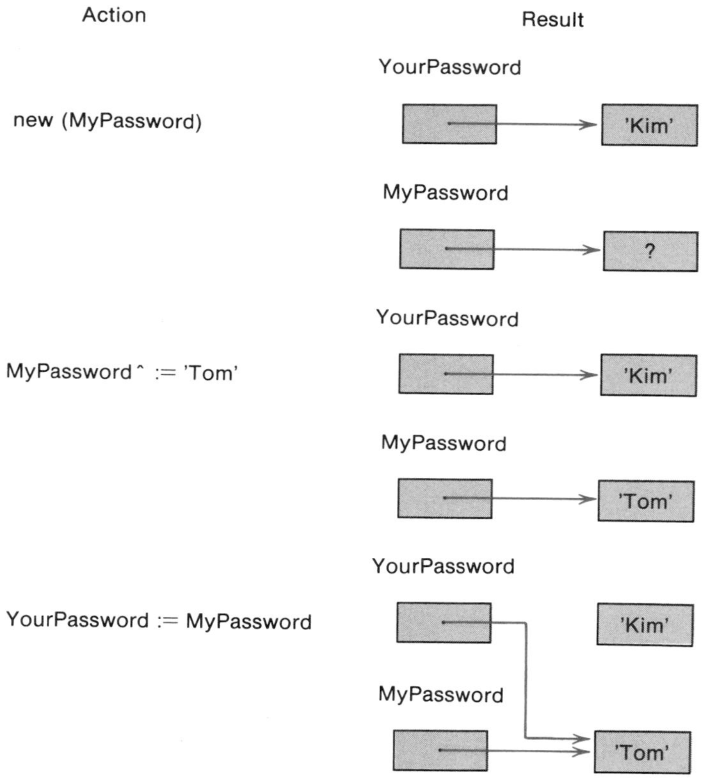

FIGURE 11.6
Changing a pointer variables

11.3.3 *Domain Types*

As a rule, the domain type of a pointer is a record. For example, we can have the following domain types:

```
type
   alfa = packed array[1..5] of char;
   ptr = ^passenger;                              (*a pointer type*)
   passenger = record                             (*domain type*)
      name: alfa;
      airline: alfa;
      ETD, ETA: alfa;                             (*departure, arrival times*)
      cities: array[1..max] of alfa;              (*route*)
      CostOfTicket: real;
      link: ptr                                   (*pointer type*)
   end;                                           (*passenger*)
   list = array[1..max] of ptr;
var
   TWAptr, NWptr, buffer; ptr;                    (*pointer variables*)
   ThisList: list;                                (*array of pointers!*)
```

TWAptr, NWptr, and buffer are examples of pointer variables that will have referenced variables which are record types. The ThisList array is interesting. Each component of the ThisList array is a pointer. We can supply two of these pointer variables with references to storage for the corresponding referenced variables in the following way:

```
new(TWAptr);                                      (*initialize TWAptr*)
new(ThisList[1]);                                 (*initialize ThisList[1]*)
```

These statements produce the results shown in Figure 11.7. The ThisList variable is an array type, not a pointer type. The elements of this array are the same pointer type, namely, ptr. This says the ThisList variable is an array of pointers. For example,

ThisList[1] references a passenger record;

and

ThisList[1]^ is the corresponding referenced variable

11.3.4 *Swapping Pointers*

The values (references) of pointer variables can be swapped. For example, we can use the new procedure to establish references for TWAptr and NWptr:

```
new(TWAptr); new(NWptr);                          (*establish references*)
```

These two statements produce the results shown in Figure 11.8. Now we can use the following assignments to swap the values of these two pointer variables:

```
buffer := TWAptr;                    (*buffer has copy of TWAptr*)
TWAptr := NWptr;                     (*TWAptr now has NWptr reference*)
NWptr := buffer;                     (*NWptr now has TWAptr reference*)
```

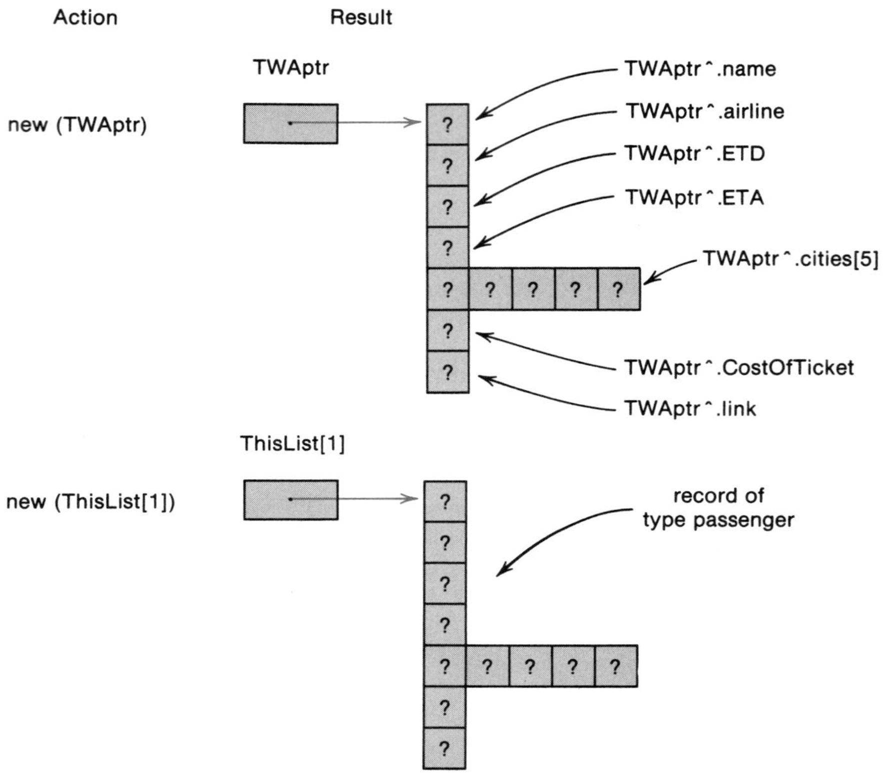

FIGURE 11.7
Pointers to records

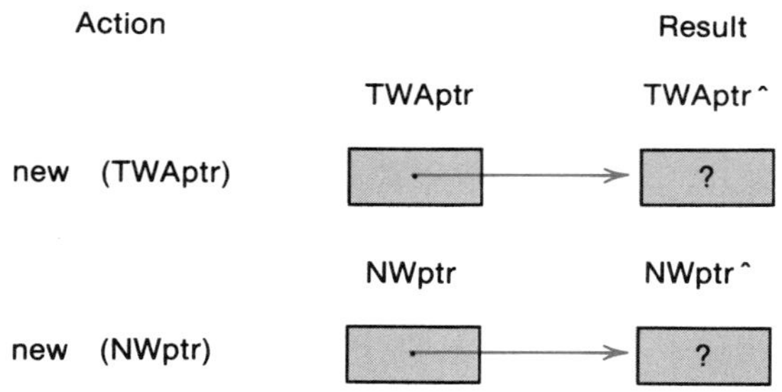

FIGURE 11.8
Creating pointers

These assignments swap the TWAptr and NWptr values. In effect, TWAptr now points to the heap storage area that was pointed to by NWptr and NWptr now points to where TWAptr was pointing. The results of these assignments is shown graphically in Figure 11.9. We bring these ideas about operations with

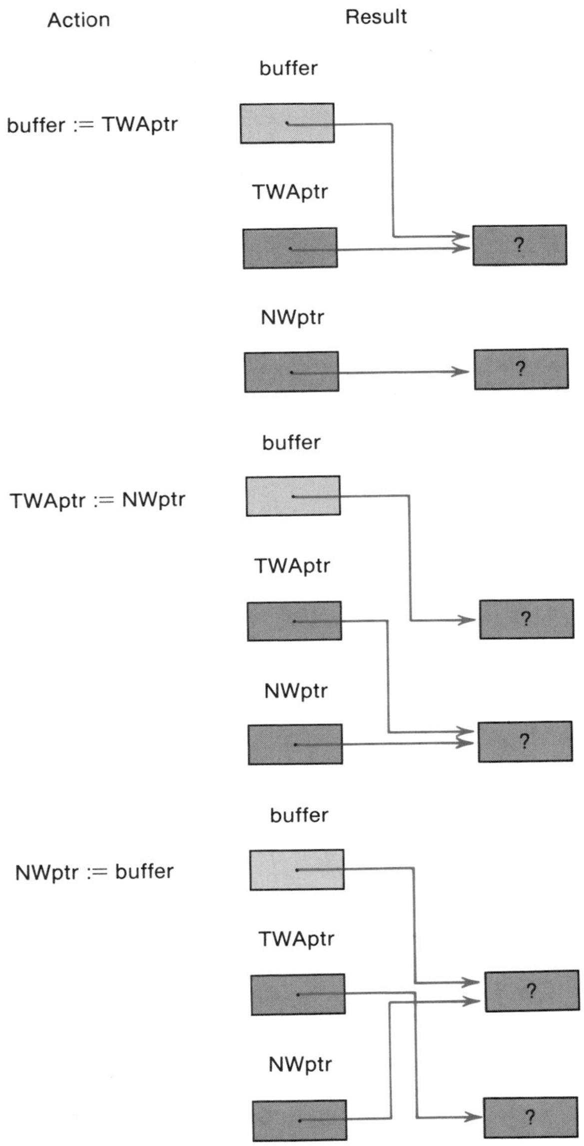

FIGURE 11.9
Swapping pointers

pointers together in a program in Figure 11.10. You might wonder why we use

```
new(third);
third^ := 'yyyyyeeeeessssss!!!!!';
```

in part (*3*) of the program in Figure 11.10. The use of the new procedure before the above assignment gives third a new reference. This means that the above assignment will not affect the referenced variable second^, which was also being referenced by third before it was given a new reference. What would be printed in part (*3*), if third were not given a new reference? The answer to this question is left as an exercise.

```
                    (*Method: Show uses of pointer variables and referenced
                                                              variables.*)

program sample(input, output);
type
   alfa = packed array[1..20] of char;
   ptr = ^node;                                              (*pointer type*)
   node = alfa;                                              (*domain type*)
   RowOfPointers = array[1..10] of ptr;                 (*array of pointers*)

 (*- - - - - - - - - - - - - - - - - - - - - - - - - - - - - - - - - - - -*)
                                          (*Show visits to memory locations:*)

procedure ShowNodes(first, second, third: ptr);
begin
   writeln(first^: 20, second^: 25, third^: 25)
end;                                                          (*ShowNodes*)

 (*- - - - - - - - - - - - - - - - - - - - - - - - - - - - - - - - - - - -*)
                                          (*Initialize and manipulate nodes:*)

procedure VisitNodes;
var
   first, second, third, buffer: ptr;               (*4 pointer variables*)
   references: RowOfPointers;                         (*array of pointers*)
   dash: integer;                                       (*for printed line*)
begin
   new(first); new(buffer);
   write('Your name?  '); readln(first^); writeln;
   write('Another name you fancy: '); readln(buffer^); writeln;
   writeln('values of referenced variables:'); writeln;
   writeln('first':15, 'second':20, 'third':20); writeln;
   for dash := 1 to 70 do write('—'); writeln;
   (*1*)
   second := first;                           (*make second point to first*)
   third := second;                                (*make third point first*)
   ShowNodes(first, second, third);
   (*2*)
   second := buffer;                         (*make second point to buffer*)
   ShowNodes(first, second, third);
```

```
  (*3*)
  new(third);                                   (*give third new reference*)
  third^ := 'yyyyyeeeeesssss!!!!!';            (*assign value to location*)
  ShowNodes(first, second, third);
  (*4*)
  buffer := first; first := third; third := buffer;        (*swap ptrs!*)
  ShowNodes(first, second, third);
  (*5*)                                     (*swap referenced variables*)
  buffer^ := first^; first^ := second^; second^ := buffer^;
  ShowNodes(first, second, third);
  (*6*)
  references[1] := first;                                (*copy pointers*)
  references[2] := references[1];
  references[3] := references[2];
  ShowNodes(references[1], references[2], references[3])
end;                                                       (*VisitNodes*)

(*-----------------------------------------------------------------*)

begin
  VisitNodes                          (*activate VisitNodes procedure*)
end.
```

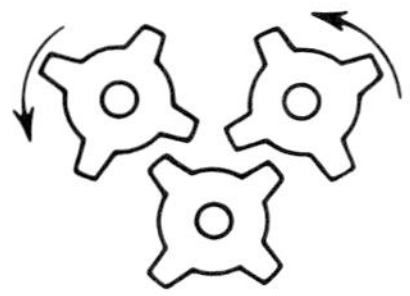

```
Your name?  Tom

Another name you fancy: Lori

values of referenced variables:
```

First	*Second*	*Third*
Tom	Tom	Tom
Tom	Lori	Tom
Tom	Lori	yyyyyeeeeesssss!!!!!
yyyyyeeeeesssss!!!!!	Lori	Tom
Lori	yyyyyeeeeesssss!!!!!	yyyyyeeeeesssss!!!!!
Lori	Lori	Lori

FIGURE 11.10 Operations with pointers

So far, we have dealt mostly with operations with pointer variables, showing how assign references and manipulate these variables. In Section 11.4 we look at how to manipulate referenced variables.

11.4 Operations with Referenced Variables

Referenced variables are treated like any of the other variables (except pointer variables) we have seen so far. They can be assigned values in the usual manner. The value of one referenced variables can be assigned to another referenced variable of the same type as follows:

```
new(TWAptr);
TWAptr^.name := 'Tom    ';                    (*assign name*)
TWAptr^.airline := 'TWA    ';                 (*assign name*)
TWAptr^:ETD := 'now    ';                     (*assign time*)
TWAptr^.ETA := 'then   ';                     (*assign time*)
NWptr^ := TWAptr^;                       (*make copy of record*)
```

These statements produce the results shown in Figure 11.11. We can also use the built-in input and output procedures with referenced variables.

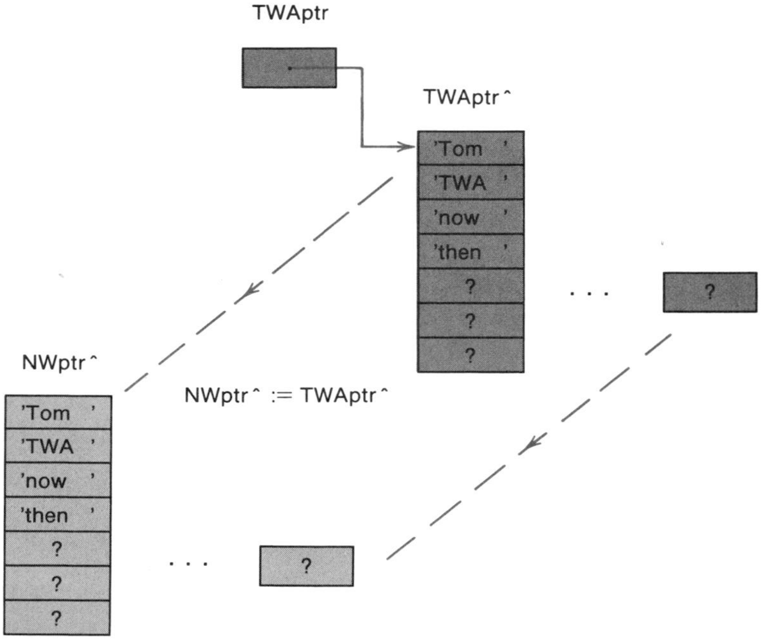

FIGURE 11.11
Copy records

11.5 Using the Built-In I/O Procedures with Referenced Variables

We can use either a read or readln procedure to assign values taken from a keyboard to referenced variables. For example, we can make the following assignments:

```
write('Enter name: '); readln(TWAptr^.name); writeln;
write('Enter airline: '); readln(TWAptr^.airline); writeln;
write('Enter ETD: '); readln(TWAptr^.ETD); writeln;
write('Enter ETA: '); readln(TWAptr^.ETA); writeln;
write('Enter ETD city: '); readln(TWAptr^.cities[1]);
```

and so on. In effect, we can use a readln statement in the usual way to assign values to referenced variables. In these statements, we have used readln statements to assign values of the fields of a record, which is the data type of the TWAptr^ referenced variable. Similarly, we can write and writeln statements to print the values of referenced variables. For example, we use the following statements to print the values of the TWAptr record that have been entered so far:

```
writeln(TWAptr^.name:20);          (*print name in column 20*)
writeln(TWAptr^.airline:20);       (*print airline in column 20*)
```

and so on.

11.6 Example: Array of Pointers

It is possible to have an array of pointers. For example, we can set up the following data types and variables:

```
type
  alfa = packed array[1..5] of char;
  ptr = ^passenger;                          (*pointer type*)
  passenger = record                         (*domain type*)
    name, airline, ETA, ETD: alfa;
    cities: array[1..max] of alfa;
    CostOfTicket: real;
    link: ptr;                               (*pointer type!*)
    end;                                     (*passenger*)
  list = array[1..max[ of ptr;               (*array type*)
var
  ThisList: list;                            (*array of pointers*)
  index: integer;                            (*array index*)
```

We can allocate storage for the components of ThisList in the following way:

```
for index := 1 to max do begin
  new(Thislist[index]);                      (*allocate storage*)
```

The results of this statement are shown graphically in Figure 11.12. The first three referenced variable for this array have the following form:

Index	Array Component	Referenced Variable
1	ThisList[1]	ThisList[1]^
2	ThisList[2]	ThisList[2]^
3	ThisList[3]	ThisList[3]^

Each of these referenced variables represents a passenger record. We can assign values to the fields of the first of these records in the following way:

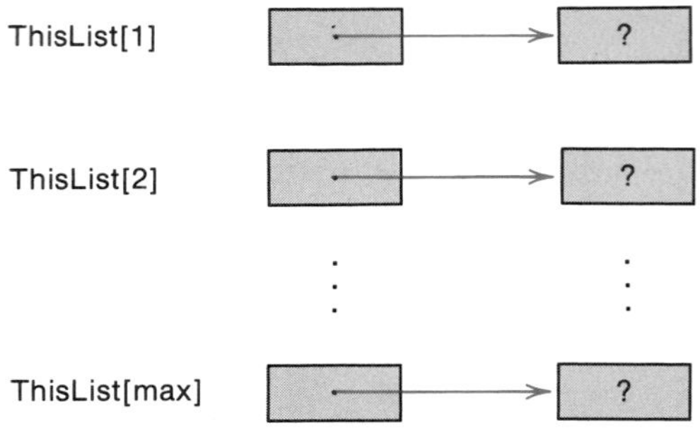

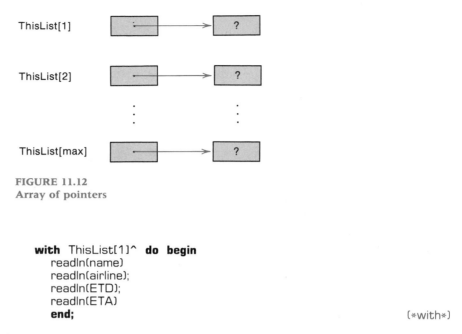

FIGURE 11.12
Array of pointers

```
   with ThisList[1]^ do begin
      readln(name)
      readln(airline);
      readln(ETD);
      readln(ETA)
      end;                                                        (*with*)
```

Similary, we can use another **with** statement to print the contents of one of these records. A program to illustrate these ideas is given in Figure 11.13. Pascal also has a built-in dispose procedure, which can be used to eliminate a reference (and possibly storage) associated with a pointer.

```
              (*Method: Set up and initialize an array of pointers.*)

program TryThis(input, output);
const
   max = 10;                                       (*maximum array size*)
   empty = '     ';                                (*shut-off mechanism*)
type
   alfa = packed array[1..5] of char;
   ptr = passenger;
   passenger = record                                    (*domain type*)
      name: alfa;
      airline: alfa;
      ETD, ETA: alfa;
      cities: array[1..max] of alfa;
      CostOfTicket: real;
      link: ptr                                        (*pointer type!*)
      end;                                                (*passenger*)
   list = array[1..max] of ptr;
```

```
(*-----------------------------------------------------*)
        (*Construct an array of pointers to passenger records*)

procedure BuildList(var ThisList: list;           (*array of pointers*)
                    var limit: integer);             (*array size*)
begin
  limit := 0;
  repeat
    limit := limit + 1;
    if limit <= max then begin
      new(ThisList[limit]);                  (*allocate heap storage*)
      with ThisList[limit]^ do begin
        write('Enter name- -a <return> to stop: ');
        readln(name); writeln;
        if name <> empty then begin
          write('Enter airline initials: '); readln(airline);
          writeln; write('Enter ETD: '); readln(ETD); writeln;
          write('Enter ETA: '); readln(ETA); writeln;
          write('Enter ETD city: '); readln(cities[1]); writeln;
          write('Enter ETA city: '); readln(cities[2]); writeln;
          write('Enter cost: '); readln(CostOfTicket); writeln
          end
        end
      end
  until (limit + 1 > max) or (ThisList[limit]^.name = empty);
  limit := limit - 1;                              (*true list size*)
end;                                                    (*BuildList*)

(*-----------------------------------------------------*)
        (*Print a copy of passenger records being pointed to*)

procedure ShowList(ThisList: list;                (*array of pointers*)
                   limit: integer);                   (*array size*)
var
  index: integer;
begin
  for index := 1 to limit do
    with ThisList[index]^ do begin
      writeln('Passenger':20, index:4);
      writeln('name':20, name:10);
      writeln('airline':20, airline:10);
      writeln('ETD, ETA':20, ETD:10, ETA:10);
      writeln('ETD city,ETA city':20,cities[1]:10,cities[2]:10);
      writeln('cost of ticket':20, CostOfTicket:10:2)
      end
end;                                                     (*ShowList*)

(*-----------------------------------------------------*)
                (*The program manager: activate procedures*)

procedure driver;
var
  PassengerList: list;                  (*array of pointers variable*)
  size: integer;                                        (*list size*)
```

```
begin
   BuildList(PassengerList, size);
   ShowList(PassengerList, size)
end;                                                        (*driver*)

  (*- - - - - - - - - - - - - - - - - - - - - - - - - - - - - - - - -*)

begin
   driver                                   (*activate driver procedure*)
end.
```

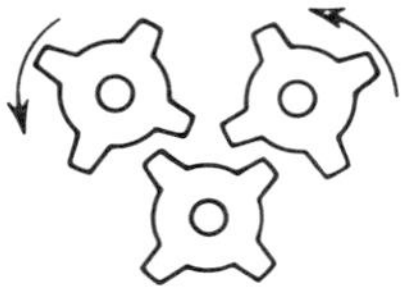

```
Enter name- -a <return> to stop: Lolita

airline initials: TWA

ETD: now

ETA: then

ETD city: NYC

ETA city: Chicago

cost: 325.45

Enter name- -a <return> to stop: Zorba

airline initials: TWA

ETD: now

ETA: 11:23 P.M.

ETD city: NYC

ETA city: San Jose

cost: 442.99

Enter name- -a <return> to stop:

          Passenger   1
               name        Lolita
            airline        TWA
           ETD, ETA        now        then
 ETD city, ETA city        NYC        Chicago
     cost of ticket            325.45
          Passenger   2
               name        Zorba
            airline        TWA
           ETD, ETA        now        11:23 P.M.
 ETD city, ETA city        NYC        San Jose
     cost of ticket            442.99
```

FIGURE 11.13 Array of pointers

11.7 The Dispose Procedure

If we use

dispose(TWAptr); (*activate dispose procedure*)

This at the very least eliminates the reference associated with the variable TWAptr. Depending on the Pascal compiler, the dispose procedure will free up the memory formerly used by a referenced variable. Memory is freed up, for example, by the dispose procedure used by IBM PC Pascal. UCSD Pascal assigns nil to a disposed pointer and it unallocates storage that is associated with a referenced variable. You will have to check your local Pascal to see exactly what your dispose procedure does. You can determine if nil is assigned to a pointer variable by the dispose procedure by trying out the following experiment:block:

Experiment 3

```
procedure check(ThisPtr: PointerType);
begin
   dispose(ThisPtr);
   if ThisPtr = nil then writeln('nil assigned!')
end;                                                    (*check*)
```

It is an error to attempt to dispose a pointer variable when its referenced variable is being accessed. For example, the following code will procedure a run-time error:

Experiment 4

```
with TWAptr^ do begin
   readln(FirstName);
                                         (*do something with TWAptr^*)
   dispose(TWAptr)                                          (*error!*)
   end;                                                      (*with*)
```

Here are some things to remember about pointers.

> **Rules of thumb with pointers:**
>
> **1. The only value a pointer variable can have is a memory address (a reference to a memory location).**
> **2. A referenced variable always consists of two parts: pointer variable identifier followed by an accent symbol (^) or up arrow.**
> **3. A referenced variable is always the domain type of the corresponding pointer type.**

4. The value of one pointer variable can be assigned to another pointer variable of the same type. Then both pointer variables will reference the same location in computer memory.

5. One referenced variable can be assigned the content of another referenced variable of the same type.

6. If a referenced variable is a record type, it can have one or more fields that are pointer types.

7. A pointer variable can be made to point to nothing by assigning nil to it.

11.8 Setting Up a Singly Linked List

Notice that the TWAptr pointer variable given earlier, for example, points to a passenger record. This record has a field that is a pointer type, namely, type ptr. We can make the link field of one passenger record point to another record of the same type using the following technique in a program body:

```
var
   ThisPassenger, ThatPassenger: ptr;            (*pointer variables*)
begin
   new(ThisPassenger);                           (*allocate storage*)
   new(ThatPassenger);                           (*allocate storage*)
   ThisPassenger^.name := 'Sally';                    (*assign name*)
   ThatPassenger^.name := 'Tom';                      (*assign name*)
   ThisPassenger^.link := ThatPassenger;             (*link records*)
   ThatPassenger^.link := nil                     (*points to nothing*)
end.                                               (*program body*)
```

In effect, the second to the last assignment of this program body makes the link field of ThisPassenger point to ThatPassenger. The two records have been linked together. The final statement of this program body makes the link field of ThatPassenger point to nothing. The results of these statements are shown graphically in Figure 11.14.

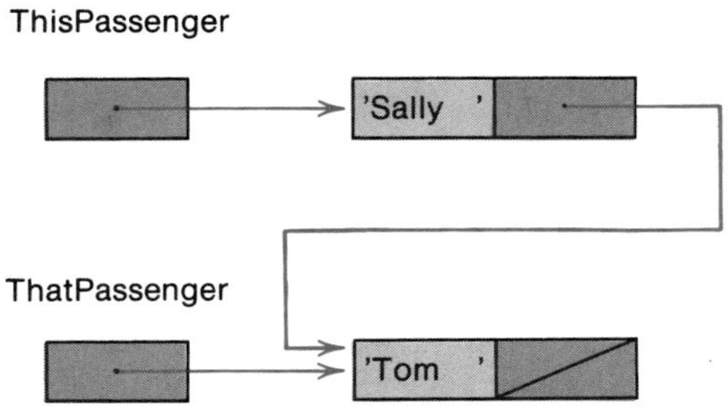

FIGURE 11.14
Linked records

This is an example of a singly linked list. The elements of a linked list are called *nodes*. A *singly linked list* consists of nodes where each node points to the next node, except the last node, which points to nil. In general, a singly linked list has the form shown in Figure 11.15.

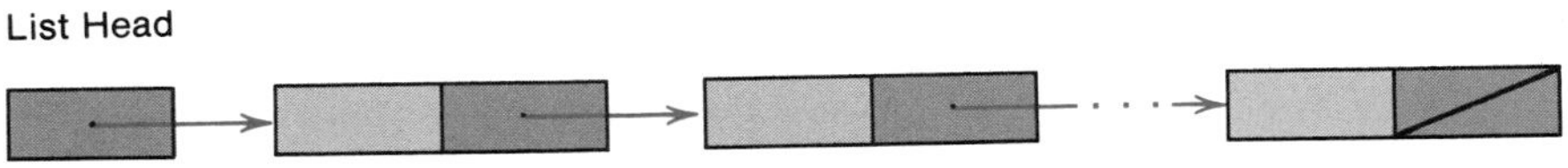

FIGURE 11.15
Singly linked list

11.9 Example: A Linked List of Names

Here is the beginning of an idea for a driver to create a singly linked list.

```
begin
   create the first two nodes of a list;
   repeat
      append next node to the list
   until list is complete;
   show a copy of the linked list
end;                                    (*driver to set up a linked list*)
```

A structure chart for a program to set up a linked list is shown in Figure 11.16.

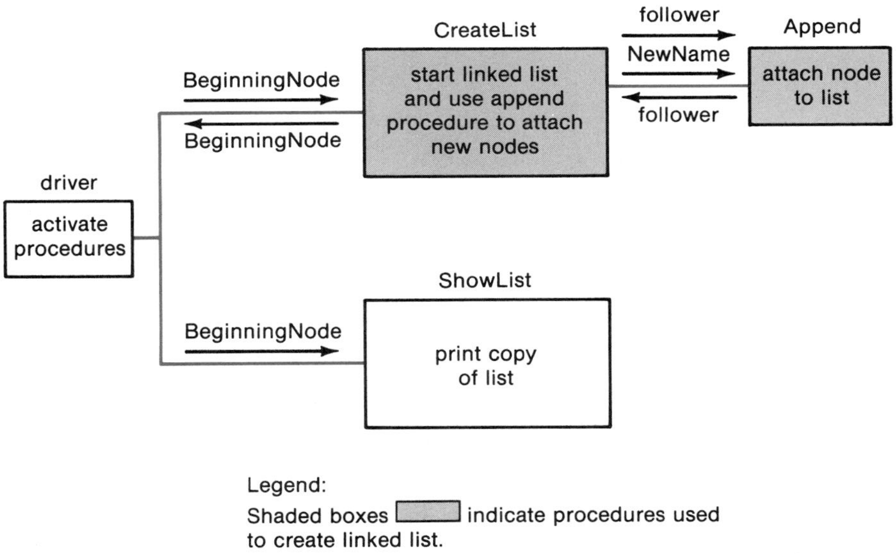

FIGURE 11.16
Structure chart for a program to create a linked list

The CreateList procedure for this program will have the following form:

```
                              (*input: sentinel, list head, list entries;
                                                       output: linked list
                        note: ListHead and next are pointer variables*)
begin
   initialize sentinel with a fixed value;
   initialize ListHead with a reference;
   assign value to List Head^.part;                    (*nonlink part*)
   initialize next with a reference;
   assign next to ListHead^.link;               (*link nodes together*)
   assign nil to next^.link;                     (*this gives a complete
                                           two-node, singly linked list*)
   repeat
      read value for next entry;
      append(next, entry)                        (*another algorithm!*)
   until entry = sentinel
end;                                         (*a CreateList algorithm*)
```

This algorithm sets up the leading two nodes of the list. Then it relies on the use of an append algorithm to attach any other nodes to the linked list. A complete two-node singly linked list is constructed before the repeat loop in this algorithm is carried out. The append algorithm can be written recursively as follows:

```
                              (*input: pointer to new node, new entry;
                                          output: extended linked list*)
begin
   assign next value to a follower pointer;
   if follower^.link = nil then begin
      assign entry to follower^.part;
      initialize a NewNode pointer variable;
      assign NewNode reference to follower^.link;
      assign NewNode reference to follower
      end                                              (*then block*)
   else
      append(follower^.link, entry)               (*self-activation*)
end;                                                     (*append*)
```

There will be no recursion inside the append algorithm, if we always activate it with the last node of the old list. This is the case with the CreateList algorithm. However, if we activate the append algorithm with the beginning node of a list, it will use recursion to search through the list for a link field with a nil value. The sentinel set up in the CreateList algorithm will be useful when we print out a list; it will give us a second way to tell when we have reached the end of a list. We show a program to illustrate the use of these methods in Figure 11.17. Notice that procedure parameters can be pointer types. These can be either variable or value parameters. This means the value of pointer variable can be passed to a procedure. (This is done in the ShowList procedure, which receives the value of the BeginningNode pointer variable in the driver procedure.) A pointer variable that has no reference (is undefined) can receive a reference from a corresponding variable parameter used by a procedure. For example, the BeginningNode in the driver procedure gets its reference from CreateList procedure. Both the append and CreateList procedures have variable parameters that are pointer types.

Notice that the ShowList procedure in this program is also recursive—and very concise. The sentinel is used to suppress printing the name field of the last node.

```
    (*Method: Append each new node to the end of a linked list.*)

program ListBuilder(input, output);
const
   sentinel = 'xxxxxyyyyy';                          (*marks end-of-list*)
type
   alfa = packed array[1..10] of char;                    (*string type*)
   ptr = ^node;                                          (*pointer type*)
   node = record                                          (*domain type*)
      name: alfa;                                         (*string type*)
      link: ptr                                          (*pointer type*)
      end;                                                     (*node*)

 (*- - - - - - - - - - - - - - - - - - - - - - - - - - - - - - - - - - - -*)
                                             (*attach new node to list:*)

procedure append(var follower: ptr;                      (*link pointer*)
                      NewName: alfa);                      (*list entry*)
var
   NewNode: ptr;                                     (*pointer variable*)
begin
   if follower^.link = nil then begin
      follower^.name := NewName;
      new(NewNode);
      follower^.link := NewNode; follower := NewNode
      end                                                  (*then block*)
   else append(follower^.link, NewName)
end;                                                         (*append*)

 (*- - - - - - - - - - - - - - - - - - - - - - - - - - - - - - - - - - - -*)
                              (*start list and extend it, if necessary:*)

procedure CreateList(var ListHead: ptr);                 (*pointer type*)
var
   next: ptr;                                        (*pointer variable*)
   entry: alfa;                                       (*string variable*)
begin
   new(ListHead); new(next);
   with ListHead^ do begin
      write('Enter name: '); readln(name); writeln;
      link := next;
      end;                                                       (*with*)
```

```
    next^.link := nil;
    repeat
       write('Enter name--xxxxxyyyyy, to stop: '); readln(entry);
       writeln;
       append(next, entry)
    until entry = sentinel
end;                                                      (*CreateList*)

(*----------------------------------------------------------------*)
                                                      (*Show linked list:*)

procedure ShowList(ListHead: ptr);                    (*value parameter*)
begin
       writeln(ListHead^.name: 20);
       if (ListHead <> nil) and (ListHead^.name <> sentinel) then
          ShowList(ListHead^.link)
end;                                                      (*ShowList*)

(*----------------------------------------------------------------*)
              (*Program manager: activate necessary procedures.*)

procedure driver;
var
    choice: integer;                                  (*control variable*)
    BeginningNode: ptr;                               (*pointer variable*)
begin
    repeat
       CreateList(BeginningNode);
       writeln; writeln('linked list:':20); writeln;
       ShowList(BeginningNode);
       write('Again?--1 = Y, 0 = N: '); readln(choice); writeln
    until choice = 0
end;                                                      (*driver*)

(*----------------------------------------------------------------*)

begin
    driver                                    (*activate driver procedure*)
end.
```

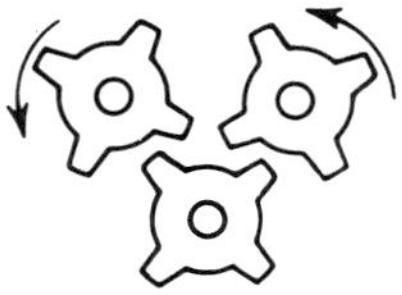

```
Enter name--xxxxxyyyyy, to stop: Lori

name: Susu

name: Carlos

name: Gandalf

name: Tomas

name: xxxxxyyyyy
```

```
linked list:

   Lori
   Susu
   Carlos
   Gandalf
   Tomas
   xxxxxyyyyy
Again?- -1 = Y, 0 = N: 0
```

FIGURE 11.17 Building a singly linked list

11.9.1 Refinement: Attaching New Nodes to an Old List

The program in Figure 11.17 does not allow us to sidestep the CreateList procedure. This means each time we build a list, we start over again with a new list. Inside the driver procedure, we can easily activate the append procedure to attach one or more new nodes to an old list. To do this, use the following algorithm:

```
begin
   assign ListHead to to a buffer pointer variable;
   repeat
      read a new entry;
      append(ListHead, entry)              (*this changes ListHead!*)
   until entry = sentinel;
   ShowList(buffer)
end;                                       (*adding nodes to old list*)
```

You will find that the new nodes are not printed by using this algorithm, since the ShowList procedure stops when it reaches a sentinel value in the name field of a node. A slight change in the ShowList procedure will make it possible to print the entire list. Try replacing 'and' by 'or' in the if conditon. This change will mean the first copy (but not the second!) of the sentinel will also be printed. You can eliminate the printing of the sentinel altogether by conditionally printing ListHead^.name, provided it is not the sentinel. This refinement is left as an exercise.

11.9.2 Refinement: Eliminating the List Sentinel

The program in Figure 11.17 can be improved and the refinement in Section 11.9.1 can be simplified by not appending the sentinel to a linked list. This can be handled inside the repeat loop of the CreateList procedure as follows:

```
repeat
   write('Enter name—xxxxxyyyyy, to stop: ');
   readln(entry);
   if entry <> sentinel then append(next, entry)
until entry = sentinel
```

Then the check on the presence of the sentinel can be dropped from the ShowList procedure. This will change (and simplify) the refinement in Section 11.9.1. This refinement is left as an exercise.

11.10 Experiment: Exploring the Heap

You are probably wondering how much heap storage you have available. The amount of heap storage available to a program will vary, depending on the computer system being used. You can try the following experiment to count the number of names you can insert into a linked list on your system:

Experiment 5

```
          (*note: This procedure uses the same pointer type defined
                              in the program in Section 11.9.2*)
procedure NewCreateList(var ListHead: ptr);
var
   next: ptr;                                  (*pointer variable*)
   entry: alfa;                                 (*string variable*)
   count: integer;                                (*node counter*)
begin
   new(ListHead); new(next);
   with ListHead↑ do begin
      write('Enter name: '); readln(name); writeln;
      link := next
      end;                                                (*with*)
   next^.link := nil; count := 0; entry := '
   repeat
      append(next, entry); count := count + 1;
      if count mod 1000 = 0 then writeln(count:20)
   until 1 > 2                                      (*endlessly*)
end;                                            (*NewCreateList*)
```

It is left as an exercise to implement this procedure in a program. Try using the program in Figure 11.17 to do this. The NewCreateList procedure was implemented in Figure 11.17 on an IBM PC and 40,000 nodes were obtained. The same procedure was implemented on a VAX-11 computer and 210,000 nodes were obtained.

11.11 Why Use Linked Lists Instead of Arrays?

Arrays are easier to work with than linked lists. However, there is a serious drawback to the declaration of an array type in Pascal. The dimension of an array type must be specified precisely. In effect, it is always necessary to specify the maximum number of cells an array will have. For this reason, arrays are space consuming. If we declare an array type with a maximum of

10,000 cells and usually need only 8500 cells, for example, then we have storage dedicated for 1500 array cells that are not used. (The extra cells are set aside to allow for all cases.) For this reason, T. Plum (1983) says arrays require a fat amount of memory (more than is usually needed). Arrays offer an inefficient way to set up lists that vary in size.

By contrast, it is not necessary to specify the number of nodes to be used in a linked list. It is available memory rather than an array size, which determines the maximum number of nodes a linked list can have. A linked list is a dynamic data structure—it can grow or shrink during the execution of a program. A linked list does not require a fat amount of memory, more memory than is usually needed to set up a list. A linked list offers an efficient way to set up lists that will vary in size.

Notice that a linked list of names will use more storage than an array with the same number of names. Each link field of a linked list of names requires storage. So in a case where a list has a fixed length, it would be better to use an array rather than a linked list. In other words, if you need to set up and maintain a list with constant length, then an array will be make more efficient use of storage.

11.12 Summary

A *pointer* is used to identify a location in computer memory. A pointer type declaration has the form

type
pointer identifier = ^domain **type**

A variable that is a pointer type gets a value by using the built-in new procedure. For example, if ThisPointer is a pointer variable, then the following statement gives ThisPointer a value:

```
new(ThisPointer);                    (*assign value to ThisPointer*)
```

The value of a pointer variable is a *reference* to a location in computer memory. The new procedure also sets up a hidden variable called a *referenced variable,* which has the following form:

form of a referenced variable = <pointer name>^

For example, ThisPointer^ is the referenced variable that corresponds to the ThisPointer variable. A *referenced variable* is used to hold a value identified by a pointer variable.

The domain type can be any of the data types we have seen so far, except another pointer type. A domain type is usually a record type. The *domain type* is the data type for a referenced variable. For example, we can have the following pointer and domain types:

```
type
  reservation = ^passenger;                    (*pointer type*)
  passenger = record                           (*domain type*)
    name: alfa;                                (*string type*)
    link: reservation                          (*pointer field*)
  end;j(*passenger*)
var
  TWA, NW: reservation;                        (*pointer variables*)
```

The referenced variables for these pointers are TWA^ and NW^. There are three ways to initialize pointer variables.

1. Use the built-in new procedure to establish a value (a reference) for a pointer variable. For example, we can use the new procedure to give the TWA pointer variable a reference as follows:

   ```
   new(TWA);                                   (*give TWA a reference*)
   ```

2. Use the nil token as follows:

   ```
   NW := nil;                                  (*assign nil value to NW*)
   ```

   Now NW points to nothing.

3. Assign the value of one pointer variable to another one. For example, we can do this with the TWA and NW pointer variables as follows:

   ```
   NW := TWA;                                  (*assign TWA reference to NW*)
   ```

Pointers are useful. They can be used to set up linked lists. This can be done where the domain type for a pointer is a record with one or more fields that are pointer types. This means the information in such records can be linked together. That is, the pointer field of one record can be made to point to the next record in a linked list. Using this technique, we can set up a singly linked list. A *singly linked list* is a list of nodes where each node points to the next node (except the last node, which points to nil).

11.13 Keywords Review

Keywords	*Related Ideas*
dispose	built-in procedure to eliminate a reference (and possibly memory) that is associated with a pointer variable.
domain type	data type of a referenced variable; it determines how much storage will be set aside for a referenced variable
dynamic data type	pointer type
heap	computer storage set aside for dynamic allocation to referenced variables
nil	a value that can be assigned to a pointer, which then points to nothing

pointer	reference to a computer memory location
type	declaration identifies pointer name and domain type
referenced variable	gives access to memory content identified by a pointer variable (it always has an up-arrow suffix)
up arrow	prefix for domain type identifier in the declaration of a pointer type; suffix for any referenced variable
singly linked list	list of nodes where each node points to the next node, except for the last node, which has a **nil** pointer

11.14 Exercises

1. What is the difference between a pointer variable and a referenced variable?

2. What is the difference between a pointer type and omain type?

The next three exercises use the following declaration:

```
type
   NewPtr  =  ^NewNode;
   NewNode  =  1672..2010
var
   p, q: NewPtrl
   x, y: NewNode;
```

3. What is the difference between *p* and *p*^?

4. Identify the pointer type and domain type for the above declaration.

5. Which of the following statements are not legal? Explain why a statement is not legal.
   a. new(*q*)
   b. new(*q*^)
   c. new(*x*)
   d. new(*x*^)
   e. *p*^ := ^*q*
   f. ^*p* := 1682
   g. dispose(*p*)
   h. dispose(*p*^)
   i. *q* := *p*
   j. *x* := 1676;
      p := *x*
   k. dispose(*x*)
   l. dispose(*x*^)
   m. *y* := 1985;
      p^ := *y* − 300
   n. *p*^ := *q*^;
   o. *x* := new(*p*)
   p. *p*^ := 1856;
   q. new(*p*) := new(*q*)

r. x := nil
s. p^ := 1800;
   dispose(p)
t. x^ := nil
u. p := nil
v. p^ := nil
w. p^ := x
   dispose(x)

6. Give a graphical interpretation of each of the following sets of statements:

a. new(p); new(q); new(t);
   p^ := 1672; q^:= 1673;
   t^ := p^;
   p^ := q^;
   q^ := t^;
b. new(p); new(q); new(t);
   p := q; q := t;
c. new(p); new(q); new(t);
   p := t; q := t;
d. new(p); new(q);
   t := p;
   p := q;
   q := t;
e. new(p); new(p); new(p)

The next two exercises use the following declarations:

```
type
   alfa = packed array[1..5] of char;
   ptr = ^node;
   node = record
      name: alfa;
      link: ptr
   end;                                          (*node*)
var
   p, q, head: ptr;
   sample: node;
   NickName: alfa;
```

7. What is the difference between head and head^ after new(head) is executed?

8. Which of the following statements are illegal? Explain why a statement is not legal.

a. new(sample);
b. p^ := string;
c. new(node);
d. p^.name := sample;
e. new(head);
f. p^.name := q^.name;
g. new(p);
   p^.link := nil;

h. p^.link := q^.link;
i. p^.link := q;
j. p^ := sample;
k. dispose(p^.link);
l. new(p^.link^.link)

9. In a circular list, the link field of the last node points to the first node of the list. Wrtie a program to build a circular list, using the following pointer type:

```
type
   ptr = ^node;
   node = record
      letter: char;
      link: ptr
      end;                                          (*node*)
```

Run your program for

a. Circular list with three nodes where each letter field has been assigned a letter of the 'yes' string. Then cycle through the list to print the following:

   yesyesyesyesyesyesyesyesyes

b. Circular list with four nodes where each letter field has been assigned a letter of the 'yes!' string. Then cycle through the list to print the following:

   yes!yes!yes!yes!yes!yes!yes!yes!

Hint. Your program should prompt for the number of times to cycle through a circular list.

10. Is a circular list also a singly linked list? Explain your answer.

11. Write a program to build a linked stack, using the NewPtr pointer type defined in the following way:

```
type
   alfa = packed array[1..11] of char;
   NewPtr = ^info;
   IRS = record
      FirstName, LastName, SSN: alfa
      end;
   info = record
      folder: IRS;
      InfoLink: NewPtr
      end;
```

That is, your program should build a linked list, where all list insertions and deletions are made at the same end. Your program should have separate procedures to push, pop, and print contents of a stack. Allow for up to 10 stack entries. In this early version of this program, your program should push entries taken from a keyboard, then pop and print (to a screen or printer) the stack entries. Run your program for

FirstName	*LastName*	*Social Security Number*
Bilboe	Baggins	521-99-0001
Susu	Baggins	521-99-0001
Stephan	Gould	323-42-0002
Tom	Seaver	421-99-0003
Jim	Hunter	221-67-0005
Bob	Gibson	991-23-0008

12. Refine the program in exercise 11 so that it takes into account the possibility of stack underflow and stack overflow. Run the refined program with
   a. Attempt to push too many stack entries
   b. Attempt to pop too many stack entries

13. Refine the program in exercise 11 so that is allows the user to do the following things:
   a. Search through a stack for an old entry using LastName as a search key (print an error message if the old entry is not found)
   b. Print designated number of entries, instead of the whole stack
   c. Tells the user how many entries are on the stack

   Using the list of entries from exercise 11, run your program to do the following things:
   d. Print record for Seaver
   e. Print top two stack entries
   f. Print top four stack entries
   g. print record for Jones;
   h. display number of entries on stack.

14. Give a graphical interpretation of the manipulatins of pointer variables and referenced variables in Figure 11.10.

15. Answer the question raised at the end of Section 11.2.4.

16. Carry out the refinement of the program in Figure 11.17 described in Section 11.8.1. Give a sample run.

17. Carry out the refinement of the program in Figure 11.17 described in Section 11.8.2. Give a sample run.

18. Implement Experiment 1, Section 11.1. Comment on the results of a run.

19. Implement Experiment 3, Section 11.6. Comment on the results of a sample run.

20. Implement Experiment 4, Section 11.6. Give sample run.

21. Implement Experiment 5, Section 11.9. Give sample run.

11.15 Review Quiz

Determine whether the following are true or false:

1. If *p* is a pointer variable with a reference, then

   writeln(*p*)

   will print the reference.
2. If *p* ^ is a referenced variable, then

   writeln(*p* ^)

   will print the reference.
3. Every pointer variable has a corresponding referenced variable.
4. The new and dispose procedures are activated with referenced variables.
5. The following assignment is illegal, if new(*p*) has not been executed beforehand on the pointer variable *p*:

   p := **nil**
6. Every pointer type has a domain type.
7. The domain type of a pointer type can be any data type, including pointer types themselves.
8. Every referenced variable has an up-arrow prefix.
9. The domain type in pointer type declaration has an up-arrow suffix.
10. In a singly linked list, the last node points to the first node.

11.16 Readings

Cooper, D. *Standard Pascal: User Reference Manual.* New York: Norton, 1983. See Chapter 12 on pointers.

Kruse, R. L. *Data Structures and Program Design.* Englewood Cliffs, NJ: Prentice-Hall, 1984. See Chapter 2 on lists.

MacLennan, B. J. *Principles of Programming Languages: Design, Evaluation and Implementation.* New York: Holt, Rinehart and Winston, 1983. See Chapter 5 on Pascal, especially pp. 206–210 on pointers.

Plum, T. *Learning to Program in C.* Englewood Cliffs, NJ: Prentice-Hall, 1983. See Chapter 7 on pointers.

CHAPTER 12

LINKED LISTS

A tree imposes a hierarchical structure on a collection of items.

Alfred V. Aho, John E. Hopcroft, Jeffrey D. Ullman, 1983

AIMS

- Distinguish between singly linked and multilinked lists.
- Introduce the key features of list processing.
- Give procedures to handle list insertions and deletions.
- Introduce binary trees that are multilinked lists.
- Show how to build and inspect a binary tree.
- Introduce insertion sorting.
- Introduce treesorts.

12.1 Introduction to Linked Lists

The structure of a singly linked list of names is shown in Figure 12.1. The structure of each node in Figure 12.1 is suggestive of the kind of structure that is needed to set up this linked list inside a computer. We can use the following pointer type to do this:

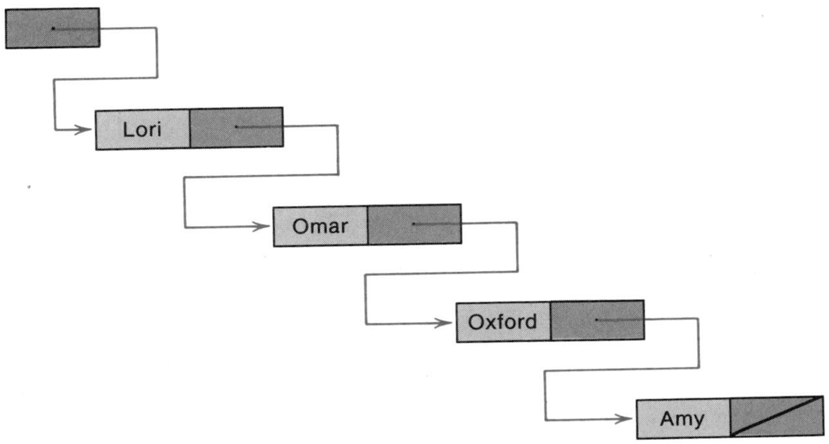

FIGURE 12.1
Linked list of names

```
type
   ListPtr = ^ListNode                          (*pointer type*)
   ListNode = record                            (*domain type*)
      name: alfa;                               (*string type*)
      link: ListPtr                             (*pointer type*)
   end;                                         (*ListNode*)
```

To put together a program to build a linked list, it is helpful first to make a sketch of the list. In other words, give a graphical interpretation of what you want before you begin writing down a formal description of the pointer type needed and the operations you will want to perform on your list. For example, you may want to doodle a bit more with the structure of the above list before you settle on the pointer type you want to use. If the list in Figure 12.1 were the beginning of a list of team players (collected information about the players on a team), then we probably would want a more detailed list like the one shown in Figure 12.2. The nodes in this linked list can be set up in a Pascal program using the following pointer type:

```
type
   alfa = packed array[1..10] of char;          (*string type*)
   beta = packed array[1..15] of char;          (*string type*)
   league = (NEast, NWest, AEast, AWest);       (*set type*)
   NewPtr = ^player                             (*pointer type*)
   player = record                              (*domain type*)
      NickName: alfa;                           (*string type*)
      LastName, FirstName: beta;                (*string types*)
      team: beta;                               (*string type*)
      place: league;                            (*set type*)
      link: NewPtr                              (*pointer type*)
      end;                                      (*player*)
```

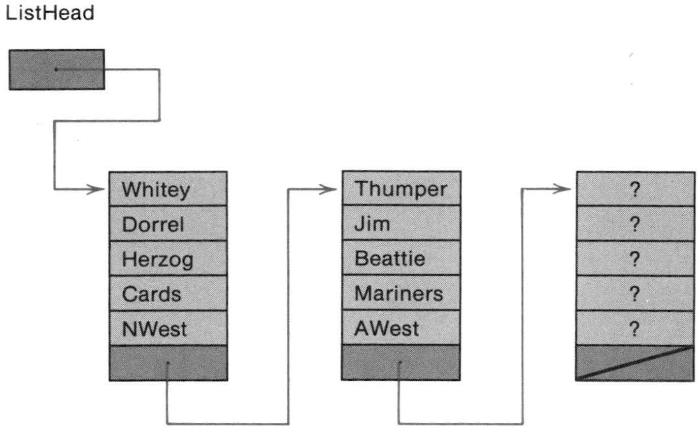

FIGURE 12.2
Linked list of team records

Refining a sketch of a linked list will mean a corresponding refinement in the type declaration for the pointer variables you need to set up your list. You can think of the sketches you make of a linked list as strategy sessions in preparation for a list processing program you will write.

The term *list processing* refers to the collection of operations normally used in working with lists. What follows is a list of these operations:

1. Creating a list (see ListCreate procedure, Figure 11.2)

2. Inspecting a list
   2.1. Printing an entire list (see ShowList, Figure 11.2)
   2.2. Printing a sublist
   2.3. Printing the content of one node

3. Insertion: putting a node into a list
   3.1. Appending a node to the end of a list (see append Procedure, Figure 11.2)
   3.2. Using a search key to determine where to make an insertion

4. Deletion: dropping reference to a node

5. Scanning (traversing) a list to find a node

6. Editing a list node (changing its content)

7. Sorting an unordered list (use method in 3.2 to do this)

In this chapter we show how to perform an insertion sort with a linked list. We also show how to delete one or more nodes from an existing linked list.

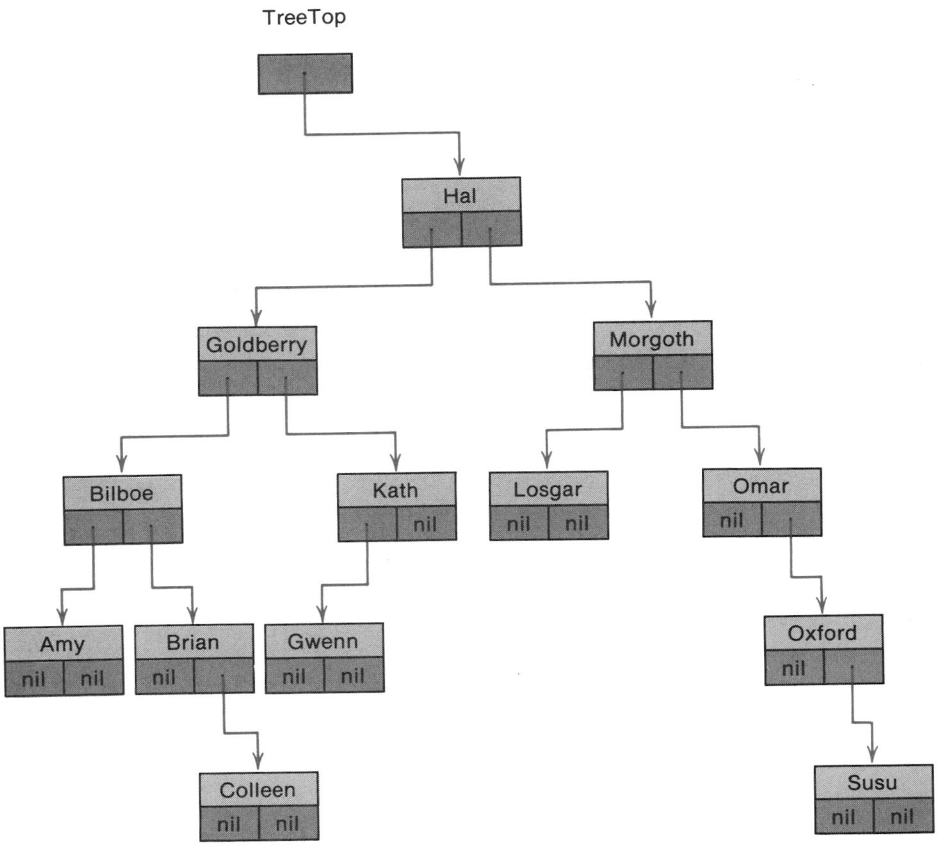

FIGURE 12.3
A name tree

So far we have dealt exclusively with singly linked lists. It is also possible to set up what are known as *multilinked lists.* In a *multilinked list,* each node has more than one pointer so that more than one list node can be referenced by a single node. An example of a multilinked list called a binary tree is shown in Figure 12.3. Again, the "picture" of a list node suggests what pointer type declaration will be needed to set up this list in a Pascal program.

```
type
   alfa = packed array[1..10] of char;          (*string type*)
   TreePtr = ^TreeNode;                         (*pointer type*)
   TreeNode = record                            (*domain type*)
      name = alfa;                              (*string type*)
      left, right: TreePtr                      (*pointer types*)
      end;                                      (*TreeNode*)
```

To set up this tree in computer memory, we can use the name field of each node to determine which node pointer to use. Here is a rule to use in constructing a name tree.

Name-tree node rule:

1. Point left, if a new name comes before the name in the current tree node.
2. Point right, if a new name comes after the name in the current tree node.

In general, the use of a tree-node rule organizes a tree into a hierarchical data structure. The beginning node of a tree is called the *root node,* which is the parent of each of the other tree nodes. In general, a tree is defined as a finite set of one or more nodes organized in the following way:

1. One node is the first parent (the root node).
2. The nodes descending from the root can be separated into nonintersecting subsets that are also trees called *subtrees.*

Each node in a tree can be thought of as a parent. In the tree in Figure 12.3, the 'Hal' identifies the root node or first parent. The children of 'Hal' are 'Goldberry' and 'Morgoth,' who are also parents. In other words, 'Goldberry' and 'Morgoth' mark the beginning of two entirely separate (disjoint) subtrees.

Level	Left Subtree	Right Subtree
1	Goldberry	Morgoth
2	Bilboe Kath	Losgar Omar
3	Amy Brian Gwenn	Oxford
4	Colleen	Susu

The root node of a tree is at level 0. The nodes immediately to the left or right of a parent node in a binary tree are called *offspring* or *children* (they are at level 1). A left node is called a *left child:* a right node, a *right child.* Terminal nodes in a tree are called *leaves.* In general we have the following definition of a binary tree:

A binary tree is either an empty tree or a tree where each node has no more then two children.

In this chapter, we show how to build and maintain a binary tree. This will lead to a TreeSort. You might be wondering why we bother using a binary tree to sort a list of records by name, for example. It turns out that a TreeSort will often be more efficient than an insertion sort using a singly linked list. We will compare the efficiency of these two sorts in this chapter.

12.2 List Insertions Using an Insertion Key

An *insertion key* is a list node field used to determine where to make an insertion in a list. For example, we can use the name field of the list of names in Figure 12.1 as an insertion key. We can do this by using the following rule: The position of a name in a list is determined alphabetically. For example, try inserting 'Gloria' into the following list of names:

Cary Colleen David Edward Gandalf Goldberry Kim

Gloria

Notice that it is the second letter of 'Gloria' which determines where to place this name in the sublist of names beginning with 'G.' This may not always be the case. For example, it is the first letter in 'Amy' that determines entirely where to make the insertion of 'Amy' into this list. Fortunately, strings can be compared in Pascal and the ordering of strings is made easy. What about inserting 'Gloria' into a linked list? A linked version of the last four names of the above list is given in Figure 12.4. To insert 'Gloria' into this list, we need to use the following steps:

1. Using 'Gloria' as the insertion key value, scan a list to determine where to make an insertion.

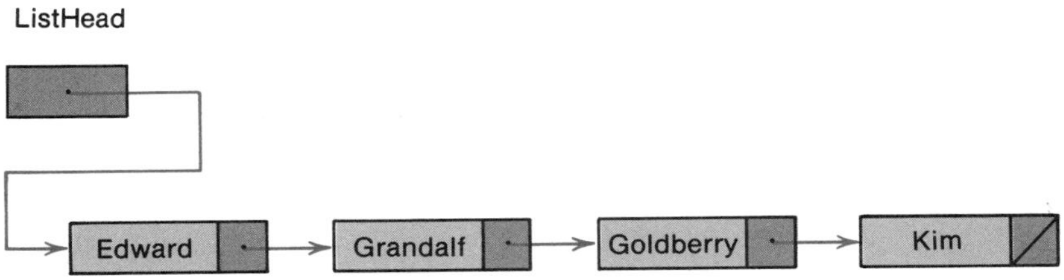

FIGURE 12.4
Singly linked list

2. Adjust the pointers in the original list as follows:
   2.1. Make the link field of the new node point to the immediately after the node with 'Gandalf' as shown in Figure 12.5.

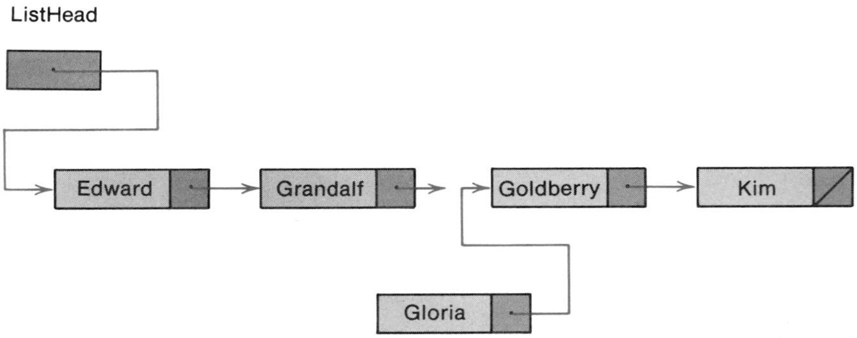

FIGURE 12.5
Start insertion into linked list

   2.2. Make the link field of the node with 'Gandalf' point to the new node as shown in Figure 12.6.

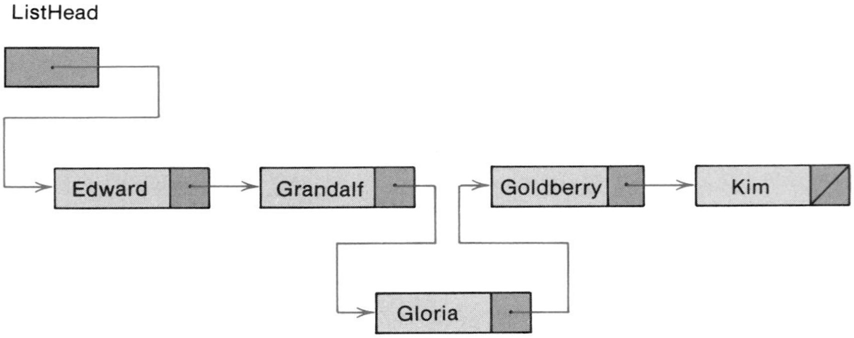

FIGURE 12.6
Final step to insert new node

We summarize the steps of this algorithm in pseudocode form as follows:

```
(*input: pointer to first node of a list;
         pointer to new node;
         two pointers that can be used to mark pairs
         of list nodes;
         search key (a name in the example);
  output: expanded list*)
```

```
begin
   assign heap storage to NewNode;
   if ListHead points to nothing (nil) then begin
      make ListHead point to NewNode;
      assign target (search key) to ListHead^.key;
      make ListHead^.link point to nothing (nil)
      end                                                        (*if*)
   else begin
      make ahead pointer point to ListHead;
      while (target >= ahead^.key) and (ahead^.link <> nil)
         do begin
               make behind point to ahead;
               make ahead point to ahead^.link         (*next node!*)
               end;                                          (*while*)
      assign target to NewNode^.key;
      make NewNode^.link point to ahead;                (*next node*)
      if ahead = ListHead then
         make ListHead point to the NewNode
      else
         make behind^.link point to the NewNode
      end                                                     (*else*)
end                                        (*list insertion algorithm*)
```

Notice that this algorithm can become the basis for an insertion sort: After each insertion, the list entries have been ordered using an insertion key value.

12.3 Example: Insertion Sorting a List of Names

We can use the following steps to set up a complete program for an insertion sort using a linked list:

```
                                            (*input: list nodes;
                                output: linked list that is ordered*)
begin
   prompt for list nodes;
   insert nodes into linked list;
   print a copy of the completed linked list
end                                              (*driver algorithm*)
```

A structure chart suggestive of how we might implement this driver algorithm is given in Figure 12.7. The CreateList procedure in this structure chart is a carry-over from Chapter 11. In the list processing program we will set up in this chapter, this procedure will have the following form:

```
                             (*input: pointer to beginning of new list;
                                            output: ordered linked list*)
begin
   assign heap storage to ListHead;
   enter search key (a name in the example);
   while KeyValue <> sentinel do begin
      InsertNode(ListHead, next, KeyValue);
      get new KeyValue
      end
end;                                     (*new CreateList procedure*)
```

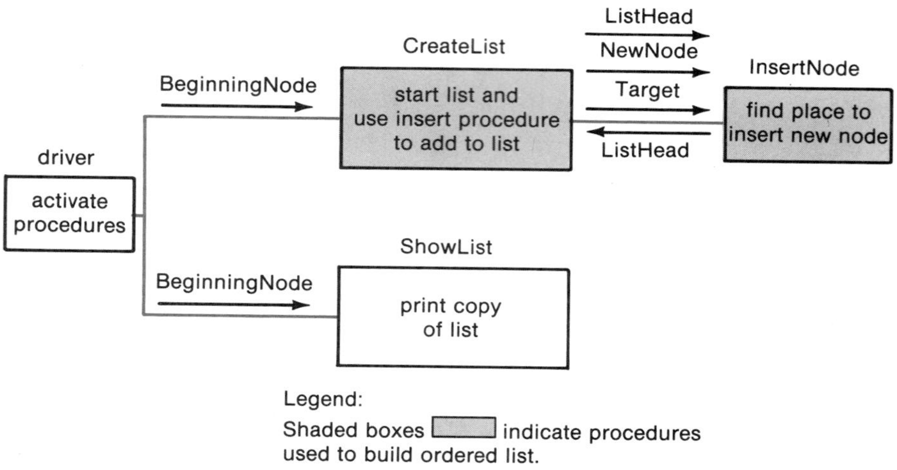

FIGURE 12.7
Structure chart for an insertion program

To set up the beginning of a list processing program, we will also develop a method of deleting nodes from an existing list. We do this in Section 12.4.

12.4 List Deletions

A search key is used to locate a node to be deleted. One of the nonlink fields of a list node will be used as a search key field. This is a node field used to detect a matchup (if there is one!) between a key value and one of a key field of one of the list nodes. Duplicates are possible—more than one key field may have the same value. So sometimes it will be necessary to use more than one search key to avoid the problem of duplicate key fields for entirely different nodes. A list of nodes for the players in a team sport is an example where the problem of duplicate search fields might arise. For example, if we choose a player's last name as the search key, there may be more than one player with the same last name. To avoid this problem, you might want to conduct a search using a player's first and last names. Care is needed in the choice of a search key.

Most of the time, a node will have more than one nonlink field, which means there will usually be a choice of more than one search key. Once a search key has been selected, a search of a list for a node to be deleted can begin. Suppose we want to delete 'Gandalf' from the list shown in Figure 12.8. Here are the steps to handle the deletion of 'Gandalf' from this list.

1. Find 'Gandalf' in the list (if it exists, there!).
2. Redirect the link field of the node before 'Gandalf' (make it point to the

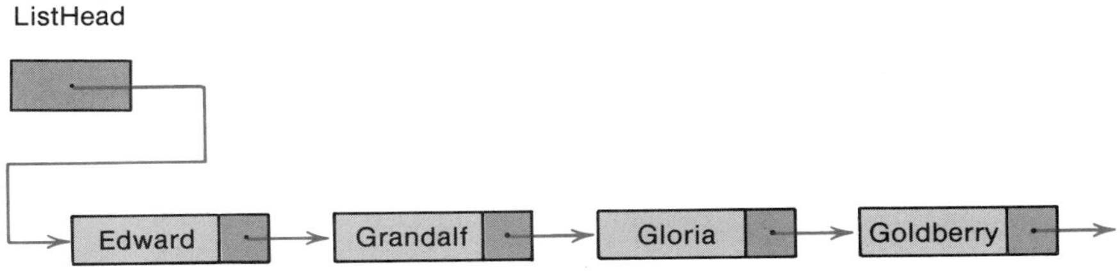

FIGURE 12.8
Sample list

node after "Gandalf") as shown in Figure 12.9. *Note:* This can be done by assigning to the link field of the node containing 'Edward' the reference held by the link field of the node containing 'Gandalf' (the node to be deleted). This makes the node containing 'Edward' point past the node containing 'Gandalf.'

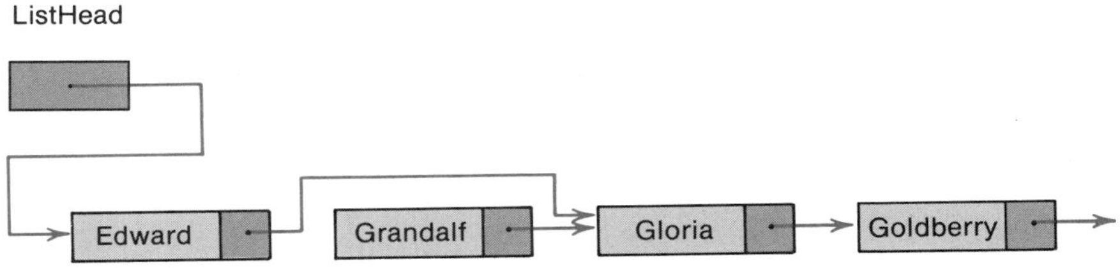

FIGURE 12.9
Redirect link of node before the one to be deleted

3. Dispose of the 'Gandalf' node, which produces the result shown in Figure 12.10.

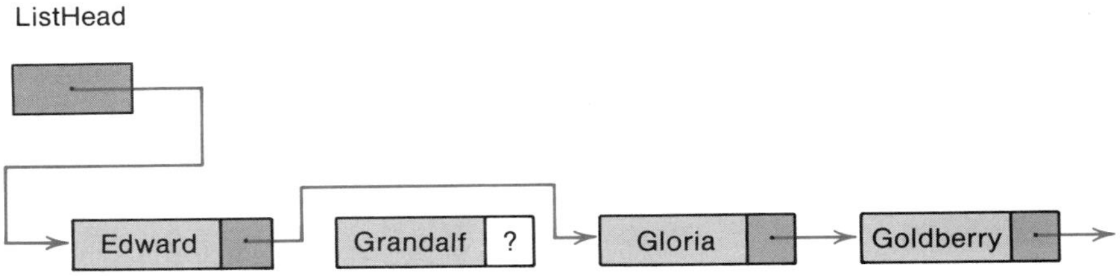

FIGURE 12.10
Dispose of a pointer

4. Assign true to a Boolean variable (call it *found*), when a node to be deleted has been found. Otherwise, if there is a search failure (you can expect this

to happen!), assign a false to found. *Note:* If you attempt to delete a node that does not exist in a list, then an error message should be printed. The found variable will tell you when to do this. If left as an exercise to develop a pseudocode interpretation of the delete procedure. To do this, you can draw on the actual Pascal code for the DeleteNode procedure given in the program in Figure 12.12.

12.5 List Processing

This gives us an expanded structure chart for a list processing program shown in Figure 12.11. The beginning of a list processing program is given in Figure 12.12.

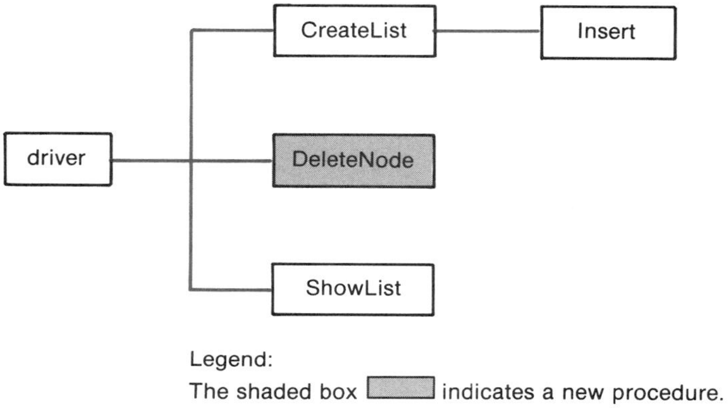

FIGURE 12.11
Expanded structure chart

```
       (*Method: Allow the user to create lists, insert new entries
                 into an existing list, delete unwanted entries, and
                                         inspect a list of names.*)

program ListBuilder(input, output);
const
   sentinel = '          ';                       (*marks end-of-list*)
type
   alfa = packed array[1..10] of char;                  (*string type*)
   ListPtr = ^ListNode;                                (*pointer type*)
   ListNode = record                                    (*domain type*)
      name: alfa;                                       (*string type*)
      link: ListPtr                                    (*pointer type*)
      end;                                                     (*node*)
```

```
(*-------------------------------------------------*)

procedure InsertNode(var ListHead, NewNode: ListPtr;    (*pointers*)
                          target: alfa);          (*name to insert*)
var
   ahead, behind: ListPtr;                    (*pointer variables*)
begin
   new(NewNode);
   if ListHead = nil then begin
      ListHead := NewNode; ListHead^.name := target;
      ListHead^.link := nil
      end
   else begin
      ahead := ListHead;
      while (target >= ahead^.name) and (ahead^.link <> nil) do begin
         behind := ahead; ahead := ahead^.link
         end                                                (*while*)
      end;                                                  (*else*)
   NewNode^.name := target;
   NewNode^.link := ahead;  (*make NewNode point to next node*)
   if ahead = ListHead then
      ListHead := NewNode
   else
      behind^.link := NewNode
end;                                                  (*InsertNode*)

(*-------------------------------------------------*)
                         (*start list and extend it, if necessary:*)

procedure CreateList(var ListHead: ListPtr);
var
   next: ListPtr;                              (*pointer variable*)
   entry: alfa;                                 (*string variable*)
begin
   new(ListHead); ListHead^.name := sentinel;
   write('Enter name--<return>, to stop: ':35); readln(entry);
   while entry <> sentinel do begin
      InsertNode(ListHead, next, entry);
      write('name: ':35); readln(entry); writeln
      end;                                                  (*while*)
end;                                                   (*CreateList*)

(*-------------------------------------------------*)
                                             (*Show linked list:*)

procedure ShowList(ListHead : ListPtr);
begin
      if ListHead = nil then
         writeln('Sorry--list is empty!')
      else begin
         if ListHead^.name <> sentinel then
            write(ListHead^.name, ' ':3);
         if ListHead^.link <> nil then
            ShowList(ListHead^.link)
         end                                                (*else*)
end;                                                   (*ShowList*)
```

```
(*-----------------------------------------------*)

procedure DeleteNode(var ListHead: ListPtr;
                         target: alfa);          (*name to delete*)
var
   ahead, behind: ListPtr;
   found: Boolean;                               (*for search failure*)
begin
   ahead := ListHead;
   if target = ahead^.name then found := true
   else begin
   found := false;
   while (target <> ahead^.name) and (ahead^.link <> nil) do begin
      behind := ahead; ahead := ahead^.link;
      if target = ahead^.name then found := true
      end                                                  (*while*)
   end;                                                    (*else*)
   if not found then writeln(target:20, ' is not in list!')
   else begin
      if ahead = ListHead then
         ListHead := ListHead^.link
      else begin
         behind.link := ahead^.link;
         dispose(ahead)
         end                                         (*inner else*)
      end                                            (*outer else*)
end;                                                 (*DeleteNode*)

(*-----------------------------------------------*)
            (*Program manager: activate necessary procedures.*)

procedure driver;
var
   choice: integer;                              (*control variable*)
   addition, deletion: alfa;                     (*string variables*)
   BeginningNode, AnotherNode: ListPtr;          (*pointer variable*)
begin
   BeginningNode := nil;
   repeat
      writeln('menu:':10);
      writeln(' ':10, '--->  1) create an ordered list;');
      writeln(' ':10, '--->  2) delete an entry;');
      writeln(' ':10, '--->  3) insert an entry;');
      writeln(' ':10, '--->  4) see list;');
      writeln(' ':10, '--->  5) exit;');
      readln(choice);
      case choice of
         1: CreateList(BeginningNode);
         2: begin
                ShowList(BeginningNode);
                writeln; writeln;
                write('Enter name to delete: ':35); readln(deletion);
                writeln;
                DeleteNode(BeginningNode, deletion)
            end;
```

```
        3: begin
                write('Enter name to insert: ':35); readln(addition);
                InsertNode(BeginningNode, AnotherNode, addition)
             end;
        4: if BeginningNode = nil then
                writeln('Whoops!--there is no list to inspect.')
             else begin
                ShowList(BeginningNode); writeln
                end;
        5:                                            (*empty statement*)
        end
     until choice = 5
end;                                                           (*driver*)

 (*-----------------------------------------------------------*)

begin
   driver                                    (*activate driver procedure*)
end.
```

```
        menu:
                ---> 1) Create an ordered list;
                ---> 2) Delete an entry;
                ---> 3) Insert an entry;
                ---> 4) See list;
                ---> 5) Exit;
4
Whoops!--there is no list to inspect.
        menu:
                ---> 1) Create an ordered list;
                ---> 2) Delete an entry;
                ---> 3) Insert an entry;
                ---> 4) See list;
                ---> 5) Exit;
1
     Enter name--<return>, to stop: Juanita
                                    name: Tomas

                                    name: Carmen

                                    name: GAndalf

                                    name: Amy

                                    name:

        menu:
                ---> 1) Create an ordered list;
                ---> 2) Delete an entry;
                ---> 3) Insert an entry;
                ---> 4) See list;
                ---> 5) Exit;
4
Amy       Carmen       GAndalf       Juanita       Tomas
```

```
        menu:
                ---> 1) Create an ordered list;
                ---> 2) Delete an entry;
                ---> 3) Insert an entry;
                ---> 4) See list;
                ---> 5) Exit;
2
Amy       Carmen      GAndalf      Juanita      Tomas

                    Enter name to delete: Gandalf

              Gandalf     is not in list!
        menu:
                ---> 1) Create an ordered list;
                ---> 2) Delete an entry;
                ---> 3) Insert an entry;
                ---> 4) See list;
                ---> 5) Exit;
2
Amy       Carmen      GAndalf      Juanita      Tomas

                    Enter name to delete: Gandalf

        menu:
                ---> 1) Create an ordered list;
                ---> 2) Delete an entry;
                ---> 3) Insert an entry;
                ---> 4) See list;
                ---> 5) Exit;
3
                    Enter name to insert: Gandalf
        menu:
                ---> 1) Create an ordered list;
                ---> 2) Delete an entry;
                ---> 3) Insert an entry;
                ---> 4) See list;
                ---> 5) Exit;
4
Amy       Carmen      Gandalf      Juanita      Tomas
        menu:
                ---> 1) Create an ordered list;
                ---> 2) Delete an entry;
                ---> 3) Insert an entry;
                ---> 4) See list;
                ---> 5) Exit;
3
                    Enter name to insert: Zorba
        menu:
                ---> 1) Create an ordered list;
                ---> 2) Delete an entry;
                ---> 3) Insert an entry;
                ---> 4) See list;
                ---> 5) Exit;
4
```

```
Amy         Carmen        Gandalf        Juanita        Tomas        Zorba
        menu:
              ---> 1) Create an ordered list;
              ---> 2) Delete an entry;
              ---> 3) Insert an entry;
              ---> 4) See list;
              ---> 5) Exit;
5
```

FIGURE 12.12 List processing

12.5.1

Refinement: Suppressing the Sentinel

The program in Figure 12.12 depends on the use of a sentinel, which goes into the name field of the first node of each linked list that is built. This sentinel shows up in the ordered list printed by the ShowList procedure. At the very least, the printing of the sentinel name should be suppressed during the activation of the ShowList procedure. This refinement is left as an exercise.

12.5.2

Refinement: Measuring the Efficiency of an Insertion Sort

The efficiency of the insertion sort in Figure 12.12 can be measured by keeping track of the comparisons made by the InsertNode procedure. Notice that each time an insertion is made, a search for a place to make an insertion always starts with the leading list node. Starting with the first node, the search continues from node to node until a place to put the target name is found. In other words, the insertion sort in the list processing program depends on a linear search technique. As a rule, it takes an average of $(n+1)/2$ comparisons to find a place to make an insertion in a list with n items. This tells us something about the efficiency of an insertion sort.

Comparisons Made by a Linear Search

List Size	*Average Number of Comparisons Made*
1	0
2	1
3	2 (probably)
.	.
.	.
n	$(n+1)/2$

Note: Sum of comparisons $= (1+1)/2 + (2+1)/2 + \ldots + (n+1)/2)$
$= (1+2+ \ldots +n)/2+=(1+1+ \ldots +1)/2$
$= n(n+1)/4 + n/2$
$= n^2/4 + 3n/4$

This says the running time an insertion sort will be close to $n^2/4$ for a list of n items.

Each time the InsertNode procedure is activated, we can keep track of the number of comparisons used before an insertion is made. This is the comparison made in the while loop of this procedure. This will mean introducing another variable parameter (call it *measure*) in this procedure. Then use the returned value of measure in the CreateList procedure to build a total number of comparisons used to complete an insertion sort. This total will vary, depending on the list of names you build. Widely scattered names will produce high comparison counts; bunched up names, low comparison counts.

It would be helpful to maintain a history of comparison totals during the running of this program. Notice that the CreateList procedure can be reactivated by the driver procedure, if you choose to build more than one list. To build a history of the comparison totals used to insertion sort each new list, set up an array of records of the following type:

```
type
  history = record
    ComparisonTotal: integer;            (*initialize after sort*)
    ListSize: integer                   (*keep track of list size*)
    end;                                             (*history*)
```

This will allow you to print out the following table:

List Number	*List Size*	*Comparisons Made*
1	?	?
2	?	?
(And so on)		

This will give you a way to measure the running time of an insertion sort. You can determine how long it takes your computer to make one comparison by looking in one of your system manuals. For example, if it takes an average of 0.78 microseconds to make one comparison on your system, then you can compute approximately how much machine time your insertion will take.

Machine time for one comparison × total comparisons

This refinement is left as an exercise. It is possible to improve on the running time an insertion sort of a list of names, for example, by storing the names in a binary tree. We show how to do this in Section 12.6.

12.6 Binary Trees

A *binary tree* is an example of a multilinked list. In a binary tree, each tree node will have two pointer fields. Here is what a tree node will look like.

```
type
   alfa = packed array[1..5] of char;
   TreePtr = ^TreeNode;                         (*pointer type*)
   TreeNode = record                            (*domain type*)
      name: alfa;                               (*nonlink field*)
      left, right: TreePtr                      (*pointer types*)
      end;                                      (*TreeNode*)
var
   ThisTree: TreePtr;                           (*tree variable*)
```

The nodes of a binary tree are organized by using an insertion key like a name. An insertion key value will dictate whether we use the left or the right link of a TreeNode. For example, we can try building a binary tree with the list of names used earlier for a singly linked list.

list: Edward, Cary, Colleen, David, Gandalf, Goldberry, Kim
first name to insert: Edward (the link fields are not used)
second name to insert—Cary:
Steps:

1. Cary comes before Edward.
2. Make left link of Edward-node point to Cary-node; third name to insert—Colleen.

Steps:

1. Colleen comes before Edward.
2. Follow left link of Edward node to Cary node.
3. Colleen comes after Cary, so
4. Make right link of Cary-node point to Colleen node.

and so on. A graphical interpretation of these steps is given in Figure 12.13. In other words, if we use the order relationship dictated by a search-key value to build a tree, the result will be an ordered tree. A program to implement this idea will have the following form:

```
                                   (*input: search-key values;
                         output: ordered list that is a binary tree*)
begin
   build tree;
   show tree
end                                     (*level 1 program idea*)
```

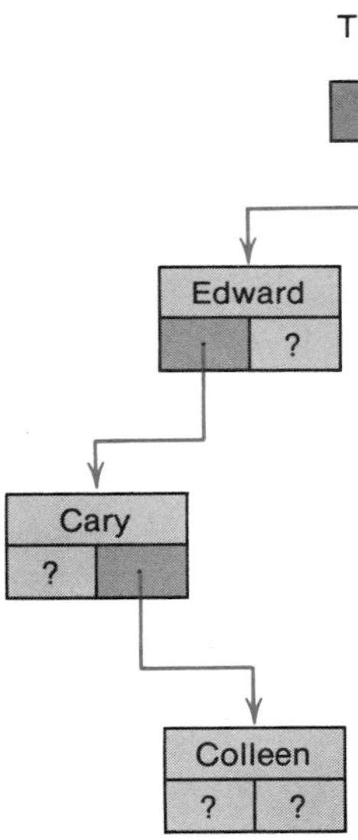

FIGURE 12.13
Beginning of a tree

The build-tree part of this program will have the following form:

```
                                              (*input: search-key values;
                                                  output: binary tree*)
begin
   make first tree node point to nothing;
   repeat
      get search-key value;
      insert into tree
   until search-key value = sentinel
end                                           (*preliminary tree builder*)
```

This tree-builder algorithm depends on the use of a tree-insertion algorithm that has the following form:

```
                                              (*input: search-key values;
                      output: multilinked list that is a binary tree*)
begin
   initialize target (search-key value);
   assign heap storage to TreeNode;
      if NewNode points to nil then begin           (*Is list empty?*)
         assign reference to NewNode;
         with NewNode^ do begin
            initialize the nonlink fields;
            assign nil to the left pointer;
            assign nil to the right pointer
            end                                             (*with*)
```

```
      begin                                        (*then block*)
   else                                        (*recursive part*)
      if target < NewNode^.SearchKey
      then insert(target, NewNode^.left)
      else insert(target, NewNode^.right)
end                                     (*tree-insertion algorithm*)
```

A structure chart for the program we are building is given in Figure 12.14. This tree-builder algorithm depends on a tree search, beginning with the tree root. If the target does not match the SearchKey field of the root node, then this algorithm activates itself in terms of either the left or the right subtree. Notice that the first self-activation eliminates half the tree from the tree search! This is a divide-and-conquer method searching for a place to make an insertion into a list. Notice that the resulting binary tree will be ordered.

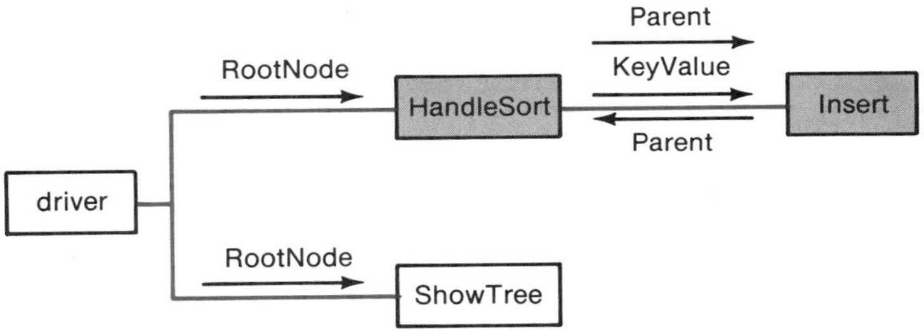

FIGURE 12.14
Structure chart for a tree-building program

12.6.1 *Printing Tree Nodes in Order*

We can print out the nonlink parts of a binary tree as an ordered list, if we use the following technique:

```
                              (*tree scan to print an ordered list*)
begin
  1. Traverse as far left as possible in tree.
  2. Print node visited (the first one will be a leaf).
  3. Traverse right and repeat steps 1 and 2
     until all nodes have been visited.
end                              (*preliminary tree scan algorithm*)
```

The idea in this algorithm is to scan as far left as possible (until we find the left-most node with a left pointer that is nil), then print the nonlink part of the left-most node. Then scan right, then left to the left-most node (a leaf, again!), then print the nonlink part of the node we are visiting. Here is a recursive procedure to do this.

```
procedure PrintTree(VisitedNode: TreePtr);
begin
   if VisitedNode <> nil then
      with VisitedNode^ do begin
         PrintTree(left);
         writeln('nonlink part = ', NameField);
         PrintTree(right)
         end                                              (*with*)
end;                                                  (*PrintTree*)
```

During this recursion, we first move as far left in the tree as we can. When the processor finds a left link that is nil, then the nonlink part gets printed. Then this procedure activates itself with the right link of the node it is visiting, which then takes the processor to the left-most node, again. Each time this procedure activates itself, the old pointer is saved on a recursion stack. Popping these old pointer values will take the processor back up the left subtree and down the right subtree.

12.6.2 *Example: TreeSorting a Name Tree*

We will put these ideas together in a program to build an ordered binary name tree. That is, the nonlink part of each tree node will be a name. A program to do this is given in Figure 12.15. There are some refinements we can make in this program to give us more information about the tree.

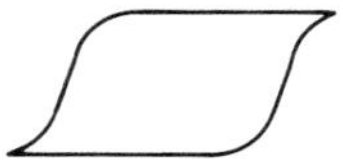

```
          (*Method: Build a binary tree using name as the insertion
                    key. Print the tree nodes in order from left
                                                      to right.*)
program NameTree(input, output);
const
   sentinel = '          ';                    (*will mark last node*)
type
   alfa = packed array[1..10] of char;               (*string type*)
   TreePtr = ^TreeNode;                             (*pointer type*)
   TreeNode = record                                 (*domain type*)
      key: alfa;                                   (*insertion key*)
      left, right: TreePtr                         (*pointer types*)
   end;                                                (*TreeNode*)

(*- - - - - - - - - - - - - - - - - - - - - - - - - - - - - - - - -*)
                                       (*Insert nodes into binary tree:*)

procedure insert(KeyValue: alfa;                   (*insertion key*)
                 var parent: TreePtr);          (*pointer variable*)
begin
   if parent = nil then begin
      new(parent);
      with parent^ do begin
         key := KeyValue;
         left := nil; right := nil
         end;                                             (*with*)
      end
```

```
    else
       if KeyValue < parent^.key then insert(KeyValue, parent^.left)
       else
          if KeyValue > parent^.key then insert(KeyValue,parent^.right)
end;                                                         (*insert*)

 (*-------------------------------------------------------------*)
                      (*Show tree nodes printed from left to right:*)

procedure ShowTree(ptr: TreePtr);                     (*a reference*)
begin
   if ptr <> nil then
      with ptr^ do begin
         ShowTree(left);
         writeln(key:25);
         ShowTree(right)
         end                                                   (*with*)
end;                                                       (*ShowTree*)

 (*-------------------------------------------------------------*)
              (*Handle data entry and activation of insert procedure:*)

procedure HandleSort(var root: TreePtr);                   (*tree top*)
var
   entry: alfa;                                      (*for tree entries*)
begin
   root := nil;
   repeat
      write(' ':20,'Entry--<return>, to stop:   '); readln(entry);
      writeln;
      if entry <> sentinel then insert(entry, root)
   until entry = sentinel
end;                                                     (*HandleSort*)

 (*-------------------------------------------------------------*)
   (*Program manager: get values needed to activate procedures*)

procedure driver;
var
   RootNode: TreePtr;                             (*pointer variable*)
   choice: integer;                               (*control variable*)
begin
   repeat
      HandleSort(RootNode);
      writeln; for choice := 1 to 70 do write('—'); writeln;
      writeln('Result of treesort:':30); writeln;
      ShowTree(RootNode);
      writeln; for choice := 1 to 70 do write('—'); writeln;
      writeln; write('Again?--1 = Y, 0 = N: ');
      readln(choice); writeln
   until choice = 0
end;                                                         (*driver*)
```

```
(*- - - - - - - - - - - - - - - - - - - - - - - - - - - - - - - - - - - - - - - - -*)

begin
   driver                                    (*activate driver procedure*)
end.

                    Entry- -<return>, to stop:   Susu
                    Entry- -<return>, to stop:   Walter
                    Entry- -<return>, to stop:   Hod
                    Entry- -<return>, to stop:   Frederick
                    Entry- -<return>, to stop:   Juan
                    Entry- -<return>, to stop:   Orson
                    Entry- -<return>, to stop:   Fidel
                    Entry- -<return>, to stop:   Wendy
                    Entry- -<return>, to stop:   Lori
                    Entry- -<return>, to stop:

          Result of TreeSort:

               Fidel
               Frederick
               Hod
               Juan
               Lori
               Orson
               Susu
               Walter
               Wendy

Again?- -1 = Y, 0 = N: 0
```

FIGURE 12.15 TreeSort

12.6.3 Refinement: Node Count

To maintain a count of the number of nodes inserted into a binary tree, we can use the following expanded version of the TreeNode type declaration:

```
type
   alfa = packed array[1..20] of char;
   TreePtr = ^TreeNode;                              (*pointer type*)
   TreeNode = record                                 (*domain type*)
      key: alfa;                                     (*string type*)
      child: (L, R, FirstParent);                    (*position indicator*)
      left, right: TreePtr                           (*pointer types*)
      end;                                           (*TreeNode*)
```

Inside the HandleSort procedure, we can maintain a record of the number of nodes being inserted into a tree. Instead of activating the insert procedure with the key parameter, we can set up a sample record of type TreeNode (call it *NewNode*). Then, the NewNode record can be built and used as an actual parameter when the insert procedure is activated. Pass the NodeCount as a parameter to CreateList. The NodeCount field of the NewNode record can be used to hold the current count of the number of nodes that have been inserted. This refinement is left as an exercise.

We can finish building the TreeNode record inside the insert procedure. We still want to initialize the child field of this record.

12.6.4

Refinement: Tagging the Offspring

We can use the child field of the NewNode record inside the insert procedure. This can be done before each self-activation by the insert procedure. If the left link is used, then child can be assigned an *L*. Assign an *R* to the child field, if a right link is used. Notice that the first NewNode passed to the insert procedure is the root node of the tree. If we give the child an initial value of First Parent inside the HandleSort procedure each time before the insert procedure is activated, then the child field of the root node will remain unchanged inside the insert procedure. This will give us a way to separate the left and right offspring of each tree we build. A separate procedure should be created (call it *PrintOffspring*) to print the left and right offspring of each binary tree we build. This refinement is left as an exercise.

12.7 Analysis of Two Sorts: Insertion Sort and TreeSort

An insertion sort takes an approximately $n^2/4$ comparisons in a list with n elements. Why? Each time an insertion is made in a linked list, the search for a place to make an insertion always starts with the first list node and moves node by node to the position where an insertion will be made. In a list with n elements it will take n comparisons (in the worst case) to find a place to make an insertion. This gives us

$$
\begin{array}{ll}
(1+1)/2 \text{ comparison} & (\text{list size} = 1) \\
+ \ (2+1)/2 \text{ comparisons} & (\text{list size} = 2) \\
+ \ (3+1)/2 \text{ comparisons} & (\text{list size} = 3) \\
+ & \\
\cdot & \\
\cdot & \\
\cdot & \\
+ \ ((n-1)+1)/2 \text{ comparisons} & (\text{list size} = n - 1) \\
+ \ (n+1)/2 \text{ comparisons} & (\text{list size} = n)
\end{array}
$$

Adding these comparisons up to complete an insertion sort in constructing an ordered list of n elements, we get

$$(1+1)/2 + (2+1)/2 + \ldots + (n+1)/2 = n^2/4 + 3n/4$$

This is for the worst case. The number of comparisons it takes to do this will vary. Even so, it is safe to assume it will take an average of $(n+1)/2$ comparisons to make an insertion in each sublist. If we assume this, we get the following count of the comparisons needed to complete an insertion sort:

Insertion sort:

Comparisons needed for an insertion sort

$$= n^2/4 + 3n/4$$

By contrast, a TreeSort is usually more efficient. Why? A divide-and-conquer approach is used in each search for a place to make an insertion. Each time an insertion is made into an ordered binary tree, we start with the root. After the first comparison we have eliminated either the right or the left subtree (half the tree!). This happens again and again in one of the subtrees. In general, it takes at most lg n (log of n base 2) comparisons to find a place to make an insertion in a binary tree. This is done with n nodes, which means it takes the following number of comparisons to complete a TreeSort:

TreeSort:

$n * \lg n$ comparisons are needed to complete construction of an ordered binary tree.

This says the running time of an insertion sort is proportional to $n^2/4$. By contrast, the running time of a TreeSort is proportional to $n * \lg n$ for a list with n elements. We leave it as exercise to compute running times for these sorts for different values of n.

12.8 Summary

An insertion sort with a linked list depends on the use of an insertion key. For example, in a linked list of names, each node has a name field that is used as the insertion key. Each time an insertion is made, a new name is compared with the name field of each existing list node until a place is found to make an insertion that will leave list names in alphabetical order.

In a multilinked list, each node has two or more link (pointer) fields. We used recursion to set up a binary tree, which is a multilinked list. In a binary tree, each node has a left and a right pointer. The insertion procedure in Figure 12.15 makes it possible to build an ordered binary tree. A tree is ordered relative to some insertion key. (We used the name field of each tree node as the insertion key.)

We also used recursion in the ShowTree procedure in Figure 12.15 to print the nodes of a tree in order from left to right. Binary trees make a good hunting ground for recursive procedures because they can be defined using a recurrence relation. Each tree node can be defined in terms of the subtree it is in. The root node is defined in terms of its offspring. The offspring in terms of their offspring and so on.

A TreeSort is more efficient than an insertion sort. An insertion sort is slower than a TreeSort because of the search technique it uses. That is, an insertion sort like the one given in Figure 12.12 always starts at the beginning of a list to find a place to make an insertion, moving from node to node until the correct place to make an insertion is found. This is called a *linear search technique*. By contrast, a TreeSort relies on a divide-and-conquer approach to find a place to insert a new TreeNode. It always starts with the root node. After the first comparison, one of the subtrees immediately below the root has been eliminated from the search. After the second comparison, one of the subtrees of the root has been eliminated. This process continues until a place is found to make an insertion. The running time of an insertion sort as a rule will be proportional to $n^2/4$. By contrast, the running time of a TreeSort will be proportional to $n * \lg n$, which is quicker.

Both linked lists and binary trees are space savers. Neither data structure takes more memory than is needed. Why? Both of these structures have no size specified beforehand. Memory is allocated in both cases only when needed to insert a new list node.

12.9 Keywords Review

Keywords	*Related Ideas*
binary tree	a tree that is either empty or where each node has no more than two offspring
insertion key	field of a list node used to determine where an insertion is to be made
insertion sort	using a linear search technique, each node is inserted into a linked list based on comparisons made between a new list entry and the insertion-key field of each node inspected
multilinked list	a list with nodes with two or more pointer fields
tree	a finite set of nodes where one node is the root node and the remaining nodes are descendents of the root node
TreeSort	using a divide-and-conquer approach, subtrees of a tree are eliminated from a search for a place to insert a new tree node. This search also depends on the use of an insertion key: Each tree node in the search has its key field compared with the key value of the node to be inserted.

12.10

Exercises

1. What is the difference between a singly linked list and a multilinked list?

2. What is the minimum number of nodes in a binary tree?

3. Is it possible to have a binary tree with one node? Explain your answer.

4. It is possible to construct a binary tree that has only right offspring from the root. Give an example of a name tree with this structure.

5. Carry out the refinement of the list processing program in Figure 12.12 described in Section 12.5.1.

6. Refine the program in Figure 12.12 so that the number of comparisons made during an insertion sort are counted. You should set up a list to hold the count for each new sort while the program is running. Then print out the individual counts and the average number of comparisons needed to complete an insertion sort. Each time a list is constructed, you should also maintain a count of the number of list elements. Then you should also print out the value of $n^2/4$ and the difference between this value and actual number of comparisons made to complete an insertion sort on that list. Print out the following table:

List Number	*List Size*	*Comparisons Made*	$n^2/4$
1	?	?	?
2	?	?	?
.	.	.	.
.	.	.	.
.	.	.	.

Give a sample run for five separate lists of names (each the same size, list = 20). *Hint:* See suggestions for keeping track of this information given in Section 12.5.2. You should try adding an additional field (call it *norm*) to the history record described in Section 12.5.2. The norm field can be used to hold the value of $n^2/4$ for each list of names you build.

7. In a game tree to represent the moves in tic-tac-toe, how many link fields must each node have?

8. Explain how the expression "divide and conquer" can be used to describe the method used in the insert procedure in Figure 12.15.

9. Write a new insertion sort program for nodes with the following type:

```
type
   ListPtr  =  ^ListNode;
   ListNode  =  record
      RndNumber: integer;
      link: ListPtr
   end;                                        (*ListNode*)
```

The nonlink part of each node will be a random number, which you will obtain for a random number generating function. Use the technique developed in exercise 7 to print a history of the number of comparisons needed each time an ordered list of random numbers is built during the running of your program. In other words, print out the same table described in exercise 7. Give a sample run where five different lists of 1000 elements are built and analyzed. *Hint:* Make ComparisonTotal type real to allow for large totals. You will also want to add an additional field (call it *norm*) of type real to hold the value $n^2/4$ for each list you build.

10. Refine the program in Figure 12.15 so that the new program prints a table like the one in exercise 6 in terms of a TreeSort. That is, you want to set up a history record like the one described in Section 12.5.2 for linked lists. Use the CreateList procedure in Figure 12.15 to construct the history record based on comparison counts used in the insert procedure. You will want to add a new field (call it *ExpectedCount*) of type real to the history record. Use this to hold the value of $n * \lg n$. This refined program should print out the following table:

List Number	*List Size*	*Comparisons Made*	$n * \lg n$

Run for your program for 10 lists of 20 names (try words from a thesaurus, for example, if you run out of names). *Hint:*

$$n * \lg n = n * ((\ln n)/(\ln 2))$$

11. Write a program to TreeSort lists of random numbers. Your program should produce the table given in exercise 10. Run your program for 10 lists of 1000 random numbers (make your machine do some work!).

12. Carry out the refinement of Figure 12.15 described in Sections 12.6.3 and 12.6.4. Give a sample run.

13. Write a program to handle airline reservations in a linked list. Use the following type declaration to do this:

```
type
  alfa = packed array[1..10] of char;
  beta = packed array[1..5] of char;
  ptr = ^passenger;
  passenger = record
    YourOrigin, YourDestination: alfa;
    FirstName, LastName: alfa;
    SeatNo, flight: beta;
    link: ptr
  end;                                         (*passenger*)
```

Your program should do the following things:

a. Allow an ordered linked list of reservations to be created.
b. Cancel a reservation in an existing list.

c. Change a reservation in an existing list.
d. Print a list of reservations already made by selected namefield or a total list.
e. Print the following statistical summary:

Origin	Number of Passengers	Destination	Number of Passengers

f. Allow reservations to be added to the list.
g. Set up a reservation file to save all reservations made.

Run your program with the following preliminary passenger list:

First Name	Last Name	Seat Number	Flight	Origin	Destination
Edsger	Dijkstra	11A	NW20	Holland	New York
Richard	Forsyth	2B	W490	London	Chicago
Alfred	Aho	17A	V901	Boston	San Francisco
Sara	Baase	5A	W490	London	San Diego
Richard	Holt	80C	NW50	Toronto	Seattle
J.	Hume	81C	NW50	Toronto	Seattle
Bill	Jones	81C	NW50	Toronto	Seattle
Craig	Nettles	27B	V532	New York	Denver

Then do the following things:
h. Delete the reservation for Jones.
i. Change the reservation for Aho to

Alfred	Aho	29B	NW876	Boston	San Francisco

(j) Add the following reservations to the existing list:

First Name	Last Name	Seat Number	Flight	Origin	Destination
Billy	Claybrook	21C	A540	New York	Minneapolis
Niklaus	Wirth	12C	NW442	Geneva	London
Lou	Piniella	22A	NW442	London	New York

k. Print out all reservations for the following places:

destination = Seattle;
origin = London

l. Save all reservations in the reservation file.
m. Print out a statistical summary for all reservations made.

12.11 Review Quiz

Determine whether the following are true or false:

1. A linked list of names takes less storage than a binary tree consisting only of the same names as those found in the linked list.
2. A divide-and-conquer approach is used in making each new insertion into an ordered linked list.
3. In terms of running time, a TreeSort is more efficient than an insertion sort.
4. TreeSorting and insertion sorting both rely on the use of a search key.
5. Every node in a binary tree has two pointer fields.
6. Both pointers in a binary tree node cannot be nil.
7. It is possible for a node in a binary tree to have two left children.
8. Every node in a binary tree that is not a leaf has at least two offspring.
9. TreeSorting uses a divide-and-conquer approach.
10. The number of nodes in either a linked list or a binary tree must be specified before either structure can be built.

12.12 Readings

Aho, A. V., Hopcroft, J. E., and Ullman, J. D. *Data Structures and Algorithms.* Reading, MA: Addison-Wesley, 1983. See Chapter 3 on trees.

Brookshear, J. G. *Computer Science: An Overview.* Reading, MA: Benjamin/Cummings, 1985. See Section 7-5 on trees.

Peters, J. F. *Pascal with Data Structures.* New York: Holt, Rinehart and Winston, 1986. See Chapter 4 on linked lists.

APPENDIX A

TABLES

TABLE A.1 ASCII Codes

	0	*16*	*32*	*48*	*64*	*80*	*96*	*112*
0	nul	dle	space	0	@	P	`	p
1	soh	dc1	!	1	A	Q	a	q
2	stx	dc2	″	2	B	R	b	r
3	etx	dc3	#	3	C	S	c	s
4	eot	dc4	$	4	D	T	d	t
5	enq	nak	%	5	E	U	e	u
6	ack	syn	&	6	F	V	f	v
7	bell	etb	′	7	G	W	g	w
8	bksp	can	(	8	H	X	h	x
9	htab	em	)	9	I	Y	i	y
10	lf	sub	*	:	J	Z	j	z
11	vtab	esc	+	;	K	[	k	{

12	ff	fs	,	<	L	\	l	|
13	cr	gs	–	=	M	]	m	}
14	so	rs	.	>	N	^	n	~
15	si	us	/	?	O	_	o	del

Legend:

ASCII = American Standard Code for Information Interchange

nul	= null	soh	= start of heading
stx	= start of text	etx	= end of text
eot	= end of transmission	enq	= enquiry
ack	= acknowledge	bell	= keyboard bell
bksp	= backspace	htab	= horizontal tab
lf	= linefeed	vtab	= vertical tab
ff	= form feed	cr	= carriage return
so	= shift out	si	= shift in
dle	= data link escape	dc1	= device control 1
dc2	= device control 2	dc3	= device control 3
dc4	= device control 4	nak	= negative acknowledge
syn	= synchronous idle	etb	= end of transmission
can	= cancel	em	= end of medium
sub	= substitute	fs	= file separator
gs	= group separator	rs	= record separator
us	= unit separator		

Note: chr(39) = ' (single quote) used in write or writeln statements to print characters. You can determine the ASCII code for a single quote, for example, by using the following arithmetic:

ASCII code = row number + column number
= 7 + 32
= 39

TABLE A.2 ASCII and EBCDIC Cross-Reference Table

Code	*ASCII*	*EBCDIC*	*Code*	*ASCII*	*EBCDIC*	*Code*	*ASCII*	*EBCDIC*
0	nul	nul	84	T		167		x
1	soh	soh	85	U		168		y
2	stx	stx	86	V		169		z

TABLE A.2 ASCII and EBCDIC Cross-Reference Table

Code	*ASCII*	*EBCDIC*	*Code*	*ASCII*	*EBCDIC*	*Code*	*ASCII*	*EBCDIC*
3	etx	etx	87	W		170		
4	eot	pf	88	X		171		
5	enq	ht	89	Y		172		
6	ack	lc	90	Z	!	173		[
7	bell	del	91	[	$	174		
8	bs		92	\	*	175		
9	ht		93	]	)	176		
10	lf	smm	94	^	;	177		
11	vt	vt	95	_		178		
12	ff	ff	96	`	–	179		
13	cr	cr	97	a	/	180		
14	so	so	98	b		181		
15	si	si	99	c		182		
16	dle	dle	100	d		183		
17	dc1	dc1	101	e		184		
18	dc2	dc2	102	f		185		
19	dc3	dc3	103	g		186		
20	dc4	res	104	h		188		
21	nak	nl	105	i		189		]
22	syn	bs	106	j	|	190		
23	etb	il	107	k	,	191		
24	can	can	108	l	%	192		{

25	em	em	109	m	—	193	A
26	sub	cc	110	n	>	194	B
27	esc	cul	111	o	?	195	C
28	fs	ifs	112	p		196	D
29	gs	igs	113	q		197	E
30	rs	irs	114	r		198	F
31	us	ius	115	s		199	G
32	space	ds	116	t		200	H
33	!	sos	117	u		201	I
34	"	fs	118	v		202	
35	#		119	w		203	
36	$	byp	120	x		204	
37	%	lf	121	y	`	205	
38	&	etb	122	z	:	206	
39	'	esc	123	{	#	207	
40	(		124	|	@	208	}
41	)		125	}	'	209	J
42	*	sm	126	~	=	210	K
43	+	cu2	127	del	"	211	L
44	,		128			212	M
45	–	enq	129		a	213	N
46	.	ack	130		b	214	O
47	/	bell	131		c	215	P
48	0		132		d	216	Q

TABLE A.2 ASCII and EBCDIC Cross-Reference Table

Code	*ASCII*	*EBCDIC*	*Code*	*ASCII*	*EBCDIC*	*Code*	*ASCII*	*EBCDIC*
49	1		133		e	217		R
50	2	syn	134		f	218		
51	3		135		g	219		
52	4	pn	136		h	220		
53	5	rs	137		i	221		
54	6	uc	138			222		
55	7	eot	139		{	223		
56	8		140			224		\
57	9		141			225		
58	:		142			226		S
59	;	cu3	143			227		T
60	<	dc4	144			228		U
61	=	nak	145		j	229		V
62	>		146		k	230		W
64	@	space	147		l	231		X
65	A		148		m	232		Y
66	B		149		n	233		Z
67	C		150		o	234		
68	D		151		p	235		
69	E		152		q	236		
70	F		153		r	237		
71	G		154			238		
72	H		155		}	239		

73	I		156			240		0
74	J		157			241		1
75	K	.	158			242		2
76	L	<	159			243		3
77	M	(	160			244		4
78	N	+	161		~	245		5
79	O	|	162		s	246		6
80	P	&	163		t	247		7
81	Q		164		u	248		8
82	R		165		v	249		9
83	S		166		w	250		

Legend:
byp = bypass
cu1 = customer use 1
cu3 = customer use 3
ds = digit select
ifs = interchange file separator
irs = interchange record separator
lc = lowercase
pf = punch out
res = restore
smm = start of manual message
tm = tape mark
cc = cursor control
cu2 = customer use 2
dle = data link escape
etb = end of transmission block
igs = interchange group separator
ius = interchange unit separator
nl = new line
pn = punch out
sm = set mode
sos = start of significance
uc = uppercase

Note: The codes in this table are in base 10.

TABLE A.3 Powers of 2 Table

2^n	n	2^{-n}
1	0	1
2	1	0.5
4	2	0.25
8	3	0.125
16	4	0.0625
32	5	0.03125
64	6	0.015625
128	7	0.0078125
256	8	0.00390625
512	9	0.001953125
1,024	10	0.0009765625
2,048	11	0.00048828125
4,096	12	0.000244140625
8,102	13	0.0001220703125
16,384	14	0.00006103515625
32,768	15	0.000030517578125
65,536	16	0.0000152587890625

TABLE A.4 Fibonacci and Lucas Numbers

$F(n)$	n	$L(n)$
0	0	2
1	1	1
1	2	3
2	3	4
3	4	7
5	5	11
8	6	18
13	7	29
21	8	47
34	9	76
55	10	123
89	11	199
144	12	322
233	13	521
377	14	843
610	15	1,364
987	16	2,207
1,597	17	3,571
2,584	18	5,778
4,181	19	9.349

6,765	20	15,127
10,946	21	24,476
17,711	22	39,603
28,657	23	64,079
46,368	24	103,682
75,368	25	167,761

TABLE A.5 February 23, 1984 weather table

	Wednesday			*Thursday Forecast*		*Friday Forecast*	
city	*low*	*high*	*pcp*	*low*	*high*	*low*	*high*
Albuquerque	21	60		28	52	23	52
Anchorage	17	30	0.02	20	29	21	29
Atlanta	41	61	0.19	39	68	38	69
Atlantic City	30	49		32	50	40	50
Billings	33	40	0.09	22	40	25	40
Bismarck	27	44		25	39	17	31
Boston	30	46		34	52	39	60
Brownville	42	75		49	72	69	71
Charlotte, NC	33	61		52	51	32	66
Chicago	32	60		33	54	31	43
Cincinatti	24	59		35	61	32	47
Cleveland	24	37		34	56	30	44
Dallas	32	70		42	68	40	58
Denver	34	64		20	45	19	43
Des Moines	33	67		31	48	25	41
Detroit	27	57		34	55	30	42
El Paso	18	67		34	68	32	61
Fairbanks	−22	−12		−16	5	−10	9
Fargo	30	43		22	33	18	28
Honolulu	70	85		70	83	70	83
Houston	46	67		39	65	48	67
Jacksonville	54	65	0.73	47	63	40	71
Kansas City	35	62		38	55	32	46
Las Vegas	48	80		34	62	32	46
Los Angeles	48	80		48	75	48	73
Louisville	29	55		33	64	38	54
Memphis	33	64		35	63	40	60
Miami Beach	36	62		64	73	51	73
Milwaukee	36	62		32	46	28	40
Nashville	26	63		32	62	35	60
New Orleans	46	64		39	66	49	69
New York	33	52		32	56	37	52

	Wednesday			Thursday Forecast		Friday Forecast	
city	low	high	pcp	low	high	low	high
Oklahoma City	33	68		38	58	31	51
Omaha	35	84		33	60	24	44
Orlando	53	76	1.44	56	69	43	74
Philadelphia	25	60		31	64	32	63
Phoenix	49	73		46	71	42	72
Portland, Ore	36	47	0.02	38	50	42	63
Rapid City	31	57		25	41	20	38
St. Louis	38	67		42	62	34	50
Salt Lake City	18	37	0.08	10	37	15	40
San Antonio	31	65		36	72	46	67
San Diego	56	59		49	68	48	87
San Francisco	43	58		43	58	43	59
Seattle	38	42		36	45	38	49
Sioux Falls	19	44		22	34	16	38
Tampa	67	75	1.15	57	66	46	72
Tuscon	38	66		36	55	36	60
Washington	32	57		36	55	36	60

APPENDIX B

PASCAL IN BRIEF

OVERVIEW

This appendix collects together the key features of Pascal. The Pascal presented in this appendix conforms with level zero of standard Pascal described in the ISO/DIS 7185 document published by the International Standards Organization (ISO). Here is the order information for this document:

Specification for Computer Programming Language Pascal
BS 6192 : 1982
British Standards Institution
2 Park Street
London W1A 2BS England

B.1 Reserved Words in Pascal

The reserved words in Pascal are as follows:

and	**array**	**begin**	**case**	**const**	**div**
do	**downto**	**else**	**end**	**file**	**for**
function	**goto**	**if**	**in**	**label**	**mod**
nil	**not**	**of**	**or**	**packed**	**procedure**
program	**record**	**repeat**	**set**	**then**	**to**
type	**until**	**var**	**while**	**with**	

Reserved words in Pascal fall into the following six groups.

special group: **program, begin, end**
declaration words: **array, const, file, function, label, packed, procedure, record, set, type, var**
statement words: **case, do, downto, else, for, goto, if, repeat, then, to, until, while, with**
operator words: **and, div, in, mod, not, or**
identifier word: **nil**

B.2 Pascal Data Types

Pascal data types fall into four groups:

dynamic: pointer
simple: Boolean, char, integer, real
structured: array, file, record, set
user-defined (ordinal types): subrange, enumeration

These data types have the following organization:

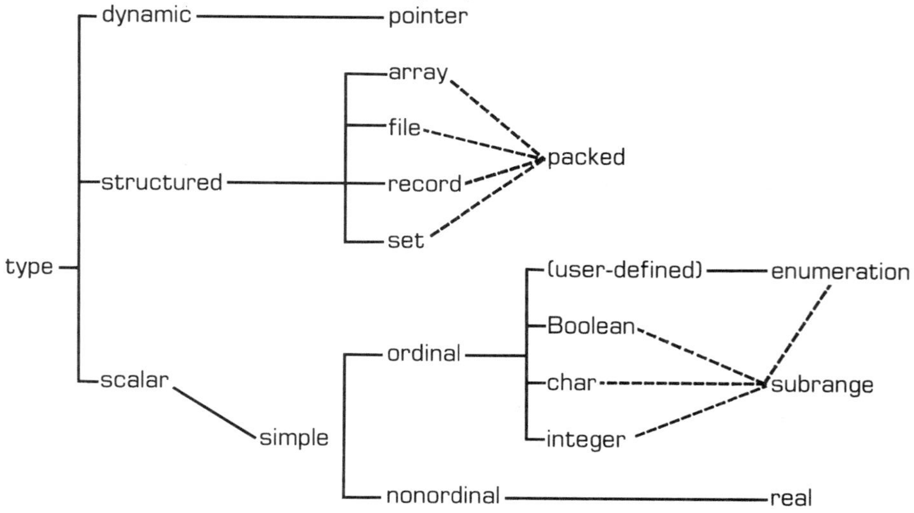

B.3 Pascal Operator Precedence

An operator specifies an operation for a machine to perform. In an expression without parentheses, a machine will use the following precedence rules to evaluate the expression, starting with level 1 (highest precedence):

Level	Operator	
1	**not**	(highest)
2	* / **div** **mod** **and**	
3	+ − **or**	
4	= <> < <= > >= **in**	
5	:=	(lowest)

Note: In an expression (without parentheses) having more than one operator on the same precedence level, the expression will be evaluated from **left to right.**

B.4 Pascal Statements

A statement specifies an action for a machine to perform. There are basically two types of Pascal statements, **simple** and **structured**. Here is how Pascal statements are organized:

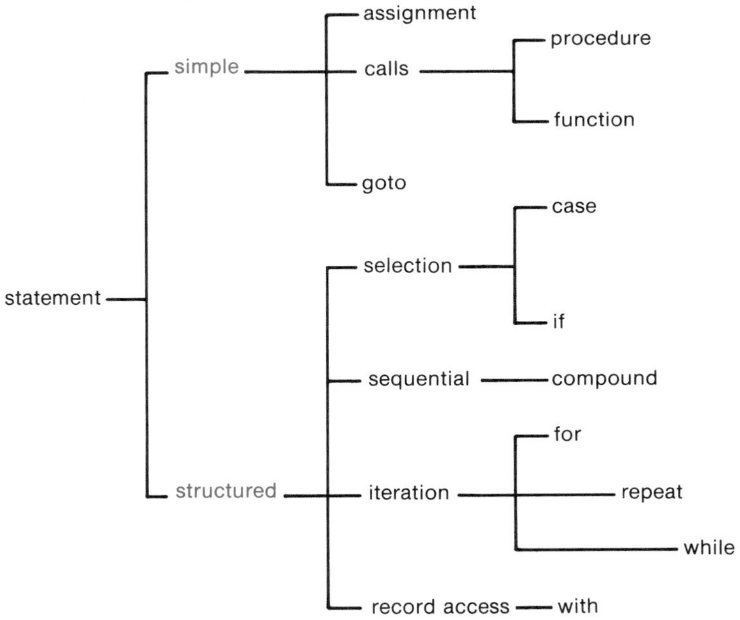

B.5 Built-in Functions

A function is a subprogram that is limited to producing a single result. Standard Pascal has built-in functions that fall into four groups, given in the following table.

Kind	*Function*
Arithmetic	abs(x), absolute value of x
	arctan(x), angle whose tangent is x, which is measured in radians
	cos(x), cosine of angle (in radians)
	sin(x), sine of angle (in radians)
	exp(x), e raised to x power
	ln(x), exponent on base e to get x
	sqr(x), x^2
	sqrt(x), $x^{1/2}$, square root
Boolean	eoln(x), checks for end-of-line in file x
	eof(x), checks for end-of-file in file x
	odd(x), checks if x is an odd number
Ordinal	chr(x), character corresponding to code x
	ord(x), position of x in scale containing x
	pred(x), predecessor of x in scale containing x
	succ(x), successor of x in scale containing x
Transfer	round(x), rounded integer value of x (a real)
	trunc(x), truncated integer value of x (a real)

B.6 Built-in Procedures

A procedure is a subprogram that specifies one or more actions for a machine to perform. Pascal has the following built-in procedures.

Group	*Procedure*
input	read, readln
output	write, writeln
dynamic	dispose(x), eliminates references to x^ and possibly frees up storage used by x^
	new(x), creates storage for pointer variable x
file	get(x), assigns current file buffer to x, if there is one
	put(x), assigns x to file buffer
	reset(x), moves file pointer to beginning of file x (prepares file x for inspection)
	rewrite(x), prepares file x for generation (this eliminates all old entries in file x, if there are any)

B.7

Backus-Naur Productions for Pascal Syntax

A *Backus-Naur production* or Backus-Naur Formalism (BNF) is used to represent the syntax of a language structure. The word **syntax** refers to the arrangements of the parts of a language structure and to the various forms a language structure can have. A BNF production will show the arrangement of the possible parts of a language structure. The following table gives the symbols used write BNF productions:

Symbols used in BNF productions

BNF symbol	*meaning*
=	reads "is defined by"
|	reads "or'
( )	grouping symbols
ab	attach (concatenate) a and b
{ }	attach zero or more items
[ ]	attach zero or 1 instance of something
' '	used to enclose a token
.	marks end of a BNF production

Here is a selection of BNF productions that you should refer to, if you are uncertain about the syntax for a Pascal structure:

```
actual-parameter = expression | variable | procedure-identifier
                   function-identifier .
actual-parameter-list = '(' actual-parameter { ',' actual-
                        parameter } ')' .
array-type = 'array' '[' index-type { ',' index-type } ']'
             'of' component-type .
assignment-statement = (variable-identifier | function-
                       identifier ) ':=' expression .
block = label-declaration-part
        constant-definition-part
        type-definition-part
        variable-declaration-part
        procedure-declaration-part
        function-declaration-part
        statement-part .
buffer-variable = file-variable-identifier '^' .
case-constant-list = case-constant { ',' case-constant } .
case-index = expression .
case-list-element = case-constant-list ':' statement .
case-statement = 'case' case-index 'of' case-list-element
                 { ';' case-list-element } [';'] 'end' .
character-string = ' ' ' character { character } ' ' ' .
compound-statement = 'begin' statement-sequence 'end' .
conditional-statement = if-statement | case-statement .
```

enumerated-type = '(' identifier-list ')' .
expression = simple-expression [relational-operator
 simple-expression] .
factor = variable-identifier | unsigned-constant | function-
 designator | set-constructor | '(' expression ')' |
 'not' factor .
field-list = [(fixed-part [';' variant-part] | variant-
 part) [';']] .
file-type = 'file' 'of' component-type .
for-statement = 'for' control-variable ':=' initial-value
 ('to' | 'downto') final-value 'do' statement .
formal-parameter-list = '(' formal-parameter-section
 { ';' formal-parameter-section } ')' .
formal-parameter-section = value-parameter-specification |
 variable-parameter-specification |
 procedure-parameter-specification |
 function-parameter-specification .
function-declaration = function-heading ';' function-block .
function-designator = function-identifier [actual-parameter-
 list] .
function-heading = 'function' identifier [formal-parameter-
 list] ':' result-type .
goto-statement = 'goto' label .
identifier = letter { letter | digit } .
identifier-list = identifier { ',' identifier } .
if-statement = 'if' Boolean-expression 'then' statement
 [else-part] .
index-type = ordinal-type .
label = digit-sequence .
label-declaration-part = ['label' label { ',' label } ';']
member-designator = expression ['..' expression] .
new-ordinal-type = enumerated-type | subrange-type .
new-pointer-type = '^' domain-type .
new-structured-type = ['packed'] unpacked-structured-type .
new-type = new-ordinal-type | ordinal-type-identifier .
ordinal-type = new-ordinal-type | ordinal-type-identifier .
procedure-declaration = procedure-heading ';' procedure-
 block .
procedure-heading = 'procedure' identifier [formal-
 parameter-list] .
program = program-heading ';' program-block .
read-parameter-list = '(' [file-variable ',' variable-
 identifier { ',' variable-identifier }
 ')' .
readln-parameter-list = ['(' (file-variable | variable-
 identifier { ',' variable-identifier }
 ')'] .
record-section = identifier-list ':' type-denoter .
record-type = 'record' field-list 'end' .
repeat-statement = 'repeat' statement-sequence 'until'
 Boolean-expression .
set-constructor = '[' [member-designator { ','
 member-designator }] ']' .
set-type = 'set' 'of' base-type .

```
simple-expression = [ sign ] term { adding-operator term } .
statement-sequence = statement { ';' statement } .
subrange-type = constant '..' constant .
term = factor { multiplying-operator factor } .
value-parameter-specification = identifier-list ':'
                                type-identifier .
variable-parameter-specification = 'var' identifier-list ':'
                                   type-identifier .
variant = case-constant-list ':' '(' field-list ')' .
variant-part = 'case' variant-selector 'of' variant { ';'
               variant } .
while-statement = 'while' Boolean-expression 'do' statement .
with-statement = 'with' record-variable-list 'do' statement .
write-parameter = expression [ ':' expression [ '
                  ':' expression ] ] .
write-parameter-list = '(' [ file-variable ',' ] write-
                       parameter { ',' write-parameter } ')' .
writeln-parameter-list = [ '(' ( file-variable | write-
                         parameter ) { ',' write-parameter } ')' ] .
```

B.8 Error Messages

The following list gives a selection of error messages typically printed as a result of syntax errors in a Pascal source text.

Message	*Remedy*
'(' expected	missing '(' in an expression with parentheses or in parameter list
')' expected	missing ')' in an expression with parentheses or in parameter list
',' expected	missing ',' in parameter list
'..' expected	missing '..' in array specification
':' expected	missing ':' variable declaration
';' expected	missing ';' needed to separate statements or to mark end of a procedure or function block
'=' expected	check constant declaration or Boolean expression
'[' expected	check array or set specification
']' expected	check array or set specification
actual parameter type does not match formal parameter:	check formal parameter type
array subscript out of range:	check subscript
bad case label	make sure case label type matches the case selector type
begin expected	check for missing **begin**

Message	*Remedy*
format expression must be type integer	make sure format number is type integer
function identifier is not assigned a value	common error: make sure you have assigned a value to a function identifier
must assign value before using variable	initialize your variables
statement ended incorrectly	check for missing semicolon
then expected	check for missing **then**
too few actual parameters	check procedure or function designator parameter list
unexpected **else** clause	common error: check for ';' following **then** statement in an **if** statement with an **else** part

B.9 Syntax Diagrams

program:

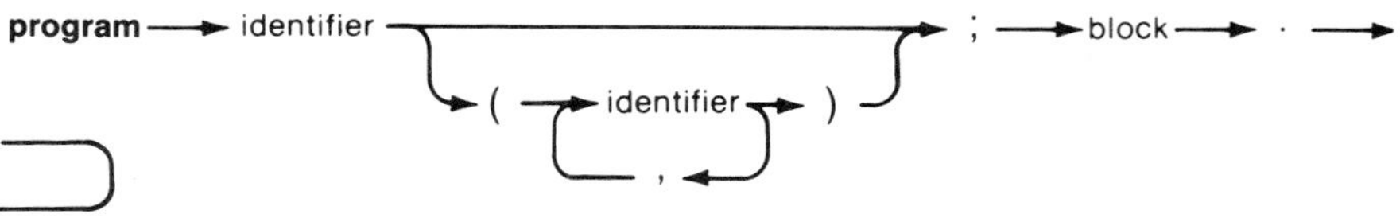

block:

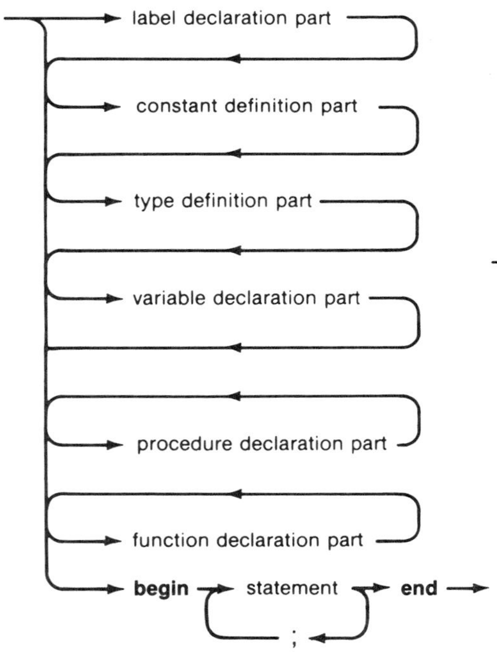

field list (generalized syntax)

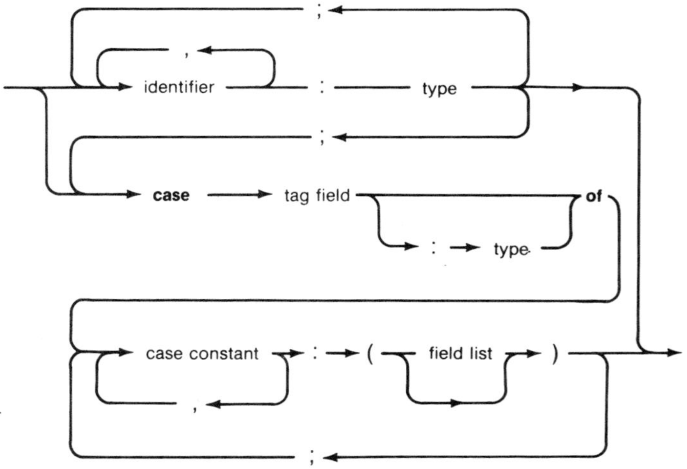

array-type:

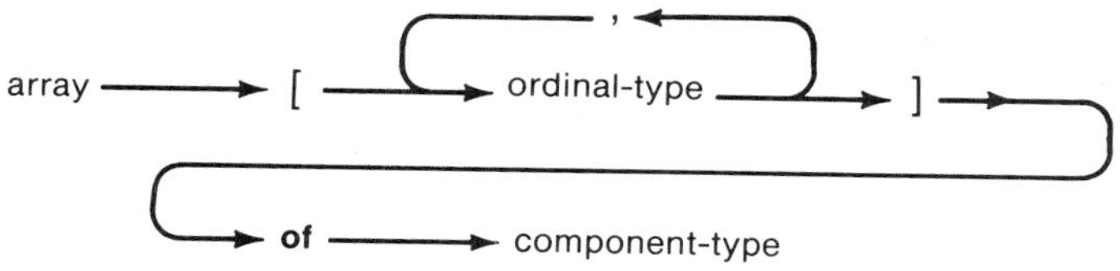

set-type:

record-type:

file-type:

compound statement:

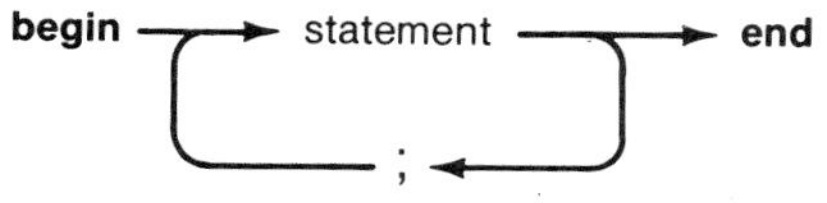

while statement syntax:

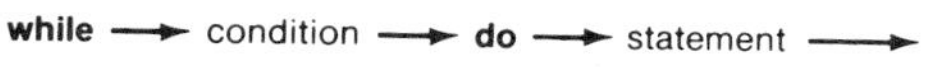

repeat statement syntax:

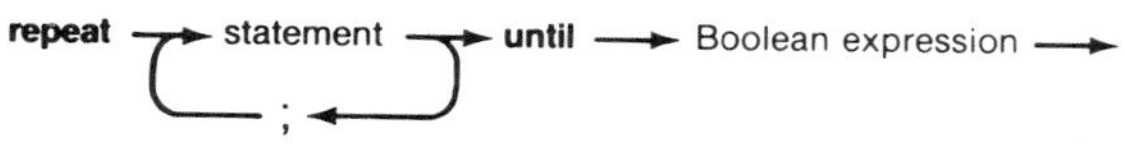

for statement syntax:

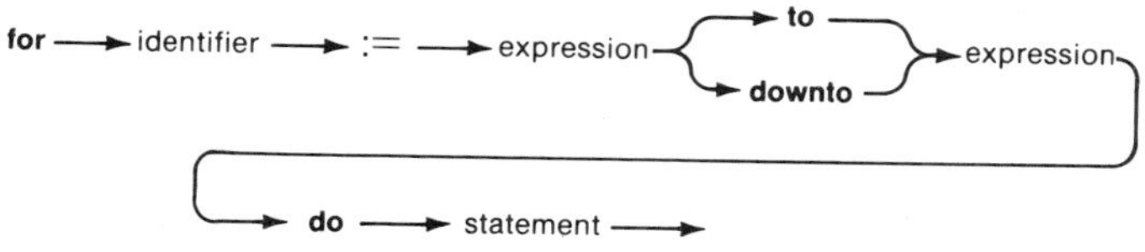

label-declaration-part:

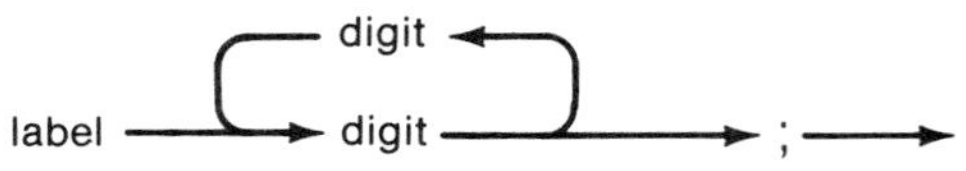

constant-declaration part:

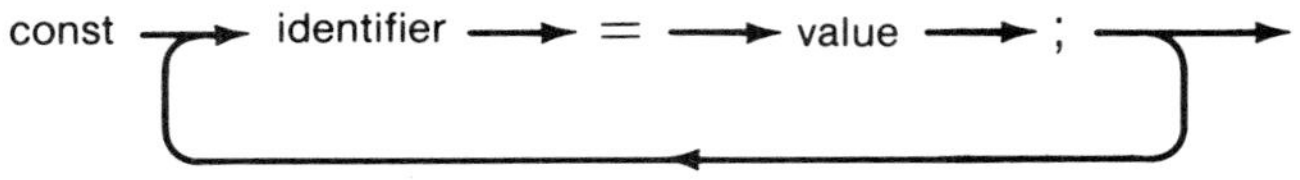

type-definition-part:

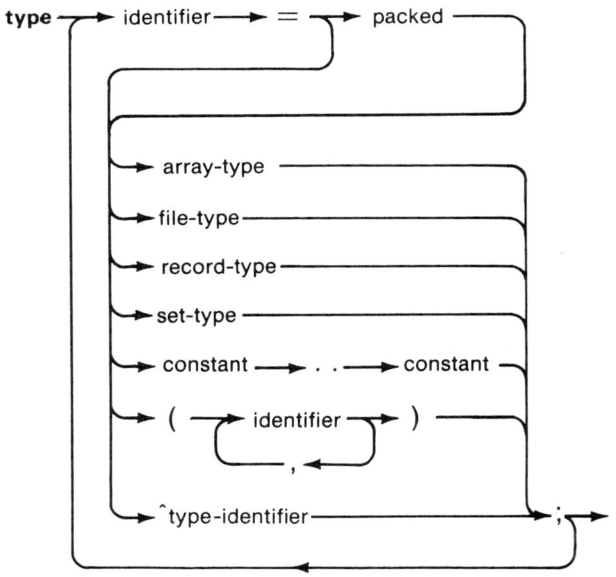

function-declaration-part:

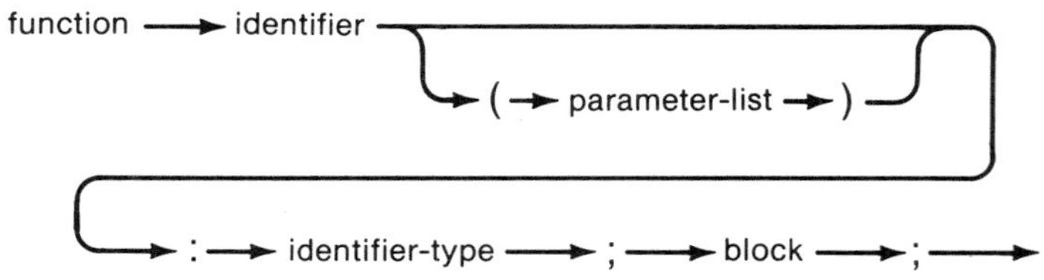

variable-declaration-part:

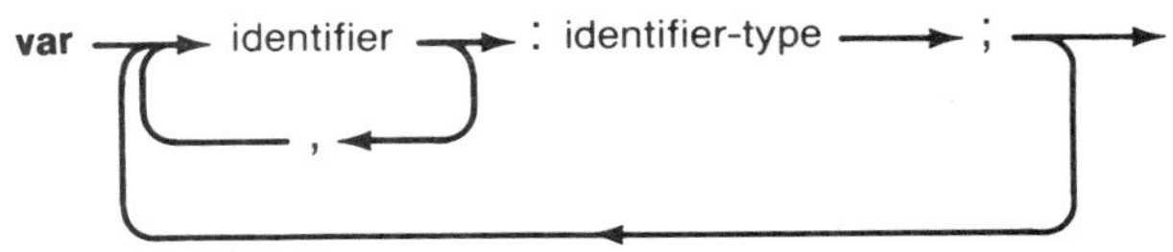

identifier:

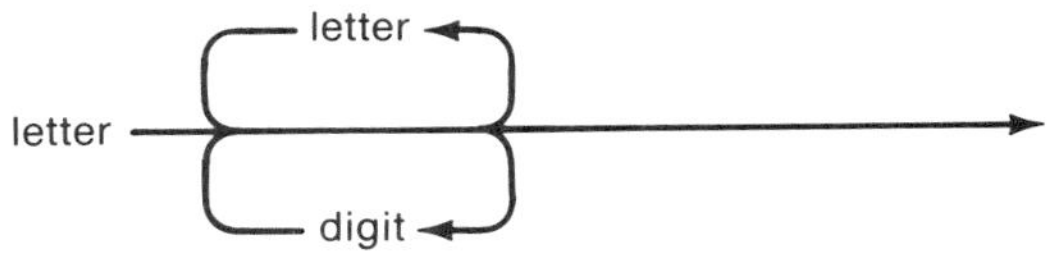

procedure-declaration-part:

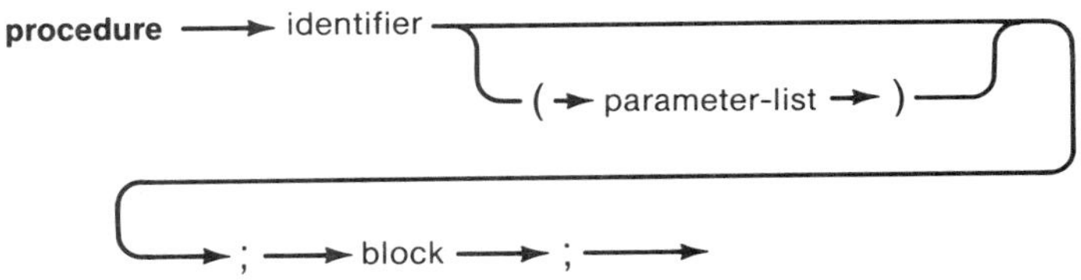

with-statement

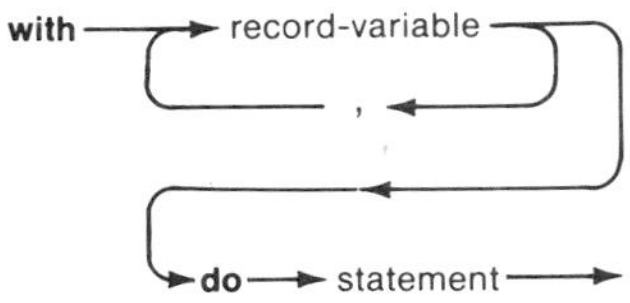

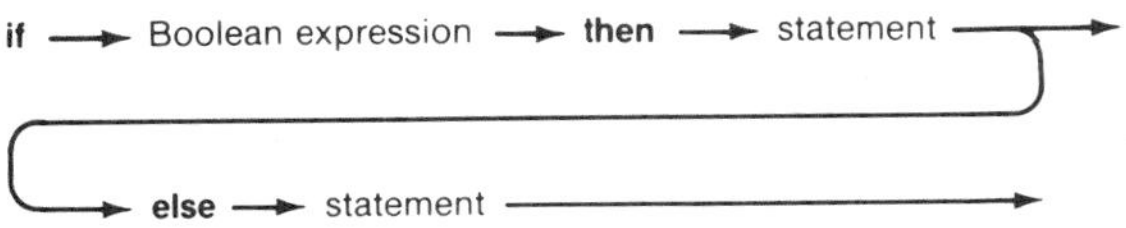

case statement:

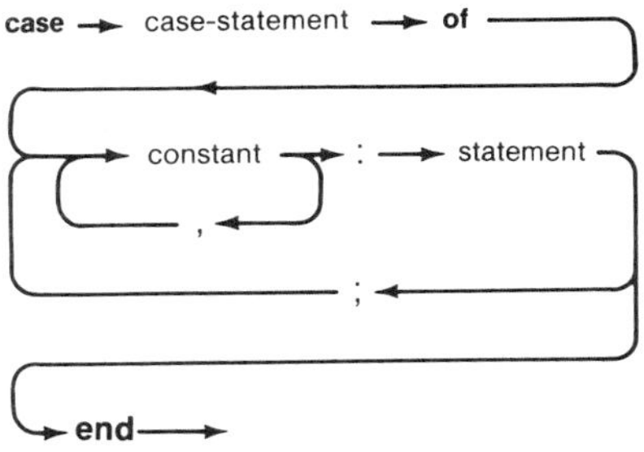

simple-expression:

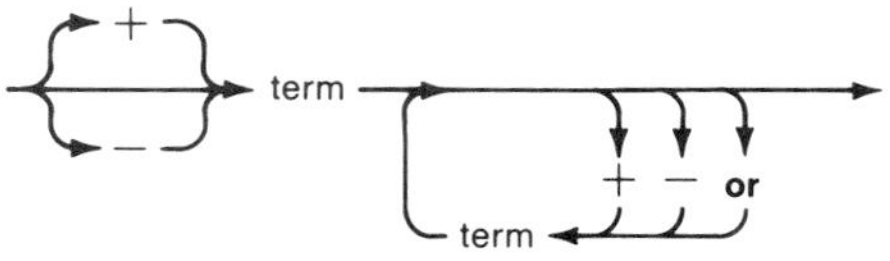

term:

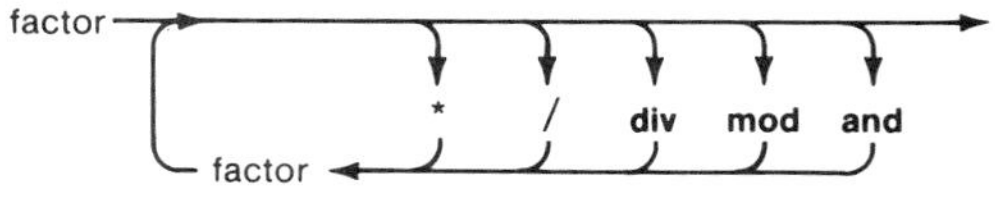

factor:

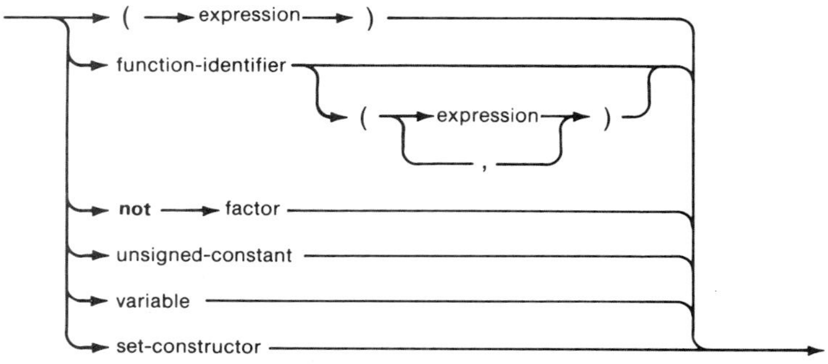

expression:

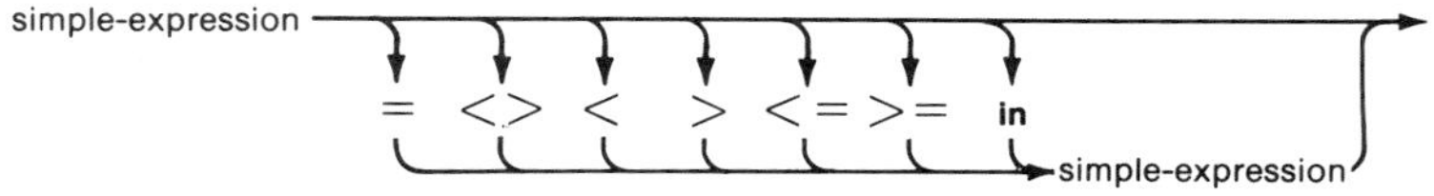

APPENDIX C.1

PASCAL EXTENSIONS

APPLE PASCAL

To implement the standard Pascal programs given in this book, the following changes will be necessary:

1. In all programs which use the built-in arithmetic functions, the mod or div operator, set up the program heading in Apple Pascal as follows:

```
(*$u apple2.system.library*)
program TryThis(input, output);
  uses TRANSCEND;
```

2. Apple Pascal does not permit function parameters, so the examples in section 7.14 should be skipped.
3. In all programs using packed arrays, use the following declaration of a StringType instead:

standard way	*Apple Pascal way*
type StringType = packed array[1..max] of char;	**type** StringType = string[max];

standard way	*non-text files* *Apple Pascal way*
write(f, item)	f^ := item; put(f)
read(f, item)	get(f); item := f^

Apple Pascal files must be closed!
use close(f, lock) to terminate use of file f.

APPENDIX C.2

IBM PASCAL

Except for chapter 9 (on files), the programs in this text can be implemented in IBM Pascal without change. To install the file-handling programs in chapter 9 on an IBM PC, the following changes will have to be made:

1. before the Pascal rewrite procedure can be used, it will be necessary to use the following IBM Pascal declaration and statements:

```
var
   FNAME : string(10);                    (*disk file name*)
   F : file of FileType;          (*make window for file F*)
```

and

```
assign(F, FNAME);                (*to associate F and FNAME*)
F.MODE := sequential;                   (*set access mode*)
rewrite(F);
```

2. before the Pascal reset procedure can be used, it will be necessary to use the following IBM Pascal statements:

```
assign(F, FNAME);             (*if it has not be done already*)
F.MODE := sequential;
reset(F);
```

3. when file-handling is complete, then use the following statement:

```
close(F)
```

APPENDIX C.3

VAX PASCAL NOTES

Except for chapter 9 (on files), the programs in this text can be implemented in VAX Pascal without change. However, in chapter 9, the following changes will have to be made to accommodate file-handling in VAX Pascal:

1. before using the Pascal rewrite procedure, use the following VAX Pascal statement:

```
open(filename, 'filename.xxx', history := unknown);
```

This is used by the VAX to set a directory file name for the new file you want to set up on the disk using the rewrite procedure.

2. before using the Pascal reset procedure in a program without the open/rewrite combination, use the following VAX Pascal statement:

```
open(filename, 'filename.xxx', history := unknown);
```

This is used by the VAX to identify a disk file which will be referred to by the Pascal reset procedure. The open/rewrite combination should be incorporated into each of the file-handling programs in chapter 13 before they are compiled on a VAX.

APPENDIX C.4

TURBO PASCAL

The Turbo Pascal compiler from Borland International consistently compiles fast, is remarkably inexpensive and easy-to-use. This Pascal compiler has some non-standard features which must be taken into account before it can be used to implement the standard Pascal programs given in this book. These features are covered in the following sections of this appendix. This appendix was prepared with the help of Professor Melchior Freund, Computer Science Department, St. John's University, Collegeville, Minnesota.

C.4.1 Turbo Standard Input/Output Switch

To use the **input** and **output** files according to the Pascal standard, Turbo provides what might best be called the Borland $B- switch. This $B- switch must be inserted as a comment immediately after a Pascal program heading in the following way:

```
program TryThisInTurbo(input, output);
(*$B-*)
         .
         .
         .
end.
```

C.4.2 Turbo Built-in Read/Write Procedures

To use Turbo to implement any of the programs given in this text, insert the Borland $B- switch comment at the top of a program as shown in the preceding section. The read, readln, write, writeln procedures can then be used as shown in this text. For example, here is a Turbo Pascal program to illustrate this idea:

```
                    (*This program picks out the largest positive integer in
                    a sequence of positive integers entered at keyboard.*)

program TryThis(input, output);
(*$B-*)
var
  ThisX, largest: integer;
begin
  largest := 0;
  repeat
    read(ThisX);
    if (ThisX > largest) then largest := ThisX
  until eoln;
  writeln; writeln;
  writeln('The largest value entered = ', largest:10)
end.
```

C.4.3 Turbo Strings

Instead of using a packed array of characters to define a string type as done in standard Pascal, Turbo follows the lead of UCSD Pascal and provides a built-in string type. In all programs in this text which set up string types using packed arrays of characters, use

```
type
  StringType = string[max];
```

instead of

```
type
  StringType = packed array[1..max] of char;
```

C.4.4 Turbo File-Handling

Turbo Pascal file-handling has some of the features found in IBM Pascal:

1. a built-in **assign** procedure to establish a directory name for a user-defined file;
2. a built-in **close** procedure to bring file-handling to an orderely halt.

   To prepare a file for generation, here are the steps to use:

3. after declaring a file variable in the standard way as shown in chapter 9, then use the following pair of statements to prepare a file for generation:

   assign(FileVariableName, 'ThisFile.xxx');
   rewrite(FileVariableName);

   or, if DirName is a string variable, then use

```
readln(DirName);
assign(FileVariableName, DirName);
rewrite(FileVariableName);
```

4. use

```
close(FileVariableName)
```

after you have finished working with a file.

5. To inspect a file, use

```
assign(FileVariableName, DirName);
reset(FileVariableName);
```

For example, here is a sample program which illustrates these Turbo file-handling ideas:

```
                              (*This program does the following things:

      1. saves a sequence of entered integers in a
         file called scores.dat;
      2. picks out the largest of the entered values
         and prints this maximum value;
      3. inspects the contents of the newly constructed
         scores.dat file.                                        *)

program NowTryThis(input, output, scores);
                                                            (*$B-*)
var
  ThisX, largest: integer;
  scores: file of integer;
begin
  assign(scores, 'scores.dat');              (*set up directory name*)
  rewrite(scores);
  largest := 0;
  repeat
    read(ThisX);
    if (ThisX > largest) then largest := ThisX;
    write(scores, ThisX)                       (*save ThisX in file*)
  until eoln;
  writeln; writeln;
  writeln('largest value = ', largest:10);
  ThisX := -1;                                 (*mark end-of-file*)
  write(scores, ThisX);                        (*save logical eof*)
  reset(scores);                     (*prepare file for inspection*)
  repeat
    read(scores, ThisX);
    writeln(ThisX:30);                           (*show file value*)
  until ThisX = -1;
  close(scores)
end.
```

Happy Turboing!

APPENDIX D

COMPUTER SYSTEMS

OVERVIEW

This appendix describes the principal components of computers, the kinds of computer system software, and various ways computers are configured (arranged). It will cover the following topics:

- Major hardware components
- Computer system software
- Machine, assembly and higher-level languages
- Types of computer systems

D.1 Major Hardware Components

A computer is a device designed to carry out instructions. The layout for a typical computer is given in the accompanying figure:

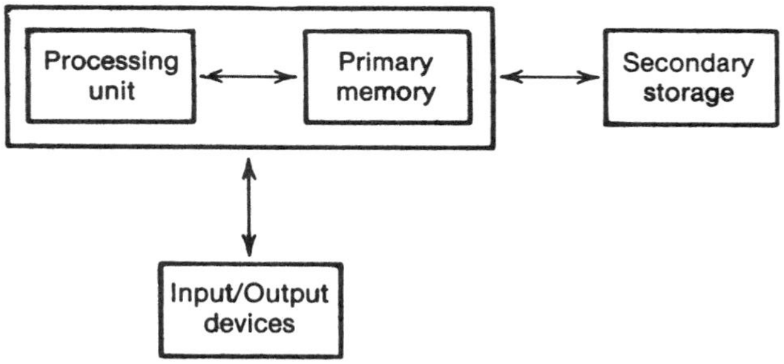

Here is how the parts of a computer work together.

Processing unit. This is usually called the CPU or central processing unit. It has two basic parts: computation unit and control unit. The CPU takes care of managing the flow of data from an input device (a keyboard, for example) or to an output device (a screen, for example). The CPU gets its instructions and data from its primary memory. Data coming from an input device must first be put into primary memory. All information stored in primary memory is in the form of bit-strings (rows of 1's and 0's). Secondary memory is used to make a copy of data and instructions stored in primary memory.

Computation unit. This is the part of the CPU that takes care of arithmetic operations and comparisons. The computation unit is also known as the **ALU** (Arithmetic and Logic Unit).

Control unit. This unit manages the flow of data to and from the parts of a computer. It also takes care of setting up the sequences of operations called for by an instruction.

Input unit. This is usually a keyboard or card reader.

Output unit. This is usually either a screen or a printer.

Primary memory. All data and instructions required by the CPU are stored in primary memory.

Secondary memory. Backup storage for data and instructions in main memory. Diskette machines, cassette machines, or disk drives are used as secondary storage units. Information is stored in files in secondary memory.

D.2 System Software

The term software refers to programs that fall into three main groups:

- Operating systems: Programs used to manage the resources of a computer
- Application programs: Compilers used to translate symbolic code into machine code (bit strings that specify actions for a machine to perform), database systems, video games, editor, etc.
- User programs: Programs written in a language like Pascal.

Basically, the term *software* refers to the nonhardware components of a computer. The term **system software** refers to operating systems and application programs like a text editor. An operating system is a collection of programs that guide and manage the operations of a computer. It is a resource manager and a control program. An operating system assists a computer in performing the following tasks:

1. Setting up a program in main memory which is ready to be run or which is waiting for some system service or removing programs from main memory.
2. Keeping track of how much CPU time is allocated to any one program on a multiuser system.

3. Preventing snags (system crashes) when programs make unreasonable requests.
4. Allocating system resources as needed by a program.
5. Making system resources accessible—taking care of user requests for a library routine like cls (clear screen) on an IBM PC or for compilers like a request for BASIC or for Pascal or for editors like EDLIN on an IBM PC or EDT on a VAX-11.
6. Taking care of system security, preventing unauthorized use of software or access to privileged areas of main memory.

Application programs make up the other chief component of computer system software. Basically, there are four types of application programs that are typically available on a computer system:

1. Assembler, which uses very simple sets of symbols to represent machine codes. An assembler is a translator. An assembly language program presents machine instructions in symbolic form which are translated into machine codes by an assembler. Because each assembly language instruction usually represents a single machine code, assembly language programs tend to make very efficient use of a machine.
2. Editor, which is a program used to prepare a source text either in assembly language or in a higher-level language like Pascal.
3. Compiler for a higher-level language, which uses ordinary language to represent sequences of machine codes. Pascal is an example of a higher-level language. A compiler is used to translate Pascal source texts into machine codes. A Pascal program, for example, is on a higher level than an assembly language program for two reasons: each instruction written in a higher level language represents a sequence of machine instructions instead of just one machine instruction; and higher-level languages like Pascal use ordinary (natural) language.
4. Data base management programs like dBase III for an IBM PC. These are programs that make it easier to set up and use files.

The combination of an operating system and application programs make up system software.

D.3 Machine, Assembly and Higher-level Languages

Machine language consists of a collection of bit strings which are used in instructions requiring no translation and which are immediately interpretable by a particular computer. A bit string is a sequence of 0's and 1's like the following one:

10000000000001010111111111110001

For example, the following bit strings are used in the machine language for a VAX-11 computer:

bit string	*symbolic form*	*meaning*
1100 000	ADDL2	add two long words (each long word is 32 bits)
1111 1011	CALLS	used to call a procedure
1101 0100	CLRL	CLEAR BITS
1101 000	MOVL	makes a copy of 32 bits in a new 32-bit location

An assembly language consists of symbols which can be used to represent machine language operators and operands. For example, ADDL2 is the symbolic form of the VAX-11 machine code operator used in addition of two long words. The long words used in the addition are the operands. For example, here is a VAX-11 assembly language instruction to add two values, each consisiting of 32 bits:

assembly language instruction	*meaning*
ADDL2 ThisX, ThisY	ThisX and ThisY each represent values occupying 32 bits of computer memory. The value of ThisY is replaced by the sum of ThisX + ThisY.

Assembly language programs are not immediately interpretable by a machine. Such program must be translated into the corresponding machine program. This translation is handled by an *assembler*. An assembly language program is considered a low-level program because each assembly language operator translates into *one* machine code. Each assembly language instruction can be represented by a single bit string, which specifies an operator and zero or more operands.

By contrast, instructions written in a higher-level programming language often correspond to more than one machine instruction, more than one bit string. Pascal is an example of a higher-level programming language. It is considered a higher level for the following reasons:

1. program instructions can correspond to more than one machine instruction;
2. language tokens are not limited to short symbols used by assembly language but rather can include reserved words imported from natural language, special symbols, and various number tokens not available on the assembly language level.

D.4

Types of Computers

A *computer system* consists of one or more CPUs connected together with a coordinated set of devices like various types of memory units, input and output units. For example, the Apple IIe is an example of a computer system with one CPU, some main memory, some form of auxiliary storage (usually one or two diskette drives), a keyboard and a monitor and, possibly, a printer. This is an example of a uniprocessing system—it relies on one CPU.

A multiprocessor computer system consists of two or more CPUs. For example, a Rainbow-100 manufactured by the Digital Equipment Corporation is an example of a small multiprocessing system. It uses an intel 8086 computer to handle arithmetic and comparisons required by a program. It delegates input and output processing to a second computer, a Zilog Z80.

Another example of a multiprocessor is the DEC 20 system, which uses one CPU for processing and a smaller PDP-11 to handle terminal input and output. The Rainbow-100 and DEC-20 are examples of *tightly coupled multiprocessors* because they share the same storage facilities (main memory and auxiliary storage devices like disk drives). By contrast, *loosely coupled multiprocessor systems* consist of autonomous computer systems with local CPUs and local storage facilities which are connected together by communication links. Examples of loosely coupled multiprocessor systems are the local area networks developed by Xerox, Digital and IBM.

APPENDIX E

SORTING AND SEARCHING

The methods of sorting and searching are collected together in this appendix. In addition, an estimate of the approximate running time of each method is given.

E.1 SEARCHING

This section presents procedures which can be used in a linear or a binary search of a list. Each search references a record which has the following definition:

```
type
  KeyType = <you pick the key type>;
  EntryType = record
    key: KeyType;
                                    (*insert other fields here*)
    end;                                        (*EntryType*)
  ListType = array[1..max] of EntryType;
```

A *list* is a sequences of records. For the sake of brevity, only contiguous lists will be considered in this appendix. A *contiguous list* is a list stored in an array. A contiguous list is also called a *bounded length list* because the array used to hold the list will always have an upper bound on the number of records which can be stored in the list. A *linear search* of a list begins at some point in the list and continues searching record-by-record until either a desired record is found or the end of the list is reached. Searching a list of records depends on a search key, which is a value which is compared with a corresponding key field of a list record. A *search key* is used to identify a list item.

The following procedure can be used to carry out a linear search of a list:

PROCEDURE 1 (LINEAR SEARCH)

```
procedure SearchList(list: ListType;
                     ListSize: integer;
                     SearchKey: KeyType;
                     var found: Boolean);
begin
  if not found
       and (ListSize <> 0) then
    if list[index].key <> SearchKey then
      SearchList(list,ListSize - 1, SearchKey, found)
    else
      found := true
end;                                                    (*SearchList*)
```

Notice two things about this procedure:

1. it must be activated with found having a value of false, which remains false if the desired list item is not found;
2. a search is carried out starting with the last list item and moves left until either the desired item is found or the beginning of the list is reached.

If we assume a list has n distinct items, then it will take an average of $(n+1)/2$ comparisons to find any one list item. This says the running time of a linear search is proportional to n. A linear search does not depend on a list being ordered. To conduct a binary search, an *ordered* list must be used. The following procedure can be used in a binary search:

PROCEDURE 2 (BINARY SEARCH)

```
procedure SearchList(list: ListType;
                     SearchKey: KeyType;
                     start, middle, tail: integer;
                     var position: integer);
begin
  if SearchKey = list[middle].key then
    position := middle
  else
    if tail >= start then begin
      middle := (start + tail) div 2;          (*divide'n'conquer*)
      if SearchKey < list[middle].key then
        SearchList(list, SearchKey,
                   start, middle, middle-1, position)
      else
        SearchList(list, SearchKey,
                   middle+1, middle, tail, position)
end;                                                    (*SearchList*)
```

Notice the following things about this procedure:

1. the list *must* be ordered;
2. this procedure must be activated with a middle value used to identify the halfway point in a list to be searched;
3. if a desired item is found, its position in the list is returned by the procedure.

This binary search procedure uses a *divide-and-conquer* approach:

```
begin
  while not found
        the middle value <> 1 do begin
    inspect the middle of the list;
    if item not found, then
     if the search key value is below the middle then
       choose the lower half as the new list to search
     else
       choose the upper half as the new list to search
    end
end                                    (*binary search algorithm*)
```

For this reason, the number of comparisons made during a binary search will be roughly equal to lg n. This is called the binary log of n, $\log_2 n$, which is can be explained as follows:

$$\text{to compute lg n, choose a number x so that } 2^x = n$$

Here are some sample computations using binary logs:

n	*lg n*	*desired exponent*
32	lg 32 = 5, since $2^5 = 32$	
64	lg 64 = 6, since $2^6 = 64$	
1024	lg 1024 = 10, since $2^{10} = 1024$	
1,000,000	lg 1,000,000 = 19.93, since $2^{19.93} = 1{,}000{,}000$	

Notice that lg x = ln x / ln 2. Check your calculator to see if it has an **ln** key (this is the natural log key).

Because the running time of a binary search *in the worst case* is lg n, this makes a binary search much, much faster than a linear search

E.2 Sorting

A list is sorted if its items are arranged in either ascending or descending order. Here are some methods of sorting:

1. bubble sort (given in this section)
2. selection sort (chapters 6 and 8)
3. quicksort (chapter 10)
4. merge sort (chapter 9 and 10)
5. insertion sort (chapter 12)
6. tree sort (chapter 12)

A bubble sort is also called a *straight exchange sort* because of its heavy dependence on exchanging list items to sort them. A bubble sort uses the following algorithm:

(*input: (contiguous) list, ListSize;
output: (ordered) list*)

```
begin
   enter list, ListSize;
   while ListSize > 1 do begin
      move largest entry to end of list;
      subtract 1 from ListSize
      end
end                                        (*Bubble sort algorithm*)
```

A bubble sort scans a list of n items n − 1 times. During each scan, it moves the record with the largest key value to the end of the list which is scanned. The largest key value is the bubble, which "rises" to the end of the list. The following Pascal procedure can be used to implement a bubble sort:

PROCEDURE 3 (BUBBLE SORT)

```
procedure BubbleSort(var list: List Type;
                         ListSize: integer);
var index: integer;
begin
   while ListSize > 1 do begin
      ListSize := ListSize - 1;
      for index := 1 to ListSize do
         if list[index].key > list[index + 1].key then
            swap(list, index)                (*hidden procedure*)
      end
end;                                         (*BubbleSort*)
```

Notice the following things about this procedure:

1. the hidden swap procedure is like the one used in the selection sort in section 6.19;
2. this procedure will run faster, if a SwapMade variable of type Boolean is used to check when a scan of the list results in no swaps (this improvement in the bubble sort is left as an exercise).
3. it takes an average of n(n − 1)/2 comparisons and n(n − 1)/2 swaps to complete a bubble sort, which makes it slow.

A selection sort is faster than a bubble sort because it depends chiefly on comparisons to sort a list. Here is a procedure to carry out a selection sort:

PROCEDURE 4 (SELECTION SORT)

```
procedure SelectionSort(var list: ListType;
                         ListSize: integer);
begin
   repeat
      place := ListSize;
      FindMax(list, ListSize, place);          (*hidden procedure*)
      swap(list, ListSize, place);             (*hidden procedure*)
      ListSize := ListSize - 1
   until ListSize = 1
end;                                            (*Selection sort*)
```

Notice the following things about this procedure:

1. FindMax is a hidden procedure which finds the position of the largest key value (this procedure is given in section 6.19);
2. swap is a hidden procedure also given in section 6.19;
3. a total of n − 1 swaps (exchanges) are used by a selection sort as opposed to about n(n − 1)/2 swaps used by a BubbleSort;
4. a total of n(n − 1)/2 comparisons are used by a selection sort.

The following procedure can be used to carry out an insertion sort:

PROCEDURE 5 (INSERTION SORT)

```
procedure InsertionSort(var list: ListType;
                        var ListSize: integer);
var entry: EntryType;
begin
  repeat
    Get(entry);                                   (*hidden procedure*)
    if entry.key <> empty then begin
      InsertItem(list, ListSize,
                 entry);                          (*hidden procedure*)
      ListSize := ListSize + 1
      end
  until (entry.key = empty)
        or (ListSize > ListMax)
end;                                              (*InsertionSort*)
```

Notice the following things about this procedure:

1. insertions are made into a contiguous list;
2. a hidden Get procedure is used to build an entry record;
3. the following hidden InsertItem procedure is used to insert a new entry:

PROCEDURE 6 (INSERT ITEM)

```
procedure InsertItem(var list: ListType;
                     index: integer;
                     item: EntryType);
begin
  while (index > 0)
        and (list[index].key > item.key) do begin
    list[index + 1] := list[index];
    index := index - 1
    end;
  index := index + 1;
  list[index] := item
end;                                              (*InsertItem*)
```

4. a constant *empty* is used to determine when to stop making insertions;
5. an average of (n + 1)/2 comparisons and swaps will be made each time an insertion is made. In terms of just comparisons, you should verify that it takes an average of $n^2/4 + 3n/4$ comparisons to complete an insertion sort. This will help you gauge the efficiency of an insertion sort.

The quick sort was invented by C. A. R. Hoare in 1962 and is another exchange sort which uses the following procedure for contiguous lists:

PROCEDURE 7 (QUICK SORTING)

```
procedure QuickSort(var list: ListType;
                        ListSize, low, high: integer);
var
   ThisLow, ThisHigh: integer;
begin
   if low < high then begin
      ThisLow := low; ThisHigh := high + 1;
      repeat
         repeat
            ThisLow := ThisLow + 1                (*scan left-to-right*)
         until (list[ThisLow].key >= list[low].key)
               or (ThisLow > ListSize);
         repeat
            ThisHigh := ThisHigh - 1              (*scan right-to-left*)
         until list[ThisHigh].key <= list[low].key;
         if ThisLow < ThisHigh then
            swap(list, ThisLow, ThisHigh)
      until ThisLow > ThisHigh;
      swap(list, low, ThisHigh);
      QuickSort(list, ListSize, low, ThisHigh - 1);
      QuickSort(list, ListSize, ThisHigh + 1, high)
      end
end;                                              (*QuickSort*)
```

A quick sort works best when the low list is close to the same size as the high list. Otherwise, in the worst case when these two sublists are always unbalanced, the running time of a quicksort is slower than a selection sort. In the best of times, when the high and low lists are consistently balanced, the running time of a quick sort is "quick!" Its running time approaches $n * \lg n$ for a list of n records in the best case.

Merge sorting is consistently fast. The recursive merge sort given in section 10.15 has a running time proportional to $n * \lg n$ in the worst case for a list of n items.

Finally, tree sorting is also consistently fast. It requires at most lg n comparisons each time an insertion is made into a binary tree. The running time of a tree sort is proportional to $n * \lg n$.

E.3 Timing Studies

The approximate running times of the searches and sorted discussed in this appendix are given in the following table:

Approximate Running times

method	*running time proportional to*	*other cases*	*growth rate*
linear search	n (worst case)	(n + 1)n/2 (average case)	linear
binary search	lg n (worst case)		logarithmic
bubble sort	n^2 (worst case)		quadratic
selection sort	n^2 (always)		quadratic
insertion sort	n^2 (average case)		quadratic
quick sort	n^2 (worst case)	nlg n (best case)	(logarithmic)
merge sort	nlg n (worst case)		logarithmic
tree sort	nlg n (worst case)		logarithmic

Note: 1) *linear growth* refers to growth along a straight line;
2) *quadratic growth,* along a curve produced by a second degree polynomial like n^2;
3) *logarithmic growth,* along a curve produced by function defined in terms of a logarithm like lg n.

APPENDIX F

SOCIAL IMPLICATIONS OF COMPUTER USE

OVERVIEW

This appendix presents some of the major issues relating to the uses of computers. Each section begins with an issue followed by a brief discussion. The purpose is to present questions for discussion and present some of the implications of each issue. The following three dominant issues are explored:

- How should computers be used?
- Which organizations are critically dependent on computers?
- As designers of programs, what are our responsibilities?

There is a list of readings in the bibliography included at the back of the book. These readings can be used to follow up on the questions raised by the sections of this appendix.

F.1 How Should Computers Be Used?

Computers give us a way to inspect and to manage the world of information. Computers can process lots of information in the twinkle of an eye. You can gauge how much information a computer can handle by how many million operations per second, or MPS, a medium-sized or large computer system can handle. For example, a VAX-11/780 can perform 0.8 MPS, whereas a Burroughs B6808-2 can handle 14 MPS and a CDC Cyber 176 can handle 42 MPS—actually 42,401,700 operations per second! That is on the slow side for some of the more recent CDC (Control Data Corporation) machines. In 1979,

CDC introduced its Cyber 203, which can perform 403 MPS (nearly half a billion operations per second!).

This means computers can process massive amounts of information in very short periods of time. Then how should computers be used? Computers are organizational tools. They are much like telescopes or microscopes, which give us access to information that otherwise would be pretty much inaccessible. However, as far as I know, nobody has ever complained about which parts of the sky telescopes inspect or which parts of the microscopic world microscopes inspect. This is not the case with computers.

The question for computers is: *What information should be inspected or managed or analyzed by computers?* It is highly probable that someday you will be in a position to decide what information gets put into a computer for analysis. For example, should all the family histories of all of the customers of a bank be put into a computer? Should information about the credit card holders for one company be shared with other companies? Should your name be put into a computerized mailing list that is sold by one company to other companies without your consent? In other words, in what ways can you safeguard the privacy of individuals in our computerized society?

F.2 Which Organizations Are Critically Dependent on Computers?

If the operations of an organization come to a standstill when its computer system fails, then that organization is critically dependent on its computer. TWA (or TransWorld Airlines) is an example of an organization that is critically dependent on its computer system to handle reservations. In a recent interview, Carl Flood, director of TWA system software, was asked if TWA was critically dependent on its computer system. Flood's reply was, "Absolutely."

TWA relies on a single IBM 9083 computer to handle all of its reservations. This computer handles an average of 7 million transactions per day. The IBM 9083 also maintains a data base (total collected passenger information files) which takes up two billion bytes of storage (or 2 gigabytes). During an ordinary day, the 9083 will process an average of 170 transactions per second. Carl Flood mentioned that the 9083 has handled up to 200 reservations in one second.

How does an organization like TWA cope with its critical dependency on its IBM 9083? It has made its main system as reliable as possible. The reliability of a computer becomes a major issue for an organization like TWA. All kinds of safeguards must be built into the system. What can cause trouble? A power failure can be a major problem. For example, in 1972 TWA had 548 power failures. In 1976, it experienced 131 power failures. So TWA has installed backup power systems to run its computer if it has a power failure.

What if the main computer goes down? TWA has a complete backup computer system to take over. TWA relies on an IBM 3033 as its backup computer system. The 3033 can handle 80 percent of the work handled by the main computer. This gets TWA by until it can get its main computer running again, whenever it fails. This is a common tactic—use a backup computer to take over if the main computer goes down. This technique is used by the space shuttle, which is also critically dependent on its computers.

The space shuttle has 5 IBM system/4 pi, model AP-101 computers. This computer can perform up to 450,000 operations per second (or about 0.5 MPS). The shuttle relies on four of these computers at any one time. The fifth system/4 is there as a backup computer in case one of the systems fails.

Can you think of any other organizations that are critically dependent on computers? Most banks are, for example. Portions of the military are. Most large businesses are critically dependent on computers. Here are some questions to raise about this problem of critical dependency:

- How should computers be built to prevent failures?
- What outside forces (electrical storms, for example) can cause computer failures?
- What are some of the ways a critically dependent organization can cope with a major failure of its main computer system?
- Are there any organizations that should not be critically dependent on computers?
- What are the advantages of a critically dependent system?
- What are the disadvantages of a critically dependent system?

F.3 As Program Designers, What Are Our Obligations?

The concept of obligation is a hidden feature of the program development cycle. It is important to consider whether a program should be written at all. You will probably be in a position some day to ask the following question: *Are there dangers in the program I am about to write?* One obvious danger in any program that prints messages on a screen or printer is this: The language used should be crystal clear and above reproach. This is a common problem that you probably have already noticed. That is, it is common for messages printed by a program to be on the sloppy side.

As a program designer, here are some questions you might want to build into the beginning of a program development cycle:

- Will this program be harmful to other people?
- What information should not be processed by your program?
- Have the rights of others been considered in the development of the new program?
- Will the new program be helpful in making responsible and intelligent decisions?

SOLUTIONS TO CHAPTER REVIEW QUIZZES

Chapter 1

questions:	1	2	3	4	5	6	7	8	9	10
answers:	T	F	F	T	F	F	F	F	T	T

Chapter 2

questions:	1	2	3	4	5	6	7	8	9	10	11	12	13	14	15
answers:	F	T	T	T	F	T	F	F	T	T	F	F	T	F	T

Chapter 3

questions:	1	2	3	4	5	6	7	8	9	10	11	12
answers:	F	F	F	T	T	F	T	F	F	T	F	F

Chapter 4

questions:	1	2	3	4	5	6	7	8	9	10
answers:	T	T	F	T	F	T	T	T	T	F

Chapter 5

questions:	1	2	3	4	5	6	7	8	9	10
answers:	T	T	T	F	T	T	T	F	F	F

Chapter 6

questions:	1	2	3	4	5	6	7	8	9	10
answers:	F	F	T	T	F	T	T	T	F	T

Chapter 7

questions:	1	2	3	4	5	6	7	8	9	10
answers:	T	F	T	F	F	T	T	F	T	T

Chapter 8

questions:	1	2	3	4	5	6	7	8	9	10
answers:	T	T	T	T	F	F	F	T	T	T

Chapter 9

questions:	1	2	3	4	5	6	7	8	9	10	11	12	13	14	15
answers:	T	F	T	T	T	T	F	F	F	F	F	T	F	F	T

Chapter 10

questions:	1	2	3	4	5	6	7	8	9	10
answers:	T	T	T	F	T	F	F	T	F	F

Chapter 11

questions:	1	2	3	4	5	6	7	8	9	10
answers:	F	F	F	F	F	T	F	T	F	F

Chapter 12

questions:	1	2	3	4	5	6	7	8	9	10
answers:	T	F	T	T	T	F	F	F	T	F

SELECTED SOLUTIONS

Chapter 1

16.

```
program question16(output);
   procedure PromptPassenger;
   begin
      writeln('How can I help you?....')
   end;                                        (*PromptPassenger*)
begin
   PromptPassenger
end.
```

17.

```
(a) assertion: repeat loop is infinite, if a < 0
    assertion: no iteration occurs in the repeat
               loop, if a >= 0
    assertion: count - ThreshHold > 0, if alarm
               sounds
(b) assertion: if weight >= 120
                  and (CalorieCount < 300) then
               no iteration occurs inside either
               repeat loop
    assertion: if weight >= 120
                  and (CalorieCount >= 300) then
               (1) iteration occurs in the inner
                   repeat loop an infinite number
                   of times and
               (2) no iteration occurs in the
                   outer repeat loop
```

Chapter 2

10. (b) Flowchart for experiment 8a:

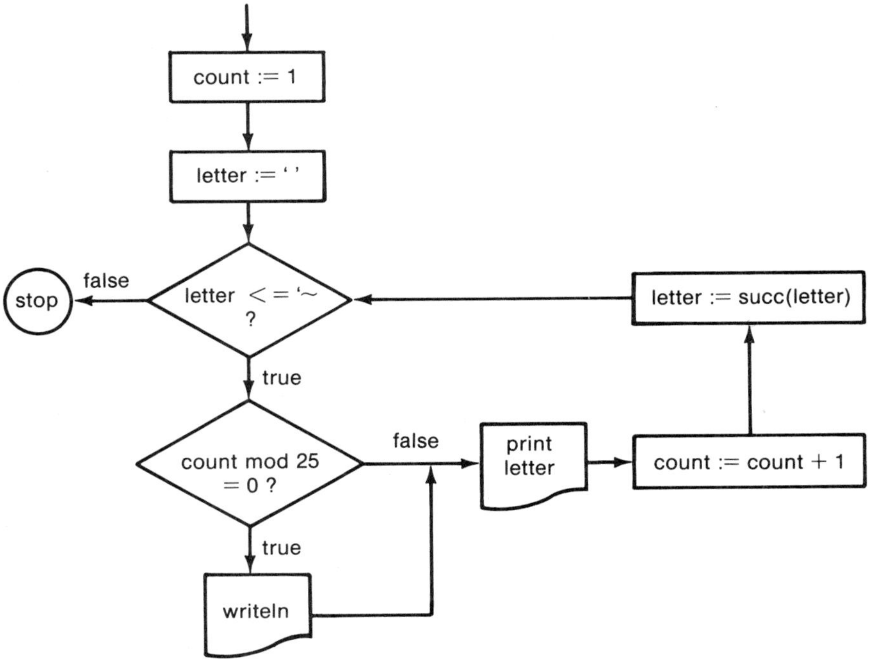

Chapter 2, Exercise 26

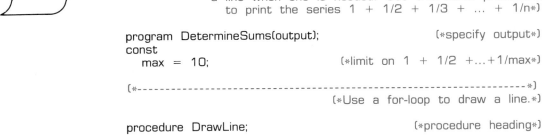

```
                     (*Ref.: Exercise 26, chapter 2 (harmonic series)
          (*Method: use one procedure to activate another one to draw
                    a line when one is needed. Use this same procedure
                      to print the series 1 + 1/2 + 1/3 + ... + 1/n*)

program DetermineSums(output);                        (*specify output*)
const
   max = 10;                                (*limit on 1 + 1/2 +...+1/max*)

(*-----------------------------------------------------------------*)
                                         (*Use a for-loop to draw a line.*)

procedure DrawLine;                                 (*procedure heading*)
const
   limit = 80;                                         (*length of line*)
var
   dash : integer;                                   (*control variable*)
begin
   for dash := 1 to limit do write('-'); writeln
end;                                                          (*DrawLine*)
```

```
(*-----------------------------------------------------------------*)
                            (*Use nested for-loops to print series.*)

procedure ShowSeries;
var
   term, DisplayTerms, copy:integer;           (*3 control variables*)
   sum : real;                                    (*holds each sum*)
begin
   DrawLine;                                    (*activate DrawLine*)
   term := 1;
   repeat
      write(' ':5);
      for DisplayTerms := 1 to term do
         write('1/', DisplayTerms:2, '+':2);           (*show terms*)
      sum := 0; copy := 1;                  (*initialize sum, copy*)
      repeat
         sum := sum + 1/copy;
         copy := copy + 1                           (*add 1 to copy*)
      until copy > term;                        (*inner repeat loop*)
      write('=     ':5,sum:10:6); writeln;
      term := term + 1                              (*add 1 to term*)
   until term > max;                            (*outer repeat loop*)
   DrawLine;                                    (*activate DrawLine*)
end;                                                  (*ShowSeries*)

(*-----------------------------------------------------------------*)

begin
   ShowSeries                       (*activate ShowSeries procedure*)
end.
```

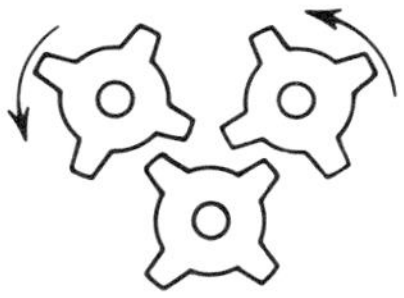

```
-----------------------------------------------------------------
-
1/ 1 + = 1.000000
1/ 1 +1/ 2 + = 1.500000
1/ 1 +1/ 2 +1/ 3 + = 1.833333
1/ 1 +1/ 2 +1/ 3 +1/ 4 + = 2.083333
1/ 1 +1/ 2 +1/ 3 +1/ 4 +1/ 5 + = 2.283334
1/ 1 +1/ 2 +1/ 3 +1/ 4 +1/ 5 +1/ 6 + = 2.450000
1/ 1 +1/ 2 +1/ 3 +1/ 4 +1/ 5 +1/ 6 +1/ 7 + = 2.592857
1/ 1 +1/ 2 +1/ 3 +1/ 4 +1/ 5 +1/ 6 +1/ 7 +1/ 8 + = 2.717857
1/ 1 +1/ 2 +1/ 3 +1/ 4 +1/ 5 +1/ 6 +1/ 7 +1/ 8 +1/ 9 + = 2.828969
1/ 1 +1/ 2 +1/ 3 +1/ 4 +1/ 5 +1/ 6 +1/ 7 +1/ 8 +1/ 9 +1/10 + =
2.928968
-----------------------------------------------------------------
```

Chapter 3, Exercise 9

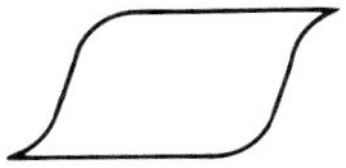

```
            (*Ref.: ch.3, exercise 9, Pascal with Program Design*)
  program e9(input,output);
    procedure ScanText(target: char;
                       var frequency: integer);
    var entry: char;
  begin
    frequency := 0;
    repeat
      read(entry);
      if entry = target then
        frequency := frequency + 1
    until eoln
  end;                                              (*ScanText*)
  procedure driver;
  var
    ThisChar: char;
    ThisCount, choice: integer;
  begin
    repeat
      write('Enter target: '); readln(ThisChar);
      writeln; write('Enter text to scan: ');
      ScanText(ThisChar, ThisCount);
      writeln; writeln;
      writeln(ThisChar:10, ' occurs ', ThisCount:4, ' times.');
      write('Again--1 = Y, 0 = N: '); readln(choice); writeln
    until choice = 0
 end;                                               (*driver*)
begin
  driver
end.
```

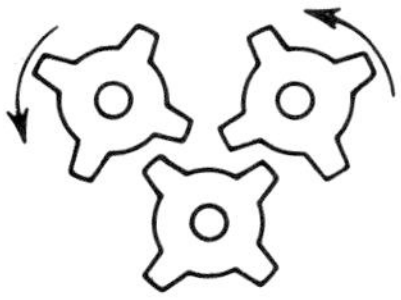

```
Enter target: t

Enter text to scan: tatumtytumtytumtoes!

         t occurs    7 times.
Again--1 = Y, 0 = N: 0
```

Chapter 3, Exercise 23

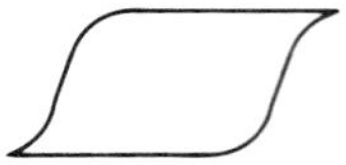

```
                    (*Ref.: Exercise 23 (Finding largest numeric entry)*)
             (*Method: Use a the built-in read procedure to scan an
                            input line of numbers and saving the largest
                                        entry in each pair compared.*)

(*--------------------------------------------------------------------*)
                                    (*Scan input line for largest number*)

  procedure FindMinMax(var largest : integer;
                       var smallest: integer;
                       next : integer);                   (*next entry*)
  begin
    largest := next; smallest := next;
    repeat
      read(next);
      if next > largest then
        largest := next;
      if next < smallest then
        smallest := next
    until eoln
  end;                                                       (*FindMax*)
(*--------------------------------------------------------------------*)
              (*Program manager: get values, activate FindMax*)
  procedure driver;
  var
    BiggestNo : integer;                                (*biggest value*)
    SmallestNo: integer;                               (*smallest value*)
    FirstNo : integer;                                     (*leading no*)
    choice : integer;                                (*control variable*)
  begin
    repeat
      writeln('Enter two or more integers on the same line:');
      read(FirstNo);
      FindMinMax(BiggestNo, SmallestNo, FirstNo);
      writeln; writeln('lgst value = ', BiggestNo:10);
      writeln; writeln('smst value = ', SmallestNo: 10);
      readln;                               (*move to next input line*)
      writeln; write('Again?--1=Y, 0=N: '); readln(choice);
      writeln; writeln
    until choice = 0
  end;                                                        (*driver*)
(*--------------------------------------------------------------------*)
begin
  driver                                   (*activate driver procedure*)
end.
```

Chapter 4

8. (a)

```
if expr = 0.5 then
   if expr = 1.0 then
      if expr = 2.0 then
         if expr = 1.6 then
            writeln('expr is close to...')
         else
            writeln('expr is interesting')
         else
            writeln('Try again!')
         else
            writeln('I believe so.');
```

(b)

```
if expr = 2 then
   if expr < 3 then
      writeln('Euler will be happy!')
   else
      if (expr > 2) and (expr < 4) then
         writeln('Perhaps!')
      else
         writeln('Mmmmm...')
else
   writeln('Which if?');
```

9. Both if-statements can be rewritten with nested case statements:

```
(a) case expr = 0.5 of
      true: case expr = 1.0 of
                 true: case expr = 2.0 of
                            true: case expr = 1.6 of
                                       true: writeln('expr is...');
                                       false: write('interesting')
                                       end;
                            false: writeln('Try again!');
                 false: writeln('I believe so');
      false:
      end;
```

```
(b) case expr = 2 of
      true: case expr < 3 of
                 true: writeln('Euler will be happy!');
                 false: case (expr > 2) and (expr < 4) of
                             true: writeln('Perhaps!');
                             false: writeln('Mmmmm...');
      false: writeln('Which if?')
      end;
```

Chapter 4, Exercise 13

```
                    (*Ref.: Chapter 4, exercise 13, use exit mechanism*)
               (*Method: Use nested loops to produce a symbol triangle
                                  which are the lower case letters*)
program ShowFloydTriangle(input, output);

(*------------------------------------------------------------*)
                                          (*print specified triangle*)

  procedure Floyd(row : integer;                     (*no. of rows*)
                  RowEntry: char);               (*beginning symbol*)

  var
    ColumnCount : integer;                        (*counts columns*)
    RowCount : integer;                        (*keep track of rows*)
  begin
    ColumnCount:= 1; RowCount := 1;
    while RowCount <= row do begin
      write(' ':15);                                   (*for margin*)
      while   ColumnCount <= RowCount do begin
        write(RowEntry:3);
        if succ(RowEntry) <= 'z' then
          RowEntry := succ(RowEntry)
        else RowEntry := 'a';
        ColumnCount := ColumnCount + 1
        end;                                    (*inner while loop*)
      ColumnCount := 1;
      RowCount := RowCount + 1;
      writeln
      end                                       (*outer while loop*)
  end;                                                    (*Floyd*)

(*------------------------------------------------------------*)
              (*Program manager: get values & activate proc.*)
  procedure driver;
  var
    choice : integer;
    first: char;
  begin
    repeat
      write('Enter no. of rows--0, to stop: ':45);
      readln(choice); writeln;
      if choice <> 0 then begin
        write('Enter first symbol: ':25); readln(first); writeln;
        writeln('Floyds letter triangle:':40); writeln;
        Floyd(choice, first)
        end
    until choice = 0                          (*exit on choice = 0*)
  end:                                                   (*driver*)
(*------------------------------------------------------------*)
begin
  driver                                (*activate driver procedure*)
end.
```

```
     Enter no. of rows--0, to stop: 5

Enter first symbol: t

       Floyds letter triangle:

       t
       u  v
       w  x  y
       z  a  b  c
       d  e  f  g  h
     Enter no. of rows--0, to stop: 20

Enter first symbol: l
       Floyds letter triangle:
     l
     m n
     o p q
     r s t u
     v w x y z
     a b c d e f
     g h i j k l m
     n o p q r s t u
     v w x y z a b c d
     e f g h i j k l m n
     o p q r s t u v w x y
     z a b c d e f g h i j k
     l m n o p q r s t u v w x
     y z a b c d e f g h i j k l
     m n o p q r s t u v w x y z a
     b o d e f g h i j k l m n   p q
       s t u v w x y z a b c d e f g h
     i j k l m n o p q r s t u v w x y z
     a b c d e f g h i j k l m n o p q r s
     t u v w x y z a b c d e f g h i j k l m
     Enter no. of rows--0, to stop: 0
```

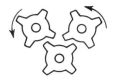

Chapter 5, Exercise 4

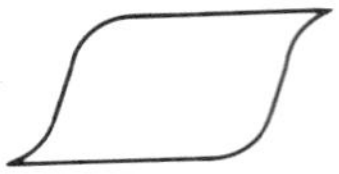

```
                                        (*Ref., Exercise 4, Chapter 5*)
                                        (*Pascal with Program Design*)

program e54(input,output);

(*---------------------------------------------------------------*)
                              (*print ASCII char. using chr( ) function*)

procedure table(low, high : integer);
var
     count : integer;

begin
     count := 0;
     repeat
        write(chr(low):5);
        low := low + 1;
        count := count +1;
        if (count mod 8) = 0 then writeln
     until low > high
end;                                                         (*table*)

(*---------------------------------------------------------------*)
                           (*program manager & activates procedure*)

procedure driver;
var
     first, last : integer;
begin
   write('Enter low, high for character range: ');
   readln(first,last); writeln;
   writeln('The character range you have selected is:');
   table(first,last);
end;

(*---------------------------------------------------------------*)

begin
     driver
end.
```

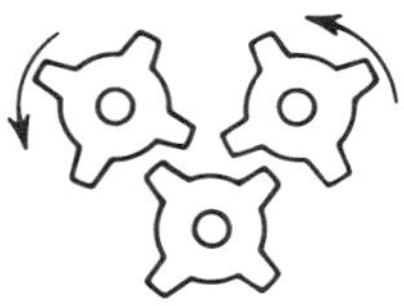

```
Enter low, high for character range:  40 101

The character range you have selected is:
     (    )    *    +    ,    -    .    /
     0    1    2    3    4    5    6    7
     8    9    :    ;    <    =    >    ?
     @    A    B    C    D    E    F    G
     H    I    J    K    L    M    N    O
     P    Q    R    S    T    U    V    W
     X    Y    Z    [    \    ]    ^    _
     '    a    b    c    d    e
```

Chapter 5, Exercise 7

```
                                        (*Ref., Exercise 7, Chapter 5*)
                                        (*Pascal with Program Design*)
program e57(input,output);

(*-----------------------------------------------------------------*)
                                (*print ASCII char. using chr( ) function*)

procedure table(values : integer);
var
     low, high, count : integer;
begin
     count := 0; high := maxint; low := -maxint;
     repeat
        writeln(' ':5,low+count:10,' ':24,high+(-1*count):11);
        count := count + 1;
     until count >= values;
     for count := 1 to 3 do writeln('.':12,'.':35);
     high := 2; low := -2;
     for count := 0 to 2 do
        writeln(' ':5,low+count:7,' ':24,high+(-1*count):11);

end;                                                          (*table)

(*-----------------------------------------------------------------*)
                                                  (*prints table header*)

procedure header;
var
     i : integer;
begin
     writeln(' ':18,'scale for type integer');
     writeln(' ':8,'low side':8,' ':26,'high side':9);
     for i := 1 to 70 do write('-'); writeln
end;                                                          (*header*)

(*-----------------------------------------------------------------*)
                            (*program manager & activates procedure*)

procedure driver;
var
     number : integer;
begin
   repeat
     repeat
        write('Enter range (<= 20):   ');
        readln(number);
     until (number > -1) and (number <21);
     writeln;
     header;
     table(number);
     write('Again? 1 = Y, 0 = N:   '); readln(number);
   until number <> 1
end;
```

```
(*---------------------------------------------------------------------*)

begin
     driver
end.
```

```
Enter range (<= 20):  21
Enter range (<= 20):  8

                       scale for type integer
          low side                                    high side
------------------------------------------------------------------

       -2147483647                               2147483647
       -2147483646                               2147483646
       -2147483645                               2147483645
       -2147483644                               2147483644
       -2147483643                               2147483643
       -2147483642                               2147483642
       -2147483641                               2147483641
       -2147483640                               2147483640
                .                                        .
                .                                        .
                .                                        .
               -2                                        2
               -1                                        1
                0                                        0
 Again? 1 = y, 0 = N:  0
```

Chapter 5, Exercise 11

```
                                         (*Ref., Exercise 11, Chapter 5*)
                                          (*Pascal with Program Design*)

program TempTable(input, output);
type
   temp = (Fahrenheit, Celsius, Kelvin, Rankine, NonScale);
(*---------------------------------------------------------------------*)
                       (*Use supplied extremes to print a temp table*)
procedure XRefTable(FirstScale, LastScale : temp;
                                    low, high, increment : real);
var
   reading : temp;
   NewX : real;
begin
   repeat
      reading := FirstScale;
      write(' ':10);                                (*leading spaces*)
```

```
      repeat
        case reading of
          Fahrenheit : write(low:8:5, ' ':10);
          Celsius :   write((5/9)*(low - 32):8:5, ' ':10);
          Kelvin: begin
                     NewX := (5/9)*(low -32);
                     write((NewX + 273.15):8:5, ' ':10)
                     end;
          Rankine: begin
                      write((low + 459.67):8:5)
                      end
          end;                                          (*case*)
        if reading <> NonScale then
          reading := succ(reading)
      until (reading = NonScale)
        or (ord(reading) > ord(LastScale));
        writeln; writeln;                     (*skip to next line*)
        low := low + increment
      until low > high
end;                                                (XRefTable*)
(*--------------------------------------------------------------*)
             (*Program manager: get values & activate procedure*)
procedure driver;
var
  LowTemp, HighTemp, Step : real;
  choice : integer;
begin
  repeat
    write('Enter low & high Fahrenheit temperatures: ');
    readln(LowTemp, HighTemp);
    write('Enter step:  '); readln(Step);
    writeln('menu:');
    writeln('--->1  all four scales');
    writeln('--->2  Fahrenheit and Celsius, only');
    writeln('--->3  Celsius and Kelvin, only');
    writeln('--->4  Fahrenheit, Celsius, and Kelvin, only');
    write('Enter choice:  '); readln(choice);
    writeln;
    writeln('Crossreference Temperature Table':40);
    case choice of
      1: begin
           write('Fahrenheit':20, 'Celsius':16, 'Kelvin':16);
           write('Rankine':16); writeln; writeln;
           XRefTable(Fahrenheit,Rankine,LowTemp,HighTemp,Step)
           end;                                 (*choice = 1*)
      2: begin
           write('Fahrenheit':20, 'Celsius':16);
           writeln; writeln;
           XRefTable(Fahrenheit,Celsius,LowTemp,HighTemp,Step)
           end;                                 (*choice = 2*)
```

```
          3: begin
                write('Celsius':18, 'Kelvin':16);
                writeln; writeln;
                XRefTable(Celsius, Kelvin, LowTemp, HighTemp, Step)
                end;                                          (*choice = 3*)
          4: begin
                write('Fahrenheit':20, 'Celsius':16, 'Kelvin':16);
                writeln; writeln;
                XRefTable(Fahrenheit,Kelvin,LowTemp,HighTemp,Step)
                end                                           (*choice = 4*)
          end                                                      (*case*)

      until 1 > 2                                           (*always false!*)
   end;                                                          (*driver*)
(*----------------------------------------------------------------*)
begin
   driver                                          (*activate driver proc.*)
end.
```

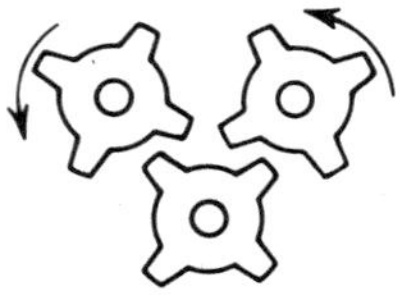

```
Enter low & high Fahrenheit temperatures: 32 34
Enter step:  .5
menu:
--->1 all four scales
--->2 Fahrenheit and Celsius, only
--->3 Celsius and Kelvin, only
--->4 Fahrenheit, Celsius, and Kelvin, only
Enter choice:  2

          Crossreference Temperature Table
             Fahrenheit              Celsius

             32.00000                0.00000

             32.50000                0.27778

             33.00000                0.55556

             33.50000                0.83333

             34.00000                1.11111

Enter low & high Fahrenheit temperatures: 32 34
Enter step:  .5
menu:
--->1 all four scales
--->2 Fahrenheit and Celsius, only
--->3 Celsius and Kelvin, only
--->4 Fahrenheit, Celsius, and Kelvin, only
Enter choice:  3
```

```
              Crossreference  Temperature  Table
                 Celsius                 Kelvin

                 0.00000             273.14999

                 0.27778             273.42776

                 0.55556             273.70554

                 0.83333             273.98334

                 1.11111             274.26111

Enter  low  &  high  Fahrenheit  temperatures:  32  34
Enter  step:   .5
menu:
--->1  all  four  scales
--->2  Fahrenheit  and  Celsius,  only
--->3  Celsius  and  Kelvin,  only
--->4  Fahrenheit,  Celsius,  and  Kelvin,  only
Enter  choice:   4

              Crossreference  Temperature  Table
                Fahrenheit                 Celsius                    Kelvin

                32.00000                0.00000                 273.14999

                32.50000                0.27778                 273.42776

                33.00000                0.55556                 273.70554

                33.50000                0.83333                 273.98334

                34.00000                1.11111                 274.26111

Enter  low  &  high  Fahrenheit  temperatures:
^Y
```

Chapter 5, Exercise 16

```
                                        (*Ref., Exercise 16, Chapter 5*)
                                         (*Pascal with Program Design*)

program e516 (input,output);

(*---------------------------------------------------------------*)

procedure BuildTable(FirstExponent, LastExponent :integer;
                     base : integer);
var
   power: real;
begin
   repeat
      power := Exp(FirstExponent * ln(base));
      writeln(power:16:0, FirstExponent, (1/power):20:10);
      FirstExponent := FirstExponent + 1
   until FirstExponent > LastExponent
end;                                                   (*BuildTable*)

(*---------------------------------------------------------------*)

procedure Header;
var
   i : integer;
begin
   writeln('Power':16,'Exponent':13,'Reciprocal':16);
   for i := 1 to 65 do write('-'); writeln
end;                                                       (*Header*)

(*---------------------------------------------------------------*)

procedure driver;
var
   Base, first, last : integer;
begin
   repeat
      write('Enter base,first and last exponents:   ');
      readln(base, first, last); writeln;
      Header;
      BuildTable(first, last, base);
      write('Again?   1=Y,0=N:    '); readln(base)
   until base <> 1
end;                                                       (*driver*)

(*---------------------------------------------------------------*)

begin
   driver
end.
```

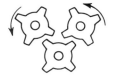

```
Enter base,first and last exponents:  2 0 15

                 Power         Exponent          Reciprocal
-------------------------------------------------------------------

                    1.             0          1.0000000000
                    2.             1          0.5000000000
                    4.             2          0.2500000000
                    8.             3          0.1250000000
                   16.             4          0.0625000000
                   32.             5          0.0312500000
                   64.             6          0.0156250000
                  128.             7          0.0078125000
                  256.             8          0.0039062500
                  512.             9          0.0019531250
                 1024.            10          0.0009765625
                 2048.            11          0.0004882813
                 4096.            12          0.0002441406
                 8192.            13          0.0001220703
                16384.            14          0.0000610352
                32768.            15          0.0000305176
Again?  1=Y,0=N:  1
Enter base,first and last exponents:  5 5 5

                 Power         Exponent          Reciprocal
-------------------------------------------------------------------
                 3125.             5          0.0003200000
Again?  1=Y,0=N:  1
Enter base,first and last exponents:  16 1 5

                 Power         Exponent          Reciprocal
-------------------------------------------------------------------
                   16.             1          0.0625000000
                  256.             2          0.0039062500
                 4096.             3          0.0002441406
                65536.             4          0.0000152588
              1048576.             5          0.0000009537
Again?  1+y,0+N:  0
```

Chapter 6, Exercise 7

```
                                         (*Ref., Exercise 7, Chapter 6;*)
                                         (*Pascal with Program Design*)

program e67(input, output);
const
   max = 500;                                 (*limit on array size*)
   empty = -1;                                           (*sentinel*)
type
   symbols = array[1..max] of integer;                 (*array type*)
```

```
(*--------------------------------------------------------------*)
                   (*Construct an array of elements of type char*)
procedure BuildArray(var info : symbols;             (*array param*)
                     var limit : integer);              (*list size*)
   begin
      limit := 0;
      repeat
         write(' ':10, 'Enter an integer--a -1, to stop:');
         limit := limit + 1;
         readln(info[limit])
      until (info[limit] = empty);
      limit := limit - 1                          (*a crucial step!*)
   end;                                              (*BuildArray*)
(*--------------------------------------------------------------*)
                                           (*draw line of hyphens*)
   procedure DrawLine;
   var
      hyphen : integer;
   begin
      writeln; for hyphen := 1 to 70 do write ('-'); writeln
   end;                                                (*DrawLine*)
(*--------------------------------------------------------------*)
                                                  (*Inspect array*)
   procedure InspectArray(info : symbols;             (*array param*)
                          max : integer);               (*extremes*)
   var
      min,space1, space2 : integer;
      count : integer;                                   (*counter*)
   begin
      space1 := 1;
      space2 := 1;
      repeat
         count := 1; min := space1 + space2;
         space1 := space2; space2 := min;
         writeln;
         writeln(' ':30, 'List elements:(interval of ',min:2,' )');
         DrawLine;                              (*activate DrawLine*)
         repeat
            write(info[min]:5);
            if (count mod 8) = 0 then writeln;
            count := count + 1;
            min := min + space2
         until min > max;
         DrawLine; writeln;
      until space2 >= 5;
      DrawLine
   end;                                              (*InspectArray*)

(*--------------------------------------------------------------*)
      (*Procedure to calculate and print average component value*)
   procedure Average(info : symbols;                  (*array param*)
                     max : integer);                     (*extremes*)
```

```
  var
     sum : integer;                          (*sum of array components*)
     min : integer;                                         (*counter*)
     ave : real;                            (*average component value*)
  begin
     min := 1; sum := 0;
     while min <= max do begin
        sum : sum + info[min];
        min := min + 1
        end;                                                  (*while*)
     ave := sum/max;                              (*calculate average*)
     writeln;
     writeln('The average component value is: ',ave:16:5);
     DrawLine
  end;                                                      (*Average*)

(*----------------------------------------------------------------*)
                (*Procedure to find smallest and largest elements*)
  procedure Find(info : symbols; max : integer;
                 var smallest, largest : integer);
  var
     min : integer;                                         (*counter*)
  begin
     smallest := info[1]; largest := info[1];     (*initialize values*)
     min := 2;
     while min <= max do begin
        if info[min] < smallest then smallest := info[min];
        if info[min] > largest then largest := info[min];
        min := min + 1
        end;                                                  (*while*)
     DrawLine;
     writeln('The smallest component value was: ', smallest:5);
     writeln('The largest component value was: ', largest:5);
     drawline; writeln;
  end;                                                         (*Find*)

(*----------------------------------------------------------------*)
                                      (*Calculates geometric mean*)
  procedure FindMean(info : symbols; max : integer;
                     var mean : real);
  var
     min : integer;
begin
     min := 1; mean := 1;
     while min <= max do begin
     mean := mean * exp(1/max * ln(info[min]));
        min := min + 1
        end;
     DrawLine;
     writeln('The geometric mean is ',mean:16:6);
     DrawLine; writeln;
  end;                                                         (*Mean*)
```

```
(*------------------------------------------------------------------*)
                    (*procedure to print range of components*)
  procedure Findrange(info : symbols; max : integer;
                       lowest, highest : integer);
  var
    range : integer;
  begin
    range := highest - lowest;
    DrawLine;
    writeln('The range is ',range:5);
    DrawLine; writeln
  end;                                               (*FindRange*)

(*------------------------------------------------------------------*)
                                    (*Finds standard deviation*)
  procedure FindDeviation(info : symbols; max : integer;
                          mean : real);
  var
    sum : real;
    standard : real;
    min : integer;
    difference : real;
  begin
    min := 1; sum := 0;
    while min <= max do begin
      difference := info[min] - mean;
      if difference < 0 then difference := -1/difference;
      sum := sum + exp(2 * ln(difference));
      min := min + 1
      end;                                              (*while*)
    standard := exp(1/2 * ln(sum/(max - 1)));
    DrawLine;
    writeln('The Standard Deviation is ', standard:16:6);
    DrawLine; writeln
  end;                                          (*FindDeviation*)

(*------------------------------------------------------------------*)
         (*Program manager : get values & activate procedure*)
  procedure driver;
  var
    quote : symbols;                          (*array variable*)
    length : integer;                             (*array size*)
    choice : integer;                       (*control variable*)
    high, low : integer;        (*highest & lowest components*)
    geometric : real;                         (*geometric mean*)
  begin
    repeat
      BuildArray(quote, length);               (*activate proc.*)
      InspectArray(quote, length);             (*print elements*)
      Average(quote,length);                    (*print average*)
      Find(quote, length, low, high);
                            (*Find smallest & largest components*)
      FindMean(quote, length, geometric):
                                     (*calculate geometric mean*)
```

```
      FindRange(quote, length, low, high);          (*find range*)
      FindDeviation(quote, length, geometric);
                                   (*finds standard deviation*)
      write(' ':10, 'Again?--1+Y, 0=N: ');readln(choice);writeln
    until choice = 0
  end;                                                (*driver*)
(*-------------------------------------------------------------*)
begin
  driver                                   (*activate driver proc.*)
end.
```

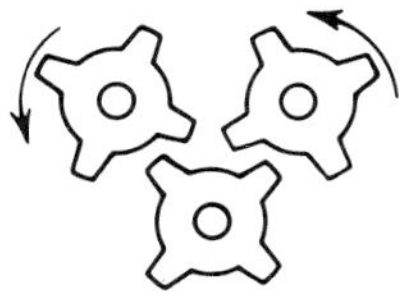

```
          Enter an integer--a —1, to stop:1
          Enter an integer--a —1, to stop:2
          Enter an integer--a —1, to stop:3
          Enter an integer--a —1, to stop:4
          Enter an integer--a —1, to stop:5
          Enter an integer--a —1, to stop:6
          Enter an integer--a —1, to stop:7
          Enter an integer--a —1, to stop:8
          Enter an integer--a —1, to stop:9
          Enter an integer--a —1, to stop:10
          Enter an integer--a —1, to stop:11
          Enter an integer--a —1, to stop:12
          Enter an integer--a —1, to stop:13
          Enter an integer--a —1, to stop:14
          Enter an integer--a —1, to stop:15
          Enter an integer--a —1, to stop:16
          Enter an integer--a —1, to stop:17
          Enter an integer--a —1, to stop:18
          Enter an integer--a —1, to stop:19
          Enter an integer--a —1, to stop:20
          Enter an integer--a —1, to stop:—1

                              List elements:(interval of   2 )

---------------------------------------------------------------
    2    4    6    8   10   12   14   16
   18   20
---------------------------------------------------------------
                              List elements:(interval of   3 )

---------------------------------------------------------------
    3    6    9   12   15   18
---------------------------------------------------------------
                              List elements:(interval of   5 )

---------------------------------------------------------------
    5   10   15   20
---------------------------------------------------------------


---------------------------------------------------------------

The average component value is:          10.50000

---------------------------------------------------------------
```

```
-------------------------------------------------------------------
The smallest component value was:       1
The largest component value was:      20

-------------------------------------------------------------------

-------------------------------------------------------------------
The geometric mean is              8,304360

-------------------------------------------------------------------

-------------------------------------------------------------------
The range is      19

-------------------------------------------------------------------

-------------------------------------------------------------------
The Standard Deviation is              5.691303

-------------------------------------------------------------------

             Again?--1=Y, 0=N: 0
```

Chapter 6, Exercise 3

```
                                        (*Exercise 3, Section 6.19.4*)
                                       (*Pascal with Program Design*)
```

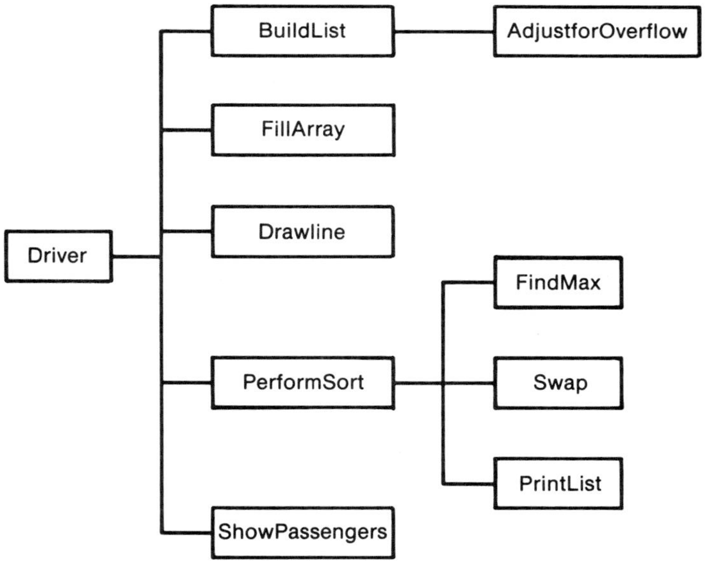

Chapter 7, Exercise 11

```
                                            (*Exercise 11, Section 7.18;*)
                                            (*Pascal with Program Design*)

program e711(input,output);
const
   max = 500;                        (*maximum number of characters*)
                                                       (*in a script*)
type
   string = array [1..max] of char;     (*note: not packed array,*)
                                           (*this is our script type*)
(*--------------------------------------------------------------*)
                                                (*scantext function*)
function scantext(script : string; target : char;
                  LastChar : char) : integer;
   var
      i,j : integer;
   begin                                                 (*function*)
   i := 1; j := 0;
   while (script[i] <> LastChar) do
      begin                                                  (*loop*)
         if (script[i] = target) then j := j + 1;
         i := i + 1
      end;                                                   (*loop*)
   scantext := j
end;                                                     (*function*)
(*--------------------------------------------------------------*)
procedure wordprocessor(var text : string);
var
   target, TextEnd : char;
   i : integer;                                (*i is local counter*)
begin                                               (*wordprocessor*)
   i := 0;                                             (*initialize*)
   if text[1] <> '?' then begin
      write('Use same text again? 1=Y,0=N: ');
      readln(i)
      end;
   writeln;
   if i = 0 then begin
      write('Enter eotxt char: ');         (*obtain eotxt character*)
      readln(TextEnd);
      writeln; writeln;
      writeln('Enter text:');                     (*prompt for text*)
      repeat                             (*read in one character at a*)
         i := i + 1;                      (*time until end of array is*)
         read(text[i])                       (*reached or eotxt found*)
      until (i = max) or (text[i] = TextEnd);
      readln                                   (*clear input buffer*)
      end;                                                     (*if*)
   writeln; writeln;
   write('Enter target: ');             (*prompt for target character*)
```

```
   readln(target);
   writeln; writeln;
   write('The target ', target ,' appears ');                    (*output*)
   writeln(scantext(text,target,TextEnd ),' times in the text.')
end;                                                      (*wordprocessor*)
(*-----------------------------------------------------------------*)
procedure driver;
   var
      ans : integer;                                (*answer to "again ?"*)
      MainText : string;
   begin                                                         (*driver*)
      MainText[1] := '?';
      repeat
         wordprocessor(Maintext);
         write ('Again?--1=Y,0=N: ');
         readln(ans)
      until ans <> 1
   end;                                                          (*driver*)
(*-----------------------------------------------------------------*)
begin                                                      (*main program*)
      driver
end.
```

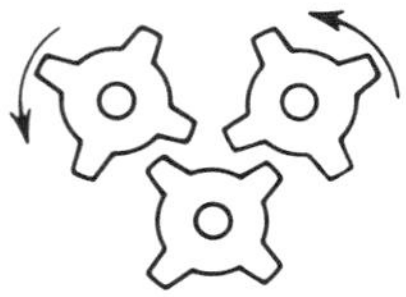

```
Enter eotxt char: *


Enter text:
     The essential methodology for data abstraction is known
as information hiding.   This approach was first proposed
by D.L. Parnas in 1972....  He proposed that the behavior
of software modules be specified completely in terms of
their external effects. Such a module hides a secret,
namely the representation of the data object that the
module manages.*


Enter target: d


The target d appears          11 times in the text.
Again?--1=Y,0=N: 1
Use same text again? 1=Y,0=N: 0

Enter eotxt char: *


Enter text:
     Old Tom in summertime walked about the meadows gathering
the buttercups, running after shadows, tickling the
bumblebees that buzzed among the flowers, sitting by the
waterside for hours upon hours.   There his beard dangled
long down into the water: up came Goldberry, the
River-woman's daughter; pulled Tom's hanging hair.    In he
```

```
went a-wallowing under the water-lilies, bubbling and
a-swallowing.*


Enter target: a


The target a appears        23 times in the text.
Again?--1=Y,0=N: 1
Use same text again? 1=Y,0=N: 1


Enter target:


The target   appears        66 times in the text.
Again?--1=Y,0=N: 1
Use same text again? 1=Y,0=N: 1


Enter target: i


The target i appears        19 times in the text.
Again?--1=Y,0=N: 0
```

Chapter 7, Exercise 18

```
                                        (*Exercise 18, Section 7.18;*)
                                        (*Pascal with Program Design*)

program e718(input,output);
type
   roll = array[1..2] of integer;
(*------------------------------------------------------------------*)
function craps(var seed : real) : integer;
begin
   seed := sqr(seed + 3.1415926535);
   seed := seed - trunc(seed);
   craps := trunc(seed *6) + 1
end;                                                         (*Rnd*)
(*------------------------------------------------------------------*)
procedure PrintDie(turn : roll);
var
   i : integer;
begin
   writeln(' ':5,'_________',' ':5,'_________');
   writeln(' ':5,'|        |',' ':5,'|        |');
   for i := 1 to 2 do
      case turn[i] of
           1: write(' ':5, '|        |');
         2,3: write(' ':5, '|     *  |');
       4,5,6: write(' ':5, '| *   *  |')
      end;                                                  (*case*)
```

```
   writeln;
   for i := 1 to 2 do
      case turn[i] of
      1,3,5: write(' ':5, '|    *    |');
        2,4: write(' ':5, '|         |');
          6: write(' ':5, '| *     * |')
         end;
   writeln;
   for i := 1 to 2 do
      case turn[i] of
          1: write(' ':5, '|         |');
        2,3: write(' ':5, '| *       |');
      4,5,6: write(' ':5, '| *     * |')
      end;
   writeln;
   writeln(' ':5, '|_________|', ' ':5, '|_________|');
   writeln; writeln;
end;                                                          (*PrintDie*)
(*---------------------------------------------------------------------*)
procedure driver;
var
   maxrolls: integer;
   seed    : real;
   dice    : roll;
   ans, sum, point : integer;
begin                                                           (*driver*)
   write('Enter a seed: '); readln(seed);
   writeln;
   repeat
      dice[1] := craps(seed); dice[2] := craps(seed);
      PrintDie(dice);
      case dice[1] + dice[2] of
         7,11: writeln('You win!!!');
      2,3,12: writeln('You Lose.');
      1,4,5,6,8,9,10: begin
                         point := dice[1] + dice[2];
                         writeln('Your point is ',point:3);
                         repeat
                            write('Enter a <return> to roll: ');
                            readln;
                            dice[1] := craps(seed);
                            dice[2] := craps(seed);
                            PrintDie(dice);
                            sum := dice[1] + dice[2];
                            if sum = 7 then writeln('You lose.');
                            if sum = point then writeln('You win!!')
                      until (sum = 7) or (sum = point)
                      end
         end;                                                     (*case*)
      write('Again? 1=Y,0=N: ');
      readln(ans); writeln
   until ans <> 1
end;                                                            (*driver*)
```

```
(*---------------------------------------------------------------------*)
begin                                                              (*main*)
   driver
end.
```

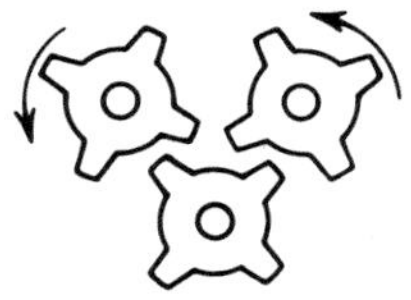

```
Enter a seed: 2.71828

*********    *********
*     * *    *       *
*   *   *    *   *   *
* *     *    *       *
*********    *********

Your point is    4
Enter a <return> to roll:

*********    *********
* *   * *    * *   * *
*       *    *   *   *
* *   * *    * *   * *
*********    *********

Enter a <return> to roll:

*********    *********
* *   * *    *     * *
* *   * *    *       *
* *   * *    * *     *
*********    *********

Enter a <return> to roll:

*********    *********
*       *    *       *
*   *   *    *   *   *
*       *    *       *
*********    *********

Enter a <return> to roll:

*********    *********
*     * *    * *   * *
*       *    *   *   *
* *     *    * *   * *
*********    *********
You lose.
Again? 1=Y,0=N: 1

*********    *********
* *   * *    * *   * *
*   *   *    *   *   *
* *   * *    * *   * *
*********    *********
Your point is   10
Enter a <return> to roll:

*********    *********
* *   * *    * *   * *
* *   * *    *       *
* *   * *    * *   * *
*********    *********
```

```
You win!!
Again? 1=Y,0=N: 1

*********    *********
*     * *    * *   * *
*       *    *   *   *
* *     *    * *   * *
*********    *********

You Win!!!
Again? 1=Y,0=N: 1

*********    *********
* *   * *    * *   * *
*       *    *       *
* *   * *    * *   * *
*********    *********

Your point is     8
Enter a <return> to roll:

*********    *********
*     * *    *     * *
*   *   *    *       *
* *     *    * *     *
*********    *********

Enter a <return> to roll:

*********    *********
*     * *    * *   * *
*   *   *    *       *
* *     *    * *   * *
*********    *********

You lose.
Again? 1=Y,0=N: 0
```

Chapter 7, Exercise 2

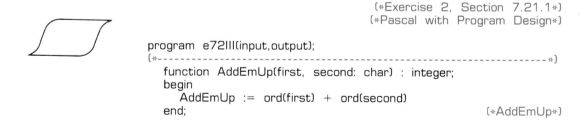

```
                                        (*Exercise 2, Section 7.21.1*)
                                        (*Pascal with Program Design*)

program e72III(input,output);
(*---------------------------------------------------------------*)
   function AddEmUp(first, second: char) : integer;
   begin
      AddEmUp := ord(first) + ord(second)
   end;                                              (*AddEmUp*)
```

```
(*-----------------------------------------------------------------*)
   function CheckChar(letter : char): boolean;
   var
      n : integer;
      int1, int2, int3, int4 : boolean;          (*allowable intervals*)
   begin
      n := ord(letter);
      int1 := (31 < n) and (n < 48);
      int2 := (57 < n) and (n < 65);
      int3 := (90 < n) and (n < 97);
      int4 := (121 < n);
      if int1 or int2 or int3 or int4 then CheckChar := true
      else begin
         writeln('UnAcceptable character.');
         CheckChar := false
         end
end;                                                    (*CheckChar*)
(*-----------------------------------------------------------------*)
   procedure Driver;
   var
      MyFirst, MySecond, YourFirst, YourSecond : char;
      MySum, YourSum : integer;
   begin
      repeat
         writeln('Allowable character are symbols.');
         write('Letter,numbers and control characters ');
         writeln('are not valid input.');
         writeln;
         repeat
            write('Enter two symbols; MyFirst, MySecond: ');
            readln(MyFirst, MySecond);
         until CheckChar(MyFirst) and CheckChar(MySecond);
         repeat
            write('Enter second set of symbols:');
            write('YourFirst, YourSecond: ');
            readln(YourFirst, YourSecond);
         until CheckChar(YourFirst) and CheckChar(YourSecond);
         writeln; writeln;
         MySum := AddEmUp(MyFirst, MySecond);
         YourSum := AddEmUp(YourFirst, YourSecond);
         if MySum < YourSum then writeln('You win!!')
            else
               if MySum > YourSum then writeln('I win!')
                  else writeln('It is a tie!!')
      until 1 > 2
   end;                                                   (*driver*)
(*-----------------------------------------------------------------*)
   begin
      driver
   end.
```

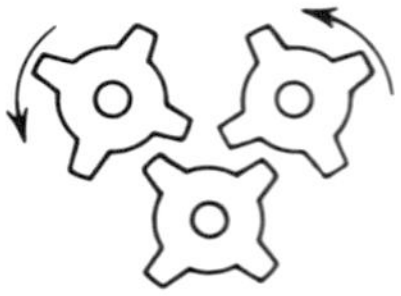

```
Allowable character are symbols.
Letter,numbers and control characters are not valid input.

Enter two symbols; MyFirst, MySecond: dd
UnAcceptable character.
Enter two symbols; MyFirst, MySecond: 33
UnAcceptable character.
Enter two symbols; MyFirst, MySecond: ^G^H
UnAcceptable character.
Enter two symbols; MyFirst, MySecond: $%
Enter second set of symbols:YourFirst, YourSecond: '\


You win!!
Allowable character are symbols.
Letter,numbers and control characters are not valid input.

Enter two symbols; MyFirst, MySecond: $%
Enter second set of symbols:YourFirst, YourSecond: '"


It is a tie!!
Allowable character are symbols.
Letter,numbers and control characters are not valid input.

Enter two symbols; MyFirst, MySecond: -_
Enter second set of symbols:YourFirst, YourSecond: =+


I win!
Allowable character are symbols.
Letter,numbers and control characters are not valid input.

Enter two symbols; MyFirst, MySecond: ^C
```

Chapter 8, Exercise 24

```
                                        (*Exercise 24, Section 8.12;*)
                                        (*Pascal with Program Design*)

program e824(input,output);
const
  max = 500;                        (*maximum number of characters*)
                                                      (*in a script*)
  max2 = 10;
type
  vowels = set of char;
  string = array [1..max] of char;
  paragraph = array[1..max2] of string;
  numbers = array[1..max2] of integer;
```

```
(*-----------------------------------------------------------------*)
procedure showresults(word : paragraph; frequency : numbers;
                      limit : integer);
var
   i, count, j, spaces : integer;
begin
   writeln('First five words':28, 'Frequency':18);
   writeln('in entered text':27,' ':10,'in text':8);
   for i := 1 to 65 do write('—'); writeln;
   for i := 1 to limit do begin
      write(' ':5);
      j := 1;
      while word[i,j] = ' ' do
         j := j + 1;                          (*ignore leading spaces*)
      spaces := 0;
      while spaces < 5 do begin
         write(word[i,j]);
         j := j + 1;
         if word[i,j] = ' ' then spaces := spaces + 1
         end;
      while j < 40 do begin
         write(' ':1);
         j := j + 1
         end;
      writeln(frequency[i]:3);
                                                         (*for*)
      end
                                                 (*showresults*)
end;
(*-----------------------------------------------------------------*)
procedure TextScanner(var count : integer;
                      var text : string;
                      targets : vowels;
                      sentinel : char);
var
   i := 0; count := 0;
   writeln('Enter text: ');
   repeat
      i := i + 1;
      read(text[i]);
      if text[i] in targets then count := count + 1
   until text[i] = sentinel
end;                                             (*TextScanner*)
(*-----------------------------------------------------------------*)
procedure driver;
   var
      frequency : numbers;
      j, i, ans : integer;
      maintext : paragraph;
      textend : char;
      maintargets : vowels;
                                                      (*driver*)
   begin
      i := 0;
      maintargets:= ['a', 'e', 'i', 'o', 'u',
                     'A', 'E', 'I', 'O', 'U'];
```

```
      repeat
         i := i + 1;
         write('Enter eotxt char: ');          (*obtain eotxt character*)
         readln(textend);
         writeln;
         TextScanner(frequency[i],maintext[i],maintargets,textend);
         write('Again?--1=Y,0=N: ');
         readln(ans)
      until ans <> 1;
      showresults(maintext, frequency, i)
   end;                                                          (*driver*)
(*-----------------------------------------------------------------*)
begin                                                    (*main program*)
   driver
end.
```

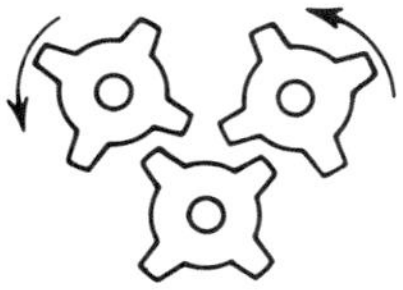

```
Enter eotxt char: *

Enter text:
        'We're going through!'   The Commander's voice was like
thin ice breaking.   He wore his full-dress uniform,
with the heavily braided white cap pulled down rakishly
over one cold gray eye.   'We can't make it, sir.   It's
spoiling for a hurricane,   if you ask me.'   'I'm not
asking you, Lieutenant Berg,' said the Commander.
'Throw on the power lights!   Rev her up to 8,5000!
We're going through!'   The pounding of the cylinders
increased:   ta-pocketa-pocketa-pocketa-pocketa-pocketa.*
Again?--1=Y,0=N: 1
Enter eotxt char: *

Enter text:
        Old Tom in summertime walked about the meadows gathering
the buttercups, running after shadows, tickling the
bumblebees that buzzed among the flowers, sitting by the
waterside for hours upon hours.   There his beard dangled
long down into the water: up came Goldberry, the
River-woman's daughter; pulled Tom's hanging hair.   In he
went a-wallowing under the water-lilies, bubbling and
a-swallowing.*
Again?--1=Y,0=N: 0
                    First five words            Frequency
                    in entered text              in text
--------------------------------------------------------------
      'We're going through!;                     138
      Old Tom in summertime walked               114
```

Chapter 8, Exercise 1

```
                                               (*Exercise 1, Section 8.15.3*)
                                               (*Pascal with Program Design*)
program e8liii(input, output);
type
  alfa = packed array[1..35] of char;
  salary = record
    name : alfa;
    earnings : real;
    case payschedule : integer of
      1 : (wage, hours, OverTime, OverTimeWage: real);
      2 : (commission, sales : real);
      3 : ( );
      4 : (rate, time, tips : real);
      5 : ( );
      6 : ( );
      7 : (MonthlySalary, MeritPay : real);
      8 : (FixedSalary, commiss, sold : real);
  end;                                                            (*salary*)
(*------------------------------------------------------------------*)
procedure BuildRecord (var sample : salary);
begin
  writeln(' ':10, 'menu:');
  writeln(' ':20, '--> 1. Hourly Wage with Over Time');
  writeln(' ':20, '--> 2. Salary Based on Commission');
  write(' ':20, '--> 3. Retirement benefits package');
  writeln(' future)');
  writeln (' ':20, '--> 4. Hourly wage plus tips');
  writeln (' ':20, '--> 5. Social Security Benefits (future)');
  writeln (' ':20, '--> 6. Medical Benefits Package (future)');
  writeln (' ':20, '--> 7. Administrator');
  writeln (' ':20, '--> 8. Ring Sales Person');
  writeln;
  write ('Enter Choice: '); readln (sample.PaySchedule);
  writeln;
  with sample do
    case PaySchedule of
      1 : begin
            write('Your Hourly Wage:   '); readln(wage);writeln;
            write('Hours Worked:   '); readln(hours); writeln;
            write('OverTime worked:   '); readln(OverTime);
            writeln;
            if OverTime = 0 then OverTimeWage := 0
            else begin
              write('OverTime wage:   '); readln(OverTimeWage);
              writeln
              end
            end;
      2 : begin
            write('Commission rate as a percent:   ');
            readln(commission); writeln;
            write('Amount Sold:   '); readln(sales); writeln
          end;
```

```
            3 : writeln;
            4 : begin
                  write('Hourly Wage:   '); readln(rate); writeln;
                  write('Hours worked:   '); readln(time); writeln;
                  write('Tips received:   '); readln(tips); writeln
                end;
            5 : writeln;
            6 : writeln;
            7 : begin
                  write('Fixed Monthly Salary:   ');
                  readln(MonthlySalary); writeln;
                  write('merit pay:   '); readln(MeritPay); writeln
                end;
            8 : begin
                  write('Fixed Monthly Salary:   ');
                  readln(FixedSalary); writeln;
                  write('Commission:   '); readln(commiss); writeln;
                  write('Sales:   '); readln(sold); writeln
                end;
        end;
        with sample do
          case PaySchedule of
            1 : earnings := wage * hours + OverTime * OverTimeWage;
            2 : earnings := commission / 100 * sales;
            3 : writeln;
            4 : earnings := rate * time + tips;
            5 : writeln;
            6 : writeln;
            7 : earnings := MonthlySalary + MeritPay;
            8 : earnings := FixedSalary + commission / 100 * sales
          end
    end;
    (*---------------------------------------------------------------*)
    procedure ShowRecord (sample : salary);
    begin
      with sample do
        case PaySchedule of
          1 : begin
                write('You have earned   ', sample.earnings:5:2);
                writeln(' dollars')
              end;
          2 : begin
                write('You have earned   ', sample.earnings:5:2);
                writeln(' dollars')
              end;
          3 : begin
                write('Retirement benefits package not yet ');
                writeln('available.')
              end;
          4 : begin
                write('You have earned   ', sample.earnings:5:2);
                writeln(' dollars')
              end;
```

```
        5 : begin
               write('Social Security benefits package not yet ');
               writeln('available.')
            end;
        6 : begin
               write('Medical Benefits package not yet ');
               writeln('available.')
            end;
        7 : begin
               write('You have earned   ', sample.earnings:5:2);
               writeln(' dollars')
            end;
        8 : begin
               write('You have earned   ', sample.earnings:5:2);
               writeln(' dollars')
            end
    end
end;
(*---------------------------------------------------------------*)
procedure driver;
var
   employee : salary;
   choice : integer;
begin
   repeat
      BuildRecord(employee);
      ShowRecord(employee);
      writeln;
      write('again?--1=Y, 0=N '); readln(choice);writeln
   until (choice = 0)
end;
(*---------------------------------------------------------------*)
begin
   driver
end.
```

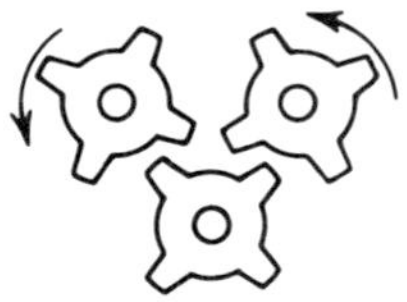

```
          menu:
                         --> 1. Hourly Wage with Over Time
                         --> 2. Salary Based on Commission
                         --> 3. Retirement benefits package (future)
                         --> 4. Hourly wage plus tips
                         --> 5. Social Security Benefits (future)
                         --> 6. Medical Benefits Package (future)
                         --> 7. Administrator
                         --> 8. Ring Sales Person

Enter Choice: 7

Fixed Monthly Salary:  2000

merit pay:  500

You have earned  2500.00 dollars

again? -- 1=Y, 0=N 1
```

```
                menu:
                         --> 1. Hourly Wage with Over Time
                         --> 2. Salary Based on Commission
                         --> 3. Retirement benefits package (future)
                         --> 4. Hourly wage plus tips
                         --> 5. Social Security Benefits (future)
                         --> 6. Medical Benefits Package (future)
                         --> 7. Administrator
                         --> 8. Ring Sales Person

Enter Choice: 8

Fixed Monthly Salary:  1000

Commission:  500

Sales:  2000

You have earned  6000.00 dollars

again? -- 1=Y, 0=N 0
```

Chapter 8, Exercise 26

```
                                          (*Exercise 26, Section 8.12;*)
                                         (*Pascal with Program Design*)
program e826(output);
type
   numbertype = 0..9;
   lettertype = 'A'..'z';
   numbers = set of numbertype;
   letters = set of lettertype;
(*-----------------------------------------------------------------*)
procedure DrawLine;
var
   i : integer;
begin
   for i := 1 to 65 do write('-');
   writeln
end;                                                      (*DrawLine*)
(*-----------------------------------------------------------------*)
procedure ShowNumberSet(digits : numbers);
var
   no : numbertype;
   first : boolean;
begin
   first := true;
   writeln('Results in the following set:'); writeln;
   write(' [':10);
```

```
   for no := 0 to 9 do
      if no in digits then
         if first then begin
            write(no:1);
            first := false
            end
         else write(',', no:1);
   writeln(']');
   DrawLine;
   writeln;
end;                                                       (*ShowNumberSet*)
(*-----------------------------------------------------------------------*)
procedure ShowLetterSet(characters : letters);
var
   ch : lettertype;
   first : boolean;
begin
   first := true;
   writeln('Results in the following set:'); writeln;
   write(' [':10);
   for ch := 'A' to 'z' do
      if ch in characters then
         if first then begin
            write(ch:1);
            first := false
            end
         else write(',', ch:1);
   writeln(']');
   DrawLine;
   writeln;
end;                                                       (*ShowLetterSet*)
(*-----------------------------------------------------------------------*)
procedure driver;
begin
   DrawLine;
   writeln;

   writeln('The intersection of [5, 6, 8] * [1, 2]');                  (*a*)
   ShowNumberSet([5, 6, 8] * [1, 2]);

   writeln('The intersection of [5, 6, 8] * [0..6]');                  (*b*)
   ShowNumberSet([5, 6, 8] * [0..6]);

   writeln('The union of [5, 6, 8] + [1, 2]');                         (*c*)
   ShowNumberSet([5, 6, 8] + [1, 2]);

   writeln('The union of [5, 6, 8] + [0..6]');                         (*d*)
   ShowNumberSet([5, 6, 8] + [0..6]);

   writeln('The intersection of [a..t] * [A..T]');                     (*e*)
   ShowLetterSet(['a'..'t'] * ['A'..'T']);

   writeln('The union of [a..t] + [A..T]');                            (*f*)
   ShowLetterSet(['a'..'t'] + ['A'..'T']);
```

```
    writeln('The intersection of [a..t] * [d..t]');                 (*g*)
    ShowLetterSet(['a'..'t'] * ['d'..'t']);

    writeln('The intersection of [a..t] * [ ]');                    (*h*)
    ShowLetterSet("'a'..'t'] * [ ]);

    writeln('The union of [a..t] + [ ]');                           (*i*)
    ShowLetterSet(['a'..'t'] + [ ]);

    writeln('The difference of [a..t] - [ ]');                      (*j*)
    ShowLetterSet(['a'..'t'] - [ ]);

    writeln('The difference of [5, 6, 7] - [1, 5]');                (*k*)
    ShowNumberSet([5, 6, 7] - [1, 5]);
    writeln('The difference of [5, 6, 7] - [0..9]');                (*l*)
    ShowNumberSet([5, 6, 7] - [0..9]);

    writeln('The difference of [a..t] - [A..T]');                   (*m*)
    ShowLetterSet(['a'..'t'] - ['A'..'T'])
end;
(*--------------------------------------------------------------------*)
begin
    driver
end.
```

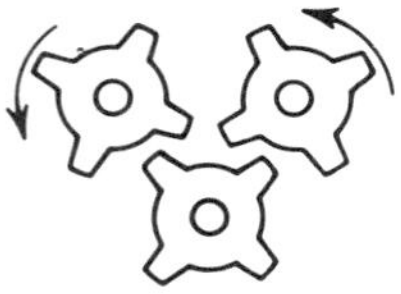

```
------------------------------------------------------------------

The intersection of [5, 6, 8] * [1, 2]
Results in the following set:

            [ ]
------------------------------------------------------------------

The intersection of [5, 6, 8] * [0..6]
Results in the following set:

            [5,6]
------------------------------------------------------------------

The union of [5, 6, 8] + [1, 2]
Results in the following set:

            [1,2,5,6,8]
------------------------------------------------------------------

The union of [5, 6, 8] + [0..6]
Results in the following set:

            [0,1,2,3,4,5,6,8]
------------------------------------------------------------------
```

```
The intersection of [a..t] * [A..T]
Results in the following set:

        [ ]
---------------------------------------------------------------

The union of [a..t] + [A..T]
Results in the following set:

        [A,B,C,D,E,F,G,H,I,J,K,L,M,N,O,P,Q,R,S,T,a,b,c,d,e,f,g,
h,i,j,k,l,m,n,o,p,q,r,s,t]
---------------------------------------------------------------

The intersection of [a..t] * [d..t]
Results in the following set:

        [d,e,f,g,h,i,j,k,l,m,n,o,p,q,r,s,t]
---------------------------------------------------------------

The intersection of [a..t] * [ ]
Results in the following set:

        [ ]
---------------------------------------------------------------

The union of [a..t] + [ ]
Results in the following set:

        [a,b,c,d,e,f,g,h,i,j,k,l,m,n,o,p,q,r,s,t]
---------------------------------------------------------------

The difference of [a..t] - [ ]
Results in the following sets:

        [a,b,c,d,e,f,g,h,i,j,k,l,m,n,o,p,q,r,s,t]
---------------------------------------------------------------

The difference of [5, 6, 7] - [1, 5]
Results in the following set:

        [6,7]
---------------------------------------------------------------

The difference of [5, 6, 7] - [0..9]
Results in the following set:

        [ ]
---------------------------------------------------------------

The difference of [a..t] - [A..T]
Results in the following set:

        [a,b,c,d,e,f,g,h,i,j,k,l,m,n,o,p,q,r,s,t]
---------------------------------------------------------------
```

Chapter 9, Exercise 1

```
                                    (*Exercise 1, Section 9.19.2*)
                                    (*Pascal with Program Design*)

program merge(input, output, a, b, NewBook);
const
   sentinel = 'xxxxxyyyyy';         (*used to mark logical end-of-file*)
type
   name = packed array[1..10] of char;
   BlackBook = file of name;                (*user-defined file type*)
var
   a, b, NewBook: BlackBook;              (*three file type variables*)

(*--------------------------------------------------------------*)
   procedure CreateFile;
   var
      list : BlackBook;
      filename : name;
   begin
      write('Enter File Name:   '); readln(filename);
      rewrite(list, filename);
      repeat
         write(' ':5,'Enter name a --->xxxxxyyyyy to stop: ');
         readln(filename);
         write(list, filename)
      until filename = sentinel
   end;                                                  (*CreateFile*)
(*--------------------------------------------------------------*)
   procedure MergeFiles(var a, b, NewBook : BlackBook;
                            fname1, fname2: name);
   begin
      reset(a, fname1); reset(b, fname2);
      rewrite(NewBook, 'fold.dat');
      write (a^ <> sentinel) and (b^ <> sentinel) do
         if a^ <= b^
         then begin
            write(newBook, a^);
            get(a)
            end
         else begin
            write(NewBook, b^);
            get(b)
            end;
      while a^ <> sentinel do
         begin
            write(NewBook, a^); get(a)
         end;
      while b^ <> sentinel do
         begin
            write(NewBook, b^); get(b)
         end;
      write(NewBook, sentinel)
   end;                                                  (*MergeFiles*)
```

```
(*-----------------------------------------------------------------*)
  procedure ShowMergedFiles(var NewBook: BlackBook);
  begin
    reset(NewBook, 'fold.dat');
    while NewBook^ <> sentinel do
      begin
        writeln(NewBook^ : 40); get(NewBook)
      end
  end;                                          (*ShowMergedFiles*)
(*-----------------------------------------------------------------*)
  procedure BuildCopy(var a,b :BlackBook);
  begin
    rewrite(a, 'copy.dat'); reset(b, 'fold.dat');
    repeat
      write(a, b^);
      get(b)
    until b^ = sentinel;
    write(a,b^)
  end;                                          (*BuildCopy*)
(*-----------------------------------------------------------------*)
  procedure driver;
  var
    file1, file2, merged : BlackBook;
    filename1, filename2 : name;
    changed : boolean;
    ans : integer;
  begin
    repeat
      writeln(' ':10, 'Menu');
      writeln(' ':10, '-->1 Create an ordered file.');
      writeln(' ':10, '-->2 Merge files');
      writeln(' ':10, '-->3 Exit');
      write(' ':5,'Enter choice:  '); readln(ans);
      writeln; writeln;
      case ans of
        1: CreateFile;
        2: begin
             write(' ':5, 'Enter file name to merge: ');
             readln(filename1);
             changed := false;
             repeat
               write(' ':5,'Enter next file to merge: ');
               readln(filename2);
               MergeFiles(file1, file2, Merged,
                       filename1, filename2);
               if not changed then begin
                 close(file1);
                 filename1 := 'copy.dat   ';
                 BuildCopy(file1, Merged);
                 changed := true
                 end;
               close(file2);
               write(' ':5,'Again?  1=Y,0=N: ');
               readln(ans); writeln; writeln;
```

```
                until ans <> 1;
                ShowMergedFiles(merged)
                end;
            3:
            end                                                     (*case*)
         until ans = 3
      end;                                                          (*driver*)
(*------------------------------------------------------------------------*)
   begin
      driver
   end.
```

```
              Menu
              -->1 Create an ordered file.
              -->2 Merge files
              -->3 Exit
        Enter choice:  1

Enter File Name:  first.dat
        Enter name a --->xxxxxyyyyy to stop: andy
        Enter name a --->xxxxxyyyyy to stop: amy
        Enter name a --->xxxxxyyyyy to stop: arthur
        Enter name a --->xxxxxyyyyy to stop: susu
        Enter name a --->xxxxxyyyyy to stop: tim
        Enter name a --->xxxxxyyyyy to stop: xxxxxyyyyy
              Menu
              -->1 Create an ordered file.
              -->2 Merge files
              -->3 Exit
        Enter choice:  1

Enter File Name:  second.dat
        Enter name a --->xxxxxyyyyy to stop: enoch
        Enter name a --->xxxxxyyyyy to stop: malachi
        Enter name a --->xxxxxyyyyy to stop: sly
        Enter name a --->xxxxxyyyyy to stop: titus
        Enter name a --->xxxxxyyyyy to stop: valery
        Enter name a --->xxxxxyyyyy to stop: william
        Enter name a --->xxxxxyyyyy to stop: xxxxxyyyyy
              Menu
              -->1 Create an ordered file.
              -->2 Merge files
              -->3 Exit
        Enter choice:  1

Enter File Name:  third.dat
        Enter name a --->xxxxxyyyyy to stop: george
        Enter name a --->xxxxxyyyyy to stop: laura
        Enter name a --->xxxxxyyyyy to stop: paul
        Enter name a --->xxxxxyyyyy to stop: rox
        Enter name a --->xxxxxyyyyy to stop: sarah
        Enter name a --->xxxxxyyyyy to stop: scott
        Enter name a --->xxxxxyyyyy to stop: xxxxxyyyyy
```

```
            Menu
            -->1 Create an ordered file.
            -->2 Merge files
            -->3 Exit
     Enter choice:  2

Enter file name to merge: first.dat
Enter next file to merge: second.dat
Again?  1=Y,0=N: 1

Enter next file to merge: third.dat
Again?  1=Y,0=N: 0

                           andy
                           amy
                           arthur
                           enoch
                           george
                           laura
                           malachi
                           paul
                           rox
                           sarah
                           scott
                           sly
                           susu
                           tim
                           titus
                           valery
                           william
            Menu
            -->1 Create an ordered file.
            -->2 Merge files
            -->3 Exit
     Enter choice:  3
```

Chapter 10, Exercise 9

```
                                          (*Exercise 9, Section 10.12*)
                                          (*Pascal with Program Design*)

part (a):
(*-----------------------------------------------------------------*)

procedure Fibonacci(count, max, a, b : integer);
  begin
    if count <= max then begin
      writeln(count:5, (a + b):10);
      Fibonacci(count + 1, max, b, a + b)
      end
  end;                                                    (*Fibonacci*)
```

```
(*-------------------------------------------------------------*)

part (b):
(*-------------------------------------------------------------*)

procedure Lucas(count,max, a, b : integer);
  begin
    if count <= max then begin
      writeln(count:5, (a + b):10);
      Lucas(count + 1, max, a, a + b)
      end
  end;                                                  (*Lucas*)

(*-------------------------------------------------------------*)
```

Chapter 10, Exercise 13

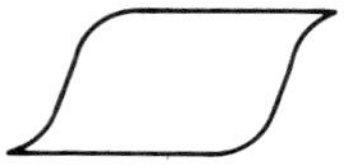

```
                                   (*Exercise 13, Section 10.12*)
                                   (*Pascal with Program Design*)

program hanoi (input,output);
type
  arr = array[1..3,1..4] of integer;
(*-------------------------------------------------------------*)
  procedure graphics (var disk : arr );
  var
    x,y : integer;
  begin
    for x := 1 to 4 do begin
      for y := 1 to 3 do
        case disk[y,x] of
          0: write ('     *     ');
          1: write ('    ***    ');
          2: write ('   *****   ');
          3: write ('  *******  ');
          4: write (' ********* ');
          end;                                        (*of case*)
        writeln;
        end;
    writeln (' *********************************');
    writeln;
  end;                                      (*end. of graphics*)

(*-------------------------------------------------------------*)

  procedure hanoi(number, pega, pegc, pegb: integer;
                  var disk : arr);
  var
    x,count: integer;
```

```
begin
   if number > 0 then begin
      hanoi(number-1, pega, pegb, pegc,disk);
      if disk [pega,1] = number then disk[pega,1] := 0
      else if disk [pega,2] = number then disk[pega,2] := 0
           else if disk [pega,3] = number then
                  disk [pega,3] := 0
                else disk [pega,4] := 0;
      if disk [pegc,4] = 0 then disk [pegc,4] := number
      else if disk [pegc,3] = 0 then disk [pegc,3] := number
           else if disk [pegc,2] = 0 then
                  disk [pegc,2] := number
                else disk [pegc,1] := number;
      graphics(DISK);
      hanoi(number—1, pegb, pegc, pega,disk)
   end
end;                                                        (*procedure*)

(*-----------------------------------------------------------------*)

procedure driver;
var
   disk : arr ;
   x: integer;
begin
   writeln('This program graphicaly shows hao the tower');
   writeln('of hanoi problem is solved with four disks.');
   writeln;
   for x := 1 to 4 do disk [1,x] := x;
   graphics(disk);
   hanoi(4,1,3,2,disk)
end;                                                        (*driver*)

(*-----------------------------------------------------------------*)
begin
   driver
end.
```

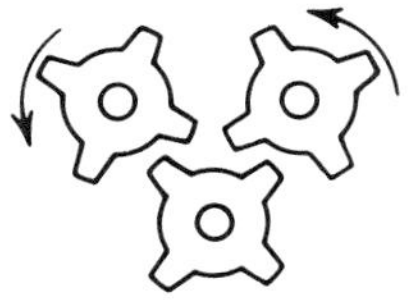

```
This program graphicaly shows hao the tower
of hanoi problem is solved with four disks.


    ***         *          *
   *****        *          *
  *******       *          *
 *********      *          *
*******************************


     *          *          *
   *****        *          *
  *******       *          *
 *********     ***         *
*******************************
```

```
    *          *          *
    *          *          *
 *******       *          *
*********     ***       *****
*******************************

    *          *          *
    *          *          *
 *******       *         ***
*********      *        *****
*******************************

    *          *          *
    *          *          *
    *          *         ***
*********   *******     *****
*******************************

    *          *          *
    *          *          *
   ***         *          *
*********   *******     *****
*******************************

    *          *          *
    *          *          *
   ***       *****        *
*********   *******       *
*******************************

    *          *          *
    *         ***         *
    *        *****        *
*********   *******       *
*******************************

    *          *          *
    *         ***         *
    *        *****        *
    *       *******   *********
*******************************

    *          *          *
    *          *          *
    *        *****       ***
    *       *******   *********
*******************************

    *          *          *
    *          *          *
    *          *         ***
  *****     *******   *********
*******************************

    *          *          *
    *          *          *
   ***         *          *
  *****     *******   *********
*******************************
```

```
    *          *          *
    *          *          *
   ***         *       *******
  *****        *      *********
*******************************

    *          *          *
    *          *          *
    *          *       *******
  *****       ***     *********
*******************************

    *          *          *
    *          *        *****
    *          *       *******
    *         ***     *********
*******************************

    *          *         ***
    *          *        *****
    *          *       *******
    *          *      *********
*******************************
```

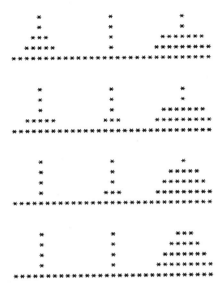

Chapter 10, Exercise 1

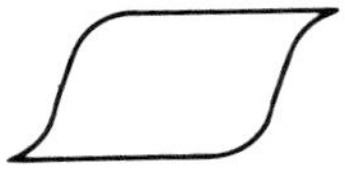

```
                                        (*Exercise 1, Section 10.14.3*)
                                        (*Pascal with Program Design*)

program BuildStrings(input, output);

const
   max = 160;                              (*maximum length of string*)
   sentinel = '*';                            (*mark end-of-string*)
type
   StringType = packed array[1..max] of char;
                                            (*use for both strings*)
(*-------------------------------------------------------------*)

   procedure concatenate(var StringA, StringB : StringType;
                                                  (*pair of strings*)
                          countA, countB : integer;
                                                  (*sizes of strings*)
                          selector : integer);   (*select characters*)
   begin
      if selector <= countB
      then begin
         StringA[countA + selector] := StringB[selector];
         con-
catenate(StringA, StringB, countA, countB, selector +1)
         end
   end;                                               (*concatenate*)
```

```
(*-----------------------------------------------------------------*)

   procedure initialize(var script : StringType;              (*a string*)
                            limit : integer);             (*size of string*)
   var
      selector : integer;
   begin
      for selector := 1 to limit do script[selector] := ' '
   end;                                                     (*initialize*)

(*-----------------------------------------------------------------*)

   procedure LengthOfString(script : StringType;      (*entered string*)
                            var tally : integer;          (*string size*)
                            count : integer);              (*holds tally*)
   begin
      if script[count] <> sentinel then begin
         tally := count;
         LengthOfString(script, tally, count + 1)     (*self-activation*)
         end                                              (*then block*)
   end;                                               (*LengthOfString*)

(*-----------------------------------------------------------------*)

   procedure BuildString(var script : StringType);            (*a string*)
   var
      i : integer;
   begin
      i := 0;
      writeln('Enter string:');
      write(' ':5);
      repeat
         i := i + 1;
         read(script[i])
      until eoln;
      script[i + 1] := sentinel;
      writeln
   end;                                                    (*BuildString*)

(*-----------------------------------------------------------------*)

   procedure ShowString(script : StringType;                  (*a string*)
                        limit : integer);              (*string length*)
   var
      selector : integer;
   begin
      selector := 0;
      writeln('Concatenated string:   ');
      repeat
         selector := selector + 1;
         if script[selector] <> sentinel then
            write(script[selector]);
      until selector = limit
   end;                                                     (*ShowString*)
```

```
(*-------------------------------------------------------------*)

procedure driver;
var
   FirstString, SecondString : StringType;   (*2 string variables*)
   FirstCount, SecondCount : integer;         (*sizes of 2 strings*)
   choice : integer;                           (*control variable*)
begin
   repeat
      BuildString(FirstString);
      LengthOfString(FirstString, FirstCount, 1);
      BuildString(SecondString);
      LengthOfString(SecondString, SecondCount, 1);
      concatenate(FirstString, SecondString, FirstCount,
                  SecondCount, 1k);
      ShowString(FirstString, FirstCount + SecondCount);
      writeln; writeln;
      write('Again?--1=Y, 0=N:   '); readln(choice); writeln;
      if FirstCount = 1
      then begin
         initialize(FirstString, FirstCount);
         initialize(SecondString, SecondCount)
         end                                         (*then block*)
   until choice = 0
end;                                                     (*driver*)

(*-------------------------------------------------------------*)

begin
   driver
end.
```

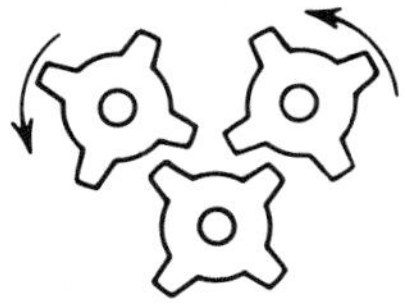

```
Enter string:
      Day broke,

Enter string:
      gray.

Concatenated string:
Day broke, gray.

Again?--1=Y, 0=N:   1

Enter string:
      Programming is designing,

Enter string:
      creating programs.

Concatenated string:
Programming is designing, creating programs.

Again?--1=Y, 0=N:   0
```

Chapter 10, Exercise 2

```
                                             (*Exercise 2, Section 10.16*)
                                            (*Pascal with Program Design*)

program QuickSortNos(input, output);
const
   empty = -1;
   max = 10000;                                        (*limit on list size*)
type
   list = array[1..max] of integer;                           (*array type*)
   table = array[1..20] of list;
(*--------------------------------------------------------------------*)
   Function Rnd(var seed : real): real;
   begin
      seed := sqr(seed + 3.1415926535);
      seed := seed - trunc(seed);
      Rnd := seed
   end;                                                            (*Rnd*)

(*--------------------------------------------------------------------*)
                                     (*Save entered numbers in an array*)
   procedure BuildList(var info : list;                     (*for numbers*)
                       high, low : integer;                (*range of Rnd*)
                       limit : integer;                       (*list size*)
                       seed : real);
   var
      number : integer;
   begin
      repeat
         number := trunc(high * Rnd(seed));
         info[limit] := number mod (high - low) + low;
         limit := limit - 1
      until limit = 0
   end;                                                      (*BuildList*)
(*--------------------------------------------------------------------*)
                                                (*Swap numbers in list*)
   procedure swap(var info : list;                             (*numbers*)
                  low : integer;                              (*list size*)
                  high : integer);                      (*number to swap*)
   var
      buffer : integer;                               (*temporary storage*)
   begin
      buffer := info[high]; info[high] := info[low];
      info[low] := buffer
   end;                                                           (*swap*)
(*--------------------------------------------------------------------*)
   procedure DrawLine;
   var
      i : integer;
   begin
      for i := 1 to 65 do write('-'); writeln;
   end;                                                       (*DrawLine*)
```

```
(*-----------------------------------------------------------------*)

  procedure PrintList(size : list;                        (*numbers*)
                      SComps, QComps : list; (*comparisons made*)
                      limit : integer);                 (*list size*)
  var
    count : integer;                              (*number selector*)
  begin
    DrawLine;
    writeln('List Size':15, 'Selection Sort':25, 'QuickSort':19);
    writeln('Comparisons':39, 'Comparisons':21);
    DrawLine;
    for count := 1 to limit do
      writeln(size[count]:13,SComps[count]:22,QComps[count]:22);
    writeln;
    DrawLine
  end;                                                  (*PrintList*)
(*-----------------------------------------------------------------*)
                                     (*quicksort of a list of numbers*)
  procedure QuickSort(var info: list;                     (*numbers*)
                      limit, low, high: integer;
                      var comps : integer);
  var
    ThisLow, ThisHigh: integer;
  begin
    if low < high then begin
      ThisLow := low; ThisHigh := high + 1;
      repeat
        repeat
          ThisLow := ThisLow + 1;
          comps := comps + 1;
        until (info[ThisLow] >= info[low]) or (ThisLow > limit);
        repeat
          ThisHigh := ThisHigh - 1;
          comps := comps + 1;
        until info[ThisHigh] <= info[low];
        if ThisLow < ThisHigh then begin
          swap(info, ThisLow, ThisHigh)
          end
      until ThisLow > ThisHigh;
      swap(info, low, ThisHigh);
      QuickSort(info, limit, low, ThisHigh - 1, comps);
      QuickSort(info, limit, ThisHigh + 1, high, comps)
      end
  end;                                                  (*QuickSort*)
(*-----------------------------------------------------------------*)
         (*Notice how the key value in FindMax is used to select
                                 the correct comparison to make.*)

  procedure FindMax(var info : list;             (*array of records*)
                    limit : integer;                   (*array size*)
                    var position : integer:        (*loc. of lgst ele.*)
                    var comps: integer); (*number of comparisons*)
```

```
var                                                        (*array index*)
   lgst, i : integer;                                      (*array index*)
begin
   lgst := info[limit]; i := 1;
   while i < limit do begin
       comps := comps + 1;
       if lgst < info[i] then begin
          lgst := info[i]; position := i
          end;                                             (*then*)
       i := i + 1
      end                                                  (*while*)
end;                                                       (*FindMax*)
(*-------------------------------------------------------------*)
          (*This procedure handles the activation of the FindMax
             and swap procedures after the user has selected a
                                                         sort key.*)

procedure PerformSort(var info : list;                (*array of records*)
                      limit : integer;
                      var comps : integer);                (*list size*)
var
   entry : integer;                                        (*choice*)
   place : integer;                             (*loc. of ele. to swap*)
begin
   comps := 0;
   repeat
      place := limit;
      FindMax(info, limit, place, comps);
      swap(info, limit, place);
      limit := limit - 1
   until limit = 1
end;                                                   (*PerformSort*)

(*-------------------------------------------------------------*)
                              (*Program manager: activate procedures*)
procedure driver;
var
   ThisList : Table;                                  (*array variable*)
   ListSize, QComparisons, SComparisons : list;
   choice, High, Low, count : integer;
   starter : real;
begin
   count := 0;
   write('Enter seed for Rnd generator: '); readln(starter);
   write('Enter range for random numbers (low, high): ');
   readln(Low, High);
   repeat
      count := count + 1;
      write('Enter size of list: '); readln(ListSize[count]);
      BuildList(ThisList[count], ListSize[count], High, Low,
                starter);
      PerformSort(ThisList[count], ListSize[count],
                  SComparisons[count]);
```

```
          QuickSort(This List[count], ListSize[count], 1,
                    ListSize[count], QComparisons[count]);
          write('Again?  1=Y,0=N: '); readln(choice)
     until choice <> 1;
     writeln;
     PrintList(ListSize, SComparisons, QComparisons, count)
  end;                                                      (*driver*)
(*-----------------------------------------------------------------*)
begin
  driver                                 (*activate driver procedure*)
end.
```

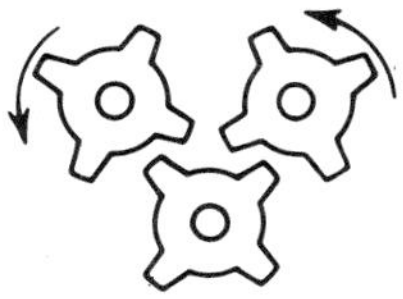

```
Enter seed for Rnd generator: 2.71828
Enter range for random numbers (low, high): 1 5000
Enter size of list: 10
Again?  1=Y,0=N: 1
Enter size of list: 100
Again?  1=Y,0=N: 1
Enter size of list: 1000
Again?  1=Y,0= N: 1
Enter size of list: 10000
Again?  1=Y,0= N: 0

-------------------------------------------------------------
        List Size        Selection Sort        QuickSort
                         Comparisons           Comparisons
-------------------------------------------------------------
               10                    45                 36
              100                  4950                649
             1000                499500               9124
            10000              49995000             129840
```

Chapter 11, Exercise 9

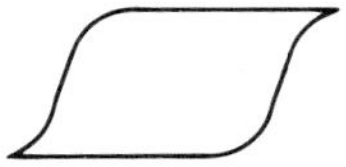

```
                                       (*Exercise 9, Section 11.13*)
                                       (*Pascal with Program Design*)

program ListBuilder(input, output);
const
    sentinel =      '*';                        (*marks end-of-list*)
type
  ptr = ^node;                                       (*pointer type*)
  node = record                                       (*domain type*)
     letter : char;                                   (*string type*)
     link : ptr                                      (*pointer type*)
     end;                                                  (*node*)
```

```
(*---------------------------------------------------------------*)
                                          (*attach new node to list:*)
procedure append(var follower : ptr;                  (*link pointer*)
                 NewChar : char);                       (*list entry*)
var
  NewNode : ptr;                                  (*pointer variable*)
begin
  if follower^.link = nil then begin
    follower^.letter := NewChar;
    new(NewNode);
    follower^.link := NewNode; follower :=NewNode
    end
  else append(follower^.link, NewChar)
end;                                                        (*append*)
(*---------------------------------------------------------------*)
                                (*start list and extend it, if necessary:*)
procedure CreateList(var ListHead : ptr);
var
  entry : char;                                    (*string variable*)
  next : ptr;                                     (*pointer variable*)
begin
  new(ListHead); new(next);
  with ListHead^ do begin
    write('Enter string: '); read(letter);
    link := next
    end;                                                      (*with*)
  repeat
    read(entry);
    append(next, entry)
  until eoln;
  next := ListHead;
  while next^.link <> nil do                      (*find end of list*)
    next := next^.link;
  next^.link := ListHead                       (*create circular list*)
end;                                                    (*CreateList*)
(*---------------------------------------------------------------*)
                                                 (*Show linked list:*)
procedure ShowList(FirstNode, ListHead : ptr; limit : integer);
begin
  if limit > 0 then begin
    write(ListHead^.letter:1);
    if ListHead^.link = FirstNode then
      ShowList(FirstNode, ListHead^.link, limit - 1)
    else ShowLIst(FirstNode, ListHead^.link, limit)
    end
end;                                                      (*ShowList*)
(*---------------------------------------------------------------*)
                  (*Program manager: activate necessary procedures.*)
procedure driver;
var
  choice : integer;                               (*control variable*)
  CyclesToPrint : integer;
  BeginningNode : ptr;                            (*pointer variable*)
```

```
begin
  repeat
    CreateList(BeginningNode);
    writeln; write(' ':5,'Print how many cycles of list? ');
    readln(CyclesToPrint); writeln; write(' ':10);
    ShowList(BeginningNode, BeginningNode, CyclesToPrint);
    writeln; writeln;
    write('Again?--1 = Y, 0 = N: '); readln(choice); writeln
  until choice = 0
end;                                                    (*driver*)
(*---------------------------------------------------------------*)
begin
  driver                                (*activate driver procedure*)
end.
```

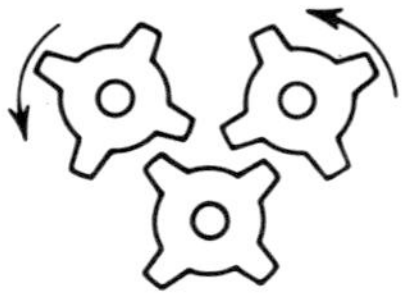

```
Enter string: yes

     Print how many cycles of list? 9

          yesyesyesyesyesyesyesyesyes

Again?--1 = Y, 0 = N: 1

Enter string: yes!

     Print how many cycles of list? 8

          yes!yes!yes!yes!yes!yes!yes!yes!

Again?--1 = Y, 0 = N: 0
```

Chapter 11, Exercise 16

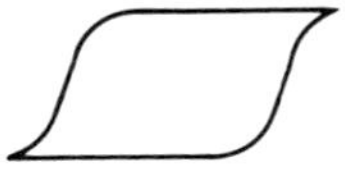

```
                                          (*Exercise 16, Section 11.13*)
                                          (*Pascal with Program Design*)

program ListBuilder(input, output);
const
   sentinel =     'xxxxxyyyyy';                     (*marks end-of-list*)
type
  alfa = packed array[1..10] of char;                   (*string type*)
  ptr = ^node;                                         (*pointer type*)
  node = record                                         (*domain type*)
    name : alfa;                                        (*string type*)
    link : ptr                                         (*pointer type*)
    end;                                                      (*node*)
(*---------------------------------------------------------------*)
                                             (*attach new node to list:*)
procedure append(var follower : ptr;                  (*link pointer*)
                     NewName : alfa;                    (*list entry*)
var
  NewNode : ptr;                                   (*pointer variable*)
```

```
begin
   if follower^.link = nil then begin
      follower^.name := NewName;
      new(NewNode);
      follower^.link := NewNode
      end
   else append(follower^.link, NewName)
end;                                                      (*append*)
(*-----------------------------------------------------------------*)
                             (*start list and extend it, if necessary:*)
procedure CreateList(var ListHead : ptr);
var
   entry : alfa;                                 (*string variable*)
   next : ptr;                                  (*pointer variable*)
begin
   new(ListHead); new(next);
   with ListHead^ do begin
      write('Enter name--xxxxxyyyyy, to stop: '); readln(name);
      writeln;
      link := next
      end;                                                  (*with*)
   repeat
      write('name: '); readln(entry); writeln;
      append(next, entry)
   until entry = sentinel;
end;                                                  (*CreateList*)
(*-----------------------------------------------------------------*)
                                                (*Show linked list:*)
procedure ShowList(ListHead : ptr);
begin
   if (ListHead <> nil) then begin
      if ListHead^.name <> sentinel then
         writeln(ListHead^.name : 20);
      ShowList(ListHead^.link)
      end
end;                                                    (*ShowList*)
(*-----------------------------------------------------------------*)
                 (*Program manager: activate necessary procedures.*)
procedure driver;
var
   choice : integer;                            (*control variable*)
   buffer,BeginningNode : ptr;                  (*pointer variable*)
   entry : alfa;
begin
   repeat
      writeln(' ':5, 'Menu');
      writeln(' ':5, '-->1. BuildList');
      writeln(' ':5, '-->2. Append to list');
      writeln(' ':5, '-->3. Exit');
      write(' ':5, 'Enter choice: '); readln(choice);
```

```
      case choice of
        1: begin
             CreateList(BeginningNode);
             writeln; writeln('linked list:':20); writeln;
             ShowList(BeginningNode)
           end;
        2: begin
             buffer := BeginningNode;
             repeat
               write(' ':5, 'Enter name-xxxxxyyyyy, to stop: ');
               readln(entry);
               append(BeginningNode,entry)
             until entry = sentinel;
             writeln; writeln('linked list:':20); writeln;
             BeginningNode := buffer;
             ShowList(BeginningNode)
           end;
        3:                                                  (*case*)
        end;
  until choice > 2
end;                                                      (*driver*)
(*-----------------------------------------------------------------*)
begin
  driver                                  (*activate driver procedure*)
end.
```

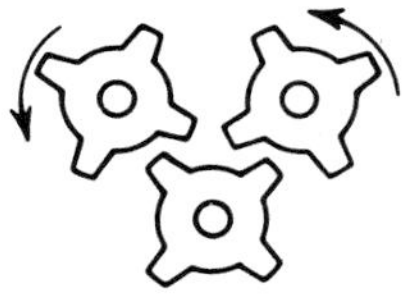

```
      Menu
      -->1. BuildList
      -->2. Append to list
      -->3. Exit
      Enter choice: 1
Enter name--xxxxxyyyyy, to stop: Lori

name: Susu

name: Carlos

name: Gandalf

name: Tomas

name:xxxxxyyyyy

          linked list:

             Lori
             Susu
             Carlos
             Gandalf
             Tomas
```

```
Menu
-->1.  BuildList
-->2.  Append to list
-->3.  Exit
Enter choice:   2
Enter name-xxxxxyyyyy, to stop:  Fred
Enter name-xxxxxyyyyy, to stop:  Alan
Enter name-xxxxxyyyyy, to stop:  George
Enter name-xxxxxyyyyy, to stop:  Laura
Enter name-xxxxxyyyyy, to stop:  xxxxxyyyyy

     linked list:

         Lori
         Susu
         Carlos
         Gandalf
         Tomas
         Fred
         Alan
         George
         Laura

Menu
-->1.  BuildList
-->2.  Append to list
-->3.  Exit
Enter choice: 3
```

Chapter 12, Exercise 6

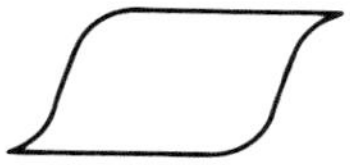

```
                                            (*Exercise 6, Section 12.10*)
                                           (*Pascal with Program Design*)
program ListBuilder(input, output);
const
    sentinel = '          ';                        (*marks end-of-list*)
type
   alfa = packed array[1..10] of char;                    (*string type*)
   ListPtr = ^ListNode;                                  (*pointer type*)
   ListNode = record                                      (*domain type*)
      name : alfa;                                        (*string type*)
      link : ListPtr                                     (*pointer type*)
      end;                                                       (*node*)
   history = record
      comparisonTotal : integer;
      ListSize : integer
      end;                                                    (*history*)
   table = array [1..10] of history;
(*-------------------------------------------------------------------*)
                         (*Find place in list to put the target string:*)

procedure InsertNode(var ListHead, NewNode: ListPtr;        (*pointers*)
                         target : alfa;                (*name to insert*)
                         var measure : integer);
```

```
var
   ahead, behind : ListPtr;                            (*pointer variables*)
begin
   new(NewNode);
   if ListHead = nil then begin
      ListHead := NewNode; ListHead^.name := target;
      ListHead^.link := nil
      end
   else begin
      ahead := ListHead;
      while (target >= ahead^.name) and (ahead^.link <> nil) do
         begin
            measure := measure + 1;
            behind := ahead; ahead := ahead^.link
         end                                                      (*while*)
      end;                                                         (*else*)
   NewNode^.name := target;
   NewNode^.link := ahead;  (*make NewNode point to next node*)
   if ahead = ListHead then
      ListHead := NewNode
   else
      behind^.link := NewNode
end;                                                         (*InsertNode*)
(*---------------------------------------------------------------*)
                              (*start list and extend it, if necessary:*)
procedure CreateList(var ListHead : ListPtr;
                     var info : history);
var
   next : ListPtr;                                    (*pointer variable*)
   entry : alfa;                                       (*string variable*)
begin
   info.ComparisonTotal := 0; info.ListSize := 0;
   new(ListHead); ListHead^.name := sentinel;
   write('Enter name--<return>, to stop: ':35); readln(entry);
   while entry <> sentinel do begin
      info.ListSize := info.ListSize + 1;
      InsertNode(ListHead, next, entry, info.ComparisonTotal);
      write('name: ':35); readln(entry);
      end;                                                        (*while*)
end;                                                         (*CreateList*)
(*---------------------------------------------------------------*)
                                                      (*Show linked list:*)
procedure ShowList(ListHead : ListPtr);
begin
      if ListHead = nil then
         writeln('Sorry--list is empty!')
      else begin
         if ListHead^.name <> sentinel then
            write(ListHead^.name, ' ':3);
         if ListHead^.link <> nil then
            ShowList(ListHead^.link)
         end                                                       (*else*)
end;                                                           (*ShowList*)
```

```
(*--------------------------------------------------------------*)
procedure DeleteNode(var ListHead: ListPtr;
                     target: alfa);
var
   ahead, behind: ListPtr;
   found : Boolean;
begin
   ahead := ListHead;
   if target = ahead^.name then found := true
   else begin
   found := false;
   while (target <> ahead^.name) and (ahead^.link <> nil) do begin
      behind := ahead; ahead := ahead^.link;
      if target = ahead^.name then found := true
      end                                               (*while*)
   end;                                                 (*else*)
   if not found then writeln(target:20, ' is not in list!')
   else begin
      if ahead = ListHead then
         ListHead := ListHead^.link
      else begin
         behind^.link := ahead^.link;
         dispose(ahead)
         end                                       (*inner else*)
      end                                          (outer else*)
end;                                               (*DeleteNode*)
(*--------------------------------------------------------------*)
          (*Program manager:  activate necessary procedures.*)
procedure driver;
var
   choice : integer;                          (*control variable*)
   addition, deletion : alfa;                 (*string variables*)
   BeginningNode, AnotherNode : ListPtr;      (*pointer variable*)
   count, Lists : integer;
   ComparisonTable : table;
begin
   BeginningNode := nil; Lists := 0;
   repeat
      writeln('menu:':10);
      writeln(' ':10, '---> 1) create an ordered list;');
      writeln(' ':10, '---> 2) delete an entry;');
      writeln(' ':10, '---> 3) insert an entry;');
      writeln(' ':10, '---> 4) see list;');
      writeln(' ':10, '---> 5) comparison table;');
      writeln(' ':10, '---> 6) exit;');
      readln(choice);
      case choice of
         1 : begin
                   Lists := Lists + 1;
                   CreateList(BeginningNode, ComparisonTable[Lists])
                end;
```

```
        2 : begin
                ShowList(BeginningNode);
                writeln; writeln;
                write('Enter name to delete: ':35); readln(deletion);
                writeln;
                DeleteNode(BeginningNode, deletion)
            end;
        3 : begin
                write('Enter name to insert: ':35); readln(addition);
                InsertNode(BeginningNode,AnotherNode,addition,count)
            end;
        4 : if BeginningNode = nil then
              writeln('Whoops!--there is no list to inspect.')
            else begin
              ShowList(BeginningNode); writeln
              end;
        5 : begin
                write('list no.':13, 'list size':13);
                writeln('comparisons made':19, 'n2/4':7);
                for count := 1 to 65 do write('-'); writeln;
                for count := 1 to Lists do
                    with ComparisonTable[count] do begin
                       write(count:10,ListSize:13,ComparisonTotal:17);
                       writeln(sqr(ListSize) div 4:11)
                       end;
             for count := 1 to 65 do write('-'); writeln
            end;
        6 :                                        (*empty statement*)
        end
      until choice = 6
end;                                                        (*driver*)
(*--------------------------------------------------------------*)
begin
   driver                                 (*activate driver procedure*)
end.
```

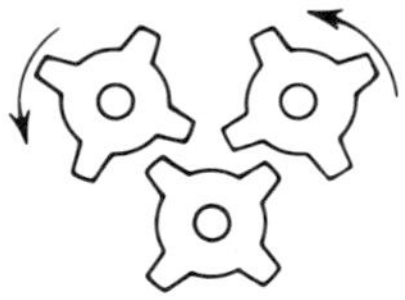

```
        menu:
              ---> 1) create an ordered list;
              ---> 2) delete an entry;
              ---> 3) insert an entry;
              ---> 4) see list;
              ---> 5) comparison table;
              ---> 6) exit;
1

      Enter name--<return>, to stop: Kristy
                               name: Ray
                               name: Dean
                               name: Wayne
                               name: Clarence
                               name: Melvin
                               name: Terry
                               name: Gary
```

```
                                          name: Roxanne
                                          name: Damian
                                          name: James
                                          name: Norman
                                          name: Gerald
                                          name: Annie
                                          name: Arnold
                                          name: Sheila
                                          name: Virgil
                                          name: William
                                          name: Thomas
                                          name: Butch
                                          name:
     menu:
          ---> 1) create an ordered list;
          ---> 2) delete an entry;
          ---> 3) insert an entry;
          ---> 4) see list;
          ---> 5) comparison table;
          ---> 6) exit;
1

     Enter name--<return>, to stop: Gerald
                                          name: Thomas
                                          name: Annie
                                          name: Gary
                                          name: James
                                          name: Terry
                                          name: Norman
                                          name: Arnold
                                          name: Sheila
                                          name: William
                                          name: Kristy
                                          name: Ray
                                          name: Roxanne
                                          name: Wayne
                                          name: Melvin
                                          name: Clarence
                                          name: Dean
                                          name: Virgil
                                          name: Butch
                                          name: Damian
                                          name:
     menu:
          ---> 1) create an ordered list;
          ---> 2) delete an entry;
          ---> 3) insert an entry;
          ---> 4) see list;
          ---> 5) comparison table;
          ---> 6) exit;
1
```

```
Enter name--<return>, to stop: Terry
                          name: Butch
                          name: Norman
                          name: James
                          name: Arnold
                          name: Dean
                          name: Virgil
                          name: Clarence
                          name: Ray
                          name: Gerald
                          name: Shelia
                          name: Roxanne
                          name: Wayne
                          name: Thomas
                          name: Damian
                          name: William
                          name: Melvin
                          name: Gary
                          name: Kristy
                          name: Annie
                          name:
 menu:
      ---> 1) create an ordered list;
      ---> 2) delete an entry;
      ---> 3) insert an entry;
      ---> 4) see list;
      ---> 5) comparison table;
      ---> 6) exit;
1

Enter name--<return>, to stop: Roxanne
                          name: Arnold
                          name: Terry
                          name: Gerald
                          name: Gary
                          name: Virgil
                          name: Annie
                          name: Ray
                          name: Melvin
                          name: Shela
                          name: Dean
                          name: Butch
                          name: William
                          name: Norman
                          name: Kristy
                          name: Thomas
                          name: Wayne
                          name: Damian
                          name: James
                          name: Clarence
                          name:
```

```
          menu:
                ---> 1) create an ordered list;
                ---> 2) delete an entry;
                ---> 3) insert an entry;
                ---> 4) see list;
                ---> 5) comparison table;
                ---> 6) exit;
1

       Enter name--<return>, to stop: Gary
                                name: Norman
                                name: William
                                name: Roxanne
                                name: Annie
                                name: Ray
                                name: Damian
                                name: Thomas
                                name: Melvin
                                name: Arnold
                                name: Terry
                                name: Shelia
                                name: Dean
                                name: Kristy
                                name: Virgil
                                name: Gerald
                                name: Clarence
                                name: Butch
                                name: Wayne
                                name: James
                                name:
          menu:
                ---> 1) create an ordered list;
                ---> 2) delete an entry;
                ---> 3) insert an entry;
                ---> 4) see list;
                ---> 5) comparison table;
                ---> 6) exit;

5
      list no.    list size        comparisons made    n2/4
-----------------------------------------------------------
         1           20                  99             100
         2           20                  93             100
         3           20                  99             100
         4           20                  94             100
         5           20                  90             100
-----------------------------------------------------------
          menu:
                ---> 1) create an ordered list;
                ---> 2) delete an entry;
                ---> 3) insert an entry;
                ---> 4) see list;
                ---> 5) comparison table;
                ---> 6) exit;
6
```

Chapter 12, Exercise 12

```
                                                (*Exercise 12, Section 12.10*)
                                                (*Pascal with Program Design*)

program NameTree(input, output);
const
   sentinel = '          ';                          (*will mark last node*)
type
   alfa = packed array[1..10] of char;                        (*string type*)
   TreePtr = ^TreeNode;                                      (*pointer type*)
   TreeNode = record                                          (*domain type*)
      key : alfa;                                           (*insertion key*)
      child : (L, R, FirstParent);                     (*position indicator*)
      left, right : TreePtr                                 (*pointer types*)
   end;                                                          (*TreeNode*)
(*-----------------------------------------------------------------------*)
                                            (*Insert nodes into binary tree:*)
procedure insert(NewNode : TreeNode;                        (*insertion key*)
                 var parent : TreePtr);                  (*pointer variable*)
begin
   if parent = nil then begin
      new(parent);
      with parent^ do begin
         key := NewNode.key; child := NewNode.child;
            left := nil; right := nil
         end;                                                        (*with*)
      end
   else
      if NewNode.key < parent^.key then begin
         NewNode.Child := L;
         insert(NewNode, parent^.left)
         end
      else
         if NewNode.key > parent^.key then begin
            NewNode.Child := R;
            insert(NewNode,parent^.right)
            end
end;                                                               (*insert*)
(*-----------------------------------------------------------------------*)
                                   (*Show tree nodes printed from left to right:*)
procedure ShowTree(ptr : TreePtr);                            (*a reference*)
begin
   if ptr <> nil then
      with ptr^ do begin
         ShowTree(left);
         writeln(key:25);
         ShowTree(right)
         end                                                         (*with*)
end;                                                             (*ShowTree*)
```

```
(*---------------------------------------------------------------*)
                  (*Show tree nodes printed from left to right:*)
procedure PrintOffSpring(ptr : Tree Ptr);           (*a reference*)
begin
   if ptr <> nil then
      with ptr^ do begin
         if ptr^.child = FirstParent then
            writeln(' ':25,key:10)
         else if ptr^.child = L then writeln(' ':5, key:10)
              else writeln(' ':45,key:10);
         PrintOffSpring(left);
         PrintOffSpring(right)
         end                                              (*with*)
end;                                            (*PrintOffSpring*)
(*---------------------------------------------------------------*)
          (*Handle data entry and activation of insert procedure:*)
procedure HandleSort(var root : TreePtr;
                     var NodeCount : integer);
var
   entry : TreeNode;                             (*for tree entries*)
begin
   NodeCount := 0;
   root := nil;
   repeat
      with entry do begin
         write(' ':20,'Entry--<return>, to stop:   ');
         readln(key);
         writeln;
         child := FirstParent;
         end;
      if entry.key <> sentinel then begin
         NodeCount := NodeCount + 1;
         insert(entry, root)
         end
   until entry.key = sentinel
end;                                               (*HandleSort*)
(*---------------------------------------------------------------*)
procedure DrawLine;
var
   choice : integer;
begin
   writeln; for choice := 1 to 60 do write('—'); writeln
end;                                                 (*DrawLine*)
(*---------------------------------------------------------------*)
        (*Program manager: get values needed to activate proc's*)
procedure driver;
var
   RootNode : TreePtr;                          (*pointer variable*)
   choice : integer;                            (*control variable*)
   NodeSize : integer;                      (*number of nodes in tree*)
```

```
begin
   repeat
      HandleSort(RootNode, NodeSize);
      DrawLine;
      writeln('Result of treesort with ',NodeSize:4,' Nodes:');
      writeln;
      ShowTree(RootNode);
      DrawLine;
      writeln('Break down of tree:');
      DrawLine;
      write('Left Nodes':15,' ':5,'Parent  Node':16, ' ':4);
      writeln('Right   Nodes':16);
      DrawLine;
      PrintOffSpring(RootNode);
      DrawLine;
      writeln; write('Again?--1 = Y, 0 = N: ');
      readln(choice); writeln
   until choice = 0
end;                                                  (*driver*)
(*--------------------------------------------------------------*)
begin
   driver                             (*activate driver procedure*)
end.
```

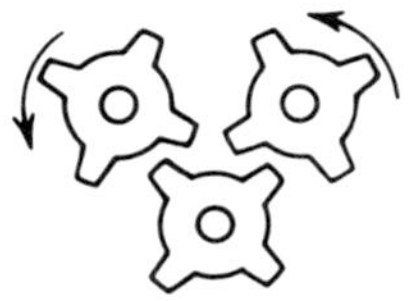

```
Entry--<return>, to stop:  Tom

Entry--<return>, to stop:  Allen

Entry--<return>, to stop:  Alice

Entry--<return>, to stop:  Joe

Entry--<return>, to stop:  Jim

Entry--<return>, to stop:  Ed

Entry--<return>, to stop:  Will

Entry--<return>, to stop:  George

Entry--<return>, to stop:  Laura

Entry--<return>, to stop:  Sarah

Entry--<return>, to stop:
```

```
-----------------------------------------------------------------
Result of treesort with    10 Nodes:

                    Alice
                    Allen
                    Ed
                    George
                    Jim
                    Joe
                    Laura
                    Sarah
                    Tom
                    Will

-----------------------------------------------------------------
Break down of tree:

-----------------------------------------------------------------
      Left Nodes              Parent ode              Right Nodes

-----------------------------------------------------------------
                             Tom
      Allen
      Alice
                                                        Joe
      Jim
      Ed
                                                        George
                                                        Laura
                                                        Sarah
                                                        Will

-----------------------------------------------------------------

Again?--1 = Y, 0 = N: 1

                             Entry--<return>, to stop:   Fred

                             Entry--<return>, to stop:   Steve

                             Entry--<return>, to stop:   Dough

                             Entry--<return>, to stop:   Larry

                             Entry--<return>, to stop:   Joe

                             Entry--<return>, to stop:   Bill

                             Entry--<return>, to stop:   Tommy

                             Entry--<return>, to stop:   Sally

                             Entry--<return>, to stop:
```

```
--------------------------------------------------------------
Result of treesort with     8 Nodes:

                    Bill
                    Dough
                    Fred
                    Joe
                    Larry
                    Sally
                    Steve
                    Tommy

--------------------------------------------------------------
Break down of tree:

--------------------------------------------------------------
      Left Nodes            Parent Node            Right Nodes

--------------------------------------------------------------
                           Fred
      Dough
      Bill
                                                   Steve
      Larry
      Joe
                                                   Sally
                                                   Tommy

--------------------------------------------------------------

Again?--1 = Y, 0 = N: 0
```

INDEX TO ALGORITHMS

INDEX TO PROCEDURES

INDEX